ONE MAN'S
AMERICA

ONE MAN'S

AMERICA

A Journalist's Search

for the Heart of

His Country

——✦——

HENRY
GRUNWALD

DOUBLEDAY

NEW YORK LONDON TORONTO SYDNEY AUCKLAND

PUBLISHED BY DOUBLEDAY
a division of Bantam Doubleday Dell Publishing Group, Inc.
1540 Broadway, New York, New York 10036

DOUBLEDAY and the portrayal of an anchor with a dolphin
are trademarks of Doubleday, a division of
Bantam Doubleday Dell Publishing Group, Inc.

Permissions information can be found on page 647.

Library of Congress Cataloging-in-Publication Data
Grunwald, Henry A. (Henry Anatole).
One man's America : a journalist's search for the heart of his
country / Henry Grunwald. — 1st ed.
p.   cm.
1. Grunwald, Henry A. (Henry, Anatole)   2. Editors—United States—
Biography.   3. United States—Civilization—1945–   4. United
States—Politics and government—1945–1989.   I. Title.
PN4874.G79A3   1997
070.4′1′092—dc20

For Louise

TABLE OF CONTENTS

Acknowledgments

Sarah Lewis joined me in May 1994 when an eye problem made reading and writing difficult. She became my indispensable link to the computer, working outrageous hours with endless patience. More than that, she was an editorial adviser and critic who asked all the right questions and offered sensitive and smart suggestions. It is almost impossible to imagine how I could have done this book without her.

Eileen Chiu Graham and Katherine L. Mihok were my researchers during essential stages of the work. Digging through my past, they came to know almost more about it than I do. They were also ingenious in tracking down the answers to countless historial questions.

Clare Mead Rosen provided important background reporting, especially on the Middle West and American intellectual history, along with highly stimulating ideas and recollections. She also conducted dozens of interviews with friends and former colleagues, whose names are listed in the source notes. I am indebted to them and to her.

Paddy Colligan and Dorothy Paulsen took over as my researchers for the last lap of this book. Drawing on their past experience at the *Time* library, they astounded me with their ability to unearth material that everyone else believed no longer existed, if it ever had.

I also had research help in specific areas from Nelida Gonzalez Cutler,

Anne Hopkins, Joan Walsh, Karen Cruz and, in Vienna, Traudl Lessing and Caroline Delval.

Nancy Kirk, my erudite, dedicated assistant since 1990, helped this book in more ways than I can enumerate, giving wise advice and encouragement. She shepherded successive drafts and took on many extra projects, freeing me to write. She also ran my office and kept the outside world at bay when possible, and when not, she handled it with charm and resourcefulness.

My wife, Louise, was my first reader and gave me shrewd comments along with loving and unfailing moral support. The book invaded her life, and she considerately made room for it. She patiently tolerated years of dinner table silences while I pondered the next chapter and interminable disappearances behind my study door. She also shared with me the excellent, perceptive journal she kept during the time I served as U.S. ambassador in Vienna.

I am grateful to my children for reading the manuscript. Peter and Mandy Grunwald provided very useful and constructive suggestions. Lisa Grunwald Adler brought her professional editing skills to bear with her zealous attention to grammar, syntax and style. However, she is not responsible for any danglers or clichés that may have reinserted themselves. All three freely supplied their recollections of our family life.

Harry Grunwald provided constant inspiration.

I'm grateful to my editors at Doubleday, successively, Herman Gollob, Deborah Futter, Casey Fuetsch and Bill Thomas, for their patient and warm support.

My friend and agent, Mort Janklow, believed in the book from the start and was a wise guide throughout.

Jason McManus, former editor in chief of Time Inc., his successor, Norman Pearlstine, and editorial director Henry Muller allowed me access to the company's library, archives and files, as well as the use of some of my writings from Time Inc. publications. I greatly appreciate their generosity. I am much indebted to many others at Time Inc.: Sheldon Czapnik, director of editorial services; Ben Lightman, chief of the library, and his successor, Lany McDonald; Elaine Felsher, Bill Hooper and Kenneth Schlesinger, keepers of the archives; Nilda Koehne of the biography files; Ben Watson of the tearsheets department; Beth Zarcone of the picture collection and their staffs.

My thanks also to the New York Society Library and its head librarian, Mark Piel, as well as my wizardly computer guru, Bruce Stark.

Many of the people I worked with over the years are mentioned in this book. Many more, inevitably, are not. I wish I could have named them all. But they will always remain in my mind, with intense gratitude for their friendship and support and for the pleasure of their company. It was a great pleasure indeed, and I am proud to have been their colleague.

—H.A.G.

FOREWORD

O<small>N SOME DAYS</small>, America seems to disappear. Looking out from the widow's walk atop my summer house in Martha's Vineyard, I see only the fog hiding Cape Cod. The land is invisible. But I know it is there, stretching from the New England dunes in a vast continuous sweep and out to the sands of the other ocean, bearing towns and cities; clapboard, steel and glass; shacks and towers; the immense fertile plains, the deserts, the timeless rivers, the restless highways. In my mind I reach out to it.

I love America because it took me in as a young refugee from the madness of wartime Europe and allowed me to make it my country. I love America because it did the same for millions of others from everywhere. I love it because it is an experiment in living and governing beyond anything dreamed of before. But I'm also disappointed by America because it seems in danger of bungling the experiment.

Loving America is complicated. It means loving not only a place and a people, but an idea; loving not merely what this nation has accomplished, but what it still promises. One should never love America uncritically. Perhaps one should never love anything or anyone uncritically. One loves people despite their faults, even sometimes *for* their faults. That is the way I love America and why I describe, as best I can, the faults along with the virtues, and the hopes that are still unfulfilled.

My story mingles the personal, the professional and the public. I spent most of my career as a journalist at *Time,* including nearly a decade as its managing editor and nearly another decade in charge of all of Time Inc.'s publications. Thus this account deals with the workings of *Time* as well as many of the events and people I observed. Always I kept searching for the meaning, the heart, of this country—my country. Even when I traveled abroad I tried to learn about America and its place in the world.

This is not another book about the decline of the United States. Nor is it a compendium of remedies to cure its ills. It is rather an attempt to retrace my journey to and through America: how I became an American and what America means today.

PART ONE

PRELUDE

IN VIENNA

CHAPTER ONE

WHEN I WAS VERY SMALL I heard about the building of the Great Western Railway in America. I confronted my governess, the darling and redoubtable "Teta." If one went to Vienna's Western Railway Station, I asked her, took a train and kept on and on—would one eventually get to America? She dismissed the question with an angry grumble, obviously not having a much more precise idea than I did about the location of the New World.

At that moment, I started my journey to America.

As long as I can remember, America loomed somewhere in the distance, as promise and question and occasionally as threat, a fantastic land of speed and technical wizardry, an unreal realm that nevertheless had real effects on my family's life and on mine.

When I grew a little older I took to sneaking into my father's study, a large, dark room, its walls lined with red plush—and with books. I had found some illustrated programs from the Casino de Paris and the Moulin Rouge; the rather chaste nudes, striking tasteful poses and wearing only strategically placed strings of pearls, were of considerable interest to a little boy of nine or ten. I kept coming back to look. During one of these stealthy forays, I took down the wrong booklet; it turned out to be a political magazine containing a drawing of a tall, angular, bespectacled man in top hat and striped pants—Woodrow Wilson dressed as Uncle Sam.

Ever since, I have imagined Uncle Sam looking a bit like Wilson; and ever since, I have been looking for the reality behind that myth-caricature.

What little we were taught in school about America was ridiculously inadequate. I learned a bit more from family sources. America was widely considered a refuge for crooks and a place of exile for black sheep of all sorts. We had a black sheep in the family, my mother's half-sister, Aunt Cilly, a lady excessively rouged and perfumed. As a girl she had been sent to America because of some scandal involving a married man. She had come back eventually, with a few idiomatic English phrases ("have a cuppa coffee," "don't worry, sweetheart") and many tales about the extravagance of American life. She assured me that no one in America ever tried to preserve or repair anything; they just threw away their possessions and bought something new.

Another informant (though not an eyewitness) was my father's brother, gentle, slightly deaf Uncle Oscar. He often pressed on me American books about how to get ahead in business, with many earnest tips about keeping well informed, looking out for new ideas and opportunities, showing self-confidence. The only trouble was that Uncle Oscar was a terrible businessman who ran Grandfather's hat factory into the ground. I was more inspired by a biography of Thomas Edison. I thought it would be wonderful to be an inventor or at least an engineer, the most typically American occupations. I longed for an American identity, and for a while I called myself Harry, which, I discovered to my delight, was an English version of my German first name, Heinz. (Years later, quite unconsciously, I would name a much loved terrier Harry.) In due course I would settle on the more formal Henry for myself. I also insisted on wearing knickerbockers, to my mind also typically American.

Another source about the United States was the books of Karl May. Without ever leaving Germany, this schoolmaster wrote countless travel-adventure books for young people. May's America was a place of good guys versus bad, Indians versus whites. May's sympathies were with the Indians, whose land, he preached, had been stolen. May's heroes were a noble Apache chief named Winnetou and an equally noble white scout known, because of his powerful fists, as Old Shatterhand. I was enthralled by the chases and ambushes, the lore about trapping and the Indians' stoic code of behavior. (May was Adolf Hitler's favorite author throughout his life, an obvious comment on the maturity of *der Führer's* intellect.)

May's stories were typical of the Wild West myth that had captured Europe. It was a daydream of release from the narrow Old World, from the mechanized, interdependent modern age that constrained individual action and from the miseries of the present.

As a child I was scarcely touched by these miseries. But I occasionally sensed them. There was, for instance, the Jittery Man. His figure always frightened me. His arms and legs shot out spastically, uncontrollably, his red face was contorted, his whole cramped frame quivered as he moved along with painful effort. He wore a gray untidy tunic with a row of medals. He was, Teta explained to me, an injured veteran. There were many such cripples (that was the word casually used) around the Vienna of my childhood. Though I never knew what became of him, he stayed in my memory as the bearer of some vague anguish, a symbol of the war.

Mostly, reminders of World War I came in the grown-ups' endless talk about its horrors and hardships. How my mother and older sister had nothing to eat but beets for weeks, while my father was away at something called "the front." How my father fell gravely ill with pneumonia and my mother managed to travel right into the restricted war zone, near what became the Yugoslav border, to get him back to Vienna and into a good hospital. This broke all regulations, but, my mother explained, "officers helped me because they were gentlemen and chivalrous toward a lady. Besides," she would add coquettishly, "I was rather pretty in those days." (She was, throughout most of her life.)

My father kept the gilt tassel of his saber as a souvenir, and once I took it to the park to play soldier. Suddenly an angry old man appeared and berated me loudly for desecrating the memory of an undoubtedly brave imperial officer. As it happened, my father had been a cavalry officer who hated horses and was attached to the supply corps; he was not especially brave and never claimed to be. He once had remarked prophetically: "Any army in which I can become a first lieutenant is bound to lose the war."

The defeat was, so I heard again and again, the end of a world. It was also the end of the old Austria, which had been a great power for four centuries. In its last incarnation as the Austro-Hungarian monarchy, a remnant of the old supranational, feudal order, it had been an agglomeration of many nationalities and races with different languages and traditions; they were held together by the relatively benign but increasingly sclerotic rule of the Habsburgs. This old order was replaced by several small, newly invented states that actually replicated the animosities and confusions of the multinational empire they supplanted.

German-speaking Austria was left alone, a truncated, tiny, impoverished country. Vienna had been an elegant, frivolous capital, part regal ballroom, part bazaar, part coffeehouse. Now it was the absurdly oversize head on a shriveled body (the population of Vienna was two million in a country of six and a half million), its graceful old baroque palaces and its newer, pompous, neoclassic buildings along the Ringstrasse equally obsolete.

Vienna was full of unemployed workers, of solid burghers who had lost their savings in war bonds, of officers who had had their stripes ripped off during the brief revolution that sent the Habsburgs into exile and established the republic. The Socialists, the "Reds," ruled in Vienna, but their uncertain grip on the government was bitterly contested by the church-oriented conservatives, the "Blacks." The fact that the disastrous war had been brought on largely by the aggressive stupidity of Austria's own rulers—and the aggressive arrogance of their German allies—only exacerbated the prevailing bitterness, self-hate, and political fratricide.

But in the midst of this ghostly scene was an artificial glow of nostalgia, a grimly sentimental pretense that the past still had meaning, that the music had not stopped.

And that is where my father played a part. For he was a librettist, the writer of books and lyrics for innumerable operettas. Today that popular art, a very distant forerunner of the musical, is largely forgotten. But it was as much a reflection of its time as Hollywood films would become later. Most Viennese operettas sang endlessly of the good old days, of loss redeemed by love. They sang of the eternal glories of Vienna, while the city shivered. They sang fortissimo of Viennese girls and the Vienna Woods. Waltzes, waltzes, waltzes—and lovely they were.

In these operettas the empire was still alive: here a Hungarian count, there a Bohemian landowner. One critic wrote sardonically about my father's best-known operetta, *Countess Maritza*, that it was counterrevolution set to music.

M̲Y FATHER'S FATHER had come to Vienna from Budapest and established himself as a hat manufacturer. Like Uncle Oscar, he was by all accounts a very poor businessman; the family was always strapped. Young Alfred, my father, held a variety of jobs and eventually went to work booking performers for a theatrical agency.

He tried his hand at writing lyrics for revues, occasionally rewriting other people's failed efforts. Someone recalled coming across him sitting on a bench in Vienna's Volksgarten, scribbling. "What are you doing?" he was asked.

"I am creating," replied my father.

He was soon creating cabaret skits and musical comedies with titles like *At the Dentist, This Far and No Further* and *The Golden Garter.* They were typical copies of French farces, with their Gay Nineties naughtiness. He teamed up with a young actor and would-be writer named Julius Brammer, and they remained partners for most of their lives. This was the era of Franz Lehár's all-time hit operetta, *The Merry Widow*, which librettists and composers tried to emulate.

When Alfred Grunwald met my mother, her solidly bourgeois family looked down on him as an unserious show business type. He had more or less picked her up when she appeared in a charity theatrical. He went backstage and gallantly offered to show the beautiful, inexperienced ingenue how to remove her makeup. Romance prevailed over parental prejudice, and the wedding took place in 1908. Three years later Alfred was doing well enough to persuade the family that, perhaps, their Minna had picked a suitable husband after all. (That rather foursquare first name was changed, ultimately, to the more fashionable and graceful Mila.)

Throughout the war years, Lieutenant Grunwald managed to keep writing. He turned out patriotic songs, including one titled *"The Mother of the Reservist."* ("Good-bye, dearest Mother, it's time to go, but please don't cry—my Emperor needs me!" As Oscar Wilde said in a different context, it took a heart of stone not to laugh at these lines.) Later, an Austrian writer, Hilde Spiel, described how, "cheerful and insouciant, the young hussars and dragoons went to their deaths in the Ukraine and the Dolomite mountains," singing not martial tunes, like their German comrades, but hit songs from the latest operettas, among them my father's.

I realized later that some people regarded operettas, those innocent musical confections, as historical symptoms, illustrating an era's disastrous flight from reality. That was particularly true of the brilliant satirist Karl Kraus: "In a way he was right," said my father, who admired him. He sometimes read aloud from Kraus's savage, unperformable chronicle play, *The Last Days of Mankind.* In the opening scene, on the day the Austrian crown prince is assassinated and the war in effect begins, some typically indolent and stupid imperial officers chatter heedlessly about this and that, including the current operettas, among them a Grunwald hit.

WE MOVED FROM a modest flat in the building owned by my mother's parents to a spacious and quite splendid apartment near the Ringstrasse. My father had become something of a celebrity; classmates asked me to get them his autograph, and so did teachers—which, however, failed to improve my grades. By then he had written librettos for the best composers in the business. Some of his works had reached Broadway, among them *Countess Maritza,* with music by the great Hungarian Emmerich Kálmán. (Reviewing the opening night, *New York Times* critic Brooks Atkinson described it as "continuously enjoyable" and the libretto "statuesque," a somewhat ambiguous compliment; the more generous *Herald Tribune* reported wild audience enthusiasm for "a resonant, handsome, graceful operetta.")

To this day, I cannot watch one of his works without feeling a little embarrassment along with affection and admiration—especially for the often brilliant lyrics. The humor was broad and naive (for those in the gallery, whom my father, not without fondness, called "the animals"). The plots obeyed the rules of the "well-made play," involving conflict, surprise and resolution, and they were full of mistaken identities and lovers' misunderstandings that a five-year-old could have resolved in two bars.

My father had no illusions about operetta's romantic clichés. Describing the requisite dramatic clash between the leading man and leading lady, he once wrote: "Now everything takes on the aspect of a tragi-musical boxing match. The music rises to a thunderous furioso—this moment is particularly dreaded by the trombone players and the horns, and it is no laughing matter for the drummers either. . . ." His librettos reflected the times. There was the lingering power of class: the prince who falls in love with the commoner but must marry a princess for the sake of the dynasty. (Snobbery spoke from the very theater programs; even if a king or a duchess had only a bit part, he or she was nonetheless listed first in the cast of characters.) There was the prevailing sense of loss: the aristocratic officer fallen on hard times who now works for a living, preferably in picturesque disguise. Again and again, love and money. Sex was never crassly shown but was perfectly evident.

Mistresses and lovers were dancing close to the edge of respectability, husbands were seeking adventure, wives were seeking revenge. Several operettas romanticized and hymned the private rooms known in Viennese-French as *chambres séparées*, which even the most respectable restaurants maintained for obvious purposes.

Later I realized that these themes were also present in the serious literature of the period, notably in the works of Arthur Schnitzler and Hugo von Hofmannsthal, which are saturated with a sweet, somewhat corrupt eroticism and the pretensions of the new rich. Vienna has always had a split personality, split between gaiety and melancholy, charm and meanness. No one knew this better than Sigmund Freud.

It came as something of a revelation to me that Professor Freud and Countess Maritza were contemporaries. Even though I went to the same grade school as Freud's granddaughter Sophie—a dark-haired little girl with merry eyes on whom I had a crush—he belonged to a sphere entirely separate from my everyday world. The Vienna-born author Frederic Morton later made the connection when he somewhat flippantly wrote that the Vienna of the period made three lasting contributions to culture: psychoanalysis, operetta and anti-Semitism.

It contributed other things as well. In fin de siècle Vienna—a period that really lasted into the early twentieth century—much of "modernity" was taking shape. By and large the avant garde condemned the present and escaped into the future, while the purveyors of entertainment ignored the present and escaped into the past.

But they also escaped to America.

"The uncle from America" was a staple of innumerable comedies and melodramas, the humble emigrant who returns a rich man. Another standard figure was the American heiress, "the dollar princess." My father used that theme for *The Duchess of Chicago*. The daughter of a metals tycoon meets the dashing ruler of a small impoverished principality in central Europe, wants to buy his castle and ends up wanting to buy him, too. It gave a picture of America as loud, crass, turbulent, dynamic. "Can you imagine what's going on in Chicago?" went one of the lyrics, approximately. "Nothing but noise and tumult. . . . And even more so in New York. Electric signs with giant letters climbing up and down; skyscrapers, Salvation Army, negroes, Indians, millionaires, missionaries, self-made men, monkeys, movie stars. . . . And the only thing that matters is the dollar check. . . ."

The main theme was the conflict between old Viennese music and jazz, between old values and new—in short, as many saw it, between Europe and America.

·   ·   ·

Aʟʟ ᴛʜɪs ᴇxɪsᴛᴇᴅ in a region quite remote from my rather lonely, cushioned, protected—too protected—world dominated by Teta, my governess.

Her real name was Marianne Stefaner, and she came from peasant stock in Alto Adige (South Tirol). I was a year old and she was in her early twenties when she joined our household. She saved my life soon afterward. We were in our country place, and I was ill with diphtheria, but the local doctor failed to diagnose it. When I seemed in extremis Teta summoned a renowned pediatrician, and thanks to his intervention, I recovered.

His willingness to rush to my bedside at a ghastly hour, it was later suggested, was at least partly due to the fact that she was having an affair with him. If so, it wasn't her last. There was the case of our gardener and his jealous wife. Then there was an Air France pilot who took off rather hastily. Plainly Teta was not lucky in love. But she was fearless, assertive, domineering. She had a dramatic flair and would recount ordinary events—losing a pocketbook, putting a fresh store clerk in his place—with her head tossed back theatrically.

Teta cheerfully woke me in the morning and patiently supervised my going to bed, playing along with the precise ritual (including many "good night's" and "till tomorrow's") I had devised to banish my fear that sleep meant never waking up. She sang to me, lustily and unfailingly off-key; her favorite was the "Toreador Song" from *Carmen*, and I was astonished when I finally heard it sung correctly at the opera. She took me to the park, where she unfortunately kept most other children away from me, judging them too rough and rude.

She took her "Muggel" (an obscure nickname she bestowed on me) for long walks, along the shiny shopping streets in the inner city and the cobbled streets of other neighborhoods, where the outdoor markets, set up for the feast day of St. Peregrine, held heaps of simple toys and souvenirs and exotic, pungent spices, fruits and nuts. On another saint's day we would survey the traditional, ubiquitous figures of St. Nicholas and the Devil, known as Niccolo and Grampus, central characters in a legend that had something to do with rewarding good children and punishing the bad.

I remember my childhood Vienna best at dusk when, shivering, one felt good to be going home through the bluish white glare of street lamps. In winter the chestnut vendors were out in force. Teta built snowmen for me, and we drove out to the Danube to watch the crunching ice floes.

Teta filled a gap left by my parents and my sister, Meta, whom I loved very much but who was eleven years older than I. On Sundays there were sometimes family excursions to the park and zoo at Schönbrunn or some other attraction near Vienna, but mostly my parents were rather remote. I would come into their still-darkened bedroom every day to give them each a ritual good-morning kiss and pick up my pocket money from my mother's night table before going off to school. I saw them often, but briefly, at the midday meal. Evenings they were usually out, and I had my supper with Teta in the nursery. Among my greatest joys were the occasions when they appeared at home unexpectedly for an impromptu dinner, bringing cold cuts and friends.

THE HOUSEHOLD REVOLVED around my father, "the Master," as the servants called him. He was especially rough on the succession of cooks, all of whom he considered crazy—an occupational deformation, he insisted, owing to the heat in the kitchen. He was a gourmand and made pronouncements like "Viennese pancakes should be so thin that you can read the day's leading editorial through them." When a dish did not measure up, he would give the terrified maid a message for the cook: "Tell her she is fired!" The execution rarely took place. Still, the turnover in the kitchen was impressive. The poor cooks usually defended themselves by arguing that they could never serve a meal on time. When my father was working, not even the thought of food could make him stop. I often waited disconsolately in the dining room while my father, next door, was pounding away at the piano—shaking the whole apartment and the one below us as well—trying to finish a new lyric.

Admittedly, a love of food was one of the things that bound us together. Like many portly Viennese, my father sinned calorically all year and then atoned for two weeks at a spa—Karlsbad, in his case—where the diet was rigid and the purgative waters, known as *sproodle*, flowed relentlessly. Once, when I was very small, I complained that my father, a poet as I understood it, never wrote any "poesy" for me. Next thing I knew, a letter arrived from Karlsbad, which began:

Not one dumpling, not one noodle,
Not one Schnitzel and no Strudel,
Sproodle, sproodle, only *sproodle*
While the band goes toodle-doodle . . .

My mother was thin, which was only one of the many differences between my parents. My father was easygoing, careless of money and hearty, though in no sense vulgar. My mother was careful, frugal and set great store by refinement. They both liked cards, but while he played tarok, a lusty central European game for three players, she enjoyed gin rummy and bridge. He tended to the sybaritic, she to the puritanical. It was only after my father's death that my mother revealed the source of their deepest conflict.

Not long after they were married, he had an affair with an actress. When my mother found out, infuriated and desperately unhappy, she moved out with my sister; things were patched up with my father's predictable promise never to see the lady again—which, predictably, he did not keep. My usually reserved mother confronted the actress, wielding a riding crop and threatened to bash her face in unless she gave up my father. Women found him attractive and charming, and he himself once told a friend that he was not really cut out for marriage. Nonetheless the marriage endured. Plainly a rift remained. My mother was upset enough to become a patient of one of Freud's disciples. She hinted that she had intended to take revenge against my father in kind but was incapable of it because, as her analyst allegedly put it, she was "hereditarily afflicted with respectability."

As for my father, he showed no symptoms of guilt. But I believe that the recurring episodes of infidelity in his librettos, and in them also the failure of "respectable" women to understand the charms of actresses and the like, represented at least a small element of apology. He reacted forcefully when my mother was courted by a rich munitions magnate (who, after being turned down, later consoled himself by marrying the beauty who came to be known as Hedy Lamarr).

All this was typical of the prevailing attitudes about sex and marriage in Austria. Maintaining marriage was important; divorce was still rare, affairs commonplace. The double standard ruled. Vienna remained a place where sensuality was never far below the surface. I constantly heard gossip about who was linked with whom and which husband or lover had found out about it. Yet with extraordinary obtuseness, the grown-ups, including my parents, assumed that children did not understand or were not interested in such talk. I was very interested indeed, but I became embarrassed by the subject and for years was unable to talk about sex or girls with my parents.

I was timid around girls, partly because I was pudgy and awkward. But, on occasion, I could be aggressive. I attended an advanced coeducational grade school, where it was customary after class for boys and girls to pair up for the walk downstairs. This pairing business assumed high significance. Once, when the girl of my choice—her name was Hilde— preferred a competitor, I was so incensed that I slapped her face resoundingly. Hilde (who went on to become a distinguished concert pianist) complained to her mother, who complained to *my* mother, who complained to Teta. A cause célèbre. I must have been six or seven, and it was the last time, despite occasional temptation, that I ever slapped a woman.

My mother thought children sensitive, and she even censored the fairy tales she read me; in her version the Wolf never devoured Little Red Riding Hood's grandmother, and Hansel and Gretel never wound up in the oven. She obviously had no inkling that the very word "oven" would, in a few years, assume a fearsome significance.

My father's shoptalk about the theater soon became more intriguing to me than fairy tales: I heard about a whole cast of characters with quaint nicknames invented by my father and his friends.

The Highway Robber was a music publisher known for his sharp dealings, Blackfoot was a manager not known for his cleanliness. Mickey Louse was the diminutive wife of a writer. The Slovak, at the time an unflattering ethnic label, was the famous Franz Lehár, who was thought to be two-faced.

They all seemed like members of a very colorful family—my family. That was especially true of "Imre" Kálmán, with whom my father collaborated on four operettas beside *Maritza*, a man of dour, notoriously pessimistic personality and great business acumen, qualities that contrasted with his romantic melodies. The partnership eventually broke up in acrimony. But they later resumed their friendship.

The theater captivated me. I was incredibly excited the first time I saw the beam from a spotlight stretching through the darkness toward the stage. My father's openings were particularly exhilarating. They were always preceded by a little ceremony when my mother gave him a small gold or silver pig for good luck (eventually a whole herd covered his desk). We would arrive at the mysterious stage door (not like civilians!). Sitting in my father's usual box, I would feel quite self-important. A quick survey of the house ("the mayor is here"), after which my father would vanish backstage. The intolerable wait for the houselights to dim. The jumping of my pulse at the downbeat to the overture. Finally the faint, sighing breeze of the rising curtain. Then the suspense until the first laughs or applause, and anxiously measuring their intensity. Watching my father take his bow along with his collaborators and the cast. Nothing in the world could be more thrilling.

I decided that I would be a playwright like my father, and I started scribbling—notes, naive aphorisms, ideas for plots, fragmentary scenes. And always in secret. I was afraid of ridicule. When I was very young, my father decided to test my rhyming ability. He asked me to fill in the missing word in a simple couplet. In rough translation it went like this:

There's something stirring in the fog.
I think it is our roving _____

After due reflection, I exclaimed triumphantly: "Doggie!" The family then and there decided that they were not raising another librettist.

. . .

YEAR AFTER YEAR, come June, the household departed for our villa in Bad Ischl near Salzburg. My father did not drive ("gentleman drivers" were still a rarity and rather sneered at), but he was ensconced in the seat next to the chauffeur; he had a special button installed on his side of the dashboard and sounded the horn constantly. Amazingly, unlike our cooks, the chauffeur stayed.

Ischl, once the favorite resort of Emperor Franz Josef, was a sort of theatrical summer colony. Pianos resounded through open windows, arguments echoed along quiet mountain walks, as new scores were composed or old scores settled. The theater folk were strictly city types, and many were Jews, but all wore the local peasant costume—lederhosen, loden jackets with stag buttons, green hats with feathers.

I loved the long summers when the family was closer. I loved our house, with its balconies encased in elaborate wooden fretwork and multicolored glass panes, where bats were apt to swoop at dusk to the terror of the women. I loved my rather hot attic bedroom, where I woke each day to the clanging of the bell at the train crossing on the other side of the river. The nearby mountain walk with its huge, black split rock known as the Hermit (I knew I was growing up when I stopped being frightened by it). The long bike rides with stops to pick wild strawberries or sweet-smelling cyclamen.

Occasionally my parents would take me to Italy or Switzerland, where I acquired a love for luxury hotels. I would stare endlessly out of the windows of the big trains with their plush compartments, trying to hold a passing image—village, farmhouse, herd of cows—with the melancholy thought that I would probably never see that scene again.

Back in Vienna I found that my life was dominated by school, and school meant terror. This was no longer the progressive grade school that witnessed my angry passion for little Hilde. This institution, a secondary school, or "gymnasium," was a gray building on a street called Stubenbastei, with echoing stone corridors and stairways, always smelling of a mixture of disinfectant, urine and sweat.

Fear was the pedagogic principle, absolute authority the constitu-

tional philosophy, threats and insults from the teachers (called "professors") the preferred mode of expression. "You have nothing but cat shit
in your brains," was the almost jovial expression favored by the bearded
German master. I dreaded athletics and was clumsy. During dodge ball I
would hide behind larger pupils to avoid being hit by the ball.

The curriculum was rigid and limited. What the textbook called
"Most Recent Times" ended in the nineteenth century, and World War
I was not mentioned (although one instructor ranted about U.S. intervention: how American tanks had unfairly turned what surely would
have been a victory for Austria and her brave allies into a terrible
defeat). Learning was strictly rote: Virgil was memorized line by line,
algebra formulas absorbed without comprehension. It was not a bad
education. But it did nothing to stimulate independent thought.

IF PEOPLE THOUGHT that the war had brought about the end of the
world, well, the world was about to end again. On New Year's Eve, as
1937 turned into 1938, Teta and I and some friends—my parents were
out—gathered to play the "pouring lead" game. One would take some
pieces of lead—sold in the shape of shamrocks, horseshoes or other lucky
objects—and melt them over a candle. The molten lead would then be
poured into a basin of cold water, where it quickly congealed in odd new
forms. Those shapes foretold the future. Did a piece look like a money
bag? That could mean riches ahead. But no, someone would argue, that
really wasn't a money bag; it was a cloud, and that meant a very rainy
year. That night I fished a twisted, spiky object out of the basin. We all
looked at it in puzzlement. Teta picked it up and examined it with
growing disgust.

"It's a swastika," she said.

CHAPTER TWO

I FIRST SAW A SWASTIKA in the kitchen of our country house, with the cook of the moment, Teta and Rudolf, the chauffeur. He took a newspaper, folded it several times, then seized a pair of scissors and started cutting into it this way and that. Suddenly Rudolf unfolded the paper and, presto, it opened up into a strange cross whose four arms ended in hooks. Laughter from the cook, indignant tut-tutting from Teta. I had no idea what a swastika was, but I thought the trick was great.

Some months later, walking with my parents, I grabbed a stick and drew on the gravel-covered ground an uncertain version of the symbol Rudolf had produced in the kitchen. My father exploded. Where and how had I learned about this? Who was responsible? How could Teta have failed to shield me from such a thing? He carried on as if I, his innocent little son, had been exposed to some obscenity.

Which, of course, I had been.

In the next few years the swastika became ubiquitous in Austria, and there was no shielding anyone from it. It appeared on walls and fences, on mountainsides, on pamphlets and posters, and eventually on the armbands of Austrian Storm Troopers, representing the local branch of Hitler's Nazi Party. Adolf Hitler, native son of Austria, came to power in

Germany in 1933. For a while he was only a vaguely disturbing name that kept coming up in the grown-ups' conversation. They called him Pemstel, slang for "brush," meaning that his mustache resembled an implement to clean toilets with. My father and his friends delighted in imitating his ranting speeches. The jokes were a defense against the horror that lay behind his words.

Soon one paid less attention to what Hitler said than to his voice, somewhere between a screech and a bellow. I heard him only on the radio or in newsreels, but I have never since experienced anything like the interaction between that voice and the sound of the crowds at his rallies, their overwhelming, abandoned scream, resembling no known human sound. It was like a vast roar from a single huge throat, blood beating behind the vocal cords, a rising vomit of rage, hate turned into joy.

Hate, mostly, of the Jews.

IT WAS SOME time before I felt that hate as a direct menace, because it took time before I understood my Jewish identity.

Ours was not an Orthodox or even a seriously Jewish household. My mother's parents had been traditional in their observance, and she clung to this for a while, but my father never cared for religion. Early on they would go to the synagogue on Yom Kippur, with my father wearing a black homburg. Eventually they stopped going, although my mother continued to fast on the Day of Atonement for the rest of her life.

She was the arbiter of faith and morals in our family, and she had a rather unconventional approach to Judaism. We did not eat kosher food, because my mother believed that the dietary laws had been conceived in primitive times. A bronze menorah stood unused and, for a long time, unexplained to me. On the other hand, Easter eggs were elaborately colored, and there was always a vast Christmas tree with candles and sparklers, not to mention presents. She never considered herself anything but a Jew, but she often pronounced, with a slightly superior smile: "There is only one religion, and that is to be good."

Even as a child I sensed that, theologically, this was rather thin.

. . .

Mʏ ꜰɪʀꜱᴛ ɪɴᴛʀᴏᴅᴜᴄᴛɪᴏɴ to any religion came from Teta, who taught me my first prayer, an abbreviated version of "Now I lay me down to sleep." On our walks she would often take me to St. Stephen's Cathedral, whose black bulk frightened me, and to her favorite church, not far from our apartment, where she would light a candle or say a brief prayer. I was put off by the bloody figure of Christ over the altar, but I liked the incense, the soft music, the solemn hush that came to define a house of worship. I was indignant when I was taken to a synagogue, where people talked noisily, prayed loudly and not in unison, kept moving about—and where the men wore hats, which seemed very disrespectful.

My formal introduction to the Old Testament began in first grade, when a teacher told us about the Bible. When she recounted the story of how Adam and Eve were driven out of the Garden of Eden, I burst into tears. I was inconsolable and, at the same time, dimly ashamed. In hindsight it seems that my reaction was entirely appropriate.

Religious education became more rigorous in high school. Twice a week our class was divided into three groups—Catholics, Protestants and Jews—for separate instruction. We Jews received the rudiments of Hebrew and the Torah from a zealous young rabbi. We were taken to the synagogue on Fridays, where, I fear, we made rude remarks about the cantor's voice and even munched sausage rolls. The place was Vienna's eighteenth-century Seitenstetten Synagogue, which was destroyed by the Nazis but has since been restored: a graceful, embracing oval under a sky blue ceiling studded with gold stars. There, after much drilling, I eventually was bar mitzvahed.

Apart from teachers or rabbis, I absorbed Judaism from "Uncle" Alex. He was one of my father's closest friends, a virtually constant presence in the household. Alexander Grünfeld was an officer in a large bank, the Creditanstalt, and was addicted to music and the theater. At almost any time he might burst into a hit tune, an aria or a few bars of a symphony, waving his arms as if to conduct.

He was something of a resident jester. If I said I was bored, which was often, he would declare in mock annoyance, "Well, I'll order up a military band for you." He used many Yiddish expressions and gave me an inkling of what I considered a strange corruption of German. Some of Alex's favorite and wonderfully sonorous words still come to mind— *mishpokhe* (relations), *metsíye* (bargain), *gevúre* (strength) and above all, *nebbish* (a hapless person).

As with so many Jews, Jewishness meant more—and less—to him than ritual and the Law. He was a passionate supporter of Zionism and gave me my first knowledge of Theodor Herzl's vision and the seemingly quixotic movement that eventually became Israel. He proudly showed me books and articles depicting the sleek modern structures of Tel Aviv and the orange groves that bloomed where there had been only desert. Alex was eloquent about how the dispersed and persecuted Jews would finally have their own homeland again, their own state and army. In those days, even among Jews, the thought of a Jewish army still evoked snickers and jokes. (Jewish sergeant issues commands in a low whisper. Officer: "How do you expect your men to obey an order they can't even hear?" Sergeant: "Don't worry, word gets around.")

Listening to Alex and dimly aware of the Nazis not far over the horizon, I shared his enthusiasm. Above all I began to learn something essential about the nature of Judaism.

Most Viennese Jews believed that Judaism was simply a religious denomination—like Protestantism, say—and if one behaved decently, one could live in peace and dignity in Austria or most other places. Later I came to understand that Judaism is *not* like other religions, that it is a unique, mysterious mixture of faith, culture and nationality, elements that cannot be unscrambled.

An amazing number of Viennese Jews, my parents included, accepted the stereotypes the Christian world had imposed. Jews were not supposed to be good at sports (although Vienna had an excellent Jewish soccer team). Things like riding and hunting and mountain climbing were what some called *goyim naches,* or pleasures for Christians. This attitude was an unconscious form of Jewish anti-Semitism.

Anti-Semitism was a familiar plague in Austria. It was based on deep-seated attitudes in the church, on the sheer isolation and ignorance of the peasants, on envy and a false sense of superiority among the petit bourgeois. The more cosmopolitan Habsburg rulers and the aristocrats had been relatively tolerant of the Jews, who grew prosperous and influential during the half century before World War I. There was a certain Austrian laxness even among the most vocal anti-Semites like Karl Lueger, the vastly popular mayor of Vienna from 1896 to 1910. He was given to making "exceptions"; "*I* decide who is a Jew and who isn't" was one of his famous sayings.

One was never for a moment unconscious of being Jewish or of who else was or wasn't. But most Viennese Jews believed in outward assimilation. Among other things this meant not giving offense by exotic dress, or alien accents, or overly ostentatious living—in short, not drawing too much attention to oneself. If there was news of someone's being involved in a scandal or a crime, my parents or one of their friends would say, "Thank God it wasn't a Jew."

That attitude went together with snobbery. Jews who gloried in the German language and culture, devotees of Goethe and Wagner, looked down on "Eastern Jews," the more recent arrivals from Russia and Poland, especially those who wore long earlocks and had heavy accents. It was those Jews, the theory went, who really caused anti-Semitism, not we respectable and, yes, refined ones. This in effect meant accepting the cliché uttered by so many anti-Semites: "Ah, but if only all Jews were like *you.* . . ."

Hitler put an end to that snobbery. The readers of Goethe and the speakers of Yiddish, the well-tailored bankers and the caftaned peddlers, the discreet ones and the loud and ostentatious ones—they were all equal in the gas chambers.

ALEX SENSED THIS, before any of us knew about the gas chambers. We did learn about the treatment of Jews in Hitler's Germany: their almost total exclusion from normal life and work, the confiscations, harassment by Gestapo and Storm Troopers, pogroms, "protective custody" and the first concentration camps. All this led to an abiding hatred of the Nazis. When word came of the explosion of the German dirigible

Hindenburg in New Jersey, my first reaction was glee at a German misfortune—until my parents reminded me, to my shame, that many innocent lives had been lost.

We were mostly preoccupied with the Depression. My father's plays were no longer performed on the once lucrative German stages. Economy measures, hardly draconian, were instituted in the family, such as getting a more modest car (a Renault replacing a Minerva, a huge luxurious oddity of Belgian make). My mother decided that times were too serious for me to be sent to dancing school, a venerable institution called Ellmayr. I pretended not to mind, but I did, a lot. My mother further thought that I had best look toward a really practical profession or trade, something that would always be needed—like plumbing supplies. Since I made a strict secret of my writing ambitions, I could not really blame her.

The Depression contributed to the move toward Anschluss, the joining of Austria with Germany. Even many anti-Nazis felt that it was the only solution to the problems of a small country that did not seem economically viable. Moreover, the anti-Nazi forces were divided. Many of the conservative "Blacks" had no use for Hitler but also loathed and feared the "Reds." They, in turn, were violently anti-Hitler but also deeply hostile toward the "Blacks." Parliament seemed paralyzed, and after a brief but bitter civil war, the conservatives seized the government and established a dictatorship, aiming to fight the Nazi fire with fire (of an admittedly lesser intensity). They tried to counter German nationalism with rhetoric about Austria as a German country, the Nazi Party with a movement called Fatherland Front, the Storm Troopers with a patriotic militia, the Home Guard, and the swastika with a cross of slightly different shape. The Austrian Nazi Party was outlawed, but the Socialists were also purged from public life, losing the government any chance of support from the workers.

The underground Nazis waged a slow terror campaign, culminating in the assassination of the Austrian chancellor, Engelbert Dollfuss, in 1934, and Hitler kept leaning mercilessly on the government in Vienna. A handful of Jews recognized the inevitable and got out. Most did not. Later on their passivity seemed incomprehensible, but, after all, Austria was their home; many, like my father, had fought for it in World War I. Besides, they still hoped the Western nations would somehow stop Hitler.

But of all the big powers, only the Soviet Union was unequivocally against Hitler. My father found solace listening to Radio Moscow and came away humming revolutionary songs played after the news broadcasts ("Come join the United Workers Front, for you are a worker, too!"), even though he was not remotely sympathetic to Communism.

Many thought that Hitler might eventually moderate his anti-Semitism. My father insisted on following his usual routine. He kept turning out operettas—simpler and less melodramatic to keep up with changing tastes, but still full of sentimentality about dear old Vienna. He also continued to write drama criticism. His last review of a serious play was published less than two months before the Nazi takeover. The play was *The Unknown Soldier* by Jean Giraudoux, a pacifist fantasy that, my father wrote bitterly, was being overtaken by harsh reality.

Shortly before eight P.M. on March 11, 1938, Chancellor Kurt von Schuschnigg went on the air to announce that he did not wish to shed "German blood" and that, "yielding to force," Austria would not resist the German army. After his final words, "God protect Austria," the lovely old Austrian anthem was heard over the radio. The Germans had used the same Haydn melody for *their* anthem, "Deutschland Über Alles," and as I listened to the music, I wondered: Is this still the Austrian anthem or already the German one?

My family and I heard this speech in stunned silence. My father said, "I didn't believe it would come to this. I still can't believe it. If only I had decided to get out. . . ." In the months and years ahead, "if only" would become a nagging, nearly intolerable refrain.

My mother said tearfully, "Oh God, what will become of us now?"

True to the code of my fifteen-year-old self, I remained stoic. Then I went into the kitchen to get a drink of water, and over the sink I started to cry. Teta was not sympathetic.

"In there you act brave," she said harshly, "and then you come out here to cry. Stop it."

I stopped. Our lives changed completely from that moment on, and so did I.

IN THIS ERA before television, the images of Hitler addressing the cheering crowds in Vienna's Heldenplatz, of the German personnel carriers rolling along the Ringstrasse, were, for us, only blurry newspaper photographs because we did not venture out.

We did watch the jubilant Austrian Storm Troopers with their red-and-black swastika banners move through our street. But the horror advanced not in marching jackboots, but with smaller, more insidious steps. The suddenly changed attitude of the concierge, the shopkeepers, the teachers, ranging from fake and forced solicitude to open contempt. The knowledge that Jews were being beaten up by Nazi bands. The fearful whispered reports about "Aryanization" of Jewish firms, meaning their takeover by non-Jews.

Our maid, Rosa, had watched Hitler's triumphal entry and reported that he was "a beautiful man." Teta almost strangled her. "Beautiful!" she screamed. "You silly goose!" And one evening Rudolf—the man who had taught me about automobiles and built model airplanes—appeared in the apartment, flushed with excitement, wearing a swastika armband. I suddenly felt a sense of distance, of otherness. Hearing that someone is a murderer or a madman has never given me the same sensation as when I learned that someone was a Nazi. They were a separate species.

I awoke in the mornings with the instant feeling that something was terribly, irreparably wrong, a dread that took hold before thought—the same feeling I would experience later after the death of someone I loved.

The danger of denunciation and betrayal was everywhere. People were arrested simply for discussing politics or saying something critical against the regime. Even at home we quickly fell into the habit of whispering or speaking in some absurd code. ("I wonder whether Uncle really managed to join Cousin So-and-so for his birthday party," which could refer to someone trying to get out of Austria or to a couple of foreign, anti-Nazi statesmen rumored to be meeting.)

Although my father was not a political figure, as a prominent Jew he could not be left alone. Two raincoated Gestapo agents appeared one day, and as my father ushered them into his study, he observed, "Feel free to look around, gentlemen. I have already destroyed anything suspicious." The remark was prompted by nervousness, not by sardonic humor. In due course he was summoned to Gestapo headquarters. For hours the household waited for news. I sat motionless, my arms, feeling at once hollow and leaden, pinned to my desk chair.

Eventually word came that he had been put under arrest along with a great many other well-known Jews. He was held in a high school gym that had been converted into a temporary prison. A lifetime later, when I was editor in chief of Time Inc., I hosted one of our usual lunches for prominent visitors. The guest was Bruno Kreisky, the Socialist chancellor of Austria, the country's outstanding political leader of the postwar period. When he was told by an aide who my father was, his voice suddenly rang across the dining room: "I was once in jail with Alfred Grunwald." For the startled audience he added, "Things were crowded, and there were two prisoners to each mattress. His father was a nice fellow, but I wish he had been thinner."

My father was sustained by daily visits from my mother, bearing a food basket, but his nourishment was the least of our worries. We were constantly afraid that he might be moved to a concentration camp.

In the meantime, I had been thrown out of my school. The new Nazi principal announced—without embarrassment, without hostility—that all Jewish students were to attend a separate school in Vienna's former Jewish ghetto. A few of our non-Jewish fellow students were indignant, but quietly; most were indifferent. The new school was crowded and disorganized, and there was little useful instruction from professors who resented having been picked to teach in the "Jew school." I persuaded my mother to let me drop out.

Even terrible times can be boring. I was bored. I did not go out much, and when I did I was usually accompanied by Teta, who by then was no longer my governess but a special housekeeper. She vowed fiercely to protect me from any Nazi bullies we might encounter.

I listened to the radio, which endlessly echoed martial music, and I read the papers, which were full of boastful rhetoric, hate-filled polemics and obvious lies uttered with a fat, infuriating conviction that gave me a permanent flesh-crawling aversion to propaganda. But I was both repelled and fascinated by a Nazi magazine for young people that occasionally drifted into the house; I sensed the insidious appeal the cause had for so many, the seduction of comradeship and regimentation and soldier playing. Would I have fallen for this appeal myself if I had not been Jewish? I don't believe so, but I cannot be sure.

For the most part, my closest friend, Bruno Zwerling, and a few other chums and I talked about politics and girls, two subjects about which we knew very little. We were eager to be diverted. Bruno reported that a neighbor in his apartment building, a lawyer, had been taken away by the Nazis and that his office had been left open and unattended. We sneaked into that office a few times, reading files about cases we did not understand, looking through personal mail and photos. We felt mildly guilty, trespassing on a life that was probably in jeopardy. But we were oddly fascinated, especially when we found, to our uncomprehending amazement, a shoebox containing a dildo.

All over Vienna, we realized dimly, there were countless such interrupted lives, big and small secrets broken open, possessions pawed over and looted—not by curious boys, but by grown men suddenly drunk with the knowledge that they could do anything they wanted.

My MOTHER HIRED a Nazi lawyer—that was still possible, if the fee was right—called Braun-Stammfest, the sort of name Dickens might have chosen. My father was eventually released from jail. But now we faced the next problem: getting out of the larger jail that Austria had become.

A new word began to dominate our lives: visa. The word signified escape, survival, safety. The search for countries willing to accept refugees from the Nazis became increasingly desperate. Crowds besieged Vienna's foreign embassies and consulates, especially that of the United States. But American visas were hard to obtain—there were limited regional quotas, plus the need for guarantees from U.S. citizens that the immigrants would not become public charges. My father thought that America was too far away, too strange.

Other possible destinations were even farther away, even stranger. What to do in Argentina or Bolivia or other hazily known or imagined places? My mother and sister spoke seriously about learning Spanish and opening a beauty salon "over there," acting out for me their putative roles as beautician and assistant.

In the end my sister and her husband, who was an industrial chemist and had worked in his father's factory, were able, much less exotically, to get to the Netherlands, where he had found a job. For my parents and myself, visas for Czechoslovakia and France became available, mostly because my father had some connections in the theater crowds of Prague and Paris.

But being allowed *in* somewhere was only slightly more difficult than being allowed *out.* The price was, in effect, the forfeiture of one's property. This involved an interminable bureaucratic process of proving what one owned, or didn't own, and of calculating what it was worth, all of which was designed simply to squeeze out as much as could be squeezed.

My father went into a deep depression as the reality sank in that he was about to be driven out of a city in which many of his lyrics had attained the status of folksongs. He also brooded about having to give up his apartment. "I can't get it through my head," he would complain, "that I have to leave my beautiful bathroom." That bathroom! Its walls covered with red brocade, gleaming with mirrors and chrome, it seemed to my father the peak of luxury, the symbol of his rise from modest circumstances.

I suddenly took part in conversations and judgments that had been strictly the province of adults. Released from silence, I became brash and considered myself the only realist in the family. Once, when my father made what seemed a particularly futile argument, "if only . . ." I called him a fool, a moment that was to haunt me for years.

At long last the bureaucratic torturers were satisfied, all documents were stamped, all approvals given, all our property seized—except our clothes and, strangely, our furniture, which we were allowed eventually to ship abroad. My mother held on to some jewelry, which she quietly turned over to Teta.

But there was a last minute hitch, and my parents decided that I had better go ahead alone. So, one day in August 1938, I made my way to the railway station (not the Western, which I once thought could take me to America, but the Eastern). I boarded a train for Czechoslovakia, where Alex would wait for me in his native town of Brno, a few hours from Vienna.

It was a moment to think about what I was leaving behind—the places where I grew up, the nursery, the playgrounds, the friends, the secret dreams and rituals of childhood, childhood itself. I felt intensely alone, with my parents back in Vienna, expecting to follow in a couple of weeks—but who could be sure? I worried about whether I would manage to make the right connection at the border. I remember crossing a maze of rail sidings and passageways, lugging my suitcase, confusion approaching panic, until, at the last minute, I was pointed toward my train by a railroad worker to whom I had desperately stammered out the only Czech words I knew: *"Prosim, pane* [please, sir], *Brno?"*

These prosaic words were my farewell to Austria.

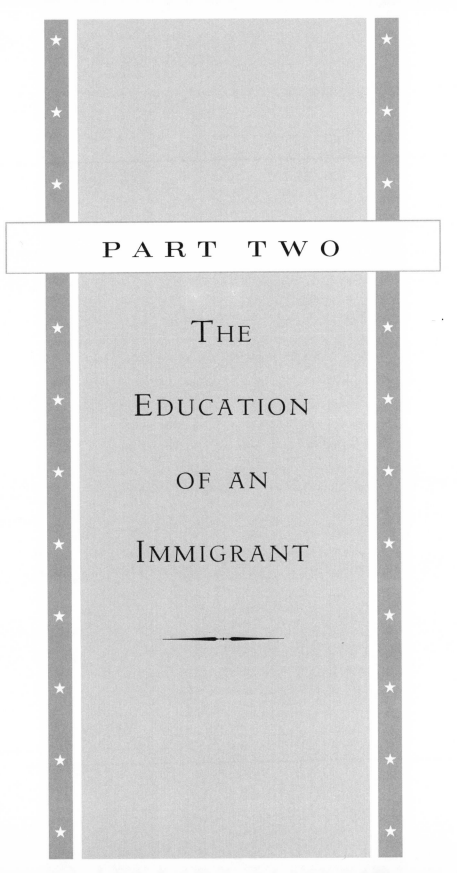

PART TWO

THE
EDUCATION
OF AN
IMMIGRANT

CHAPTER THREE

M‍Y PARENTS EVENTUALLY DID GET OUT of Vienna and joined me in Czechoslovakia, a proud democracy that still looked wealthy and comfortable on the surface, even though it was already threatened by Hitler.

We felt wonderfully liberated in Czechoslovakia. It was extraordinary, after months of fearful whispering, to be able to speak freely anytime, anywhere. Yet despite our relief at being there—we were staying with distant relatives—we knew we now were homeless.

Unexpectedly one day, Teta arrived. Dramatically she held open her coat and pointed to the lining: she had sewn into it some of the jewels she had been given by my mother, who now tried on her diamond engagement ring. She seemed amazed, puzzled, as if she had found something she didn't quite recognize. (Today the ring belongs to my daughter-in-law, Rebecca Rasmussen, to whom its provenance is fascinating.)

Teta had taken a serious risk, and when she returned to Vienna the Gestapo, perhaps tipped by an informer, gave her a hard time. But she admitted nothing and was eventually left alone. "These idiots," she told me years later, "they didn't know who they were dealing with."

After a few weeks in Czechoslovakia we moved on to France, where we felt safer from the Nazis. During two years in Paris I learned French,

I learned at least something about the soul of the city, and I learned how to be a refugee. The last was by far the most important.

My father had a very small amount of money outside Austria—in Switzerland, of course, the sort of emergency nest egg that most Europeans of any means tried to keep there; my father's, I was told, took the picturesque form of American Gold Eagles. But he was reluctant to touch that resource, so we relied mostly on what few royalties were still coming in from performances of his works in Europe, outside the Nazi domain. We just managed to get by. Still, we were true refugees: uprooted, insecure, tolerated but not welcome, at the mercy of the "authorities."

The first rule for the refugee is to accept that condition. The second is to do everything in one's power to acquire some legal, stamped piece of paper; I have rarely felt such intense joy and relief as when, after much maneuvering and petitioning, the police finally sent us our little green *cartes d'identité*, confirming not only our identity but our right to exist. Other lessons are to stay unencumbered by too many possessions (we would ignore this, to our regret) and to be inconspicuous.

The French were not enamored of Jews, and they loathed the sound of German. Intensely aware of this, I would feel hotly embarrassed when I sat in some sidewalk café on the Champs-Elysées—the Colisée or the Marignan—while my parents and their friends would converse in loud, usually agitated German, drawing glances from the passersby.

This gave me an additional incentive to learn French. I enrolled in the admirable institution the Alliance Française, where I nearly mastered the relentlessly logical but insanely intricate laws of French grammar. I also fell—silently—in love with an English beauty in my class named Jean Moncrieff, whose looks anticipated Grace Kelly's.

Yet somehow the routine of daily life in our small furnished apartment in Passy, a modest middle-class neighborhood, created a faint illusion of being at home. Living in very close quarters, the pressures of refugee existence, the uncertain future, enervated my parents and made them irritable. There were many bitter fights over what struck me as trivialities. Their quarrels sometimes upset me to the point of tears;

invariably blaming his wife, my father would shout: "Now see what you have done to the child!" These episodes reinforced my apparently inborn dread of confrontations.

But Paris offered compensations. Shopping for baguettes and crème fraîche, raiding the lending library for the latest Simenon, and traveling about on the métro, I discovered the bourgeois, sybaritic city, cynical and often mean beneath its beauty. I loved it (how could one not?) and refused to believe what my elders whispered about the decadence of the French Establishment—this minister drunk after eleven every morning, that leading editor on the payroll of some industry or, worse, some foreign government.

Then came the Munich meeting where French premier Édouard Daladier joined Neville Chamberlain in delivering Czechoslovakia to Hitler.

If the First World War was caused by arrogance, almost by boredom with peace, the Second was caused by cowardice, by the failure of France and Britain—and the United States—to face down Hitler. I would eagerly search the French and international press for strong anti-Hitler, antiappeasement editorials or speeches and read them aloud at the dinner table. The radio, too, brought some encouragement, especially anti-Nazi broadcasts beamed at Germany. (Announcer: "Good night, *mein Führer*. . . . And if you have trouble sleeping, why don't you try counting . . . counting the countries you invaded, the peoples you suppressed, the men and women and children you murdered. . . .")

Germany invaded Poland on September 1, and two days later France and Britain declared war on Germany. At first it was almost an anticlimax, what came to be known as the phony war, the massed Allied and Nazi armies facing each other without moving. Back in Paris there were few signs of war, despite mobilization and occasional air raid alerts (in the cellar below our apartment, the building's owner appeared in silk dressing gown and ascot, receiving the sleepy, rumpled tenants like a perfect host). Ignoring the lesson about not accumulating material possessions, my parents had rented a flat and crammed it full of the furniture that had arrived from Vienna.

I continued to pursue my secret passion for writing, scribbling constantly in a notebook or pounding away on my cherished typewriter.

My father, meanwhile, was dreaming of Hollywood. For him, as for most other émigré writers, Hollywood was El Dorado, even though they had sneered at the film business. Through some spurious grapevine, mostly imaginary reports would reach the émigré cafés—Frank Capra was looking for a script, James Stewart needed a new part—and the writers would go back to their cheap flats to rummage through their trunks and brains for something marketable. They seldom, if ever, found it. America was becoming the ultimate hope, the supreme refuge.

My father had changed his mind about it being too strange and had cast about for contacts in the United States. He decided to try to reach the legendary J.J. Shubert, who, with his brother, Lee, owned or controlled about two-thirds of the theaters in New York and was, as one of my father's titles might have put it, the King of Broadway. He liked Viennese operettas and had successfully produced several of my father's. Couldn't J.J., my father now wrote in a letter to him, use Alfred Grunwald as an adviser for operetta productions? Shubert replied that he failed to see "how you could fit into a proposition here in America." Tastes had changed. "I know you are having a hard time there, but it would be hopeless and impossible to try and relieve the situation of so many unfortunate people."

Two or three other, similar rejections showed how difficult it would be to get the guarantees of support required for a visa. Even with such guarantees, under the quota system the waiting list appeared endless. The magnificent American embassy near the Place de la Concorde seemed unapproachable, as if surrounded by invisible rays.

But, tantalizingly, American music and artifacts and advertisements were everywhere. Someone gave me a Coca-Cola pocket calendar bearing the picture of a slightly plump, sexy American girl, sitting on a rock; the object became a talisman for me and the girl a sort of American Lorelei.

In a more serious vein my father read me a poem by Goethe that expressed Europe's early idealization of America (in rhymes I will not try to render in English):

America, you're better off
Than this old continent of ours,
You have no ruined castles,
And no ancient basalts.
You are not disturbed in your innermost self,
By useless remembrance
And pointless strife.

I had started to learn English as a child, my first teacher being a cousin of my father's, a round, radiantly sweet little woman who gave rather inadequate lessons for a living.

In Paris my tutor was an Englishwoman of considerably more authority. Mrs. Livingstone chose *Gone With the Wind* as our textbook. The opening line ("Scarlett O'Hara was not beautiful . . .") remained lodged in my mind. The novel gave me my first simple information about the Civil War, with a certain bias toward the South that would take me some time to adjust.

I looked for America in Hollywood movies. They showed a mechanized, rather frantic country, not so much romantic as sentimental, often extolling goodness but also (in the gangster melodramas) glamorizing evil. Their most important message came through their style and their humor. These traits were epitomized by the screwball comedies of the thirties and by the Fred Astaire–Ginger Rogers movies. For years in my imagination, New York was Fred and Ginger gliding across the glittering roofs of skyscrapers, in a city as young, as ageless, as they.

And there was in American movies a bantering, good-humored irreverence that implied a special ease, between men and women, bosses and employees, politicians and voters—the shrug of equality in the face of hierarchy, the great American grin of freedom in the face of authority.

THE FRENCH GOVERNMENT declared all German and Austrian nationals to be enemy aliens, refugees included. All males over the age of sixteen must be interned.

My father went off to an internment camp at Bourg-Lastic in the

Auvergne. He didn't have a bad time of it, worked on a camp revue with other theatrical inmates and was released after a few weeks through the intervention of French friends. But I would soon be old enough to be interned as well, and we were afraid that I would be trapped in a camp if the Germans advanced. Our faith in the impregnability of France's famed defense fortifications, the Maginot Line, was beginning to waver.

My mother hit on a stratagem. She found a private clinic for nervous disorders whose head was willing to help out by admitting me as a patient. For the sake of the staff I tried to play my part, walking through the garden, looking melancholy—I hoped—and occasionally talking to myself and gesticulating wildly. I recognized that I must have been pretty unconvincing when I witnessed the real thing. I had observed a dark-haired young man with an angelic face who had carried on—and I was a little jealous—an obvious romance with a beautiful fellow patient. Suddenly one day he fell down, started pounding the ground with his fists and kept screaming, "Ah the women . . . the women and the little children . . . they are killing them . . . the women, the children . . ."

In those days I saw everything as a potential play or movie, so I developed a plot. Fellow hides in asylum, feigning mental illness. Gradually begins to feel comfortable in the place and comes to prefer it to horrible world outside. When it's time for him to leave, he refuses, throwing insane fit. Audience never knows whether he is faking in order to stay in or whether he's really gone crazy. . . .

I never tried to write it. I left the place, by walking out when it became clear that the authorities had more urgent worries than enemy aliens.

On May 10, 1940, the Germans began to turn the Maginot Line through the simple expedient of crashing through neutral Belgium and the Netherlands. That evening a friend, the son of a well-known Viennese composer and collaborator of my father's, phoned as we were at dinner in our Paris apartment to say that he and his wife were getting out of the city, by car. Would we like to come along? Without preparation, even without much discussion, my parents and I got up from dinner, left the dishes on the table, left everything else except for a couple of small bags (and my typewriter and a part of my stamp collection, which I insisted on taking along). Then we walked out of the apartment. We piled into our friend's car, a small Peugeot, and headed south, away from the German armies.

We drove along jammed highways and across countless roadblocks. Standing guard at one of them, an elderly policeman examined our documents and became suspicious of our alien birthplaces. There ensued a bizarre scene as my father and his friend, standing on a war-choked highway with the smell of panic in the air, began crooning one of my father's songs—a waltz—in order somehow to anchor our identity in the international community of art. *"Ah,"* said the policeman after a few bars, *"je me souviens qu'on aimait danser à cette musique-là"* ("I remember we used to like to dance to that tune"), and waved us through with a broad smile.

As we continued south we kept hearing reports of the seemingly impossible: the much vaunted, supposedly proud French army had ignominiously collapsed.

After five days and nights, during which we slept in barns, fields or on the roadside, we arrived in Biarritz, its resort palaces and every other conceivable form of lodging overrun with refugees. Many carried beautiful leather suitcases with the colorful stickers of luxury hotels; now this luggage had somehow begun to look shabby.

We kept slipping into cocktail lounges frequented by foreign diplomats. Some of those diplomats proved to be benignly corrupt. A Portuguese second or third secretary was willing to sell, not entire visas—that was too dangerous—but at least the imprint of the embassy seal, which, after payment of a steep bribe, was furtively stamped into our passports.

My father and I traveled to a remote part of town and in a toy shop bought a child's printing set. Back in our rented room, having locked the door and posted my mother as a lookout, we carefully set up in rubber type the wording of a real Portuguese visa, copied from one that had been obtained by a lucky friend. We then printed the text above the stamp, and my father, after dozens of practice runs, copied the official signatures with considerable flourish.

We were hoping to use the forged visas to get to Lisbon via Spain (as it turned out, Spain closed its border and crossing the Pyrenees illegally on foot was an alternative the unathletic Grunwalds rejected).

Next we tried to exit by sea. A hundred-odd frightened, querulous fellow refugees had gathered under a crane in the harbor, imperfectly sheltered from the rain. Someone noticed that I was carrying a typewriter, and I was drafted to write a petition to the port commander to let us go aboard the last freighter (". . . last hope . . . our fate is in your hands . . ."). Finally we got aboard the *Cap Figalo,* no thanks to my eloquence, but because my father waved some franc notes in the right direction.

We spent the nights in the hold of the freighter, bound for Morocco, surrounded by people moaning, vomiting, crying out in their nightmares or merely chattering ceaselessly. I tried to silence some particularly noisy fellow passengers by shouting, *"Ta gueule!"* ("Shut your face!")—a vulgarism that bothered my parents more than the hard planks on which they were trying to sleep.

When I saw the movie *Casablanca* some years later, with its aura of adventurous romance, I could not identify it with the rather prosaic place where we landed.

As we waited for some chance to get to the United States a consuming worry was the fate of my sister and brother-in-law. Having moved to the Netherlands, they were trapped by the advancing Germans. We abruptly stopped hearing from them, knew nothing of their whereabouts and had no idea whether they were alive or dead.

Eventually we worked the miracle of a visitor's visa to Canada and, on the strength of that, transit visa number 86 to America. The American consul who issued it was a tall, gangling man named Willard Quincy Stanton, who shocked me by putting his feet on his desk. To him I shall be forever grateful.

We reached Lisbon and there managed to get a booking on the USS *Exeter,* due to sail in mid-September to New York.

I watched from an upper deck as she slowly pulled away from her moorings. I focused on the widening strip of blue water between ship and shore, thinking, I must remember this sight. That shore—it's Europe receding, I am leaving Europe.

The *Exeter* was compact, sleek, beautiful, all wood paneling and brass and soft pastel carpets. To accommodate extra passengers, mostly refugees, one of the dining rooms had been fitted out with cots. But my parents and I actually had a tiny cabin to ourselves. Once we were even invited to the captain's table, where I sat next to a blue-haired lady who said she came from Massachusetts, a word I thought I would never be able to pronounce.

By way of homework I read a book, *États-Unis 39*, a rather hasty but engaging journal of a U.S. tour by the distinguished French writer André Maurois. He reported on the glories of griddle cakes and relishes, on barbers costumed like operetta figures, on Major Bowes's *Amateur Hour*, the immensely popular radio program that to Maurois represented the embodiment of the American Cinderella myth.

The book showed me, tantalizingly, how little I knew about the strange country we were approaching.

Finally came the moment when, sailing into New York Harbor, we saw the Statue of Liberty, that great cast-iron cliché, a sight no less moving because I expected to be moved. Someone recited the inscription, the famous Emma Lazarus poem ("The wretched refuse of your teeming shore . . ."). My English was not nearly good enough then for me to realize that it is quite condescending and quite bad poetry.

As we were about to dock I thought we should tip the steward, and my parents instructed me, frugally, to give him a dollar. "We don't take dollar tips," said the steward icily. It seemed to me an unfortunate note on which to arrive, but the embarrassment was quickly neutralized by the excitement of seeing the Manhattan skyline. It was unbelievable, slightly frightening, oddly human in its irregularity, beautiful in a way no European notion of beauty could encompass.

So we had done it. We had got away from the Nazis, had avoided concentration camps and strafings on the road and so many other perils that had become sickeningly commonplace, and had reached the long-dreamed-of haven. We had been unbelievably lucky. I was convinced that my life so far had been a prelude, a preparation for my coming to the United States.

It was an oppressively hot day, and I was offered a Coca-Cola. I hated it.

And so began my real American education.

CHAPTER FOUR

EVERY IMMIGRANT LEADS A DOUBLE LIFE. Every immigrant has a double identity and a double vision, suspended between an old and a new home, an old and a new self.

The very notion of a new home is absurd, as impossible as the notion of new parents. One's parents *are* who they are; one's home *is* what it is. It is one's birthplace, ratified by memory. It is the nursery wallpaper, the family dining room, the stories and songs that surround one's growing up.

Yet home, like parentage, must be legitimized through love; otherwise it is only an accident of geography or biology. Most immigrants to America received little love in their homelands or saw it betrayed; whether they starved in Ireland, or were persecuted in czarist Russia and Nazi Germany, or, later, were driven into the sea in Vietnam, they did not abandon their countries—their countries abandoned them. In America they sought not only a new life, but a new love.

So did my parents and I.

But the immigrant also seeks knowledge. Every immigrant is a permanent student of his substitute home, of its customs and rules, its public as well as its secret dreams.

I will always think of New York as it was to me in those days as the true, the ideal, New York. It really did look as if Fred and Ginger might be dancing somewhere across the rooftops. It had its grim and dirty corners, as I would find out soon enough. But it struck me as luxurious, open, safe—and, often literally, dizzying.

My first impressions were, predictably, size and speed. The Paris métro, seemed, in retrospect, tame compared with the New York subway and its express trains. That very word suggested "real" trains thundering between cities and countries, but here somehow trapped underground.

Although I studied maps, I could not quite grasp the city. It was so big—it seemed as if one could simply disappear forever—and it had no center. European cities were concentric, having grown behind walls and fortifications around the square, the palace, the dome, the town hall. In New York these were missing or turned up in some unexpected place. Uptown and downtown were strange concepts, functions of the boring but logical metropolitan grid. Everything seemed to be in flux. Rich and poor neighborhoods were strangely mixed; how could luxurious Park Avenue suddenly turn into a slum? Within a block or two of the most sumptuous edifices—apartment buildings with canopies and uniformed doormen seen in Europe only in front of grand hotels—you could find impermanent-looking two-story structures with grubby shops. The city had no predictable categories: pharmacies sold food, supermarkets sold books, stores seemed to open and close whenever they chose, day blended into neon-lit night.

But New York had, along with the relentless pace and excitement, a curious sweetness. Trolleys were still running along Broadway, their rattling wheels and clanging bells reassuring and homey. The Third Avenue el still stood, its ungainly iron girders creating mysterious shadowy recesses below, while the trains above looked old and tame exposed to daylight, their thunder somehow muted, like empty threats. The double-decker buses on Fifth Avenue were my favorites; climbing up the narrow steps and sitting upstairs seemed romantic, especially if you were riding an open-top model with the wind on your face. In the midst of city traffic, you could still catch glimpses of the river and the luminous sky above it. And you were reminded of the ocean as the sounds of horns from ships in the harbor drifted in, mournful but inviting.

. . .

We quickly discovered that most refugees from Europe were living in Washington Heights or on the West Side of Manhattan, between the Sixties and Nineties. That is where we found temporary lodgings, in a large apartment just off Broadway that had been converted into a rooming house. I liked it, liked the remnants of its old luxury, liked the common dining room presided over by a magnificent-looking black woman whose daily question at breakfast, "How do you like your eggs?" seemed to symbolize heady choices and opulence. But, "Too expensive," my father announced, and after a week or so we moved to a furnished room in a brownstone on West End Avenue, with a lovely bay window, a kitchenette and a tiny alcove, where I slept. The rent was modest, but even so, our livelihood was precarious.

My father's diminishing Gold Eagles were transferred to New York, and I accompanied him to the Chase Bank on Pine Street, where he would turn them into a mundane, modest bank account. Walking along those deep Wall Street canyons, I felt small and overwhelmed, more so than I had ever felt before the dark looming shapes of St. Stephen's or the Hermit. But I also felt excited by the business of his opening an account, which certified a degree of normalcy and security.

My father became obsessed with the desire to resume his old trade, not only to earn money, but to recapture some of his success and reputation. But he was a writer who had lost his language—his English was eager but shaky. He had also been deprived of his cultural habitat, of audience tastes and theatrical fashions he understood.

I, too, was impatient to start making a living, but at seventeen I had no marketable skills and the first order of business was to improve my English.

Despite the past efforts of Aunt Kate and Mrs. Livingstone, when I arrived in the United States my English was just passable. Rereading a few of my extant letters today, I am amused and oddly touched by the writer's desperate attempts to translate literally German colloquialisms into English ("come forward" for "get ahead"), by the faulty syntax, the misspellings. My editing hand twitches.

After a few weeks in New York I enrolled in an English class for immigrants, sponsored by a Jewish philanthropic organization in Times Square. It was the kind of class described memorably by Leo Rosten in *The Education of H*y*m*a*n K*a*p*l*a*n.*

Unfortunately my class had no hilarious Kaplan to offer, or anything else interesting, so I dropped out, moved a few blocks south and continued my studies in the movie theaters on Forty-second Street (not yet given over to pornography), where I would usually sit through one or two double features (at twenty-five cents). It was a great year—*Philadelphia Story, Rebecca, The Bank Dick, Pride and Prejudice.* I was intrigued by the growing number of anti-Nazi films, which gave a lot of employment to Jewish refugees often playing blond German beasts, and stunned by Chaplin's *The Great Dictator,* amazed that it was possible to laugh at Hitler.

As language instruction the movies were supplemented by radio, newspapers, advertisements, talk overheard in the street. The variety of foreign and native accents in New York—from Russian rumble to Italian singsong, from Brooklyn diphthongs to Long Island lockjaw—would have taxed Henry Higgins. They hopelessly confused me. But I kept up an obsessive effort to wallow in English. I read and listened like a spy. Not until I started to dream in English did I feel that I was really getting a grip on the language.

Meanwhile I continued to write plays, still in German and still in secret. This was not easy in our one-room apartment. So I found a shop where typewriters could be used on the premises, financing the rental by liquidating part of the stamp collection I had brought from Vienna. I turned out what I considered a romantic comedy about a girl who has a notion of the ideal man but eventually settles for someone quite different. I wanted an unbiased opinion, so I mailed the manuscript to my father, giving a phony name and asking for his judgment.

The brown envelope arrived, and I maneuvered him into reading the script. His verdict: "Well, it's pretty immature, but it shows some promise." At which point, in a rather dramatic revelation scene, I unveiled the writer's identity and my ambitions. My father was delighted and astonished. "I had no idea that you were drawn to the muses," he said, and noted that he, too, had written his first play at seventeen—it had actually been produced and became a big hit.

He thought my play needed work, and he considered taking a hand himself. But the idea of my aiming straight at a career as a playwright seemed daunting, given my youth and my uncertain grip on English. Surely I must complete my education first. Given our very meager resources, I needed to start earning money and aimed for something more practical and steady. The answer was journalism. I thought there would be time for plays on the side, or later.

Our circle had always included many journalists, but my mother retained a certain skepticism about the press and probably would still have preferred the plumbing supply business for me.

At a secondhand furniture store on Fourteenth Street, my father had bought an old, scarred, wooden desk with a flip top. His Royal typewriter was screwed into the top, which could be reversed to make the machine disappear in a space below. But it disappeared only at night. During much of the day he was busy typing.

He wrote to contacts and potential contacts, trying to promote revivals of his works or adaptations. He wrote to agents and producers, or would-be producers, many on the remote fringes of show business (including one entrepreneur memorably named Captain Jefferson Davis Cohn). He wrote to J.J. Shubert, despite his earlier rejection. He wrote to composers and librettists, hoping to enlist them as collaborators: Jerome Kern, Oscar Hammerstein (who had adapted one of his musicals for a London production). He wrote to Mike Todd, L. B. Mayer, Ernst Lubitsch. Almost every letter contained the key sentence "I believe my name may not be entirely unknown to you," words that still give me a shiver of pity. These ritual phrases were followed by a sampling of his operetta titles and a reference to past glory—for instance, one of his prose plays produced on Broadway by the great David Belasco.

He even wrote to Otto von Habsburg, the pretender to the Austro-Hungarian throne who was then living in the United States and, according to a monarchist friend, had Hollywood connections, which he said he would be willing to use for a Viennese writer. My father was instructed to phrase the letter in the archaic, subservient style that he knew well from those old librettos about princely romance: "Your Majesty! Most Gracious Lord and Emperor! . . . I am informed that Your Majesty has deigned to express his all-highest interest . . ." Evidently Otto's connections were not enough to command the all-highest interest of Hollywood, for nothing came of it.

Nothing came of the other letters, either. People often replied politely (or pompously, as in the case of Jerome Kern: "Your name, attached to many fine works, has for years been held in my estimation. . . . I am glad to evince interest in reading your latest, but I have heavy commitments," etc.).

Tantalized as my father was by the world of popular entertainment in America, he did not manage to enter it. He could not find the password—or, simply, the words.

He fought hard to master English. He refused to touch German books. He listened religiously to the radio: Eddie Cantor and Fred Allen and Jack Benny. He typed long lists of American idioms. He tried to convince himself—and potential producers—that he was writing competent English dialogue and lyrics, but he never could get them right. He might try to rhyme "Brooklyn" with "queen," "kitsch" with "bridge."

Most of my father's émigré writer friends were in the same predicament. Despite their gratitude to America for taking them in, many felt alienated. They complained about lack of respect for intellect, especially European intellect. Lawyers and doctors deplored the difficult exams they had to pass before they could practice in the United States. One physician friend of ours composed a wry lament:

The merest babes chant this refrain:
"Papa flunked his test again!"

"God damn Columbus!" was a humorous tag line, almost a greeting, among disgruntled émigrés. They talked a lot about how important and wealthy they had been back in Germany or Austria. Their nostalgic boasts inspired a self-deprecating joke. Two dachshunds meet on Broadway. First dachshund: "You are looking very well." Second dachshund: "You should have seen me back in Berlin. There I was a St. Bernard."

They flocked together in certain restaurants, especially in a pastry shop called Éclair, which became a close equivalent of a Viennese café. Many New Yorkers didn't much care for this refugee invasion. I did not like being a refugee. I found myself telling Americans that my family and I had "always traveled a lot," as if that somehow made us not so much refugees as cosmopolitan globe-trotters. I soon recognized how ridiculous this was, but I still wanted as little as possible to do with refugeedom, with the foreign enclaves that struck me as self-imposed ghettos.

I continued to explore the city and came to know New York's special hours. One was around eleven o'clock, sidewalks glistening in the sun and the girls marching along, their legs moving with precise morning energy under their dresses; although my experience was limited, I felt that no other women I had ever seen had quite the same stride. At dusk people hurried a little more than usual, as if to secret destinations. The sharp outlines of the buildings began to blur, and the lights came on; I was amazed that they stayed on indefinitely, luminously dotting the night sky.

I also began to distinguish the scents of New York: hot dogs (or chestnuts in the winter) on street corners, earth and leaves in the parks, beer outside bars, popcorn outside movie theaters, perfume outside department stores—and gasoline everywhere.

It was quite a while before I saw any settings that might have been appropriate for Fred and Ginger. The Starlight Roof, the Stork Club, El Morocco or the Ambassador ("formal after ten o'clock") were known to me only from ads or newspaper columns. But New York gave me a sense of miraculous glamour, symbolized by Rockefeller Center, a temple of luxurious modernity.

The corner drugstore was a second home, with its bewildering range of merchandise, its crowded counters and smoothly revolving stools, its quick, slangily efficient soda jerks (the appellation seemed, at first, terribly rude). I was fascinated by the candy stores, with their arrays of chewing gum and oddly named sweets (Hershey's Kisses, Baby Ruth), their mingled smells of tobacco and newsprint, their comfortably musty phone booths; the Childs and Schrafft's restaurant chains, with their aproned waitresses bearing blue-plate specials and lavishly constructed ice-cream sodas, one of the greatest American inventions. And the Automat! It was a never-ending source of delight to newcomers, who had never seen food behind little glass windows or paid for it with coins clicking into slots—both a convenience and a hilarious, Chaplinesque self-parody of America on the go.

New York's mayor Fiorello La Guardia seemed to embody the city— brash, irreverent, yet humane, funny and tireless. With his squashed face he looked like Pulcinella. He ran an efficient and clean city government and even an honest police department. He was unlike any political figure known to Europe, riding fire engines and reading the comics on the radio so that the kids would not miss any installments during a newspaper strike.

The comics! How could grown-ups seriously follow the daily adventures of Little Orphan Annie and Dick Tracy, not to mention Superman? Wasn't Superman something out of Nietzsche and vaguely associated with Nazi theories about the German master race? Using that concept, however indirectly, as the basis for a comic strip seemed silly, childish. But, I concluded, it was surely far better than using the concept as the basis for a murderous tyranny. I sensed, without as yet being able to define it, America's ability to domesticate menace and shrink giants.

The main theme, the common denominator, was freedom.

One felt very little fear, and no hesitation, about walking anywhere at any time; my first experiences with what was quaintly called necking took place well after dark in Central Park. There, and in the other parks—Riverside, Fort Tryon—the very layouts proclaimed freedom: no manicured flower beds, no rigid *allées,* but an attempt to replicate unforced nature; no old women with big leather bags, as in the parks of Vienna, selling tickets if you wanted to sit down.

The atmosphere of service, even deference, to the individual citizen was startling. Policemen, always menacing figures in my childhood, were actually friendly; officials, while still bureaucrats, at least were not tyrants. I went to the free symphony concerts in Lewisohn Stadium and the medieval oasis of the Cloisters, wandered in the vast seascape of Jones Beach with its handsome bathhouses, art deco signs and brave attempts at neatness (garbage cans looked like ships' funnels). In Europe such institutions were more grudging, touched by the arrogance of government or Socialist patronage. All this seemed absent here, or present only in milder form.

European cities were ruled by "don'ts" and "can'ts." Don't step on the grass (it took me months before I would comfortably do so in Central Park). Don't walk into buildings without permission. Don't talk to strangers. Don't talk back to important people. You can't take a streetcar after certain hours, can't shop in the evening or on Sundays, can't casually return things you bought. In Europe the presumption was that everything was forbidden unless specifically allowed; in America, it seemed, everything was allowed unless it was specifically forbidden—and not much was.

I visited the 1939–40 New York World's Fair a few weeks before it closed. It was a monument to the cult of progress, a carnival of industry as well as a real carnival, boastful and hopeful. America willed itself to believe in the future.

A seventeen-year-old refugee from a continent rife with murder and betrayal, I had reason to be skeptical about the promises of progress. But I, too, was willing myself to be an optimist, if only in defiance of my elders. The history of Europe, of Judaism, of their own lives, had taught my parents to be frugal with their trust and sparing with their hopes. But as much as they were capable of it, they put their hope and trust in America. And so did I.

The feeling acquired a label, oddly enough, in a barbershop on Broadway. As I took my seat, I groped for sleeves in the sheet flung about me (that is what I had become accustomed to in France), and the barber correctly sized me up as a foreigner. He said reprovingly, "You're in God's country now, son." It was the first time I'd heard the expression, and it seemed quaint. But I was to realize that it was merely a colloquial version of the entirely serious conviction that America had a special destiny.

CHAPTER FIVE

THE UNITED STATES of 1940 had half as many people as today, augmented that year by 70,756 immigrants, including the Grunwalds. Life expectancy was about a decade less, and only about 5 percent earned college degrees.

On the other hand, there were only 5 percent of today's major crimes and divorces. Nearly a quarter of all Americans still lived on farms. The moral standards the country professed were small-town standards. Four-letter words could not be printed even by Hemingway, and some of Faulkner's work was banned in the especially puritanical enclave of Boston. Movies were "voluntarily" censored by the studios. "Hell" and "damn" could not be used on radio. House detectives were on the prowl for "illicit" couples in hotels. Homosexuality was taboo, and just about the most enlightened attitude toward it considered it an illness that deserved therapy.

The day I landed in America, the papers carried the obituary of Philip Diel, ninety-six, a retired New Jersey farmer who had fought at Antietam and Gettysburg (where he heard Lincoln's address) and who was in Ford's Theater when the president was shot. To the generation of Franklin Roosevelt's parents, the Civil War was virtually a contemporary event.

Above all, the Depression was still felt in people's bones: the biggest blow to America's self-confidence, its faith in free enterprise and in the transcendent virtue of individual effort.

I befriended an American boy about my age whose father had committed suicide because of the crash. He talked about it sadly, but almost with a sense of shame rather than sorrow. As with war, some people remembered the worst of the Depression with something approaching nostalgia, as having produced a certain solidarity in misery.

It suddenly occurred to me that Americans of the Depression era were also refugees. Like my parents and their friends, they were haunted by loss and spoke of the good old days. Of course they were still in their own country, but they didn't have the comfort of blaming a diabolic set of villains, like the Nazis.

I struggled to understand how this disaster, this great fall from grace, could have happened to the vast, powerful and rich United States.

The New Deal seemed like a marvelous instrument of redemption. As I read about it I thought it must also have been a great adventure, especially the Hundred Days of what sounded like a gigantic wave of improvisation. I had visions of brain trusters sitting around in the small hours, drafting legislation on the backs of envelopes. But I soon realized that not everybody had that benign a view of the New Deal.

During my first few months in America the country was engrossed in the spectacle of Wendell Willkie running against Franklin Roosevelt, who was seeking a third presidential term ("unprecedented," the papers invariably noted). I was only dimly aware of the difference between Democrats and Republicans; I was so ignorant of Anglo-Saxon political history that I hardly knew about Whigs and Tories.

The turbulent campaign was both oddly cheerful and startlingly bitter. Somewhere I heard a campaign song, to the tune of "God Bless America," which contained the words "God damn Republicans." This seemed a little shocking. But there was something almost jovial about it, compared to the Nazi hymns still echoing in my ears.

My family and I knew next to nothing about Willkie. But we knew all about FDR, or at least we knew what we thought mattered: that he was against Hitler. "Roosevelt-and-Churchill" had become almost a single name. During our flight we had often listened on crackling short-wave radios to those two voices: Roosevelt's serene cadences, Churchill's defiant growl, both condemning the latter-day barbarians. In the simplistic logic of the newly arrived refugees, anyone who was against Roosevelt must be bad.

With some bewilderment I listened to Willkie attack Roosevelt and the New Deal for using near totalitarian methods and to Roosevelt, just as demagogic, flaying "selfish seekers for power and riches and glory."

My parents and I tried to keep up with the campaign but listened especially to the war news. It was odd to find the events that had driven us from Europe discussed and judged by strangers. This, we half felt, was *our* disaster; *we* were the experts on it. We were afraid that many Americans still did not understand the Nazi threat and dreaded U.S. isolationism. In a Madison Square Garden speech, Roosevelt excoriated the Republicans and in particular three isolationist congressmen, Joe Martin, Bruce Barton and Hamilton Fish. Derisively, repeatedly, he intoned their names. My parents and I, sitting around the radio, gleefully joined the chorus along with FDR and the Garden crowd: "Martin, B-a-a-arton and Fish . . ." We wrongly suspected Willkie of belonging to the isolationist camp.

A family friend, an émigré journalist who was writing for German-language papers in the United States, told us that Willkie was backed by someone named Henry Luce, editor in chief of *Time* and some other magazines. It was the first time I had heard the name. In the mid-1930s, our friend reported, it had been a fan of Mussolini's and had even been rather benign in some of its stories on Hitler. But since then Luce had become a passionate advocate of American intervention on the side of the Allies, as he would make ringingly clear in his famous *Life* editorial in early 1941, "The American Century."

My parents and I were frightened by some pro-Nazi groups. Father Coughlin, the rabid "radio priest," spoke of the Nazis' sacred war against Bolsheviks and Jews, called the New Deal the Jew Deal and declared: "When we get through with the Jews in America, they will think that the treatment they received in Germany was nothing." We were told not to take Coughlin seriously, that he was a fringe figure; but he commanded a steady radio audience of between thirty million and fifty million people. It seemed incredible that this effusion of hate and stupidity was possible in America.

More respectable and therefore troubling was Representative Martin Dies, who headed the House Committee for the Investigation of Un-American Activities. He was quoted in the papers: "We must ignore the tears of sobbing sentimentalists and internationalists, and we must permanently close, lock and bar the gates of our country to new immigration waves and then throw the keys away." When a proposal was introduced in Congress to admit ten thousand refugee children from Europe, even Roosevelt didn't have the courage or power to support it.

I came to understand that this antialien feeling did not really invalidate America's unique attitude toward the immigrant. Throughout history, exile was seen as a calamity. America turned it into a triumph and placed the immigrant at the center of a national epic, even though in every generation there were eruptions of anti-immigrant passions. It was one of those deeply troubling American contradictions with which I would often struggle.

I would come to see anti-immigration feelings and isolationism against the background of deep disillusionment following World War I, which, after all, had accomplished nothing—certainly not a world "safe for democracy." I also came to understand America's visceral distaste for the corruptions, the cynicism, the dynastic quarrels, of the Old World.

This understanding came to me only gradually, of course, in bits and pieces. I acquired my first halfway methodical view of American history at Haaren High School in Manhattan.

HISTORY, AS WE had been taught in Europe, was a succession of battles and dynasties, in which ordinary people were shadowy generalizations. American history was an adventure story, in which plain citizens—lawyers, farmers—were among the leading characters. I found it hard to imagine a European political manifesto mentioning "happiness." That simply seemed like a private, not a public, word.

In European history land had been a finite quantity, and its conquest meant wrestling it from some monarch. In America, at least for a time, land had seemed endless, and its conquest meant wresting it from nature. And, of course, from the Indians. It was astonishing to find that the Indians were not Karl May stick figures but real, along with their white counterparts. Sitting Bull, Tecumseh, Daniel Boone, Buffalo Bill—there they were, certified historical characters, just as genuine as George Washington. Americans didn't feel guilty then about the country's treatment of the Indians. I put it down with a shrug to the sort of clash between cultures—one advanced, one arrested in time—that happened before and would happen again.

I began to sense some permanent American themes. The strong strain of individualism. The frequent reference to inventions and their impact, the frequent "panics," referring not to natural disasters or war, but to business. The lasting political conflict between elitism and populism, strong central government and states' rights.

It was incredible that slavery had existed less than a century ago. It was incompatible with everything we were being taught about American ideals: yet another, and the greatest, of those American contradictions.

The authors were unabashed about noting the dominant English influence in the early United States, but they were expansive and not condescending about the role played by immigrants. Each chapter in our principal history text began with questions, and I was particularly amused by "Do you know anyone who came to this country from Europe? Why did he come?" The alchemy of the melting pot was unquestioned.

I sometimes wondered: Can this ever be *my* history? The thought evoked in my mind an odd echo of the Passover service in which the impudent son who questions the purpose of the holiday is firmly told that "the Lord led *me* out of Egypt." Did Patrick Henry rebel for *me*, was Gettysburg fought for *me*? Somehow the questions seemed preposterous. Yet I came to believe that the answer was yes: America had always seen itself as a venture undertaken for all mankind.

. . .

I ENTERED THE senior class of Haaren High School late in 1940 and
graduated a term and a half later, in June of the following year. Haaren.
Formerly known as DeWitt Clinton. Tenth Avenue and Fifty-ninth
Street, on the fringes of Hell's Kitchen, not all that hellish in those days.
The large brick building, built in 1903, was wondrously ornate in the
imitation Dutch colonial style: shields and bas-reliefs, an eagle over the
entrance, small sculpted representations of gowned scholars, looking a
little like the figures that move in and out of the recesses of medieval
clocks. Today it is the John Jay College of Criminal Justice, its land-
marked shell preserved and cleaned to an incongruous shine.

Haaren was, to my surprise, a community. It offered not only student
publications and clubs, but even a student government with opposing
parties and elections—although what that government was supposed to
do was never very clear. It had something called assembly, where the
Pledge of Allegiance was recited every day and entertainments occasionally took place; I was startled and moved one morning when a student
stood on stage and in a sweet Irish tenor sang "I'll Take You Home
Again, Kathleen," which seemed to have nothing to do with school.
There was, of course, a school song, to the tune of "Pomp and Circumstance," which thrilled me, although I didn't know that it was by Elgar
and had not been composed especially for Haaren.

All these obvious and trivial elements of life in an American school
were utterly strange and exciting to me. The students were mostly lower
middle class or working class—not that those terms were used. Many
had Italian or other foreign names, and about a third of them were
black. It was my first contact with large numbers of blacks, and I found
it routine. They sat together in the cafeteria, but there was no strong
sense of separateness or strangeness. Perhaps that was because everything and everyone was so strange, so far from my experience, that a
black face did not really make much difference.

What did make a difference was girls. It was a little unsettling—
pleasantly unsettling—to spend so much time with so many females. I
was intensely aware of their voices, their gestures, their conscious or

unconscious flirtatiousness and, in most cases, their earnestness. I didn't "date" (a word I found absurd); I was too reticent and much too grimly bent on schoolwork.

I formed one friendship at Haaren that has lasted to this day. It started during gym, which I hated as much as I had in Vienna. Often I would sneak away from the exercises in progress and climb to the elevated running track, a good hiding place. One day I bumped into a serious, dark-haired young man who was hiding there, too. His name was Lucian Heichler. He was also Viennese, the son of a doctor, and he disliked athletics as much as I did. We took to each other immediately. We discovered that we both admired *Faust* and deplored knowing of no really good English translation; we decided to attempt our own translation, at the rate of two lines a day (we barely got into the "Prologue in the Theater" before we quit). We talked and walked endlessly; sometimes, on cold winter evenings when we did not yet feel like going home, we would go to Horn & Hardart for warmth and conversation. Over a single five-cent cup of coffee we would discuss life and girls; the talk was mostly theory, although Lucian was always falling in love and I, being all of two years older, slipped into the role of fatherly adviser. It was a role I would adopt in many situations in the future; like the running track, it was, I found, a good hiding place.

IN CONTRAST WITH my miserable grades in Vienna, I was suddenly a star pupil at Haaren. In fact, so were most of the other refugee students—there were perhaps fifty out of several hundred—who were mildly resented by the American students for crowding the top of the honor roll. We did well partly because academic standards were lower than in almost any Gymnasium back in Austria or Germany. Most of my fellow pupils at Haaren seemed shockingly ignorant—about the world, about history, about literature.

I realized that in Europe quite a few of these students would by now have been diverted into trade schools, with their lower intellectual demands and social cachet. I also got an inkling of a certain breezy anti-intellectualism. My classmates often called me smart, but if there was a

compliment in those words, there was an even stronger, mocking suggestion of dealing with someone rather weird.

But again the all-important fact was freedom: the freedom to think
for oneself, to question. In my Vienna school, students had been rooted
to one classroom and the teachers came to lecture. Here, it was the
students who moved about, noisily roaming the corridors on the way to
different rooms and teachers. That was a metaphor for this American
school—roaming was encouraged intellectually as well.

In Vienna the teachers considered us to be idiots until proved otherwise. In America they considered us to be intelligent until proved otherwise. I acquired drive and ambition I never had before; I was determined to fight back against what had happened to us, to retrieve our loss
by making a place for myself in this new universe. The experiences of
the past two years had in a sense woken me up. Being tossed out of one's
home wonderfully concentrates the mind.

MY SHORT STAY at Haaren dramatically improved my English by
subjecting me to total immersion. English is notoriously illogical. Its
pronunciation and spelling are wildly inconsistent; all foreigners must
sooner or later rebel against having to distinguish between "rough" and
"though," "read" (present tense) and "read" (past tense). Its grammar is
loose and flexible. I picked up the rules from what I read and heard,
until they became instinctive to me. I learned to react to a split infini-
tive as I would to a false note from a singer or the screech of a knife on a
plate. I spotted and denounced dangling participles before I knew the
term (nowadays hardly anyone seems to know it).

I found English liberating. I had never been comfortable with German. Partly this was the fault of our regimented schooling and the way
language was policed in the classroom (despite the vulgarity of some of
the teachers) and even in the nursery. Certain words were forbidden,
certain expressions considered in poor taste. In New York I was uncon-
strained by such old inhibitions, by the old censorship of shame.

This gave me a heady freedom in using language, but it also led to
some difficulties. I had to learn that "Christ!" was not a devout exclama-

tion and that there was a difference between "darn" and "damn." Once, when I proudly read a short story I had written to an American friend of my parents, I caused consternation because I had innocently used "son of a bitch" when I meant "son of a gun." I quickly understood the relative offensive caliber, but it took longer to realize that the former was, in the right circumstances, highly useful, while the latter was quaint and out-dated.

With a few classmates, I started a student magazine. It was called *Variety,* consisted of eighteen typewritten mimeographed pages and lasted for two issues. I listed myself as editor in chief, a title I would again hold on my college newspaper, but thereafter not until forty years later. Among my contributions to *Variety* were an editorial on the fall of France with lots of drumrolls and a story bringing *Cyrano* up-to-date (Roxanne goes off with a football hero).

My grasp of idiom and slang were still feeble—the formalities of a language are easier to learn than its informalities. How really impolite was "can it"? How out of date was "button your lip"? What was the difference between "well-heeled" and "well-fixed," "sissy" and "panty-waist"? I became addicted to P. G. Wodehouse and had to discover that "my dear chap" and "I say" were not American English—and that the prose written by the columnist Walter Winchell was not English at all, though inventive in a ghastly sort of way ("splitsville," "infanticipating").

I gleefully pounced on expressions that utterly delighted me ("You could have knocked me down with a feather," "Lady Luck"), only to discover that they were clichés, their gilt rubbed off by excessive use. That was, I argued in a school composition, very unfair. "My greatest ambition is to give a phrase to the English language that will be hack-neyed as hell, a real cliché, fifty years from now." That did not happen.

With joy I discovered the New York Public Library at Forty-second Street and the cozy, slightly musty neighborhood branch where moth-erly librarians marked your library card with little date stamps mounted on the ends of pencils. Voracious, indiscriminate, I would take out six or eight books a week. I tried to sift the differences between the powerful clumsiness of Dreiser and the staccato virility of Hemingway. I settled with special delight into James Thurber's mad but somehow rational landscape, into Damon Runyon's caricature Broadway and Ludwig Bemelman's grand hotel full of eccentrics.

Soon I realized that I had to find my way not only into the country's language, but into its imagination. The fairy tales of my childhood, sanitized or otherwise, were not the fairy tales that Americans remembered. Quotations from *Alice in Wonderland* went right past me. The business of catching up was disorganized and disorienting; I encountered Winnie-the-Pooh well after Socrates, Mary Poppins well after Hester Prynne.

But there were some advantages. The lack of chronology enabled me to discover the miracles of Shakespeare (I knew only some of his plays, in German translation) not with a schoolboy's grudging incomprehension, but with a near adult's understanding and thus with far greater pleasure.

Just as most lovers believe that they were destined for each other, I developed an almost mystical conviction that somehow I was meant for the English language and no other. Joseph Conrad, who began learning English at twenty, considered it "the speech of my secret choice" and had "a strange and overpowering feeling that it had always been an inherent part of myself."

I felt the same way.

CHAPTER SIX

Having received my Haaren diploma to the now familiar strains of "Pomp and Circumstance," I took a summer job as an office boy for a department store supplier and started looking for a college, preferably one with a journalism school.

My parents begged me not to leave New York, and them. After what they had been through, they were entitled to my emotional support. So I did not consider out-of-town schools, and I was too ignorant to know the difference—academic or social—between Ivy League and other colleges. The choice in New York came down to Columbia or New York University. I picked NYU because it had an under-graduate journalism program, which would enable me to finish faster.

So I arrived one morning in Washington Square, accompanied by my father, who was prompted either by a sense of ceremony or by curiosity. He surveyed the scene briefly and left me at the main entrance; NYU didn't remotely resemble what either of us had imagined an American college to look like.

It was housed in a jumble of office buildings, reconverted factories and other old, more or less renovated structures. It had no campus. Or rather, its campus was Washington Square Park, a little too modest in proportion to the massive, noble arch, but inviting, with its benches and bits of greenery, its population of shoeshine men, chess players and derelicts.

NYU's pride was uptown, the "Heights" campus at 181st Street, over-looking the Hudson—hence the university's absurd hymn, "O grim gray Palisades, thy shadows / Upon the rippling Hudson fall . . ." It looked like a real university, but it made no money (and was finally sold off in 1973 for its valuable real estate). To stay solvent, NYU depended on the downtown schools, in those days attended largely by subway commuters.

I became fond of the grungy buildings, the "student affairs" offices with their creaky floors, the dyspeptically green-walled cafeteria grandly called "Commons." There were a few attempts at imitating "real" cam-pus life, even including some Greek letter societies in whose disorderly quarters I learned to drink Scotch. I also discovered Greenwich Village, which lapped onto the university like a pungent sea.

And then there was education.

I found intellectual freedom and experimentation. I often turned in exam papers in the form of fables, playlets or poems. Much of my college education became entertainment to me.

NYU was a long way from its present academic distinction; the cur-riculum was full of superficial survey courses and generally undemand-ing (I was allowed to fulfill my science requirement by taking three credits in meteorology). There were many offerings in what one classics instructor acidly termed "the social so-called sciences." I was arrogant about those. During a discussion in sociology, a formidable female stu-dent dismissed something I said, in tones of utmost contempt: "But that's a *value judgment!*" Hers struck me as a voice of doom. Value judgments, I thought, were precisely what was needed in the world and what I wanted.

I eventually switched my major to philosophy. The journalism courses, which had drawn me to NYU in the first place, I soon found to be a waste of time.

I WAS LUCKY TO be able to study with two distinguished philosophers, Sidney Hook and James Burnham, and they made lasting impressions on me. In appearance as in background, they could hardly have been more different. Hook: small, bristling mustache. Amused eyes. Abrupt body movements inside his dark, slightly rumpled suit. Rasping voice, Brooklyn accent, barely controlled passion. Burnham: smooth faced, prim lipped, Brooks Brothers suits, dry voice with a slight WASP whine (although, in fact, he was a Roman Catholic). He showed not passion, but strong, slightly detached conviction. Hook grew up in Williamsburg, Brooklyn, where in the years before World War I, Jews ("sheenies") were often attacked by Irish or Italian gangs, though deadly violence was rare. Young Sidney ("Four Eyes" because he wore glasses) went to public school, and he told me that the discipline and the rote learning imposed by martinet teachers were not very different from what I had experienced in Vienna.

Burnham came from a wealthy midwestern family and had studied at Princeton. Both had been drawn to Marxism, largely because of the suffering caused by the Depression and the conviction that conventional capitalism or even the New Deal could not cope with the crisis. Both had broken with Marxism by the time I studied with them and continued to fight Communism all their lives. Hook remained a dedicated believer in Democratic Socialism; Burnham became convinced that Socialism in any form was unworkable. He was a brilliant Cassandra who was often wrong; in *The Managerial Revolution* he falsely assumed that the new managerial class would establish worldwide totalitarian rule. He accurately foresaw the eventual collapse of the Marxist system but felt that the United States would need a much tougher policy than "containment" to bring this about.

Hook was less given to vast apocalyptic predictions. He fought in the trenches for his vision of democracy and humane education and against all dogmatism.

A teacher, Hook once said, is a sculptor in snow: he is remembered only by the generations that have seen him in action. The memory of Hook in action does not melt easily. Unlike Burnham, who rarely left his desk while lecturing, Hook paced and gesticulated. He used logic with the speed, ease and sureness of judo. He would pounce on a faulty argument with the triumphant cry "Tautology!" or the ringing accusation "Non sequitur!" It was sheer pleasure to watch him demonstrate a valid syllogism, the parts clicking into place like the tumblers of a smooth, solid lock—or have him explode an invalid one, the components collapsing in a heap of nonsense.

He had no use for metaphysics and its traditional project of defining a body of natural moral law based on self-evident, absolute and universal truths.

Hook found "no shred of valid evidence for the existence of an immortal soul" and described himself as an open-minded atheist. Moral standards, he argued, like his mentor John Dewey, had to be based on scientific, rational examination of their logical implications and probable consequences. I never saw how this method could establish a solid ethical basis for action; consequences, implications—by what standards could they be measured? That merely pushed the question back another step, toward the need for stable, universal values, the existence of which Hook denied. Otherwise, as traditional philosophers argued, values became mere opinions, mere emotional preferences.

On the other hand, the attempts of the metaphysicians to derive from the nature of man a system of universal laws and principles, or to prove the existence of God, did not completely convince me either.

The metaphysicians were attempting a sort of Indian rope trick, trying to climb on their rational, finite arguments toward something infinite, while the pragmatists were like Baron Munchausen, pulling himself out of a swamp by his own hair to reach, if not dry land, at least a raft. In the end I always sided with the metaphysicians, but it seemed to me that their position ultimately required faith beyond the most scrupulous work of reason.

Later I would delve a bit more deeply into such questions, through reading, especially some of the countless books by Mortimer Adler, whom Hook denounced as a new medievalist. I did not get to know him until several years after I left college, but in my mind he became, with Hook and Burnham, part of a great trio of teachers.

He and Hook had much in common. Hook had the same faith in the supreme efficacy of reason as Adler, but Adler seemed to feel that once a logical argument had been made, only fools could fail to see its authority. He would proceed to demolish error, but his eyes looked sad and pained.

As a student at Columbia under John Dewey, Adler had heckled him in class. Once he cited a passage of Dewey's writing and declared: "There is certainly nothing of the love of God in this utterance." Goaded past endurance, the great man jumped to his feet and shouted: "Nobody is going to tell *me* how to love God!" When Adler as a young man met Gertrude Stein, she submitted to his hectoring for a while, then hit him on the head several times with her fist and shouted: "Adler, I won't argue with you anymore!"

Later, when he was presiding over an extraordinary eight-year project called the *Syntopicon*, a two-volume superindex to the Great Ideas as found in the Great Books, I came upon him at the University of Chicago, in a rambling building known as Index House. He was drilling fifty or so academic staff members. His pep talk went something like this: "Aristotle and Aquinas are doing fine, but Kant, Descartes, Plotinus, must catch up! . . ." Adler set a quota for the indexing of a certain number of Great Ideas each week, and deadlines were proclaimed in terse bulletins ("Oct. 22—God").

Adler, with his colleague Robert Hutchins, advocated a rigorous core curriculum based on the Great Books. He argued that American education was becoming a large racket, producing students chaotically informed and "viciously indoctrinated with the local prejudices of professors and their textbooks" instead of being taught lasting ideals. This was at the heart of the controversy about progressive education, with its emphasis on electives, on "learning by doing," on stimulating creativity rather than merely imparting knowledge by rote. High school and college curriculums began to sprout electives like Health and Safety (meaning that a student would learn how to "mend a fuse, walk across a street and avoid VD"), Exploring the Occult, Great Sleuths, Science Fiction and the American Teenager.

Adler was never taken quite seriously by the academic guild. But he remained faithful to the Great Books idea and expanded the list to include more twentieth-century authors. In more than forty-eight books he took on freedom, love, knowledge, capitalism, socialism—and on and

on. His most typical title, perhaps, was *Aristotle for Everybody;*
lieved that philosophy is indeed for everybody.

Was THAT REALLY true? I thought so. The yearning for stable values
in an era of continuous upheaval was felt everywhere. Growing numbers
of Americans were left with the flexible, elusive tenets of pragmatism,
even if they might only vaguely understand the term. Right and wrong,
they were told more and more often, were matters of personal prefer-
ence. "What's right for *you* is not what's right for *me*" was becoming the
almost universal argument. " 'I believe,' " said the Catholic theologian
Ronald Knox, "has been replaced by 'I feel.' " I heard about a history
professor who argued that he didn't like Hitler, that he had faith in
democracy, but no one could *prove* that Hitler was bad and democracy
was good.

Sidney Hook thought he could, in pragmatic terms—without appeal
to the moral law or other higher authority. At times Hook, lacking the
crutches available to believers, seemed like a very solitary figure.

Toward the end of his life he wondered whether intelligence was
enough for the virtuous life. What, he asked, without finding an answer,
was the source of moral courage? Perhaps the answer is simply courage—although I can hear him shout, "Tautology!"

Campus LIFE AT NYU was exhilarating and just as important as my
formal schooling. I worked on the student paper, the *Washington Square
Bulletin,* and eventually, in my senior year, became its editor. I inflicted
pretentious play and opera reviews on my helpless readers. I also wrote
ringing editorials; in one I criticized my future boss's wife, Clare Boothe
Luce, for allegedly isolationist opinions; to ridicule internationalist zeal,
she had coined the word "globaloney," and I countered with a ghastly
coinage: "isolucionism."

Not for a long time would I have the satisfaction and authority I felt
while dummying up a *Bulletin* front page with a heavy black grease
pencil. A special pleasure was closing the paper, which involved a night

at a nearby print shop ("going on issue" was the jargon for this), reading proof, cutting stories to fit and, on the frequent occasions when the foreman was drunk, actually setting headlines. It was great to struggle wearily out of the shop into a gray New York dawn, the page forms all locked up, the aroma of printer's ink and hot lead in my senses. I should have realized, but didn't as yet, that journalism would not be a temporary phase in my life, that I was hooked for good.

Then there was Greenwich Village. Its great days were past. Edna St. Vincent Millay was no longer around to burn her candle at both ends. Dylan Thomas had not yet arrived. But Henry Miller was still a resident, surrounded by his halo of scandal, as were Willem de Kooning and Franz Kline. All of them, of course, mere colorful rumors to me and other kibitzing students. Lesser artists were still extolling or explaining their masterpieces and cadging drinks in countless saloons. There was excitement left, despite the heavy admixture of uptown and out-of-town bourgeois: poetry readings in grimy walk-ups, O'Neill plays at the Provincetown Theater and jazz. Above all, jazz. My ear, used to the waltz and opera, had become attuned to it.

Nick's. The Village Vanguard. Le Jazz Hot. And the eating and drinking joints: Ed Winston's for beer and the jukebox; Eddie's Aurora for spaghetti followed by (the waiter's singsong dessert offer never varied) "spumoni, tortoni or cheesecake," which are madeleines to my memory. One fellow student, a young man improbably named Marcy Tinkle, would often discourse on how we were really majoring in Greenwich Village.

M ARCY WAS PART of a group of friends that gave me a sense of belonging. We would meet for lunch at a regular table, behind a broad pillar in Commons. Our number included two aspiring actresses, and we often read plays aloud over our hamburgers; my favorite part was Sheridan Whiteside in *The Man Who Came to Dinner*, but I was a terrible actor.

Lucian, my gym-hating companion from Haaren, who was also at NYU, was part of the group. I formed several other deep and lasting friendships at NYU, notably with a fascinating girl named Rinna Grossman, whose Russian-born father was a Zionist leader. She had been raised in London and had a cutting British accent and an equally cutting sense of irony. For obscure reasons, she gave me the nickname "Cookie."

I grew equally close to two remarkable brothers, Noah and Eli Karlin, whose background, coincidentally, had some similarities with Rinna's. Their mother and three uncles had come to Britain from Russia via Palestine. One of the uncles, Serge, had grown very rich in business in England and was the feared and revered head of the clan. Their divorced mother had managed to send the boys to Eton and brought them to New York when war broke out. Adored by her sons, she looked like an elegant witch with long red fingernails, overpowering charm and a fatal tendency to live far beyond her means.

Noah was short, feisty, sentimental under a hard exterior; Eli, eighteen months his junior, was tall, dreamy looking and tougher than he seemed. They were frighteningly bright, bumptious in their Etonian self-assurance and continuous talkers. Noah wanted to be a journalist and politician (I told him that he really wanted to be Disraeli when he grew up), but eventually he went into business with his rich uncle back in England. Eli planned to be a writer, took a Ph.D. in philosophy—a field in which he was worlds ahead of me—but also ended up in business.

The most important member of our group was a reed-slim girl with warm brown eyes and an irrepressibly enthusiastic nature. Her name was Beverly Suser, and she would eventually become my wife. Long before then, she contributed mightily to my American education.

Her father, of Russian origin, had been a horse breeder in the Transvaal, in South Africa. While the family, including two daughters and two sons, paid a long visit to New York, the younger boy died of diphtheria. His mother was so distraught that she could not bear to leave the country in which her little boy was buried, and she persuaded her husband to sell out his spread in South Africa and move to the United States. They lived in a large, sunny apartment on Riverside Drive, wondrously cluttered because Johanna Suser incessantly haunted auction houses and found beauty or interest where few others could discern it;

until I saw her collection, I had never understood the word "tchotchkes."
Max Suser loved horses, indeed all animals, and nature; he was not a
city man. He did reasonably well in New York real estate, but he was
too honest and trusting for that business. His heart was not in it. That
was plain from his large, callused hands, accustomed to rough reins, and
his faraway look, accustomed to the wide distances of the veld. His wife
was large, pillowy, spoiled (by him and the whole family), with the
incongruous vanity of a once very pretty girl who still sees herself that
way. In many respects she had a better head for business than he; she
opened a dress shop on Lexington Avenue and made a success of it.

Beverly, the only sibling to be born in the United States, had been
raised to be strong, self-confident, straightforward and kind: those were
the qualities her father believed in above all others. She had gone
through a New York public education, and she was free of snobbery; she
would mention her high school (Julia Richman) more proudly than
someone else might have cited an exclusive girls' academy. She was
cheerful about helping out in her mother's shop, and she discovered that
she had a knack for selling. She radiated the deeply American belief
that she could accomplish anything she put her mind to and that others
could as well.

As editor of her high school paper, she had eluded Secret Service
agents at the Waldorf by using fire stairs and managed to get an interview with Eleanor Roosevelt; on another occasion she bagged Madam
Chiang Kai-shek. She would cite these exploits as simple models of how
to get ahead. When a New York paper ran a feature about her, she
complained that the journalists she had met "are all so old—at least
forty—and bald or gray. Just no pep at all, and they could hardly get
around." Her ambition, like mine, was writing, and she had a breezy,
staccato style.

Our courtship started rather slowly, initially without much enthusiasm on her part. "Don't talk yourself into anything," she said briskly
early on, when I made some awkward romantic declarations. She softened gradually, and we began to see a lot of each other, sharing a
malted at a soda joint called Sid's, or eating at Eddie's Aurora, or exchanging life stories on a bench in Washington Square Park. We were

drawn to each other, but neither of us had much free time, and besides, we felt bound by the prevailing rules about sex.

Before I met Beverly, NYU had already provided my first introduction to these rules, a generation away from the great sexual revolution of the sixties. Given my sheltered upbringing and my earnest refugee years, my explorations were limited and timid, but I found the accepted mores baffling and absurd.

I had heard, of course, like everyone else, that America had had a sexual revolution in the Roaring Twenties, when the present generation's parents had rebelled against *their* parents and morals had been loosened by the automobile plus bootleg whiskey. Later surveys claimed that by the forties premarital sex was quite widespread. But it seemed to me that my fellow students—especially the females—were still dominated by puritanism and middle-class respectability. The girls were always haunted by fear of pregnancy. Yet "necking" and "petting" (I never quite got used to these juvenile words) were universal and governed by certain familiar rituals. The geography and topography of the body were staked out inch by inch, with (sometimes flexible) borderlines crisscrossing the anatomy; there were detailed rules as to what was permissible short of consummation. Everybody seemed to agree that restraint was desirable but also expected it to be challenged.

All this was surrounded by public, almost civic discussion, with magazine articles and books offering views on how far a nice girl could go and where or how to draw the line. Somehow, the duty of defending and maintaining the moral order was invariably imposed on the female. "Remember that the average man will go as far as you let him go," said a typical manual. "A man is only as bad as the woman he is with."

Europe was in some ways stricter about sex, in other ways much freer, or at any rate more realistic. A young French instructor with whom I compared notes agreed: "American girls often let you go almost as far as possible and then flatly say no. With a French girl, either she smacks your face and sends you away, or you have won." I thought I detected around me a desire, which I would come to regard as very American, to have things both ways—titillation as well as morality, abandon as well as virtue.

． ． ．

ABOUT HALFWAY THROUGH my college years, we began hearing more stories of the Nazi concentration camps. There were terrible accounts of gas chambers and mass crematoriums. We heard in circuitous ways that many of our relatives and friends had been taken to the camps, including Alex, whom we had vainly tried to bring to America. One of my closest childhood friends was the nephew of a conductor at the Metropolitan Opera; I got in touch with the maestro, Fritz Stiedry, who knew only that the boy and his family had disappeared. But mostly we worried about my sister and her husband, from whom we still had heard no word. It was all too easy to imagine what might have happened to them.

I slept badly and had nightmares. The waking nightmares were worse; riding in a packed subway, I would visualize those cattle cars I had heard about, jammed with Jews destined for the camps. I tried to keep all this to myself, not even telling close friends. I managed to go on with my NYU routine, although my grades suffered.

But my mother, deeply concerned herself, sensed that something was wrong. She may have been alerted by the fact that I was eating less than usual, an extraordinary and alarming symptom, and had become quite thin (for the only time in my life; in photos from that period I seem downright ethereal). She immediately argued that I should get some help and proposed that I see a Viennese therapist she knew. I reluctantly agreed.

I found it curious that I was about to be placed into the hands—however indirectly—of that legendary, unreal figure, my schoolmate Sophie Freud's grandfather. I also thought it ironic that the episode in the French clinic was in a way being reenacted, but for genuine cause.

Dr. Blumberg, as I shall call him (I have forgotten—blocked?—his actual name), lived and practiced in a brownstone not far from our apartment. He was a short, bald man with a furtive manner. I assumed that I would wind up on a couch and would be taken through the obligatory (I thought) questions about childhood and parents, leading up gradually to the revelation of Oedipal conflicts, of neurosis and guilt lurking behind my fears. I didn't like the prospect; yet I was mildly disappointed when Dr. Blumberg, instead of directing me to a couch, waved me to a steel chair facing his desk and started asking rather routine questions about how I felt and why.

His attitude struck me as both patronizing and hostile. He seemed to suggest, without saying so, that my feelings were quite natural, given the horrible events in Europe, and yet somehow self-indulgent. After only two or three sessions, I grew restless and rebellious. Then something else happened that overshadowed my problems with Dr. Blumberg.

I had registered for the draft and looked forward to being in the army. When I passed servicemen on the street I imagined myself in their uniform. But my parents dreaded the prospect. As they saw it, this could mean losing their son after having probably lost their daughter. When I argued that I owed this service to America they agreed intellectually but not emotionally. After months of waiting, I was called up and reported for my physical. I became part of a herd of chilly, naked young men, most of them joking feebly as they moved from doctor to doctor. But then a total surprise: one of the examiners informed me that he had found a heart murmur. The verdict was 4F.

I was badly shaken. I knew my parents would be greatly alarmed at the diagnosis—the very word "heart" in the medical sense, was frightening to them. They would worry and fuss and watch me incessantly. Instinctively I decided not to tell them the truth and instead made up some story about my (undeniably) flat feet. I was unreasonably annoyed with them when they were glad. For me, it only reinforced my remorse at having escaped the Nazis unscathed and made me feel distant from an America galvanized and consumed by war. I found it painful to hear war news, to read casualty figures, to see pictures of American soldiers in combat. Above all, I felt separated from my generation and even more of an outsider. Years later I came across a quotation from Dr. Johnson that I found apt: "Every man thinks meanly of himself for not having been a soldier."

These feelings should have been grist for Blumberg. But instead of making me want to take it all to him, the experience somehow had the opposite effect. The doctor's dark office, the slowly and slyly probing questions, my own "condition," seemed small and unreal. I simply quit the therapy, and after some arguments my mother gave up. I coped with my emotional problems as best I could on my own, and I gradually regained my equilibrium. I was much helped by Beverly's soothing and cheerful companionship. I worked hard in school to improve my grades and impatiently looked toward my graduation, in June 1944, wondering what I would do afterward.

One day I had a conversation with Noah that was to shape my life. "Listen, I've answered an ad for a part-time job," he said. "They just hired me as a copy boy. It's easy work, you are around interesting people. You get to make free telephone calls, and you earn a little money. Pocket money, but still . . . I think you could get a job there, too."

"Just where is there?" I asked.

"Oh, *Time* magazine," said Noah.

PART THREE

TIME,

MAIN STREET,

HOLLYWOOD

CHAPTER SEVEN

A BUZZER SOUNDED INSISTENTLY. I looked up at the black box on the wall and saw the number "01," which I had just learned denoted the office of the managing editor. Three or four of us were lounging around the copy boys' desk—scarred, boxlike tables arranged in a horseshoe. Nobody moved, until one of the boys turned to me and said authoritatively, "You might as well get your feet wet."

I headed across the copy room, a large, irregular clearing at the intersection of two corridors with many desks and typewriters and glass-walled cubbyholes, and toward the open door in the corner. The little typed card on the door frame said T. S. Matthews, the name of the managing editor of *Time*. I had never seen him, but as I walked nervously into the big office, I somehow knew that the man behind the desk was not Matthews. He had thinning hair, a slightly pointed nose and formidably vaulting eyebrows. He looked vaguely familiar; I must have seen his picture somewhere.

"Where are the morning papers?" he asked sharply.

I had no idea, muttered something apologetic and headed out the door.

Henry Luce had given up directly editing *Time* long ago, but he was still completely in charge and descended from the executive floor once a year or so to take over the managing editor's duties for a couple of weeks; it was his way of keeping his hand in and staying in touch with the staff. That evening—my first at *Time*—the copy boy who was supposed to fetch the early editions of the morning papers had not shown up, and nobody had remembered to delegate that chore. I raced to the elevator and out of the Time & Life Building (the "old" one on Rockefeller Plaza) to the corner of Fiftieth and Sixth, scooped up the papers and was back in Luce's office in minutes. As I placed the papers on his desk, he did not look up, grunted what could have been taken as thanks and thrust himself at the front page of *The New York Times* with savage curiosity.

It was my first, hardly momentous encounter with Henry Luce.

I had followed Noah's suggestion and applied for a copy boy's job at *Time*. I had been interviewed by a tall, lanky, very New England woman named Content Peckham, chief of the copy desk. Supervising the unruly crew of copy boys plainly irritated her (she would shortly become boss of the magazine's researchers). She acted like a formidable, mildly profane headmistress. "Goddamn it," she told me, "we spend money like a bunch of drunken sailors around here, but on some things we are pretty stingy." Like copy boys' pay. She offered me a job working three nights a week, at $4.50 a night. I took it. Years later she described what I had looked like to her (dark suit, dark five o'clock shadow, black briefcase) and added, "My God, you scared me into hiring you." In fact, of course, I had been far more scared than she.

My duties were not demanding. They included tearing stories out of newspapers with the help of long steel rulers, stories that had previously been marked by a team of "news markers" (much information used in *Time* in those days was lifted from other publications or books). We copy boys also made "sets"—stacking alternating layers of yellow typing paper and carbon sheets, for all stories had to be typed with thirteen carbon copies, in the pre-Xerox, precomputer era.

We rounded up dinner orders from the staff, conveyed them to the nearby Schrafft's on Fifth Avenue and toted back the yellow cardboard boxes full of ham-on-ryes and Cokes. There were trips to Grand Central with heavy pouches of pictures and copy to be dispatched to the printing plant in Chicago and errands of all sorts. Few of them were as interesting as the one requested by a writer who phoned in at a late hour, asking that I go to his desk, pick up a small paper bag I would find there and bring it to the apartment of one of the researchers, where, he said, he was having a drink. I followed instructions but in the taxi traveling uptown could not resist looking inside the bag; it contained a pair of lacy black garters. All in a night's work, I thought.

Copy boys—and copy girls, as they were then guiltlessly called—were a mixed, rather intriguing and studious crew. Our group included a smart and patient Indian immigrant, a student at St. John's University who was working toward a doctorate in psychology, the rather arrogant son of a U.S. Army general, a newspaper publisher's niece who was pretty but slightly cross-eyed and whom I mortally offended by telling her (truthfully) that I thought this made her even prettier.

The best part of the job was carrying mail and copy around the two editorial floors—best because it gave me a chance to read the copy as I went. My fellow copy boys accused me of editing the stories in my head during my rounds, and they were not far wrong. Once I actually rewrote a cover story I didn't like and showed my version to the original author; with near saintly patience he sat me down and explained why in his view my effort was not an improvement over his. The incident has been rendered somewhat differently by my former colleague Jason McManus. According to his account, I was hovering over the writer as he was typing, until I suddenly saw these words appearing: "Kid, if you don't cut this out, I'll break every bone in your body." I allegedly retreated, muttering, "Cliché!" This version may be true in spirit, but it is, alas, fictitious.

I must have seemed full of chutzpah and quite pretentious, an impression surely reinforced by the fact that I often arrived at work wearing a homburg. In a novel about *Time* called *The Big Wheel*, John Brooks, a *Time* writer who moved on to *The New Yorker*, had a character he later admitted was partly a caricature of me; Henry La Pointe was brash, ambitious, offensive, and, though born in the United States, kept talking about the crowned heads of Europe he had met. Even if I had met any, such talk would never have occurred to me. I wanted to be part of the "team," awkwardly trying out phrases like "Well, I guess we'll be closing late tonight." But at the end of a totally silent elevator ride alongside the managing editor, I would say good night—and then wonder whether I had really spoken to T. S. Matthews or only to the elevator man.

At first the busy people around me, groaning over typewriters or purposefully striding along the corridors clutching clipboards, struck me as almost indistinguishable from one another. They, in turn, scarcely knew my name; I was sometimes tempted to whip out my *Time* employee identity card. One very great man, Bob Boyd, who was in charge of makeup, production and other chores later performed by a whole crew with computers, called me Buster. He didn't fix my name in his mind until one night when everyone else had left and news came over the AP machine of some coup in a minor Latin American country. Aware of my literary ambitions, Boyd asked me to write three lines on the event—and they actually got into print.

I enjoyed the camaraderie of the copy boys' desk, the endless palaver—Noah superciliously defending the British empire—and Miss Peckham striding past on her long, lovely legs and raking us with some tirade: "I see we're overstaffed. Goddamn it, this is a magazine, not a discussion group."

But I grew restless. I sent a petition to the personnel director, pleading for some spot in the company that would "involve a little more brainwork and a little less footwork." I kept hearing rumors about Time Inc.'s developing new publications, and I brashly decided to join the game. I wrote a prospectus for a new magazine to be called *Ideas* and a proposal for a global daily, which I sent to one of Luce's assistants, who in turn sent it to my immediate boss, Content Peckham. "Perhaps this guy belongs in Promotion," she scribbled on it, "or maybe on the moon."

Having graduated from NYU by now, I felt I had lots of leisure and took on some more part-time work, as a writer-reporter with a labor newspaper, the *Trade Union Courier*. The boss soon offered to hire me full-time, but covering union locals or writing editorials on the minimum wage failed to thrill me. I would miss the excitement I felt even on the fringes of *Time*. So I left the paper and became a full-time copy boy on the magazine. Noah was still there, and our friendship deepened. A few years later he wrote me nostalgically, from London, to recall the "leisurely lunches (while someone else ran copy) at which the nature and meaning of the world could be transformed several times over by our sophomoric philosophy; the sessions over highballs and hard-boiled eggs in dim bars while glorious castles rose into the air on the basis of a small but regular paycheck." Occasionally we had double dates, during which, I am afraid, I was apt to recite T. S. Eliot, whose poetry hypnotized me. But *Prufrock*, I found, was not apt to induce a romantic mood.

I was increasingly preoccupied with my sister's fate, about which we still knew nothing. She became linked with a particular part of my copy boy chores: watching AP machines. We copy boys wrestled the endless reams of paper that flowed into big baskets, ripped off and distributed the dispatches and got hell if we missed an important bulletin. I liked being alone with the machines in the semidark, windowless, soundproof little room, jungle hot; the incessant clatter, like a loud, mechanical heartbeat, symbolized the news business to me. I liked reading the datelines, feeling a link to distant places and to the war. Somehow this made it more immediate than the neat, very well written stories that appeared in *Time* the following week under the heading "World Battlefronts." But it also increased my anxiety. I would wander into the wire room to scan every dispatch for news of the Netherlands, looking for clues, however indirect, to the fate of Meta and Walter.

I$_F$ I WAS CONNECTED to current events in the outside world, working at *Time* also linked me to the past. *Time* was then more than two decades old, something of an American institution, and I eagerly explored its origins.

When *Time* started, the atom was still unsplit. So were most marriages. Movies were silent, and a "byte," however you spelled it, had to do with food, not information. In headlines, "holocaust" was only a word for a large fire. The juxtaposition of "man" and "moon" was strictly fantasy.

The story of *Time*'s founding had become legend: How two Yale sophomores—Henry R. Luce and Briton Hadden—developed the notion of a tightly written weekly news digest.

How they raised $100,000, mostly from family and friends. How they recruited a tiny staff of inexperienced college graduates and one or two near professionals, supplemented occasionally by debutantes for clerical work. The first scrawny issue was dated March 3, 1923.

Luce and Hadden were an odd pair. Hadden grew up in Brooklyn, the son of a stockbroker; he was habitually frivolous and iconoclastic about the Establishment, including business, and dreamed of being a baseball player.

Luce was raised in China, the son of a Presbyterian missionary, was intensely serious, as well as respectful toward business, and apparently harbored some ambition to become president of the United States. He idealized America. Years later he regretted not having had an American hometown and added that when he was asked, " 'Where were you born? Where did you grow up?' I would give anything if I could say casually, 'Oskaloosa, Iowa.' "

The distinct personalities of the partners were clearly evident in the early *Time*, though Hadden's predominated at first, because he acted as editor until his death from a streptococcus infection in 1929 at the age of thirty-one. The early issues of *Time* were quite un-American, if measured by the pieties of Oskaloosa. It was irreverent and occasionally cynical. It was also blunt, even graceless, in the way it pushed facts at the reader. A *Time* specialty was the more or less colorful detail often omitted from standard newspaper reports: the menu at a state dinner, the vintage of the wine with which the food (in the inevitable phrase) was "washed down," the color of the president's necktie.

A little later the magazine developed what came to be known as *Time* style, with its piled-on descriptive adjectives, as in "jut-jawed, haystack-haired Henry Wallace." Some people never appeared without a certain identifying refrain, as in "Senator James Thomas Heflin, who mortally hates and fears the Roman Pope."

People didn't simply die; instead, "Death, as it must to all men, came to So-and-So." For obscure reasons, sentences were inverted to the point

Teta and I (aka Muggel), circa 1925. (PERSONAL COLLECTION OF HENRY GRUNWALD)

My mother and my sister Meta, circa 1918. (Personal collection of Henry Grunwald)

My sister Meta and I in
Bad Ischl, circa 1928.
(PERSONAL COLLECTION OF
HENRY GRUNWALD)

At the table in our Vienna
dining room, scribbling
while waiting for lunch.
(PERSONAL COLLECTION OF
HENRY GRUNWALD)

My father, third from the left, in Austrian native costume, with his fellow librettist, Julius Brammer, the composer Emmerich Kálmán (seated), and his friend "Uncle" Alex in Bad Ischl in the mid-twenties. (PERSONAL COLLECTION OF HENRY GRUNWALD)

Countess Maritza in its original Vienna production, 1924.

As editor of the NYU student newspaper, the *Washington Square Bulletin*, I (far right) treat the managing board to milk shakes. My Coca-Cola dream girl watches from on high.

(Photo reprinted courtesy of New York University, *Washington Square College Bulletin*)

Refugee portrait of my father.

(Personal collection of Henry Grunwald)

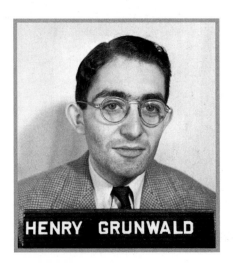

My first *Time* mug shot when I went to work as a copy boy.

(Photo reprinted courtesy of Time Inc.)

Back to back, not eye to eye: Otto Fuerbringer and T. S. Matthews at the 1948 Republican convention in Philadelphia.
(© ROY STEVENS/TIME INC. PICTURE COLLECTION)

Henry and Clare Luce in Spain, Easter 1952.
(PHOTO BY DMITRI KESSEL, *LIFE* MAGAZINE, © TIME INC.)

Roy Alexander, *Time* managing editor from 1949 to 1960.
(Photo by Alfred Eisenstaedt, *Life* magazine, © Time Inc.)

Time foreign news staff in 1948: Max Ways (front row center), me (second from right),
Mark Vishniak (middle row far right). (Photo by Herb Gehr, *Life* magazine, © Time Inc.)

of self-parody: "A ghastly ghoul prowled around a cemetery not far from Paris. Into family chapels went he, robbery of the dead intent upon." ("Backwards ran sentences until reeled the mind," wrote *The New Yorker*'s Wolcott Gibbs in a classic spoof.)

Time insisted on printing middle names in full, which did not please everybody. Walter P. Chrysler, who prided himself on being a rugged, ex-mechanic, was furious when *Time* revealed that the middle initial stood for Percy. In a face-saving deal *Time* agreed to omit the Percy, except once a year.

The magazine was apt to deal with America like a somewhat supercilious observer reporting on the natives. When, on its founding in 1925, *The New Yorker* announced that it would not be "for the old lady in Dubuque," Hadden ordered up a story that featured a fictitious Old Lady from D. who scathingly denounced *The New Yorker*'s reverse provincialism.

All of this put a certain unsettling distance not only between *Time* and the reader, but between *Time* and the rest of the American press. In the magazine's early years, much of that press, as I later perceived it, was still part of a largely rural country of vast, lonely spaces, where people sat reading the *Satevepost* (as *Time* invariably called it) by lamplight or listening to crystal radio sets. By its nature and style, *Time* proclaimed that it was different. *Time* did not offend against the basic American values, especially the cult of success ("The bitch goddess sat in the outer office," Luce once said). But it was not a cozy Main Street magazine, either. For all its collegiate brattiness, the early *Time* reflected the transformation of America after World War I—not the longed-for "normalcy," but a dizzying tumble into the twentieth century.

BY THE TIME I arrived, *Time* had become much more serious. The war had darkened its tone. It had also forced the magazine to cease being a rewrite sheet (Luce's phrase) and to deploy its own correspondents. But *Time*'s new seriousness was a relative matter; it did not entirely eliminate the oddities of its style, and it scarcely diminished the peculiarities of some of its staff. Many of the people I had at first considered nondescript were in fact eccentrics.

There was Winthrop Sargent, the music critic, who had played second violin under Toscanini and was an impressive hypochondriac; among other things, he needed to be immobile for twenty minutes after meals to aid his digestion, and at night he required six bottles of beer to sleep. His editor reported that he said he hated music. Robert Fitzgerald, later renowned as a poet and translator of the *Iliad,* who wrote art, was apt to keep his mouth shut for long periods, grinding his teeth in fury; they were, it was reported, quite worn down. Wilder Hobson, who oversaw several cultural sections, listened to jazz records and worked with his shoes off, invariably revealing huge holes in his socks.

In this gallery of odd characters a standout was James Agee, the film critic. He was otherworldly to the point of often leaving his paychecks uncashed in his desk drawer; he was gentle and sweet souled, his power-ful body padding along the corridors on soft, silent feet. He spoke in a hush and was a marvelous talker, though eloquent in arguing that talk-ing was the enemy of writing. But, especially when he was drinking, which was often, he was capable of frightening, violent rages if he encountered what he considered injustice, insult or philistine bad taste; at an office party I once saw him try to beat up the publisher.

Probably the strangest of all the characters on the magazine was the foreign news editor, a rotund, gray-haired man with a twinkle in his eyes that somehow did not go with his plain black or gray suits, his funereal ties and his habit—unusual on the magazine—of keeping his office door closed. I had heard about him but failed to pay much atten-tion until I decided that I wanted to become a *Time* writer and started submitting "shorts" to various editors—brief items culled and rewritten from the newspapers.

I showed one to the foreign news editor; it reported the opening of phone links between K'un-ming, China, and Calcutta, India. I got some-one to translate "Hello, hello . . ." into Mandarin and "Calcutta call-ing!" into Hindi.

"Pretty clever," said Whittaker Chambers. "I'll run it. And you might try again."

I did, and after a few weeks Chambers mentioned me to Matthews, who called me into his office.

"You have been writing some items for Whittaker Chambers," he said in a neutral tone. I nodded nervously. "He thinks they are quite good. Whittaker believes you should have a formal tryout as a writer."

"That would be wonderful!"

"However," continued Matthews, looking at me severely down his sharply carved nose, "if you don't pass muster, I can't give you your old job back."

I was willing to take that chance.

I HAVE SAID THAT every immigrant leads a double life, between past and present, and so did I. My American present was based in Rockefeller Center. My immigrant past was based in West Seventieth Street. We had moved there, into a slightly larger furnished apartment—ground-floor rear, dim, facing a bedraggled garden, sagging couch that bore a permanent stain carefully covered with a throw by my mother. Noise from the old steam pipes and a wheezing refrigerator would mingle with the sounds of my father's typewriter or, occasionally, his second-hand upright piano.

To supplement our income, including my own modest contributions, my mother took in piecework, embroidering and crocheting. A particular specialty became a head covering then fashionable, the snood. Piles of these objects as well as mounds of yarn covered most surfaces in the apartment.

The place depressed me, so I spent as much time as I could in the Time & Life Building. One can hardly be sentimental about an office building, but I developed a strong attachment to it; I had become accustomed to the sight of the circular information booth in the lobby known as the fishbowl, where one met people to go to lunch; to the oddly appealing scent of freshly waxed corridors on a warm summer night; to the sudden hint of surprising dawn through the windows. The *Time* offices were scarcely luxurious, but bright with the steel-and-glass vistas of Rockefeller Center, radiating energy and exhilarating action. The

Seventieth Street apartment was filled with uncertain hopes, memories, worry.

Time was reality to me; to my father, reality was his desk on Seventieth Street. I still wanted to be a playwright, but I had become absorbed by the journalist's trade; for him there was no trade besides show business. I tried to understand American politics and society; he tried to understand the American public and its tastes in entertainment. The names that mattered to me were Whittaker Chambers or Tom Matthews; the names that preoccupied him were, still and always, Cole Porter, Oscar Hammerstein, Irving Berlin. He would have been surprised to learn that Berlin, in late 1939, had written but not published a salute to Vienna that could have been by Grunwald:

> The waltz of old Vienna
> Has gone beyond recall
> Vanish from most ev'ry house
> Kalman and Lehar and Strauss

> The waltz of old Vienna
> You heard at ev'ry ball
> They still play them it's true
> But the feeling is false
> You can't do the goose step to a waltz.

Despite the earlier rejection, my father turned to J.J. Shubert again and again. J.J. was truculent and in his younger days had often slugged actors or aides who disagreed with him. He was also notoriously stingy. My father loved the story of how, during the highly successful run of *Countess Maritza*, one dancer asked for an additional pair of bloomers; the pair she wore in the first act, she argued, didn't match her second-act costume. The problem was submitted to J.J. "If she has the kind of legs where the audience notices what color her bloomers are," ruled J.J., "it don't make a damn bit of difference what color her bloomers are."

By now, Shubert had mellowed somewhat. When he had a flop,

which was often, my father was apt to write, suggesting that J.J. would have done better with one of *his* projects, and he would propose another one. Given J.J.'s reputation, his attitude was relatively benign. His two- or three-line replies were usually negative, but he encouraged my father just enough—now inviting him to drop by for a chat, then agreeing to listen to a score—to keep him hoping.

Despite many experiments with new forms, for the most part dismissed by my father as "Pirandellirium," the stage was still dominated by the "well-made" and realistic play, and most playwrights still felt bound by the unities of time and place. This reflected the ideal of an orderly, rational society where cause and effect were calculable, the belief that somehow life could be divided into acts and scenes in predictable sequence—even though such a society never existed. It was the era of Robert Sherwood, Elmer Rice, Maxwell Anderson (a conventional playwright despite his flights of prose poetry) and Kaufman and Hart. Writers like Philip Barry and S. N. Behrman still produced drawing-room comedies, even though the drawing room itself had become almost as unreal as the great hall of a medieval castle.

My father found comfort in the familiar construction and devices. Once he took me to a melodrama titled *Johnny Belinda,* and he quickly noted a shotgun hanging on the wall of the rural kitchen set. He told me: "If you see a farmer's gun on the wall in the first act, you can be sure that it will go off before the final curtain." It did, and he was delighted by this small affirmation that the laws of the theater were intact.

But he failed to understand that even conventionally constructed American plays were animated by a natural, informal spirit and peopled by lifelike characters, in contrast with the contrivances of the old French school, in which "situation" was everything and character served plot rather than the reverse. He loved but could not quite grasp American humor and was baffled, for instance, by *Arsenic and Old Lace;* how could twelve murders be a laughing matter? Above all, he could not quite cope with the American musical, with its exuberance and irreverence; he was shocked to find that one scene of the great hit *DuBarry Was a Lady* took place in a men's room. He tried at every turn to convince himself that the new fashions were only the old fashions refurbished; he dismissed *Lady in the Dark* as just an operetta with psychoanalysis thrown in. But even he realized that *Oklahoma!* had marked the start of a truly new dispensation.

He continued his struggle with English, but it was a losing battle. Occasionally he enlisted me to help correct a letter or even a scene in a play. He was apt to argue with me and with the language; "But why can't I say it *this* way?"

He attempted to Americanize some of his old "merchandise." A satirical operetta about Cleopatra was rechristened *Egypt's First Lady* and offered to Mae West; a Montmartre romance was transferred to Greenwich Village, and wouldn't it be just right for Deanna Durbin? He knew that all these projects were what he called soap bubbles, but he kept trying.

An avid moviegoer, he was enchanted by American films and would analyze them endlessly. He tried his hand at movie treatments, with subjects ranging from Adolphe Saxe, the inventor of the saxophone, to Wall Street. An agent suggested to him that a good story might be found in the hapless Maximilian, the Austrian archduke who (briefly) became emperor of Mexico. My father produced a plot in twenty-four hours: Viennese nobleman at Maximilian's court falls for a patriotic Mexican girl, who considers him the enemy, etc. Hollywood was no more receptive to this than to his other ideas. "Too continental," he was told by a Fox executive, "and that means old, stale, uninteresting."

Finally one theatrical producer grew enthusiastic about his libretto involving the 1872 visit of Johann Strauss to the United States, about which he had done voluminous research. Strauss had been invited to conduct a series of concerts for a Peace Jubilee in Boston. The opening event was a monster affair, with a newly built concert hall holding one hundred thousand people, an orchestra of more than one thousand musicians and a chorus of twenty thousand. Strauss had twenty assistant conductors, and a cannon shot marked the downbeat to "The Blue Danube." Posters of Strauss wearing a crown as the Waltz King were plastered all over town; hundreds of women besieged him for locks of his hair—which were provided by a Newfoundland dog. All in all it seemed like promising material.

Unfortunately for my father, the producer had writing ambitions and reworked the original libretto with another author, despite endless, detailed memos from my father. The composer, an old collaborator of my father's, logically enough was supposed to put together a score from Strauss's own melodies but kept substituting more and more of his own music.

I had not quite believed in the reality of the project that had sprouted from my father's old Royal, till I saw *Mr. Strauss Goes to Boston* on the theater marquee and the printed program. (The most interesting name listed was that of George Balanchine, who choreographed the show.) For the Broadway opening at the Century Theater, my parents and I tried to reenact, as best we could, those first-night rituals I remembered from my childhood, including my mother's gift of a new good-luck piglet.

The charm didn't work. The reviews ranged from patronizing to devastating, so much so that my father felt lucky he was credited only with providing the original story. Of course he was convinced that his own libretto would have made the show succeed instead of closing after twelve performances; for months and even years afterward he churned out letters retracing every scene, showing how humor and suspense had been sacrificed in the new, amateurish version, etc. A letter along such lines went to Louis Kronenberger, the superb *Time* theater critic who had also panned the show. By then I was writing for the magazine, and I sat in an office close to Kronenberger's, but we were careful not to mention the letter.

M Y PARENTS AND I endlessly and anxiously discussed Meta and Walter, not wanting to believe that they were dead. We read and dissected all news items about the Nazi occupation of the Netherlands, which were not reassuring. By early 1945, as the Allies fought their way through Holland, our suspense had become feverish. On March 10 the AP machines finally carried the news that the Netherlands had been liberated. My parents sent an inquiry through the Red Cross. Within a week we had our reply. It was the word we had desperately hoped for during nearly five years of silence but had no longer quite believed in: Meta and Walter were alive and well. "It's a miracle," my mother kept saying tearfully. "A miracle."

A FEW WEEKS LATER we received an extraordinary thirty-page letter from my sister, in which she described her ordeal. I read it aloud to my parents. Here in our shabby but secure living room, in a rich and vibrant city, in the midst of our everyday world—my father's shadowy hopes of placing plays, my ambitions to get ahead at *Time*—the letter suddenly brought to life the world of war and terror. It also brought to life my memories of Meta and Walter: she—short, slightly pudgy, with soft brown eyes to match her sentimentality, melancholy hovering beneath the cheerful surface, and a goodness and courage I did not yet fully appreciate; he—unemotional, realistic, stoic and proud of it, with a fine, history-obsessed mind aided by a formidable memory, and no less courageous.

Meta's chronicle began with the German invasion of Holland in 1940, the annihilation of Rotterdam by German bombs, the paralyzing fear and the "knowledge that we were trapped again, for the second time in Hitler's hands." Thousands of Jews committed suicide rather than fall into Nazi hands. Actually things were relatively calm for a year, but then the Nazi occupiers turned increasingly brutal and began mass roundups of Jews. Meta told of the day they had to put on the yellow star and how people, friends and strangers alike, greeted them effusively in the street to demonstrate against what the Dutch considered an outrage. The only chance now was to go underground, or "underwater," as the Dutch put it.

From then on, Meta's story glowed with a series of vignettes of quietly heroic Dutch people of every sort who sheltered the two fugitives at extreme risk to themselves of torture and death. An underground leader known as Oom (Uncle) Jim gave them forged Dutch documents, and they assumed different identities, painstakingly living every detail, including the celebration of their new birthdays. They both worked for the underground, Walter forging documents, Meta typing and distributing news bulletins she took from BBC broadcasts, mindful that merely listening to such broadcasts or even owning a radio was punishable by death.

One day, on a train between Leiden and The Hague, Meta ran into one of the frequent raids conducted by the Gestapo to catch illegals. A sharp agent recognized her identity papers as forgeries, and she was arrested. She had checked a parcel at the station, which, she suddenly realized, might tip the Gestapo to her real identity and lead them to Walter; she managed to swallow the parcel check, determined not to reveal the truth about herself, especially that she was Jewish. Under interrogation she pretended to be English; she reinvented herself as one Mary Nicholson, daughter of a well-known playwright. Luckily the Germans who dealt with her knew no English and decided to investigate her story through neutral agencies. Meanwhile she was held in prison.

Alone in her cell, she deciphered the dates, names and mottoes that previous inmates had scratched into the wall: "The Lord is my shepherd." "Always answer, 'I don't know.' " "Keep smiling." *"Quand on n'a pas ce qu'on aime, il faut aimer ce qu'on a* [If you don't have what you love, you must love what you have]." "Long live the Queen." With a nail she found on the floor, she added her own message to the others: *"Sterkte* [strength]." Lying on her cot that night, she was desperately worried about Walter. "My right hand tried to trace his face on the wall, his eyes, nose, mouth and chin," she wrote. "Yes, that's it. Finally, not so alone any more, I fell asleep."

Her account of prison existence brought to life the guards and officers, some kind, some brutal; her fellow prisoners, who were mostly Jewish, and her shame when she denied her Jewishness even with them (most of them didn't believe her anyway); their camaraderie, their attempts at humor, their daydreams of "afterward," of how they would celebrate their freedom ("white dinner jackets for our men, evening gowns for us, champagne . . .").

One night they heard a fusillade in the courtyard; they knew through the grapevine that seventeen members of the underground were being executed. They heard the screams of a young girl: "What have you done to my fiancé! Oh, let me die with him, let me die." And a harsh voice in reply: "You should be ashamed of yourself. Eighteen years old and wants to die!"

Suddenly a male prisoner was heard breaking into the "Marseillaise," and within minutes the whole prison was singing it, followed by the Dutch anthem, "God Save the King" and "The Star-Spangled Banner."

Following the Allied invasion of Normandy, the prison was ordered evacuated, before Meta's story had been checked out. Within hours she and the other prisoners were on a train headed east, toward the camps. She decided that if she had to die, she would rather die in Holland, "among these good and gentle people." The train was the kind that had individual doors on each compartment; at night, as the other prisoners covered their mouths so that no instinctive cry would alert the guards, Meta opened her compartment door, stepped on the running board and let herself fall.

As she hit the ground, she was sure that she was dying. But no; bleeding, in pain, she managed to scramble to a nearby house, whose owners fetched a doctor and a representative of the underground. He was suspicious of her, and she of him. Next morning he reappeared with "something to give you strength." He placed a Bible into her hands and said: "Come, trust me. I trust you." The underground hid her with a family in another part of the country and notified Walter of her escape; but it would have been too dangerous to bring them together. That did not happen until ten months later, when it was considered safe for Walter to join her. The Allied offensive went slowly, and the retreating Germans were savage; at one point Meta and Walter spent ten shivering hours under the floorboards of their house while the SS searched overhead. Then, finally, Allied troops entered their village, and "we and some of our neighbors triumphantly lifted them to our shoulders."

The most moving passage in the long letter concerned a message to Walter that Meta had smuggled out of prison: a tiny piece of paper wedged in with the stays of a corset worn by a prisoner who was being released. If she was killed in prison or in a camp, she wrote, "please tell Mother and Father that I died in an air raid. That would be less painful for them." The three of us cried as I read these lines.

Meta concluded with the words "Greet America for us. We hope to see it some day." Two years later they came to New York to stay.

CHAPTER EIGHT

AFTER FOUR MONTHS OF TRYING OUT as a writer, I was hired for good and made the masthead of the November 12, 1945, issue. The fact that *Time*'s vaunted checking system had failed and my name was misspelled—Greenwald—only slightly dimmed my pride, or my father's.

My appearance on the masthead gave me a strong sense of identity, of belonging. For a long time to come, I would occasionally glance at my name—right there between Frederick Gruin and Barker T. Hartshorn—to make sure it was still there. I remember that masthead as I remember the class roll from my school days.

Some years before, William Saroyan had created a stage character who sold *Time* subscriptions door to door, reciting mellifluous masthead names. The potential subscribers were enthralled and I could understand the feeling.

In the *Time* system, writers relied on reams of material assembled by researchers plus cables from *Time* correspondents. Often so much paper landed on the writer's desk that he almost literally had to dig himself out. His story went to the department senior editor, who might scrawl the dreaded words "See me" on the bottom. That meant a confrontation in which the editor would demand revisions with more or less comprehensible instructions. Or else he might revise or rewrite the piece himself.

Then it was the managing editor's turn for some further fiddling, plus questions and comments in the margin. Even those cryptic picture captions, over which writers labored as if they were composing haiku, were edited and reedited.

Finally the researchers moved in. They were, and remained for decades, exclusively female. They did not have private offices or even cubicles then, but worked together in open areas known as bullpens. Their boss, Content Peckham, insisted that they wear gloves and stockings even in summer ("and even if you have good legs"), but at least she did not require hats, as was the rule at *Vogue*. Since even in those relatively innocent times the streets of New York at night were not considered very safe for women, researchers who had to work late were conveyed home in limousines; my college friend Rinna Grossman, who in the meantime had also joined *Time*, dubbed them "chastity chariots."

The researchers included some memorable types. There was Blanche Finn, who came out of the labor movement and talked like a longshoreman (she also looked a little like one), her milder words to a copy boy or junior writer being "Hey, sonny, what the hell do you think you are doing?" There was Manon Gaulin, a Frenchwoman who kept a horse in New Jersey and, it was said, rode people just as hard; she resembled Charles de Gaulle both in looks and authoritative manner. There was Lili Lesin, a German with a Dietrich-like voice and very large bosoms of which she was rather proud; once, in the elevator, she found an editor of another magazine staring at them fixedly and she growled: "That's right, I've got three." There was Judith Friedberg, formidable and fearless, who once was assigned to cover Winston Churchill's arrival in New York and had herself hoisted by rope up the side of the *Queen Mary* to get a better look (her report began: "First came the puff of smoke, then the cigar, then the Prime Minister"). Although researchers did some local reporting they were barred for years from becoming full-fledged correspondents or writers, to their fury and frustration. Yet they were important to *Time* as guardians of its cult of facts; they bore the ultimate responsibility for accuracy, and every time a mistake was detected in print an orange-colored "errors report" was circulated by Content Peckham, with a clear statement as to who was to blame. The researchers were, Luce once said, "veritable vestal virgins whom levitous writers cajole in vain, and managing editors learn humbly to appease."

The system was an enormous luxury for a writer, allowing one to turn out copy without stopping to look up facts, thanks to the magic words "to kome," or "TK" for short. Thus one might put down: "In year KOMING, Napoleon met the Czar on a raft in the middle of KOMING river." The researcher was expected to find and fill in the missing information. A *Time* writer named Edward Kennedy imagined how the system would cope with the Second Coming:

Is Christ Episcopalian, as is rumored,
Did the Holy Ghost matriculate at Yale?
God the Father, to my knowledge, never went to any college,
But call Vassar on the Virgin, without fail. . . .

From what bakery came the loaves in loaves and fishes?
When the water changed to wine, the vintage see;
For the Virgin Birth, however, there is need for small
    endeavor—
Let Researchers drop their Research and See Me.

At the end of the week the researcher had a chance to get her own back, when she had to certify, with a pencil dot over every word, that the story was correct. Acrimonious battles ensued with the writer (sloppy! irresponsible!) trying to get away with something considered wrong by the researcher (pedantic! literal-minded!). Often the battles ended in compromises, or "weasels," with ambiguous language that might be "checkable" but not necessarily true.

The hours were brutal; early in the work week (beginning Thursday in those days) the pace was slack but turned into late-night or all-night sieges as the Monday close approached. The wife of one writer, A. T. Baker, complained in a letter to Matthews: "I can think of only three jobs that are important enough to work such an exhausting amount of hours: an obstetrician in an understaffed hospital or town; the President of any country; a general in time of war. I think it is ridiculous to go at such a killing pace just to get out a weekly newsmagazine, even though a good one."

Nevertheless, I loved it.

I loved it because of the satisfaction that comes—along with much agony—from working under pressure and against deadlines. One writer, in an office near mine, literally tore his hair out, in large handfuls, as he worked. Another, dissatisfied with a cover story he was writing, tossed all twenty-odd pages out the window. I was forced to test and develop my skills as if they were muscles.

The first significant pieces I wrote were about the Nuremberg war crimes trials, and this gave me an extraordinary sensation. Here were the dreaded nightmare figures who had loomed over me for years, a mixed bag of scoundrels, brutes, soldiers, bureaucrats and bourgeois, having been swept into the dock, on trial for their lives. Like many people, I had been uneasy about the retroactive nature of the law under which they were being tried; it was, I thought at first, just the victor's customary vengeance, dressed up in judicial robes. But I convinced myself that the Nazi horrors required a formal reckoning of a kind that had never happened before. The American prosecutor, Robert Jackson, it seemed to me, was civilization incarnate, wearing (I noted with *Time*'s customary attention to detail) a cutaway and gray-striped trousers for the great occasion.

The act of writing stories that would be read by an audience of several million momentarily brought together two people: the apprentice journalist to whom Nuremberg was a public event and the refugee to whom Nuremberg was part of personal history. As I added an adjective here (no, something stronger!) or looked for the right pejorative noun there (is that tough enough?), I felt that I was judging these men before the judges. In my mind I was punishing them, eradicating them, even before the hangman would. It gave me, for the first time, the sense of power that comes with journalism—an often spurious and dangerous feeling.

Even in those fledgling days I was disturbed that someone's pencil stroke could eliminate my description of a sunset, say, and obliterate the work of a night or week; this, rather than just the lack of a byline, constituted the *Time* writer's true anonymity. Besides, I was still clinging to my dream of being a playwright, a notion that was always present, like the knowledge of some valuable object locked away in a safe. But I experienced, just often enough, those rare moments when the right ideas, the right words, suddenly appear in your mind: for seconds your head swims, you feel the intoxication that otherwise comes with the thin air of high altitudes. To get paid for it, praised for it, to see my words (or most of them) in print within a few days—that was powerful balm for discontent.

Many of the writers really wanted to be doing something else, or thought they did. Few truly creative ones stayed on *Time* for very long; John Hersey, John O'Hara, Irving Howe, John McPhee, Calvin Trillin and John Gregory Dunne, among others, eventually fled. But some remained longer, mostly for the money, but not entirely so. I found that, mixed with the discontent, the complaints, the ritualistic announcements that, by God, one should quit and write a novel (or a play, in my case), or perhaps run a country weekly, there was much pride in craft and much loyalty to *Time,* though it was gauche to show it too openly.

It was possible, within limits, to guard one's individuality as a *Time* writer and to use one's imagination. That was true, for example, of Paul O'Neil, who wrote a classic piece called "The Last Traffic Jam," which ended with the vision of all the cars on all the streets and highways having finally come to a complete halt and America, incorrigible, getting ready "to lay boards across the tops of a billion sedans and start all over again."

And it was particularly true of James Agee, who not only reviewed movies for *Time* (as well as the *Nation)* for seven years, but was also *Time*'s house poet, with license to write about almost anything he wanted, and did so brilliantly while respecting the magazine's discipline. No one else was capable of a line like this, from a cover story on the devastating communal riots in India: "The world, with one war still red under its nails and another beating in its belly . . ."

Whittaker Chambers, especially, urged on me the belief that one could maintain some personal sounds within the tightly conducted *Time* chorus. He tried to prove it to me when he allowed me to start an otherwise mundane story about some UN meeting with the words "It was the hour of cocktails and small fears . . ." Matthews sent the story back with the remark "Means what?"

"I know what it means," replied Chambers, and the line stayed.

AFTER WORKING FOR Whittaker Chambers for several months, I still knew very little about him. In one of those outbursts of managerial efficiency that occurred occasionally even in those innocent years before the rise of the MBA, someone at *Time* had the notion of sending a questionnaire to all employees to see what past experience or special expertise might be useful to the magazine. Word went around that Whittaker Chambers had listed, among other things, foreign editor of the Communist *Daily Worker.* I wasn't sure whether to laugh at this as some grim joke or to take it seriously. I realized, like everybody else on the magazine, that Chambers was a fierce anti-Communist. But as the newest and youngest staff member, I was unaware of his Communist past.

He had been hired as a book reviewer in 1939, through the intervention of a friend on the staff. He always insisted that he got the job because he began a trial review of a war book with the words "One bomby day in June . . ." He was an excellent critic, but he inserted his political opinions into most of his reviews.

Matthews and other editors thought he was obsessive on the subject of Communism but were captivated by his writing skill and knowledge. Luce also came to admire him; he was promoted to senior editor and put in charge of the entire Back-of-the-Book, including such ideologically useful departments as press, education, religion. But what Chambers really wanted was to get his hands on the Foreign News section. He finally did in 1944, several months before I arrived at the magazine. It was the start of a fierce intramural conflict that was a parochial version of the bitter and intricate battle seething in the outside world.

The immediate question was whether the wartime alliance with the

Soviet Union could and should continue into peacetime. Beneath that question were larger issues: the very meaning of Communism and Americanism, the question of whether hostile ideas should ever be treated as hostile acts in a democracy.

I knew, of course, that throughout the thirties the Soviet Union had passionate champions in the United States, and not only Party members or fellow travelers. Many people were sincerely convinced that the Great Depression marked the end of capitalism and that Communist Russia had developed a superior system. Many also saw the Soviets as the only force willing to resist the Nazis; they reminded me of my father listening eagerly to those anti-Hitler broadcasts from Radio Moscow. In 1932 a group of distinguished writers, including Sherwood Anderson, Erskine Caldwell, Upton Sinclair, John Dos Passos and Edmund Wilson, had declared the Soviet Union to be "the moral top of the world where the light never really goes out." In August 1939 another group of four hundred liberal intellectuals extolled the Soviet Union as a "bulwark" of peace.

A few days after this manifesto appeared, Stalin concluded his nonaggression pact with Hitler. Except for a few diehards, most people saw this as a rank betrayal of all the "progressive" aims the Communists claimed to stand for. It was as if the pope had been unmasked as an atheist; many of the disillusioned faithful left the Communist church.

When, three years later, Hitler tore up the pact and attacked Russia, the Soviets were all at once fighting alongside the United States and many past Soviet supporters managed to shed their earlier shame. Even Winston Churchill said that if Hitler invaded hell, he would at least make a favorable reference to the devil in the House of Commons. In many quarters Stalin was seen no longer as the devil, but as our brave ally and his country as a member of the club called "the democracies." Typical was the movie *Mission to Moscow*, based on the book by Joseph E. Davies, who had served as U.S. ambassador to the Soviet Union in 1937–38. In that film the Soviet Union was a robust paradise, Stalin was good old Uncle Joe, Leon Trotsky a collaborator of the Nazis and the infamous purge trials a stern but just procedure. James Agee called it almost the first Soviet production from an American studio. Skeptics, mindful that the Soviet regime was still a tyranny that kept millions in labor camps, were widely dismissed as malevolent saboteurs of impending peace.

Chambers felt, with some reason, that he was surrounded by more or less dedicated left-wingers or by well-meaning but naive liberals who shared the widespread illusions about the Soviets. That category, in his view, included most of the foreign correspondents, who were apt to defend or rationalize Soviet policies.

As he edited the stories written mostly from their dispatches, he followed the *Time* system with special enthusiasm, often ignoring or altering the original reporting. He might change the emphasis, pick and choose certain facts while discarding others. Once he wrote an entire story about ideological developments in Hungary without any reporting from anyone; challenged by a researcher, he replied: "I *know* what they are thinking, I *know* what they are talking about in the cafés of Budapest."

His *Time* pages told of the advance of Communism throughout Eastern Europe, backed by the occupying Red Army, and asserted that Stalin's "ambiguous political purposes . . . were giving the creeps" to all but Communists and "unrealistic men of good will." A few years later, such statements would seem tame and obvious. But at the time, many correspondents found them outrageous. The telex machines positively quivered with protests from the people in the field, including John Hersey, then a *Time* correspondent in Moscow, who charged that his words were "torn from the context" and fitted into *Time*'s "vicious" editorial bias. Other correspondents made similar complaints. John Shaw Billings, Luce's deputy, looked into the situation and reported what was obvious: Chambers saw the Soviet Union and Communism as bent on gaining world power, while the correspondents disagreed, "unanimously reporting Russia as a peace-loving nation."

Even more heated was the conflict over China. Everyone knew that Luce, the missionary's son, was deeply devoted to the country of his birth. Young staff members felt sophisticated when they recalled that his Hotchkiss nickname had been "Chink." At the same time, a certain hush often accompanied mention of China, or Chiang Kai-shek.

To me, China, unlike Europe, was an abstraction. In my childhood, the European image of China was even more mythical than that of America. In the amusement park in Vienna's Prater, a giant "China-man" had towered over my favorite carousel; for obscure reasons he was called Calafati, and I never ceased to marvel at his queue, which was many yards long. He represented only a sideshow vision of China, but the "serious" vision wasn't all that serious, either; the French Enlighten-ment philosophers had used a largely imaginary China as a kind of rational model commonwealth, the better to condemn their own society.

As for the American view, it was far more realistic but also shot through with a great deal of myth; it had always alternated between demonization or idealization, between the Yellow Peril and *The Good Earth.*

Brutally invaded by Japan in 1931, China had fought bravely for its independence and with the outbreak of World War II became a cher-ished ally against the Axis. China's generalissimo Chiang Kai-shek was considered a hero by most Americans. He was a Christian, he said the right things about democracy, he was married to a beautiful woman who had been educated in the United States.

Luce did not ignore the shortcomings of Chiang's regime, criticized it and urged reform, though he tended to blame the defects on the years of desperate war and Communist opposition. But he still admired the "Gimo" and agitated for him both inside and outside of the magazine.

Luce's—and *Time*'s—man in China was the brilliant young Theo-dore White, whom Luce had met and hired during a 1941 trip to Chungking. In a sense, Luce both invented and adopted White. At first White was, if anything, a more passionate Chiang devotee than Luce himself, but he became gradually disillusioned with the regime's ineffi-ciency and corruption. He came to admire the Chinese Communists in their northern stronghold of Yenan for their spartan virtues, and like many China experts, he felt that Mao Tse-tung's followers were a differ-ent, not a "real" brand of Communists—"margarine Communist," they were sometimes called—and that basically they were pragmatic, demo-cratic-minded reformers. Luce kept wrestling with White—and I be-lieve often with himself. At one point he sent a memo to some of his senior colleagues, raising the possibility that his China policy was in "serious error" and asking for "advice and counsel." He allowed himself to be reassured. He and White kept arguing by cable. The situation finally exploded over a cover story in November 1944 on General Joseph ("Vinegar Joe") Stilwell, the American military commander in China, who loathed Chiang, considered him "an ignorant, illiterate, peasant son-of-a-bitch," habitually referred to him as "the Peanut" and wrote sophomoric doggerel about him. Eventually Chiang insisted on Stilwell's recall.

The cover story on these events was written by Fred Gruin, my future masthead neighbor, a calm, careful alumnus of *The New York Times.* The story was edited, of course, by Whittaker Chambers.

The finished version argued that Chiang should not be forced into a coalition with the Communists (as advocated by White and many others); that the Communists' "totalitarian features," such as secret police and political detention camps, were consistently ignored by American reports; that Chiang in Chungking ran a dictatorship to safeguard "the last vestiges of democratic principles" in China. White was enraged by the story and eventually quit.

"I was wondering," he observed later, "whether it was my proprietor or I who was mad."

From London, my friend Noah kept up a running commentary on *Time*'s offenses. He recalled his great-grandmother in Russia who would get her son to read the newspapers to her and invariably asked only one question: "Is it good for the Jews?" Noah continued: "In much the same way all *Time* editors go into a trance on any subject, and ask themselves: " 'Is it good for Chiang Kai-shek?' "

Luce believed—and would continue to believe—that Chiang's ultimate defeat had not been inevitable. "I was there," he often said, referring to a visit in 1945, "and I trust my judgment as a reporter."

In hindsight, it is clear that he was mistaken. But it is just as clear that many China experts (why were they always called "China hands"?) and journalists were equally mistaken in believing that a successful coalition with the Communists would have been possible, or in sizing up the Chinese Communists as a breed of democratic reformers.

In 1984, after White had returned to China for a two-month tour, I allotted him thirteen pages of *Time* to report what he found. I was now editor in chief, and I felt that in a way I was compensating for the reams of copy he never got into the magazine during the Luce years. When I first knew him he looked like a terrier with spectacles; now he looked more like an owl. White had long been a best-selling author and had mellowed. He wrote with love and perception of the people's past suffering and the turmoil of change. He still felt that China was a mystery, but he saw some hope that, step by slow step, the country could move toward a better, freer condition. He also wrote that Mao had undoubtedly been mad.

I asked him: "Don't you think that the seeds of madness were there all along?"

"You mean," he countered sharply, "should I have spotted them back in the forties? I don't see how anyone could have. But you are really asking me whether I was wrong back then. Well, I don't think so."

THE OFFICE BATTLES of the forties continued. Chambers would ignore, as much as he could, staff members he considered in the enemy camp. Occasionally he would call someone in and ask bluntly: "Where do you stand? Which side are you on?"

Blitzed by complaints about Chambers, Luce rendered a typically Solomonic decision. He strongly backed Chambers on his handling of China and of events in Europe, arguing that Chambers had counteracted strong propaganda designed to "smother honest reporting of Russian policy." But he sought to pacify some of his best correspondents by conceding that Chambers might have failed to distinguish between specifically Communist policies and "general revolutionary, leftist or simply chaotic trends." A little later Luce created a new section, "International," which would handle most large policy stories. It was eventually edited by a brilliant newcomer, Max Ways. Chambers continued to head a narrower foreign news department.

In his own way, he still had the last word. Just after the end of the

1945 Yalta Conference, Chambers wrote—and persuaded Matthews to publish—a brilliant political fantasy entitled "The Ghosts on the Roof."

The shades of Czar Nicholas II and his family, who had been shot to death by the Bolshevik revolutionaries in 1917, alight on the roof of their old summer palace at Yalta, where the conference is in progress. They want to know what the Big Three are up to. On the roof they meet Clio, the Muse of History. It turns out that the czar has become a Marxist and is a devoted fan of Stalin's. "What statesmanship! What vision! What power! . . . Stalin has made Russia great again." In large part he did so, the czar explains, by using a new "device for blowing up other countries from within"—Communism. With rising enthusiasm the czar and czarina enumerate Stalin's conquests—the Baltic states, Poland, Rumania and on and on.

Clio interjects: "All right-thinking people now agree that Russia is a mighty friend of democracy. Stalin has become a conservative."

The czarina retorts: "Between two systems of society, which embody diametrically opposed moral and political principles, even peace may be only a tactic of struggle."

"Ghosts on the Roof" provoked a furious reaction; letters to *Time* ran heavily against the piece. Inside the Time & Life Building many people fumed, gathered in small groups to grumble. On the other hand, there was much rejoicing among Chambers loyalists; a little band drifted one by one into his office, and someone brought a bottle to toast the Ghosts.

ONE NIGHT OVER drinks in a nearby bar, a researcher I liked very much named Mira, a refugee from Poland, turned to me earnestly. "Henry, I hope you won't come too much under the influence of Whittaker Chambers," she said, and went on for the better part of an hour to explain what was wrong with his "fanatical" anti-Communism.

I wasn't moved by her arguments because I was already strongly anti-Communist. Even back on the NYU student newspaper I had written fiery editorials against the Young Communist League.

Gradually I became part of what some ironically called the Chambers cell, although very much a junior member. Initially I was far more interested in his role as my editor than in his politics.

He was immensely skillful, though he rewrote too much. He worked with a huge, thick pencil—black lead, shining red on the outside—a brand then made specially for *Time*. His short fingers could scarcely grasp it, but he enjoyed wielding it like a weapon, especially when he savagely scrawled "Kill" on a story he decided to drop. Most other editors used "NR" for "not running," but Chambers preferred the lethal-action verb.

But he was unfailingly patient and kind with a novice. Once, when I was hopelessly stuck in a cover story on Tito, Chambers took me to the movies, which seemed like an outrageous waste of time with deadline approaching; but it did allay my panic.

At its best, his own writing style had a poetic simplicity, but sometimes it verged on the apocalyptic. He could get away with it, but when I tried to imitate him, the result was embarrassing. His editorial advice tended to be elliptical. From his Communist experience he had acquired a habit of theorizing and categorizing; once, when he read a story I had started with a pretentious quote from Auden, he leaned back, eyes twinkling, and declared, "Ah, the literary fallacy," as he might have said, some years before, "Ah, a bourgeois deviation."

Yet he loved literary allusions. He usually greeted Rinna Grossman, one of his favorite staff members, with a slightly altered quote from Marlowe: "Holla, ye pampered jade of Asia." When some event occurred that would undoubtedly please left-wingers, he would recite a treasured line: "Picture the lewd delight, under the hill tonight . . ."

He had a chuckly sense of humor that sometimes tended to the black. A few of us liked to lunch at a Dutch restaurant across the street that served *nasi goreng*, a spicy mixture of rice, meat or shrimp and vegetables, accompanied by *krupuk*, large, crisp, shrimp crackers. "Indonesian ears," he would invariably call them, and fantasize that in some colonial massacre all these ears had been cut off, frozen and turned into a major export.

Occasionally he would tell stories about his life, clearly selected with an eye for color. There was the time, after he finished high school, when he ran away from home and lived in the French Quarter of New Orleans, supporting himself doing odd jobs. He stayed in the same house as "One-Eyed Annie," a very ugly prostitute, and her pimp.

He also enjoyed telling how he first saw his future wife, Esther Shemitz. It was during a demonstration in support of a textile workers' strike in Passaic, New Jersey. The police tried to keep the strikers shut inside a factory hall, but finally the doors burst open and the strikers stormed out, seemingly led by a slender, black-haired girl. "Get that bitch in the brown beret!" Chambers would imitate a cop's angry voice. She was in Passaic to cover the strike for a pacifist publication, he would explain, and added proudly, "The cops rushed at her, swinging their clubs, but she marched right on."

Such TALES GAVE only a few tantalizing glimpses of his past. Chambers thought that his family represented "in miniature the whole crisis of the middle class." But the family was hardly typical.

Whittaker's mother had grown up in prosperity, but her family lost its money and she found herself expelled from what she always remembered as a girlhood paradise. His father was a commercial artist, not quite a failure and not quite a success, an uncommunicative and unloving man who for several years abandoned his family; during that period Whittaker's mother slept with an ax under the bed. *Her* mother, who lived with the family, hallucinated about the house being filled with gas and often threatened everybody with a knife. Whittaker, a strong boy, was usually assigned to wrest the knife from her, leading to struggles that left small, permanent scars on his hands.

There were other scars. Despite his physical strength, Whittaker (he was christened Jay Vivian but loathed those names and substituted his mother's maiden name) was a thin-skinned child who could never shrug off cruelty or injustice. He would never forget a schoolyard prank in which three boys relieved themselves on a lollipop and then offered it to an unsuspecting fourth; "I think it was at that point," he noted later, "that I developed a deep distrust of the human race."

Whittaker's younger brother, Richard, was an alcoholic who drifted in and out of the Chambers house, trailing despair at the cruelty, stupidity, materialism and power lust of their dying world. Richard eventually killed himself, leaving his brother riddled with grief and guilt.

By the time I knew him, he had settled on a farm near Westminster, Maryland, from where he commuted weekly to Manhattan. The farm was run by his wife and a hired man, but Chambers pitched in whenever he could. I had a hard time imagining that split existence, could not quite visualize him in overalls, milking his cows or racking hay. But he was never more open and serene than when he told us about the small crises and triumphs of the farm, never more warm and loving than when he spoke of his children. Only rarely did he allude to his Quaker religion—he had joined the Society of Friends shortly after his break with the Party, hence his dark suits and black tie.

Yet he had not escaped the conspiratorial attitudes of his Communist past. In restaurants he would usually look for a table against the wall or, even better, in a corner. An establishment called Hicks on Fifth Avenue, where I occasionally joined him for an ice-cream soda, had two entrances, and he would try to find a table from which he could keep an eye on both. It was a habit that he had developed in the days when he had just broken with the Party and lived in hiding, fearing for his life.

Sometimes we took walks, and we would discuss music or politics, and he would occasionally try out his fairly fluent German. Once, after an especially interesting ramble, I sent him a quote from *Faust*, a work he admired as much as I: *"Mit Euch, Herr Doktor, zu spazieren, ist ehrenvoll und bringt Gewinn* [To walk with you, Doctor, is an honor and profitable]."

I received a note in return: "No, no, Henry, though it was kindly meant. I am of that to which my plain dress is testimony. If you would understand what you are dealing with, I commend to you the lines of Robert Barclay [an often persecuted convert to the Quaker faith]: 'For, when I came into the silent assemblies of God's people, I felt a secret power among them which touches my heart; and as I gave way unto it, I found the evil weakening in me and the good raised up. . . .' But not honor and profit."

When I made some observation he considered apt, he would squint at

me and say, "Now how did you know that?" It was flattering for someone more than twenty years his junior.

Every now and then, Chambers made allusions or dropped hints
about people he had known in the Party. Once I wandered into his office
and he looked up from a newspaper. "Alger Hiss," he said, pointing to
the story he had been reading. It referred to some news that Hiss had
made in his role as general secretary of the United Nations founding
conference. "He is a Communist, you know."

"Oh really?"

"Yes," said Chambers. "And still he keeps getting these important
jobs. But that's a long story."

The name Alger Hiss meant nothing to me, and I let it pass.

CHAPTER NINE

I HAD BEEN WRITING for *Time* only a little over a year, but I was developing a slight case of claustrophobia. Of course there was New York all around me, with its theaters and concert halls, its political and intellectual prize rings. But what of the world beyond?

I wanted to get out, to see, to listen, to touch. I was not thinking of Europe or Asia. Des Moines or Cincinnati or Omaha sounded more compelling to me than Chungking, let alone Paris.

After some nervous hesitation I went to see Roy Alexander, the managing editor's deputy. "I'd like to suggest something. I hope it isn't too far out of line." Actually, I was sure that it was.

"Shoot," said "Alex."

"I'd like a little time off, on top of my vacation, to travel."

"Travel *where?*" he asked, plainly astonished and expecting me to name some exotic spots.

"The Midwest," I said. "I think it would be good for my American education."

Alex reflected for a few moments. "Yeah, it probably would be," he said. "I'll even throw in some expense money."

So, with a modest but habit-forming expense account, I set out on the first of many trips across America. I headed west, into the heartland, an expression—cliché!—that was still new to me.

I began my expedition in Chicago, having taken a sleeper from New York on the *Liberty Limited.* Those were the last years of the great trains—the *Super Chief* and the *Twentieth Century Limited,* the *Zephyr,* the *Comet,* the *Meadowlark,* with their air of barely restrained power, their rhythm of rattling ease, their aroma of plush and diesel fuel.

I arrived early, before my room at the Hotel Knickerbocker was ready, and wandered over to Lake Shore Drive. A morning mist was rising from the water, lightly shrouding the high, gleaming fronts of the buildings in a veil of purity. Elated, I strolled on and, within a few blocks, found myself behind the facade: in shabby, murky, garbage-strewn side streets suggesting anything but purity.

It was a stunning contrast that reappeared all over the city: the gothic commercial cathedral that is the Tribune Tower (in which are embedded, I learned, "chunks" of other worthy buildings like the Taj Mahal) and the tawdry, raucous saloons near the Loop; the classic opulence of the art institute and the reeking stockyards. The city's fast growth had left raw edges: rural wooden telephone poles, low buildings that looked unfinished. All this seemed only to heighten the atmosphere of untamed energy and drive.

Did I really feel this, or was I merely looking through a scrim of familiar caricatures—for instance, my father's operetta of long ago ("And in Chicago, have you any idea what's going on? Nothing but noise and tumult . . ."), or the legendary Chicago I had heard and read about, the domain of Al Capone and *The Front Page* and Sandburg's "Hog Butcher for the World . . . stormy, husky, brawling, city of the big shoulders"?

The answer was: Both. Myth and reality were inextricably mixed.

Curious echoes of the past caught up with me. I was told to meet someone in a house on Go-eethy Street, the local pronunciation of Goethe, and suddenly the poet-sage of Weimar appeared to my imagination in bizarre midwestern disguise. The sense of dislocation was even stronger when, passing a Chinese restaurant on Dearborn Street, I heard familiar music: though the raw air a loudspeaker was blasting "Play, Gypsies" from *Countess Maritza* at the bustling pre-Christmas crowds; a few people actually hummed along.

Afterward I went to a coffee shop, put nickels in the jukebox and listened to some American songs. I was not sure why I did this. Perhaps I was trying to demonstrate (but to whom other than myself?) that I now belonged in another world.

I moved on, north by northwest.

I WAS NOT prepared for the land. I had grown up within sight of mountains: a presence both inspiring and monitory, drawing one's eye upward to the line between rock and sky.

In Europe and on the East Coast of America I had come to know the ocean: the beach, serene or grim, continuously transformed by the play of the tides; the mystery of how water—mere liquid—could suddenly become an unstoppable force.

In spite of what I had heard and read about the romance of prairies or pampas, I assumed that flatland must be dull. And so I found it, at first. Mountains and sea emanate drama, danger, even hints of death. The land of the Midwest spoke of steady, persistent, monotonous everyday life. I felt no mystery, no menace—until I learned about the sudden assaults of twisters and blizzards, drought and flood.

I saw the regular progression of the fields in their precise rectangles, the scattered farms and towns as if dropped at random into the expanse stretching from horizon to horizon.

As the train window framed almost the same picture hour after hour—silo and windmill, road and field—I gradually sensed the magic of those distances, of the sheer, immense stretch of the soil. It was the overwhelming illustration of what I had learned in my history books about land as a key to the American story.

Today many would argue that land is far less significant except as a food producer and that its expanse has been shrunk by technology. The national saga of how it was conquered and civilized seems meaningless in decaying cities choked with crime and poverty. Yet in the Midwest land retains a powerful hold. It still determines the American sense of scale. In Europe nature is a fenced and neatly tended garden, and towns are as tightly packed and orderly as cemeteries. In the United

States nature seems unstoppable and towns are unpredictable, haphazard, free.

Eᴀʀʟʏ ᴏɴᴇ ᴍᴏʀɴɪɴɢ, in an upper berth on a train going from Des Moines to St. Louis, I woke with a start and heard myself say out loud: "Main Street." I had read the Sinclair Lewis book some years before but had not thought of it again until that moment. I decided that I would find the original Main Street and see what had become of it since Lewis had described it nearly thirty years before. After a very short stay in St. Louis, during which I picked up a copy of the book, I turned around and headed back up north.

Much as I enjoyed Lewis—I had read almost everything he had written—I realized that, Nobel Prize notwithstanding, he was mostly a caricaturist. But as such he was also a very sharp observer.

Sinclair Lewis had called his birthplace of Sauk Centre, Minnesota, Gopher Prairie. The novel had carried its bigotries and family secrets, its sturdy faith and ridiculous foibles to the outside world. "Main Street is the climax of civilization," Lewis had written with heavy irony. "That this Ford car might stand in front of the Bon Ton store, Hannibal invaded Rome and Erasmus wrote in Oxford cloisters. What Ole Jensen the grocer says to Ezra Stowbody the banker is the new law for London, Prague and the unprofitable isles of the sea. . . ."

It seemed to me, as I reread the passage on the train, that events had put truth into this flight of mockery. The United States had won World War II. It had not done so alone, of course, but it was now the only democratic country with strength and wealth to spare. America really did stand for the values embodied by Erasmus, and it did have a decisive influence on London, Prague and "the unprofitable isles."

I arrived the day before Christmas, and my first impression of the town was how small it was, how seemingly lost in the wintry desolation of the high plains. I was struck, as I have been again and again in many American settings, by the absence of gradation or transition; the prairie reached within a few yards of the town, earth or mire almost directly abutting front doors or store counters or altars.

The Palmer House ("Steam Heat, Hot and Cold Running Water, First Class Bar Room in Connection") was still the shabby structure with rickety chairs in the lobby that Lewis had described as the Minniemashie House, but it had acquired a shining cash register; the dining room, once a "jungle of stained tablecloths and catsup bottles," now had a bright red lunch counter and, I discovered, served sophisticated olives before meals.

I found my way to the *Sauk Centre Herald* and introduced myself to its editor, a short, thin, pale-faced man with knowing eyes named Chuck Rathe, who readily agreed to be my guide, though he was slightly puzzled by my self-imposed assignment. It was my first experience with one of the joyful fringe benefits of journalism; countless times since, in strange towns, I have sought out another journalist, invariably finding help, information, bright conversation over a few drinks and, in general, the camaraderie of the trade.

Walking into a shop or up to a front porch and asking people about their businesses, their lives, their past, was not easy, given my shyness with strangers—it required determination. But people were welcoming and patient, if a little curious about this young outsider with horn-rimmed glasses who asked questions in accents that evoked the East Coast, if not something more distant (according to neutral testimony, my speech by then was fairly standard Atlantic, with some British inflections left over from my Paris tutor and only a trace of German gutturals). For their part, the citizens of Sauk Centre seemed to have an accent, too; "out" and "about" sounded like "oat" and "a boat."

Main Street seemed scarcely longer than when Lewis's heroine, Carol Kennicott, measured it in a short, panicky walk, and it still consisted chiefly of flat, impermanent-looking two-story buildings, their wood occasionally thinly disguised by stucco. The greatest transformation had taken place in the corner drugstore. "A greasy marble soda fountain and pawed-over heaps of toothbrushes and combs [along with] nostrums for consumption" had been replaced by chrome fixtures and a neat, antiseptic variety of toys, household goods, film and Kleenex. Over it all hovered the picture of a white-sweatered Coca-Cola girl (a bit thinner than the one on my Paris calendar) looking down benignly as if to bless a country united by national brands.

I was looking for the old conservative pieties, and they certainly were there: belief in Christianity (mostly Protestant), Republicanism, business and virginity. But orthodoxy had been weakened, and even virginity seemed to have become a relative term. Ben DuBois, president of the First State Bank, was a Democrat who wrote a New Deal–ish column he published as advertising in the *Herald.* He invited me to have Christmas dinner with his family, and over the turkey (which I had not yet learned to like) he did his best to shock, with casual statements like "My great-aunt was one of the most notorious prostitutes in Syracuse, N.Y." He boasted that he did not believe in churches, quoted Montaigne and Marx, proclaimed the need for a strong government role in the economy—but at the same time deplored increasing regimentation.

While some of his iconoclasm was merely playful, DuBois did represent a certain undercurrent of doubt on Main Street, as well as its ability to assimilate heresy. Even Lewis, once loathed for his savage portrayal of the town, was now a local hero, his insults ignored. If Main Street had a faith, it was not simple.

Despite the victorious war, and the Midwest's huge contribution to it, I noticed little sense of triumph. There had been widespread predictions of recession and unemployment. Even though that had not happened, the concern lingered, reinforced by a series of strikes.

America was at the apex of its power, but the Midwest—like much of the rest of the country—didn't see it that way. Sauk Centre fretted about problems of "readjustment" and was groping to come to terms with the world. Some in the Economists' Club, a regular gathering of about a dozen prominent townspeople, advocated free trade ("I say pull down all the walls"), others disagreed, and argued that the United States needed tariffs to avoid competing with cheap labor ("Do you want to work for twenty cents a day?").

There was worry that collectivized Russia could outproduce America. Inevitably the debate turned to Communism.

"What we need is to stand up to them."

"Nonsense. You just see where it gets us."

"The people are just like us. They want the same things we want."

"Only difference is, they have one cartel in Russia, and we have several. I don't think Communism is morally wrong." This from a veteran. His father, a grocer, retorted: "You can't be a Communist without being an atheist."

"We don't have to worry about Communism," said DuBois, "if we can make our system work right here."

This exchange anticipated issues that would echo in national debates for decades. It also failed to anticipate many. There was no mention of women's rights, or the environment, or blacks. Only a handful of "Negroes" lived in Sauk Centre, and they were not considered a "problem."

HISTORY WAS NOT much in evidence. To most midwesterners a century was a very long time, which set them apart from southerners, who were still apt to refight Bull Run or the Wilderness Campaign, not to mention Europeans, who still argued passionately about the French Revolution or some glorious victory in an ancient war. (Years later, visiting Poland for the first time, I was puzzled that people seemed visibly stirred when they heard my name. The effect was caused by the Battle of Grunwald, so labeled for a village where Polish armies defeated the Teutonic Knights in 1410, a triumph still proudly remembered and celebrated in Poland.)

As I came to know more about the Midwest, I understood that the region was far more diverse than it first appeared, with deeply different political, social and religious traditions. Much of what had been progressive in predominantly agrarian midwest communities seemed to be the opposite in a highly industrialized, interdependent society. Midwest farmers clung to self-reliance, individualism, enterprise—but also to price supports. Visiting farms in Illinois, Minnesota, Iowa, I was struck by the huge distinction inherent in the words "peasant" and "farmer." As a youngster in Austria I had known peasants; they embodied a narrow, stolid mentality, both servile and cunning. When I spoke to them I almost automatically chose simple words and my voice sounded, in my own ears, artificially folksy. The gap between peasant and bourgeois was huge.

By contrast, the American farmer was independent and self-assured. Yes, he might be prejudiced about many things, and his life was certainly more isolated than that of city dwellers. But he was probably surer of his position, of his freedom and equality. I saw little of the old pitchfork radicalism that had so often erupted in bad times. Even on the smaller spreads that had not yet become mass-production enterprises, the farmer now was a manager in overalls, a bourgeois who happened to be driving a reaper.

But his life was changing; he was beginning to live in a new country. Insularity was eroding, perhaps not primarily because America was discovering the world, but because it was discovering—or rediscovering—itself.

Like weight being redistributed, a great shift was beginning in the population. That was a sequel to a migration from the land to the cities that had begun eighty years before. Blacks were streaming north in search of a better life. The bus stations I saw seemed haphazard, impermanent, grubby. But it was moving to watch black families get off the Greyhounds or Trailways, carrying cardboard suitcases and bundles tied with string. They watched for relatives who were supposed to meet them, their faces reflecting fatigue, hope and anxiety: the same look of immigrants landing on American piers.

The country was also about to discover a new sense of community, thanks to the stirrings of television. Once, at dusk, during a later trip, I walked into a farmhouse in Minnesota. It was dark except for one source of flickering light—a television set. An old woman was watching intently, oblivious of the surrounding gloom, obviously drawing warmth from this new type of hearth. Television, I realized, was a *presence* in the house, an antidote to loneliness and a wholly new link with a once remote world.

The midwesterners I met were still apt to see their part of the country as the "real America" and to dismiss other regions as backward and ignorant (the South), beautiful but crazy (the West) or ruined by aristocrats (the East). A Des Moines businessman slyly asked me if I knew the full quotation from which Horace Greeley's famous advice, "Go west, young man," was taken. I didn't. He triumphantly recited: ". . . and grow up with the country, away from these eastern idlers and imbeciles."

But a measure of cosmopolitanism was setting in. Within a few years Kansas would repeal Prohibition, which had been on the books since 1881, defying William Allen White's prediction that "they'll vote dry as long as they can stagger to the polls." Farmers were reading *The Wall Street Journal,* their wives were reading *Vogue* and the kids were sneaking comic books. The G.I. Bill meant that a college degree was no longer elitist. Travel agencies offered package trips to Europe; the Grand Tour was being democratized and mass-produced.

I was quite sentimental about the Midwest and still am. I even tend to agree that it represents "the real America," although I know that this is irrational because there are many different "real" Americas. The region's ugliness and narrowness Lewis complained about would find new forms. But first impressions, like first loves, never quite let you go. The Midwest, for all the changes that have transformed it since, will always be the place I found during my first voyage there, a place vast, open, strong, and embodying both parts of the cliché: heart and land.

CHAPTER TEN

THE MIDWEST REINFORCED MY BELIEF that the United States is the closest thing to a classless society that ever existed; but this makes the remaining class distinctions (and they will always remain, anywhere) more subtle and harder to read than in places where class is openly, assertively displayed. The result, I found, was a social topography to which there are very few maps.

The absence of rules, or their ambiguity, was unsettling. If an Emily Post was needed as an arbiter of manners, it could only mean that there were no fixed manners. Could one really trust, and should one emulate, the general informality? I had grown up in societies in which calling someone *du* or *tú* meant the height of intimacy or condescension. In the beginning I found it impossible to call my superiors at *Time* Tom or Roy, and I even addressed some of the older researchers as "Miss."

Titles, I noticed, were rare (Ph.D.'s did not put "Dr." on their calling cards!). Rank was not stressed, boss and clerk seemed to wear much the same suits and drove much the same cars. I slowly grasped that beneath middle-class uniforms and uniformity lurked significant distinctions, that identical-looking suits could be quite different, that the distance between the East Side and West Side of Manhattan was not measured merely in city blocks, that there were hierarchies and tribes, great names and lowly names, old money and new.

All this made fitting in both easier and more difficult. Above all, I wanted to fit in. Even as a child I was not gregarious, inclined to observe silently from the edges of a room. I didn't like it, but at first I didn't know how to overcome it. The experience of being chased from my birthplace into an uncertain world taught me that I could not afford shyness if I wanted that place in line, that visa—or that assignment.

The journalistic world in New York was divided into clans, and *The New Yorker* clan had little to do with *The New York Times* clan, for instance, and neither mixed much with the *Time* people. It took me a while to feel part of our clan.

Opportunities for this were provided by countless office parties; by a semiofficial hangout on Forty-eighth Street just across from our building called the Three Gs, which featured generous drinks, terrible food, sickening green walls; and by the annual company picnic at some nearby country club, inevitably known as *"Time* Out." Aside from the small and special cluster in college, I have never been able to form new friendships easily. With men, that is; my closest friends have been women, often without any sexual involvement. But at *Time* I did find a circle of companions.

There was Robert McLaughlin, a talented fiction writer (his story, "A Short Wait Between Trains," was a much anthologized classic) who was at the magazine strictly for the regular salary, turned out fast, competent copy—almost without looking, I sometimes felt—and struggled to control much inner anger. Douglas Auchincloss, who had worked in psychological warfare and—a natural extension—in advertising, combined a passionate interest in religion with an equally passionate and much requited interest in women. His copy was always excellent and always late. Chris Merillat, a buttoned-down ex-marine from the Midwest with a laugh that he barely allowed to struggle to the surface, as if he were trying to suppress some ill-mannered eruption. He had great curiosity about history's odd corners and would later spend years working on a book about St. Thomas the Apostle, the "Doubting Thomas." Roger Hewlett, a former actor and would-be playwright with a Lincolnesque, *jolie-laide* face. He had an invigorating gift for parody. The wonderfully named Solie Tootle, a dazzlingly blond researcher, who piloted her own plane and always looked as if she were ready to break out the champagne. With Rinna Grossman as a sort of group leader, we used to lunch together, often picnic style at someone's apartment, and inevitably became known around the office as the Lunch Bunch.

The group made me feel at ease and helped teach me something about that complex American social structure I had found so puzzling. I came to understand what Ivy Leaguers were (contrary to a widespread impression, they didn't constitute a majority on the staff), and that a midwesterner could have an impeccable eastern veneer without being phony, and that the right, easy style could make acceptable what would have been vulgar in anyone else—and that in most situations these things didn't matter at all, but somehow, in some, they did.

I began to discover the infinite gradations of snobbery, as well as a phenomenon especially hard for a European to appreciate: reverse snobbery, with its delight in understated dress and decor often indistinguishable from shabbiness. During a visit to Tanglewood, I was a guest (courtesy of a Boston correspondent) at a distinguished club whose furnishings might have been accepted only with hesitation by the Good Will.

I also learned that the old, European, aristocratic contempt for "trade," of which I'd had more than a whiff in my childhood, was rare in America, partly because there was no convincing aristocracy; there was social anti-Babbittry and ideological anticapitalism, but these were more than made up for by the businessman's self-regard. At *Time* the people from the "business side," circulation and advertising types headed by the publisher, mixed with us occasionally; at one point, however, Matthews had forbidden the publisher to enter the editorial floor without his express permission. They were a separate tribe: permanent smiles, enamel complexions, but—in those days—an almost touching, if perhaps grudging, deference to "you guys who put out this terrific book."

The editorial staff was rather inbred, a condition reinforced by our peculiar week, which separated us from the rest of the city; we worked Saturdays and Sundays and had Tuesdays and Wednesdays off. The young wife of one editor once told Luce she wished he would change the schedule so that people would be free on Sundays. Why? he wanted to know. "Because," was the reply, "I am too young to give up dancing." Luce was puzzled. "Why can't you dance on Tuesdays?" he asked.

The Time & Life Building and its immediate vicinity seemed surrounded by an invisible bubble under which people drank, ate and very often slept with each other. Office affairs were pervasive. They were usually discreet, especially by later standards, but one quickly learned to read the signs: the near simultaneous exits from the office by this writer or that researcher, the long disappearances, the notes sent back and forth. When I took over my new writer's desk, recently vacated by someone who had moved to another office, I found a stack of love letters he had carelessly left behind.

Sometimes discretion wore thin; we all kept hearing stories. There was the one, for instance, about an editor who was chasing a researcher around his cluttered office and was just about to land her on the couch when she saw some books scattered there and cried out: "Oh no! Not on top of the Jewish encyclopedia!" Sometimes there were tears and scenes. In one public incident a researcher, a small, exotic blonde with the face of a lascivious doll, accosted a writer in a much traveled corridor and screamed at him for not leaving his wife as he had promised. (We were astonished, because we had always considered him rather square.)

Affairs occasionally led to divorces. One party to a messy separation, broke and with no place to live, spent many nights sleeping at his desk, to the outrage of the cleaning women. Several colleagues married *Time* researchers. I sometimes had the impression that, somehow, all of life was taking place in the office.

IN THE EARLY fifties my editor and mentor after Chambers was Max Ways, a graduate of Philadelphia and Baltimore newspapers. His father had been H. L. Mencken's first editor, and Max, who was capable of Menckenesque anger at stupidity and prejudice, often quoted the great curmudgeon. "Injustice is not so hard to bear," was one of his favorite lines, "it's justice that really hurts." Max had worked as an analyst of enemy economies for the Joint Chiefs of Staff and had strong views on economic matters, passionately arguing, for example, that the U.S. Postal Service should be privatized.

I did not think that he was very impressed by me at first. Eventually he became quite complimentary about my work and told me later that I had actually begun to win him over in conversation when I said that the British were masters of creative hypocrisy. He liked that phrase. His subtle mind delighted in paradox; when Tito broke with Stalin, for example, he argued that the rift occurred not because the two were so different, but because they were so alike. He was given to arcane historical and philosophical allusions; he might hold forth, for example, on the Gnostics, an ancient conglomeration of sects believing in the power of secret knowledge, whom he compared to modern intellectuals.

As an editor Max was relentlessly logical about how an article should be constructed, and his intensity was often expressed in body language. He might rear back abruptly in his chair when he found a transition too harsh or twist his torso to illustrate a whole new direction for a story. Hair flying upward, eyes peering over the rims of his glasses, he would struggle for the right term to explain what he meant. Often he merely managed to say, "The story needs . . ." and give a twist or wave of the hand, like an orchestra conductor. I learned to read those gestures after a while; when I failed he would mercilessly rewrite my copy.

Though he had come late to the *Time* culture, he quickly absorbed the highly formalized craft of *Time* writing, in those days governed by as many rules as the art of *Die Meistersinger*. Much of the old *Time* style was gone, living on mostly in parodies. But quite a few traces remained. "Great & good friend" was still the accepted euphemism for lover, and America's leading newspaper was invariably the "good, gray *New York Times*."

New *Time* writers, myself included, took pains to master "tycoon" and "pundit" and the use of professional appellations, as in "Ecdysiast Gypsy Rose Lee" or merely "Busdriver Smith." We gleefully pounced on contractions like cinemogul. The pages were still populated by newshounds (or hens), moppets, and socialites. The magazine still liked its characters to be dynamic; they strode rather than walked, plumped for rather than chose, whacked rather than merely beat, made whopping rather than just big profits.

We worshiped words, played with them, laughed over them, made fools of ourselves with them. *Time* liked unusual headings: for instance, "Peripatetics" for stories about the international movements of diplomats; we tried to come up with new ones (I once proposed "Threnodies," which was rejected as too gloomy).

I struggled endlessly with my leads, trying to be especially clever and arresting; this could take days, and I realized that it was just an excuse to avoid the real, painful business of writing. I confess that I can still recite some of my favorites ("The Democrats have nothing to cheer but fear itself.")

But the essence of *Time* writing was not words but structure. One of the simplest reasons for the success of the newsmagazine formula is that it avoids the deadly "inverted pyramid" form of daily newspaper articles (most important fact first, additional facts in descending order of significance) and instead tells events as far as possible in chronological sequence. But that is only a general principle; it doesn't tell you just how to put a particular story together. I struggled week after week with the problems of organization—for instance, avoiding clunky transitions and devices like "to repeat" or "as already stated above." It sounds simple, but it isn't.

Sometimes, when I went to bed near dawn in the midst of an especially difficult cover story, its pieces would assume almost physical shape in my mind, and between waking and sleeping, I feverishly moved them about in endless combinations.

OVER ALL OUR struggles hovered T. S. Matthews—T.S.M., irreverently rendered as "tism" by Rinna Grossman—always deferred to as supreme arbiter of style, taste and values. My knowledge of New England prep schools was confined to hearsay and fiction, but I imagined Matthews in a headmasterly role.

Matthews was born in Cincinnati, educated at Princeton and Oxford;

there was little of his hometown to be found in his stiff manner and laconic, precise speech. His father was an Episcopal bishop, his mother a Procter & Gamble heiress, and he was comfortable neither with God nor with mammon. As a young man he wanted to be a poet, became a book reviewer for the *New Republic*, where he worked under Edmund Wilson. After Wilson left he was persuaded by a friend at *Time* to join the staff as a writer.

At first he couldn't take the magazine seriously; it was run, he thought, by "smart, ignorant boys." On every piece of his copy, he observed, he could have written: "I do not like my work." Years later, embittered after a falling-out with Luce, he wrote me from England: "I feel that *Time* writers are in somewhat the same case as New York subway riders who have never experienced the London underground: they have had a hard life and have no reason to think that there could be a better."

Matthews was aloof, formal. The weekly staff tea parties he forced himself to give in his office were agony both to him and to his guests. His deafness increased his distance from people. He was slightly old-fashioned in his speech; when he promised me a raise, he said that I could "expect a betterment." ("A betterment yet!" Noah exclaimed sarcastically when I told him about it.) He was a snob, less in a social than in an aesthetic sense. Once a young cousin of his whom I had come to know brought his new fiancée to the office to meet Matthews. She was a charming girl of Russian-Jewish background. "The dirty-fingernail type" was Matthews's reported judgment.

I wondered whether he was anti-Semitic. I had encountered the social *Gentleman's Agreement* form some years earlier, when I went to a travel bureau to make a reservation at a Florida hotel and was told that it was restricted. I did not know what that meant but found out soon enough. It was a shock, but I concluded—perhaps a little too easily—that it was not very frightening compared with the lethal anti-Semitism of Europe. Matthews certainly had a sense that Jews were different and was capable of arrogant generalizations (he might say things like "Why do they hurt their own cause by being so shrill, by protesting any and all slights?"). But I came to believe that he was fundamentally decent.

Years after he had left *Time* he covered the trial in Jerusalem of the kidnapped SS leader Adolf Eichmann, and he developed a deep respect and affection for Israel. In those later years I also came to see his wry humor, his vulnerability and his permanent sense of guilt.

But when I served under him (I use the "served" advisedly), very much his junior as well as a junior on *Time,* we had almost nothing in common; we met only on the shared ground of words.

He was a masterly editor for whom good English was a cult. He hated prolixity; once, over a rare lunch, we discussed writers, and I admitted to admiring Maugham. Half-dismissively, half-admiringly, Matthews said, "Oh, he just knows what to leave out." Matthews, plying his editing pencil, also knew what to leave out, as his writers learned to their sorrow but ultimately to their benefit. His style was matched only by the unvarying precision of his handwriting. He was famed and feared for his devastating marginal notes on copy, such as "Sounds like Choctaw. Try it in English." On another occasion he noted: "This story is badly researched, written, edited and typed." (I feel that he never surpassed his *Fortune* colleague Eric Hodgins, who once wrote on a manuscript, "This substantially subtracts from the sum of human knowledge.")

When he finally, reluctantly, put his initials, T.S.M., in the upper-right-hand corner, it was, to his writers, a major seal of approval. Outright praise from him was rare and treasured. Once, when he put "Good" on one of my stories and on second reading crossed that out and changed it to "excellent," I felt as if I had won a Pulitzer.

It was Matthews who eradicated most of the old *Time* style, kept some distinguished writers on the magazine and attracted new ones. He brought taste and judgment to the cultural pages, an accomplishment on a magazine whose first issue had speculated that T. S. Eliot's *Wasteland* might be a hoax.

Nevertheless the magazine was still held in contempt by most intellectuals—and by people who wanted to pass for intellectuals. What made them really angry was the rise of what Dwight Macdonald would call "Midcult."

Scandal sheets and women's magazines need not be taken seriously.

But magazines like *Time* had intellectual pretensions and were therefore threatening. Macdonald, who once worked for *Fortune* and considered Luce "by no means the worst" of American journalistic entrepreneurs, argued that Midcult "has it both ways; it pretends to respect the standards of High Culture while in fact it waters them down and vulgarizes them."

Thus *Time*, in its much advertised effort to be "curt, clear, concise," was accused of oversimplifying complex situations. True enough—but compared to what? Certainly compared to the better literary or scholarly journals, but not compared to most of the press, or "Masscult." Especially in the coverage of the arts, religion, education, science, *Time* took up stories most newspapers and popular magazines never touched. No other publication approaching a mass circulation (*Time* sold some 1.5 million copies a year in the late 1940s) would have carried the equivalent of *Time*'s cover stories about Arnold Toynbee or Reinhold Niebuhr or C. S. Lewis or T. S. Eliot (no longer considered a hoax) or Joyce Carey or Augustus John. When critics complained that such stories were middlebrow, they forgot that for most American newspaper readers, middlebrow was a step up.

Another charge was that *Time* was snotty and smart-alecky, often hurtful to people. Certainly true, although the complaint could be carried to the edge of paranoia, as it was by Matthews's former boss Edmund Wilson, who wrote that *Time*'s "jeering rancor" reduced most people it wrote about to "infra-human" manikins who "pop up their absurd little faces in front of the lenses of the Luce photographers."

The most serious complaint about *Time* was that it was politically slanted and biased. Again, true. At the outset Luce and Hadden had decided that there would be no editorial page in the magazine and that analysis and opinion would be mixed in with the news, as it always had been until the beginning of the twentieth century. The relatively new but already sacred convention of separating fact from opinion is largely phony, because it implies that anything that isn't an editorial or a signed column is factual. In reality any news story is slanted in a dozen ways, by the selection of facts, by emphasizing some details over others, by the attribution of views to named or unnamed sources of the reporter's choosing. Much of the time readers who complain about bias in a story are really complaining that the bias is not their own.

The magazine's aim, the young founders had announced in their prospectus, would not be objectivity but fairness: presenting both sides of a case and indicating which side struck the editors as more persuasive. But "on-the-one-hand, on-the-other-hand" journalism, of course, was boring, and besides, Luce considered it irresponsible; *Time,* he felt, had a duty to show where it stood.

But that duty was apt to be expressed by the use of loaded words. For similar actions, a favored politician might be described as hard-hitting, an unfavored one as brutal; what might be thoughtful in one would be bumbling in another. So sometimes the fairness principle prevailed; often it did not. Over the years this situation would get worse; it would also get better. During Matthews's tenure, it caused him much pain and much conflict with Luce.

In response to a sharp memo from H.R.L., T.S.M. replied, "You have written it as if to dogs, not to human beings. . . ." Luce apologized, and Matthews noted later, "I can't imagine Beaverbrook or McCormick, or any press lord you can mention, tolerating that kind of talk from one of his subordinates."

Matthews was a liberal, more or less, but he judged politics, like everything else, essentially on the basis of aesthetics. In his view most politicians were boorish, stupid and tasteless; the very act of running for president, he once told me, showed that a man must be power mad—or simply mad—and thus should be disqualified by the very act of running.

Matthews was less a journalist than a literary man. Some years later, when my son, Peter, was born, he remarked, "Perhaps he will grow up to be a better journalist than either of us, or perhaps something even better than a journalist." The professional journalists on the magazine, people who had been trained on dailies, respected his gift of style but resented him for being too arty, too snobby. He also struck some as being sanctimonious. "He should have been a bishop," snarled Max Ways, a Catholic. "But in *his* church, not in mine."

The most journalistic of the anti-Matthews group was Roy Alexander, a Jesuit-trained Catholic ("the Jebbies seem to have a lot of influence around here," he would say). He seemed simple: cheery, brisk, slightly profane. He was, in fact, highly complex. The son of an opera singer, he was a lifelong devotee of the man he called Joe Green, meaning Giuseppe Verdi; he was the magazine's top authority on Latin quotations and knew more theology than anyone around except Luce. He was one of the few people I have ever known who really believed in an afterlife; he looked forward to it, he said, because then he would know all the answers. He had been a military pilot, was a friend of Lindbergh's, had risen to a top job on the *St. Louis Post-Dispatch.*

He liked to move quickly. When an editor pleaded with him to hold a story for another week to make it better, Alex would invariably say no, with the admonition "Only one thing grows in the hand." But he understood that *Time* was not a newspaper and had the limitations of a weekly; crossing his hands behind his head, tilting back his chair and looking out through small, uncomfortably shrewd eyes, he would pronounce, "A newsmagazine with a scoop is like a whore with a baby."

Gradually Matthews's position was becoming shaky. He had been drinking heavily; he would have several martinis for lunch (usually at the nearby Hotel New Weston, whose restaurant offered a fourth martini free after the first three) and then return to the office, swallow mouthfuls of Gelusil, and pass out on his couch for a while. In the evening he would drink more while working. He would feel fine at the time but terrible in the morning. ("No gentleman ever feels very well in the morning," as someone once remarked.) The hangover was an accepted part of the culture, and not only at *Time.* Realizing that he couldn't go on drinking and do his job, he went on the wagon temporarily but knew, as he wrote later, that he was fundamentally dissatisfied with his job and "couldn't go on doing it indefinitely without some sort of drug to keep me quiet." To his sister he once said, "Better a bottle in front of me than a frontal lobotomy"—an uncharacteristically awful joke.

Eventually he took a leave of absence to travel in Europe and, from a distance, take a whole new look at *Time.* During the trip Matthews's wife fell ill; she would die within a few months, of cancer. On his return

Luce gently moved him upstairs with the title of editor, while the real power would be in the hands of his former deputy, Roy Alexander, who now became managing editor. He had been a good executive officer to Matthews, but he grabbed power when he saw the chance. Matthews, a spectacularly poor office politician, did not at first understand the real situation; he felt Luce had done him a favor and thanked him for being "as generous and heartening as only you can be."

I came to appreciate Alexander's sturdiness, his essential kindness, but at first I was wary of him because I revered Matthews and felt that under Alex, all T.S.M.-inspired attempts to give the magazine a modicum of literary distinction would vanish.

AFTER FIVE YEARS at *Time*, I was vaguely dissatisfied.

When Matthews invited ideas and criticism from the staff, I complained about the shallowness of some stories, insufficient enterprise in developing new subjects. I called *Time* middle-aged, though it was a year younger than I, and arrogantly pronounced: "To be mature is an achievement. To be middle-aged is unforgivable."

Above all, I felt that *Time* had become too familiar. Through war and peace, depression or recovery, disaster or triumph, *Time* chronicled the world in one-column measure, and no event, however momentous, had yet pushed the magazine beyond that measure or enlarged the neat little one-column headlines beyond their uniform size (14-pt. Vogue bold). Immutably the magazine opened with National Affairs which in turn always opened with The President's Week, and marched on to Foreign News and all the other regular departments, with only rare alterations. Change was overdue, as there was bound to be a revolution in journalism—or, strictly speaking, another revolution, if *Time* represented an earlier one.

Yet the thought of change was also threatening. I had a recurring dream: I open the magazine and it looks totally different. The classic architecture—column after column, like a Greek temple—has been smashed. Type comes in all sizes, fat and thin; it runs all over the page, in lines long and short. Pictures have burst their neat little black frames and grown to monstrous shapes. Special features, different and obscure headings, have broken up the department structure that used to be as reliable as a calendar.

The image was prophetic, because it came very close to describing what eventually happened to the magazine. But at the time, was it a hopeful dream or a nightmare? It was both. Much as I advocated reform, the steady, weekly sameness of *Time* obviously gave me a reassuring sense of stability—as it surely did the reader. Life was unpredictable, but not the way *Time* framed it. Chaos is the normal state of affairs, but *Time* tried to impose order—an artificial order—on chaos.

Matthews told me that he agreed with my criticism but was in no position to do anything about it. Luce dispatched him to London to explore the possibility of a British version of *Time*. When at length he got the news that Luce had decided against the project, Matthews cabled: "Why did you keep me standing on tiptoe so long when you weren't going to kiss me?"

He settled in Britain, bitter about *Time*. I looked forward to his periodic visits, for I was deeply fond of him. He took to writing sad, if not despairing, poetry, which he published privately and regularly sent to his friends for Christmas. But he lost none of his editorial acerbity. At his funeral in Princeton in 1991, I heard the instructions he had left for the service. "I should like to have the 19th Psalm read (not sung) ['The heavens declare the glory of God . . .']. The text I want is in the Book of Common Prayer, not the King James version. I'd like to have this great poem recited by a trained reader of verse—not in mincing chancel tones nor with oratorical vulgarity. . . . And I want this psalm read by a single voice, not in the dreary antiphonal between the precise priest and the slurred, shamefaced muttering of the congregation."

CHAPTER ELEVEN

JUST AS I WAS GRUMBLING about familiarity and routine, something unpredictable happened. While I was still regularly writing about foreign affairs, I was given an occasional special assignment. Perhaps because my bosses knew vaguely about my father's line of work, and because I often talked about my interest in the theater, these assignments were mostly in the entertainment area.

In 1947 I was asked to write a cover story about Oscar Hammerstein. In the past my father had considered Hammerstein his counterpart in America and thus an equal. Now he saw him as a man to whom he wrote deferential letters, a figure on top of a world he could not reach. When I told him about the *Time* assignment he said to me with a touch of sarcasm: "Maybe you should ask him how he thinks he would have done if he had been thrown out of America and tried to make a living as a librettist in Vienna or Berlin."

Mostly *Time* writers did not meet the people they profiled, but I asked permission to interview Hammerstein myself. As I walked into his suite at the Ritz in Boston, where a new show was trying out, I clutched the carefully prepared "query" of the sort that usually went to correspondents: a list of questions I had drawn up. I was still a novice in the interviewer's game of probing and feinting.

Hammerstein turned out to be the gentlest of men, pleasantly awkward, with the build of a mellowed ex–football player, a shy but warm smile often creeping out from under his permanent worried frown. We talked about his early operettas of the cloak-and-daguerreotype era, such as *Rose Marie* and *Desert Song*, which had been as corny as anything produced in Vienna, and his classic *Show Boat*. He recalled his long years of failure, during which, thanks to some "inner conceit," he'd stubbornly refused to give up.

Hammerstein was modest about his role in the revolution of the musical theater; he had led it away from bathos or farce toward the natural characters and simple, unaffected language of *Oklahoma!* and *Carousel*.

The new show, *Allegro*, was even simpler. It was about a young physician who falls in love with the wrong girl, then the right girl, and along the way learns about the evils of greed. It would not be a hit, but Hammerstein saw the musical as a reflection of his own life and philosophy. "The sophisticates have let us down. This is a time for hope." It was the outlook of a man, perhaps naive, who wrote so many of America's great songs and expressed much of the country's optimism on the eve of the fifties.

Just before leaving, I said: "I believe you know my father, or at least of him."

"Of course," Hammerstein said politely. "I think we met once when I visited Vienna, and we have corresponded. I hope he is well."

"Yes, thank you," I said lamely, wanting to add: "No, not really. He wants to be *you*, and he can't be."

H OLLYWOOD WAS NEXT. A year after the Hammerstein project I was assigned to write a cover story on Olivia De Havilland, who had just finished shooting *The Snake Pit*. Leaving behind all those stories about whither the UN or what next for British Socialism (not to mention an exceptionally cold New York winter), I flew to California. I was to join forces with a *Time* Los Angeles correspondent, Ed Rees, who had been assigned to report the article, although he was actually an aviation specialist. ("It figures," he said. "Her cousin manufactures planes. He makes the De Havilland bomber.")

At first this legendary place seemed disappointingly mundane, suggesting a garish Main Street with palm trees. But what exactly was Hollywood? I discovered, of course, that it was not Los Angeles, and I decided to see something of the city before exploring the movie enclaves. Despite all advance warnings, I tried walking. In the late afternoon I started out from Beverly Hills in the direction of downtown Los Angeles. I walked for miles, well into the night, along endless avenues: a concrete desert, interrupted again and again by neighborhood clusters, sometimes tawdry, sometimes oddly charming, like urban oases. I had an amused vision of being lost forever, disappearing.

Finally, overwhelmed and exhausted in the small hours, I caught a streetcar back to Beverly Hills. The ride was strangely cozy and quiet; the bright red car, not unlike the trams of my childhood, seemed to be rattling in place on a movie set, and the passing, often rustic landscape looked as if it were being scrolled past the windows.

For years Hollywood had been the remote magic lantern from which I drew so many of my early images of America. Now, suddenly, here I was, hearing those mythical names of stars and directors and producers casually mentioned. Ed suggested that we could see almost anyone I wanted, thanks to *Time*'s clout.

The movie industry was even more eager than usual for publicity, because it was in a slump. The old Hollywood was nearing the end of its gaudy empire, but it didn't know that yet. For the moment the studio system was still in force, consisting of scattered dukedoms hierarchically organized; even a visitor could quickly see the rigid dividing lines between extras and bit players, featured players and stars, cheap writers and expensive writers and, enthroned above all, the omnipotent studio head. One of the best was the producer of *The Snake Pit* and chief of the 20th Century–Fox studios, Darryl Zanuck.

I knew the basic facts: midwestern, school dropout, pulp writer, assistant to Mack Sennett in the silent era, author of endless scripts for the dog star Rin Tin Tin, production chief for Warner Brothers at twenty-seven. Short, physically reckless as a polo player and big-game hunter, he was also courageous professionally. In seventeen years as the creative tyrant of 20th Century–Fox, he uniquely combined profitability and quality. He was once quoted as saying that the secret of his success was to "make good shit." Many of his films deserved a higher rating than that, notably *The Grapes of Wrath*, the searing screen version of the Steinbeck novel. Despite such exceptions, Hollywood, then, was like Detroit before the fall; its products were large, reliable, not very adventurous, and in tune with the customers' tastes—until the customers decided otherwise.

Zanuck agreed to see me, and I found him, surrounded by underlings, pacing in front of his office bungalow, wearing a Tyrolean hat, swinging his famous sawed-off polo mallet for emphasis while puffing a huge cigar through his slightly Bugs Bunny–ish teeth. He wanted to talk about how difficult and daring a decision it had been to make *The Snake Pit*, which was based on a good but depressing novel about insanity and appalling conditions in mental hospitals. "Everybody thought *I* was crazy to want to make this picture, including my wife," he said. "Believe me, it was a hell of a gamble, even though you fellows from New York may not be all that impressed." I noticed the strange defensiveness that even the most successful Hollywood figures showed toward the East.

Just as I was about to be dismissed, Zanuck asked me where I came from, and I told him. The mention of Vienna seemed to provoke a gleam in his eye. "You know Mike Curtiz, the director?" Of course I had heard of the man who had directed *Casablanca*. "He is Hungarian, you know," Zanuck went on. "In fact, he fought in the Austro-Hungarian army during the first war. I served in the American Expeditionary Force. Listen to an extraordinary story."

As he told it, during some fierce, close-in fighting on the western front, he captured an Austro-Hungarian soldier. But the fellow was strong, slashed at Zanuck with his bayonet (he illustrated by swinging his mallet) and badly cut his leg before escaping. Years later, when Zanuck was production chief at Warners, he met a director named Curtiz; the man had a strong Hungarian accent and seemed vaguely familiar. Sure enough, he was the soldier who had gotten away! His real name was Kertész. When he recognized Zanuck, he fell on his knees and tried to kiss the wound he had inflicted. "Here, I'll show you," said Zanuck, starting to roll up his trousers. "People wouldn't believe this if I put it in a movie, would they?"

"Fantastic!" I said stupidly; it was a word I would find myself using constantly in Hollywood. But there was something in the faces of Zanuck's entourage that made me suspicious.

Suddenly Zanuck burst out laughing. "You swallowed it, didn't you?" He was delighted. Curtiz-Kertész had indeed been in the Austro-Hungarian army, as Zanuck had been in the American Expeditionary Force, but the rest was an elaborate fiction he loved to try on visitors.

In the following days I saw something of Zanuck at work—his fabled, interminable story conferences, at which he enacted whole scenes; his fanatic attention to detail, expressed in an endless stream of memos. *The Snake Pit* certainly had benefited from attention to detail, his and everyone else's. It was a brave and excellent film. Appropriately enough for Hollywood, I thought, it dealt with reality and illusion, albeit in its extreme form. It gave a picture of life inside a state institution that was harrowingly realistic—and not only for its day. The director, Anatole Litvak, had carefully studied Camarillo State Hospital, had even placed microphones in several wards to record the cries and muttering of the sleeping patients and faithfully reproduced them for the movie sound track. Olivia De Havilland had also spent time in the hospital. As I interviewed her, remembering my own weeks in that French sanatorium, I was especially fascinated by the stories she told me about her encounters in the institution: for instance, the seemingly rational woman who suddenly declared that she had to get home to join her dead son, who was "still in the crypt in the dining room."

I was struck by the Hollywood contrast between painstaking, dedicated craftsmanship and the extravagance, both material and emotional, that surrounded it. Olivia De Havilland was a thorough, almost obsessive professional from an aristocratic British family. Despite her outward timidity, one could sense, beneath her round angelic face, a second face of hard, sharp planes. She had an engaging elegance of spirit. Days after our interview she sent me a message: "I think I told you that I felt great pity for the patients in the institution. I'd like to revise that. 'Pity' is a condescending word. Let's say I felt a great surge of compassion. We are all victims of life, and these people simply were the hardest-pressed."

I saw her again years later, in Paris, where she then lived in energetic semiretirement. With a group of friends we found ourselves at a discotheque, Castel. When I pleaded that I was too old for this kind of dancing, Livvie, several years older than I, dragged me onto the floor and said: "Nonsense. Allowing yourself to get old is just being lazy."

TWO OTHER ACTRESSES who have lingered in my memory were more typical, in that they had come from lowly circumstances and had reinvented themselves, with some help from the studio illusionists. Self-creation appealed to the very American idea of life in which any metamorphosis is possible.

One of the two was Ava Gardner. I met her a few years later. By then the press had decided that Hollywood was going through not only a business crisis, but a glamour crisis. *Time* planned a cover story on Ava Gardner, who, it was thought, might possess enough of that old magic—though scant acting ability—to lead the movies out of their sex doldrums. I joined the Hollywood correspondent, by then Jim Murray, who, following what seemed to be a pattern of nontypecasting, was more interested in sports than in show business (he later became a popular sports columnist for the *Los Angeles Times*).

Ava Gardner, a sharecropper's daughter from North Carolina, had been married to Mickey Rooney and the bandleader Artie Shaw and was getting ready to marry Frank Sinatra as soon as he got a divorce. Among innumerable lovers there had been Howard Hughes and a bullfighter who published a book of poetry about her ("In my breast you will still remain / With a throbbing that recalls you . . ."). Altogether a pretty exhilarating assignment.

Jim Murray and I took Ava to dinner at an Italian restaurant; an MGM press agent, George Nichols, had insisted on joining us, presumably to see that Ava behaved herself. He was only partly successful. She spoke freely about her reputation as a sexpot—quite well deserved, she insisted. "People think I am the type who would take the busboy out back," she said, eyeing the young waiter who was serving our table. "Well, I just might." The waiter blushed till his face almost matched the color of the spaghetti sauce.

"Fantastic," I said—that word again. Nichols tried to change the subject.

Ava became increasingly irritated by him. She winked at me and announced that she was going to the john. I excused myself to do the same. Without exchanging a word, we headed out of the restaurant and got into her car. She was the most reckless driver I have ever known, but after a hair-raising and heart-stopping ride, we arrived at her house and proceeded to attack a bottle of Courvoisier. She had just kicked off her shoes and started dancing slowly on the coffee table (Grunwald: "Fantastic!") when Nichols arrived, panting and fuming, accompanied by a highly amused Jim Murray. The evening dwindled after that.

Photographs, including the romantic *Time* cover, rarely did her justice. They failed to capture the true expression on her face, which was both inviting and expectant, as if she were always waiting for something exciting to happen. And I suppose she was. She ended up in London, boozy and middle-aged. Before she died at sixty-seven, she said: "I'm just a miserable lonely woman who should never have been a film star."

A few days after my first meeting with Ava, a press agent friend of mine asked if I wanted to go to a studio wrap party. Of course I said yes. The sound stage we entered was huge and confusing. Under the glaring lights, the crowd was packed. But I suddenly sensed something odd about it, and after a few moments I realized what it was: there were no women present. The picture, explained my friend, was a war drama and had an all-male cast.

"Goddammit," I complained, "my first studio party and you pick an all-male movie! When can we get out of here?" At that moment a path opened in the crowd and, on the arm of a studio executive, there approached a sweet and spectacular blonde, full body swaying slightly, her mouth half-open, her eyes at once shy and merry. The executive brought her over and introduced Marilyn Monroe.

My friend said, with a laugh, that I had just complained about the absence of women on the set.

"I guess," said Marilyn in the girlish half whisper that someday would be as famous as Dietrich's growl, "God sent me to make it up to you."

It was the beginning of a short, warm and, unfortunately, platonic friendship. I worked up the courage to take her dancing that evening, and we agreed to meet again if she came east. I thought there were two things she wanted above all else: kindness and intellect. She needed to be treated well and to be taken seriously. At our first dinner in New York she talked about books, and I undoubtedly sounded a bit superior, throwing titles around. In that small voice she asked: "Have you read *Catcher in the Rye?*"

To my considerable embarrassment, I had not, and she proceeded to describe it to me. I read it the next day and wrote her a thank-you note, adding, truthfully, that I had become an instant Salinger addict. I found later that small gestures like thank-you notes melted her.

At that time she had had only a few minor movie parts, most notably "Miss Casswell," the aspiring actress and bimbo in *All About Eve.* She was thought to be the personal property of Joe Schenck, the elderly founder of 20th Century–Fox. I saw her a few more times before she was swept away in the Hollywood maelstrom and eventually married Joe DiMaggio. While that match did not exactly fit my belief that she yearned for intellect, it was the perfect symbolic union of the only two types Americans really worship: sports heroes and movie stars.

We met again once, after the marriage to DiMaggio broke up. We talked about her early life—the foster homes, her mother's mental breakdown, the orphanage, the first marriage, all those rather desperate, Dickens-in-California stories that would become familiar as her legend grew. Suddenly she asked me shyly: "Do you know Arthur Miller?" I said that I knew his work but had met him only briefly. "Don't you think the plays are *wonderful?*" she breathed with intense awe.

I replied that I thought so about *Death of a Salesman* but had reservations about some of the others.

She grew impatient and sharply reiterated that they were wonderful.

Quiet again, she confided: "I just met him again. Years ago, we were once introduced at a Hollywood party. He just sat there, looking at me, holding my toe." She wiggled her foot. "My *toe!*"

She was obviously in love with him. I felt the unreasonable if inevitable pang of jealousy and wished her well. I suspected that Miller was too heavy for her, too much the Jeremiah, but at last she had her intellectual.

Years later I edited a collection of critical essays on Salinger, and I somehow kept thinking of her. By now she had become the star who was, in Norman Mailer's words, "every man's love affair with America, [our] sweet angel of sex." But she was also the star who was neurotic, calculating, temperamental, chronically late, both childish and imperious, taking on and then shedding courtiers; she was adored as well as hated. "She has breasts like granite and a brain like Swiss cheese, full of holes," said Billy Wilder.

I could not ever accept that cruel description. In my mind there has always been a link between Marilyn and Holden Caulfield. She had that same quality of intelligent naiveté, the willingness to ask ingenuous questions. "Where do the ducks in Central Park go in winter?" could have been a Marilyn query. Like Holden, she had a way of trying to capture elusive meanings with a vague, all-purpose phrase. Marilyn: "Somebody is always trying to get a sort of chunk out of you, or *something.*" Holden: "She looked so damn nice, the way she kept going around and around in her blue coat *and all.*"

Like Holden, Marilyn was a rebel against the meanness of the world; unlike him, she knew how to compromise with it and use it. But Holden, I am sure, would not have pronounced his ultimate censure over her; he would not have called her a phony. She wasn't, to me. I found her enchanting and natural. She was much stronger than Holden, at least for a while, but ultimately doomed like him.

BEFORE I LEFT for Hollywood for the first time, I learned later, Matthews had said: "He'll never come back." Well, I did come back, but I kept thinking about Hollywood, so totally absorbed in the process of creating fictions. The air seemed filled with a constant buzz of ideas, plots, angles, characters: imagination on the assembly line. I remembered the movie ideas I had jotted down in Paris, along with my juvenile plays and stories, and I actually resurrected one concept. It had to do with the Unknown Soldier. I wrote a one-page proposal and sent it to Dore Schary, then head of MGM, whom I had met. A few days later my phone rang and the caller introduced himself as an MGM executive. "Mr. Schary has read your outline," he said. "We like it. We would like to acquire it."

My reply should have been, "We are delighted," but I was too stunned even to ask, "How much?" As it turned out, MGM paid me $5,000, a sizable sum in those days. The picture was never made. Still, the coup might have been enough to encourage me to try for a screenwriting career. I was not seriously tempted. Why not? If I still thought I could write plays, why not movies? I believe I had become more committed to *Time* and to journalism than I realized. Also, I was put off by everything that was unstable and bizarre about Hollywood.

The conventional wisdom is that only about one-tenth of what you hear about Hollywood is accurate. I came to a drastically different conclusion: that absolutely anything you hear about Hollywood, no matter how fantastic, is true. And if it isn't now, it will be. Nevertheless, given Hollywood's role in the imagination of America and the world, I thought that it had to be taken seriously.

THERE WAS ONE organization that took Hollywood very seriously, the House Committee on Un-American Activities. Beginning in the late 1930s and resuming in the late 1940s, it investigated the film business. The committee also looked into radio and TV, inspiring a publication called *Red Channels,* a list of "potential subversives."

The probe was often absurd. One early investigator charged that Shirley Temple, age nine, had helped Communism by sending a greeting to the French newspaper *Ce Soir,* which was Communist.

During a hearing on the Federal Theatre, a leftish project hated by foes of the New Deal, a witness quoted Shakespeare's contemporary, Christopher Marlowe. "Is he a Communist?" asked a congressman from Alabama. To the committee, Communism apparently was timeless. Representative John Rankin of Mississippi declared that "Communism hounded and persecuted our Savior during his earthly ministry [and] inspired his crucifixion."

In a different vein, Rankin delighted in revealing the real names of movie stars, which "we found out": Danny Kaye was really David Daniel Kaminski, Eddie Cantor was Edward Israel Iskowitz, Edward G. Robinson was Emmanuel Goldenberg. I was intrigued by these revelations, as an immigrant whose father had sometimes talked about changing our name from Grunwald to Greenwood or Granville. (My old friend Bruno Zwerling had transformed himself into Bryan Sterling). Rankin's intent was obvious. The committee, he said, was trying to save America from "the horrible fate the Communists have meted out to the unfortunate Christian people of Europe." Rankin had once referred to the columnist Walter Winchell as a "little kike."

During the Hollywood hearings, "friendly" witnesses testified about how Communists had infiltrated the Screen Writers Guild. The famous Hollywood Ten, as "unfriendly" witnesses, defiantly refused to answer questions fully about their past affiliations or to name names of colleagues who might have been Communists. The ten, who were indeed Communists, were under Party instruction to remain silent and present themselves as champions of democracy, which they did fulsomely. They were dismissed by their studios, cited for contempt of Congress and eventually went to jail. Others avoided jail by taking the Fifth Amendment against self-incrimination and were widely described as "Fifth Amendment Communists."

Many notable figures, including Humphrey Bogart and Frank Sinatra, had strongly criticized the committee for its methods, which damaged many innocents.

In my own Hollywood rounds I got a whiff of all this. I had often been irritated by the sentimental anticapitalism in many movies (money-makers were always villains), but I could not take Hollywood's version very seriously. Still, the politicians who flailed against Hollywood recognized an uneasy mood in the country. In questioning the great American dream machine, they were reflecting a basic anxiety about the U.S. position in a confusing and increasingly hostile world.

PART FOUR

IRON

CURTAINS

———————◆———————

CHAPTER TWELVE

THE PARTY CONVENTION scheduled for the summer of 1948 in Philadelphia filled the Republicans—including Luce—with great hopes of recapturing the White House.

Harry Truman looked, as one Republican jibe had it, like a "gone goose." "To err is Truman" was the mildest of the insults. He was attacked not only as an old machine politician but as being soft on Communism. Moreover, the Democrats were divided. Henry Wallace, former vice president, agriculture and commerce secretary, had formed a liberal third party, which, it was thought, would cost Truman many votes. A strong civil rights plank that liberals had managed to write into the Democratic platform would prompt the defection of a sizable southern contingent, the Dixiecrats. Even many Democratic leaders thought they would lose the election.

I was curious about the convention. So I asked Roy Alexander if I might tag along with the large group of writers and editors who were going to Philadelphia. The experience gave me a lasting affection for that unique, political rite—jamboree, jubilee, circus, Fourth of July parade, public debate, secret conclave.

On the third night of the convention I tried to keep score on a tally sheet, but I had a hard time concentrating because the booming names of the states kept evoking pictures of the country in my mind. Arizona,

Arkansas, Colorado . . . It was history. . . . Kansas, Kentucky, Maine
. . . It was also poetry of a sort. The voices from the floor spoke with
the many accents of a continent, corny but genuine in their local pride.
"Georgia, the empire state of the South . . . The great, free state of
Maryland . . . Virginia, the cradle of democracy . . ."

The show, like democracy, was neither smooth nor pure nor dignified
nor comfortable. But its great, heartening attraction was people: the
thousands of faces above their fluttering cardboard fans, constantly in
motion, arranged in disorderly, unregimented rows. It didn't matter
whether they were Republicans or Democrats. To me, it was America
itself sitting there under the banners and the lights, America in shirtsleeves and suspenders.

Main Street, or at least the Midwest, furnished a third of the delegates and the major contenders for the presidency: Robert Taft of Ohio,
Harold Stassen of Minnesota, Arthur Vandenberg of Michigan. Even the
governor of New York, Tom Dewey, it was carefully noted in the nominating speech, was "born and raised in our great Midwest." The region
was heavily represented among the presiders, the handlers, the strategists. Despite the hardly reticent presence of the Californians, the Texans, the New Englanders, the robust booster spirit of the Midwest predominated in the hall.

Rebecca West said the crowd reminded her of country folk gamboling
on the village green. Republican conventions, I would find, were invariably better dressed and more staid than Democratic conventions, but
there was more than enough gamboling. Still mindful of the solemnity
or the grim ideological passions of European politics, I was bemused by
the silly hats, the organ thunder and the giant din of the bands, the
"spontaneous" demonstrations, clouds of balloons rising to the distant
ceiling, a girl in a canoe borne by four marines. The efforts for Taft
were wildly unlikely, considering the candidate's persimmon personality. They included a hotel fashion show with models wearing pink
elephants on their garters and a baby elephant called Eva, imported as a
mascot from India. The great Meyer Berger of *The New York Times*
interviewed Eva, looking for hints to the convention's outcome.

Yet there was real political machinery underneath all the folderol and real, if highly imperfect, democracy. It was one of the last "real" conventions, because it still made genuine decisions.

I had the impression that a shout or a speech, some sudden storm of emotion, some shift of mood on the floor, could sway the final choice. Things were never quite so spontaneous as they seemed. Decisions were made by a dozen or so key politicians. But nothing was really predetermined, and there was genuine suspense.

Reporters sweated in the tropical, un-air-conditioned hall. They kept trolling for bits of information that would be outdated in hours. *Time* operated with its customary inclination to overkill: a correspondent for every major candidate, plus some general-assignment reporters, plus that troupe of writers and editors from New York, headed by the managing editor. Their dispatches were destined for the very writers who were watching the proceedings from the press gallery and who would head back to New York the day before the presidential nominations to start writing their stories. That arrangement seemed strangely roundabout to outsiders, but it was dictated by the newsmagazine system.

In addition to the individual reports, *Time* correspondents were required to produce a chronological running account of events as seen from the press gallery: speeches, demonstrations, incidents. A reporter would hammer away at his portable for half an hour or so, then pass it to the next fellow. I felt thrilled and important when the typewriter came my way for the first time and, occasionally scanning the hall through binoculars, I typed useless trivia: "Up on the rostrum, Charlie Halleck drones on about the great opportunity for the G.O.P. . . . Chairman Joe Martin, looking fiercely bored, seems to shrink into his chair. . . . A commotion over in the Illinois delegation, presumably an impromptu caucus. . . . Every other delegate seems to be mopping his face with a paper towel: no wonder the toilets have run out of them. . . ."

Even more exciting was my moment to dangle one of the scarce floor passes around my neck and wander along the aisles, among the delegates. I recognized some of the party chieftains from their press photographs—Herbert Brownell of New York, Dewey's top adviser, a well-tailored, low-key lawyer who suggested an usher in a fashionable

Protestant church; William Knowland of California, a massive man with the shoulders (and the mind) of a bull; James Duff of Pennsylvania, boyish looking in his mid-sixties, with incandescent red hair and electric blue eyes. Now and then I would ask a question, trying to decide which of several familiar categories best suited them: the conspiratorial operators, the bland, smooth-faced strategists, the glad-handers, the domineering bosses or the would-be statesmen.

The rationale for *Time*'s saturation effort, which resulted in many thousands of words beyond what would be printed, was that, as a weekly, the magazine would have to offer an organized package that contained analysis and summary, plus telling detail not found in the dailies. But what really mattered to me, and to most of my colleagues, was the exhilaration of being close to events, of slipping into the web of plan and accident, of routine and ardor, that is politics. There were clear signs that the way in which conventions would henceforth be reported—and conducted—was changing. *Life* and NBC had teamed up to cover the event, and politicians were constantly interviewed in an improvised studio; most of them looked ghastly, although a makeup man was hastily recruited from Charles of the Ritz. TV cameras were still monstrously heavy and were much harder to haul around than Eva the elephant. Besides, the convention was seen live only on the eastern seaboard. But I knew that things would never be quite the same again when I saw Dewey arriving at the convention center on a television set in the press gallery well before he was visible in the hall. Henceforth, half-ashamed, print reporters would often have to take their information straight off the tube. Even the best-written "human interest" vignettes would have a hard time competing with the camera's chance view of a delegate snoring, a security guard arresting a pickpocket who protested he was a loyal Republican, an ancient politico reminiscing about the old days, when booze and obscenities flowed generously and when a floor fight often meant a fistfight.

What was not yet wholly clear was the way in which television would change the very nature of conventions. In the future, conventions would be wide open to the outside, and politicians would play not to the delegates, but to the country. A speaker who was ignored in the hall might command an audience on TV. What one saw in the hall would be quite different from what one saw on the screen; the very colors and sounds would be less real in the reality of the auditorium than in the reality of the screen.

But that summer in Philadelphia, when the rooms were still smoke filled and the contests for votes in the big hall were real, it all seemed to matter, and it did.

Polls on the eve of the convention showed Truman lagging behind the major Republican contenders. The Republicans were so confident that they even trotted out Herbert Hoover without embarrassment. He was then seventy-four, and I thought I was seeing a fleshy ghost, a character who had been time warped out of his despised niche in history. The convention gave him a sixteen-minute ovation, his failures wiped away in an effusion of unrepentant nostalgia.

If Hoover brought the delegates to a sentimental glow, Clare Boothe Luce whipped them into fighting spirit. On the opening night, the congresswoman from Connecticut all but declared victory. Her hair shimmering in the spotlight, her pearls as bright as her voice, she was the Republicans' blond Pasionaria. The Democrats, she charged, could thrive only on crisis, and she denounced their presidents as "troubadours of trouble, crooners of catastrophe"—setting a Republican style of alliteration later perfected by Spiro Agnew's brilliant speechwriter William Safire, who attacked the nattering nabobs of negativism. (With a sudden pang of embarrassment, I recalled my feeble and unfunny undergraduate potshot at her five years or so before.) She also took on Henry Wallace, who advocated a soft line toward the Soviets; "Red Hank," Clare called him gleefully and, alluding to one of ventriloquist Edgar Bergen's puppets, "Stalin's Mortimer Snerd." (Wallace himself later realized that his third party had been heavily infiltrated by Communists.)

I am sure Clare Luce meant what she said, but to my mind she was too brilliant, too studied, and that gave her performance an air of brittle insincerity. The crowd, however, loved her delectable malice. She was a rarity, a woman of real political importance. Only a small percentage of the delegates were female. One other woman delegate spoke, gingerly, about women as guardians of the family and creatures who know "the cost of life as men never know it."

CLARE LUCE'S HUSBAND had come along with the *Time* contingent. He enjoyed holding bull sessions with his troops or presiding at lunches with some of the convention's principal actors. But of course he was one of the actors himself. As a leading Republican who had worked so hard to send Wendell Willkie to the White House, he now displayed his party's rosy flush of new hope. But he was also involved in a fight over the direction and meaning of the GOP. The issue was isolationism.

To me, a quite junior writer, Luce was a remote figure, glimpsed only occasionally—slim, elegant, almost always hatted (he was said to be embarrassed by his thinning hair), long, tapered fingers nervously holding a cigarette. It was known that he favored the reluctant Vandenberg, chairman of the Senate Foreign Relations Committee and a convert from isolationism who now held a missionary belief in America's international responsibility that paralleled Luce's own.

After the second ballot, a *Time* reporter told me, Luce rushed up to his friend Roy Roberts, president of the *Kansas City Star,* and insisted, "Roy, you've got to swing Kansas and Missouri behind Arthur on the third." It was plainly too late, and Roberts brusquely refused to try, adding, "Harry, Arthur doesn't have a prayer." Perhaps in retribution, Roberts was described in *Time*'s convention story as "pachydermatous."

Before Tom Dewey was finally nominated—and sent on his way toward one of the great upsets in American politics—the old isolationist wing of the party staged a last-ditch rally around Taft.

But isolationism was crumbling, and what caused its decay was the cold war. The never-ending battle between "moderate" and "conservative" Republicans was taking a new turn. Taft notwithstanding, the conservatives would be defined no longer by isolationism, but by super-interventionism, as long as it could be shown to be anti-Communist. Truman had undertaken aid to Greece and Turkey to avoid a Communist takeover (in the "doctrine" that would bear his name), had launched the Marshall Plan and, in order to preempt Republican criticism, had set up a program requiring loyalty oaths from federal employees. Yet Truman was still denounced for having given away too much to Stalin at the Potsdam Conference and for not being vigilant enough toward subversion at home. The attacks were almost interchangeable. "We shall drive out every Red and pink on the federal payroll." "If Joseph Stalin could vote in the next election, he would not vote Republican."

With such rhetoric in mind, some revisionist historians have claimed that after World War II the United States was eager to find another enemy. To my mind that is untrue. As I witnessed during my midwestern trip, Americans were impatient to disband their armies, supported the slashing of defense budgets and hoped to be left alone by the Soviets.

Apologists for Moscow charged the United States with being the expansionist power and gradually encircling the Soviets militarily. From time to time Stalin would speak about accommodation. But in a speech barely a year after Yalta, Stalin denounced coexistence with the capitalist West and rededicated himself to world revolution. Supreme Court Justice William O. Douglas thought it was the "declaration of World War III." It was, in fact, the declaration of the cold war.

CHAPTER THIRTEEN

In "The Revolutionist's Handbook," an appendix to *Man and Superman*, assuming the voice of his modernized Don Juan, Jack Tanner, George Bernard Shaw wrote: "Any person under thirty, who, having any knowledge of the existing social order, is not a revolutionist, is an inferior." So why was I not drawn to Communism and never had been? I had often wondered about that. Wasn't it a character flaw not to go through a radical phase? Given the world's untold misery, wasn't revolution almost a moral imperative?

Perhaps my attitude was explained by the rest of Shaw's quotation: "AND YET Revolutions have never lightened the burden of tyranny: they have only shifted it to another shoulder." I pounced on that line with the joy of recognition.

My earliest impressions of Communism were inextricably interwoven with my impressions of Nazism. First there had been the massed red flags carried by the marching ranks of demonstrators singing the "Internationale" as they moved through our street in Vienna. I watched from a little balcony of our apartment, just as I would soon watch the swastika flags being carried past, the anthem then being the "Horst Wessel" song. (A much inferior tune, I thought.)

As I became politically more aware, I understood the distinction.

Communism had sprung from a desperate reaction against the misery and chaos that the Industrial Revolution had caused. It was the great foe of Nazism, which to some extent had been invented to fight it; Communism did not have death camps (or so we thought at the time); it was not nationalist, but international minded; it was somehow idealistic.

But my dominant emotion, after our expulsion from Austria, was a sense of loss: the loss of what seemed in retrospect an idyllic childhood. Such a sense of loss led others toward revolution, representing the desire for revenge or justice, or both. But my desire was different: somehow to recapture and restore that lost idyll. Communism as I glimpsed it early on, with its enforced equality and sweaty cult of the proletariat was hardly the instrument of such restoration.

THE YEAR 1948 happened to be the one hundredth anniversary of the publication by Karl Marx and Friedrich Engels of the *Communist Manifesto*. That had given me an idea, and I suggested to Max Ways that *Time* do a cover story on Marx. I thought it was a good journalistic notion, but I also felt that it would allow me to learn something. Writing about a subject, I had already discovered, was the best way to study it.

When I proposed the notion to Max he reared back in his chair. He was almost twenty years my senior, and I had the feeling that he did not think a twenty-five-year-old was up to writing even a merely journalistic history of Marxism.

"You know we don't like to put dead people on the cover."

I reminded him that *Time* had broken the taboo when it ran Hitler on the cover after he died in his bunker amid the Götterdämmerung of the Third Reich. Eventually I won Max over.

I did not follow the usual procedure of leaving the background work entirely to a researcher. Instead I moved into the reading room of the New York Public Library. I had brought along an antediluvian recording machine—it used little green disks—to dictate, in a whisper, notes from my reading. More efficient, I thought smugly, than Marx's scribbling away in the British Museum. At the end of the first day, foolishly not having tested the device earlier, I was appalled to find that it had not recorded a single word. I carried on with yellow pads and pencils.

My aim was to learn more about the origins of Communism and especially about the American reaction to it. Not much of my background research ended up in the story, published in early 1948. The piece rather desperately tried to come to grips with the Marxist dialectic, which struck me as a very uncertain guide to understanding the world, a swaying intellectual rope bridge stretched across a chasm.

Max Ways rewrote large parts of the story and in the process removed all my pounding, Chambers-like references to crisis and tragedy and history that suggested bulletins from Armageddon. But the exercise did benefit my education. It gave me an almost personal sense of Karl Marx, the idealistic, arrogant, choleric German Jew who could write romantic love poems to his aristocratic wife and vicious polemic attacks on his enemies; the tender, playful father who would not lower himself to take a bourgeois job that might have moved his family out of their poverty-ridden refugee existence in London. He was consumed by his writing and his revolutionary intrigues. One episode among the countless incidents of his life especially lodged itself in my memory, perhaps because I was already trained by *Time* to seize on the telling anecdote. Once, riding on a bus, Marx saw a commotion in front of a pub, with a woman shrieking: "Murder! Murder!" Marx stormed off the bus and found a man apparently battering his wife. Violence against women (or animals) drove Marx wild. He hurled himself into the fray to save the woman, only to find that the man was merely trying to take his tippling spouse home from the pub. As soon as Marx intervened, the woman sided with her husband and both started beating the black-bearded intruder, while a street crowd closed in, muttering about damn foreigners. I thought the incident said a lot about Marx: combative, irate at injustice, a born autocrat supremely sure of knowing who and what was right, and frustrated in his efforts. His life illustrated for me the hauntingly thin and perhaps accidental line between crank and prophet, crackpot and genius.

The *Communist Manifesto*, I learned, was published in the United States in 1871, more than twenty years after it appeared in Europe. The Frontier was still the great reality. The immense feat of establishing the

United States, securing it and expanding it beyond all familiar horizons, was still felt as a *contemporary* American achievement.

That feeling persisted into the era of American industrialization. I discovered unhappily that "foreign" and "subversive" had been almost automatically equated, because the majority of radicals were immigrants. In Europe Communism was a stone hurled from across the street; in America it was considered an infection carried from across the ocean.

Despite a long tradition of native radicalism, Friedrich Engels complained, Americans were "tremendously backward in theory" and far too practical minded and "matter-of-fact." The awful conditions of the workers in American cities in the 1870s were gradually ameliorated by nonideological unions and by capitalists who, however grudgingly, went along with their demands for reform.

The United States was itself the embodiment of a successful revolution; a rebellion against *it* had to be seen as counterrevolutionary (not that Americans used such terms). The loud glorification of America, I realized, masked lingering uncertainty about the fate of this still new country.

My explorations of the Communist past led me into long dialogues with a man named Mark Vishniak, who had been hired some years before by Tom Matthews to set up a "Russian desk" at *Time* to help penetrate the walls of silence or disinformation surrounding the Soviet Union. Day after day, Vishniak, a short, fussy, passionate man who was sixty-five in 1948, would dig through masses of Soviet newspapers, magazines, books and broadcast transcripts, looking for clues to trends and decisions buried in the tundras of Party-line prose. He produced regular summaries of events for the editors; he wrote them in Russian, to be translated by a Russian-born assistant whose English was better than his. Their arguments over his interpretations and her translations would resound in the corridors, like echoes of an Eisenstein sound track.

Vishniak was a remnant of history. He had been a law professor in Moscow, an ardent Social Democrat, and after the Russian Revolution he became a member of Alexander Kerensky's provisional government. When Lenin and his Bolsheviks swept Kerensky aside, Vishniak escaped to the West. He firmly believed that Marxism was compatible with democracy, that Lenin represented a perversion of Marx, and Stalin a perversion of Lenin; I argued that, on the contrary, they were logical extensions of one another. I saw Marxism as just another Utopia. What always struck me in my reading, from Thomas More to Edward Bellamy was the utter inhumanity of their imaginary communities even as humanity was extolled, the abolition of freedom even if freedom was claimed. All Utopias are bound to become totalitarian when carried into practice. I was certain that only tyranny could ultimately maintain complete equality and some arbitrary regimen of the good life to be led by the New Man.

MANY OF AMERICA'S fears about Communism were based on real enough causes, notably the discovery in the late 1940s of an elaborate espionage network bent on handing Moscow the formulas and methods for producing atomic bombs. The network included two British scientists, Alan Nunn May and Klaus Fuchs, and Julius and Ethel Rosenberg, of whose guilt I was convinced, despite a tireless campaign to the contrary. The Soviets undoubtedly would have managed to build atomic weapons anyway, but probably not as early as they did.

The American reaction was a long way from the civics classes at Haaren High. The pure principle that no political opinion, no political party, however odious, should be suppressed had been battered for some time. Under Truman's loyalty program, the FBI began a massive investigation of government employees, an inquisition without normal or consistent rules of evidence. Simply mixing with people who belonged to a Communist or Communist-front organization (the attorney general published a continually updated list) could stamp someone a security risk. "Guilt by association" entered the language.

Supporters of the loyalty program argued that the Communists represented more than just another opinion or party and that they were in fact a conspiracy to overthrow the American democratic system. Whittaker Chambers, among others, held that the United States was, in effect, at war with Communism, justifying the infringement of some civil liberties. To me the remarkable thing was not how many people accepted this, but how many rejected it.

My friends at *Time* and I argued about all this endlessly, often bitterly, usually with Scotch lubricating our reason. One fairly typical, late-night bull session particularly stayed in my memory. Someone asked angrily: "After all, who started it?" That sounded like a naive, playground sort of question, but to my mind it wasn't.

"Who started it?" repeated Bob McLaughlin just as angrily. "Capitalism did, by setting up a brutal new system, by sweating and starving and exploiting the workers."

"Grinding the faces of the poor," muttered Auchincloss. "Dark Satanic mills and all that."

McLaughlin ignored the irony. "Precisely. That was the initial 'aggression.' Communism was simply a defense, a defense of the victims."

"But that was a hundred years ago," I argued. "Don't you see that capitalism has changed completely since then? And Communism is far more brutal than capitalism at its worst."

Communism, I argued, constituted a massive offensive whose aims were reiterated every day around the world in a thousand styles and accents. How could Americans be expected *not* to react with anger and fear?

It is a basic liberal tenet that motives matter, that one must make allowances for and understand what drives people, that even an ax murderer deserves to have extenuating circumstances weighed—poverty, or abuse by cruel parents, or other forms of conditioning. Yet few liberals were willing to extend that kind of understanding to anti-Communism.

This was about to be demonstrated in a spectacular and divisive contest.

CHAPTER FOURTEEN

THAT AUGUST IN 1948 I was spending a vacation at the Wauwinet House on Nantucket. (I had not yet switched my permanent summer allegiance to the other island, Martha's Vineyard.) When I came back from the beach around midday, the owner, Bob Backus, looked at me oddly and asked, "Do you know a man named Whittaker Chambers?"

"Of course. He used to be my boss. We both work for *Time.*"

"What's he like?"

"That's not easy to say. I happen to be devoted to him. . . . Why do you ask?" I was puzzled because Backus was not normally inquisitive.

He silently pointed to a stack of *New York Times* that had just arrived. A banner headline read:

RED "UNDERGROUND" IN FEDERAL POSTS ALLEGED BY EDITOR . . .

EX-COMMUNIST NAMES ALGER HISS, THEN IN STATE DEPARTMENT . . .

The story told how Whittaker Chambers, a senior editor at *Time* magazine and "admitted former Communist," had testified under subpoena before the House Un-American Activities Committee on Communists in the government. He described himself as a former member of the underground organization of the Communist Party. The "apparatus" to which he had been attached was "developed" by one Harold Ware, a son of the renowned and lusty Communist leader Ella Reeve ("Mother") Bloor, sometimes known as the sweetheart of the movement. The group's purpose, said Chambers, was infiltration of the government, not "primarily" espionage, although that was "certainly one of its eventual objectives."

He was further quoted as saying, "Disloyalty is a matter of principle with every member of the Communist Party. [It] exists for the specific purpose of overthrowing the government."

Among the people Chambers named as belonging to the group was Alger Hiss, who had served for ten distinguished years in the State Department, most recently in the important post of director of special political affairs. Currently he was president of the highly respected Carnegie Endowment for International Peace.

Suddenly I recalled that occasion in his office, nearly three years before, when Chambers had said almost casually that a man named Alger Hiss was a Communist.

The story in the *Times* reported that Chambers cited other names, including Alger Hiss's brother, Donald, also a former State Department official, now in private law practice. The brothers, according to an accompanying story, vehemently denied the charges. There were other denials, and some no-comments.

Thus began the "Hiss case," which for years would loom over most political discussion in the United States. It was the cold war reduced to a human drama. It was a mystery story as well as a morality play. It gave rise to innumerable conspiracy theories, caused fury beyond all reason and pitted charges of treason against charges of fakery and Fascism. It was later seen as a major political stepping-stone for Richard Nixon, who was a member of HUAC. It was a political litmus test about how you defined Americanism or assessed Communism. Like the Dreyfus affair, it defined an era. It involved conflicts not only of politics but of class and even of religion. It was, in the minds of many, part of a larger struggle for the soul of America, perhaps of the world.

· · ·

THE MAN WHOSE picture appeared in the *Times*—double chin, rumpled shirt, eyes turned upward as if in search of some elusive memory—had undergone the subtle metamorphosis that happens when people who are familiar to you become performers on a public stage.

This was no longer quite the same man who had given me my first break on *Time,* the pudgy, benign, if slightly mysterious editor who helpfully discussed my work and joined me and other writers for lunch and joked with us and told stories. He now was a universally visible prophet who spoke in a solemn vocabulary about crisis and danger, an accuser, a narrator of sinister plots. And he was a man who gradually revealed a dark, tortured, often distasteful side of his own life.

The congressmen hardly knew what to make of him. He struck notes of philosophy and religion, used words like "history" and "tragedy" as they had hardly been heard before in this hearing room.

Chambers had come to Communism gradually. He had worked as a laborer, helping to build a Washington street railway, literally bloodying his hands and living in squalor; fellow workers had helped him, which gave him a sense of the camaraderie of the proletariat.

During a trip to Europe in the 1920s, observing the misery and hectic escapism, he became convinced that the world was going through a deadly crisis. Only Communism seemed to have a practical cure.

He described how he had worked first in the "open" Party, then underground. He evoked the strange world of revolutionary bureaucracy, of political ambushes and personal infighting, the iron ideological control from the top, the paradox that people who are sincerely outraged by the injustices of society would endlessly submit to the injustices of the Party. He described the subculture of secrecy: the false names and papers, the passwords and codes and mail drops. But eventually, he said, his experience convinced him that Marxism really meant slavery and spiritual night.

For a year after his break with the Party, fearing his former comrades would try to kill him, he was "sleeping by day and watching through the night with gun or revolver within easy reach." He and his wife, testified Chambers, had been close friends of Hiss and his wife. Before

Chambers made his break, he said, he pleaded vainly with Hiss to leave the Party also.

In 1939 he had told his story to Assistant Secretary of State Adolph Berle, who had promised to take action—but nothing had happened. Going to the government with his information, said Chambers, was "a simple act of war, like the shooting of an armed enemy in combat. At that moment in history, I was one of the few men on this side of the battle who could perform this service." Since his defection he had tried to live "an industrious and God-fearing life."

I was sure that Chambers was telling the truth. But as I followed his testimony, I felt—as I would often in the future—that he sounded theatrical. It made me uncomfortable. It was a matter of style, not substance. But I could understand why that style alienated many people and caused them to distrust what Chambers was saying.

Hiss asked to appear before the committee. The difference between him and his accuser was almost cartoonlike, oversimplified like a morality play. Hiss recited his dazzling record: Johns Hopkins University, Harvard Law School, law clerk to Justice Oliver Wendell Holmes, counsel to the Senate's Nye Committee investigating the World War I role of the munitions industry ("merchants of death"), stints with the Agricultural Adjustment Administration and the Justice Department, followed by his State Department positions and his role at Yalta, where he had helped draft the final agreement. Later he would submit a list of "personages of recognized stature under whom or with whom I worked in Government" that ran to four pages. "Ask them," challenged Hiss, "if they ever found in me anything except the highest adherence to duty and honor." Hiss was the consummate Establishment figure. He had an open face and spoke with the WASP grace that covers firm self-assurance with a light wrap of modesty.

Chambers, by almost too perfect contrast, was a man with a mottled past who had worked in a political underworld, switched loyalties, or, as Hiss himself would later put it, "a confessed former Communist and traitor to his country." He was a rumpled, unprepossessing figure whose fleshy softness seemed at odds with the melodramatic lines delivered in a flat monotone.

Hiss vigorously denied any Communist affiliation or even sympathy and asserted that "so far as I know" he had never "laid eyes" on Chambers. Shown photographs, he said he did not recognize him and professed himself totally puzzled by Chambers's motives in making the charges.

Some members of the panel—including Rankin—congratulated Hiss because he seemed so utterly convincing. It looked as if the committee had been taken in by an impostor, and one member remarked, "We have been had. We are ruined." But, at least in part thanks to arguments by Nixon (who later said he thought that Hiss had sounded "a little too mouthy"), it was decided to have one more go at Chambers.

In executive session Chambers gave an amazing list of details about Hiss, his wife, his servants, his household, to support his claim of friendship with the Hisses. Conceivably Chambers might have found out the facts about the Hiss family without the close relationship he claimed, but this was very hard to believe. As the case developed, many of these details would become almost legendary, sounding like chapter headings in an implausible novel. Among them, the "Bokhara Rug," the "Ford Model A," the "Prothonotary Warbler" and, later, the "Woodstock N230099 Typewriter" and the "Pumpkin Papers." (A short book could be written about the saga of the typewriter alone—who owned it and when, who tried to find it and who tried *not* to find it.) Chambers testified that Hiss had regularly contributed money to the Communist Party, although he was not an "open" member. Chambers said he had once received a Bokhara rug as a token of gratitude from the head of the Communist underground in the United States and had passed it on to Hiss. Chambers also said that he had stayed in the Hiss apartment, rent free. He recalled an old Ford that he said Hiss had turned over to the Party in case it might still be useful to some poor organizer. A subcommittee under Nixon recalled Hiss and tried out the details on him. Hiss confirmed all, but with different and innocuous explanations. He changed his story about never having known Chambers, saying he *might* have known him, but under the name of George Crosley, a freelance writer with whom he had been briefly acquainted in the thirties. He described him as something of a deadbeat and sponger, to whom he had sublet the Hiss apartment and "thrown in" an old Ford car. Crosley defaulted on the rent, said Hiss, and also failed to pay back some small loans, but gave Hiss a rug he had received from "some wealthy patron" as partial compensation. (Eventually the committee staff produced documents to show that rather than giving the Ford to "Crosley," Hiss had transferred ownership to a used-car dealership, from which, later evidence showed, it immediately found its way to a member of the Communist Party.)

Then there was the matter of the warbler. Chambers had described how Hiss, a dedicated bird-watcher, once told him excitedly that he had spotted a rare prothonotary warbler along the Potomac. In the course of the questioning a committee member more or less casually slid into the topic of bird-watching and asked Hiss whether he had ever seen a prothonotary warbler. Yes indeed, replied Hiss with enthusiasm, "right here on the Potomac."

In a surprise confrontation arranged by the committee, in a hotel suite, the two men faced each other. Could Hiss identify Chambers as Crosley? Hiss first asked Chambers to speak. Then he asked him to open his mouth, so that he could check on what he recalled as Crosley's bad teeth. ("There must have been considerable dental work done," said Hiss, which Chambers confirmed.) Hiss then asked to hear more of Chambers's voice, and the *Time* senior editor began reading from a copy of *Newsweek* handed to him by a committee member with a sense of humor. In the end Hiss made the identification.

At one point, when Hiss asked him rhetorically how he could claim to have stayed in the Hiss apartment without having rented it, Chambers said, "Very simply, Alger. You were a Communist and I was a Communist."

Before the session was over, Hiss challenged Chambers to repeat his accusations in a forum other than the committee, where they would not be privileged against a slander suit. Chambers did so, on the TV program *Meet the Press.* After several weeks, amid mounting impatience by his supporters, Hiss sued.

•   •   •

THE HISS CASE was becoming an obsessive topic of conversation. At countless cocktail and dinner parties I found myself proclaiming defiantly and defensively "I am a friend of Whittaker Chambers." The statement was usually greeted with mockery, if people thought I was merely stupid; or anger, if people thought I was as evil as Chambers himself.

Partly it was a matter of politics; to some, Chambers was merely involved in a plot to besmirch the legacy of the New Deal. Partly it was a matter of snobbery, of both the social and moral variety. Informers were distasteful, no matter what their cause. Above all, it was a matter of anti-anti-Communism. People who considered themselves progressive and enlightened loathed "Red-baiting." Did spies and traitors exist? Of course, but surely all this stuff was terribly exaggerated; words like "conspiracy," "infiltration," "apparat" drew sardonic, superior smiles. In descending order, the case for Hiss went: (1) he was not a Communist at all but probably, at most, a member of a Marxist study group; but (2) if he *had* been a Communist in his youth, so what? Certainly he was not a spy; but (3) if he *had* turned over some papers, they weren't all that important. The same kind of argument went on constantly in the *Time* offices. The majority of the staff distrusted Chambers's testimony, their attitudes ranging from vague suspicion to outright contempt. He was defended by a small group of loyalists, myself included.

When Hiss's lawyers demanded that Chambers turn over any pertinent papers or other documents, the case took a sensational new turn. Chambers produced a sheaf of papers that his nephew had hidden at his request some years before, when he quit the Party. Chambers said he had forgotten about them. They included sixty-five typewritten pages, copies of classified State Department cables that he said Hiss had given to him. There were also four sheets in handwriting later identified as Hiss's, summarizing other State documents. This seemed to be evidence of espionage by Hiss and flatly contradicted Chambers's explicit earlier testimony that espionage had not been involved and that no papers had been passed.

Why had he lied? To shield Hiss, said Chambers, to spare him even

greater harm than his initial testimony would inflict ("There are degrees of injury"). I was sure that Chambers meant it. But at the same
time he must have also been trying to shield himself by avoiding the
admission of espionage—although legally he was not at risk, as the
statute of limitations had expired.

The papers were not the only things he had given to his nephew for
safekeeping. There were also several rolls of developed and undeveloped
microfilm, some of which later proved also to be copies of confidential
State Department documents. To keep some ammunition in reserve,
Chambers did not give the film to the Hiss lawyers along with the
papers but took it to his farm. Eventually, in the presence of a committee investigator, he produced the rolls of film from a hollow pumpkin,
where he had hidden them for one night. Why the pumpkin? Chambers
would explain that he had seen what he took to be Hiss investigators
prowling about the farm, and the pumpkin made a perfect, innocuous
hiding place. But it clearly also provided a theatrical touch he enjoyed.
He was inspired, he later recalled, by a Soviet movie in which underground Communists had transported arms inside papier-mâché figures,
one of them a pumpkin-shaped god of Fate.

It was not known at the time that shortly afterward Chambers tried
to commit suicide by inhaling cyanide fumes but failed. He was exhausted, desperate, and suspected that he might be indicted for having
committed perjury in denying espionage. Instead, faced with the State
Department documents, a grand jury indicted Hiss for perjury. Specifically he was charged with lying when he denied having had contact
with Chambers after a certain date and again when he denied giving
Chambers classified papers. Experts, including Hiss's own, had determined that the papers were copied on a Woodstock typewriter, a machine once owned by the Hisses and later given to the family of their
maid. But asked to explain the copies, Hiss merely said, "Until the day I
die, I shall wonder how Whittaker Chambers got into my house to use
my typewriter."

Several members of the grand jury laughed. It was no laughing matter to Hiss's supporters. They were certain that Chambers had obtained
the documents from someone other than Hiss and had then copied them

himself on the Woodstock. Since no remotely plausible theory was ever produced about how this might have been accomplished, the Hiss defense team later suggested that a duplicate machine with identical characteristics might have been constructed by Chambers; but it would take experts hired by Hiss well over a year to build a fake Woodstock that, in the end, approximated but did not duplicate the original. Still, Hiss maintained that he was the victim of "forgery by typewriter."

As for the summaries in Hiss's own hand, they were explained as notes Hiss made for briefing his State Department superior at the time, though that superior flatly contradicted this and their contents were not connected with Hiss's usual area of responsibility.

I FOLLOWED EVERY step of the proceedings, every advance and setback of the Chambers cause, not only in the daily press, but through superb reporting by one of the best correspondents I have known, Jim Bell, who covered the trials for *Time*. Like all Chambers partisans—and foes—at *Time*, I waited impatiently for his daily reports and, forgetting any other activity, pounced on them as soon as a copy boy dropped them into my "in" box. In later years Bell and I often traveled together, and I was invariably struck by his possession of an invisible divining rod for falsehood (less elegantly known as a shit detector) and by his ability to grasp the most intricate situations in various foreign countries he did not know. In many ways the Hiss-Chambers case was a foreign country to him, but he quickly mastered its geography and psychology.

Bell provided insight and the kind of detail that fed one's imagination more than television would. There was the prosecutor, towering Tom Murphy, who looked like a combination of a Coldstream Guard and a chipmunk. The defense attorney, Lloyd Paul Stryker, who shouted, whispered, cried and overflowed with mother and home, patriotism and the Bible ("Yea, though I walk through the valley of death I shall not fear, for I am with Alger Hiss"). Hiss himself, neat and youthful: "His fingernails, while carefully filed, were down near the quick."

Chambers, as Bell described him, was imperturbable under Stryker's assault, sometimes sad, never combative; the lawyer's tactic was to recite what he called the "teenants" (he meant tenets) of Communism to show that as a Party member Chambers had been ready to lie, cheat, conspire, take false names—all of which Chambers calmly conceded. "In the tropics," Stryker at one point told the jury, "when a leper walks in the streets, the cry is heard before him: 'Unclean! Unclean!' I say to you, 'Unclean!' at the approach of this moral leper."

Esther Chambers, unlike her husband, was not built to let this sort of thing pour over her calmly. Stryker confronted her with a school application she had once made for their daughter, Ellen, at a time when Chambers was still "a criminal, secret conspirator" and she misrepresented him "as a decent citizen. . . ." Esther Chambers, reported Bell, half rose out of her seat, eyes flashing, and shouted: "I resent that! My husband *is* a decent citizen. A great man!"

She also told of the Chamberses' relationship with the Hisses in minute detail—joint trips and outings to the movies, the time the Chambers baby boy wet a rug in the Hiss house and Priscilla gave her a fine, soft towel as a diaper (she still had the towel).

In the end the jury was deadlocked, having voted eight to four for conviction. The image that stayed most vividly in my mind from Bell's account of the first trial was that of Chambers during recesses, alone in a bare room with two straight-backed chairs and an unused desk. "No one came to talk to him. He looked out over the city and thought."

BELL CONTINUED HIS reporting when the second trial opened four months after the first ended. Except for a more experienced judge, Henry Warren Goddard, and a less theatrical defense lawyer, Claude Cross, the cast was much the same.

The diplomatic cables Chambers said he had received from Hiss were read into the record (at the first trial the State Department had objected to their introduction on security grounds even after all those years). Dating from before World War II, they dealt with troop movements, arms shipments, negotiations, intrigue, and reflected fateful indecision at the Fascist threat. The cables were important at the time, but oddly archaic now. "As they droned through the courtroom," reported Bell, "as the distant events and people were retold—Hitler, Chamberlain, Spain, the Sino-Japanese war—one had the feeling of listening to one of those nightmare radio programs, walking down a long corridor, with hollow, disconnected voices all around."

As he had during the first trial, Dr. Carl Binger, a psychiatrist, testified—on the basis of what he was told about Chambers by the defense and a study of his writings—that Chambers had a "psychopathic personality." Murphy effectively demolished that testimony.

Finally Bell described the moments following the guilty verdict (Hiss would be sentenced to five years in prison): "The defendant's face paled. His wife's right cheek twitched. Cross was white. A young member of the defense team wiped tears away. The courtroom emptied except for the lawyers. The chair in which Priscilla Hiss had sat presented a picture. There, in grotesque imitation of life, lay two slightly soiled white gloves. The right glove was clasping the left. On the red leather chair, they seemed to be the limp hands of someone long dead."

A MIASMA OF NASTY rumors hovered over Chambers—that he was a drunk, that he had been in jail or in a mental institution, that he was a homosexual.

Ironically this was one rumor that was based on truth. Chambers had told the FBI, it was revealed years later, that between 1933 or 1934 and 1938 he had had numerous casual homosexual experiences. His first partner taught him "an experience I did not know existed." For four or five years he "fought a wavering battle against this affliction." In 1938, when he broke with the Party, he also, "with God's help . . . managed to break myself of my homosexual tendencies and since that time I have been a model husband and father."

As far as I could tell from my discussions with colleagues, no one at *Time* knew about this part of his past. Nothing about Chambers gave me the slightest inkling. The revelation did not change my estimation of him but gave me an even greater sense of the emotional torment that this man had undergone in his life.

. . .

THROUGHOUT THE HEARINGS and the trials I had been only occasionally in touch with Chambers. Soon after the case broke, Chambers had offered his resignation to spare Time Inc. embarrassment, and well before the trial started the company accepted it, in a brief, cold announcement. I was dismayed by its tone and told Chambers so in a heartfelt letter. Later I would ask Jim Bell: "When you see Whit please tell him that I'm thinking of him." It was not enough, but I was following a misguided instinct of reticence.

Three years after the end of the second trial, Chambers published his autobiography, *Witness*, an agonizing self-revelation that deeply affected me. In some ways the book brought Chambers closer, yet it also made him more remote, as happens with people whose extraordinary experiences one can never share.

He dealt with his inner struggles, his slowly growing conviction that he had followed a false promise of salvation, and his decision, first, to risk his life by breaking with the Party, and then to risk his newly comfortable existence by revealing his past, thereby "reluctantly, grudgingly, step by step . . . destroying himself that this country and the faith by which it lives may continue to exist. . . . I do not know any way to explain why God's grace touches a man who seems unworthy of it. But neither do I know any other way to explain how a man like myself—tarnished by life, unprepossessing, not brave—could prevail so far against the powers of the world arrayed almost solidly against him. . . ."

I wrote Chambers a letter and told him that even as a very minor figure in his life, I should have—many of us should have—given him more sympathy and support. (Incredibly, I still addressed him as "Mr. Chambers," but he of all people probably understood that formality; he always referred to his hired man as Mr. Pennington.) *Witness* had literally moved me, I added, in the sense that after reading it, I was not quite the same person as before. In the book's ending he had given a picture of the aging Whittaker and Esther compared to Philemon and

Baucis, the devoted couple of Greek mythology who begged the gods to die at the same time and were turned into a pair of trees growing close together. That passage prompted me to write that love was an unacknowledged theme of the book: the desperate lack of love in his childhood, the insufficient or futile love of his brother, the love turned to rage and hate that marked the Communist, the love of God, ultimately the realization that even in the midst of disaster, love is the only salvation. I now realized, I wrote, that in a way he had tried to take the burden of our times onto his shoulders, while the rest of us talked about it.

He replied to my solemn letter just as solemnly: "I accept your points in the way that you make them, and say: Yes, that is right. But because you make them it is no longer possible to feel any sadness that this should be so; only a peace that someone knows it is so. I think that is all that is needed in this strange experience."

I did not tell him that there were also many things about the book that troubled me, especially the sometimes bathetic style, the self-dramatization, as in the lines about giving his life so that his country might live.

Chambers wrote with a tortured intensity that sounded off-key in this land of indomitable optimism; it was almost un-American, said Arthur Schlesinger, who called Chambers a figure out of Dostoyevsky, not William Dean Howells.

To Chambers, the common sin of capitalists and Communists was materialism, although the Communist variety of that sin was worse. He seemed to be yearning for a time before the Industrial Revolution, even before the Enlightenment.

As it happened, I was assigned by *Time* to write a story rounding up the reviews of *Witness*. I was incensed because many were nasty. (*Time* itself had reviewed the book sympathetically and at length.) What I submitted was more of a polemic than a news story. It was thrown out and replaced by a neutral compendium of quotations from various reviews, an exercise I attacked as spineless in a steaming memo to my editors. But I realized later that they had been right because my piece had been far too emotional.

On balance I had to admit that most of the reviews were fair. All took the book seriously; almost all were impressed by its genuine anguish, its intellectual sweep and literary skill; but almost all had difficulty—as did I—with Chambers's insistence on Christianity as the only real antidote to Communism. My old mentor Sidney Hook, the proud secular humanist, made the most eloquent case against that view. It was a harsh case within a respectful review.

He called the book one of the most significant autobiographies of the twentieth century, which threw more light than any other work on the nature of Communism and on what fatally attracted men of good will to its altars. He felt that it was bound to prove to any reasonable person that Chambers was telling the truth. (He later described him as a man of honor.) Hook agreed with Chambers that Communism was not an "honestly avowed heresy," but an international conspiracy waging undeclared war against democracy. But he violently rejected the notion that man must either worship God or Stalin; many people worship both.

The review took me back to Hook's classroom. I almost saw him up on the platform, mustache bristling, hands chopping the air.

Yet Chambers was right in asserting that the conflict *was* one of faiths, not just economic or social systems. I shared some of his horror of the crimes that had been committed in the name of reason. I was also only too aware of the fiery abominations that had happened in the name of faith.

But I thought there had to be some spiritual foundation, deeper and stronger than enlightened goodwill, psychology, education and reasonably distributed material comforts. The issue was precisely this: how to understand human beings. I came across a statement by Reinhold Niebuhr that struck me as dazzling in its rightness. Niebuhr, hardly a reactionary or an apologist for capitalism, had written: "Communism is so cruel and so fanatical because it has a completely erroneous conception of human nature. Living by the illusion that the abolition of a social institution [property] will redeem man of all sin, it naturally feels justified in using any means which will attain this end." He added: "These illusions are merely a hard variety of the soft illusions [of] Christian and secular sentimentalists." But you did not have to be a religious absolutist or a mystic to see that there was a deep yearning for something beyond the values T. S. Eliot had caricatured in his imagined epitaph for modern Western civilization:

> Here were decent godless people:
> Their only monument the asphalt road
> And a thousand lost golf balls.

On the more limited issue of whether Chambers or Hiss was telling the truth, a majority of the critics, like Hook and Schlesinger, seemed convinced by *Witness*. I believe Hiss decided to help the Soviet Union from purely idealistic motives—like Whittaker Chambers and so many others, including the British spies Burgess and MacLean. What unconscious reasons—love-hate of country and family, revenge for unknown injuries—might have been part of his motivation is a question beyond anyone's capacity to judge. As far as I know, Hiss was never subjected to the outrageous, secondhand psychoanalysis that some supposedly respectable practitioners inflicted on Chambers.

But for many people, his innocence remained a passionately held article of faith. It could not be shaken by *Witness*, nor by Allen Weinstein's 1978 book, *Perjury*, a painstaking review that makes an overwhelming case for Hiss's guilt. (When Weinstein interviewed me, he made it clear that he had actually set out to prove Hiss blameless but was led irresistibly to the opposite conclusion.) To his defenders Hiss was a gentleman martyr. Sidney Hook told of a Columbia professor who declared: "Even if Hiss himself were to confess his guilt, I wouldn't believe it."

Ironically, some people on the Right were not exactly enamored of Chambers, either. Yes, his charges fitted in with their own, much cruder view of the Communist conspiracy. But he blamed the shortcomings of America for much of the Communists' success, not a palatable argument for superpatriots. The more simplistic members of the Right could not forgive him for having been a Communist, no matter how repentant he was now. Typical was the splenetic columnist Westbrook Pegler, who contemptuously referred to Chambers as a "backslid Bolshevik" and described him in a bad parody of the despised magazine's language as "fat-faced, vapid Senior Editor of *Time*, New York smear sheet. . . ."

For me, one heartening reaction to *Witness* came from my old friend Lucian, who by then had finished a stint as an army historian and had entered the U.S. foreign service. He had decided long ago that Hiss was lying but had retained his view of Chambers as unsavory, egotistical, neurotic. Having read the book, he wrote, "I am doing penance. Of course he is an egoist, but he is also a great and lovable man. I do not find that he has sought refuge in an extreme mysticism. He seems to be honestly and simply religious. I do feel that he is still giving too much credit to the philosophy, teaching, ideas of Communism. He still takes that rot too seriously. . . ."

One of the most haunting things about Chambers's original testimony was his statement that, when he defected from the Communist Party, he thought he was leaving the winning and joining the losing side. Even though he was determined to warn America "so that it might continue to exist," he suspected the attempt would be futile and that Communism would be victorious.

We now know how wrong he was.

In the minds of many people the Hiss case was never really closed. Late in 1992 the press suddenly carried news that Alger Hiss had been exonerated by Moscow. A Russian military historian, General Dmitri A. Volkogonov, was quoted as saying that Hiss "was never an agent of the intelligence services of the Soviet Union." This generated big news stories and editorials about Hiss's victimization and vindication.

Six weeks later Volkogonov recanted. He had not been "properly understood" and had never meant to give Hiss a full clearance. He had reported only his failure to find incriminating documents in his brief search and added that documents could exist in other archives or have been destroyed. In 1996 the U.S. National Security Agency released a batch of intercepted messages from Soviet spies in the United States to Moscow; one 1945 message referred to an agent in the State Department, code-named "Ales," who was almost certainly Alger Hiss.

. . .

In 1991 I had experienced a personal postscript to the Hiss affair. While working on this book, I decided to get in touch with Hiss. Through a mutual friend I sent a message that I wanted to talk to him and followed up with a letter.

I wrote that as a friend of Whittaker Chambers's I would not be surprised if he turned down my request. But after all these years, I continued, I wanted to take another look at the past and clarify some things in my mind. Word came back: Okay, but Hiss did not feel up to a face-to-face meeting and suggested a phone conversation.

I knew that since his release from prison in 1954 Hiss had made a meager living as a salesman for a printing company and, eventually, a consulting lawyer. He had written a book, *In the Court of Public Opinion,* in which he protested his innocence, but in a curiously impersonal and dispassionate way, almost as if he were presenting a lawyer's brief for someone else. I knew that he and Priscilla were separated in 1959, that she had died in 1984, that he had remarried, and that he was ill with emphysema. At eighty-six he was nearly blind; friends often came to read to him.

On the phone, in October 1991, his voice sounded weak; he often paused for breath, and halfway through the thirty-minute talk he said he must rest and asked me to call him back after fifteen minutes.

To ease into the conversation, I began by talking about world events. His opinions were standard liberal, entirely respectable, and would have been unremarkable on the op-ed page of *The New York Times.* He was surprised by the swift collapse of Communism. The chief cause, as he saw it, was to be found in the excesses of Stalin, "who did more to damage the Soviet Union than the German army." It appeared to many people that Socialism in general had collapsed as a theory, but he doubted that. Socialism was still viable and, he suggested, desirable.

The United States had certainly contributed enormously to the unraveling of the Soviet empire. As soon as Truman had the atomic bomb, "we applied pressure that they could not withstand." Truman also "frightened Stalin by attempts at undermining Soviet policies [through]

CIA-type operations." A more benign relationship probably would have been possible, especially if death had not removed Roosevelt, who saw the chance for "cold-blooded cooperation."

In hastening the end of the cold war, the United States paid a high price in neglecting domestic problems. He was "disheartened" by the country's callous attitude toward the underclass; "as a New Dealer, I find this shameful." He thought we were "done with" McCarthyism but expected trouble from the "insensitivity to suffering by large numbers and a reliance on repression rather than openhandedness." He saw a danger "of our becoming a divided nation, something like the Romans with the proles and the rest of society."

Finally: Did he care to say anything about the Hiss case? Without hesitation he took up the subject. Essentially he offered two arguments: Chambers (1) had been coached by the FBI; and (2) was a psychopath.

Hiss mentioned a recent biography of J. Edgar Hoover that indicated Chambers had spent far more time with the FBI than previously known. "It's clear that he came to know what was wanted of him." Oddly, he offered a comparison with Britain's Labour prime minister Harold Wilson, who according to Hiss was attacked and smeared by the British Secret Service because "he was too Socialist." Almost casually he said: "It's one of the things [people who make policy] have to expect."

Was he bitter about the Hiss case? "It's not a happy memory, but it wouldn't do me any good to be bitter."

Hiss was understated, detached, utterly consistent in his role as the stoic but suffering servant of the truth. I could understand all over again why so many people had believed him. But the substance of what he said about the Hiss case was an insult to any average intelligence. The comparison with Harold Wilson was preposterous. As for FBI coaching, I found it difficult to imagine that even Hoover's best efforts could have gathered the amount of detailed personal information over many years that Chambers displayed in his testimony.

By an odd coincidence, on the evening of my conversation with Hiss I had been invited to the annual dinner of the Pumpkin Papers Irregulars, an informal conservative group that meets on Halloween to commemorate the celebrated pumpkin and what it symbolized. The main speaker was Jeane Kirkpatrick, who feelingly evoked past Communist fabrications and pointed out how long these lies had been defended by anti-anti-Communists. She recalled past prophets (including Chambers) who had predicted the victory of Communism, and—understandably—she gloated over its defeat. At one point she said: "Whatever may have been wrong with this year from the perspective of the likes of you and me, can you imagine what this year must have been like for Alger Hiss?" Laughter, cheers.

Having talked only that morning to the feeble, blind old man with the quavering, ghostly voice, I found the glee somewhat misplaced; Chambers, I was sure, would have felt the same way. The fact remained that Hiss had served a deadly cause.

CHAPTER FIFTEEN

My PARENTS FOLLOWED MY CAREER at *Time* with pride. But my father observed it all as if through a scrim. His main preoccupation, his near obsession, was the work he invented for himself.

He had realized long ago that he needed American collaborators, and he worked with a seemingly endless series of playwrights, most of them second- or third-raters, some of them amateurs. Despite the constant disappointments, he refused to give up. He went on typing and typing. "Work is my drug," he would say, and, "Optimism is my last capital."

One day word came via an agent that Rudolf Friml, the aging but still highly regarded composer of such American operetta antiques as *Rose Marie* and *The Vagabond King*, had accepted a new libretto of my father's. Surely this was the breakthrough at last. Then Friml changed his mind. He was afraid that the story, which had something to do with a revolution against the dictator of a small, unnamed Latin American country, might offend friendly governments. My father went into a frenzy of letter writing, arguing in indignant capitals that the world "has just been through a bloody war to eliminate DICTATORSHIP and defend DEMOCRACY!" Why should anyone worry, he sputtered, about offending some remaining dictatorships, like Argentina or Franco's Spain? His protests, of course, brought no results.

He kept working. The scripts piled up. I pitied him—and it is terrible to pity a father. I also admired his refusal to stop trying. But his mood began to turn dark and bitter. He called Hollywood a pesthole of bad taste that deserved to be A-bombed, and he was especially caustic about successful fellow émigrés; Billy Wilder was a second-rate Berlin scribbler, the great Max Reinhardt, whom he actually admired and under whose management one of his plays had been produced, was now "Maxi Goldman" (his original name) and "always overrated." Everything was luck and accident; otherwise how could stardom have come to Hedy Lamarr, who had no talent, or Paul Henreid, the hero of *Casablanca*, who had not impressed him back in Vienna when he was an understudy and bit player in some Grunwald works.

He quarreled with long-standing friends and colleagues, rehearsing ancient grievances and disputes. "You have become a sour bus," protested an old crony whose English was worse than his.

He grew uncharacteristically boastful. In an epic battle with one choleric and, I suspected, alcoholic American collaborator, he proclaimed: "You should thank Hitler for having sent you an author of international standing to work with!" "You are an international liar about your standing and your work," came the venomous reply. "Remember, you are not an American yet. You are not fit to be a citizen!"

That threat notwithstanding, the Grunwalds were naturalized. On November 29, 1948, my parents and I journeyed to the U.S. courthouse in Foley Square. In an imposing, wood-paneled chamber, beneath elaborate carvings—scales of justice, pen-and-scroll for scholarship, oil lamp for wisdom—perhaps two hundred immigrants were assembled. The robed judge administered the oath of citizenship, and the mixed chorus of many accents repeated the words: "I hereby declare on oath that I absolutely and entirely renounce and abjure all allegiance and fidelity to any foreign prince, potentate, state or sovereignty . . ." I had long since felt myself an American and had overcome the typical refugee's feeling that only a piece of paper can give security and identity. Still, like the wedding of a couple who have already lived together, the ceremony changed something: it meant an emotion validated, a loyalty formalized.

My father was very proud of his citizenship. "I am a Yankee now," he said.

. . .

Meanwhile messages reached him from Austria, where his plays were being performed again, urging him to come home. My father replied politely that he longed to see Austria again—someday, on a visit. He was less polite with friends who had returned. "I can scarcely imagine you giving a dinner party in the garden of your old house," he wrote to one, "gorging on *Backhandel* [fried chicken] with ghosts in a ghost town. Does it give you great satisfaction to see that old Nazi gang? The Viennese always were a two-faced lot, anti-Semites of the meanest and stupidest sort."

Yet he felt kindly toward non-Jewish Austrian friends who, he knew, had also been victimized. He wrote a new, sentimental song about Vienna (with music by the composer of the classic "Vienna, City of My Dreams"). Consistency was never his greatest virtue. I think he might have mellowed about Austria, had there been time.

My mother, still good-looking but with her fine features like a slowly dissolving photograph of the youthful face I remembered, ran our little household efficiently and stoically. Occasionally she grumbled—about the dingy apartment, the noisy refrigerator that kept her awake, her rheumatism. She took great joy from my sister and brother-in-law, who in the meantime had arrived in America and lived nearby. (Meta worked as a seamstress at Bergdorf's, even though Walter had found a good job in his field of industrial chemistry.) I disliked the apartment as much as she did, but I knew that my parents would be very hurt if I moved out. Besides, staying there saved money. I continued to be pulled back and forth by my life at home and my life in the office. At home I was still often a child—my mother would fret: "Do you have to work so hard? Must you come home so late?" In the office I was an adult professional, involved in a big, powerful organization and, through it, in the world at large.

In 1949 my parents finally decided to move to a bright flat in Forest Hills. I took a furnished apartment in the East Sixties. But then my father had a serious heart attack, and following my mother's entreaties, I moved in with them again. He complained that he no longer had much energy at the typewriter, but he managed to keep some of his old sense of humor. Examining the doctor's bills, he said: "The cost of living is high in America, but the cost of dying is higher." A stroke was next; for months he could neither speak nor write. In a sense he lost his language for a second time, and he painfully, doggedly, worked to regain it. Emaciated, sitting on a folding chair on a patch of lawn behind the apartment house in Forest Hills, he struggled to learn to speak again, half laughing and half crying when the words came out wrong. He covered sheet after sheet of paper with awkward letters, eventually forming disjointed phrases.

Finally desperate, he swallowed a bottle of sleeping pills. Perhaps foolishly, but instinctively, I urged his doctor to revive him. He died a few weeks later, on February 24, 1951, a week after his sixty-seventh birthday. The undertakers slipped a body bag over his diminished frame, strapped it onto a trolley and took him out in the service elevator. I accompanied him. We went through the rear exit of the building, past the smelly garbage bins waiting to be picked up. I watched on the sidewalk while he was being trundled into the hearse.

I was pleased that *Time* ran an item in its "Milestones" section ("DIED. Alfred Grunwald, 67, Vienna-born librettist" . . .), along with equally crisp notes on the passing of a Pillsbury of the flour Pillsburys, an Underwood of the typewriter Underwoods, and a Sicilian-born fruit-and-vegetable tycoon.

MY MOTHER TOOK it hard. During my father's illness she had been his tireless and uncomplaining nurse. Now she felt without purpose. "I'm no good at playing the role of a lonely woman," she would say. Given my rough hours at *Time* and my occasional trips, my mother did not see much of me, and she resented that. I wrote a story for *Time* about the younger generation, based on reporting by several correspondents, who found that youth was not very rebellious, either against society or authority or even Mom and Pop. "Why insult the folks?" said one student. "They shouldn't be blamed for everything." My mother picked out the quote. She said somewhat sarcastically: "Very nice that you think the parents are not responsible for the hard times young people have to go through."

Eventually she developed a small social life of her own, and she took a job in a trade publishing firm, where she did clerical work, having taught herself to type. The job made her feel useful and independent.

But she talked constantly about missing my father and how her apartment reminded her of him. "It holds the sound of his voice, his footsteps, his calling my name," she wrote me when I was away on a trip. "I hurry home as if he were still waiting for me." The words made me wonder, given what I knew by then about the big rift in their past and recalling the bitter quarrels I had cringingly witnessed over the years. Was this pretense? Revisionism? Self-pity? Yes, all of that, I decided, but at the same time also genuine: part of the contradictory reality of love.

MY FIRST REACTION, amid the grief over my father's death, was an impulse to strike back, as it were: to get married and create new life. But I did not feel ready for that. Beverly and I had drifted apart for a couple of years after college, then, in our mid-twenties, started seeing each other again and soon became very close. She was working as an editor in a publishing firm owned by relatives, an outfit specializing in comic books. We would meet after work, in a bar near the Time & Life Building, where we were simply called "the kids" by the Irish bartender. Over straight Scotch we would exchange war stories about our jobs. I would go on about the latest editing outrage committed by one or the other of my bosses or my latest triumph over some fellow writer I considered a rival. She, much more entertainingly, would tell me how she was coping with the impossible Ham Fisher, creator of *Joe Palooka* and the brilliant Al Capp, father of *L'il Abner*. We would discuss our ambitions, and we got to know the cast of characters in each other's lives.

She had a fresh, winsome face and a permanent radiance. Her disposition was invincibly sunny. But she also had her stubborn side. She felt that her own opinion could validate any judgment, and when she said "I just don't like that man" or "that play," no further justification was required. That, too, like her belief that anything was possible, struck me as a very American trait. I had never felt so totally content and so happy with anyone before; I once told her that she made me feel as if my heart were wrapped in cotton wool.

Why not get married? She never pressed me, and I could not decide. I sometimes discussed this dilemma with a girl I had befriended, in a nonromantic way, at *Time,* where she worked on the cable desk. I found her fascinating, because she firmly accepted the existence of hell. An Irish Catholic, she had been raised "by the nuns," who had inculcated in her the belief in what she called "the hot pot." Clever and funny, she liked to analyze my problems. "I know what's the matter with you," she would say. "What you are lusting for is Cecily Smythe-Heatherstone with the finishing-school lockjaw and the single strand of pearls. You don't want Sally in Our Alley. You don't want Riverside Drive."

As I leafed through the engagement or wedding announcements in the society pages, I often wondered about those cool blondes from Foxcroft or Madeira, whose fathers always seemed to be stockbrokers and who always had two addresses, Fifth Avenue and Southampton or Bar Harbor. The debutantes I met occasionally at *Time* or at parties were not much to my liking, but still, I had a mental image—completely immature, and I knew it—of the ideal female, who was of course a version of Katharine Hepburn.

But there was a deeper reason for my long hesitation: I felt hemmed in. I had been under my parents' rule for years, tied down by their love and their fears. I had studied hard, I was working hard, and much as I enjoyed it, there was little time to be venturesome or irresponsible. I loved Beverly very much, but she represented another tie, another obligation. I wanted to be free—for how long I was not sure. As I told my hell-fearing friend, "I want to be on all the gangplanks on all the ships between here and Shanghai. Or maybe Cherbourg."

FOR YEARS AFTER coming to the United States I simply wanted to be an American, nothing but an American, wanted to put Europe out of my mind, even out of my background. But I found that this was impossible. Europe retained a strong hold on my emotions.

I still saw Europe as the embodiment of the past, much of it evil, the remnant of a once magnificent order that had lapsed into decay. It was the breeder of endless wars and finally of the incomprehensible horror of Nazism. It seemed the antithesis of America.

Yet another part of the truth came to the surface, as I watched Europe struggling up from the bloody rubble of World War II and trying to rebuild a civilization. I watched at a safe distance, with my best approximation of the journalist's detachment. But I had not been able to feel detached from the soul-piercing, nightmare images and stories of the concentration camps. Nor could I feel indifferent to the postwar panorama of destruction, hunger, economic and political chaos, the misery of the uprooted (DPs, for displaced persons, was the new shorthand). In the midst of all this, Europe seemed to call to me.

The feeling was often stirred by some random episodes: the news, for instance, of shivering Berliners cutting down the trees in their beloved Tiergarten for firewood. Sometimes the message came to me through novels or movies. The scene in Rossellini's *Open City* when the character played by Anna Magnani is shot by German occupiers and a priest holds her corpse in a reverse pietà, gave me a sense of Europe's acceptance of fate and yet also of its gift for survival.

Increasingly I recalled the European culture I had tasted in my childhood. When colleagues or friends took trips to Europe, I found myself offering advice about what to look for and asking questions. They ranged from the high political (whatever happened to the pan-European movement?) to the trivial (did they still have tea dancing?). Once, when a friend from the Midwest was about to embark on a first European grand tour in a distinctly breezy and carefree mood, I was moved to one of my occasional attempts at poetry:

. . . And you are not afraid to go?
Why no,
Of course not, and why should you be?
For you go free

Of memory and measure.
You take no tears for sunken private treasure,
No pictures dark behind your lids.
And if the auctioneer should ask for bids—
For tapestries (but slightly stained with blood),
For gilded walls (still slightly damp after the latest flood),
For crown (a pearl is missing), for throne (the king is lost)—
You will not stop to estimate the cost
In currency of half-remembered self,
But you will quickly buy the things that fit your shelf,
Giving your innocence in fond exchange,
Reject the others as a bit too strange,
Too dubious for the house built on your certain plain,
And turn away with small suspicion of the nagging pain
That clings insistent, faithful, serflike to the things you bought.
And yet, my friend, take thought.
The marble dust sprinkling that weed
Is seed.
The church beneath that broken dome
Is home.
That portrait of a queen or peasant shrew
Is you.

Overdramatic, no doubt, but I *was* stirred by the fate of Europe and by its links to America: the new civilization, after all, had sprung from the old. "Europe, the mother of us all" was a phrase that kept going through my mind. I wanted to go back and have a look at my origins.

My father's illness had made long trips difficult. Now, despite the new emotional claims of my mother's widowhood, I was eager to get out. I had recently been appointed a senior editor—not very senior at twenty-eight—and for some time I would alternate between writing and editing. Matthews had tried to keep me from getting too smug by warning: "Don't think that you are joining the Union League." But the promotion did encourage me to suggest a lengthy European trip. Again, as with my previous attack of wanderlust, *Time* was generous. Roy

Alexander suggested that I work in *Time*'s London bureau for a while and allowed me, after that, to go out scouting various countries for my and the magazine's enlightenment.

I said a painful good-bye to Beverly. I told her that I was not sure whether I would come back to her. I realized that she was deeply hurt and very unhappy, but I felt an overwhelming need to be on my own. So, in October 1951 I sailed for England. My mother saw me off at the pier, fretting that in the rush of departure I had forgotten my warm overcoat.

I felt some apprehension about what I would find out during this journey of rediscovery, about Europe and perhaps about myself.

As the *Nieuw Amsterdam* docked at Southampton, I remembered the moments, eleven years before, when the overcrowded *Exeter* with its anxious human cargo pulled out of Lisbon harbor, and I almost hypnotically fixed my eyes on the receding European shore. The reverse movement toward this bustling British pier made me feel far less intense. I was no longer a refugee setting out toward a strange world, but an American citizen and what, in a way, every refugee wants to be: a tourist.

When the immigration officer asked the reason for my coming to the United Kingdom, I felt inordinately pleased to be able to say, journalism—which may be the ultimate tourism.

CHAPTER SIXTEEN

TIME's LONDON BUREAU had chosen to put me up at Brown's Hotel, a ramshackle, venerable institution, inhabited, or so it seemed, mostly by retired colonels and tweedy ladies from the counties. Brown's introduced me to being "awakened with tea," involving a liveried factotum silently shimmering (as Wodehouse put it) into one's room bearing the steaming symbol of morning and renewal.

More serious phases of my British education were undertaken by Andre Laguerre, the magazine's London bureau chief. Laguerre was the bilingual and brilliant son of a French diplomat and an Englishwoman and had served as press chief to Charles de Gaulle in his British wartime exile. A passionate devotee of baseball and horse racing, Laguerre also had a superb grasp of politics, which he saw as combining the former's strategic intricacies with the latter's speed and heart. Taciturnity was almost a religion with him. Much later, when he ran *Sports Illustrated*, he would sit stonily through the regular luncheon seminars with Time Inc.'s editors, conducted first by Henry Luce, then by his successor Hedley Donovan; while other participants tried hard to shine, Andre was silent, week after week, year after year, speaking only when asked a question.

He presided efficiently over the London office, then a shabby, freezing warren in Soho's Dean Street, approached through a gauntlet of friendly, overage whores. Andre's real headquarters was the pub around the corner, the Bath House, where he consumed vast quantities of beer or Scotch (depending on the hour) without ever impairing his deadly accuracy at darts or his powers of ratiocination. He indoctrinated me in the current British situation. A general election was under way that was, in effect, the first major referendum on the Labour government. It had carried out a social revolution, but Britain was still beset by shortages, unemployment and a gray mood.

A few days after my arrival I was reunited with my friend Noah. Having gone to work for his uncle, he was about to marry a charming cousin—he somehow seemed unable or unwilling to leave the sheltering circle of his clan. We celebrated over dinner at his uncle's very posh establishment in Belgrave Square. Then Noah, a Tory volunteer worker, took me out canvassing. He was wearing a blue Tory rosette on his oldest overcoat, and we set out by taxi to the East End. Deep in Labour territory, we walked from house to small, dingy house, "knocking-up" the residents. Usually one look at the blue on Noah's lapel was enough to evoke the words "We're Labour!" followed by a slammed door. But some of the householders were willing to listen to his low-key pitch and to accept the literature he was carrying. The pamphlets were long and dull.

Next day, in Chiselhurst, a dormitory constituency fourteen miles from London, I had my first introduction to British class structure. At Conservative headquarters, most of the volunteers could have come from the lounge at Brown's; the accents were not uniform, but a certain modulated gentility prevailed.

At Labour headquarters clothes were shabbier, faces both angrier and more tired, accents harsher and (to my untutored ear) more mysterious. It didn't take much imagination to read in these people the evidence of decades of deprivation, shivering nights and unhealthy diets, long vigils on the picket line. Over a feeble electric fire I asked the local chairman what he did for a living. I had never heard a simple statement uttered so meaningfully. "I'm a wheelwright," he said, making it sound like both a boast and a curse. The Labour Party was still dominated by the craftworker's view of the world, distrustful of machines as creators of unemployment, hostile to industry. In the end, the Tories won narrowly and the aging Winston Churchill was returned to power.

I took away a deep sense of how serious the British were about their politics. Their corrosive class resentments—so different from the situation in the United States, I thought—did not keep them from respecting and playing by the rules. I gained a new appreciation of "His Majesty's Loyal Opposition," a phrase that had always thrilled me, because in my earliest political experience opposition had never been loyal.

Rereading some of my cables, notes and letters from those days, I find that I was infatuated with England. I brashly concluded that Britain was sailing down the drain with colors flying, pretty good discipline on board, all hands singing "Rule, Britannia." But I also believed that the end was a long way off.

AFTER MY MONTH-LONG London stint I decided on a side trip to Scandinavia. Its high point came when a Finnish-American journalist, Paul Sjerblom, insisted that I must attend a reindeer roundup in Lapland. We left our safe cab, and I presently found myself semihorizontal on a reindeer sled, at first partnered by a friendly Lapp, then—as he hopped off—terrifyingly alone, clinging desperately to the reins and staring at the jiggling rump of the uncontrollable animal ahead of me.

It was a wild, enchanted ride through trackless forests, over ditches, tree stumps, and sometimes, it seemed, straight through space.

Another experience was less idyllic. The iron curtain ran along the Finnish border, and I wanted to see it. After a lengthy trek through the snow, I found myself peering at barbed-wire barriers, bold warning signs and Russian border guards. I was acting like a typical cold war sightseer. It was, I realized, a rather pointless exercise, as if by merely looking really hard, one could somehow penetrate a hidden and horrendous reality. One of the Russian soldiers stared back at me through binoculars, and I half imagined that he looked more puzzled than hostile.

. . .

ALL THIS, I knew, had been a detour, a delaying tactic. My real journey was to Germany and Austria.

I had never been in Germany before, but for as long as I could remember it had loomed as a huge diabolical presence. I had regarded Germany's utter defeat as just retribution. But my emotions could not stay that simple. There were competing images: horrifying pictures of the concentration camps, as they were seized and liberated by Allied troops; pictures of bombed-out German cities, of survivors scrambling for food among the debris; of the once goosestepping Hitler Youth transformed into shuffling orphans. The scenes of German suffering in no way balanced the bestial enormity of the Holocaust. But they did stir, almost in spite of myself, flickers of pity.

Neither revenge nor pity, however, is a sensible guide to policy. U.S. and other Western leaders rejected the proposal by Treasury Secretary Henry Morgenthau to deindustrialize Germany; they remembered the savage reaction that economic and political punishment had produced in the humiliated Germany after World War I. Besides, the Soviets were plundering their occupation zone in East Germany and were openly aiming for a reunited Germany under Communist rule. Hence the Western determination to rebuild the shattered country. By now that rebuilding had succeeded to an amazing degree. Most of the cities had been restored, the rubble having been cleared laboriously, piece by piece, much of it worked into new structures. In Cologne, one of the few places where reconstruction was slow, the magnificent cathedral rose in contrast with the surrounding moonscape of ruins. Yet even the rubble had an orderly, neatly stacked look; I had the impression that it was being dusted once a week.

A visitor from outer space would have easily concluded that Germany was the victor. Germans, I found, could scarcely believe that food was still rationed in Britain. Yet little about the colorful and well-stocked shops, crowded streets and neatly dressed people suggested ease. Hard work, beginning virtually the day the bombs stopped falling, had helped create this prosperity; hard work kept it expanding.

As I watched these scenes I kept wondering: Where were those legions of marching Storm Troopers, those massed flags, those hate-roaring crowds, the whole swastika-crowned dance of death? Were they really gone, as Hitler's bunker was gone, covered over by innocuous gravel? Had they really been replaced by these diligent citizens, these busy, mundane streets and squares, this flourishing commerce? Could monstrosity ever really give way to *Alltag*—commonplace, quotidian life? I found myself staring at ordinary Germans, trying to penetrate that mystery. I knew that the old horrors were still inside them, somewhere under their clothes, under their skin, behind their foreheads. But I could not truly feel it, could not truly connect these banal, average people with the inhuman, murderous robots they had been.

Or many of them had been. Which ones in particular was always a nagging question.

I moved about Germany rather hectically. I went to Bonn, the new seat of government, still bucolic and provincial, the birthplace of Beethoven (as everybody insisted on telling you, as if certifying that Germany was a civilized country, after all).

I went to stately but pudgy Munich; in one of those brawling beer halls, now oddly tame, Hitler had launched his movement. And to old Hanseatic, sea-sprayed Hamburg, whose solid elegance was interrupted by the grimly erotic Reeperbahn, where sin seemed a duty.

Alongside returning prosperity, misery remained, including a severe housing shortage. Combined with an equally severe shortage of males, the situation produced some odd social arrangements. I met a "family" consisting of two middle-aged women sharing one man and one apartment.

West Germany was burdened by nearly nine million refugees, mostly of German origin, who had fled or been expelled from the Communist East. Most had been taken in and settled or helped to emigrate. But between forty thousand and fifty thousand displaced people were still quartered in more than one hundred camps or left to roam the streets.

I saw one "residual group" (as bureaucratic jargon had it) in a refugee camp in Bavaria: families from Poland and other iron curtain countries cooped up in squalid barracks, the mixture of boredom and despair as distinctive as the stale air. They had no idea what would become of them, and most had even stopped daydreaming about some hoped-for destination. "At least here we are warm," said one young girl from Czechoslovakia, "and we are fed."

I felt that sense of identification and remorse that I would always experience around refugees, in this century of refugees. I was, after all, also a displaced person; although I had managed to be re-placed to a secure home, only a few years and enormous luck separated me from their fate.

FINALLY BERLIN. A driver employed by *Time* who displayed his city's typical air of having seen everything and of being prepared for anything, gave me a tour. The high point was the Kaiser Wilhelm Gedachtnis Kirche, the memorial church that had deliberately not been rebuilt; it remained a permanent reminder of the war, pointing upward like the stump of a crudely amputated arm.

Until now my most compelling images had been formed by the great airlift, when the Soviets blockaded the city. Berlin, located deep inside the Soviet zone, was a separate enclave administered by the four powers, with road and rail access from the West supposedly guaranteed. By barring that access, the Soviets had tried to starve the city into submission and force out the Western powers. In one of the decisive acts of the cold war, the United States had determined to supply Berlin by air, and for weeks that drama had fascinated me. I had almost been able to hear the constant roar of those C-47s and C-54s filling every ear in the city. I had imagined that I could listen in on the happy, efficient chatter of the G.I. air controllers ("That's flour coming in on EC 72. . . . Roger. . . . Ease her down"). The resolution of the Americans had seemed to merge with the courage of the Berliners. After twelve months the Soviets gave up and lifted the siege.

By the time I arrived two years later people were still not allowed to leave the city without Soviet permission. Berliners suffered from severe claustrophobia, aggravated by languishing business and high unemployment. Yet the spirit of defiance was alive. They accepted their imprisonment, as they accepted the city's East-West split with relatively good cheer.

The two parts of Berlin had separate laws, governments, police and fire fighters, phone and postal services, currencies. But circulation within the city limits was still fairly easy. The underground continued un-hindered. When the trains passed the border between the zones, the lights would flicker out for a few moments as they were switched from one electrical system to the other. To a newcomer like myself, that momentary darkness symbolically separated two worlds.

THE COLD WAR was causing a major reversal: the transformation of Germany from America's occupied enemy to its ally. The United States was pressing West Germany to rearm, with tireless support from Chan-cellor Konrad Adenauer.

The Soviets fulminated against this policy, and it was not popular in West Germany, either. The most serious opponents were the Socialists, whose leader was habitually identified by *Time* as "one-armed, one-legged Kurt Schumacher." That flip description covered a fearful amount of German history. Schumacher had lost his right arm on the Russian front in World War I and his left leg after a decade in Hitler's concentration camps.

In his Bonn office I found him a thin, cadaverous man, grimly punc-tuating his impassioned words with thrusts from his bony left hand. A firm anti-Nazi, he was a German patriot who wanted an independent, neutral Germany. "I believe neutrality is the only way to reunite our fatherland. Why should Russia be expected to let go of East Germany, if the prospect is that it would become part of a militarist, capitalist, anti-Soviet country?" Despite widespread fears of a new German national-ism, I thought the greater danger was a kind of passivity, a moralistic neutralism through which Germany might allow itself to drift toward Moscow, or at least assume an illusory middle position between the superpowers.

Adenauer fought patiently, brilliantly, against this trend. He was sev-enty-five, and I was disappointed that he declined an interview, because

I thought it might well be my last chance to see him. As it turned out I met him ten years later, when he was still chancellor. Schumacher was dead by then, and so, it seemed, was the argument for a neutral Germany.

Adenauer, the flat-voiced, Catholic politician from the Rhineland, appeared to me the very antithesis of the familiar image of braying Prussian authority. He discussed the politics of Europe with the outlook of a visionary and the sure grasp of a ward leader. Waxen faced, weary, infinitely patient, ready to maneuver without ever losing sight of his goal, the greatest German statesman of this century represented a lesson about true strength, which requires mind more than muscle, and cunning in the service of principle.

Even the existence of an Adenauer, the embodiment of the "good German," could not stop me thinking of Nazism. I was, after all, a Jew in Germany a mere six years after the end of the Holocaust. By the time of my visit the postwar "denazification" process had largely ceased and the Nuremberg war crime files were formally closed.

But I happened across two figures who had been prominent in those files. In the case of Franz von Papen my contact was indirect, through his son. The aristocratic cavalry officer and diplomat, who during the death throes of the Weimar Republic had served briefly as chancellor and had done much to bring Hitler to power, had been acquitted of war crimes charges. The younger Franz von Papen was a public relations operative working for, among other Ruhr firms, the huge Mannesmann concern, manufacturers of pipes and other steel products. I had gone to see him because I wanted to get a picture of the German business scene and *Time*'s Bonn bureau thought that he could give me some useful leads. Smoothly affable toward a member of the American press, he was eager to put me in touch with Ruhr executives. "You will find these to be intelligent, sophisticated gentlemen," he said. "They are open-minded and generous. It's our smaller businessmen who are greedy and narrow."

The men I met through him approximated his description. Many of them had backed Hitler's rise to power, and most had worked hard to supply his war machine. But to a man they now claimed to deplore what

Hitler had done to Germany (what he had done to the rest of the world was mentioned less often).

As for young Von Papen, facing him, I kept thinking of his father, who, as Hitler's ambassador in Vienna, had worked hard to soften up Austria for the German takeover. He was at Hitler's side when *der Führer* entered Vienna. Memories of the Anschluss rose in me, of our exile, of Meta and Walter's suffering. I was enraged by this man's blandness about the past. But I had acquired enough journalistic discipline to suppress the angry things I could have said. I merely ventured a bit of sarcasm: "And how is your famous father?" I asked.

The sarcasm was lost on his son. "Oh, he is quietly in retirement," came the reply. "He is doing some writing, to set the record straight. He was never really for Hitler, you know. Besides, he is angry that the German government has denied him a pension."

I bitterly thought of my own father's last years. Old Von Papen lived almost two more decades and died at eighty-nine, having fought in vain for his pension.

The other Nuremberg survivor, with whom I dealt directly, was Hjalmar Schacht, universally described as Germany's financial wizard, who had served the Kaiser, the Weimar Republic and the Third Reich. He had helped provide the regime's financial underpinnings and had been an ardent supporter of Hitler's, although his relations with *der Führer* eventually became strained; in the dock at Nuremberg he declared, "I could have killed him personally if given the chance." When a film about the Holocaust was shown in the courtroom, displaying pile after pile of corpses in gruesome variety, Schacht turned his back on the screen.

Acquitted, he went to work as a writer and international economic consultant. He had just finished a report on the Indonesian economy that my editors in New York wanted to see, so I duly called on him in Hamburg. At seventy-five he was spry, jovial, supremely self-confident, with the sly, round face of a wooden puppet. He mused about Hitler's terrible misjudgments both in war and economics ("The man didn't understand finance") and offered to show me the Indonesia report, for a hefty fee. "After all," he said, beaming, "I must build a new existence for myself." I had the considerable pleasure of turning him down. I found it eerie to be in the presence of a man who had served Hitler, worked with him, dined with him, undoubtedly laughed with him. I had no reason to disagree with the Nuremberg judges who had found him innocent of war crimes, but I could not forget how he had literally turned his back on those crimes.

I was glad when the time came to leave Germany. I had not felt horror; oddly, that sentiment had been stronger at a distance. But I experienced a deep unease, a kind of vertigo caused by looking from an increasingly normal present into the abysses of the past. I also felt irritation over something more mundane: the mounting arrogance shown by most people I met. Defeat had given the Germans the bleak security of having hit rock bottom. Their economic comeback gave them a feeling of superiority over the victors.

I CONDUCTED THE Von Papen and Schacht interviews in English because both spoke it fluently. But throughout my time in Germany I was often uncertain about which language to speak. During a decade in America I had used very little German; most of the time even my parents and I spoke English with each other. Here I resorted to my somewhat rusty German only rarely, when dealing with someone who lacked English. Even then I sometimes used an interpreter, for accuracy, and perhaps more so because I was so eager to assert my status as an American.

That feeling became even stronger as I left Germany for Austria. At the border crossing, when I showed my passport and answered a few routine questions in German, I actually tried to exaggerate my Americanized pronunciation. I realized quickly how childish that was, but it was a symptom of trying to cope with my identity, with my old half-remembered self.

My train, from the border to Vienna, traversed the same countryside that I had looked out on as a child, the same rushing landscape that I

used to fix on with the thought that I would never see it again. But I
tried to pretend that I was on my way to just another city I would
inspect for *Time*.

That attempt collapsed the moment I alighted at the Westbahnhof,
the old Western Railway Station. I was surrounded by the same smells
of coal dust and sausages in the cold, sharp, winter air. Presently I
looked out from a rattling taxi, at the same streets and monuments,
somehow amazed that they were all still there.

I began to see with double vision. Childhood images were superimposed on present views, and they did not coincide. Everything now
seemed absurdly smaller, the streets narrower, the buildings lower, the
distances shorter; what I recalled as a long walk had become just a brief
stroll, and the park where I had played, spacious in my memory, was
scarcely more than patches of grass divided by a few paths.

Everything seemed shabbier. I remembered the city in color; the
present hue seemed gray. Parts of Vienna were still in rubble, but much
had been repaired or rebuilt, including the venerable Hotel Sacher and
St. Stephen's Cathedral, its new roof too bright to look natural. The
other churches, patched and more their humble selves, still drew wor-
shipers to prayer before fading altars, favoring even passersby with generous whiffs of incense. The baroque palaces stood as before, if somewhat dilapidated, their portals still seeming to wait for carriages that
never came.

I made my nostalgic rounds; I did memories as a tourist does monuments. Our old apartment building, its facade badly decayed, was de-
faced with a huge commercial sign. The amusement park in the Prater,
its attractions much diminished. Calafati, the giant Chinaman who had
loomed over a carousel, was gone, having burned to cinders in a 1945
bombing raid. But the big Ferris wheel that starred in *The Third Man*
was still there, revolving slowly. Also still present was the *Wat-
schenmann*, literally "the slapping man," a fat effigy whose ears you
could box with all your available strength for a few pennies, a cheap
outlet for pent-up fury; over the decades he must have silently accumulated quite a fever chart of Viennese rage.

My nostalgia was limited by a certain selective reticence. I am not sure by what principle it functioned, but I avoided some encounters, perhaps sensing that they might be painful. I went to see my old gymnasium with its sad, crumbling front, but I barely stuck my head inside the dank lobby; not until years later would I actually revisit the school. I also made no effort to find any of my old classmates or teachers. As for family, I had not a single surviving relative in Vienna.

But there was Teta. My reunion with her was explosive. I had written her about my impending arrival, and she came to my hotel room, impatiently bursting through the door, laughing, weeping, uttering cries of astonishment: "I can't believe it! . . . You're really here . . . Jesus-Maria, you're so big!" She had aged only slightly and was as peasant strong and melodramatic as ever, eyes gleaming, arms rising heavenward in enthusiasm, indignation or amazement. Again and again she hugged me, then pushed me away to get a better look, staring at me in a mixture of pride and disbelief that her "Muggel" was now twenty-nine and a man. She had married a retired railway official with a small government pension, a gentle man much older than she—he was now in his nineties and nearly senile. "Lord, when I married him, I didn't think he'd live this long," she said in her blunt way. But she nursed him devotedly and rarely left his side.

We retraced some of our old walks, looking for every corner, square, passage or cozy bench we remembered. She was bursting with stories about the hardships of the war years—mostly hunger and cold. Her hatred of the Nazis was now supplanted by her loathing of the Russians—thieves and rapists, most of them, as far as she was concerned. Did I realize that for many nights after the Red Army moved in, Viennese women slept on the roofs of their buildings, hoping the Russian soldiers would be too lazy to climb the stairs? "I was lucky; they never came near me," she growled, adding fiercely: "But lucky for them, too. I would have taught them a lesson!"

Mostly she was full of questions about my mother and my sister, whom she wanted desperately to see again, and full of memories of the good old days. I loved her very much, but I also realized that apart from reminiscences and news about the family, I had little to talk to her about. We were separated by the simple, heartbreaking distance between childhood and adulthood. But I felt protective toward the woman who had always been so protective of me. Later my sister and I helped support her with regular payments from my father's royalties.

I found myself doing things that as a boy had seemed very adult to me. I took up cigars. I went to a famous haberdasher (Knize) to buy ties and had suits made to order at bargain prices (the dollar was strong). I dined at restaurants that had always sounded glamorous (they were, in fact, not very glamorous, but I adored the rich food that, absurdly, I then still considered the best in Europe). I dropped into a nightclub, the Moulin Rouge, whose rotating red windmill sign had once symbolized forbidden wickedness; I sat through second-rate cabaret acts and observed clusters of rather pathetic hostesses waiting for action. The head-waiter approached me with the classic question: "Does the gentleman desire a lady?" I bought the usual bottle of expensive fake champagne for a scrawny, sad blonde who frantically wanted to know all about New York.

At every turn I encountered my father. The dance band at the Moulin Rouge, like other bands and every barroom pianist in town, played the songs to which he had written the lyrics; vocalists crooned his words. The manager at my hotel remembered him. "He was a fine gentleman," he said. "What a pity he could not have come back to Vienna." I thought but chose not to say: "What makes you think he would have wanted to?"

At a political cabaret I was startled and amused by an anti-Communist parody titled *Comrade Maritza (Maritza* again!), whose hero was no longer a count, but a commissar yearning for the past ("Play gypsies, dance gypsies . . . I too was once a rich and happy bourgeois . . ."). Naturally I also went to the Theater an der Wien, where most of my father's operettas had been produced, now given over to opera, since the bombed-out Oper on the Ringstrasse had not yet been resurrected.

I visited the former star-manager of the Theater an der Wien, who used to sing lead tenor roles and was now fat and bald but still full of energy. He was running a sort of operetta school and invited me to a student performance of one of my father's works. The leading comedi-enne was a lovely, aspiring actress playing a middle-aged spinster; neither wig nor costume could hide her youthful magnetism. I would see a great deal of her during my stay in Austria, although I found that Beverly was still constantly in my mind.

As in Germany, I asked myself what had become of the mean little bureaucrats with swastika buttons in their lapels, the hate-filled informers, the Gestapo men who had routinely sent Vienna's Jews into exile or to the camps. Surely most of them still had to be here, passing me in the street, ushering me to my theater seat, waiting on me in shops with that ineffable Viennese mixture of servility and resentment.

There had been denazification proceedings, but they had not gone very far. For the Viennese, denazification took forms quite remote from politics or law: the relentless reenactment of *Gemütlichkeit*, the worshipful devouring of confectioner's masterpieces at Demel's. Above all, it took the form of two glib arguments: we couldn't help it because we were forced to go along; and, we suffered, too.

The ultimate refuge of the Viennese was being Viennese. They were as flattering and title mad as ever (I was instantly promoted to Herr Editor in Chief). Foreign detractors had always accused them of lacking character, and many Viennese more or less jovially agreed. I knew that I could never live among them again permanently or trust them again—with a few notable exceptions. Yet I found that I could not hate them. Was that lack of character in myself?

At any rate, the absence of hate did not bring a sense of belonging.

In Vienna, under Four Power occupation, the cold war was somewhat less harsh than elsewhere. But suspicion was part of the ambience. The gray man with pince-nez at the next café table, who kept looking at the entrance over his newspaper: was he merely a retired university professor or a spy? Or both? The barmaid who kept asking about my work, my travel plans: was she merely being friendly or was she reporting to the Soviets on the movements of Americans?

I began to feel that Vienna was hosting a masquerade ball—the masked ball having always been a symbol of this city's concealed emotions. I was embarrassed by my imaginings. "Don't worry," said an

American of vague official connections who, I had been assured, worked for the CIA. "Everybody feels that way in Vienna after a while."

Lucrative illegal arms sales to the satellites kept a horde of operators, or *Schieber* (literally, "pushers"), in luxury; they could be spotted everywhere, especially in the fancier nightclubs, sporting silk shirts and bejeweled blondes. The lives of ordinary Austrians were pinched but moderately comfortable. They ate well because food was subsidized, partly through U.S. loans. Austria had a startling ability somehow to survive by luck and by what the Viennese call *Durchwusteln*, or "muddling through."

The mood was symbolized by Chancellor Leopold Figl, a little man with a farming background, who had been the head of the Austrian Peasants' Union. A strong anti-Nazi, he had spent six years in a German concentration camp. Despite his well-tailored black morning coat, he looked incongruous in the magnificent chamber from which Metternich had fought to preserve an empire. For that matter I, too, must have seemed incongruous, interviewing him in somewhat halting German.

"Well, maybe we eat a little too much," he replied with a disarming smile to a question about whether Austrians were living too well. "Perhaps we shouldn't have spent all this money importing pork for Christmas. But what are you going to do with these Viennese—they've got to have their pork once in a while. But we're going to keep it down to once a week—that's all! Let them eat beef!" Unconscious of any Marie Antoinette echoes, the chancellor's press chief broke in with a spirited defense of pork as a psychological weapon against the Communists. Deeply serious: "Don't forget that every single piece of roast pork we eat here makes a tremendous impression in Prague."

Before leaving Austria, I had to make a pilgrimage to Ischl. The winter weather made it seem even more desolate than I had feared: dead trees, unkempt lawns, muddy paths, stained and decomposing walls. Our villa still stood, but it had been partitioned into rental apartments; its wooden balconies were nearly falling down, their fretwork splintered and their colored glass panes broken and patched, the garden weed swamped, the little gazebo gone. The river still sparkled in the winter sun, the bridges stood and the bell at the rail crossing still clanged when trains approached, but somehow it sounded shrill, quite different from the soft and golden morning tone in my memory.

I had a reunion with Rudolf, who had settled in Ischl. He looked wizened, although he must have been only in his forties. He spoke bitterly of his wife, who had run off with another man, and sadly about my father, whose letters he had proudly kept. He read me a few passages. "Good old Austria had the same experience with Herr Hitler as you did with your wife," my father had written. "It was shamelessly deceived. Looking back, I can only ask: why did all this have to happen?"

Moving about Germany and Austria as an American editor, I again recognized the heady but hazardous sense of power that accompanies the journalist's role.

A little later I was offered the chance to become *Time*'s Moscow correspondent and turned it down. *Time*, while praising my voluminous reporting in Europe, had printed very little of it. The New York office was remarkably tolerant of my somewhat querulous messages about unused or, as I saw it, mangled contributions. I didn't like having my work slashed at a three-thousand-mile distance, even though (or perhaps because) I myself had often inflicted such treatment on correspondents and would continue to in the future. I opted for the editor's role, concluding that it was more blessed to cut than to be cut.

Besides, I was still determined to become a playwright and still pretended to myself that journalism was only a way station. Had I been more honest, I would have admitted that I had become thoroughly seduced by journalism and attached to *Time*, for what it offered me by way of security and standing.

My trip was coming to an end, and I was pulled back to America by several forces. One was my mother, who throughout my trip had continued to write, each sad letter a claim to my affection, a summons. She asked me to find her a certain silver cake server in the Vienna shops as well as a good edition of Lessing's plays, and she admonished me to be sure to visit the Albertina, with its matchless collection of drawings. She kept asking whether she ought to send me my warm overcoat. She complained, while disclaiming any intention to complain, about my long absence. "I don't live for my children, I only live *because* of my children," she wrote, with the maternal genius for inducing guilt.

Above all, she mourned my father. I was moved by her evident pain. I knew that what awaited me in New York was her melancholy embrace, her grievance about not sharing sufficiently in my life. Part of me resented her claims and wanted to stay away. But I was also drawn back to her, for despite our frictions, she was home.

Another force drawing me back was Beverly. I had missed her badly from the moment I sailed. I sent her little presents along the way. She had decided to visit South Africa, where she had hordes of relatives. She sent me accounts of the family, of politics, of apartheid, of the natural wonders of the land. One day she informed me that she had become involved with a young doctor, who wanted to marry her. My initial reaction was to wish her luck. But eventually the news produced the predictable and classic reaction in me: I wanted her back and told her so in a long cable. I realized how essential she was in my life. Her acceptance of me, her devotion, had bolstered my self-confidence. Above all she created a sense of well-being and contentment that I did not want to be without. In other words, I loved her.

I was also drawn back by America. The U.S. influence in Europe was all-pervasive, but I concluded that even America would not be able to save the Continent from gradual oblivion. I did not foresee Europe's later, brave attempt to reinvent itself. Before setting out on my trip, I had wondered whether my birthplace would reclaim me. It did not. The cause was not merely the Nazi experience, but the American experience. Through American lenses Vienna seemed not only physically small, but intellectually and psychologically cramped, ultimately alien, despite my continued susceptibility to three-quarter time and baroque. I knew that I would never stop responding to European culture: the stone hymns of its architecture, the devotion of its craftsmanship, the rituals of its cuisines, the stubborn endurance of its family life. But a basic link to my origins had been broken forever. On my flight back to the United States

I remembered a long-ago German movie about the construction of a platform in the mid-Atlantic that would enable planes to refuel. I often used to think that, metaphorically, I lived on such a platform, halfway between the continents. But now, back in New York, I felt that I had left that precarious float and had, once and for all, landed in America.

CHAPTER SEVENTEEN

I CAME HOME to McCarthyism in full fury. I had to face up to a dark side of the country in a way that I had not done earlier. I also had to face up to something in myself: a tendency to see both sides of an issue, which can be, but is not always, a virtue. All that had gone before—the loyalty probes, the HUAC hearings, the Hollywood investigation—climaxed in the "McCarthy era."

Joseph McCarthy retroactively annexed the Hiss case. He invoked it constantly, giving rise to the widespread notion that he and Whittaker Chambers were much the same morally and politically, that Chambers was a McCarthyite who had read Dostoyevsky. That was quite false.

Chambers's compassion for his enemies, his notion that Communism represented a judgment on the West's own shortcomings, were as alien to McCarthy as the philosophers' stone or the Hindu concept of karma.

Like a venomous Wizard of Oz, McCarthy played to an ever-ready belief in conspiracy. Communism was indeed a conspiracy; but McCarthy grotesquely oversimplified and trivialized it, thus threatening the very cause he supposedly championed.

I did not come to this realization immediately. I took seriously a defense of McCarthy by a strange character named Willi Schlamm. Born in Poland, raised in Vienna and a gifted editor in Prague, he had been a Communist before turning to the Right. He had come to the United States in 1938, taught himself English and within three years was working for *Fortune.* He became a sort of ideological counselor to Luce. Short, with the high forehead and back-brushed hair I associated with Viennese café intellectuals, Schlamm could be courtly; he regularly brought lilies of the valley to female employees. Later he left to help found, with William Buckley, the *National Review.* He was a virulent advocate of "rolling back" the Soviets in Europe rather than just containing them, which at the time I found persuasive.

At Time Inc. he floated in a sphere far above me. But once, at some office function, I had a chance to speak to him about McCarthy. "He may be a bit rough, but he takes ideas seriously," said Schlamm. "He knows that ideas have consequences. Marxism is a deadly poison, and a whole generation of our intellectuals has absorbed it." Turning away, he muttered: *"La trahison des clercs!"*

La trahison des what? I asked myself. I suppose I should have known the reference. Next day, resorting to one of the great luxuries offered its writers by *Time,* I asked a researcher to look it up. "The Treason of the Intellectuals" turned out to be a mildly notorious polemical essay published in 1928 by the French philosopher-novelist Julien Benda, in which he argued that the "clerks" (in the medieval sense of the word, or what he called the "priests of the mind") had abandoned their traditional, selfless service to truth and justice. Instead, argued Benda, they had taken up materialism, pragmatism and worship of the nation and the state. I saw later that he had touched, only narrowly, on a broad subject: the modern intellectuals' role as the permanent opposition to the Establishment.

But Benda's title stuck in my mind. It fit some of my concerns: the lingering belief by many intellectuals that the Left was progressive and that the Soviet Union stood for peace; the anti-anti-Communism I had encountered during the Hiss-Chambers furor and still kept encountering.

"McCarthy is a Fascist," my brother-in-law, Walter, said one evening at dinner. I defended him against this charge. The Fascist label, I argued, should not be used lightly—especially not by someone like Walter who had barely survived the real thing. To me Fascism meant, above all, brutality as a routine, violence as a system of government.

McCarthy and his followers hardly made such distinctions about their targets: Communists, fellow travelers, dupes, liberals, whatever. A handful of self-appointed investigators published blacklists of supposed subversives active in TV news, the entertainment world, education, the press. A mere accusation or suspicion was enough to get people fired.

A right-wing columnist labeled my colleague Douglas Auchincloss a pinko who should have been fired from the magazine. His offense: membership in "the American Roundtable on India," denounced as a Communist front. Another case, resembling countless others, involved that most lighthearted and innocent of entertainments Johann Strauss's *Die Fledermaus*. The comedian Jack Gilford, who had been accused of being close to some Communist fronts, had been hired by the Metropolitan Opera to play the comic jailer Frosch, in an English-language version. His performance was brilliant. But when the production went on tour, in city after city the American Legion protested. As Rudolf Bing, the Met's general manager later recalled, they accused "Gilford and the Metropolitan and me and probably Johann Strauss of God knows what." Bing stuck with Gilford ("We had enough casting problems without letting outsiders dictate whom we could hire," he told me). In similar situations most other managements caved in.

For about two years after my return from Europe I floated between various writing and editing assignments, but I was not directly involved in our McCarthy coverage. *Time* attacked McCarthy from the start, notwithstanding the strange judgment by W. A. Swanberg, in his extremely biased 1972 biography of Luce, that the "Lucepress . . . gave McCarthy more support than opposition." *Time*'s attitude was foreshadowed by a story in March 1950 that declared that "loud-mouthed Joe McCarthy . . . had made a wretched burlesque of the serious and necessary business of loyalty checkups." A *Life* editorial urged readers "not to join in the McCarthy lynching bee," and added: "It is right to fight Communism; it is wrong, wicked, to smear people indiscriminately, most of whom are good Americans."

Luce condemned McCarthy, but not always as passionately as his editors. In memos that filtered down to me, he said it was important to note that probably a majority of Americans approved of McCarthy and that liberals for years had practiced their own form of McCarthyism by turning "practically every businessman" into a villain. *Time* said as much and suggested that the press actually helped McCarthy by paying too much attention to him.

That was a favorite argument of Max Ways, who by then had moved on to edit National Affairs. I would often find him in his office, shaking his head over some front-page story reporting McCarthy's latest onslaught and hissing through his dentures: "Those fools! They're just building him up."

Eighteen months after McCarthy's first charges about Communists in the State Department, in February 1950, Luce instructed *Life*'s editorial writer that "it was about time to hit [him] hard" again, which the magazine did. Soon afterward *Time* ran a cover story on "Demagogue McCarthy," which its subject denounced as "prostitution of the freedom of the press."

I found that watching and listening to McCarthy induced a permanent shudder, like the screeching of chalk on blackboard. He was singularly unprepossessing: pugnacious chin, shifty eyes, snarling mouth, nasal, threatening tones. When he was pleased with a joke or an ironic twist, he went into a compulsive, simpering chuckle, gurgling as a drowning man might if a drowning man were trying to laugh. His accusations became so reckless that he threatened to discredit even moderate and discriminating opponents of Communism—guilt by association in a different sense. He described Owen Lattimore, a middle-level academic who had often acted as adviser to the State Department and was vehemently against Chiang Kai-shek, as a top Soviet agent in the United States. Within days McCarthy found it necessary to reduce the charge to "security risk." Yet he went right on trying to find other Lattimores, including, in his view, Secretary of State Dean Acheson. I considered Acheson's policy in Asia too conventional. But McCarthy was absurd when he attacked Acheson, the consummate mandarin of the Establishment, as "a procurer of pinks and punks in the State Department." Meanwhile, a kind of intellectual blacklist developed: subjects that were dangerous to teach in the classroom or present on the screen. In Houston schools *Robin Hood* was banned, the outlaw's policy of taking from the rich and giving to the poor being plainly Marxist.

Americans were fighting again, in a remote and bleak part of the world. The Korean War was oddly suspended between eras. It was still surrounded by some of the spirit of "the good war," which had ended five years before. But its goals were less clear, and U.S. power no longer was irresistible. North Korea's invasion of the south was backed by China and the Soviet Union; Beijing's vast manpower and Moscow's atomic bomb imposed unaccustomed limits on what the United States could do. During stints in the Foreign News section I seemed always to be writing, with conviction, about how America needed "the will to win." But the fighting produced only stalemate. General Douglas MacArthur wanted to break it by attacking China, an unacceptable risk. From London Noah berated me for *Time*'s sympathetic treatment of MacArthur: "I saw no mention of the time the general walked on water, or is that only one of his minor miracles?" I explained in reply that the war created enormous frustration among Americans. This fed the McCarthyite suspicion that some sort of domestic villainy must be to blame.

While *Time* continued to criticize the Democratic administration, it also continued to castigate McCarthy. He accused *Time* of merely throwing "pebbles" at Communism while actually "rendering almost unlimited service to the Communist cause." He appealed to advertisers to boycott *Time*, without much effect, but a great many of his followers, including Walter Winchell, berated the magazine as a pink encampment. I found it odd, and reassuring, to see *Time* attacked both from the Left and the Right.

Sometimes the magazine seemed to be backtracking, when it criticized McCarthy's critics and liberals for still underestimating the Communist menace. But *Time* remained plainly anti-McCarthy, calling him reckless, indecent and a liability to the country. I had come to loathe McCarthy and sympathized with his victims; but I also disliked those whom I regarded as phony victims, playing at martyrdom.

Chief among these was the playwright Lillian Hellman. A well-known and consistent supporter of Stalinism, she was summoned to appear before the House Un-American Activities Committee in 1952. She wrote a letter saying that she was ready to testify about anything concerning herself, but that she would not bear witness against others and hence would plead the Fifth Amendment. (In fact, once she testified about herself, she could not then have invoked the Fifth Amendment about others.) Her letter won much attention, especially the ringing pronouncement "I will not cut my conscience to fit this year's fashions." Hellman and her admirers presented this as a great act of courage, but I felt that like others, she took the Fifth to stay out of jail.

More than two decades later Hellman further celebrated her bravery in a short, widely praised memoir, *Scoundrel Time*. Hellman accused liberal intellectuals, many of them former friends, of being partly responsible for what she considered the direct progression from Chambers to McCarthy to Nixon to Vietnam. She blamed them for not speaking out against McCarthyism (many, of course, had), and she asserted gratuitously that most of them, as children of "timid immigrants" who had made good, were determined to safeguard their success "at any cost."

In the same vein she denounced as despicable opportunists all those who chose to testify before the committee. Some indeed had sounded revoltingly obsequious, but Hellman totally ignored the fact that many testified not to follow "fashion" or to avoid trouble, but out of conviction.

The most revealing sentence in *Scoundrel Time* mentioned in passing the "sins of Stalin Communism—and there were plenty of sins and plenty that for a long time I mistakenly denied." That casual subclause was the only admission in the book of her past mistakes and Communism's crimes. Yet, as Sidney Hook pointed out, she had either defended or been silent about the Moscow purge trials, the Nazi-Soviet pact, the Soviet invasions of Finland and Poland, the Katyn massacre of Polish officers by the Soviets, the overthrow of the Czech democratic government and the crushing of the Hungarian uprising, the building of the Berlin Wall, the incarceration of Russian dissidents in asylums, and Soviet anti-Semitism. In a TV interview Hellman said she had not criticized the Soviet Union's leaders because they had never done anything to her, and she lived here, not there. Yet, Hook scathingly observed, she had not lived in Spain but had criticized Franco, had not lived in Germany but had criticized Hitler.

In the 1970s I would meet Lillian Hellman occasionally on Martha's Vineyard, where we both had summer houses and shared many friends. She was tiny, feminine, with an ugly, basilisk face. She was legendary for a kind of terrorist's charm, a mixture of humor and rage, warmth and bitchiness, with a child's total and peremptory self-absorption. People relished stories about her: the time she was not invited to a party for the visiting Frank Sinatra and she phoned the police with an anonymous tip that a bomb had been planted on his yacht, thereby disrupting the whole evening. When we talked, it was warily. Once she held forth on Luce, Clare, *Time* and their "reactionary" politics. On another occasion I brought up *Scoundrel Time*. "In your fascinating book," I began with an interviewer's routine flattery (well, it *was* fascinating in its way), "you wrote that facts are facts and yet . . ." And I started to make a point about her misstatements. She stared as if amazed that anyone would bring up such a thing, compressed her lips and turned away. I felt rather cheated of the invective I had expected.

I last saw her at a party a few years before her death in 1984, when she was ill with bronchial complications from her incessant smoking, nearly blind and partly paralyzed by a stroke. She had to be helped into the room, and swathed in black, she momentarily created the impression of a corpse being carried in. Embers of the old rages still seemed to be inside her. But we exchanged only a few polite sentences before I drifted away; it seemed somehow indecent to be near someone I still disliked despite her pitiful condition.

Later, reading Peter Feibleman's engaging memoir, *Lilly*, I decided that she had been a monster with some redeeming traits. Nobody, after all, could be all bad who said of the movie *Julia*, based on one of her stories, that it was "up to its ass in good taste"; or who, when asked at a meeting whether she had endorsed gay liberation, replied: "The forms of fucking don't need my endorsement."

Mary McCarthy once, accurately, called her a liar, inviting a libel suit. But she may have been one of those liars who after a while no longer know they are lying, because they make their own truth.

.   .   .

ANOTHER, AND FAR more important, playwright who came up against McCarthyism was Arthur Miller. I saw him often at parties and found him honest as well as painfully solemn. Although a left-winger, he was less given to Stalinist causes than Hellman. He too was brought before the committee, in 1956. When asked whether a certain writer had been present at a Communist meeting years before, he refused to answer, although he had not pleaded the Fifth Amendment, thus risking jail. (He was convicted of contempt of Congress, but the conviction was reversed on appeal.)

Miller's anti-anti-Communism became most vivid for me not through his politics, but through his play *The Crucible*. It was a simplistic morality play. In Miller's account of a Salem witch trial, good was all good and evil was all evil; he did not admit the inevitable mixture of the two.

The play was an obvious metaphor for McCarthyism. I was troubled by the suggestion that Communism, like witches, was somehow unreal and, beyond that, by the oddly limited and unimaginative view of the nature of evil.

ABOUT HALFWAY THROUGH the McCarthy era, in 1952, the country faced another presidential election. The Democrats held their convention in the big arena of the Chicago stockyards, its approaches and corridors reeking faintly of blood and offal. The nominee was Adlai Stevenson, a reluctant knight who had wanted to run only if he would face Robert Taft rather than Dwight Eisenhower. Then the Republicans nominated Ike, with strong backing from Luce. (*Time* printed an influential story that showed state by state why Taft would be unable to win the election.) But Stevenson accepted the nomination anyway.

I watched his acceptance speech from the press gallery, sitting next to Matthews. It was close to two A.M. when the candidate took the podium in the dazzling glare, facing the banners, the litter, the smoke—the usual convention hall scene. But it was not the usual convention speech.

Rereading it decades later, I found it remarkably full of clichés and bombast. "If this cup may not pass away from me, except I drink it, Thy will be done." The comparison to Jesus Christ seemed lightly blasphemous and downright arrogant in its humility. But even the bathos was somehow ennobled by touches of grace.

In the huge hall he seemed a slight figure, and he created the impression of bouncing up on the balls of his feet to project himself beyond the podium. But the high-pitched voice was compelling. The journalists, veterans and novices alike, were mesmerized as he went on. "Triumph over the great enemies of man—war, poverty and tyranny . . . Thick walls of ignorance and mistrust . . . must be directly stormed by the hosts of courage, of morality. . . . Better we lose the election than mislead the people; and better we lose than misgovern the people. . . ."

Matthews and I were on our feet, staring at each other a bit wildly. To him Stevenson was an old friend and Princeton classmate, to me merely a public figure. But I believe our emotions were engaged in much the same way. Stevenson was so much more literate than other politicians and more stylish. In tone, language, attitude, he deliberately set himself off against all politicians and especially that vulgarian (as he then seemed) Harry Truman, whom he loathed.

But what would ultimately matter far more was the contrast with Eisenhower, and that contrast was not to Stevenson's advantage. To most Americans he would become the archetypal "egghead," but also something more: an essentially accurate perception that Stevenson was indecisive, his agonized brooding often hidden behind a clever quip. (The comedian Mort Sahl joked that Stevenson was like a Unitarian who believed in the Ten Suggestions, and that if he were a Klansman, he would burn question marks.)

Soon after the conventions, Luce gave a lunch for Jock Whitney, the rich and powerful owner of the *New York Herald Tribune*, who was an early, staunch Eisenhower backer. Several *Time* writers had been invited who would not ordinarily be at table with Luce and the likes of Whitney. As the talk wound around to what the Eisenhower strategy might be and how to improve his rhetoric, it suddenly occurred to me that the impeccably friendly but observant Whitney was here as a talent scout: speechwriters were needed for Ike, and he was looking over some of Harry's guys. I was flattered to be included, but the nod would go to Emmet Hughes.

Hughes had come to the magazine about the same time as I, after a brief career as press attaché and military intelligence analyst at the U.S. embassy in Madrid. We pounded our typewriters in adjoining offices before he went abroad as a correspondent. He had a darkly handsome, finely sculpted face and a subtle mind. I admired his eloquent, slightly florid writing and his imaginative eye. He had a knack for finding symbolic significance in the smallest details; in the cafés along Rome's Via Veneto, he reported, white-coated waiters snipped the hard edges off the omelets being served, while thousands of Romans lived in hunger and poverty—evidence to him of a bourgeois decadence that made converts for the Italian Communists.

Now he was back in New York, and soon after the "audition" lunch he joined Eisenhower as a speechwriter (and later as assistant in the White House). It was Hughes who persuaded Ike to promise that, if elected, he would personally try to end the Korean stalemate ("I shall go to Korea"), a powerful element in Ike's eventual smashing election victory.

A month before the election I spent some time with the Eisenhower campaign in the Midwest, joining the *Time* correspondent covering Ike and the rest of the traveling press. It was my first exposure to the traditional campaign train that even then was becoming a relic. Its steam-age pace tried desperately to accommodate the new technology. TV producers in gray double-breasted suits, stopwatches dangling from black ribbons around their necks, roamed the aisles. Delicate antennas quivered atop reporters' walkie-talkies like feelers on strange insects. But electronic communications were limited, and panting Western Union messengers still collected dispatches to be dropped off at the next telegraph office. I felt that the whole train was a self-contained capsule, oddly sealed off from the outside world, from the landscape passing behind glass.

But every now and then the capsule would break open and the outside became real. At a typical whistle-stop in Wisconsin, the train pulled into the depot. Most of the reporters stayed aboard—they would hear the candidate's remarks over loudspeakers, not that they expected any surprises. But I made my way to the platform with a handful of correspondents. I was delighted by the scene: grain elevator, warehouses, glimpses of Sears or Montgomery Ward. The fire brigade's brass band. Hand-lettered signs ("We Like Ike!"). Cheerful crowds—overalls or business suits, aprons or cloth coats. Children everywhere, scampering along the roofs of train sheds, squatting in trees, hanging precariously from semaphores, both awed and irreverent. It was my chance to get a close look at Ike, who spent most of the time secluded in his private car. Now he emerged, grinning, looking quite natural in mufti, and took his place behind the shaky lectern at the rear of the train. He referred to his campaign as a crusade, but he did not come across as a crusader. He sounded like the local mayor or banker, garbling his sentences like a Rotary speaker who had lost his text. His pronunciation was uncertain ("fatchist," "prestidge"). The townspeople beamed at him with proprietary smiles. Ike was excruciatingly careful not to take on McCarthy directly. I knew from Emmet Hughes that Ike despised him but "didn't want to get into a pissing contest with that skunk." Hughes, among many others, was disappointed by Ike's caution, but I thought that it was probably the right strategy. By his restraint, Ike appealed to the country's underlying common sense that could coexist with phobia. Many people regarded McCarthyism as a patriotic duty, but Ike, the unquestioned patriot, emanated a reassuring quality, a soothing boredom that allayed fear and suspicion.

At *TIME* THE Eisenhower-Stevenson campaign provoked an intramural conflict. The magazine was fairly blatant in backing Ike. Following tradition, *Time* was to run successive cover stories on the candidates just before the election. Stevenson was first. Otto Fuerbringer, the assistant managing editor, had volunteered to write the story. Like Roy Alexander, Fuerbringer was an alumnus of the *St. Louis Post-Dispatch*, an extraordinarily able and intelligent journalist and a dedicated Republican. His story was passed by Max Ways, then senior editor for National Affairs, and went to Matthews for "top editing." (By then Matthews had been eased upstairs but retained the right to edit cover stories.) He found Fuerbringer's piece, as he would put it later, a clumsy but murderously malign attack. Carbon copies of the draft had been passed around, and everyone waited for the inevitable blowup. Matthews rewrote much of the article. When, after perhaps two hours, a copy boy carried the story back to the typists, I wandered to the copy desk and looked it over. Page after page showed passages crossed out, with new language written between the typed lines in Matthews's meticulous hand. Where things got too crowded for that method, Matthews had written inserts on pieces of paper that were pinned to the original and dangled from the copy like little flags. The published story was bland and mildly favorable to Stevenson.

Luce intervened. He sent a memo about the following week's cover on Eisenhower; he would be "pleased," he said, to handle the final editing of the story himself. This was of more than routine interest to me, as I had been assigned to write that piece.

So the cover story, always a rather nervous-making exercise, became something of an act of state. "We've got to play it pretty straight," said Max Ways in prepping me. "But we should come down hard on this business that Ike is just a military man with no political experience. That's nonsense. And of course we've got to lay out his stand on the issues. As for McCarthy—well, you know . . ." And he gave one of his cryptic conductor's waves.

The piece I turned out indeed stressed Ike's political skills as demonstrated while he was in command of the Allied forces. To show that many people mistakenly thought of him as merely a soldier, I quoted a taxi driver who had said to me: "But after all, he's just a hero." It was a good line, but quoting taxi drivers was stooping pretty low—even worse than quoting chestnut vendors in Paris. (Bob McLaughlin once wrote a sarcastic postcard from France about what "the best minds among the chestnut vendors" were saying about international issues.) The piece duly explained Ike's middle-of-the-road positions and was painfully cautious about his painfully cautious handling of McCarthy. No warts were acknowledged. When Luce received the story, he hardly put a pencil to it.

The article was slanted, but it was not outrageous, and it did not do violence to my own views. Besides, I told myself that I was merely a craftsman, like a carpenter who would build a chest or a table to specifications. I was not ashamed of this attitude, nor was I proud of it. It was never a matter of writing falsehoods, but of emphasis, tone, judgment. I would often chafe under guidelines handed down, and I would often argue, sometimes even successfully. But as a very new editor I understood and accepted the rules of the game. It was some time before I had enough clout to break the rules, let alone make some new ones of my own (including a ban on quoting taxi drivers or chestnut vendors).

As for Eisenhower, I had become genuinely convinced that he would make a better president than Stevenson. Much as I still admired his intellect and literary graces, Stevenson did not strike me as decisive enough to lead, and I did not think he could successfully defang McCarthy. For a time it was not clear that Ike could, either.

Some Eisenhower advisers were impatient with his caution about McCarthy, especially C. D. Jackson, another Time Inc.–er lent to the White House. C. D. was an executive of ducal bearing and great shrewdness. Once, during a visit to New York, he told me in confidence: "Much as I admire Ike, he does need a lot of propping up. We've zippered the toga of Republican leadership on his shoulders, but now we have to keep the zipper shut."

I occasionally discussed McCarthy with Whittaker Chambers, who to my regret was also reluctant to criticize him publicly, although he told me that he considered McCarthy a guerrilla and that the political Right must not tie itself to him.

The atmosphere was gradually changing. A harbinger was Ed Murrow's famous broadcast in early 1954, which presented a devastating image of McCarthy, consisting largely of TV footage of the senator's own words and actions. Eyebrows arched earnestly, Murrow concluded in his deep, pulpit baritone: "We will not walk in fear, one of another. . . . We cannot defend freedom abroad by deserting it at home. . . ."

I watched the program with a group of friends, most of them convinced anti-Communists who had long been willing to give McCarthy the benefit of the doubt. But we were all deeply affected by Murrow's broadcast, and so was the country. In the meantime McCarthy had committed the fatal error of accusing the U.S. Army of suppressing evidence of espionage. The charge was based mostly on the case of an army dentist, Major Irving Peress. He was probably a Communist, and army intelligence had raised questions about him, but he was promoted and honorably discharged. For this, McCarthy savaged the army as if treason were rampant. Thus began the Army-McCarthy hearings, which kept Joe on camera for an incredible thirty-six days in the first national TV morality play.

Certain TV images worked more powerfully against McCarthy than any amount of reasoned criticism. Joe's incessant, nasally aggressive interruptions: "Mr. Chairman, Mr. Chairman . . . point of order!" The attack on the committee itself for unwittingly helping the Communists. The constant, whispered advice from Roy Cohn, the brilliant young counsel to the committee, with his soulful but sinister eyes. The image was not helped by Cohn's handsome young protégé, David Schine, a volunteer consultant to the committee; when Schine was drafted Cohn went to absurd lengths to protect him from the hardships of military life, such as getting him off KP duty. "Cohn and Schine" began to sound like an old vaudeville team.

Finally, the emergence of Joseph Welch, the fey, elderly Boston lawyer who acted as counsel for the army. He had the classic appeal of the apparent weakling who turns out to be a champion and contributed the most famous line of the hearings: "I never really gauged your cruelty or your recklessness. . . . Have you no sense of decency, sir, at long last? . . ."

Within six months of the end of the hearings, after bitter debate, the Senate voted to censure McCarthy for abusing the subcommittee and thus violating senatorial ethics and tending "to bring the Senate into dishonor and disrepute, to obstruct the Constitutional processes of the Senate." The vote was sixty-seven to twenty-two. The fever had broken.

During his few remaining years (he died in 1957), McCarthy was uncomprehending, baffled how he, yesterday's hero, had been abandoned. The year after his censure he asked a reporter what he could do to get back in the public's good graces. What if he declared that he had seen the error of his ways, that he now felt no one should be stopped from saying what they believed? It was a stunningly naive idea. But then, I was convinced that McCarthyism was, as much as anything else, a form of naiveté about the world.

One of the worst aspects of McCarthyism was its implication that all America needed to do in the service of freedom was to fight Communism. That was simply not true. As Sidney Hook would have put it, and probably did while trying to teach logic to his beginning philosophy students, the defeat of Communism was a necessary but not a sufficient condition for the triumph of freedom.

PART FIVE

A KIND OF

VICTORIAN

ERA

CHAPTER EIGHTEEN

In RETROSPECT it seems puzzling how McCarthyism could have been part of a decade that later was considered the last idyllic and serene era in America. It was, after all, the time of *Leave It to Beaver* and *Father Knows Best*, of Doris Day's permanent virginity and Mitch Miller's sing-along sentimentality, new suburbs that were regarded as Edens with barbecue pits. In a way, McCarthy's followers felt that they were defending *Leave It to Beaver* against Communism. The split-level ranch house was a bunker. A design critic, Thomas Hine, thought he could detect Joe McCarthy's face glaring from the fierce front grills of those early fifties cars, although later he found the chrome "mouths" softened and widened into an Eisenhower smile. I often imagined Ike as Queen Victoria, a diadem over that broad forehead.

The fifties were a brief version of Britain's Victorian era. Pax Americana certainly was a successor to Pax Britannica. U.S. troops stood guard in Europe and Asia, U.S.-led alliances spanned the globe, U.S. commerce and technology followed the flag, and vice versa. There were other parallels: godliness seemed next to busyness (as well as business). Propriety reigned, widely confused with morality. But beneath the seemingly solid surface, rebels were at work.

I had often felt that life for me had not yet quite started. Now the overture was clearly finished. I became a husband and a father—and thus a good citizen of the fifties.

Following my cabled entreaties plus lengthy telephone calls, Beverly returned from South Africa in a forgiving mood. She and I were married in January 1953, in a small wedding at one of our favorite places, the Plaza Hotel in New York. We blended right into the romantic imperative. Just as the United States insisted, at least in theory, that everyone must have equal economic and social chances, so it insisted that everyone must have equal romantic chances. It was quite a radical idea: the populism of Eros.

I remember holding forth about this a few nights before our wedding, in our usual pub (the bartender was delighted to hear that "the kids" were getting married and offered free drinks). I recalled that in Europe or, for that matter, earlier in the United States, marriage often had to do with family property, or social standing, or power. Nowadays in America the idea of marriage for motives other than love was downright repellent.

Beverly looked at me quizzically. "But you *do* love me?" she said. "You're not trying to get out of it?"

"One, of course I do, and two, of course I'm not," I replied. "I'm just theorizing."

I saw a paradox surrounding all this. Despite the emphasis on romance, marriage was almost a civic obligation. Remaining single seemed antisocial and un-American.

Getting married, we found, was like being embraced by some vast fraternity. Everywhere advertisements unceasingly displayed the idealized American family. Husband and wife beamed at each other in the bathroom (hot-water heaters), at a christening in church (Bodiform pews), on a train, with the message "Why don't you take her with you on that next business trip?" (Union Pacific). The solid family appeared even in the bomb shelter, illustrating "How to Survive an Atomic Bomb" (Mutual of Omaha).

The churches proclaimed: "The family that prays together stays together." In the TV world not only were all happy families alike, but all families were happy.

Unlike trout fishing or chess, marriage, I believed, did not have to be, nor indeed could it be, taught. But here was that strange and wonderful

American conviction that one could learn anything. Typical of that, I thought, were those ads: "Learn to Dance in a Day." (Having missed out on dancing school in Vienna, I had actually enrolled at the Dale Dance Studio on Broadway, a neon-garish establishment with mirrored rooms where a petite and determined instructor named Trudy taught me a passable fox-trot and rumba but failed with the tango. It all took a lot more than a day.)

Marriage had become the subject of earnest counseling, as part of a growing advice industry. Beverly and I saw (and happily ignored) endless articles on how to make marriage succeed. The consensus was that it took *work;* bliss didn't just happen—you had to make an effort. "It all sounds sort of grim," I remember telling her. "Almost like heavy lifting."

"Ah, pooh," she said, using one of her favorite expletives. "It's all either nonsense or else just common sense." One morning she looked up from the *Times* and said: "Here's an expert who thinks that marriage difficulties must be treated as mutual problems. In other words, he says, both partners must be involved. You can't put the burden on just one. *This is news?"*

But some, like Dale Carnegie, the vastly popular prophet of self-assertion *(How to Win Friends and Influence People)* cast wives in an almost ludicrously inferior role. Some of his rules, ostensibly addressed to men, were incredibly patronizing toward women: "Don't criticize," or only gently so, and "Don't forget to be appreciative" about the "little woman's" cooking or clothes; also, give "the little girl" a hand when she needs it.

I found this attitude much too condescending, but I did not fully realize how untenable it really was. I respected women's intellect, and I thought too much of it was being wasted in our society. Yet I was rather complacent about the limits *Time* put on its female employees and thought it quite natural if women chose home over careers, as Beverly had. I soon came to realize that the fate of American women was highly complicated and constantly questioned; in a sense it was emblematic of the contradictions inherent in the decade, if not in America itself.

. . .

 MY EUROPEAN TRIP had given me a new and somewhat dramatic perspective on the American woman. As the world saw her, she seemed to roam the globe fearlessly and heedlessly; the snows of the Himalayas and the mud of the Nile were strewn with ashes from her cigarettes and lipstick-smudged tissues from her handbag. Weavers by the Ganges spun cloth to reveal her matchless figure, while whalers in northern seas and rubber planters in steamy Malaya labored to produce the restraints should that figure become too bounteous. In the great, half-dead cities of Greece and Italy, her high heels clicked energetically along history's cobblestones. She was seen as dominating her men, who, it was thought, could say with Cato the Censor: "We rule the world, but our women rule us."

That view was widely shared at home. Yet it did not fit in with the image of "the little woman" or, for that matter, with the women at *Time*. It may not be fair to use them as female exemplars of the decade, but they did represent the "career girl."

Some were more or less comfortably settled into their unmarried lives. Some were well-balanced working wives. But many seemed a little lost. As I learned over confessional drinks, they were always finding themselves. They hankered for careers, but for marriage as well. Many were from the Midwest, their clear eyes still dazzled by New York but their cheerily egalitarian temperaments determined not to be too impressed. They all seemed to live in small furnished apartments, often brownstone walk-ups, which contained prints or museum reproductions, chintz, a few souvenirs from home, and at least one comfortable armchair frankly dedicated to male visitors. They kept French cookbooks and exotic spices in the kitchenette, and they cooked demonstratively; in my bachelor years I ate many an overly ambitious dinner on shaky bridge tables, by candlelight, with carefully introduced wine ("I hope you like it. I asked for a good bottle"). Their emotional lives were complicated; I was aware of several short, unhappy marriages but more frequently unhappy love affairs, quite a few of them with married men. They confided in me because they found me a good, patient listener. I respected their confidences, and even after all these years I prefer not to use their real names.

There was Zoe, tall, gangling and yet graceful as a giraffe, who went off to San Francisco and what she later described as a "demotic marriage." Her husband was an indolent but violent would-be writer who beat her. She divorced after giving birth to a baby girl.

There was Ingrid, a deeply serious, Nordic-looking amazon who found *Time* too superficial and went off on what she intended as a wild European fling with a boyfriend from Bombay. She returned months later and confided to me that "too much freedom is bad for human beings. We just don't know how to cope with it. We need schedules, constraints, to get things done."

There was Renee, a curious mixture of gaiety and religiosity who announced one day that she was about to become a nun. *Time* gave her a vast going-away party that was awash in liquor and confusion—after all, how did one act when confronted with a future Bride of Christ? Four days later Renee was back; the convent, she said, only slightly abashed, was not what she had expected.

There was Grace, the gentle and studious daughter of a prominent lawyer who had come to *Time* straight from Vassar and in short order fallen in love with an utterly charming and unprincipled married man (well, perhaps he wasn't *totally* unprincipled: "Having more than two affairs simultaneously is disgusting," he once observed). He promised to leave his wife for Grace but didn't. I would see her week after week, walking along with small, precise steps, a kind of patient hurt in her doe eyes (the description inescapably applied), maintaining a straight-spined gravitas. After several years she gave up, left the magazine and allowed her mother to take her to Europe, the classic nineteenth-century treatment for broken hearts. She sent me long Grand Tour letters animated by a sense of humor as modest and careful as her handwriting. "I still love my boy with my whole heart (bad)," she wrote, "but I no longer pine to come home (good)."

Grace's vaguely Edith Wharton–like story, or the stories of the other *Time* women, of course, could have happened—and did—in other generations. But they illustrated the dilemmas that still seemed relatively new in the fifties: the difficulty in being accepted in careers, the conflict between job and marriage, the confusions of sexual freedom.

These thoughts prompted me to propose a *Time* article about the American woman, one of those national pulse-taking exercises. The correspondents, who usually hated working on such "roundups," pitched in enthusiastically and assembled an instructive gallery of American females.

At one extreme was the Huntress, literally: a freckle-faced, muscular girl from Montana who had shot every animal in Africa, liked to display snapshots of herself bending over bleeding carcasses and had, in the censorious words of the reporter who described her, "failed somehow to be a woman." She might have served as the model for Ludwig Bemelmans, when he had one of his characters say that American women are "beautiful to look at, and they have the soul of a tennis player or a cash register. They do not love the dog, neither the grandfather, neither the child, least of all the husband—not even the lover." Despite women's still very limited and lowly presence in business and the professions, many men were afraid of women pushing into careers. A minister observed, in language rather suggestive for a cleric, that "man has been unhorsed; woman wants him back in the saddle and resents his inability to remount."

Catholic theologians saw a revolt against the image of Mary, sociologists a revolt against the home, and psychologists a revolt against the will to live—a kind of death wish.

At the opposite extreme of the Huntress, women were trying desperately to prove their femininity: a Washington bachelor described how, when he had caught the flu, women acquaintances descended on him in droves, bearing groceries, hot beef broth, sherry, doctors' telephone numbers, and even cleaned his apartment.

The article about the American woman, as it happened, never saw the light of print. I don't remember why; possibly it was too inconclusive, pointing in too many directions. But it reflected the American reality at the time.

A few years later *Time* commissioned a study of what the 1955 male graduates of twenty American colleges wanted in a wife. They emphatically did not want a "career girl," nor did they want an "empty shell," as one Princetonian put it, but her activities should involve charities—and even that preferably later, with the children grown up. The sociologist David Riesman studied the survey and observed that what these men seemed to want was "a presentable date." The class of 1955, he went on, simply wanted the family to replace the fraternity, but he wondered whether the girls would want those boys. "After all, Grace Kelly has had a career and has married a prince."

In 1956 *McCall's* published "The Mother Who Ran Away," about a woman who found being a happy housewife so stressful that she suffered a breakdown and amnesia (yet, at least as the magazine told it, the cure was just more togetherness). This episode, like others, amounted to only a small sign of what one writer called the crack in the picture window, although perhaps it was, more accurately, a crack in the mirror—the mirror of happy self-congratulation.

There were other cracks. In 1953 Simone de Beauvoir's long feminist tract, *The Second Sex,* was published in the United States. I had read about it when it appeared in France four years earlier, and I expected to dislike it. From what I had read and heard about her, she came across as a modern, Marxist version of Mme. de Staël, with less humor and charm. Her lover-partner was Jean-Paul Sartre, the guru of existentialism, and together they formed the intellectual world's most fashionable couple. Her main thesis seemed to be a gross and annoying oversimplification: that man had enslaved woman. But the book was far more subtle and sensitive than I had expected, written with more anguish than anger. I might groan at her statement that the woman in love is condemned to fear and servility; yet she unmistakably knew what love felt like and seemed to long for it. Not until much later did it become clear that she had been quite submissive toward men, especially Sartre.

In fact she was struggling with the big feminist dilemma: how perfectly justified demands for professional and social equality are apt to slide into a hopeless rebellion against biology. The book was reviewed skeptically by both male and female critics, but its message slowly spread and took hold. It would burst forth in more popular, less intellectual form a decade later in Betty Friedan's *The Feminine Mystique.*

• • •

THE SAME YEAR *The Second Sex* appeared in the United States, Alfred Kinsey suggested that "the little woman" was not quite what she was so fondly taken for. His *Sexual Behavior in the Human Female* was considered much more shocking than his study of male sexual behavior six years earlier, because in the lingering Victorian perception women were much "nicer" than men and much less driven by sexual appetites. But the second "Kinsey Report" contradicted that.

By then Kinsey had become something of a figure in American folklore. A zoologist, he had started literally with the birds and the bees, then turned to people. He and three colleagues traveled the United States, interviewing 5,300 men and 5,940 women; their lengthy answers were carefully coded and stored under top-secret conditions in the antiseptic offices of the Institute for Sex Research, which shared an old, ivy-covered Indiana University building with the Department of Home Economics.

When I edited a *Time* cover story on Kinsey I learned about some of his apparent contradictions. He had built up a huge collection of pornography, yet he was a devoted and resolutely faithful husband—indeed rather square. A compulsive worker, he was unassuming, publicity shy and yet had a considerable talent for public relations. Journalists who interviewed him usually agreed not to report on his work until he gave his assent; he had achieved this docility by persuading the reporters to become part of his study and detail their sexual histories, which had given them a sense of responsibility, not to say complicity. I asked a *Time* correspondent whether this had happened to him. "He never suggested it," said the reporter with regret. "And I was quite ready to tell him all."

Kinsey's findings were, for their day, startling. Almost half the women had sex before marriage (compared with 83 percent of the men). A quarter had extramarital affairs (compared with half the men). Virtually all younger women engaged in "petting," more than half to the point of orgasm. Kinsey's research refuted the widespread view that between one-third and two-thirds of American women were frigid; he said, in effect, that there were no frigid women—only clumsy men. According to his numbers, women between twenty-one and forty attained orgasm 84 percent to 90 percent of the time. (After reading this, an irreverent copy boy walked into my office and suggested a headline for our story: "Come One, Come All." I regretfully rejected it.)

I had some reservations about Kinsey's canvas of the American bedroom. He quite properly declared that as a scientist he was not concerned with moral issues, only with measurements. But along with the measurements came certain messages about what was natural or normal. If a man was sexually aroused by seeing a streetcar, according to Kinsey, that might simply be caused by some past association with a "desirable sexual partner" and no more difficult to explain than another man being excited by a woman undressing. I thought of this as the *Streetcar Named Desire* argument; the principle was that any act was "biologically normal" if performed by people, or animals, especially in large numbers. The British anthropologist Geoffrey Gorer called this "justification by numbers," which he considered "in some ways the fundamental democratic fallacy. . . . If a few people do or think something, it may be wrong; but if a lot of people do or think it, then it is obviously right. . . ."

To Henry Pitney Van Dusen, who as head of Union Theological Seminary was a major Protestant oracle, the Kinsey Report suggested "deteriorating morals" approximating the "worst decadence of the Roman empire."

Such criticism notwithstanding, Kinsey's work greatly helped to change the U.S. perception of women and of sex. It provided much of the psychological ammunition for the sexual revolution in the sixties.

Among other consequences that can be fairly attributed to Kinsey was one of America's great publishing successes. Hugh Hefner was twenty-two and a psychology major at the University of Illinois when he came across the first Kinsey Report. It gave him the idea for a magazine that would fight prudery and hypocrisy. Five years later he launched *Playboy* with a few thousand borrowed dollars.

I saw the first issue early in 1954. The senior editor then in charge of *Time*'s "Press" section, Joe Purtell, showed it to me, half amused, half embarrassed. He told me that it had sold an astonishing fifty thousand copies at fifty cents a copy. *Life* then cost twenty cents. The magazine reminded me of the first strip show I had seen, in Pittsburgh (Mayor Fiorello La Guardia had banned such entertainments in New York). There was something both coarse and innocent about the spectacle at the Casino Theater: the awkward chorus line, the third-rate tenor, the awful comedians, the genuinely erotic striptease. During the intermission the candy butcher peddled "the finest milk chocolates and chewy bonbons," along with "this little forbidden book from Paris, France, full of the spiciest stories ever published. And I'll throw in a-b-s-olutely free this sen-sational picture—it shows a young lady on what they call a chayze lounge and you will notice that she has no clothes on. . . ."

As I looked through *Playboy* I told Joe: "I don't know anything about Hefner, but isn't he trying to be a candy butcher in print? He's got the bonbons—all that stuff about the good life. He's got the spicy stories, even if they are old. And he's got the nudie pictures."

"Yes, but *his* pictures deliver a lot more than those pathetic old French postcards," replied Joe, "or, for that matter, than any other girlie magazine around."

It was true. That first issue delivered a nude photo of Marilyn Monroe. Hefner had bought it for $500 from a calendar company; she had been paid $50 for posing, four years before, when she was unemployed in Hollywood. The picture seemed oddly familiar—perhaps, like most American men, I had imagined the details. In his introduction to the first issue Hefner wrote: "We enjoy mixing up cocktails and an hors d'oeuvre or two, putting a little mood music on the phonograph and inviting a female acquaintance for a quiet discussion on Picasso, Nietzsche, jazz, sex." I laughed out loud at the notion of Nietzschean foreplay. Yet perhaps Hefner had given his magazine the right intellectual patron in the German philosopher who observed that "man's attribute is will, woman's attribute is willingness."

I did not take the magazine seriously at first; it was three years later that *Time* took notice, when *Playboy* was becoming the cornerstone of an empire of pleasure. The magazine purveyed more and more first-rate writers along with first-rate skin. But the skin was preternaturally smooth and unblemished. Hefner wanted his nudes to look wholesome, like the girl next door who just happened to be undressed and whom you could imagine taking home to Mom after she put her clothes back on. (Pubic hair did not appear in the magazine till 1971.)

Hefner had started a seemingly endless series of articles on "the *Playboy* philosophy." He inveighed against archaic statutes banning sodomy and other "unnatural" acts, and he argued that the law had no business seeking to regulate behavior between "consenting adults." Once in the sixties, Peter Bird Martin, a jolly, highly versatile *Time* editor, told me: "You know, Hefner really sees himself as another Luce."

He had a point. Hefner was a kind of anti-Luce, as earnest about the gospel of hedonism as Luce was about the gospels of Christianity and America. He was a reverse Puritan. My friend Frank Gibney, who had been a fine correspondent and editor for both *Time* and *Life,* worked as a top executive at Hefner's new magazine, *Show Business Illustrated,* in the early sixties. He too compared Hefner with Luce—he saw the same driving commitment to his magazine, the same earnestness. "But Hef is narrow," added Frank. "He simply doesn't have Harry's insatiable curiosity about the world at large."

Once, at an office party, I mustered the courage to ask Luce what he thought about being compared with Hefner. His eyebrows shot upward. "What, what? Who said it?" he asked. While I was still groping for some evasion, he rushed on. "Never mind. I suppose some people would assume I should take it as a compliment," he said with a rare touch of irony. "I think the notion is silly don't you?" Some years later, when I visited Hefner at his Playboy mansion in Los Angeles, I put the comparison to him. He was amused but flattered. He would not want to put himself in the same category, he said, but yes, he guessed they had both recognized a trend and need in American society and identified a demand in the marketplace. "I have also been compared to Billy Graham," he went on, echoing what he had told a *Time* correspondent earlier. "They say I'm an evangelist. But I'm not trying to spread a new religion. I just want to see to it that certain things get said that need to be said."

He spoke quietly, serenely, puffing away at his pipe. His absorption in the magazine was clear from the way he discussed it, feature by feature; like every creative editor, he believed in his own intuitive understanding of the audience and despised the notion of making magazines according to market surveys.

We talked in a comfortable lounge with touches of an amusement arcade; I recall electronic toys and slot machines in the background. Hefner clearly delighted in the sybaritic settings he had created for himself. I kept looking for signs of sensuality or other powerful appetites in him and could not detect any.

When I visited the first Playboy Club, in Chicago, the place struck me as not really erotic. The "bunnies" in their preposterous costumes, with their fluffy tails and rabbit ears and uplifted, outthrust bosoms—but untouchable—seemed to have escaped from some lecherous nursery. (I had read that as a child Hughie had been separated from an especially loved blanket decorated with bunnies, and I wondered what could be made of this by an imaginative shrink or scenarist. Was the bunny his Rosebud?) In the early seventies, when *Time* did a long story on Hefner and his new competitors in skin publishing, it inadvertently upset his domestic arrangements, which involved regular commuting between Chicago and Los Angeles. The story was accompanied by a picture of Hef watching a movie, relaxing on a double chaise, flanked by a Wedgwood bowl full of popcorn and by his Chicago girlfriend, Karen Christy, cuddling close. Ensconced in the Los Angeles mansion, his much longer established girlfriend, Barbi Benton (his *maîtresse en titre,* as the French used to say, his "mistress of record"), had not suspected his serious involvement with Karen until she saw the picture. The shock was intensified by a crack in the story to the effect that Hefner had always been a "two-of-everything consumer." Barbi exploded, and although Hefner managed to patch things up, his captain's paradise was never quite the same again.

Two years after the birth of *Playboy* another American institution was unveiled: Disneyland. I am not sure when I began making a connection between the two, but it did occur to me eventually that the realms of Playboy and playpen were linked. *Playboy* was the Disney-land of sex. Hefner extolled the innocence of sin; Disney extolled the innocence of innocence. Hefner and Disney, midwesterners with origins not far from Main Street, both with a passion for cartooning, had built their own cartoon worlds that had become vast, successful enterprises. But ultimately, the Disney fantasy would prove more enduring than the Hefner fantasy. *Playboy* survived, but it was overtaken by the sexual revolution it helped prepare. In an increasingly X-rated American culture, the *Playboy* philosopher became a bore; the shiniest centerfolds could not compete with the porn movies spilling from the shelves at the corner video store.

The Disney theme parks, on the other hand, lasted and grew, their talisman being the purity, if not the holiness, of childhood. Increasingly America was talked about as a child-centered society.

Beverly and I really became parts of that society when our three children were born. My mother had not been delighted by my marriage. She had nothing in common with Beverly's family. But Beverly's natural warmth, reinforced by skillful efforts, won her over. My mother gradually began to make a life for herself, with friends of her own, bridge, concerts, charity work, an occasional trip and close ties to my gentle, patient sister, Meta. Just as she was approaching a measure of serenity, she was told that she had to undergo minor surgery. The seemingly harmless operation was followed by the appearance of an embolism, which, I became convinced, was treated ineptly by the small private hospital my mother had chosen at her doctor's advice. As the danger became clear, one of Beverly's sisters remembered that we had brought back a souvenir from a recent trip to Rome: a rosary blessed by the pope. An observant Jew but modern, usually rational, she phoned us and shouted furiously: "Throw that thing away! Throw it away!" Beverly did, to my surprise; I was less given to superstition, or at least not in a sense that regarded the papal touch as a menace to Jews.

Two days before Christmas 1953, my mother died, quietly and undramatically. Meta, distraught as she was, nevertheless reminded me of an incident from my childhood. It seems that the mother of one of Meta's girlfriends, a rather large and slightly disheveled person named Mrs. Stein, had come to visit. Asked for a description of the occasion, I observed: "Meta is a girl, Mrs. Stein is a woman, and my mother is a lady." Laughing and crying, Meta said: "You were right. She died like a lady, too."

She had not lived to see the birth of our son, Peter, less than two years later. At the insistence of Beverly's family, we arranged a *bris* for him, a ritual circumcision. I had never witnessed one, but I more or less knew what to expect, and I dreaded the prospect: the chanted prayers, the *mohel* wielding the silver knife, the whole ceremony of a baby's induction into the tribe. I thought of it as rather barbaric, and I fortified myself with several stiff drinks at a nearby bar. The bartender, apparently noticing that I was somewhat distraught, asked me what was the matter. I told him that I had just become the father of a boy. *"L'Chaim,"* said the bartender, though he was Irish. "To life," he added, as if I might need a translation. He poured another Scotch on the house. I calmed down and became suffused with the joy, pride and dread of fatherhood. My continuing American education from now on merged with the education and raising of my American children.

WHEN MY FIRST grandchild, Elizabeth Adler, was born in 1992, I took off my library shelves a book with a well-worn blue plastic cover. I gave it to Elizabeth's mother, my younger daughter, Lisa, with the inscription "This is not exactly the Family Bible, but it did help raise you and your siblings. So I hope it will give you a sense of continuity." The book was *Baby and Child Care* by Dr. Benjamin Spock. It first appeared in 1946, but throughout the following decade and far beyond, it was indeed a bible for millions of families, and a symbol of the whole society's attitude toward the child.

In my own early years, I knew, the greatest danger to infants was considered to be germs; by now it was neurosis. Physical antisepsis had been replaced by emotional hygiene. The ruling principle used to be discipline; the best American pediatricians had prescribed strict timetables for sleeping, toilet training and feeding. Picking up a crying baby and giving it an unscheduled swig was considered a serious mistake. Spock, a popular pediatrician in New York noted for his warm rapport with children—and mothers—did not start the rebellion against such rigidity, but he soon led it. Inflexible schedules, he argued, can be downright damaging. By all means hug them and kiss them, he wrote, because they need it. Discipline is important, he advised, but love more so. This gave rise to the familiar charge that Spock was the great instigator of "permissiveness," which would eventually become a significant public issue. By the mid-fifties Spock himself admitted that permissiveness had gotten out of hand with "certain parents," and while he refused to "shoulder all the blame," he set about revising his book. Later editions would put considerably more stress on discipline and order. Children should be taught, he asserted, that they are in the world not for their own satisfaction and must be given "a moral sense."

Spock arrived in our household a little ahead of Peter. "He uses 'at the same time' and 'on the other hand' too often," I complained to Beverly. "He's always pointing you in two directions at once—love *and* discipline, take it easy *but* be watchful and so on."

"What's wrong with that?" said Beverly. "You're always talking about how we've got to balance freedom and order."

She had me there. Besides, unlike me, she saw no problem with Spock's injunction to trust one's instincts, because that is precisely what she did in almost all situations. Her Spock-sanctioned self-assurance about what was good for infants made it easier for me to cede to her full authority over the nursery. While our children were babies (our son was born in 1955, our daughters Mandy and Lisa in 1957 and 1959), I shirked what later would be regarded as a father's obligatory share in nurturing. I left that largely to Beverly and to a nurse I insisted on hiring, even though it strained our budget. I participated in very few midnight bottle parties, never changed a diaper and only occasionally was in the applauding audience during a potty performance. But expectations were different then.

It was not until we moved, for half a year, in 1956, to West Redding, Connecticut, that I learned that "child-centered" had another dimension. The town was about an hour and forty minutes from Grand Central. In New York children had to compete with all the excitements and dodge all the dangers of urban life. Here life seemed to be arranged for and around them. The mayor of nearby Stamford had run for reelection on a "happy kids" platform. The terrain seemed overrun by the cheerful, noisy horde of baby boomers and their somewhat older siblings, tall in the saddles of their bikes, triumphant in their—or their parents'— cars. Like their elders, they acted in groups that kept flowing together, in a kind of breezy collective; privacy was suspect and solitude discouraged. By all accounts school resembled a permanent summer camp, increasingly overcrowded and understaffed by underprepared teachers. The people we met seemed to spend an extraordinary amount of time and energy organizing their children's piano or dancing or riding lessons. The members of the older generation, having experienced the deprivations of the Depression and World War II, were now trying to give their offspring the things they had missed. "We are the slaves of our children," the wife of one neighbor, the executive of a successful snack-food company, often said. She was only half joking. There was an undercurrent of anxiety that the kids might not get enough attention or affection, that they might feel rejected or, worse, reject their parents; in what Spock described as a reversal of attitudes and values, children were almost formally granted the right to judge their elders. When our own children were older, I would myself become very much aware of the little judges in our midst.

WHAT HAD LANDED me amid the idylls, such as they were, of the suburbs? It was my continuing desire to be a playwright. This desire was part of me, habitual, obsessive, half dream, half ache. I was still unable to go to the theater without feeling the old excitement at the rising of the curtain, without the stabbing conviction that I must be part of this stage world. Throughout my years at *Time* I had continued to toy with ideas for plays, putting down outlines and pages of dialogue. My models varied, but most of all I wanted to be Shaw. I worked up a plot I considered Shavian, about the world's last capitalist who is kept around by the victorious Communists as a permanent warning against capitalist evils—he is made to live in the grand old style, and guided tours through his mansion explain the vicious luxuries that the revolution had eliminated—and I had a marvelous time writing the guide's lines: "We now enter the library, traditional lair of the tyrannical head of the house. Behind this massive, ornately carved desk dating from the period of maximum bourgeois extravagance, the typical capitalist pored over his plans for exploitation and conquest. . . . This way, please. . . . We move into the drawing room. Note the decadently upholstered furniture, where overfed and empty-headed drones used to . . ."

Eventually, after discarding themes involving a sixteenth-century miracle faker and a twentieth-century worker priest, I concluded that I should stick to characters and situations I knew. I decided to write a play whose action would take place entirely during an office party. I had an outline in mind that owed a lot to some of the women I knew at *Time*, especially Grace and her unhappy love affair. The outline was not complete, but I decided I must take the plunge. I asked for a six-months leave of absence from the magazine. Before we left, Grace, who had no idea that she was to be the model for my heroine, gave us a farewell party. One of the guests, on hearing my plan, declared: "No great play has ever been written in Connecticut."

I was at my desk early every morning. I wrote endless notes, fleshing out characters, contriving scenes. Occasionally I would seek guidance from an excellent self-help book by the critic Walter Kerr, all too aptly titled *How Not to Write a Play*. I turned out reams of dialogue, but the plot somehow wouldn't come together. I could never quite decide just what should happen to my people. I knew, of course, that conflict was the essence of drama, but conflict was precisely what I had trouble with. I seemed to shy away from it in my imagination as I did in my life; the little boy who had cried at the expulsion of Adam and Eve apparently had not completely disappeared. When I mentioned to Beverly that I was not sure how to do something dramatic with my two main characters, she said: "Why couldn't they have sex?"

I was rather shocked. "On *stage?*" I asked.

"Why not?" she replied.

It seemed too crass to me; I wanted to keep the action more subtle, moody, something suggesting updated Chekhov. Actually, I realized later, what I was heading for was only William Inge. I kept hammering away at my typewriter, at my brain, and got nowhere; no convincing plot emerged.

"It's impossible," I told Beverly one evening. "I can't do it before going back to *Time*. I failed."

She had realized all this long ago, I believe, but she said loyally: "You haven't failed. You just haven't finished."

I pretended to accept that and told myself—and others—that I would continue working on the play. But I really knew better; there was no play to finish, only disjointed and lifeless fragments. For years I would still occasionally jot down ideas for plays or movies. But I had to face the fact that my dream had been a false dream, obviously prompted by a desire to emulate my father, and that I was just not cut out for the work. It was a harsh disappointment, and I kept looking for explanations. When I first tried my hand at writing plays, I did not know enough to be inhibited; later I had read a great deal and developed a critical faculty. Except in rare individuals, that is the enemy of creativity. But I believe my difficulty went deeper. I simply lacked dramatic talent, just as some people don't have an ear for music or an eye for art. But at bottom didn't this involve a lack of courage, a fear of failing, of exposing oneself? In contrast, journalism, or any kind of nonfiction writing, provided a safety net of information or a chance to hide behind facts.

At any rate, we ended our suburban interlude and returned to the urban version of middle-class contentment that then seemed natural in the city and throughout America.

ALL ECONOMIC STATISTICS pointed to constantly rising prosperity. An essential part of that atmosphere was the American automobile. *Time* was infatuated with automobiles, and not mainly, as cynics claim, because Detroit was such a heavy advertiser, but because the internal combustion engine was seen as driving the American economy, if not the American dream.

I still remember my amazement, when I arrived in America, to find ordinary people driving and owning cars. The automotive hoopla was connected in my mind with one all-important fact—the American worker increasingly thought of himself as middle class. The very meaning of "middle class" was being expanded beyond all past definitions. I thought that was great. It did not occur to me that ever-rising expectations might someday not be fulfilled. Beverly and I were living in an apartment (rent-controlled) on East Seventy-second Street. We were not saving much, and I certainly knew that we were not rich. But in some strange way I felt we had pretty much everything the rich had, and I believe this was a typical mood. It was about that time that I began paying attention to national income statistics, and I found that my *Time* salary of $20,000 in the mid-fifties put me in the top 5 percent of incomes. I was gratified but a little shocked; the average income seemed pretty low. But it was rising steadily, which accounted for the relative lack of dissatisfaction among those lower in the earnings table.

I thought that I was doing all right with mammon; but I was not so sure about that other force to which the fifties were so devoted—God.

CHAPTER NINETEEN

ONE DAY IN THE FALL OF 1953 Beverly and I were making our way through what was still known as Idlewild Airport when we ran into Luce. His wife, Clare, had been appointed by Eisenhower to be U.S. ambassador to Italy. Luce spent about half his time in Rome, but he often dashed to New York to look after the magazines, and he was now heading back. "Absolutely everybody is turning up in Rome," he said. "Why are *you* going?"

With some satisfaction I was able to say: "I'm going to see the pope."

I had been assigned to write a cover story on Pius XII, which Luce had no reason to know. Later, during the flight, he came to the tourist section and invited us to dinner at the American ambassador's residence. When Beverly and I arrived at the Villa Taverna we found him in the magnificent stone front hall, pacing from column to column, a phrase book in his hand. He was doggedly trying to learn Italian. "No one is here yet, so maybe I could press you into service," he said, handing the book to Beverly. "Give me a little quiz." She did. I suppose he would have earned a C; he had no ear for languages.

The dinner turned into something of a seminar on the pope. A few years before, Clare had undergone a highly publicized conversion to Roman Catholicism, and she had become a fiery advocate of her new faith. A famous joke had her emerging from an audience with the pope, who was heard to say: "But Mrs. Luce, I'm already a Catholic." In reality, since the United States did not have diplomatic relations with the Holy See, she had to keep her distance from the pontiff. One of the dinner guests was Sol Levitas, a courageous Democratic Socialist perpetually at war with the Communists and all forms of totalitarianism. He raised the question why the pope had not acted against Hitler and done more to protect the Jews of Europe from Nazi persecution. Clare, cool and beautiful, argued that he was a diplomat by training and a priest by inclination who saw it as his first duty not to create martyrs, but to keep the church alive. The church itself had been attacked by the Nazis, she pointed out, and many priests had protected Jews. Levitas was not convinced.

Both Luces gave the pope great credit for intervening in Italian politics by announcing that Communists and their supporters would be denied the sacraments. But Luce grumbled that the pontiff did not really seem to understand or appreciate capitalism.

Next day Beverly and I set out for Castel Gandolfo, the pope's summer residence, where he often lingered into the late fall. Belatedly warned about the dress code for papal audiences, she had hastily acquired a veil, which now dangled incongruously from her black pillbox hat. We were accompanied by *Time*'s longtime Vatican correspondent, William Rospigliosi, an Italian prince, Cambridge-educated and anglicized from accent to furled umbrella. In the seventeenth century one of his ancestors, Giulio Rospigliosi, had worn the crown of St. Peter as Clement IX. During the drive through the Alban hills, Bill entertained us with Vatican news and gossip. Bill told of the pope's extremely ascetic life, his meager diet ("when he really needs a good beefsteak to build up his strength"), his solitary household supervised by a German-born nun who was sometimes irreverently known in Rome as La Papessa. I eventually included this detail in my story. Some people took offense. Luce later let me know that the story was okay, but that the reference to La Papessa was not "gentlemanly." It was the only time I heard that term applied to journalistic practice.

We had been granted a "special audience," a category below "private" and usually including a dozen or so people. In the damask-walled, cherub-bedecked reception room at Gandolfo, a chamberlain in flowing robes surveyed the nervously waiting group; with the huge leather book in his hands he suggested a recording angel. Suddenly a thin, white-clad figure stood before us, seeming to have materialized rather than entered. I was aware of a striking contrast between the simplicity of this apparition and the marble opulence of the summer Vatican. Briskly the pope started to make the rounds of the room, with the chamberlain reading each caller's nationality from the book. Most were American, and most were deeply moved, some to tears ("Your Holiness, I have been waiting for this moment all my life"). The pope spoke almost diffidently, in careful English, occasionally in French. "Where are you from? . . . What is your work? . . . You head a Catholic Boys Club? Very important!" Everyone knelt to kiss his ring. As he approached Beverly and me, I suddenly faced the dilemma of whether, as a Jew, I should kneel or not. Beverly curtsied, which she evidently thought would not unduly provoke Jehovah. I touched the floor with one knee but did not kiss the ring. I had some trouble rising again, but with obvious practice and surprising strength, the pope smoothly helped me up. I conveyed greetings from Mrs. Luce and identified myself as a journalist. "We bless your work," said the pope. Hardly a momentous exchange. But there was something about his aura, the radiant smile lighting the gaunt face and the fragile yet erect figure (he was then seventy-seven) that I found very moving. Just before he left he spread his arms wide, wider than seemed possible, as if he were trying to embrace the whole room, if not the world.

I was also moved by historical echoes. I could not help thinking that among this man's predecessors were the popes who had faced Attila on his march to Rome, preached the First Crusade against Islam, excommunicated Martin Luther, humbled Emperor Henry IV at Canossa, been taken prisoner by Napoleon.

RELIGION WAS BOOMING in the United States. In 1954 Congress revised the Pledge of Allegiance by inserting the deity; the familiar for-

mula became "one nation, *under God,* indivisible, with liberty and justice for all." After reeling for years under the attacks of Darwinism and
scientific skepticism, the churches were resurgent. Gallup estimated that
by the mid-fifties nearly 80 percent of all Americans were church members, or at least declared themselves so, a sharp increase from earlier
decades.

I had much to learn about the American forms of Christianity. In
Europe theological differences—and fantasies—were often brutally repressed as heresy; America was still alive with a restless religious imagination and rampant spiritual free enterprise. To me religion had always
been a force out of the past; the very notion that the founder of a faith
could have lived in the twentieth century, like Mary Baker Eddy,
seemed almost as strange as Christian Science's view of illness as an
illusory state. What was I to make of Jehovah's Witnesses, who believed
that Christ had assumed power in heaven in 1914, that precisely 144,000
people would be saved? Or the Mormons, with their belief that for a
thousand years the New World had harbored a now vanished people,
related to both American Indians and Jews, that had been visited by the
Savior? I could scarcely cope with a prophet named Smith or an American stopover by Jesus.

One of the oddest figures in the current gallery of American religious
leaders was Norman Vincent Peale, a former journalist who had found
that trade morally objectional and had taken to the pulpit. He was the
minister of happy talk, the Dale Carnegie of religion. From Manhattan's
Fifth Avenue Marble Collegiate Church he preached a gospel to millions
that would have been unrecognizable to that church's rigid Dutch Reform founders. In his sermons and his book *The Power of Positive
Thinking* he taught that salvation was easy, requiring optimism, self-
reliance and a bit of willpower. Among his topics: "Believe in Yourself,"
"How to Have Constant Energy," "How to Create Your Own Happiness." Far from resisting Freud, like so many other ministers, Peale
enthusiastically took up depth psychology and launched a therapy service. His partner in this enterprise was a psychiatrist whose name could
have been invented by Oscar Wilde: Dr. Smiley Blanton. Peale's fre-

quent references to prayer (or "prayer power") showed that God was still part of his doctrine, but increasingly He sounded like a partner—often a business partner.

At the very time the "feel good" gospel flourished, a totally different and opposite religious trend was evident in the United States: neoorthodoxy. Its chief spokesman was Reinhold Niebuhr, the Evangelical pastor and theologian who loomed behind the optimistic pulpits as the Old Testament prophets had loomed behind the vainglorious thrones. The gist of his message was that faith in human perfectibility and automatic progress is a delusion and that Christianity means nothing without a belief in original sin. Niebuhr saw life as a kind of permanent Lent, essentially tragic, a situation in which the Christian must nevertheless cling to his faith. The notion of life as paradoxical or tragic, I thought, was deeply alien to the American way of thinking. But it was the kind of message Luce insisted the public must occasionally hear, just as he insisted on putting Niebuhr and other leading theologians on *Time*'s cover. But not even *Time* and *Life* could turn Niebuhr into a popular prophet. The intellectual gulf between him and a Norman Vincent Peale was almost ludicrously wide. But Peale was right about one thing: the widespread desire for spiritual sustenance. As he put it: "Where there is a hunger, there must come a feeding."

A feeding of a very different sort was offered not by a minister, but by the British historian Arnold Toynbee. In 1954 he published the last four volumes of his massive *Study of History*. At Luce's request I read them and gave him a report. Toynbee's thesis was that Western civilization could prevent its decay only through religion. Unlike Gibbon, who believed that the Roman Empire had been destroyed by Christianity, Toynbee argued that the danger was not civilization being supplanted by the church, but the church being supplanted by civilization. His message essentially was: "Hang on and pray." This formulation, he wrote, had come to him during a dream in which he was clasping the foot of the crucifix over the high altar in the Abbey of Ampleforth and a voice said: *"Amplexus expecta!"* ("Cling and wait!")

I met Toynbee during one of his stays in New York. Over tea at the staid old Hotel Brevoort (it was a little like having tea with Gibbon or

Carlisle) he expounded his views, including a remarkably benign reference to Luce's "American Century." He was precise in speech, donnish, with light, fluttering eyelids and a seemingly transparent face. I reminded him of a passage in his last volume in which he had given a confession of personal faith that included "Christ Adonis, Christ Osiris," Buddha, "tender-hearted Muhammad," Confucius. He instantly remembered the passage and went on quoting: "Mother Mary, Mother Isis, Mother Cybele, Mother Ishtar . . . by whatsoever name we bless thee for bringing Our Savior into the World." This pantheistic melange could hardly be accepted by Christian theologians or preachers. It was certainly not accepted by Billy Graham.

I encountered Graham in 1957 during his first New York crusade. When he came to lunch at *Time* I was not quite prepared for his height, which seemed to burst the tall door frame as he entered, or his intense blue eyes, or his earnest modesty. At table he said grace, which rarely happened in the corporate dining rooms of the Time & Life Building, where the nearest thing to prayer was an appeal, on some issue, to Henry Luce. New York, Graham thought, might be "ready for God."

Graham was knowing about the evangelist's trade: the power of music at his meetings, how to select the right sermon from his collection of five hundred, the danger of overdoing the evocations of hellfire. But I could not detect any cynicism in him. At times he sounded rather simple. Recalling his crusade in New Orleans a few years before, and seeking to illustrate the sinfulness of that city, he related the story of a man who had been enticed to a hotel room by a bar girl. "He was a little drunk, I suppose, and fell asleep," said Graham, continuing dramatically: "And do you know what happened? When he woke up the next morning, the girl was gone, and so was all his money!" Graham told this as if it were the most unusual, the most outlandish incident. I found it hard to reconcile such naiveté with his appeal to millions in some of the worldliest cities, including London. Eventually I concluded that it was his very naiveté that was at the core of his attraction, because it was a kind of guarantee of his genuineness.

I went to see him several times at Madison Square Garden, which for the occasion was quite transformed: no cigarette or beer fumes and a subdued, respectful audience. Prowling the podium, pounding a Bible, Graham shouted: "You are guilty! You are guilty!" But then he would lower the intensity with the reassurance that Scripture contained all the necessary balm for humanity's ills. Finally came the "invitation": "I'm going to ask you to do something that I've seen people do all over the world. I've seen the congressman, the governor, the film star. I've seen lords and ladies. I've seen professors. I'm going to ask every one of you tonight to say: 'Billy, I will give myself to Christ, as Savior and Lord. I want to be born again. . . .' Just get up out of your seat and come now. Quickly, right now. . . ."

And they did get up, and they did come. The music swelled. Hundreds moved forward slowly and solemnly. Guided toward the platform by well-trained volunteer counselors, they looked deeply serious and some downright beatific. I listened to myself carefully for any inner whispers or palpitations, any instinct to respond to Graham's "invitation," but I felt none. I was only a sympathetic observer.

Graham was sharply attacked in some quarters. The intellectual and liberal *Christian Century* complained that his crusade was so overwhelmingly organized that it had no regard for the "caprice of the Holy Spirit." Many critics believed that Graham was just another Peale, although in my view he was far more serious. He was also often compared with that other enormously popular preacher, Fulton Sheen, which was not quite right, either.

Bishop Fulton J. Sheen was the best-known Catholic proselytizer of his day, who brought into or returned to the fold, among many others, Clare Luce, Henry Ford II, the violin virtuoso Fritz Kreisler, the iconoclastic journalist Heywood Broun, and Louis Budenz, a leading Communist and editor of the *Daily Worker*. He also gathered in many more obscure souls—one could imagine notches on his crosier—and he was the star of a weekly half-hour TV show, *Life Is Worth Living*, in which he competed successfully in the same time slot with Milton Berle's vastly popular comedy show (inevitably the contest was known as Uncle Miltie versus Uncle Fultie). He was a passionate critic of Marx,

Freud and what he considered the lax morality of liberalism. Many saw him merely as a holy huckster, among them Tom Matthews, who despised him, with a mixture of Protestant conviction and Episcopalian snobbery. With glee he told me: "To put it simply, I think Sheen is a son of a bitch." That made me only more curious about him.

A year or so before my trip to Rome, I had arranged to attend one of Sheen's telecasts in the studio audience. The program originated in a Broadway theater, the Adelphi, and that was fitting, for Sheen was a brilliant and completely theatrical performer. It was an extraordinary show. The usual buildup, the disembodied voice announcing, "Five seconds, five!" and then: "His Excellency, Fulton J. Sheen." He strode calmly from the wings and leaned into the rising wind of applause. He was in full bishop's regalia: purple biretta, purple-piped black cassock, billowing purple cape. As he walked about the set, representing a study with a small statue of the Virgin and a large American flag, he swished the cape expertly, fingering the chain of his large gold pectoral cross. He would hunch his shoulders and pleadingly spread his arms; he ogled the camera, made love to it. His voice was insinuating, soft, sometimes almost boyish, but with occasional hints of thunder. He spoke flawlessly, without cue cards. Occasionally he used a blackboard to set down key words or simple diagrams. When Sheen was through with a point, the blackboard would be wiped clean, out of camera range, by a stagehand whom Sheen always cutely referred to as "my angel."

Later I was intrigued by the contrast and the similarities between him and Billy Graham. Both condemned what Sheen described as Western civilization's recent view of Christ as weak and effeminate, and Graham derided the view of Christ as a jolly Santa Claus. Both affirmed the reality of the devil, but not the horns-and-sulfur caricature; to Graham he was "a prince of lofty stature and unlimited cunning," and in Sheen's view he came "disguised as the Great Humanitarian." Both denounced the nation's sins, especially materialism. Sheen came across as a dark angel, Graham as a blond athlete temporarily encased in a business suit. Sheen gave the impression that he was arguing his case, Graham that no argument was possible.

I went to interview Sheen for a *Time* piece a few weeks after the broadcast. We talked in his study in the small, red brick house on East Thirty-eighth Street in Manhattan where he lived and worked. At close range his eyes were his most remarkable feature: iris and pupil almost merging into single, shining black disks, creating the impression of hypnotic penetration. I found it hard to look for long into those eyes. He sat next to a large, purring, window air conditioner, but Sheen's purr was louder. His rhetoric and his gestures were only slightly reduced from his television persona. When he talked about Freud (sex) versus Adler (power) versus Jung (collective unconscious), he was just as glib as on the air.

He reminisced about his early years in Peoria and his ordination when he still looked so young that he was mistaken for an altar boy. I wanted to know how conversion happens, how it was done. People usually turn to the church because of some physical or spiritual crisis, he explained, or some intellectual crisis, which he defined as dissatisfaction with their "own ordinariness." Sometimes the most ardent anti-Catholics are the closest to conversion, because "hatred indicates interest." When giving instruction, he never stressed emotion and discouraged mystical belief: no "leap of faith." Even when people said they believed in God, he would insist on drilling them in the several logical proofs of the existence of God. He told me that he could usually sense after the first couple of hours of instruction whether someone would eventually "make it" or not.

This was a phase in my life when I was strongly attracted to Catholicism. Years later I mentioned this to William Buckley, who had become a friend, and he observed: "Henry, it's not too late. Why don't you pope it?" My impulse had complex causes. The Nazi experience had certainly confirmed my Jewish identity with a vengeance, but it had also taught me the truth of the Yiddish saying *"Schwer zu sein a Yid."* ("It's hard being a Jew.") Besides, in America I encountered a kind of Judaism I had not known before. While American society made it easy for Jews to become assimilated and to shed their traditions, as many did, I also found a kind of aggressive clannishness among Jews that I was not used to. They tended to ask about everyone, from a new senator to a new boyfriend, "Is he Jewish?" They applied that ancient question "Is it good for the Jews?" to virtually every public event. This was true of Beverly's family, as well as people much further removed than the Susers from the immigrant past. Much of this attitude, I realized, had to do with Israel, which for many American Jews had become identical with Judaism as a whole, and the old query now seemed interchangeable with "Is it good for Israel?"

I began brooding about the spiritual content of Judaism. There was something magnificent about the insistence that every act of daily life, every bite eaten, every step taken, must be sanctified and regulated by the Law. At the same time I was impatient with the endless prescriptions and prohibitions, few of which I had ever observed, but which, I thought, were about superficialities rather than essentials, about form rather than faith. True, the prophets' messages had often been deeply spiritual. Micah had given Jews the simplest and greatest command: To "do justly, to love mercy and to walk humbly with thy God." Isaiah spoke of that God as "the Prince of Peace." But Judaism involved a perpetual contest between the Law and the prophets, and in that contest the Law seemed to have the upper hand.

I had rarely attended a seder before, and when I joined Beverly's family for the Passover observance I was bothered, as I would be later at my son's *bris*, by its clannish nature: just us and the Lord. He was treated as the head of the tribe, rather than the God of all mankind. I had a particularly hard time with the ten plagues visited by Him on the Egyptians, especially the killing of the firstborn. After each mention of a plague, the participants took a drop of wine out of their glasses and splashed it on their plates. Did the wine stand for blood? No, I was told, wine was a symbol of pleasure, so that diminishing our wine signified curbing our pleasure at our foes' defeat. I found this unconvincing and was offended by the delight with which even the youngest children at the table kept this count of the divine acts of terror. I began to think more seriously than I had before about Christianity. Despite centuries of persecutions and violence in the name of God, I believed that Christianity offered more of a universal and loving spirit than Judaism.

I was attracted to the Catholic Church not only by the operatic quality of its rituals, but, far more seriously, by its promise of absolute moral authority and intellectual certainty. The negative side of this was narrowness and bigotry in parts of the church. But Catholicism also offered forbearance, tolerance of human frailty. I saw it in some Catholic writers who knew that saintliness could be found in very imperfect vessels. One such writer was Georges Bernanos. His *Diary of a Country Priest* was the story of a young, awkward, often inept pastor who nevertheless clings to his religion and brings it to at least a few others. This version of Christianity was not optimistic, yet it affirmed, almost in spite of itself, hope and grace.

I encountered a more complex version of such faith in Jacques Maritain, the neo-Thomist philosopher who taught at Princeton throughout the fifties. I met him at a large dinner honoring Mortimer Adler's Great Books program. He was a slight, somewhat stooped figure with a cap of white hair above his delicate face. I cannot claim that I came close to a full understanding of Maritain, let alone his master Thomas Aquinas. Adler (Clare Luce called him a "Peeping Thomist"), a friend and disciple of Maritain's, encouraged me to try. I did grasp that Maritain, like Aquinas, saw no conflict between faith and reason. He wanted "intelligence to be taken from the Devil and returned to God." I was intrigued to learn that he had been raised in a Protestantism he found feeble and had been converted to Catholicism (together with his Jewish wife) in a search for absolutes. I recognized the urge.

During much of my trip to Rome I had thought of Sheen and often played with the notion of asking him, on my return, to give me instruction, if only as an experiment, to see if it would take. In the end I decided against it; I realized that it would be a waste of time and, in some basic sense, dishonest. My problem was not only with Christianity and Catholicism, but with religious faith in general. Rationally I was convinced that the universe without God made no sense, but that simply was not the same as believing. I felt the need for faith, I envied those who had it, but I also knew that I could not argue myself, or be argued, into faith.

Sheen said often that the reason one man accepts "the truth" and another does not stems not only from divine grace, but from human will. I recognized that I lacked both the gift of grace and the real will to accept Sheen's truth and that I had only flirted with the idea. I understood that to reject the supernatural out of hand was just another form of ignorance and that modern science believes in phenomena that in other times were called miraculous, but that still did not mean I could accept, for instance, transubstantiation or the virgin birth or the divinity of Christ. Sheen liked to speak about the Hound of Heaven relentlessly pursuing the human soul, quoting the poem by Francis Thompson ("I fled Him, down the nights and down the days; / I fled Him, down the arches of the years . . .") I had to conclude that I was simply not fleeing, and was not being pursued, by the Hound of Heaven.

Just as I could not argue myself into becoming a Christian, I could not argue myself out of being a Jew. Being Jewish involves both more and less than faith. For all my reservations about Judaism, and despite my failure to obey its rules, I ultimately could not abandon it. Especially after the Holocaust, I felt that it would be shameful to try to deny my heritage. While I deplored Jewish tribalism, I was somehow bound by it. Eventually my attitude toward Judaism would become far more positive. I came to understand that ritual was not empty but helped keep Judaism alive against all odds, that the Jewish tradition contained a moral force that reached far beyond the tribe. In one of the notes to myself I occasionally jotted down to clarify my thinking, I wrote: "I am not a comfortable Jew. I am not comfortable in a synagogue, I am not comfortable at the Seder table. It all seems somehow Oriental. Just as it did in my childhood, religion to me still means organ music and hushed cathedrals. Yet, to make things even more difficult, I don't like the services of the Reform Jews either. The organ music doesn't *belong*, somehow, nor do the stained glass windows, and the bare heads are just as strange there as hats or yarmulkes would be in church. And the almost total absence of Hebrew in the prayers reminds me (as would the Mass without Latin) of the awkwardness of Italian opera in English. I suppose there is no satisfying me. And yet, when all is said and done, I simply *know* that I am Jewish. Even if I truly experienced a spiritual transformation, which obviously I did not, I would never be completely sure whether in some part of me, I was not acting like those Jews I used to hear about as a child who were 'baptized' simply for convenience, to escape the burden of being Jewish. Not that it is really a burden in America. I find myself paraphrasing (no doubt blasphemously) the words of Jehovah: I am what I am."

CHAPTER TWENTY

DURING THE LATTER PART OF THE FIFTIES I came to know Henry Luce better. He always displayed a distinctly old-fashioned courtesy. When he wanted to see one of us, he never sent a summons by his secretary but insisted on picking up the telephone himself and saying, albeit brusquely, "Could you come up?" If one of his "senior colleagues" was in the hospital, Luce would usually dispatch a handwritten note and a flower arrangement (after an appendectomy I received a bunch of red roses). His single most important quality was curiosity. He had no small talk and, instead, asked questions. Some people thought it was a joke when they heard that before a Luce visit correspondents would ride to the airport and back to anticipate possible questions from the editor in chief ("What's that factory? . . . When was that church built?"), but it was true. Like the correspondents, I quickly learned that if I didn't know the answer to a question, I must never try to fudge but simply admit ignorance. It was possible to argue with him, and in fact, he welcomed it, but only if one had one's facts and logic absolutely straight.

He was the autocrat of the luncheon table; his regular lunches with his editors (I was occasionally included), at which he never seemed to pay the least attention to the food, were seminars; his relentless questions alternated with his own views and pronouncements. When he took a trip he usually wrote a report, which would then be discussed at the table. Luce's observations ranged from the cosmic to the trivial (French prime minister Pierre Mendès-France had worn, when they met, a very badly cut brown suit). He was almost impossible to interrupt, partly because he was growing hard of hearing, partly because he was always so intent on his subject. Waiting for a momentary pause and jumping in required infallible timing—and some courage.

I was no intimate of his, but he used me occasionally for special chores, as when he asked me to report on the Toynbee volumes. Another time he had me ghostwrite a speech about China and, by way of preparation, reminisced at length about his childhood there. Trying to assume Luce's voice about China, of all subjects, proved too much of a challenge. He tore apart my draft with great professional skill and gusto. He felt that the text had gone on too long before getting to a major emotional flourish and said, "I have to come sooner." It was not the kind of expression one was apt to hear from Luce, but he was so deeply involved with his subject that his guard was down. That happened rarely. At a dinner party, after the press had started writing about the possibility of a birth control pill, Luce speculated what it might do to American mores and predicted that it would lead to much more sexual license. "Even now," he said, "people seem to accept adultery much more readily than when I was a young man." His words were detached and almost clinical. None of us had the slightest idea that at the time he was himself deeply involved in a passionate affair with a young woman close to thirty years his junior—and an employee of his, at that. She was Lady Jean Campbell, granddaughter of Luce's friend and fellow press baron, Lord Beaverbrook. She was working at *Life* as a photo researcher. Jean was one of the most charming women I ever met, with velvet brown eyes, a soothingly melodious voice and a free-ranging mind. Luce fell deeply in love with Jean and wanted to marry her. The affair lasted for at least two years before most people in the Time & Life Building—or Clare—knew anything about it. It was, by Jean's own later account, an idyllic romance; her picture of Luce was of a totally different man from the one known to his public or his colleagues: tender, sentimental, poetic, funny and even fond of good food. The romance was ultimately ended by Clare, whose rage frightened Luce. She made it clear to Harry that she would never give him a divorce. When news of the affair reached the papers, most of the staff was amazed. Only Luce's oldest and closest associates knew that both Harry and Clare had had affairs before.

For the rest of us, it was a little like finding out about a parent's infidelity. Despite their essentially unhappy marriage, Harry and Clare were obviously linked by a strong bond of companionship that seemed to grow stronger after the affair with Lady Jean was over. Some years later, after Luce's death, Beverly and I had dinner with Clare, and she mused about her marriage and marriage in general. Harry, she said, had not been easy to live with. "He was often so busy that when I wanted a decision for a dinner party or a trip, I would send a memo to his secretary." She conceded that there had been graver difficulties than that, but she had grown rather mellow about them. Alluding to the Jean Campbell episode, she said, rather patronizingly, making it sound far less serious than it obviously had been: "That's the way men are. They get older and they go a little crazy. You just have to give them room, you just have to ride it out." But her best line on the affair had been spoken earlier: "If Harry marries Jean and I marry Lord Beaverbrook, I would become Harry's grandmother."

I WAS NOW EDITING a group of Back of the Book sections. Luce's interest in culture was wide-ranging and often surprising, even though he was most deeply concerned with domestic politics and foreign affairs. He was especially fascinated by international law, and at story conferences I often dutifully relayed his suggestions in that area. Two irreverent *Time* writers, Calvin (Bud) Trillin and John Gregory Dunne, would invariably chant, imitating parrots: "Law and peace! Law and peace!"

Luce was often told that people read *Time* from back to front, because they thought that the cultural departments were less politically opinionated and offered more information not easily found elsewhere. He was partly annoyed by such comments and partly flattered. The rest of the press often did not satisfy readers who, in their new suburbs, were eager to be, and to be seen as, sophisticated. That left a big opportunity for *Time*. Every week we were barraged with files from correspondents, reports from researchers and masses of publications designed to give us the flavor of the creative scene, of the intellectual fashions and battles.

Some of us spoke self-mockingly about being in the culture corner, but we liked it. "The back" was nearly a self-contained community within *Time*. Our mainstays were several highly gifted writers. It was a period of great advances in medicine and science—the beginnings of organ replacements, space travel, computers—and the chief interpreters of these wonders were an odd pair. Gilbert Cant, who wrote Medicine, was British born and a former naval war correspondent who cultivated a seadog manner (a barked, "Cant!" was his usual way of answering the phone). He had a passion for bird-watching and cutting contempt for anyone who dared to consider the pastime as somehow soft. He was constantly at war with fellow journalists whose view of the medical profession was too rosy. (His favorite quotation was Arthur Hugh Clough's "Thou shalt not kill; but needst not strive / Officiously to keep alive.")

Jonathan Norton Leonard, who wrote Science, was a New Englander who strongly believed in his power to explain and persuade. He liked to recall that his first salaried job had been that of censor for the classified ads in *The New York Times:* "When I saw a 'Positions Wanted' item that read, 'Young girl, inexperienced, will do anything,' it was my task to call up that young girl and make clear to her she might be misunderstood." At *Time* he had more complicated explaining to do. He was fascinated by space but deprecated the prospect of manned space flight because, in his view, the crews would be totally controlled by teams and computers on the ground. "They might as well use chimps," he would say.

Another engaging pair of writers resided in the Books department. The man who faced the massive output of print week after week, with weary skepticism, was Max Gissen. He scanned almost a hundred new books a week and took careful notes in a small, spiky hand. At a weekly conference with his senior editor (me) and other reviewers and researchers, he would go over a list of perhaps twenty titles he had found worth considering, telling what each was about. By the end of the recital, when I would assign five or six for review, everyone was in a haze of drowsiness. But Max plowed on; he felt even authors who would never be reviewed deserved these moments of attention.

Max's fellow critic was Ted Kalem, originally Theodore Kalemkierides. The son of immigrant parents, he spoke only Greek as a small child but made up for it later with a passion for English that occasionally led him to excess. He was a shameless punster ("a moth-Eton travesty of an English country school"). Like Jim Agee, he combined great sweetness with rage—rage at incompetence, pretension, dullness, and what he came to regard as his underpaid condition.

In Gissen's and Kalem's view the decade was not exactly a golden age of literature, but in hindsight it shines. Faulkner and Hemingway were still writing, O'Hara was going strong, Mailer had emerged, as had Bellow, Cheever, Styron and Malamud. Ever since being introduced to his work by Marilyn Monroe, I was especially taken with J. D. Salinger. When I launched a cover story about him, he proved harder to report on than the pope or the head of the KGB. He lived like a hermit in Cornish, New Hampshire. To find information about him we deployed a dragnet of correspondents, which was supplemented by an enterprising researcher, Martha Murphy. (Later, as Martha Duffy, she became one of *Time*'s outstanding cultural editors.) She drove to New Hampshire to stake out Salinger and almost literally ran into him on a dirt road, driving in the other direction. She followed him to the nearby post office, where she confronted him and asked if they could talk. He stared at her in shock, ran back wordlessly to his Jeep, swung the vehicle around and took off. We nevertheless pieced together a fairly good story. When it appeared, Salinger went to the local paper store and bought up all the copies of *Time*, explaining that he did not want his neighbors reading about him. The shop's owner immediately reordered a lot more copies and sold all of them.

Vladimir Nabokov was far less elusive at least physically. Spiritually and intellectually he was as hard to pin down as the butterflies he hunted, and just as shimmeringly complex. I came to know him in New York and later visited him after he settled in Switzerland. He was passionate about his craft and about many other things, some rather surprising. He loved comic strips and could go on in great detail about the adventures of Buzz Sawyer and his amnesiac wife. Nabokov could become so excited in conversation that his eyes would fill with tears, which he would wipe away with his handkerchief. He was the politest man I ever met, with manners transported from his aristocratic childhood in prerevolutionary Russia, formal yet natural. Once Beverly and I gave a dinner party in his honor and he had to back out at the last minute because of the flu. After he recovered he paid a call on us (that was the phrase he used) to apologize. "A note would not have been adequate," he said. "And certainly not the telephone. It's too impersonal, too disembodied." His ceremoniousness formed an intriguing contrast with the wild fantasies of his fiction. Although he seemed haunted by the past and by memory, he scorned émigrés who mourned their lost riches, and I told him the joke about the refugee dachshund who said he had been a St. Bernard in the old country. Nabokov chuckled, but like many witty men, he did not have much patience with other people's humor. He played games with reality as well as with words. His evocation in *Lolita* of roadside America was utterly convincing and yet purely impressionistic. "It had taken me some forty years to invent Russia and Western Europe" he wrote. "And now I was faced by the task of inventing America." But, invincibly genuine and original, he did not have to invent himself.

ONE OF MY favorite departments was Music. The writer was a short, angelic-looking former combat pilot named Carter Harman. Before coming to *Time* he had been a promising second-string critic on *The New York Times* but managed to break the string. Covering concerts, he sometimes liked to leave at intermission to get a head start on his writing but always had a friend to report to him any important developments. Once he left a recital by the great Kirsten Flagstad at midpoint and wrote a glowing review. Next morning he was appalled to discover, on the front page of the rival *Herald Tribune,* that Flagstad had fallen flat on her face during the second half, having tripped over a rug. His friend had failed him. The friend was a rising young soprano named

Beverly Sills, who had left early because Flagstad had given her a head-ache.

Carter and I both loved opera and we gave it a lot of space in *Time*, even though Luce considered it hopelessly absurd. He did get to the Metropolitan Opera occasionally for social reasons. I rarely heard him so scathing as when he discussed *Die Fledermaus* and its preposterous plot (I wondered what he would have made of my father's librettos). I loved opera, not despite its irrationality, but in large measure because of it. The music illuminated the words as nothing else could. Theoretically straight drama was more real, but, as Shaw argued, the superior intensity of musical expression makes opera far more real.

Occasionally, after Beverly and I had attended a performance, I would return to finish up some work at the office, in black tie. This gave rise to the canard that I was sporting an opera cape. Not true; alas, I am not built for it (I am five feet six and have been accurately described as pear-shaped).

The fifties were a great operatic age. There was the infinitely thrilling Callas, whose brilliant vocal acting was surrounded by suspense: one could never quite know how she would sound hitting the next high note or whether she would hit it at all; her rival Renata Tebaldi ("The other one," Callas called her), whose invariably beautiful voice I found far less interesting; Richard Tucker, with his glorious bronze tenor; Cesare Siepi, Don Giovanni incarnate; Mario del Monaco, the closest thing possible to an Italian heldentenor; and, among the relative newcomers, Leontyne Price, a black Madonna. The undisputed ruler of the operatic realm in New York was Rudolf Bing, the Met's general manager, a true impresario. A Viennese, he had made a name at the Glyndebourne and Edinburgh festivals and become a British citizen, a fact he signaled by wearing a bowler and invariably taking tea at four. It was over tea, at the Plaza, that I first met him. He had summoned me to voice a complaint but disarmed me by observing that I was known at the Met as the only journalist who paid for his tickets. Then he got down to business: "Mr. Grunwald, I really must urge you to stop making fun of our artists."

Time occasionally wrote unflatteringly about the height of short tenors or the width of fat sopranos. I defended this practice. Of course opera depended on the willing, even eager, suspension of disbelief, but there were limits; the physiques of certain singers spoiled any illusion of romance. Bing was unconvinced. "When you are dealing with a glorious voice like Jan Peerce's, what does it matter if we have to place him on a couple of steps so that he won't be singing directly at Mme. Milanov's *poitrine?*"

The conversation ended inconclusively; as we parted, Bing more than half-seriously suggested that music critics should be licensed, and I tried to explain about the First Amendment. Still, I decided to ease up on the physical comments, and I discovered that Bing was also bothered as I was by some of the shapes on his stage. Some years later *Time* reported that under his regime there were far fewer "love duets between a bandy-legged tenor and an overstuffed love seat"; the average size of the women's costumes had shrunk from twenty to fourteen. I would see more of Bing after the Met's move to the "new house," the hideous, modified-Fascist structure at Lincoln Center. Bing often asked Beverly and me to be in his box. He was a gracious host, although he watched the performance intently, sometimes moving his arms along with the maestro in the pit, usually a little off the beat. He ran the Met autocratically, but mostly with good manners. His wit was catty. Once someone joked that when Met ballerinas get too old to dance, they become typists. Bing said: "Oh, really? I thought it was the other way 'round." When he learned that Leonard Bernstein was conducting Beethoven's *Missa Solemnis,* Bing said to me: "I suppose it should be retitled *Mitzvah Solemnis.*" He encouraged formality. He once phoned me, before some special occasion, to insist, "Mr. Grunwald, you *will* wear tails tonight," and when I protested that I didn't own any, he gave me the name of a good rental place. Despite his elitism, it was in Bing's time that the Met opened up to a much wider audience.

GOING THROUGH MASSES of old paper in preparation for writing this book, I came across a long file from *Time*'s music researcher, the formidable Dorothea Bourne, formidable because she towered over both

Carter Harman and me and because, as an interviewer, she was a living and relentless tape recorder; her reports were overwhelming. This one was about the jazz pianist Dave Brubeck. It was dotted with notes and questions in an unfamiliar hand. "How? . . . Why? . . . You speak of rules; what *are* the rules? . . . You say he knows what hecklers look like; what *do* they look like?" The notes, I thought, were quite pesky, and I wondered who had written them. I suddenly realized with a shock that the handwriting was mine. The report and the notes brought back not only myself as an eager young editor, but Brubeck as an astonishing young jazz musician.

I did not find the distance from the Metropolitan Opera to the New York jazz clubs particularly forbidding. Some of the performers I had heard in my college days were still around, as were Armstrong and Ellington and Benny Goodman. But a whole new brigade of younger artists had come along, and the most compelling was Brubeck. Carter Harman had led me to him, and I heard him at Basin Street and later in Carnegie Hall. More than most performers he hated hecklers and boozy, inattentive audiences; he had an almost mystical feeling about the people he played for. "If you play only for your own ego and not for other people, you soon get sick of yourself." He was given to bouts of discouragement when he felt he no longer wanted to play—he was all of thirty-three when I met him. "Then—well, I have to make money, and something will turn up that makes me think I can go on." He admired and perhaps envied people who drew strength from meditation ("saints or something") and thought that perhaps similar strength could come from intense music making. "If you think of creativity as coming from God, then you can't burn yourself out." Raised as a Presbyterian on a California cattle ranch, Brubeck was seriously drawn to Catholicism; he later converted, wrote a mass and other sacred music. The Brubeck quartet played highly complex, contrapuntal music. As he bent his tall, gangling body over the keyboard, staring down at his hands, occasionally shaking his large head from side to side, he seemed to be searching for some secret pattern. He thought of playing jazz as composition, but where "Stravinsky has all year to think of the next note, we have to think of it in a second." He regarded jazz philosophically, even politically. Fascist and Communist regimes, he pointed out, habitually cracked down on jazz, and he felt that jazz should be part of American propaganda abroad. Jazz, he argued, was the embodiment of the American spirit; it was the freest music, but contained by discipline.

As he said this, one night after a performance, I grew excited. Here it was again, the theme that so often preoccupied me and that I seemed to find everywhere, even in Spock, now even in jazz. "You are talking about the pull between freedom and order," I said rather solemnly, as if I had just made a big discovery.

"Of course," Brubeck replied in a tone suggesting wonderment that anybody would be surprised by such an obvious fact. "That's what it's all about." His large hands made a sweeping gesture that seemed to include art, life, democracy.

And why not? I had always believed that changes in musical forms indicate changes in society. (Hardly an original idea; Plato, among others, had said it.) The storms and effusions of the romantic composers signaled the end of eighteenth-century order and balance. When the waltz appeared, with couples clutching each other instead of decorously, ceremonially moving about in minuet or gavotte, people were scandalized, and understandably; the Johann Strausses were not exactly avatars of social revolution, but their rhythms did indicate new mores and an almost uncontrollable exuberance.

Even as Brubeck was making his cool, brainy music, in dissent from the older, more conventional jazz and from the bland, familiar pop sounds, a different kind of dissent began to be heard. It was less brainy than glandular.

One of its earliest exponents was Elvis Presley. He was news to me before he was music: news that he was causing riots, that teenage girls flung themselves at him en masse and carved his name into their skin, that his performances were lewd because he gyrated like a stripper: Elvis the Pelvis. *Time* called him a sexhibitionist. Critics were devastating: "No discernible singing ability," "amateurish," "stereotyped." Indignation extended to rock in general. Boston banned it from dance halls, and other cities imposed similar prohibitions. An organ of the Catholic Church condemned rock as embodying paganism. I could not quite see, at first, what the fuss was about. But though the tunes were banal and his delivery whiny, there was a certain appeal in the husky-rough-velvety tone and the dropped syllables suggesting secret words withheld. I remember my fox-trot-tempered feet being literally convulsed by Presley's "Jailhouse Rock." Most people still considered rock and roll a passing fad, and if it signaled a social upheaval, that was certainly not yet evident.

IN 1956 *TIME* declared peace between America and its intellectuals. "The Reconciliation," read the cover line. The story announced that after decades of hostility toward American society, and after years of McCarthyite attacks on eggheads, intellectuals were close to resuming a constructive role. "Many have come at last to realize that they are true and proud participants in the American Dream." In typical fashion we sent out correspondents in search of representative intellectuals and their views. The reporters went to places as far afield as Ischia in the Bay of Naples, where the melancholy W. H. Auden was interviewed in a rustic villa, and Missoula, Montana, where the curmudgeonly Leslie Fiedler, professor of English at Montana State, held forth. The rough consensus was that the failure of liberal optimism, exemplified by the Holocaust and the cold war, had indeed altered the relationship between America and its intellectuals.

The face on the cover for this story was the finely cast visage of Jacques Barzun, the Columbia University historian, a somewhat offbeat choice. I had met him several years before when I moonlighted an article for *Life* about the 1848 revolutions. He was a consultant to the magazine. Lean and elegant, gravely polite, he looked distressed that he might be inflicting pain as he pointed out several mistakes in my manuscript. The pencil in his hand suggested a scalpel, which he worked with the gentlest and most accurate care.

One of the things that had commended Barzun as a *Time* cover subject was that he disliked existentialism—he considered it something of a fraud. Luce loathed Sartre, the archexistentialist, because he could not accept the notion that life is essentially absurd. I had a hard time

with it, too, but I grudgingly admired the bravado in the other half of
Sartre's proposition, that despite life's absurdity, one must act. "Human
life," Luce said repeatedly, "is tragic and triumphant and also comic but
never absurd." Barzun felt the same way.

He was French born and had come to the United States as a young
boy, and had the immigrant's special love for America—a love I knew
so well. He summed it up in a quote from F. Scott Fitzgerald: "America
is a willingness of the heart."

What *Time*'s and other accounts downplayed was that many intellectuals were still emphatically unreconciled, among them C. Wright Mills,
the sociologist from Texas who rode to his Columbia lectures on a
motorcycle and excoriated the American *Power Elite*, and Paul Goodman, who described himself as a "community anarchist" and attacked
the corruption, mendacity and stupidity of America, summing up his
indictment in the title of his best-known book, *Growing Up Absurd.* The
most typical intellectual protest, soon taken up by the press, was against
"conformity." But often that complaint was not truly radical. Many
Americans began to worry about their conformity the way Frenchmen
worry about their livers. Among the first to call attention to the condition was David Riesman in *The Lonely Crowd,* which classified societies
and individuals as inner-directed and other-directed. People in the first
category have a sort of inner gyroscope that guides them toward fixed
goals; people in the second have an antenna that picks up signals from
others. The United States was becoming an other-directed society, said
Riesman, in which the most desirable qualities were adaptability and
the knack of getting along with one's fellows. Children "are supposed to
learn democracy by underplaying the skills of intellect and overplaying
the skills of gregariousness." (Shades of West Redding, I thought as I
read this.) For a while, "Are you inner-directed or other-directed?" became a sort of cocktail party game.

Probably not by accident, Time Inc. produced two writers who shared
the Riesman vision. One was W. H. Whyte, author of *The Organization
Man,* which described the American corporation as the ultimate other-
directed community, the "citadel of belongingness." Initiative was sti-

fled, as Whyte saw it, not by tyrannical bosses, but by groupthink. He did not advocate the overthrow of the corporation but merely urged the "organization man" to protect his individuality by fighting within the system, sticking up for his opinions and occasionally committing small acts of resistance, especially thwarting personality tests.

"Holly" Whyte was an editor on *Fortune,* and I talked to him occasionally. He had an elongated face reminiscent of Klimt's women and a quietly sardonic manner. He offered two pieces of advice highly valuable to a writer: first, you must start out with a hypothesis to get you going, but you must not hesitate to throw it out when it doesn't fit anymore; second, neatness is an overrated virtue, and messiness, especially early in a project, is almost indispensable.

The other writer was Sloan Wilson, author of *The Man in the Gray Flannel Suit,* a highly successful novel about corporate opportunism versus idealism, rat race versus family. It was not a very good book, but by putting the organization man into a recognizable costume, Wilson created a character—or at least an enduring label—that gave life to Riesman's and Whyte's theories.

Wilson had worked for Roy Larsen, president of Time Inc., one of Luce's earliest partners and something of a genius in the art of selling magazines. One morning, Wilson recalled, "I looked in the mirror and saw that I was wearing a homburg." He quit to write his novel, one of whose principal characters was modeled on Larsen, a man who combined touching courtesy and obsessive energy with frequent infidelity to his formidable wife (offered a chance to censor some possibly compromising passages in Wilson's manuscript, Larsen declined). I met Wilson a few years after the book's publication; he had the build of a ski instructor and handsome, open, slightly weak features that could not quite match the rippling jaw muscles of Gregory Peck, who had played his Wilson character in the movie. He recalled how the famous flannel suit had been suggested to him as proper attire by a Time Inc. executive, who added that he should get it at Brooks Brothers. "When I argued that I couldn't afford it, the fellow advised me to go to the boys' department, which was much cheaper—and carried very large sizes."

Riesman, Whyte and Wilson were earnest and quite polite in their attacks, but ruder and noisier protesters against conformity were massing: the Beats.

In 1955, THE year in which, among other things, Lawrence Welk began his weekly TV show, Jim Henson created Kermit the Frog, Patrick Dennis published *Auntie Mame*, the twenty-nine-year-old Allen Ginsberg wrote his long poem *Howl*.

> I saw the best minds of my generation
> destroyed by madness, starving hysterical naked,
> dragging themselves through the negro streets at
> dawn looking for an angry fix . . .

Howl, suggesting Whitman with obscenities, became the hymn of the Beats and Ginsberg became their patron saint. In the gingerly way then required, the press conveyed that he was a homosexual, and a scruffy one at that. On being introduced to him, it was reported, the poet Edith Sitwell, who had the air of a medieval chatelaine, observed: "My, you *do* smell bad." He argued that every American had a constitutional right to take drugs and announced that the Beat generation was a religious phenomenon, its name standing not for beat as in tired or abject, but for Beatitude.

As a devotee of T. S. Eliot, Yeats and Hopkins, I did not much care for *Howl*. I found it wild, naive, self-indulgent, occasionally repellent; yet there were passages that affected me with the sheer power of their fury and despair. My old colleague Paul O'Neil, the marvelous writer who had envisioned *The Last Traffic Jam*, thought that Ginsberg, "even at his most unreasonable, communicates excitement like a voice yelling from inside a police car."

In his 1956 poem *America* ("Go fuck yourself with your atom bomb"), Ginsberg almost identified *Time* with the country, and not by way of flattery:

Are you going to let your emotional life be run by Time
   Magazine?
I'm obsessed with Time Magazine . . .
Its cover stares at me every time I slink past the corner candy
   store . . .
It's always telling me about responsibility. Businessmen are
   serious.
Movie producers are serious. Everybody's serious but me . . .

Later I was startled to find that many people thought the Beat movement had been put on the map by the publicity it received in *Time* and *Life*. Actually the magazines were slow to discover the movement. We were earnestly and self-importantly concerned that a *Time* cover might give premature attention to an unworthy subject. He, she or it "isn't worth it," or at least not yet, was the frequent refrain during the weekly conferences convened to discuss future cover subjects (the Beats never did make it).

When Jack Kerouac's *On the Road* appeared in 1957, we took it seriously but mixed condescension and contempt: "The book's importance lies in [the] attempt to create a rationale for the fevered young who twitch around the nation's jukeboxes and brawl pointlessly in the midnight streets." Not many other critics were much more favorable.

During a Chicago visit I attended a memorable cocktail party, given by a rich Chicago financier for Ginsberg, Peter Orlovsky ("Ginsberg's intimate friend," as *Time* put it) and Gregory Corso ("who boasts that he has never combed his hair").

ORLOVSKY: "I'm Peter Orlovsky. I'm very fine and happy and crazy as a wild flower."
GINSBERG: "I'm Allen Ginsberg, and I'm crazy like a daisy."
CORSO (after being asked by a guest for a comment): "Fried shoes. Like it means nothing. It's all a big laughing bowl and we are caught in it. A scary laughing bowl."

It was not a bad description of the Beat phenomenon itself. Most of the country considered it a laughing matter. The dirty, bearded Beatnik in frayed sandals became a humorous figure in TV situation comedies; live specimens to jazz up parties were offered by Rent-a-Beatnik services.

But not everyone was amused. Norman Podhoretz, editor of *Commentary*, diagnosed the Beats as embodying a "revolt of all the forces hostile to civilization itself—a movement of brute stupidity and know-nothingism that is trying to take over the country from [the] middle class." The harsh condemnation reminded me, once again, of Holden Caulfield and how he provoked some people with his sense that the world was phony, meretricious and loveless. I had always been struck by the almost personal anger with which mature critics berated him as a whining spoiled brat. The phonies whom Holden hated, argued one such critic, John Aldridge, "constitute a fair average of what the culture affords. They are part of the truth which Holden does not see." But it was precisely "what the culture affords" that Holden rebelled against. So did the Beats. Up to a point despair must be respected, even if it seems unearned.

But up to what point? What made them ultimately futile, it seemed to me, was not that they condemned a materialist society, but that they lacked a real understanding of that materialism or of the limits that must exist in any functioning society. For most of them, mewling and aimless, Beatdom was not a heroic enterprise, but an escape, as were drugs.

Lawrence Ferlinghetti, I thought, was one of their better poets; yet even he could write a silly passage:

> [He] is a kind of carpenter
> from some square-type place
>   like Galilee
>   and he starts wailing and claiming . . .
>   . . . the cat
>   who really laid it on us
>   is his Dad
> . . . They stretch him on the Tree to cool . . .

During a visit to San Francisco late in the decade, I went to the City Lights bookstore, which Ferlinghetti had founded. On the edge of Chinatown, it was a marvelously cramped and cluttered wedge of space, the walls lined with paperbacks and the basement bearing cryptic inscriptions left by earlier tenants, a group of Holy Rollers ("Remember Lot's Wife," "In Adam All Die," "You Are Your Father"). Ferlinghetti presided over the emporium, a tall, lean figure in corduroys, with serene blue eyes. He had once worked in the mailroom at *Time*, at about the time I was a copy boy, which, in my mind, at least, established a certain bond between us. Ferlinghetti later reminisced in a letter to me about his mailroom days. Having returned from World War II, in which he had commanded a convoy-escort vessel during the Normandy invasion, he tried to land a publishing or newspaper job. Although he held a journalism degree, he found nothing and took that mailroom job as a possible stepping-stone to editorial work. "I was hoping I could somehow work my way up to Copy Boy, an exalted position in my eyes," he wrote me. "As it turned out, I never even got to *see* the inside of any editorial office," and he eventually quit and went on to Columbia University, the Sorbonne—and poetry. As for the *Time* mailroom, "We were a sad crew given to goldbricking and nose picking, not to mention reading all exposed mail addressed to the editorial department. Mutiny was our constant theme, given our feeling of being enslaved belowdecks. I don't think we performed any acts of sabotage, but the corporate giant towering above us was definitely something we wanted to defeat with our slingshots (I guess I'm still trying)."

What intrigued me especially during my visit to the City Lights was the people who crowded the shop, not to buy books but to gawk at a slightly weird celebrity, take in atmosphere and perhaps move on to another Beat landmark, the Coexistence Bagel Shop. The Beats had been taken up not only by the wealthy, social truffle hunters like the ones at that Chicago cocktail party, but by much of the public—and that is where the "mass media" did play their role. Beat phrases derived from the jazz world—cat, cool, dig, cop-out, funky, turning on—entered the American idiom, as did the all-purpose, mindless interjection "like." Most American cities were dotted by Beat coffeehouses. A book about the Beats, *The Holy Barbarians*, by Lawrence Lipton, became a best-seller, as did *The Dharma Bums* by Kerouac. MGM made a (terrible) movie called *The Beat Generation.* I was impressed and bemused by America's extraordinary ability to assimilate dissent and insult, to turn defiance into fashion or entertainment.

Far more than the rambling mutiny of the Beats, two events broke through the surface complacency of the waning Eisenhower years. Though wildly dissimilar, each in its own way blotted America's self-image. One was the quiz scandals, the other was *Sputnik.*

By the second half of the decade, the once homey and modest quiz shows had turned into vastly lucrative show biz enterprises. Radio's *$64 Question* had become TV's *$64,000 Question.* By far the most popular of the contestants, on an NBC program called *Twenty-One,* was Charles Van Doren, at thirty-eight an archangelically handsome English instructor at Columbia and scion of a great intellectual dynasty; along with his father, the distinguished poet-professor Mark, the Van Doren family bristled with literary stars. Yet Charles managed to convey an all-American simplicity, as he struggled, sweated and groaned inside the contestant's "isolation booth," talking to himself ("Let's see, the aria comes at the end of a party given by . . . what's her name? . . ."), flaying his brain for answers. The range of his knowledge seemed dazzling. His father observed: "I have no idea where he learned all these things." Mortimer Adler, who had known Charles since he was a boy, said he was "aghast that anyone would have this kind of information in his head. I just can't believe it isn't a mental burden." I knew Charles, having met him some years before through mutual friends; drinking and talking with him, I found him charming but slightly remote. While he was clearly very bright, I saw no evidence of the demonic photographic memory later attributed to him. I assigned an excellent *Time* researcher, Jean Sulzberger, to investigate the quiz show phenomenon. We ended up running a story addressing the question "Are the quiz shows rigged?" Our answer was: Yes, up to a point. We concluded that the producers, through long preliminary interviews, were aware of what the contestants knew or didn't know and so could let them win or make them lose. It was a typical case of a bad half-truth hiding a far worse truth. A contestant who had been maneuvered into taking a fall came forward to say that all questions and answers had been fed to contestants in advance. By then Van Doren was off the show, having won $129,000 and a juicy NBC contract for appearances as a resident sage. For close to a year NBC and the producers vehemently denied the charge; so did Van Doren before a grand jury. Not until a Congressional committee began to investigate did he confess. His mea culpa struck me as smarmy and unconvincing (he said that he had hoped to instill a love for education in the young). The movie that later chronicled all this was excellent but overly sympathetic to Van Doren.

There was no doubt that Americans felt betrayed. Perhaps some people were not surprised that you couldn't trust an intellectual like Van Doren. But it was unsettling to think that you had been cheated by those beaming, amusing masters of ceremony—almost as likable as "Uncle Miltie" Berle himself. What did that say about all TV, the beloved national entertainer in the American living room?

Sputnik was infinitely more important than the tawdry quiz show debacle, though for most people not as personal or immediate. For years America had felt secure in its technological superiority over the rest of the world and especially those menacing but backward Soviets. Surely in space exploration, with its need for sophisticated computers, they couldn't compete with the United States. Yet now they accomplished something the United States had wanted to do for years: they had launched a 184-lb. satellite into orbit. By contrast, the thinly funded U.S. Vanguard project had hoped to lift a satellite less than one-eighth that weight. Moscow's feat meant that the Soviet Union must have a ballistic missile powered by a rocket as big as anything the United States had produced. It took a while for the significance of the news to crystallize.

"Listen now," one radio announcer said, "for the sound which forevermore separates the old from the new." And they did listen, across America, to the *beep-beep-beep* from Sputnik as it circled the globe more than five hundred miles up at 18,000 MPH. The insistent, eerie *beep* meant many things. It meant a potential military threat, which Nikita Khrushchev quickly and crassly pointed out. It meant a reproach to U.S. intelligence services, which had been taken by surprise; to U.S. policy makers, who had shown no great sense of urgency about space; to a system that was not turning out enough mathematicians or physicists.

To some it meant national soul-searching; it was time, said Senator Styles Bridges, to be less concerned with "the height of the tail fins of the new car" or the "depth of pile of the new rug" than with the depth of American patriotism and education. Sputnik reinforced a growing belief that American kids were badly schooled (*Why Johnny Can't Read* came out in 1955), largely because of progressive "life adjustment" education. Calls grew louder for going "back to basics."

So attention was once again focused on the younger generation. Somehow, despite worries about lax education, and the Beat phenomenon, the most frequent accusation was still that the young were hopelessly conformist. They were called the silent generation or the brainwashed generation, without heroes or villains and no axes to grind—all the axes had supposedly turned into buried hatchets. "There's not a rebel among you!" proclaimed political scientist Hans Morgenthau. Wallace Stegner of Stanford said he wanted to tell his students: "My God, *feel* something. . . . Plunge, look alive, go boom!"

Toward the end of the decade I was asked by NYU to give a talk to its Phi Beta Kappa chapter. Looking back at my own college years, I felt that the ground had shifted and guessed—perhaps wishfully—that the pragmatism and relativism so fashionable then were played out. Their version of society had been too simple; we were due, I thought, for a view more complex, more mysterious, perhaps more religious. I did not quite trust the universal diagnosis of "conformity," certainly not as a lasting condition; I recalled another "silent generation," in Europe after the Napoleonic Wars, which preceded the revolution of 1848. Facing my NYU audience of Phi Bets, I tried to imagine future rebels among them. It wasn't easy, but I told them: "I would like to think that the quality in you that is called conformist is really something else—a form of waiting for some new understanding. Right now we seem to be in a strange kind of interregnum or intermission. But sooner or later the intermission will be over." I certainly did not suspect the spectacular extent to which the young—and America—would obey Professor Stegner and go boom. But it would not happen right away; first came Camelot.

CHAPTER TWENTY-ONE

No one who saw John Kennedy's inauguration can forget the presence on the platform of the aged Robert Frost, in shambling dignity, starting to read a poem he had written for the occasion. Blinded by the sun, he had to leave off after three lines and instead recited, from memory, one of his famous poems, "The Gift Outright" ("The land was ours before we were the land's . . ."). But the unheard lines were later printed, and they summed up the glistening promise so many saw in Kennedy:

It makes the prophet in us all presage
The glory of a next Augustan Age
Of a power leading from its strength and pride,
Of young ambition eager to be tried . . .
A golden age of poetry and power
Of which this noonday's the beginning hour.

It was not to be an Augustan, a golden age, and almost certainly would not have been even if John Kennedy had lived and been re-elected. But it remains amazing and heartbreaking to recall the extravagant hopes Kennedy stirred in America. I was not sure how much he could actually accomplish, but I was swept up in the excitement of the Kennedy romance—and that is what it was.

The New Frontier coincided with a new regime at *Time* and a new phase in my career. After ten years as managing editor, an unsurpassed record, Roy Alexander went upstairs as an assistant to Luce. Otto Fuerbringer, Alexander's longtime deputy, became managing editor. As for myself, much as I had loved the culture corner, I had grown restless after a decade on and off, and I told Fuerbringer so. Editors were moved around fairly often, and I felt I had built up enough credit to ask for a new assignment. "Well, I guess you have had a pretty long run there," said Otto, adding carefully, "What would you like to do?"

I told him that I had become increasingly fascinated by American politics and that I thought I had learned enough about it by now to edit the Nation section. Otto shook his head. "I think not. But how about foreign news? That's where you began as a writer, and given your background, it's logical." Of course I jumped at the chance; and in September 1961 I took over the World section.

When a press agent phoned me to pitch a new singer, I stopped him cold, explaining that I was no longer handling the back of the book but was in charge of the world. Unfazed, the publicist went right on: "Well, we represent some terrific countries, too."

Thus, throughout the American travail of the early 1960s, professionally I concentrated on foreign affairs. It sometimes made me feel as if I were looking back at the United States from abroad, which gave me a special sense of poignancy.

TOWARD THE END of Ike's Victorian era, unease and dissatisfaction were palpable. Many people had become bored with Ike—and boredom is one of the great, underrated driving forces in history. America was ready for John Kennedy.

The Kennedy legend has become so vast, with so many layers of glorification and denigration, that it almost requires an archaeological dig to retrieve the original impression made by John Fitzgerald Kennedy. The first Kennedy name I became aware of was old Joe's. During our exodus from Europe my family and I had read about a multimillionaire named Joseph P. Kennedy, U.S. ambassador to London, who proclaimed that the West really had no quarrel with Hitler and should do business with him. For some time, until I learned more about the vagaries of politics, it was a mystery to me how this nasty isolationist could be Franklin Roosevelt's envoy and partisan. I found it equally surprising that Joe could be the father of the apparently enlightened Jack.

At first young Kennedy, campaigning for Congress, came across as something of a lightweight, relying mostly on charm. He looked almost like a teenager, with a shock of hair falling over his forehead. But he was, *Time*'s correspondents noted, already an expert at the "Irish switch," which involves shaking one person's hand while talking to another. (Jack's maternal grandfather, John Francis "Honey Fitz" Fitzpatrick, notorious mayor of Boston, reputedly could, at the same time, smile at a third.)

During his courtship of Jacqueline Bouvier, he was pictured at Hyannisport, in shorts, skipping stones along the water, evoking Huck Finn.

In late 1959 I met him for the first time in a private room at Manhattan's '21' Club. Kennedy had not yet formally declared, but there was little doubt that he would run for the presidency in 1960. Lunching with several *Time* journalists, he had an easy urbanity toward his hosts and the waiters alike that went beyond the politician's practiced bonhomie. His posture was very straight but graceful, giving no hint of his back troubles. ("Oh, the daring young man on the flying trapeze . . . ," a slightly drunk colleague of mine crooned under his breath. "His movements are graceful, etc.") I found something odd about his smile; it came only from his lips, while the eyes remained reserved and rather cold. His already famous voice, that mixture of Boston honk and Irish drawl, was infectious even over the lunch table; he reminded me a little of FDR in the way he bit off clauses and sentences. He spoke candidly about his difficulties as a potential candidate. The Senate, he said, was a poor track to run for the presidency, because with every vote you antagonize somebody, and he listed some of his controversial votes. I realized that in the process of reciting problems, he was also reminding us of his independence.

For the most part he was serene and ironic about himself. "My people tell me that I'm very disorganized," he said. "They claim also that I'm a terrible driver and never carry cash. I keep writing notes to myself, which I lose all the time. I really don't know that I'll make it till 1960!"

He did, of course, and won the nomination at the Democratic convention in Los Angeles on the first ballot. That night Luce and Luce's son, Henry III ("Hank"), watched the acceptance speech on TV with Joseph Kennedy, an old friend of Harry's. Joe Kennedy wondered how *Time* would treat the candidate. Luce had known Jack since he was a boy and had written a flattering introduction to young Kennedy's precocious book, *Why England Slept.* So far the magazine had been benign. Luce told Joe that in domestic policy he realized Jack would have to take a liberal line (although Joe protested: "Harry, you know goddamn well that no son of mine could ever be a goddamn liberal"). But in foreign policy, Luce went on, "if Jack shows any signs of going soft on Communism, we will clobber him."

Joe replied: "You don't have to worry about that."

On the same occasion Joe asked Harry whether Jack's career didn't inspire him to have his own boy, Hank, go into politics—why not buy him a congressional seat? Luce was shocked. "But you can't do that," he told his old friend, who knew better.

Soon after the nomination Kennedy again met with a group of editors at the Time & Life Building in New York. George Hunt of *Life* asked him why he wanted to be president. Kennedy said instantly: "Because that's where the real authority is." This Willie ("That's where the money is") Sutton answer was as obvious as it was disarming. Hedley Donovan, Luce's deputy observed later that perhaps Kennedy should have been asked, "Authority to do what?" but thought it would have been a pity to make Kennedy clutter up his reply with campaign platitudes.

Every American election, it has been said, is a contest between the past and the future. This seemed especially true of the 1960 campaign.

Kennedy argued that the Democrats must make a fresh start or be left behind by history, like the Whigs. His program was the fairly standard, moderate-liberal litany, but he ran on the virtue of youth, which still struck a lot of people as a relatively new idea. I sometimes found it hard to remember that Richard Nixon was just four years Kennedy's senior; he sounded, and apparently *wanted* to sound, older. Nixon ran on experience: eight creditable years as Ike's vice president and a thorough familiarity with world affairs. But all his experience and stature faded in the famous TV debates, during which he often was defensive, uncertain, ill at ease in his skin.

I had been sympathetic to Nixon since his role in the Hiss case, and I did not share the idea of him as a reckless Red-baiter. Yet I felt that something was missing in him, and, surprisingly, I found that view shared by Whittaker Chambers, whom I saw occasionally whenever he visited New York. Early in 1960 Nixon had asked him to lunch. Chambers came away unhappy. Though he had every reason to support him, Chambers felt that Nixon lacked deep conviction and sweeping vision. "He's probably the best the Republicans have got," he told me. "But it may not be enough. I rather pity him."

Kennedy won by the narrowest of margins (0.17 percent of the popular vote), but that fact was swept aside by the glee that surrounded the building of the Kennedy administration.

His regime turned out to be an odd hybrid, somewhat schizophrenic. John Kennedy continued to sound belligerent toward Communism, but he wanted to seem pacific to the world. He believed in military strength, but he also warned that Americans had to prevail in the shadowy wars of subversion and in what became known as the struggle for hearts and minds. Kennedy wanted to be a combination of the Good Samaritan and Machiavelli, the sponsor both of the Peace Corps and of the Green Berets. This mixture greatly appealed to me; I thought it was just what was needed. But it was also dangerous unless handled with sure intelligence, as became all too clear within eighty-seven days of Kennedy's inauguration, at the Bay of Pigs.

The scheme of sending a force of Cuban exiles against Castro had been taken over from the Eisenhower administration but weakened. Kennedy wanted to make it seem as if the United States were scarcely involved, and he curtailed critical air support for the invaders. The resulting debacle sobered Kennedy, who only weeks before had boasted, "Sure, the presidency is a tough job, but I don't know anybody better suited to do it." After the disastrous defeat of the invaders, Kennedy brooded alone in the Rose Garden. The American public was remarkably generous toward him and gave him credit for assuming full responsibility. That struck me as naive because there was no way in which the president could escape responsibility in such a situation (even though aides were busy blaming the CIA and the military). Kennedy remained hypersensitive on the issue. A *Fortune* article, excerpted in *Time*, exposing some of the mistakes made in the Cuban adventure, was denounced publicly by Kennedy as "the most inaccurate story I ever read." In fact, the piece contained some relatively minor errors.

Luce never really resented Kennedy's tantrums. "I like Jack," he said. "He always seduces me." I felt equally attracted to Kennedy. I and millions of others probably saw in him what we would have wanted to be ourselves. With what approached a fan's attention I followed his progress, especially his 1961 European trip with its mood swings from the jubilant romp in Paris to the sobering confrontation with Khrushchev in Vienna.

Reading our correspondents' files, I thought I detected, in Kennedy's progress, a thread of fragility: the president after arriving at the Quai d'Orsay, being rushed to the bathroom and into a gilded tub of steaming water to ease his back pains; Kennedy sitting in his shorts on the homeward-bound plane, telling aides about his Vienna confrontation, clearly shaken.

It was widely assumed that Khrushchev had read weakness in the young president, but in the fall of 1962 he learned better.

Khrushchev later said that he had decided to place Russian missiles in Cuba only for defensive purposes and to give Americans some of their own medicine, since U.S. missiles ringed the Soviet Union. The Cuban missile crisis began in silence and largely hidden from the press. Finally

Kennedy told the nation the facts, announced he had declared a blockade and issued an ultimatum to Moscow to withdraw the missiles. In the end Khrushchev backed down.

Although some critics later complained that Kennedy had promised not to invade Cuba and quietly removed some (obsolete) U.S. missiles from Turkey, I thought it was a significant cold war victory for the United States. It was also a frightening passage. Ironically, in the missile age it really did not make a huge difference whether we faced long-range missiles 5,700 miles from Washington in Omsk or shorter-range missiles 1,130 miles away in Cuba. But their proximity was nevertheless unsettling, because of their effect on the imagination.

It was probably the one time that many Americans seriously thought that nuclear war might be imminent. People bought handguns and rifles (to fight off looters after an attack?) and stocked up on groceries. A friend in San Francisco told how her mother had called to say good-bye before moving to the mountains and advised her to transfer her bank account, although where to was not clear. Hedley Donovan recalled wondering on the commuter train from Long Island whether he and his friends would be around the next day. He displayed his optimism by announcing that he had just purchased a new roll of subway tokens. There was a rash of civil defense meetings, briefings and announcements. It was the start of a modest boom in bomb shelters, and newspapers ran lists of what to take with you below. I am embarrassed to recall that I suggested to my friend Max Schuster, one of the founders of the Simon & Schuster publishing firm, a bomb shelter anthology of uplifting and entertaining reading, an idea he wisely turned down with an indignant shudder. Despite the many apocalyptic scenarios long in circulation, I, like most people, had never been able to accept the reality of a nuclear war—no doubt a self-protective failure of imagination. I was impatient with journalists and pop psychologists who blamed all kinds of disorders, from juvenile delinquency to alcoholism, on the threat of the bomb. But now the threat was harder to ignore. I remember watching the evening news with my son, Peter, then seven, who was looking in puzzlement at the images of those long tubes in the intelligence photographs of the missiles.

"I'm nervous," he said precociously.

"Don't worry," I told him. "This fellow Khrushchev is a bully, but he won't do anything."

"Why not?" asked Peter.

"Because he knows that if he hurts us, we'll hurt him," I replied. I did not add that grown-ups called this notion MAD, for mutual assured destruction.

My reassurance seemed less convincing, at least to me, when maps of New York City appeared on the TV screen, showing the effects of a possible nuclear attack, with ground zero at Times Square. We did not know it then, of course, but Khrushchev later admitted thinking that he had enough missiles in Cuba "to destroy New York, Chicago and the other huge industrial cities, not to mention a little village like Washington." That night I looked in on Peter, Mandy and Lisa as they slept. I suppose my face must have been rather grave, because Beverly said with that formidable certainty of hers: "I know what you are thinking. It's not going to happen."

During the crisis Kennedy asked Luce and Otto Fuerbringer to come to the White House for a special briefing. Oddly enough, Luce remembered the long silences more than whatever was said. But he came away convinced that the president considered a nuclear conflict quite possible. Before opting for a blockade, Kennedy had seriously thought about sending U.S. troops into Cuba but feared that this might provoke Soviet retaliation in Berlin, and war. Fuerbringer recalled Kennedy's saying, "We just might have to throw one." Politically Kennedy saw the crisis as a setback because it seemed to vindicate the hard-liners, including Luce, who had urged getting tough with Castro. "You were right about Cuba," he told Luce as they parted.

THE MEETING WAS a further measure of Kennedy's preoccupation with the press. No president before him had been as conscious of his public image. He granted special access to favored reporters and froze out others.

Kennedy was especially obsessed with *Time* because, as he said often, it was very influential among swing voters. He received an early copy of the magazine on Sunday night, and as often as not, by the next morning he was on the phone complaining to the Washington bureau. Kennedy considered Fuerbringer hostile—with good reason. Fuerbringer, a Republican by tradition and conviction, intensely disliked Kennedy; I suspect he was annoyed that he could not look down on him as he had on Truman for his crudeness and Stevenson for his softness. During most of the election campaign Fuerbringer had been ill and away from his desk; he magazine had been run by his deputy, Thomas Griffith. "Griff," who began life in a Seattle orphanage, was a lucid and literate journalist, a civilized gadfly, who had recently published a remarkable book, *The Waist-High Culture*, in which he criticized what he saw as America's intellectual and cultural mediocrity. Liberal but judicious, as acting managing editor he kept the political coverage strikingly fair and balanced. The tone began to change when Fuerbringer returned to his post shortly before the inauguration. To Hugh Sidey, who was covering Kennedy, the president-elect complained, not wholly in jest, "You have failed me. You assured me this man was at death's door."

When the magazine reported that Kennedy had posed for *Gentleman's Quarterly*, the president was furious. He had *not*—they'd simply run his picture, Kennedy insisted to Hugh Sidey, who had been summoned to the Oval Office. As it happened, Colonel John Glenn had just splashed down in his space capsule from his orbital flight on February 20, 1962, and the president was on the telephone to congratulate him, with Sidey sitting across his desk. Sidey later regaled me and other colleagues with an account of how the president, in a version of the "Irish switch," spoke warmly to Glenn one moment, then swung back to Sidey, giving him hell about the *GQ* affair.

Kennedy was intrigued when an invitation reached him early in 1963 to attend a huge *Time* celebration of its fortieth anniversary. The grandiose notion was to invite all the people who had appeared on the cover of *Time* since its founding—or as many as were alive and could be assembled in a suitable space. Kennedy pondered for weeks whether or not he should accept. In the end he didn't, because, he explained to

Sidey, he didn't want people to think that he was currying favor with the Luce publications. He missed quite a party.

As the festivities got under way, a certain star drew her daughter aside, saying reflectively, throatily: "Take a good look around, darling, drink it all in—you will never see anything like it again." Bette Davis was right. The event in May 1963 marked the height of *Time*'s power and self-assurance, but it also defined a period in the United States. It was, perhaps, the final burst of an era in which America still felt itself at the top of the world.

Luce had favored a big bash for the fortieth, rather than waiting for the fiftieth anniversary, because, as Clare Luce quoted him later: "I don't expect to be around for that one." He was only sixty-five, but he had had his first heart attack in 1958, a closely guarded secret; as it turned out, his prediction was right.

A special staff was recruited within the company to plan the party, with much of Time Inc., from top brass to copy boys, kibitzing. Many of us made a game of browsing through scrapbooks of the more than two thousand past covers, which had a hypnotic effect on me. First there were, in black-and-white drawings, mostly forgotten faces that could have been the basis for a trivia quiz. Who was (1) Leo H. Baekeland? (2) Zachary Lansdowne? (3) Capt. Robert Dollar?* But some names jumped out: Roosevelt and Trotsky and Rudyard Kipling and Hearst and Orville Wright and Einstein and Hitler.

Alas, many of the subjects were unavailable; researchers went to work to divide the dead from the quick. Many living but obscure subjects were dropped, and there were some peremptory challenges of people who had incurred the hostility of Time Inc. or vice versa. Inevitably quite a few notables came to mind who somehow had never made the

---

* Answers: (1) Baekeland: U.S. industrial chemist who helped found the modern plastics industry; (2) Lansdowne: American dirigible ace killed flying in bad weather in 1925; (3) Dollar: Scottish-born, poor immigrant, shipping magnate, founder of Dollar Lines.

cover—for instance, Jean-Paul Sartre, Albert Camus, Ralph Ellison, Alexander Calder, Jackson Pollock, Arnold Schönberg and Malcolm X. I suggested, unsuccessfully, that there might be a separate banquet for some of them—*Time*'s own *salon des refusés*.

As it turned out, no foreign heads of state or government came. Luce asked one of the editors to summarize for him the "more interesting regrets." Chancellor Konrad Adenauer, who in the German *Who's Who* listed his selection as *Time*'s 1953 Man of the Year under "decorations," had originally accepted, then changed his mind, sending a flowery tribute to America and the magazine. Charles de Gaulle had an aide decline, with a less flowery but still quite handsome salute. The queen of Greece, whom Luce adored ("My favorite queen," he called her), was detained by a celebration of her own: the centenary of the Greek dynasty. Some uncrowned heads also couldn't make it. Jacques Cousteau would be at the bottom of the sea, Albert Schweitzer too busy in his jungle clinic. Ike Eisenhower, ungratefully, refused to give up a previous engagement at the Masters' golf tournament in Augusta. From General Paul Harkin came a dark omen; as chief of the U.S. Military Assistance Command, he explained, he was too busy "trying to find solutions to our many problems here in Vietnam."

Some researchers, writers and editors, myself included, were drafted to write background notes to help Luce and the other designated toastmasters with their introductions—all cover subjects were to be presented—and to provide conversational fodder for the various table hosts. The reports were stamped "confidential" for good reason. Of Winthrop Aldrich, head of Rockefeller Center, the notes said: "Pretty good water colorist, pretty lousy Ambassador to London, notorious skirt-chaser." Senator Barry Goldwater: "Shrewd, smart and ignorant." Norman Chandler, head of the Times-Mirror Company: "Los Angeles is narrow-based, a cow-town, and in large respect, the L.A. *Times* and Norman Chandler are to blame." Henry Cabot Lodge: "Though once *Time* correspondent in Washington, tends to address journalists as, 'My good man.' " Within days of the event the intelligence was still being updated by breathless bulletins ("Mrs. Winston Guest is expecting a baby").

Press coverage was formidable: nearly one journalist for each of the 284 "cover guests," not counting *Time*'s own correspondents. *Time* executives and editors shepherded guests to the Waldorf-Astoria. I drew escort duty for Adlai Stevenson and Olivia De Havilland. Stevenson was the U.S. ambassador to the UN. He was by then fairly benign about *Time* and the notorious cover story on him back in 1952. "Worse things have been written about me since," he said ruefully.

Inevitably, the evening was oriented less to the future than to the past. "A living waxworks," cracked Bob Hope, one of the masters of ceremonies. Later John Dos Passos recalled the phrase that froze "unspoken on every tongue: 'By God, I thought you were dead.' " There were ample reminders of U.S. military achievements, from Douglas MacArthur to Omar Bradley; the seemingly ever-rising GNP was symbolized by a clutch of businessmen, including Henry Ford II, G.M. board chairman Frederic Donner, Conrad Hilton, David Ogilvy, William Paley and David Sarnoff. Survivors of the New Deal mingled with slightly fresher Republicans. Among other intriguing juxtapositions, Elizabeth Arden, the cosmetics queen and racing stable owner, rubbed shoulders with the jockey Eddie Arcaro, Ethel Merman with Perle Mesta, the superhostess she had portrayed on stage. I was particularly struck by Senator Hubert Humphrey dancing badly (I thought) with Ginger Rogers, the dream girl of my adolescence just beginning to turn chubby; I tried but failed to cut in. Also present, though I did not meet them that night, were the tennis champion Dick Savitt and his young wife, Louise.

Henry Luce was triumphant, mellow and, as the lead-off toastmaster, generous in his introductions; he managed to make some historical points in a conciliatory vein. Presenting Henry Wallace, former Red menace and vice president, Luce referred to his own famous slogan and declared: "Someone said, 'The American Century'; no, he said, " 'The Century of the Common Man'—perhaps both were partly right." The only member of the Kennedy clan in attendance was Senator Edward Kennedy, who had made the cover as part of a family group portrait. At thirty-one, he was slender and handsome and spoken of warmly in the background material (exuberant, patient, sensitive), with no hint of future blemishes. The administration was represented by Secretary of State Dean Rusk, rushing the season in a white dinner jacket, and by Vice President Lyndon Johnson.

The Johnson appearance involved some suspense. Shortly before zero hour, *Time*'s Washington bureau chief, John Steele, while dressing in his New York hotel room, received a phone call from Johnson. He was awfully sorry, he said, and yes, he had promised to come to the *Time* dinner, but it turned out he really had to go to his daughter Luci's Girl Scout meeting that night. Would Steele apologize to Mr. Luce? He truly regretted this, etc.

The journalist and the politician had known each other for years. "Oh, Lyndon," replied Steele, "go fuck yourself," and hung up.

Within moments, as Steele told me later, the vice president was back on the line. "John," he said, "I guess I can't do this to you." When Johnson made his late entrance at the Waldorf, Luce announced him: "Himself is here!"

Jack Kennedy sent a message that was read by Time Inc. president Jim Linen, a chubby and boundlessly dynamic optimist who somehow managed to make even Kennedy's barbs sound complimentary. After paying tribute to Luce's role as an innovative editor, the president went on: *"Time* has instructed, entertained, confused and infuriated its readers for nearly half a century. Like most Americans, I do not always agree with *Time*, but I almost always read it." Kennedy added that he thought he had lately detected in the magazine "those more mature qualities appropriate to an institution entering its forties—a certain mellowness of tone, a greater tolerance of human frailty and most astonishing of all, an occasional hint of fallibility. . . ."

The principal speaker of the long, long evening was someone only Luce could have wanted for such an occasion: the ponderous German-born theologian Paul Tillich, whose topic was "The Human Condition in Relation to the Anniversary Celebration of *Time* Magazine." In his rather Teutonic rhythm he asserted that the essence of the human condition is ambiguity, "the inseparable mixture of good and evil, of true and false, of creative and destructive forces." *(Time*, of all publications, was not fond of ambiguity.) One must recognize, said Tillich, that all institutions, including American democracy, and all achievements, even perfection itself, are ambiguous. (Later in the evening, bumping into Mortimer Adler, I asked him if Tillich hadn't committed a logical error by in effect saying that perfection wasn't perfect. "Not necessarily," Mortimer replied cryptically, and was off to the men's room.) It was very heavy going, especially after filet de boeuf au foie gras. It occurred to me that Tillich was playing the role of the prophet warning of the frailty of all power and glory. Surely Tillich meant to tell Luce, *Time,* the self-satisfied audience of achievers and America in general not to let success make them too arrogant, too confident of fate. It was, in hindsight, a very appropriate moment for such a warning. Indeed it might have applied to the absent president.

In the next few months Kennedy had another moment of triumph, when he stood at the Berlin Wall and proclaimed that, spiritually, all free people were citizens of the divided city (*"Ich bin ein Berliner"*). A considerably less shining episode involved Vietnam and the death of President Ngo Dinh Diem, an early link in the long chain of fatal miscalculations that would follow.

The diminutive Diem had been a courageous nationalist leader fighting against the imperial French rulers as well as against the Communists; "Follow me if I advance! Kill me if I retreat! Revenge me if I die!" had been his call to his men. President of South Vietnam ever since the split between North and South in 1954, Diem was a member of a strong Roman Catholic clan; one of his brothers was archbishop of Hue; another brother, Ngo Dinh Nhu, was the regime's ideologist and chief of the secret police. A passionate anti-Communist, Diem was increasingly accused of being dictatorial, disorganized, isolated. He was anathema to the country's Buddhists. Some Buddhist monks had taken to a grisly form of protest against Diem's rule by dousing themselves with gasoline and publicly immolating themselves. It was becoming the conventional, sophisticated wisdom in Washington that Diem, long backed by the

United States, was so unpopular and autocratic that he actually hampered the fight against Communism and that a more sensitive, democratic-minded leader was needed.

A special demon to Diem's opponents—and most of the American press—was Madame Ngo Dinh Nhu, his sister-in-law, widely seen as the incarnation of everything that was wrong with his regime, in which she wielded considerable power. She had married Ngo Dinh Nhu when she was sixteen and adopted her husband's Catholic religion. "The sacraments," she liked to say, "are my moral vitamins." She fought for women's rights and managed to outlaw concubinage, prostitution, taxi dancing, adultery, abortion and (except by official permission) divorce.

In the fall of 1963 she toured the United States and came to visit *Time*. It was one of the rare occasions when Clare Boothe Luce appeared in the Time & Life Building. She greatly admired Madame Nhu, and they had much in common: they were both beautiful, intelligent, hard, feminist, anti-Communist and Catholic. Madame Nhu was widely described as a dragon lady, but I thought dragon fly would be more appropriate; she was tiny, standing not much more than five feet, with a delicate, doll-like, slightly pouty face. Her small talk included the odd information that Vietnamese never drink milk but feed it to the pigs; she added ironically: "It's just our tradition, not anti-American."

Her more serious views by now were familiar. Americans were "Ivanhoes" forever in love with the underdog but confused about just who the underdog was. In Vietnam the Communists certainly were not, nor were the Buddhists. She called them "provocateurs in monk's robes," who had been (it was one of her more famous lines) "intoxicated and barbecued." Throughout, Clare Luce uncharacteristically confined herself to a supporting role. She did defend Diem's nepotism in making his brother, Madame Nhu's husband, head of the secret police. After all, Clare argued, Bobby Kennedy as attorney general ran America's "secret police," the FBI.

Madame Nhu was in San Francisco when word came that a military coup had unseated Diem and her husband. She observed that it could not have happened "without American incitement or backing." She lashed out, bitterly. Within hours word came that the brothers had been killed. There was little doubt even at the time that the Kennedy administration had promoted the coup. I thought that, at the very least, Kennedy had played Henry II to Diem's Becket ("Will no one rid me of this troublesome priest?"). When he heard of Diem's assassination, he was reportedly shocked. "What did he expect?" remarked General Maxwell Taylor, former chairman of the Joint Chiefs of Staff.

The coup against Diem marked an ultimate failure of the Machiavellian side of Kennedy's policy. Nor was it the last time that the United States found it hard to reach inside another country to establish the sort of government it wanted. These attempts always reminded me of the robot arms that handled dangerous chemicals behind a safety shield. But nations are not laboratories. Diem was followed not by the hoped-for democratic leader, but by a series of military strongmen, some of them ciphers, others reasonably resolute. All would ultimately fail.

KENNEDY MOVED THE United States more deeply into the Vietnam War; the notion that had he lived he would have pulled America out of that conflict never struck me as convincing. He set us on the way to the moon, though we did not yet know that we would get there. At home he started more than he was able to finish, including the crusade for civil rights, to which he came late and reluctantly. He had to be pushed by events, and by his brother Bobby, to defy the southern segregationists in the Democratic Party. Despite my attraction to Kennedy, I had little enthusiasm for the swimming-pool horseplay at Hickory Hill and for the infusion of show business and the "rat pack" into the White House atmosphere.

Along with the ingratiating exterior came signs of ruthlessness and the glib assumption of privilege. But Kennedy made it all attractive—perhaps achieving not "poetry and power," as Frost had put it, but charm and power. I felt that for all its egalitarianism America had a secret hankering for aristocracy—why else the endless fascination with the British royals? The Kennedys' background, even the whiff of corrupt machine politics, reassuringly suggested that they were not snobbish, that somehow they were—though it was an oxymoron—self-made aristocrats. Jack Kennedy brought out a joy and exuberance that had not been seen in politics before. He was above all else a lover—and I do not refer to his philandering. (The best-informed journalists knew very little about that at the time.) Wooing America, and the world, was second nature, along with the passion and the artifice that are always part of wooing. That was his strength as well as his weakness. Love may not be a reliable force in politics, but part of me loved America loving Kennedy.

On November 22, 1963, Henry Luce was presiding over one of his regular lunches with editors of his magazines in a private dining room on the forty-seventh floor of the Time & Life Building. The topic was the U.S. economy, and my mind was wandering when, about halfway through the meal, we were jolted by a ringing telephone in the corner. Otto Fuerbringer went to answer it and came back looking grim and disbelieving. "The president," he said, "has been shot."

Luce was literally in midsentence; as usual he was a hard man to interrupt, and he continued saying a few more words on the economy before he ran down. It was impossible for any of us to take in the news immediately. Then there was the desperate hope that the shooting was not fatal. But after a few minutes the headwaiter came in and said in one of those odd phrases that stay forever in the memory: "Gentlemen, the president is on his way out." Kennedy's death was confirmed at 2:00 P.M. EST.

I hastily finished the martini I had been nursing and joined the silent exodus from the dining room. No matter how we felt, we had magazines to put out—and now quite different magazines. Back in my office I found comfort by getting down to work: tearing up the existing layouts of my World section, sending queries to correspondents in the field for foreign reaction. Behind everyone's professional "the show must go on" demeanor, there was real grief. A German-born researcher burst into my office, in tears. She was weeping not only for the president, but crying in rage about a conversation between two writers she had just overheard.

"Can you imagine," she said between sobs, "those bastards were talking about the stock market, how the market would react. How can they, at a time like this!"

The *Time* cover for that week, already on press, was to have been the jazz pianist Thelonius Monk. A poll among *Time* staffers and readers undoubtedly would have chosen John Kennedy as the cover. Surely this was one of those rare occasions when the *Time* tradition of not putting dead people on the cover might be broken. But, unhesitatingly, Fuerbringer ruled that the week's cover would be the next president, Lyndon Johnson, as a symbol of the nation's continuity. To colleagues who pleaded for Kennedy, he said firmly, "The king is dead, long live the king." The cover had long since been engraved; a standby portrait of the vice president was always on hand. It was a ghastly picture, with a huge shield of the Republic in the background. I thought the heraldic eagle looked rather better than Lyndon, who wore that half-grin he so frequently displayed on the least appropriate occasions. Some editors were crowding around Otto's desk, looking at the picture, and I wondered aloud over the appropriateness of showing a smiling Lyndon Johnson. "He's *not* smiling!" Otto said angrily. At the very least, I felt, Johnson looked smug and self-satisfied. Perhaps the picture was appropriate after all.

As it turned out, the thirteen-page *Time* story was clearly overshadowed by other coverage and especially by television. The images, from Jacqueline Kennedy's blood-spattered suit to the riderless horse in the funeral cortege, showed, as never before, the power of television to draw the nation into a circle of shared experience. It was not information, but emotion, and it foreshadowed how in future people would learn about and react to the world. On the press plane back from Dallas to Washington, as colleagues told it, the reporters listlessly tried writing on their portable typewriters but did not get very far. "We needed to talk, to say something," one observed later. "Yet we had nothing to say to each other." The words would come later, millions of them, but in the first moments and hours mere language was inadequate.

I felt physical pain at the thought of the country, of how America could have spewed forth such an event. But I also felt a personal loss.

Although I had known Kennedy only slightly, he had that quality, shared by all stars, of giving people a sense of intimacy. Otto's words "The king is dead" continued to ring through my mind, but in altered form. I kept thinking of a book by the wonderful Mary Renault, *The King Must Die*. It had to do with the ancient custom of putting a king to death at the end of a certain harvest cycle, or at the approach of his infirmity, in order to propitiate the gods. "The king must die," I kept scribbling on a notepad, without quite knowing why. I felt that in some mystical way the nation from time to time had to put its heroes to death, literally or symbolically. I looked for Renault's book and, browsing, found a half-remembered passage. "I recalled what a man had told me," the narrator said, "about a land where the custom is the same. He said that in all those parts there is no rite in the year that moves and holds the people like the death of the King. 'They see him,' this man said, 'at the height of fortune, sitting in glory, wearing gold; and coming on him, sometimes unknown and secret, sometimes marked by the omens before all the people, is the one who brings his fate. . . .' "

Lee Harvey Oswald, who brought Kennedy's fate, was a mystery; no one knew his motive. Two days later the pathetic, clownish Jack Ruby shot and killed Oswald at the Dallas police station in full view of the TV cameras—revenge reduced to grim farce. Almost instantly the conspiracy theories began. Could Oswald have acted alone, or was he part of a plot? After a week or so I tried to put down my own thoughts. "It seems that people have a hard time accepting the notion that so terrible an act was the result of obscure hate and mad happenstance. It seems somehow outrageous, an insult to life. It is easier to find a pattern, however evil. The ancients in Mary Renault believed in fate. We no longer do. Kennedy's murder is a reassertion of fate. America still rejects the idea of fate but we need to find some meaning in the outrageous and senseless. And so we seek explanations in conspiracy."

When the Warren Commission report appeared I was persuaded by it despite its many inconsistencies. But I had not been prepared for what the report brought to light: a half-crazed political underworld full of corrosive paranoia.

Kennedy's murder altered the atmosphere like an unstable electric charge suddenly loose in the air. Dissent and political strife no longer seemed safely contained within established rules. Every mishap now seemed more ominous, and even good news was shadowed by doubt. In short, "the sixties" had begun.

PART SIX

OVERTURNING

THE

COUNTRY

CHAPTER TWENTY-TWO

In AMERICA AND THE WORLD it was the Kennedy-Johnson era. In the small universe of *Time* it was the Fuerbringer era.

In some quarters Fuerbringer was known as "the Iron Chancellor" for his Germanic ancestry and autocratic manner. One researcher, Clare Mead, who had been a nun for ten years but reentered the world because she had found church discipline too severe, observed after one week's exposure to Fuerbringer: "For this I left the convent?" Years later, during a reminiscing session, Tom Matthews asserted that Fuerbringer had "tortured" me. I did not see it that way. He rode me hard and could be devastating about the copy I produced. He patronized me, but on the whole he was fair about my work. I admired his formidable range of knowledge ("He knows everything," said Luce) and his stunningly accurate memory. He was extraordinarily well organized, a relentless clean-desk man, unlike myself, and he hardly ever toted the usual heavy briefcase home with him at night. Occasionally he could be seen carrying an ostentatiously thin manila envelope with one or two stories inside for overnight reading. "There is no reason at all why paper should overwhelm anyone," he often said rather smugly.

He was tall, athletic, handsome. He never lost his temper and rarely dropped his smile, even when rendering a crushing judgment. When he was enthusiastic about something his eyes would glisten with pleasure.

What he was most often enthusiastic about was politics; he took a passionate interest in the maneuvers, ploys and counterploys from Capitol Hill to statehouses. Forecasting politicians' chances was an absorbing parlor game to him.

Fuerbringer modernized *Time* in many ways. He expanded the range of subjects covered, and, not least, he replaced the traditional lineup of cover illustrators, of whom the only interesting one had been Boris Artzybasheff, a Russian émigré with a unique imagination; in his hands a German submarine commander would become a sea serpent, an American repairman would be seen riding a snail. Otto brought in modern artists, one or two quite awful, but most distinguished and exciting.

That reach for what was fashionable and new, but not *too new*, was typical. Fuerbringer struck me as the personification of a certain kind of American, sophisticated but within safe limits. That mist would come into his eyes when he talked about growing American worldliness, including foreign travel and "little black-tie dinners." He invented a *Time* section called Modern Living, to cover food and wines and style and the good American life in general, which I edited before my foreign assignment, while I half suspected that anything labeled "modern" was already passé. He took culture seriously—he was appalled when I told him that *The Philadelphia Story* was one of my favorite movies. He put the likes of Ingmar Bergman and Le Corbusier on the cover.

Fuerbringer was proud of his Harvard degree and proud of his heritage. His grandfather had been a founder of the Missouri Synod of the Lutheran Church, his father president of the church-sponsored Concordia College in St. Louis. He loathed the term "Bible Belt" and banned it from the magazine. He saw himself as independent of the boss, but on many issues he was more Lucean than Luce. Like Luce, he strongly backed an active American role in the world.

Although that role had become familiar since World War II, Luce and most other *Time* editors thought it needed constant reinforcing. To that end, the Time-Life News Service employed over a hundred full-time foreign correspondents and three hundred stringers to serve all the company's magazines. It took a vast communication network to handle the flow of information between the field and New York—batteries of telex machines, several news desks. The language of these exchanges was fairly standard English, although in the not too distant past cable companies had charged by the word, which led imaginative editors to invent money-saving contractions, as in "Pariswarding" for "I'm headed for Paris" and "steptaking" for taking steps. According to legend, a wire service correspondent had begged for a salary increase for two years and finally got a negligible boost, which prompted his reply, "Upstick your raise asswards." By now *Time* no longer used cablese except in rare instances (as, for example, "outspaced," meaning that a story had been dropped for lack of space).

One day Otto Fuerbringer turned to me and said, "Your job reminds me of a conductor, let's say Leonard Bernstein." I was puzzled. "You can wave your baton and in comes Berlin. Another wave and Singapore is heard from. And so on." Since in my secret Walter Mitty dreams I often saw myself as a symphony conductor, the comparison was pleasing, but excessively fanciful. Each week the correspondents would suggest stories—far more than we could use. As foreign editor I would pick some of them, occasionally making new suggestions of my own. It was then the task of the foreign news service under the chief of correspondents to carry out the reporting.

The organization of the Time-Life News Service had not essentially changed since the early days. It was still not technically part of *Time* magazine but, through the chief of correspondents, reported directly to Henry Luce. Neither I nor the managing editor could fire a correspondent or even reassign him; on the other hand, correspondents did not have the power to add or delete a single word of copy. This caused frustration and led to innumerable squabbles, large and small. I recall with particular fondness a typical incident involving Paris bureau chief Curtis Prendergast, who had accompanied Charles de Gaulle on a trip to Corsica. He complained bitterly that the published story did not contain even a footnote about the fact that Napoleon had been conceived there.

Most correspondents nevertheless tolerated the system because of its compensations. The lifestyle was lavish. For years the Paris bureau was located in a palatial building on the Place de la Concorde just across from the Ministry of the Navy, and standing at those tall windows overlooking the Egyptian obelisk might well give an American journalist a certain sense of imperial power. Most bureaus had their own cars and drivers, many of them legendary characters who could be relied on to perform every sort of service. Expense accounts were generous; in one case the question arose whether the cost of moving the mistress and the horse of one reassigned correspondent could be charged to the office. Granted. Another reporter put on his expense account the single and unelaborated statement "Trip down the Nile, $25,000." Granted, but correspondent subsequently fired. Items like "orchids and caviar for Maria Callas, as well as pâté for her poodle" raised no accountant's eyebrow. In most foreign capitals the Time-Life bureau chief held a quite exalted social position, and entertaining local notables was considered part of the necessary business of maintaining contacts. Most of the correspondents were dedicated, talented and colorful. There was Robert Neville, who wrote his dispatches in longhand (one could almost imagine the quill), standing up at a tall desk in tribute to his bad back and to Hemingway's example. There was Dave Richardson, who had a severe stammer, which aroused so much sympathy in his interview subjects that they told him far more than they had intended. There was Honor Balfour, a pink-cheeked, round-faced, cheery woman who had stood for Parliament as a Liberal and spoke of Winston and Harold and Hugh as if they were members of the family.

The chief of correspondents after 1962 was Richard Clurman, who had come to *Time* from *Commentary* magazine. He had a great sense of news and of people, and he was an ideal boss, invariably standing up for his troops against any outrages that might be committed by the New York editors. His charming wife, Shirley, a shrewd observer of people and an earth mother type even when she was a girl, had been a classmate of Ann Brokaw, the daughter of Clare Luce, who had been tragically killed in a car crash. The Clurmans and the Luces became close friends, but as far as I could tell, Clurman never abused that friendship in the countless office battles he had to fight or mediate. Some people are always remembered through a single image, and my defining image of Dick Clurman was the sight of him in a lavish suite at the Ritz in Paris on his return from a Vietnam trip, still wearing his jungle jacket, which oddly clashed with the brocaded Louis XV background, notebooks and pens spilling from his pockets, while waiters set up a bar and other flunkies installed a special telephone line. Wherever Dick went, even when he was in the hospital for an operation, his own telephone line would instantly follow. A cartoonist would render Dick with at least four wristwatches, to show the time everywhere in his vast empire on which the sun never set, a telephone receiver permanently attached to his ear; Dick, above all others, was the man for whom the cellular telephone would later be invented. Brash under a suave exterior, he made it his business to know everybody and was a cosmic interviewer ("Now what would it really take to end famine in India?") and never stopped interviewing, even at dinner parties, where he was notorious for clinking his glass early in the meal and starting a symposium. He and Fuerbringer were almost inevitable enemies, partly because of the divided authority between the magazine and the news service, partly for political reasons; Clurman was much more liberal. Despite this he became a close friend and sailing partner of the conservative superman William Buckley; Clurman, wrote Buckley, is a fearless cutter of Gordian knots, one of the world's most organized men and, although Jewish, the possessor of a Calvinist conscience, a man who will do anything for a friend provided he remains free "to tell you what a damn fool you had been."

THE COLD WAR, by now, had become a familiar and frozen pattern. This was an era of retreating colonialism with new nations emerging almost daily, or so it seemed. The spectacle was becoming standard: a grimly cheerful member of some old regime, preferably a royal, handing over power to a bemedaled black or brown politician, old flag down, new flag up, the dirge of the old national anthem and the still unsteady clarion calls of the new (it was a great time for composers of national anthems).

The revolt against colonialism had become a great psychodrama. The most influential coauthor of that drama was Frantz Fanon. A black writer and psychiatrist born in Martinique, he published a scorching diatribe entitled *The Wretched of the Earth*. His devil was Europe, whose scandalous opulence had been built from "the sweat and the dead bodies of Negroes, Arabs, Indians and the yellow races." As for the United States, a former colony that set out to overtake Europe, "it had become a monster," full of the mother continent's "taints, sickness and inhumanity." Fanon prescribed violence as a "cleansing force." I never thought that the colonial system could or should survive, but I also felt that Fanon's case was fantastically overdrawn. Europe's mastery, it seemed to me, was due not chiefly to greed and cruelty, but also to a series of creative surges—the Renaissance, the Industrial Revolution. I was especially angered by the indictment of the United States, which except for relatively brief periods had never been a colonial power and had often sided with Third World independence movements against its European allies. Moreover, all too often the newly freed peoples, once brothers in subjugation, began to fight each other. The retreat of the old empires prompted the Soviet Union and China to try to fill the vacuum. This became another phase of the cold war and a major subject for American journalism.

My World section was given much space by Fuerbringer, including cover space. I never once heard a word of protest from "the business side" that this or that cover character involved in some distant coup or menacing trend might not sell all that many copies of *Time* on the newsstand. *Time* functioned on the absolute assumption that it must give the readers what they needed to know even if they found it tough going.

When I took over the World section, *Time*'s foreign coverage had become far more earnest than in the past, with less emphasis on exotic customs or quaint incidents. A notorious exception would come in 1966. Ghana's Communist-leaning dictator, Kwame Nkrumah, had been deposed, and, it was reported, soldiers were eating the animals in his private zoo. This inspired Jason McManus, then a highly promising *Time* writer (and Rhodes scholar) to indulge a deep, incurable love of puns. With two colleagues he concocted a piece that began: "Somehow the old eland was missing. Neither hide nor hare of him had been seen since the day that Kwame Nkrumah had been ostrichized, accused of being the biggest cheetah in Ghana, but safaris anyone knew, no fowl play was involved." The entire story went on like that. It had been intended as a joke, but in a bizarre mood, Fuerbringer decided to print it. I happened to be traveling in Africa at the time, and the piece did not enhance my welcome in Ghana. After I left I cabled McManus, borrowing his title, "Fangs a lot!"

Even without such pun-ditry we could still rely on a lively, familiar cast of characters, whose personal traits we liked to reiterate. There was Charles de Gaulle, usually *Le Grand Charles,* who led France as if it were still a great power. There was General Francisco Franco, very slowly moving Spain into the twentieth century; we always delighted in pointing to his legendary bladder control, which drove his colleagues to despair during endless cabinet meetings. Among the newer members of this stock company were Hussein of Jordan, in his twenties but on his way to becoming the PLK (plucky little king), and Prince Sihanouk of Cambodia, who played the saxophone and whom we frequently referred to as "Snookie." In a category by himself was Nikita Khrushchev, who seemed to be banging the world over its head with his missiles as he had banged his shoe on a UN desk some years before.

THE SOVIET UNION, Russia, Moscow, Moscow, Moscow—the words had been in my ears incessantly for most of my life. Some months after the missile crisis I decided that I must see Russia. Almost every Westerner's first view of it is unforgettable, and so was mine.

The Kremlin was an almost brutal history lesson, a magnificent, preposterous conglomeration of all periods, for centuries added to, altered grandly, patched. Somehow with the gold clouds of its cupolas floating overhead, it seemed uniquely right. Nothing else in Russia did.

I was taken in hand by Israel Shenker, the Time-Life bureau chief, a scholarly, ironic correspondent who had advised me to travel as a tourist because foreign journalists rarely received permission to move outside of Moscow. He himself had tried vainly to visit other parts of the Soviet Union; once when he asked to go to Odessa "to see the sunset," his request was denied by a bureaucrat with the comment: "It's the same sunset in Moscow." Shenker's translator and sidekick, and my frequent

guide, was Paul Shikman, whose American father had been a dedicated
Communist and decided to move to Russia shortly after the Revolution.
Warned by friends that he might starve, he replied: "There will always
be potatoes." As it happened, his son, Paul, recalled, "During the famine
there weren't even potatoes." Paul had grown up as a Russian but spoke
excellent English laced with oddly antiquated American slang ("He's a
corker"; "It's the bees knees"). Unlike his father, he was deeply skeptical
about Communism but never said so openly when he was indoors,
where the secret police might have planted bugs. Instead, when translat-
ing or repeating official propaganda, he would raise his eyebrows, roll
his eyes or speak with ironic fervor.

Roaming about the city with Shenker or Shikman, I found it virtually
impossible to spot a wall anywhere, old or new, that was not cracked or
peeling. Recently built apartment houses were falling apart even before
tenants moved in. This fact was already a cliché but nonetheless striking
against Khrushchev's boast that the Soviets would soon overtake the
West.

In the vast GUM department store, whose high, arched ceiling gave it
a cathedral-like air, people gathered around merchandise (plentiful but
shoddy), touching it almost reverently.

I fully understood—for the first time—how much our Western world
cared for and coddled the individual. In the West not only ads, but goods
and services tried to please me, appealed to me, hence talked to me. In
the Soviet Union things did not talk to people. The Soviets struck me as
unwilling Spartans, but the vast majority accepted the system, in a
strange devotion to mere forms. The lowliest lunchroom had a cut-glass
chandelier, supposedly lending dignity to its grimy surroundings. My
suite at the Hotel National in Moscow contained a grand piano covered
with a white bedsheet. The top of the instrument was missing, and it
was hopelessly out of tune. But wasn't it splendid to have a grand piano
in your room? Less innocently, such delusion applied to politics and
foreign policy. You called something peace or progress, and for gullible
millions, it was.

Surprisingly, Stalin was much in evidence as a scapegoat. Was the
economy backward? Stalin held us back. Were officials timid? Stalin

Whittaker
Chambers editing.
(PHOTO BY
ALFRED EISENSTAEDT,
LIFE MAGAZINE, © TIME INC.)

At the Iron Curtain in
Finland, 1952.
(PHOTO REPRINTED COURTESY
OF TIME INC.)

With Clare Boothe Luce at the 1972 Democratic convention in Miami Beach.
(PHOTO © 1972, JUDITH GEFTER)

With Marilyn at a party at New York's '21' Club. (PHOTO © SAM SHAW)

At South Vietnamese army base, 1969. (PERSONAL COLLECTION OF HENRY GRUNWALD)

With Frank McCullough at Tayninh, South Vietnam, in 1964.

Breaking a precedent.
Robert Kennedy on the
cover (June 14, 1968) after
his assassination.

With Gloria Steinem at the
1976 Leadership Conference in
Washington, D.C.

Essie Lee.
(© WALTER DARAN/TIME INC. PICTURE
COLLECTION)

Alwyn Lee.
(© VELIO CIONI/TIME INC. PICTURE
COLLECTION)

Johanna Davis.
(© SIMON NATHAN/TIME INC. PICTURE
COLLECTION)

The family on Martha's Vineyard: Beverly (next to me), Lisa, Mandy and Peter. On the table, our wire fox terrier, Bravo. (PERSONAL COLLECTION OF HENRY GRUNWALD)

Lobsters à la Castro: Beverly in the kitchen with Fidel. Havana, Cuba, 1980. (© DAVID HUME KENNERLY)

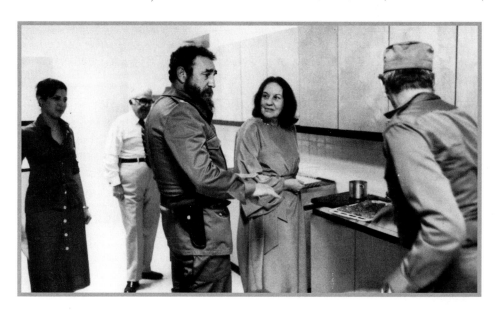

Interviewing Nixon, 1971. From left, White House correspondent Jerrold Schecter, me, Hedley Donovan, the President and Hugh Sidey. (PERSONAL COLLECTION OF HENRY GRUNWALD)

Interviewing Gerald Ford, 1975. Running out of time? (PERSONAL COLLECTION OF HENRY GRUNWALD)

taught them fear. Stalin caused terrible damage, but things were differ-ent now. I mentioned to Paul Shikman that Stalin, after all, had been made possible by the system. How could they be so sure that the Stalin years would not happen again? "There is no system," said Paul (we were outdoors). "Whoever is on top runs Communism in his own way."

I still found much paranoia about the outside world, especially about Germany. I asked a Russian journalist what he thought would happen in Berlin. "Germany will not be reunited," he told me, "until we have some genius at the head of our government who will realize it is not worth holding on to a few more million reluctant people. But Khru-shchev cannot do this, nor his immediate successor." At the time, no-body had heard of Mikhail Gorbachev. Conditions in Russia made me angry at a regime, so arrogant in its self-praise and so often praised by sympathizers in the West, that was keeping its people in such misery.

Day after day I had the sense of being watched and distrusted. Like almost all travelers, I experienced an enormous sense of relief at leaving. When I climbed aboard the outbound Scandinavian Airlines plane at the Moscow Airport, saw the trim flight attendants and felt the crackle of American, English and French newspapers, I was truly moved—perhaps even more so because of a particularly graphic reminder of what I was leaving behind. My sister-in-law, Sally, collected foreign hotel keys. The key from the National was old, ornate, bronze, and had a tassel attached. I put it in my pocket as I was leaving the hotel, thinking it would make a nice addition to her collection. As I was about to board the plane, two plainclothesmen stopped me and asked for the key.

On my return to New York someone identifying himself as working for the CIA called and asked to see me. He turned out to be a short, quite sad-looking man, with a scarred, old-fashioned briefcase, and he wanted to know what I could tell him about the Soviet Union. I did not consider it outrageous for a journalist to talk to the CIA, but I did not think I could tell him anything the agency did not know. I gave him a brief version of my impressions. From his disappointed manner I gath-ered he thought I was holding things back and that he had hoped for secrets. But the most important fact about the Soviet Union was no longer secret: the great Communist experiment in Russia was a failure.

Khrushchev's successor, Leonid Brezhnev, that heavy-footed political hulk, was offended by a *Time* cover story on him, which carried the banner "Breadlines in Utopia" and described him as "tough as a T beam and elusive as a Black Sea eel." The Time-Life Moscow bureau was closed down and not allowed to reopen for nearly five years. During the increasingly ossified Brezhnev regime, the cold war assumed a certain stability. America's preoccupation with Communism shifted from Moscow to the third world, especially Vietnam.

In THE LAST months of the Kennedy administration the fighting in Vietnam still seemed distant and unreal; *Time* referred to it as the "dirty little war in Asia." But it had already aroused passionate opposition. Most American correspondents in Saigon were pessimistic about the war and especially about the Diem regime. That led to a furious conflict between Fuerbringer and Charles Mohr, who was covering Southeast Asia for *Time*. Looking deceptively mild with his sandy blond hair and eyelashes and milky complexion, Mohr was a passionate reporter who had previously been *Time*'s White House correspondent. He was a star and a favorite of Luce's. Along with everyone else, I considered Mohr a superb journalist, but I had recently been involved in a brush with him over a cover story about Madame Nhu. In a letter that could be described only as hysterical and insulting, he argued that the story had been too kind to the Diem regime, had ignored his conviction that it was a disaster, and in effect he called Fuerbringer and other editors in New York fools and knaves. In my response I grew almost as overheated as Mohr, arguing that the story had been reasonably balanced and that Mohr was close to paranoia. That was a word also used by Clurman, although he defended Mohr's reporting. I attributed Mohr's attitude to what I had heard about the poisonous, hothouse atmosphere of Saigon. The episode was a replay, in different circumstances, of the old controversy over Chiang Kai-shek. Again, Luce and many others backed the regime that most journalists considered inept and corrupt; and again, without being able to suggest a convincing alternative.

The fact that the Pentagon and U.S. headquarters in Saigon were consistently optimistic about the course of the war, while the Saigon correspondents were consistently pessimistic, kept nagging at Fuerbringer. He virtually dictated a story for the Press section, accusing the Saigon press corps of sitting around the bar of the Hotel Caravelle, drinking in, along with the Scotch, each other's "convictions, information, misinformation and grievances," while ignoring any positive developments in the war. The story infuriated Mohr, and he resigned. He already had another job offer from *The New York Times*. Years later David Halberstam, who himself had been in Saigon as a *New York Times* correspondent, wrote, in *The Powers That Be* that in the view of many *Time* staffers some of the ensuing damage might have been avoided if I had not been on vacation. Previously, wrote Halberstam, I had prevented in-house bloodshed over Vietnam by "keeping Fuerbringer unhappy, and Mohr unhappy, though, of course, keeping Fuerbringer less unhappy than Mohr." That description was probably accurate enough, being another way of saying that I strove for balance in the way I edited our stories. But even if I had not been away, as World editor I probably would not have had much influence over a story in the Press section, given the compartmentalized structure of the magazine.

After a Clurman mission to Saigon, Luce agreed that the original account had been unfair and authorized a further Press story. At a session involving Luce, Fuerbringer and Clurman, the article was hammered out. The finished story contained a retraction of sorts and suggested that *Time* had been wrong. According to both Fuerbringer and Clurman, Luce approved the story by putting his initials on it; but in other respects their versions differed sharply.

According to Clurman, Fuerbringer, saw this story as a direct attack on his reputation and authority and, later, behind Luce's back, removed some of the language containing the quasi retraction. Clurman was stunned. So was Luce, according to Clurman, who quoted the boss as saying, "How could he have done it!" Fuerbringer denied this version.

The whole imbroglio represented more than the endemic hostility between New York and the correspondents: the internecine war reflected the growing, agonizing conflict in the nation over Vietnam. Even the best and the brightest, in David Halberstam's phrase, were conditioned by the patterns of World War II, which was seen as a permanent warning against appeasing aggression, and by the Korean War, which had dramatized, for most Americans, the Communists' drive for power in Asia. I recall bitter arguments about whether the war in Vietnam involved civil or international hostilities. In one sense the fighting between the South Vietnamese government and the Communist guerrillas, the Viet Cong, was indeed a civil war; but it was also an international conflict because the 1954 Geneva Conference had divided North and South Vietnam in an arrangement the Communists agreed to but never really accepted. The guerrillas were heavily supported by North Vietnam, which, in turn, was backed by Moscow and Beijing. I was a hawk in those days and believed firmly in the widely accepted domino theory, which held that if South Vietnam fell, the rest of Indochina would fall as well. That, in turn, would greatly weaken, if not destroy, the U.S. position in Asia.

There were, of course, some dissenting views, but few were persuaded by the occasional argument from journalists and academics that the key to the struggle in Vietnam was not Communism but nationalism and that North Vietnam's leader, Ho Chi Minh, was not a Moscow or Beijing puppet but an independent nationalist like Tito. It certainly did not persuade me.

When Lyndon Johnson took office there were fifteen thousand "advisers" in Vietnam. By mid-1964 there were twenty-five thousand Americans on the ground. Johnson had become determined to step up the American role, even though he had positioned himself as a man of peace in his 1964 reelection campaign against Barry Goldwater, who sounded far more bellicose. Luce, who thought that a greater U.S. effort (with an American "pro-consul," as he once put it) was needed in Vietnam, nevertheless backed Johnson against Goldwater.

In April 1964 Luce resigned as editor in chief, retaining the title of editorial chairman. His successor, Hedley Donovan, was fiercely independent, but when *Life* came out for Johnson I was convinced that this reflected not only Donovan's but Luce's view. *Life* argued that Goldwater's views on Communism were inaccurate and alarmist and that Johnson had been a good president so far, notably in getting a civil rights bill and a tax cut through Congress. Clare Luce backed Goldwater, a disagreement with her husband that titillated the press and the Time Inc. staff.

In the meantime I was becoming increasingly curious about Vietnam. As a teenager I had had a vague and fantastic view of it. My father, who hardly ever missed an exotic locale, wrote an operetta set in Saigon. It was called *Dschainah* and dealt with a dancing girl and a French officer whose romance owed something to *Madame Butterfly*. One lyric that stuck in my mind for years, from a chorus of French sailors, went, "Whether we are menaced by the yellow Chink or the Jap, we will give our lives for the fatherland." Since then my picture of Vietnam had become considerably more realistic. I had been dealing with the country from a distance and through other people's eyes. Now I wanted very much to see it for myself. In June 1964 I set out on a trip around Asia, with Vietnam and Laos as my chief destinations.

THE FIGHTING IN Laos had actually drawn more attention in the United States than the conflict in Vietnam. Before Eisenhower left the White House he had warned Kennedy that "Laos was the key to the entire area of Southeast Asia." Like Vietnam, Laos was beset by Communist insurgents, the Pathet Lao. The country was ruled by three factions, each headed by a prince: the Communists, the Rightists and the Neutralists. They were constantly maneuvering, forming and dissolving coalitions and fighting each other intermittently, mostly on a plateau known as the Plain of Jars, so named because it was dotted with prehistoric vessels. After landing in Vientiane, I had not even entered the airport building when I was cheerfully informed by our local stringer that a coup seemed to be in the works. The explanation was surrealistic. Some factions were disgruntled over the recent closing of the national lottery—or was it a gambling casino?—and the resulting decrease in various incomes for various pockets.

To my regret, no coup occurred while I was in Laos, although it easily could have. Vientiane was a village, a place of shacks and temples in sad disrepair. During a fifteen-minute walk I passed drab little villas with rustic shutters, reminiscent of very small-town France, belonging to the cabinet, the high command and the leaders of every faction. My escort was *Time*'s stringer, an Englishwoman named Estelle Holt, who looked a little like Mary Poppins except that she had gone rather native. Once, when asked how she had come to Laos, she simply replied: "I drove." She had, indeed, made the trip by car with a friend, first settling in Bhutan, drawn to Laos for mysterious reasons. She was a familiar figure in Vientiane in her cotton blouse and skirt, rubber flip-flops on her feet ("I'm not sure she actually owned a pair of shoes," said a friend). Though not a journalist by training, she became a press groupie and started stringing for various news organizations. She spoke Laotian, adored the people and thought Laos the center of the universe. She lived in a Chinese brothel because it was cheap; the girls loved her and made her into a mascot. As we moved along she gave a running commentary. "The minister of defense lives over there," she told me, pointing across the muddy street at one of these sleepy little dwellings; then, a few feet farther on, "The chief of staff." It was all so close that I felt a Laotian coup might be arranged by opening the shutters, leaning out of the window and yelling across the street.

In the evening I made the required pilgrimage to the Green Latrine, a tavern where, in a fine spirit of democracy, anyone might be seen doing the *lamvong*, a twistlike folk dance, including cabinet ministers, U.S. Marine guards from the embassy and CIA spooks. Several nights before my visit the place had been damaged by a grenade. But it had been thrown by someone's jealous mistress rather than a Pathet Lao agent.

After dropping in at the Latrine, I was not in the mood to crawl behind the mosquito netting of the Settha Palace Hotel, otherwise known as the Bungalow, a grim establishment in which dubious drinking water was supplied in gin bottles and the air-conditioning was within a degree of Alaska. (It occurred to me that half of Somerset Maugham's stories could not have happened if air-conditioning had been available in his day.) So the place to go after the Latrine was the Strip, a row of rustic, dimly lit bars, well staffed with hostesses. In one establishment the madame eagerly greeted the American visitor, chased away all the girls and insisted on talking politics for a good half hour. One of the most engaging customs on the Strip was for each girl to come up to a man in turn and solemnly shake his hand. If he wanted only a drink or two, there was no resentment, no pushing. But then there was very little pushing about anything at that time in Laos. I was intrigued by the handful of Americans and Europeans who had settled in Vientiane. One of them told me: "You don't have to resort to opium—by the way, you can get it anywhere—to be hooked by this place. It's lethargic and unchallenging, and you don't have to live up to anything or anyone—not even yourself."

However unfairly, I could not help feeling that Laos was a make-believe country, fighting a make-believe war, and that it was only a sideshow to Vietnam.

O n   m y   t h i r d   night in Saigon I dreamed that I had discovered the solution to the Vietnamese dilemma. It was brilliant and simple, and I was about to put it down on paper—but somehow it kept slipping away. In the first moments after waking up, I was still excited by that near revelation and frustrated by its elusiveness.

Feeling a little embarrassed, I spoke about it to Frank McCulloch, who covered Vietnam for *Time*. "Hell," said Frank, "everybody in Saigon has that dream." McCulloch had it regularly. So did diplomats and other members of the press. Even Robert Sherrod, renowned Time-Life correspondent during World War II, had the dream when he visited Vietnam. Malcolm Browne, then of the AP, told me that the dream stopped when he went to the United States for a month but resumed on his return.

Everyone in Saigon seemed to be drawing diagrams. It was an automatic gesture of trying to provide a pattern of order where none existed. After an excellent French dinner at L'Amiral, the foreign minister, Phan Huy Quat, turned over the menus and started drawing. "A" marked safe areas, "B" in between, "C" Viet Cong–held areas. He proposed surrounding a given area with troops, broadcasting appeals for the non-Communist populations to come out, setting up receiving posts and then opening up with artillery. After one area had been cleared, move on to the next. It was another variation of the basic plan, call it pacification or clear-and-hold or whatever, that had been tried before. Other diagrams: a shape like an L appeared on the menu, one bar symbolizing the necessary military effort and the other representing the required political effort. I had already heard it proved conclusively that the war could not be won without a political solution and equally conclusively that there could be no political solution until the war was won. With a quick stroke someone at the table turned the L into a triangle by adding a third bar, standing for what—administration? propaganda?

Next morning, looking down from a shuddering helicopter, I saw no diagrams on the land. There were only irregularly shaped paddies of varying shades of gray and silver—lovely, intangible, somehow soporific. The young PFC who rode shotgun on the chopper had a hard time staying awake as he bent over his machine gun, which he sternly pointed below, at nothing in particular.

We were in Tayninh province about fifty miles from Saigon, headed for a Vietnamese special forces camp near Black Bridge Mountain. There had been heavy fighting in the area. We were accompanied by an American escort officer, a lieutenant colonel who had obviously been passed over for promotion once too often; he had a two-day beard and quite clearly a monstrous hangover. About halfway to the camp the pilot announced that we would "come in hot," meaning that there was combat. The lieutenant colonel yelled into McCulloch's ear, pointing at me, "Who is this guy?" McCulloch gave my name, but the lieutenant colonel went on impatiently: "I don't mean his name, I mean what does he *do?*"

"He's the foreign editor of *Time.*"

"You mean *Time* magazine?"

"Yeah."

"Oh, *shit!*"

We landed unscathed, but the escort officer could hardly wait to get us out of there. The camp somewhat resembled an old western cavalry post, only less secure looking. A jeep arrived containing two dead Vietnamese soldiers and five live ones, who shared the vehicle with the corpses casually, almost indifferently. The extraordinary thing, I thought, was that these sad-looking soldiers were still fighting at all, however badly underpaid, or unpaid, and uncertainly led, in a country that had been at war since they were born.

We moved on to the still incompletely fortified village of Suoi Cao, which was supposed to be something of a model and a key to how the war could be won. It had neat, new houses, an infirmary, a six-room school, a new market—quite clearly capable of giving the peasants a better life than they had ever had. If, that is, the Vietnamese army could provide security and banish fear. The place struck me as an island, unconnected with the rest of the country, especially Saigon.

Returning to the capital a few days later was a shock. I did not like the city, with its rather absurd, pseudo-Romanesque, red brick cathedral and its once graceful but increasingly garish boulevards. I was put off by its seeming indifference to the war. Middle-class professionals and intellectuals I met struck me as cynical, without deep loyalty to anything, full of high phrases about the needs of the peasants they scarcely knew and automatically critical of any regime in power.

Some of them called for a neutral South Vietnam to end the war but had few illusions that such a solution would lead to anything but a Communist takeover. One lawyer said: "That wouldn't be the end of the world for us. After all, the Communists would need us, the educated elite, if you will, to help run the country." I decided that this crowd was hopeless and not representative of the many South Vietnamese who were genuinely against the Communists.

Prime Minister Nguyen Khanh felt the same way about "this elite." "I sometimes think we should withdraw all our troops from Saigon. Then the Communists would move in and these people would finally get a taste of what it is really like."

Khanh was a roly-poly general of thirty-seven with a goatee and a brash self-confident manner. He had seized power from Diem's immediate and ineffectual successor, General Duong Van Minh ("Big Minh"), but had left him in place as a figurehead chief of state. When I met him Khanh had just seen a report quoting President Johnson as saying something about an honorable peace, and it upset him greatly: "If the U.S. wants an honorable peace, they had better not count on General Khanh.

An honorable peace in Vietnam means negotiation, which in turn means neutralism. The end result would be slavery." Despite his obvious intelligence and vigor, and the possibility that he was the best leader South Vietnam could produce at the moment, Khanh was not really convincing. Inevitably I had to compare him to the magnificent stuffed tiger at the entrance to his office. He was out thirteen months later.

The man I expected to be more impressive, and on whom great American hopes were placed, was General William Westmoreland, formerly deputy commander of U.S. forces in Vietnam and just appointed to the top post. He was strikingly sad looking, even when he smiled. I had been warned that his strongest explicative was something like "dad-gum," but he did not resort even to that. At first he spoke less about the military situation than about the political dilemmas in Saigon, which clearly baffled him. On the military side his message was simple: more American troops.

He spoke warmly of the South Vietnamese forces but said he had been thinking about bringing in bugles and whistles for them, for communications and morale. As for the morale of the Americans, he pleaded earnestly for more USO appearances. In the next few years, throughout the controversies about the war and Westmoreland's performance, I could not forget how appalled I felt to hear the American commander in Vietnam speak seriously about the difference Bob Hope, say, or Nancy Sinatra might make to the war. It seemed to me that perhaps the "elite" of Saigon were not alone in a sense of unreality.

That feeling was shared by *Time*'s correspondents in Saigon, two remarkable journalists. Frank McCulloch was a Nevadan who had been a bush league pitcher (a scouting report for the St. Louis Cardinals read: "Fast but wild. Watch"), had held a variety of newspaper jobs from the Winnemucca, Nevada, *Humboldt Daily Star* to the *Los Angeles Times* and had served as a marine sergeant in World War II and Korea. The Saigon street urchins called him "buddha" because he shaved his head bald, which he found convenient in the Asian climate. With one of Vietnam's prominent Buddhists, Thich Tri Quang, he would compare the relative merits of an electric shaver and a blade razor. Before he left

Vietnam in 1968 he had outlasted three ambassadors, two U.S. military commanders and seven Vietnamese heads of government. He was a relentless reporter, scrupulously fair and very brave.

For James Wilde, brave was hardly the word; foolhardy was more appropriate. A Canadian, Wilde was an unabashed war lover who managed to combine that fervor with a melancholy compassion for war's victims. He had a somewhat cadaverous face with a beaked nose under a floppy bush hat, drank too much, liked his opium and spoke in poetic cadences spiked with obscenities. He addressed people he respected, and some he did not, with the all-purpose honorific of "Doctor." Although a modest man, he had great faith in his power of survival. Once, on patrol with South Vietnamese troops, he was, as usual, yards ahead of the soldiers making their way through brush-covered territory. Suddenly Wilde began to sink into the ground, farther and farther, until he was visible only from the waist up. He had sunk into a Viet Cong snare known as a "spider trap." The South Vietnamese stood frozen as a gun-toting Viet Cong appeared about ten or fifteen feet away from the trapped Wilde. The two stared at each other for a few moments, and then the Viet Cong turned and took off. As Wilde told it later, "I looked that guy dead in the eye, Doctor, that's why he fled." A year or so after my visit he was with the Fifth Vietnamese Airborne Battalion when it ran into an ambush. He spent forty-eight hours in a drenching monsoon, helping to load 453 dead, including six U.S. advisers, onto helicopters. As he described it in a terse cable: "Water running from their slack mouths, swollen legs and arms that keep coming off, rotten with rain. Feet popped off one large U.S. army sergeant while dragging him to the whirlybird. Scared near to shitting all the time since could feel Viet Cong watching from nearby treeline. Stench of death massaged my skin."

In Vietnam I realized that visiting firemen from New York who dropped in to "look at the war" (there would be many more after my visit) were a burden for McCulloch, Wilde and the many other *Time* correspondents who would move in and out. The most difficult part, McCulloch explained, was not keeping them from getting killed, but persuading them, in a few short days, that this was a different war from any the United States had fought before, a war in which territory, superiority of arms and equipment did not count.

I believe they persuaded me, at least to some extent. At that time McCulloch still thought that South Vietnam could prevail with better leadership and more good old American know-how, but he also felt the Pentagon and the U.S. command in Saigon underestimated the difficulties. After all, according to U.S. intelligence (which McCulloch did not really trust), the Viet Cong had forty thousand men under arms while the South Vietnamese had more than ten times as many. So why weren't we winning? Wilde had an answer for that, which he would regularly repeat to future visitors, including a disturbed Henry Luce: "Nothing will change, Doctor, until there are some South Vietnamese out there with fire in their guts."

Fire in their guts or not, I concluded, South Vietnam could not make it without the war's being expanded to the North to stop the relentless influx of Viet Cong reinforcements. (U.S. officials feared that a massive move against the North would bring in the Chinese.) Some American military experts persuaded me—quite mistakenly, as it would become clear—that the North could be successfully contained without massive intervention, merely with small but well-targeted surgical air strikes. But I felt that even with action against the North, a stalemate was the best we could hope for.

In a report to my colleagues at *Time* back in New York, I said: "The trouble is that we tend to look at the situation in flat either/or terms. Defeat in Vietnam is easily defined. But victory is far less easily defined and certainly not, I fear, in terms of unconditional surrender, lick-the-bastards-once-and-for-all. Victory, to me, means hanging on and achieving a standoff with the North. A pretty modest definition of victory? I wonder whether the United States is really willing to pay the price for a more ambitious one."

In order to hang on and achieve a standoff, I felt that the United States had to continue the war. The following year, in a new *Time* section called Essay that Fuerbringer asked me to edit, we made that point. The piece conceded that the Viet Cong were partly motivated by nationalism and that to some extent this was a civil war, but it reiterated the domino theory and the need to resist Communism, which, despite the growing Moscow-Peking split, was still an international, aggressive force. The essay was titled "The Right War at the Right Time," and I considered it a good provocative head, then. Opponents of the war and critics of the magazine would not let me forget it.

One of my lasting impressions as I left Vietnam was the quality of the people we had sent there. It was quite startling to find a hulking professional American army colonel, who had spent most of his military life in this or that U.S. Army base, suddenly transported into the Vietnamese jungle, worrying about village schools and hospitals, improvising tactics for an impossible guerrilla war and, not incidentally, showing genuine pride in and affection for his Vietnamese charges. Some of this benign quality would remain with the U.S. forces to the very end; much of it would be buried by the growing bitterness and cruelty—on both sides— as the fighting steadily increased and thousands of unhappy draftees poured into the bloody fields of 'Nam.

AFTER LAOS AND Vietnam I made other stops. The great story in the area was the tremendous success of the free economies in Thailand, Malaysia and Hong Kong. Granting all the differences, this success resembled the triumph of free economies in Western Europe, which had set up a kind of magnet or force field that was pulling at and weakening the Communist systems of the Soviet Union and Eastern Europe.

I thought of this in Hong Kong, that enclave of feverish commercialism topped by fog-shrouded, dreamlike towers. I drove out of the city and into the silent, treeless New Territories along the Chinese border. The sleepy frontier station, with its small railway bridge, its highly polished British policemen and its sullen Red Chinese soldiers on the other side, made a singularly quiet border. I wondered whether that border would someday be crossed by an invading force—the force of the free market.

My other impression had to do with concepts I heard so much about: face, and Asia's imperviousness to Western reason. The importance of face had declined considerably, I thought, and in some situations America was more preoccupied with it than the Asians. I also thought that perhaps it was not the Asians who were impervious to Western reason, but we ourselves who were not applying it. I sensed a profound realism in Asia, which made Americans seem positively romantic and deluded. This applied, I reluctantly believed, to the U.S. refusal to recognize Communist China. I could see withholding diplomatic relations for a while as a bargaining ploy, but I always felt that recognizing an existing, functioning regime merely meant recognizing reality, not moral approval. I did not yet connect this rejection of realism with U.S. policy on Vietnam. Gradually, in the months and years ahead, the very word "Vietnam" assumed different undertones; it was no longer a geographic term, but a symbolic name for a growing nightmare.

CHAPTER TWENTY-THREE

I HAD A SENSE that America was getting away from me. On all sides I saw attempts to overturn the country, its values, its promise, even its history.

Images and slogans flicker through my memory as if illuminated by the psychedelic flashes of lightning in some vast disco. "Hey, hey, LBJ, how many kids did you kill today?" echoed by "Ho, Ho, Ho Chi Minh, the NLF is gonna win." Sit-ins and love-ins. Mace and marijuana. "Where Have All the Flowers Gone?" but also "I always hold my flower in a clenched fist." Bra burning and draft card burning. "Burn, Baby, Burn." If there was a pattern, it was love alternating with hate, idealism blending into rage. And increasingly the rage was black.

The struggle for black equality had, of course, started long before Vietnam, and it stirred me much more deeply. I was unconsciously making a distinction between the civil rights movement and the other forces of protest. There was some justification for this distinction, because the black movement's grievances and aims struck me as clearer, sharper, more in the center of the American conscience. It certainly troubled my own conscience.

For years, like most people living in the North, I considered "the Negro problem" mainly a southern affair. And the South baffled me. I had never forgotten my first glimpse—literally a glimpse—when, during a train ride to Florida years before, I opened my window shade and saw "White" and "Colored" signs on a toilet in a passing railroad station. I found it almost impossible to square the whole ghastly system based on the "separation of the races"—the segregated schools, buses and theaters and the political disenfranchisement of blacks—with American democracy. In 1963 the nation witnessed the days of rage in Birmingham. The Reverend Martin Luther King Jr., who at thirty-four was emerging as the most compelling black leader in the United States, had organized a series of demonstrations to protest segregation in the city. True to his Gandhian beliefs, he wanted the demonstrations to be peaceful, but violence erupted. The scenes were unforgettable: police dogs savaging demonstrators, water from firehoses slamming blacks against walls, hundreds of children arrested after having tried to integrate white churches, a woman lying on the ground with a policeman's knee pressing into her throat. How could these scenes be squared with the glow of Camelot, with the image of a country that saw itself as the champion of freedom and humanity throughout the world?

Two concepts helped me, to some extent, in resolving that awful dilemma. One was expressed in the phrase "tragedy of history." I considered the South a truly tragic—perhaps the only tragic—region of the United States. I felt that it had been enslaved by slavery longer than other parts of the world, not only because of greed and moral corruption, but because of geographic isolation. I knew from European history that defeat—for example, the defeat of Germany in World War I—could leave a corrosive legacy; I understood that something similar had happened to the South in the Civil War, resulting in its doomed resistance to the modern world.

Moreover, I thought, things were manifestly and steadily improving. And this was my second relatively comforting concept: continuous reform. Even in Birmingham there were the first signs of movement, however modest, toward desegregation. Voter registration drives began to give political power to blacks. Gradually schools seemed to be opening up, despite the agonizingly slow advances since the *Brown* decision. *Time* cited some further instances of progress, some pathetically trivial; for instance, starters at Miami's municipal golf courses no longer asked a trio of white men if they would accept a Negro fourth. There seemed to be a growing alliance against segregation between blacks and whites, symbolized by rallies, marches and, not least, the "Freedom Riders," who were continuing their dangerous forays. A climax of hope was reached at the March on Washington when two hundred thousand blacks and whites, holding hands and singing, streamed from the Washington Monument to the Lincoln Memorial. King's famous speech ("I have a dream") was so eloquent that the words themselves almost became a substitute for action, somehow conveying accomplishment rather than merely a promise. Watching on TV, I found myself temporarily forgetting that the great peroration—"Free at last! Free at last! Thank God Almighty, we are free at last!"—described only a hope still unfulfilled. King was far from the best speaker I had ever heard; many other orators were more polished and more naturally dramatic. But his occasional flatness of tone and his somewhat blunt, dull features added to his total earnestness and conviction. King had summed up the black condition in another, more homely way when, in a Los Angeles talk, he quoted an old slave preacher: "We ain't what we ought to be and we ain't what we want to be and we ain't what we're going to be. But thank God, we ain't what we was."

Years later, when I recalled that optimistic view, a black *Time* reporter said critically: "You were just a meliorist." I had been called worse things. But the expectations kept clashing with disappointment. Even during the planning of the great March on Washington, there had been mounting criticism of King's gradualist and nonviolent philosophy. New black leaders emerged over the next few years, far less comfortable and comforting in white eyes than Martin Luther King. I could easily imagine sitting down with King and discussing what I took to be the common goal of all right-thinking Americans to bring about black equality. I could not quite imagine this with the hard, hostile new set of black spokesmen who, to a great extent, rejected the white world. They were men like Stokely Carmichael, the founder of the Student Nonviolent Coordinating Committee: a philosophy major from Howard University who was still in his teens when he emerged as one of the fiercest agitators for black power. He would tell black audiences: "[We are] building a movement that will smash everything Western civilization has created." Huey P. Newton, a highly intelligent thug who co-founded the Black Panthers, was another. Although the organization would turn out to have an underside of crime and brutality, many blacks idolized the Panthers. So did many white liberals, some of whom were thrilled to be flirting with real outlaws. Leonard and Felicia Bernstein gave their notorious party to raise funds for twenty-one jailed Black Panthers, an event that was chronicled by Tom Wolfe under the memorable heading of *Radical Chic*. Wolfe had a wonderful time describing the barricades of Park Avenue, with a Black Panther "field marshal" preaching the overthrow of the system amid the Roquefort canapés and massed silver-framed photographs. The Panthers survived radical chic, but radical chic scarcely survived the party. News of the event provoked an extraordinary amount of indignation. A *New York Times* editorial fumed: "Emergence of the Black Panthers as the romanticized darlings of the politico-cultural jet set is an affront to the majority of black Americans." The anger of the *Times* and other well-meaning supporters of civil rights was understandable; they were deeply threatened by a mounting attack on the very idea of integration by militants who asserted that blacks were superior to whites and should live apart from them.

That was the message of the Black Muslims. For a long time I found it impossible to take them seriously. They were led by a bizarre old man, Elijah Muhammad (born Elijah Poole), who habitually referred to "the white devils" and whose lavish way of life did not, in the eyes of his followers, detract from his prophetic power. His teachings sounded like a ghastly copy of white racism and a weird echo of the vicious slogan "Let them go back to Africa." American blacks, with their umbilical ties to Christian churches, it seemed to me, had nothing to do with Islam. Yet Black Muslims could not be ignored, and I learned this partly from Gordon Parks, the brilliant *Life* photographer with whom I had become friendly. Parks was a star in the white world not only as a photographer, but, later, as a writer, filmmaker and composer. He had spent months covering the Muslims for *Life* and had become close to Malcolm X, Elijah Muhammad's magnetic and dangerous lieutenant. Malcolm was not yet a legend; the press saw him mostly as an unashamed demagogue whose gospel was hatred. Gordon was impressed by the Muslims' emphasis on discipline, their insistence on right living and their programs for practical education. He was also impressed by Malcolm and his scorching anger against whites and moderate blacks: Malcolm condemned the March on Washington as a gimmick, a shot of Novocain, which, when it wore off, would leave only worse pain behind. But Gordon could not accept the Muslims, who would lead blacks into a separate state. "A lot of white men have helped me in my career, including several Jews," he once told me. "I won't repudiate them. I could no more do that than I could shed my black skin." But he did feel a kinship with the Muslims. "Although I won't allow them to be my keeper," he wrote, "I am inherently their brother." He also wrote in *Life:* "I've always had faith in America, but I have also been angry—even bitter. It is now time for America to justify this belief I have in her, to show me I have not believed in vain."

The "Novocain" of the March on Washington did wear off; a year later came the Harlem riots. The trouble started in an all too typical way, when a fifteen-year-old black high school student with a knife was shot and killed by a white cop near a school in a mostly white Manhattan neighborhood. For five nights blacks in Harlem attacked police, hurled Molotov cocktails, broke store windows and looted. It was mild, as riots went (1 dead, about 150 people injured), but black anger and white fears were intense. In a Harlem church James Farmer of CORE said: "I saw New York's night of Birmingham horror!" Although the violence did not spill beyond the borders of black communities, Manhattanites were jittery. Forty blocks uptown from my safe East Side apartment, the fighting was close but far enough away to keep me from personal risk. I could not help being relieved that the violence was not happening in *my* neighborhood, but at the same time that relief made me feel guilty.

To me, as to most white New Yorkers, Harlem was essentially unknown and very nearly forbidden territory. During my early years in New York I would still occasionally go to some jazz club in search of the remnants of the old Harlem of the 1920s, the Harlem of the Savoy Ballroom, the Cotton Club, Duke Ellington and Billie Holiday. Most of that scene had vanished years ago. Coming home from a trip to Connecticut or Westchester, I would sometimes get off at the 125th Street station instead of going all the way down to Grand Central. Given the crime in Harlem, it was always a nervous experience, looking for a taxi to take me home. After a while I decided that the time saved was not worth it. I usually saw Harlem only from the window of those suburban trains, a drab blur interrupted occasionally by the bright colors of wall posters, the passage too swift to identify human shapes or faces. Press coverage of Harlem was modest, generally confined to crime and politics.

The riot compelled new attention. I read about what, of course, I knew existed but did not often focus on: the rat-infested, crumbling tenements, the idle youngsters, the dope pushers, the hostile white cops, the rackets both black and white.

I knew hardly anybody who lived in Harlem. I did know Albert Murray, a fine writer, who was strong and humorous, and his wife, Mozelle; he would go on to celebrate his own life as well as the black experience and black music in America in such books as *South to a Very Old Place* and *Stomping the Blues*. Beverly and I had met them at a party, and the four of us occasionally had dinner at each other's apartments. I sometimes told Beverly that we should have more black friends, and she agreed. But we realized that an effort to meet and cultivate them would have seemed artificial. I earnestly examined my feelings, and within the inevitable limits of self-knowledge, I did not detect any prejudice. I did find curiosity and the unease caused by a sense of differentness. The inescapable truth was that, as I had seen during my first contacts with blacks in high school, we lived separate lives.

The "black problem" was not just a southern problem, as I had once thought. The North achieved through indifference very nearly what the South achieved through Jim Crow. Malcolm X had a point when he said, "When I speak of the South, I mean south of Canada. The whole U.S. is the South."

Some of the blacks with whom I worked at *Time* expressed the conflicting forces that were tearing at America. Few blacks were working on the magazine or elsewhere in the press, despite considerable efforts to recruit them; the pool of qualified candidates was small, partly because journalism, unlike the law or other professions, had long been considered out of their reach. One black writer felt so alien in the Time & Life Building, and so sure that "they" were out to get him, that he carried a knife to work. Others came to feel quite at home, among them Joe Boyce, son of an Episcopal priest, who had been a policeman in Chicago before turning to journalism. Though in no sense a radical, he admired the Panthers and other militants because it took courage "to call for blacks to be responsible for their own destiny, to no longer strive for approval of whites." Soft-spoken, with a face that could be both angelic and mischievous, he could speak movingly about the moral good in people and how patience would bring it out. Years later he reflected that patience had not been quite enough and that blacks were still not near equal treatment in the white world: "You see, the civil rights movement fell short because integration never worked. And that was because it was never about integration with us, it was about desegregation. That's very different."

Jack White had a harder edge and a less soothing appearance; he was lean, handsome, with heavy-lidded eyes that seemed to hide anger underneath. As a student at Swarthmore he was arrested and jailed during a civil rights demonstration. The local paper wrote a story about "the arrest of twelve bearded Communists," when none wore beards, three were girls and only one was a Communist sympathizer. Then and there White decided that he wanted to be a journalist. He realized "that sometimes how something is reported is more important than the event." After a few years on *The Washington Post* and a civil rights publication, he came to *Time,* whose reporting of black America he considered "often haughty and paternalistic." In his view it was a matter not of prejudice, but of ignorance. The point would be illustrated at the time of the Attica prison riot in 1971, when the magazine wrote of an "anonymous poem, crude but touching in its would-be heroics" that was being passed around by the prisoners to buck up their courage. It went: "If we must die, let it not be like hogs / Hunted and penned in an inglorious spot. . . . / If we must die, O let us nobly die. . . ." The poem was actually the work of a major black American poet, Claude McKay. White saw this, accurately enough, as a sign that *Time* writers, like most educated whites, had scant knowledge of black culture. "As a young man I really thought there would be a black revolution in America that would result in the overthrow of the existing order. I can't remember what was going to take its place; there was no thought-out notion of that." But he rejected black separatism. He came to feel, in hindsight, that the radicals who wanted to "tear down America" had missed the boat: "We need a revolution of personal values. The choices we make for ourselves determine what happens to us. You can't come into the white world with a chip on your shoulder. You have to learn the skill of getting along with white people and still keeping your self-respect and not lose your mind." White did get along, did keep his self-respect and did not lose his mind. Looking back, he once told me, "For people like us, the educated black middle class, life has never been better." Yet in some ways things have gotten tougher, and not only for the black urban poor: "As we get closer to the goal, the goal is defended more fiercely."

I remembered what White had said about our ignorance of black life—or at least our ghetto life—a few years later when Hedley Donovan decided that we needed a closer look. The result was a two-day tour of the South Bronx and adjoining neighborhoods, an urban war zone devastated by arson and gang fighting, with miles of burned-out tenements inevitably evoking bombed cities. The itinerary read in part: "9:00 A.M.: 48th Precinct, headquarters for both the Police Command and the Borough's Arson Squad. 10:00 A.M.: Criminal Court. We'll meet with Judge Antonio Figuero, a black Puerto Rican and a local elder. . . . 2:00 P.M.: Visit to low-income and middle-income housing projects. . . . 5:00 P.M.: Meeting with two or three members of the Savage Skulls." It was a rather naive, domestic version of the *Time* News Tours, and the territory we tried to explore was in many ways more alien than the foreign countries we usually visited. None of us had any illusion that this two-day excursion could give us more than a glimpse of reality. But even a glimpse seemed better than just watching these scenes on television or reading about them.

Our group of six was led by the New York bureau chief, Laurence Barrett, a native of another part of the Bronx, and we traveled in a comfortable van. Barrett had told us to omit neckties and jackets in order not to look too conspicuous, a suggestion ignored by Donovan. We spoke to social workers, policemen, judges and shopkeepers. All of them told stories of crime, drugs, poverty and despair. All of them declared their determination to help rebuild this blighted area. Members of the gang Savage Skulls had promised to meet us in a saloon near Southern Boulevard. They failed to show up, probably because the meeting had been set up by a policeman who worked with gangs and because plainclothes cops shadowed us not so discreetly. Hedley was highly irritated, in a manner I had witnessed on trips to Russia and the Middle East, when Aleksei Kosygin and Yasir Arafat failed to keep their appointments. "I've been stood up by better people than the Savage Skulls," he observed as he sipped his beer out of the bottle, trying to blend into the landscape.

Next day we visited Riker's Island, the notorious prison in the East River. As we walked through the oppressive cell blocks, which echoed with a permanent, angry hum, we were watched by the inmates who had been allowed outside their tiny cells for exercise. Some looked amazed, some amused, but most were indifferent. We were instructed to stick together. I occasionally fell behind, however, not quite up to Hedley's long-legged pace. "I had this sudden vision of *Time*'s managing editor being taken hostage," Larry Barrett recalled later. "The question would be not 'Who lost China?' but 'Who lost Grunwald?' And the answer would be 'Barrett!' "

I had a somewhat different experience in East St. Louis, where I and a colleague moved less obtrusively. Crossing the bridge from prosperous and lively St. Louis, within sight of the city's graceful arch, I felt as if I were moving into a quarantined area. Yet there was lots of action, lots of hope. The slum was in the grip of convulsive urban renewal programs: various plucky, black self-help groups, Rube Goldberg structures of federal aid, new housing, new clinics, a maze of model cities projects.

Yes, there was progress, but blacks and whites were operating on different clocks. It was almost as if the ancient clichés about the races had been reversed: the dynamic, impatient white man, who wants everything done instantly, was now begging for patience; the slow, lackadaisical black man, who had no sense of urgency, now demanded everything at once. On balance I was encouraged that in many cases black-white dealings were less like warfare than like bargaining sessions. I thought it conceivable that many liberal blacks, like white blue-collar workers, might turn conservative someday. The thought was premature.

In 1965 Watts exploded. I visited the area later and could hardly believe that these neat houses, these seemingly quiet, palm-dotted streets, a setting that might be envied by millions elsewhere in the world, could have been the breeding ground for such rage. Two years after Watts came the Newark riots, with twenty-six people dead.

Six days later it was Detroit's turn. Blacks stormed through the streets, looting stores and torching buildings (most of them black owned). Lyndon Johnson reluctantly sent in federal troops. After more than a week the toll was put at forty-three killed, five thousand people homeless, more than one thousand buildings and nearly three thousand businesses destroyed. Explanations of why it had happened ranged from conspiracy theories about outside agitators to the standard diagnosis that black despair was to blame. "We have left some Americans behind," said Walter Reuther, head of the United Auto Workers. "Those Americans do not feel a part of society and therefore don't behave like responsible people."

True enough, I thought. Yet most of the looters arrested were not unemployed, not from the most miserable parts of the black community. Tens of millions of federal dollars had been poured into Detroit by a highly sympathetic administration.

I remembered the theory that revolutions happen not when things are at their worst, but when conditions are getting better. LBJ certainly earned no thanks from black extremists. H. Rap Brown called the president "a wild mad dog, an outlaw from Texas" for sending "honky cracker federal troops into Negro communities to kill black people." In a famous line he pronounced violence as American as cherry pie.

· · ·

I BEGAN TO READ James Baldwin, who in 1963 had published his overpowering jeremiad, *The Fire Next Time*. "At the root of the Negro problem," Baldwin wrote, "is the necessity of the white man to find a way of living with the Negro in order to live with himself. . . ." Years later James Baldwin came to lunch at the Time & Life Building. By then he was a celebrated writer and was living much of the time in Paris. But he was still the nervous creature of almost fetuslike fragility, and he was as incensed about the black condition as ever.

"Perhaps the best way to tell you what I mean," he began in his melodious tones, "is to tell you that I have been in your kitchens." Our group alternately stared at him or at the crisp tablecloths, the gleaming china and silver in front of us. "My mother was a cleaning woman, you see, and sometimes when I was a child, she would take me with her when she went to clean your kitchens. So I have seen your kitchens, you know, but you have never seen mine." As my colleague Otto Friedrich later reminisced, he was "passionate, witty, rueful, prophetic." Baldwin recalled that there came a point in his youth when he "could not discover any principled reason for not becoming a criminal" because he was "icily determined never to make my peace with the ghetto and to die and go to Hell before I would let any white man spit on me." When he was a boy, he told us, blacks wanted to escape being black by trying to straighten their "nappy" hair with hard brushes and pomades. "One was always being mercilessly scrubbed and polished as if in hope that the stain could thus be washed away. . . . But," said Baldwin, "no more": blacks would no longer succumb to the white image of them and of what was beautiful.

"This," he said, "had everything to do with the rise of Africa in world affairs. At the time that I was growing up, Negroes in this country were taught to be ashamed of Africa. We were told that Africa had never contributed anything to civilization." He rejected the Black Muslim notion of racial separatism, and he did not agree with Malcolm X's pronouncement that "Africa is my home." But he nevertheless asserted the new pride many blacks felt in the continent of their origin.

It was one thing, it seemed to me, to emphasize neglected black history, but it was preposterous to claim—as some black nationalists did—that science and algebra required "a black perspective" or that studying Swahili was as important for young American blacks as mastering English. Al Murray said: "I see no point in learning Swahili, Afro haircuts and quaint costumes. I'm not about to go sifting for my African ancestors. For my purpose, I go back to 1619 or whenever it was that cargo of the first twenty blacks was dropped in Virginia. Once they came here, they became Americans and you had the birth of the blues—let us say—which the Africans have no connection with. The essence of the black experience in America is in that art form. African music doesn't vary. They don't riff."

I realized that Murray's view was becoming unfashionable, but I found it convincing. It was reinforced for me during an Africa trip Beverly and I took in 1966.

I KEPT LOOKING for that past African civilization that, Baldwin and others argued, had been so shamefully ignored by the West. I found one example of it in Ethiopia. Addis Ababa seemed suspended in an era of mud huts and strolling goats with an overlay of Mercedes limousines. Everywhere street hawkers sold scrolls depicting the saga of the queen of Sheba journeying to King Solomon. Emperor Haile Selassie was still on the throne he had first occupied thirty-six years before; he was only fifty-four but seemed much older. I dimly remembered him from my childhood, when I had seen newsreels as he stood before the League of Nations, pleading in vain against Mussolini's invasion. He was as straight backed as a statue, naturally dignified, shrewd and totally unembarrassed in defending his kingdom's minimal progress toward modernity. "Freedom," he said, "is dangerous." I asked him about the changes he had seen since the beginning of his long reign. His dried mask of a face smiled, and he said with quite a touch of biblical poetry: "I have seen the great become small, the small become great; I have seen good destroy evil and evil destroy good. I have seen how little history changes." Then he rose and gestured toward a bookshelf at his back: "To really answer your question, I would have to read all those volumes." He pointed to a set of the Great Books series edited by Robert Hutchins and Mortimer Adler. Suddenly I imagined Mortimer's stocky, ripe form behind the emperor's spear-thin figure, quoting Aristotle. I failed to see how the past represented by the emperor could be pertinent to blacks in the modern world.

A similar thought struck me when we were shown around the Zimbabwe ruins (from which the new name for Rhodesia was later taken). No one was sure who had built this temple city, probably in the fifteenth century. It had been skillfully erected without mortar. But as my guides pointed to these mysterious remains in pride, as evidence of a glorious past, I reflected that these structures, for all their grandeur, dated from a time when the Pyramids were ancient, when the Acropolis was old, and when Chartres was no longer new. I could not fight down a sense of Western superiority and had to remind myself that civilizations develop at different paces.

When whites arrived in Africa in significant numbers during the fifteenth and sixteenth centuries, most of the continent had reached roughly the Iron Age. Since then the growth of technology and culture in Africa had been sharply limited. It was easy, and surely accurate in part, to blame the brutal shocks of the slave trade and the deliberate retarding policies of the colonial powers. I rejected the argument, heard over and over again from whites during my trip, that the Africans were unfit to create advanced societies. But I also rejected the notion pressed by some black nationalists that African civilization was just as advanced as the West's, only different. We were still some years away from the spurious claims that black Africa via Egypt was really the source of European civilization. For the present, Africa and the West intermingled in curious ways.

In Lagos I found a Jewish stage director from Berlin who had lived among the Yorubas as a quasi chief and believed his wife had been saved from cancer by the tribe's juju. In Abidjan a white psychiatrist referred certain cases he could not cope with to a juju man. The juju man, in turn, sent mental cases beyond the power of his magic to the psychiatrist.

If the African past offered a single legacy, it was tribalism. That was

the very antithesis of a modern society, and many African leaders themselves deplored it. Jomo Kenyatta, the Mau Mau leader who was now
president of Kenya and the very incarnation of the tribal father figure,
told me with a majestic sweep of his ceremonial fly whisk: "Tribalism
will disappear with education and development." I am not sure that he
meant it, but if so, he was wrong. The tribe, with its reassuring sense of
identity and community, endured. Officials in modern offices, modern
clothes and modern cars would say casually about each other, "He is a
Yoruba," or, "He is a Hausa." It was as if every African bore an invisible
identification mark on his face—invisible only to untutored Western
eyes.

We found a different kind of tribalism in South Africa. For years I
had heard from Beverly about life in South Africa, which she herself
had known only from her parents' stories and from the trip she had
taken there before our marriage. Her accounts had contained many
themes: the romance of the veldt and beautiful horses and endless land
on her father's spread, of which he still dreamed on Riverside Drive in
Manhattan; the blacks and their loyalty and their responses to kindness,
all reminiscent of certain idyllic versions of the old South, but also their
brutal exploitation in the cities and their serflike condition imposed by
apartheid. One of Beverly's uncles was a Johannesburg physician, another sat in the South African parliament, a member of the United
Party, a timidly liberal organization dominated by South Africans of
English origin as against the Afrikaner Nationalists who ran the government. The uncles and their families were good people and typical of the
Jewish community, largely anglicized and cautiously progressive. They
conceded that the apartheid system was bad but felt that it could be
changed only gradually because the blacks weren't ready for power.
Everything—the veldt and the hills, the motor cars, the modern factories and the busy shopping streets—was shadowed by the race question.

Yet the majority of South Africans constructed a separate reality far
more fantastic than anything I had experienced in black Africa. There
was a quality of logical insanity about the whole scheme of the "homelands," or separate ministates in which the blacks were supposed to be
segregated on a fraction of South Africa's land.

The exquisite, birdlike novelist Nadine Gordimer said of the home-land strategy: "While other countries want to detribalize, our government, in effect, wants to retribalize. The policy is to turn the blacks into foreigners in their own country."

Talking to blacks, Beverly and I found, was as difficult as talking to Russians in the Soviet Union; there was a similar pall of fear, with informers and Special Branch agents assumed to be lurking everywhere. I was reminded of the Soviets' internal passports by the infamous system of "passbooks," which had to be carried by blacks at all times. The ultimate irony was that whites themselves had now been ordered to carry identity books, suggesting that the jailer had become entwined inextricably with the jailed.

Because *Time* was considered too critical of the regime, the magazine was not allowed to have a bureau or a full-time American correspondent throughout most of the sixties. We returned to South Africa in 1976, when *Time* was allowed to reopen a bureau.

I did not believe that "one man, one vote" was possible in the near future, but I thought that some system of weighted voting would happen. I wrote as much in *Time,* and that statement made headlines in the South African press; fortunately some papers also quoted my scathing criticism of the regime. I recalled what one of Beverly's uncles had told us during our earlier trip: "We are trying to hold down this force of the black man in our country with all our might. And we can probably do it in our lifetime. But it's bound to burst out someday, and in a terrible way. We are buying time for ourselves at the expense of our children and grandchildren." He would not have believed it possible, nor would I have, that within the time of his children a black man named Nelson Mandela, then in jail, would be president of South Africa after a one-man, one-vote election.

Both trips left me with the renewed conviction that black nationalism was ultimately a dead end for American blacks. Taken to its logical end, it could lead only to a black version of apartheid.

CHAPTER TWENTY-FOUR

O NE ISSUE ON WHICH MORE WHITES were beginning to agree with blacks, in the late sixties, was Vietnam. Disproportionate numbers of blacks were fighting, lacking the college exemptions of white middle-class youth. Black leaders felt that the money spent for the war could be better used in the ghettos.

"No Vietnamese ever called me nigger" was a slogan often seen on placards at peace demonstrations. The statement hardly stood up as a logical argument, but it contained emotional logic. It was now widely said that the war overseas and poverty at home were linked. The charge was that both sprang from the same basic moral flaws in American society, especially racism.

I thought the argument was glib and wrongheaded. The war was motivated by a certain conception of the Communist threat that had little to do with racial feelings. The misery of the inner cities was caused by many complex factors of which racism was an undeniable but limited part.

Still, the antiwar movement and the civil rights movement seemed to converge. The black protest increasingly became a model for other causes, and whites who felt victimized saw themselves symbolically as blacks. Norman Mailer had pointed the way in his 1957 essay "The

White Negro," in which he compared the status of the "hipster," as outsider and outcast, to the fate of the blacks. Feminists were making similar comparisons. The writer Paul Goodman complained that his homosexuality "made me a nigger."

It was martyrdom by association, borrowed victimhood. There was also borrowed revolution. The word was used frantically, and much too casually, especially by journalists. The black, the youth, the feminist, the musical, the sexual, the environmental revolution. Occasionally they seemed to converge into one large rebellion, but mostly they were separate streams of marchers moving in their own parades.

Those parades kept demanding attention through their chants and shouts and slogans—and especially their music. When I first heard the Beatles, on records, they did not exactly suggest a radical new era. Fuerbringer proposed them as Men of the Year for 1965, and I thought he was joking. (The eventual choice was General William Westmoreland.) I was surprised when later I read about a large student protest rally at the University of California, Berkeley, where some of the leaders started to sing the old union hymn "Solidarity Forever." Since hardly anyone knew the words, the crowd jubilantly burst into "We All Live in a Yellow Submarine." It was too easy to assume that this song represented the extent of youthful rebellion.

Bob Dylan was a different matter. I was captivated by his lyricism even as I was startled by his radical preachments. In his most prophetic song, "The Times They Are A-Changin'," he expressed a sweeping antiauthority mood when he told "senators and congressmen" that if they couldn't help, they should get out of the way. He addressed parents similarly, telling them not to criticize what they could not understand—"Your sons and your daughters are beyond your command. . . ."

Innumerable similar warnings were conveyed by other artists. The message aside, I could not grasp why groups had to be called Jefferson Airplane, the Grateful Dead, the Doors, Moby Grape and Procul Harum. If, as I always believed, changes in music were linked to changes in society, we were headed for a spell of bedlam.

In the mid-sixties I visited my first discotheque, Arthur, in Manhattan. The place was jammed, dark, with Mondrianish wall decorations barely discernible in the gloom, and the sound was overwhelming, all-enveloping, like massed drums wired directly into the brain.

At his concerts Jimi Hendrix simulated sex and orgasm with various musical instruments, climaxing by smashing his guitar and setting it on fire. I saw Jim Morrison and the Doors on television—on *The Ed Sullivan Show*—which bravely tried to keep up with the times. In his hoarse, colorless voice he sang "Light My Fire," to my ears a monotonous, organ-grinder tune: he had been instructed by the squeamish Sullivan to bowdlerize some of the lyrics that suggested getting high on sex and drugs. He disobeyed.

By comparison, Elvis's gyrations, a decade ago, seemed almost touchingly innocent.

SEX WAS INCREASINGLY seen in political terms as the ultimate weapon of freedom; I thought that was placing too heavy and serious a burden on it. I found it fascinating that sociologists and more or less progressive clergymen were attempting to construct new standards. They came down to "situation ethics" typified by Lester A. Kirkendall, who declared in *Premarital Intercourse and Interpersonal Relationships:* "The moral decision will be the one which works toward the creation of trust, confidence and integrity in relationships." Of what possible practical use could such advice be to people, young or otherwise, in real life?

Dr. Alan Guttmacher, the venerable crusader for Planned Parenthood, told an audience of tenth- and twelfth-graders that they must have "a feeling of sexual responsibility. Don't enter premarital sex lightly. Enter it after deep and searching thought. If in doubt, don't. Premarital sex should be entered into as a faithful episode. You choose your mate carefully and remain faithful at the time." He also admonished them to use effective protection. When I read that quote I thought it was very close to what a psychologist had called "permissiveness with affection." I told Beverly: "What this morality comes down to is love plus contraceptives, love for a while, anyway." Soon afterward we happened to meet Guttmacher at the house of mutual friends. Beverly confronted him at once: "I'm very glad you told them, 'If in doubt, don't,' " she said. "But how are young people supposed to know when they feel responsible? Are they really going to stop and think deep thoughts while they are wrestling on the living room sofa? And what do you mean by 'faithful at the time'? Is that faithful for three days or three weeks or what?"

Guttmacher, a tall, white-haired, avuncular man, answered gently: "I know it sounds a little vague and it puts quite a burden on the young. But what's the alternative? If you tell them it is terrible to have sex before marriage, most of them won't listen to you, and they will just lie to you about what they're doing."

My own upbringing had been in a time and place where the rules were rigidly proclaimed and quietly broken. I thought of my college years when they were absurdly, desperately bent, but I always believed that society needed a certain amount of hypocrisy to function. Perhaps rules were only a kind of bargaining position with one's conscience, but they still made for a degree of restraint. Or so it seemed. At the time of the Guttmacher conversation, our children were thirteen, eleven and nine, so the subject was still theoretical for us—although not much longer.

In traditional sexist fashion, during the next few years I was not particularly concerned about what our son, Peter, might be up to but felt quite differently about his sisters. Even as a child Mandy had a way of keeping her life to herself; not so Lisa, the youngest. By the time she was about to graduate from high school, Lisa informed us that she had fallen in love with a young man who lived out of town and had invited him to commencement. She then approached Beverly and me separately to ask whether he could stay in her room during his visit. As it turned out we told her exactly the same thing, without previous consultation: we didn't object on moral grounds, but we didn't like the idea aesthetically. What did I mean by that? Lisa wanted to know. I was about to say, "You don't do this sort of thing in your parents' house," but I realized that the inevitable retort would be: "So you would prefer we did it somewhere else behind your back?" Besides, I knew that appealing to aesthetics was a cop-out, masking a deeper moral ambiguity. Part of me was motivated by the atavistic instinct to protect my daughter from this

marauding stranger; part of me was saddened by my child's growing up
and into the joyful and painful chaos of life. At the same time, I had to
face it: my moral convictions were simply no longer strong enough to
say flatly: "This is wrong." I gave in, and so did Beverly. After Lisa and
the boy, with elaborate casualness, retired to her room, we faced each
other in the living room.

"I don't believe we're letting her do this," I said.

"What else could we do, really?" said Beverly. "I didn't tell you at the
time, but three years ago she came to me and asked about boys and sex
and was it all right to go to bed with them. Some of her friends boasted
that they had. I told her it could be a wonderful thing, but that she
should wait. I told her love should be part of it."

" 'Permissiveness with affection,' " I quoted. "Are you telling me that
this is love down the hall? That they thought about it deeply and
responsibly, as old Guttmacher says they should?"

"I don't know," said Beverly. "They probably believed they did."

The romance lasted for a few months. In our eyes the episode was
typical of what was being experienced by countless parents who surren-
dered to the inevitable in much the same way. I also understood that the
dilemma went far beyond sex. A great many members of my generation
were morally uncertain about other issues and did not really believe in,
or live by, all the principles we professed. The young sensed it and
trapped us in our own contradictions.

This was evident again and again in their protest movements and
especially in the campus rebellion.

THE TIME & LIFE Building sometimes struck me as an embattled
tower assaulted by howling winds of disturbing new forces. As journalists—the average age of the editorial staff was probably around forty—
we tried manfully, if not desperately, to keep track of what was going on
in America, like weathermen dutifully taking notes on a storm in progress. (The word "weathermen" would eventually assume a special and
ominous significance.)

In 1966 *Time* put on its cover, without illustration, in big black type, the question "Is God Dead?" The story explored the crisis of religious faith, the spread of atheism (including Christian atheism) and the effect doubt might have in stimulating new belief. The answer to the cover's question was, "No, not really," but it outraged countless readers. Peter was then a student at Manhattan's Collegiate School, which held a daily chapel session, although its religious character had been planed down to mere interdenominational pieties. To his horror and embarrassment, he heard the headmaster thunder from the pulpit against *Time* magazine's blasphemy, which to him was tantamount to having his father denounced as the devil.

For 1966 the magazine chose, as the Man of the Year, the "under 25" generation. The cover portrait showed a conspicuously clean-cut, young white man, in shirt and tie with a short haircut, and behind him a pretty, perfectly coiffed and made-up white girl, and behind her a black and an Asian. The story accurately pointed to the generation's diversity and overall prosperity but took a wildly optimistic view of the Man of the Year's prospects: "He is the man who will land on the moon, cure cancer and the common cold, lay out blight-proof, smog-free cities, enrich the underdeveloped world and, no doubt, write finis to poverty and war." As it turned out, only one of these predictions came true. The story duly noted the slogans "Don't trust anyone over thirty" and "Tell it like it is." It reported, "No adult can or will tell them what earlier generations were told: this is God, this is Good, this is Art, that is Not Done." But it took a remarkably innocent view, including some howlers, such as the statement that despite the pill, the mating habits of the young hadn't changed much and that the new no-touch dancing was asexual. The story also gave a rather bizarre description of the American soldier in Vietnam: "From the moment he arrives (usually aboard a comfortable troop ship), he is swiftly moved into and out of combat in planes, helicopters or trucks. He has a camera, transistor, hot meals and regular mail. If he is hit, he can be hospitalized in 20 minutes; if he gets nervous, there are chaplains and psychiatrists on call. It is little wonder that he fights so well." I was not involved in that story, nor in the one we did a mere six months later. (If I had been, I'm not sure they would have shown much more insight.)

The second piece was a story on the hippies. The cover picture offered a psychedelic mélange of long hair, love beads and guitars. The article quoted Toynbee to the effect that the hippies were "a red warning light for the American way of life." Mostly the piece tried, with almost touching earnestness, to provide a guide to hippiedom for the square reader and the presumably baffled country out there. It explained the derivation of the word from the old "hep" and gave definitions of such terms as "crashing" and "rapping" and "spaced" and a kind of *Baedeker* to Haight Ashbury, the San Francisco mecca of hippiedom. As in the previous story, there was much stress on idealism: "It could be argued that in their independence of material possessions and their emphasis on peacefulness and honesty, hippies lead considerably more virtuous lives than the great majority of their fellow citizens." But where the earlier story had barely alluded to drugs, this one bravely tried to face up to the phenomenon from pot to LSD, from "libidinal kicks" to "eucharistic" attempts to find God. The reporting was, at times, highly naive: "Once the [pot user] learns the number of puffs necessary to reach his 'high' he rarely takes more." I knew from observation that this was not accurate. I myself smoked marijuana from time to time and found it mildly pleasant but could never really develop a taste for it. To my over forty sensibility it simply could not replace the dry martini.

THE STORMS OUTSIDE did not often penetrate the Time & Life Building. Yes, there were miniskirts, long hair and the occasional smell of pot in the stairwells. There were heated debates, especially about Vietnam, but few signs of rebellion. An exception was Andrew Kopkind, a young correspondent and writer who went on to become one of the authentic radical journalists of the decade. He was a pleasant, well-mannered young man with fleshy features and a somewhat protuberant, moist lower lip that gave him a petulant air. He came from that impeccable suburb Greenwich, Connecticut, where his father was a prominent Republican who had been outraged, as Andy recalled, when his son was spotted at a Stevenson rally. I was startled when he informed me, one day in 1965, that he was quitting.

He was dissatisfied with his job and with *Time*, which he said encouraged a kind of distancing and cynicism and seemed to rob him of the capacity to care. Writing or reporting for *Time*, he felt, was like being a junior executive for Hunt's Foods or Unilever or any other large corporation. Although he had always been a "leftie," he had gone to work for *Time* because there had seemed to be no alternative to a mainstream career. During his San Francisco assignment the budding Free Speech Movement at Berkeley, just across the bay, had felt far away. "I thought it was just a bunch of kids, and I wasn't interested in it. Just panty raids, a little bit more than that." But he was gradually won over. "It wasn't Vietnam," he recalled later. "It wasn't issues, but the possibilities of action and of people working to effect change in their own lives. I got very interested in organizing, in people organizing; young, very confident, relatively unsophisticated, yet very sophisticated in certain ways." After he left *Time* Kopkind went to work for the *New Republic* and covered the civil rights struggles in Selma. What gripped him "wasn't hearing Martin speak at the church or anything like that. It was the organizers of the sharecroppers and how they were helping people to transform their lives. And I thought to myself, this was exactly what I'd been thinking of all my life. A couple of months later I asked, Is anybody doing this up north? They said to go over and see this guy Tom Hayden in Newark. I spent five days there and that really got me involved."

I regretted Kopkind's leaving because I liked him and considered him very talented. At first I classified him as a familiar type, the young rebel against his well-to-do, middle-class background. That was accurate enough, but there was some new accent to his radicalism. I gradually began to explore the intellectual background and leadership of what was becoming known as the New Left.

I kept hearing more about Tom Hayden, generally regarded as its spiritual father. Hayden came from a modest, middle-class, midwestern background and started his education at a Roman Catholic School in Michigan, where the notorious Father Coughlin was pastor. The nuns, he later recalled, "would make you kneel in a Christian position and then beat you to teach you a Christian lesson. It didn't work. But those

nuns were in robes and you felt you couldn't rebel." Hayden made up
for it later. He became a founder of the Students for a Democratic
Society, and in 1962, while a graduate student at Ann Arbor, he unveiled a long manifesto before a meeting in Port Huron, Michigan.
Much revised, the "Port Huron Statement" became the charter of the
New Left. Solemn and turgid, it recited the evils of American society,
the misdeeds and corruption of the political parties, government, the
military and business. It called for a new politics. I was troubled by the
vague, airy demands for the end of poverty and for universal brotherhood unaccompanied by realistic solutions. As for what was perhaps the
manifesto's central prescription, participatory democracy, I considered it
wrongheaded and impractical; modern society, I thought, was too vast
and too complicated to permit governments along the lines of the town
meeting or the Greek city-state.

C. Wright Mills, the iconoclastic sociologist who died of a heart attack
at forty-six, was a strong influence on Hayden. Mills's picture of a bored,
alienated nation evoked Hayden's father, "proud in his starched white
collar, occupying his accountant's niche above the union work force and
below the real decision makers, penciling in numbers by day, drinking
in front of the television at night, muttering about the world to no one
in particular."

I understood why Hayden and other New Leftists were drawn to
Mills, but I resented their attempt to adopt Camus. I did not think they
deserved him, and his tragedian's cloak seemed entirely too large for
them. I had been fascinated by Camus's *The Plague,* his parable of the
Nazi occupation of France, and by "The Myth of Sisyphus," his haunting
essay on the human condition. I was captivated by Camus's inability to
accept formal religion while recognizing the need for religion. Unlike
Sartre, he had recognized the evil of Communism. Like Sartre, he believed in the absurdity of life, a concept that could be shallow, and even
vulgar, as expressed by many others, but assumed in his works a certain
heroic quality. His existentialist insistence that despite this absurdity
one must act, one must keep pushing the stone up the hill even if it
inevitably rolls down again, seemed convincing in his words but hollow
as rendered by Hayden and other New Left activists.

My darkest bête noire among the gurus of the New Left was Herbert Marcuse, a German-born academic who had come to the United States as a refugee from the Nazis in 1934, at the age of forty-six, and taught at various universities, ending up as professor of philosophy at the University of California at San Diego. He emerged from almost total obscurity only when the New Left took him up. His reputation became international; demonstrating students in Rome carried banners reading: "Marx, Marcuse, Mao."

Many followers of the New Left simply saw freedom as the absence of restraints. The shrill insistence on "freedom *now*," "peace *now*" and "nonnegotiable demands" struck me as a tantrum rather than a revolution: the anarchy of the kindergarten.

Marcuse, by contrast, was much more sophisticated and insidious. He was truly Orwellian in his message that what most Americans consider to be freedom is really a technique of control and subjugation. In a society of "total administration," he wrote, "the exercise of political rights (such as voting, letter-writing to the press, Senators, etc., protest demonstrations . . .)" only strengthen the system by creating the illusion of democratic institutions.

True lovers of humanity, Marcuse argued, had the right and duty to suppress all those not of the Left. People with wrong ideas should be denied "freedom of speech and assembly." Marcuse's message had practical consequences. The writer and educator Lionel Abel quoted a University of Buffalo graduate student who explained why demonstrations and protests had succeeded: "Our movement wasn't organized democratically. We kicked the Dow [recruiting] people off the campus though they had every right to be there." It was Marcuse, this student added, who more than anyone else "gave us the intellectual courage to be intolerant." John Dewey's disciple Sidney Hook attacked Marcuse in a debate at Rutgers University: Would he prefer blacks (and others) to be free to choose their own way of life? Or would he prefer them not to be free if what they chose was, in Marcuse's eyes, the wrong, bourgeois and consumerist values? Marcuse replied: "I would prefer that the blacks did not have the right to choose wrongly." While Dewey would not have approved of Marcuse, it seemed to me that Dewey's relativism had prepared the ground for Marcuse and undermined the standards needed to resist his ideas.

LUCE WAS STILL very much a presence and a voice in the Time & Life Building, even though he and Clare spent a great deal of time in their house in Phoenix. He remained curious about everything new. He and Clare even tried LSD, with the guidance of a psychiatrist friend. "It's the most wonderful thing," he said afterward. "You look at that glass on the table and see shimmering colors on either side of it." He also reported that he heard magnificent music and thought that a certain cactus he had never liked suddenly looked beautiful.

Still, he was puzzled and troubled by much of what was happening on the American scene. Driving through the Haight Ashbury district, he looked at the oddly dressed youths and asked the *Time* correspondent who accompanied him, "What are their goals? What are their motives?" Another time I ran into him in the lobby of the Time & Life Building, and he took me off to a coffee shop and said: "I want to talk to you about this alienation business. Everybody is talking about how the young are alienated. I don't get it. Have you ever felt alienated?"

"No, not really," I replied. But then I had been young two decades before. I was about to add that I had often felt alienated as a refugee, but Luce was already rushing to another subject. I also could have added that I was once again getting restless at *Time,* and did not see where my career was leading, and occasionally, desultorily, I looked for other jobs. Once, I even put out feelers when I heard that the head of a network news division might be leaving, though I was hardly qualified for that post. I sometimes discussed my situation with Ben Sonnenberg, who had befriended me; he liked to include in his circle younger men whom he considered promising; besides, his daughter, Helen Tucker, and Beverly were close friends.

The son of poor Russian immigrants, Sonnenberg had moved quickly through journalism and public relations work for charities to commercial publicity and re-created himself as an Edwardian gentleman. He wore bowler hats and shirts with white stiff collars and checked dickeys, evoking a Max Beerbohm cartoon. For some years he had practiced his trade only among the largest corporations and richest individuals; he had made enough money to live in a magnificent thirty-seven-room mansion on Gramercy Park South. He liked to suggest that he knew everybody's secrets and probably did, his conversation running along the lines of "You know, of course, that she was a high-priced hooker before she ran into the count." His speech was florid and not above mixed metaphors. He once said, "I supply the Listerine to the commercial dandruff on the shoulders of corporations." In his later years he told me: "I'm really in the immortality business. There are these old men who want to find interesting ways to be remembered and are willing to pay millions for it. I supply the ideas." (One of his ideas involved the banker Robert Lehman's gift of a superior art collection to the Metropolitan Museum of Art, where it occupies the Lehman Wing, surely immortality of sorts.)

During our occasional lunches Ben would offer career advice, which was always enigmatic. "Henry," he might say, "there's this girl walking down the street in a red dress, swinging her hips. All the boys are after her. The trouble with you is that you don't wear a red dress." What he meant to say, of course, was that I was not aggressive enough in promoting myself. "You're doing it the hard way," he said, another time. "From what I hear, you just work hard and you're good at what you do, but . . ." He left the words dangling in midair, plainly conveying that this wasn't enough. He just shook his head, and his walrus mustache seemed to droop even more than usual.

For years I had not really aspired to the top job at *Time*, but one day I realized, looking at the likely competition, that it might well be within reach, after Fuerbringer had his run. Two other contenders had been eliminated by Fuerbringer, who had persuaded Luce to move them to *Life*. Clearly his own choice to succeed him eventually was James Keogh, an able journalist from Omaha, Nebraska, as conservative in outlook as Fuerbringer but not nearly as imaginative. I considered him somewhat square and once described him, unkindly, as the Lawrence Welk of *Time* magazine. Nevertheless he represented real competition.

I discussed my ambitions with Beverly, who was skeptical. As she had told a close friend, "He's short; let's face it, he's fat; and he's Jewish. Can you see him as a boss of all those WASPs at *Time*?" When I heard about the remark I confronted her with it, indignantly brushing aside the relevance of my height or shape but conceding that my Jewishness might indeed be an obstacle. There were relatively few Jews on the editorial staff and virtually none on the business side. I talked about this with Dick Clurman, himself a Jew. "Harry isn't anti-Semitic," said Dick. "It's just that he hasn't known many Jews. He has a sense of their being different, but that is not the same as prejudice. He often asks me about this or that issue: 'What do you think of it as a Jew?' I always have to tell him that I don't think 'as a Jew.' "

Where a sense of people being different ends and prejudice begins is a very thorny question. But Luce was genuinely interested in Judaism and fairly ignorant about it. Once he asked me to look at an article someone had submitted involving an Israeli high-court decision about what constitutes a Jew. The writer felt that the decision was narrow, exclusive, nationalistic, and did a disservice to Judaism, a "universal religion." I'm afraid I was moved to send Luce a memo, of almost Talmudic length and complexity, trying to explain that Judaism was a mixture of faith, race and nationality and that subtracting any one element would destroy the whole. Judaism was *not* a universal religion except in the sense that Jews, dispersed across the world, might be seen as living reminders of the one God and witnesses to the Old Testament. Or, perhaps, I added, just as a creative irritant. I do not recall whether Luce ever read or reacted to my attempt to educate him, but he was angered that in some quarters he was considered anti-Semitic. Long afterward Clare told me Harry was really bothered by the accusation. "I remember one day he came home looking very happy and said, 'I've just met a bright young Jew named Grunwald who works for *Time* and will someday take that monkey off my back.' "

At the time of those lunches with Clurman I had little idea of how Luce felt about me, but one day I received an invitation to dinner from him at his Fifth Avenue apartment. The conversation—we were alone—was relaxed, or as relaxed as it ever could be with Luce. He talked foreign policy while I felt cramped with suspense. Finally he said:

"A little bird tells me that you are very restless." The little bird obviously had been Clurman. I admitted that I was, not quite knowing where I was headed.

"Don't take this as a formal offer yet, but how would you like to be the managing editor of *Fortune*?"

I said I was surprised and flattered but didn't really think that I would be right for the job and vice versa. Luce did not insist. Getting back to the subject of *Time*, I said, "I'm sure Otto is going to be around for quite some time still, but afterward it seems to me Jim Keogh is clearly in line for the job." Thinking of Ben Sonnenberg, I felt that this was about as much "red dress" as I could display. After a few moments Luce said: "I don't think you should take that for granted."

It was a clear signal that I was at least in the running. I left the apartment elated. I couldn't wait to tell Beverly the news and called her from the corner telephone. A year and a half later I was appointed assistant managing editor of *Time*, alongside Jim Keogh. Now our competition for the top job on the magazine, managing editor, was on in earnest.

In my new job I performed various editing chores, supervised the preparation of cover art and sometimes filled in for Fuerbringer when he was away. In February 1967 Henry Luce died of a heart attack. My son, Peter, then thirteen, said: "You loved Mr. Luce, didn't you, Daddy?" Saddened and shocked, I realized I had. Amazingly, Fuerbringer, echoing his decision regarding John Kennedy's death, thought that Luce should not be on the *Time* cover. But the reaction on all sides, including the Luce family, was indignant. Prodded by Donovan, Fuerbringer gave in. So, for the first and only time, Luce's face appeared on the magazine he had created.

The funeral took place at the Madison Avenue Presbyterian Church, and the main eulogy was spoken by Dr. David Read, Luce's pastor. After the predictable tribute to Luce's role in America, Read spoke at length about Luce as a man of faith and his quite literal belief in Christ that lay behind his lifelong fascination with theologians, including, Read noted, Teilhard de Chardin. I remembered Luce discussing enthusiastically Teilhard's notion that, as a result of vast new knowledge, we were headed for a great breakthrough toward a new order of being and that man was now partly in charge of his own evolution. That suggested a collaboration between man and God, and it occurred to me that Luce had seen himself—I believe without blasphemy—as God's collaborator.

From Hedley Donovan came the most apt words: "He was endlessly dissatisfied with the state of his own knowledge, with the performance of his magazines, with the performance of his country. And he saw clear remedies for the glaring gaps and ills; he was a malcontent of profound and unswerving optimism."

At the end of the service, walking toward the exit, pushed by the crowd, I found myself next to Clare Luce. Her stepson, Hank, was with her, but she took my arm for extra support; I was surprised because we were not close. Considering what I knew about their quite separate lives, let alone his affair with Lady Jean, she impressed me as more shaken than I had expected. As we neared the doors Clare removed her arm, visibly pulled herself together, straightened her shoulders and walked out into the blaze of the photographers' flash bulbs, a lifelong trouper and star.

In the flood of tributes and evaluations, critics continued to insist that he had almost single-handedly started the cold war and was mainly responsible for Washington's China policy, a preposterous exaggeration. Inevitably he was described as the last American press lord. He was also one of the increasingly rare public figures who combined a high degree of intellect with earnest piety and unembarrassed idealism about his country. Andrew Heiskell later said that Luce died at the right time because "the principles that had guided us for decades had eroded so much as to be meaningless," not for all Americans, but for enough of them to make it a different country. "In today's America," said Heiskell, "Harry would have been miserable." But Luce had continued to believe in America's mission. In his last speech given shortly before he died, at the University of California at Santa Barbara, Luce noted that a constitution was being written in Saigon that would include guarantees of freedom of expression and an independent judiciary. "Nothing of this sort is anywhere to be found in Asian tradition," said Luce. He affirmed his belief that democracy, as defined and championed by America, would prevail. Clearly he still believed in the American Century. Some thought that his death coincided with and symbolized its end and that it was expiring amid the bloodletting in Vietnam and the uproar at home. I did not think that the American Century was over, but maintaining that concept in 1967 was infinitely more difficult than when Luce first proclaimed it as a rallying cry for what would become America's triumphant role in World War II.

Chapter Twenty-five

W̲ITH LUCE'S DEATH Hedley Donovan came fully into his own. He was to remain in his post as editor in chief for fifteen years. He was tall, handsome, with ice blue eyes that could be disconcerting in their piercing clarity. The son of a Minnesota mining engineer who did not retire until the age of ninety-one, Hedley seemed indestructible and full of the virtues of his home state, which he remembered as an idyll of strength, honesty, self-reliance and opportunity. A Rhodes scholar and World War II naval intelligence officer based in Washington, he came to Time Inc. about the same time I did and rose to the managing editorship of *Fortune* in a short seven years. While he was Luce's deputy and then editor in chief, I often came into contact with him. He was straightforward, fair and utterly firm in his convictions, which were, if anything, harder to shake than Luce's. When he disapproved of something in a piece of copy, he would say mildly, "I have a bother with this," which I found more chilling than any harsher criticism. "Foolish" was one of his favorite words of condemnation, more devastating than an obscenity would have been (I never heard him use one). Among the things he considered most foolish, and against which he crusaded tirelessly, were implausible and unanchored statistics, such as how many man-hours were lost each year to the common cold.

He knew exactly who he was and despised personal publicity as unseemly and unnecessary. He and I shared a love of opera, but I could never quite keep up with his passion for betting, the more complicated the parlays the better. He had a great gift of silence; during lunches with him I would at first try to fill the long pauses with nervous conversation until I learned better. He was a man of massive calm, and I sometimes fantasized how he would react to Judgment Day. I imagined being summoned to his office by his secretary, and after a long, wordless stretch, while weeping and wailing and gnashing of teeth rose from the distant street below, he would fix me with those cold eyes and say: "Well, what do you think? Is it worth a cover story?"

One of his hobbies was moving boulders on the beach in front of his house in Sands Point, Long Island. Shades of Sisyphus? He would have rejected the comparison as too pessimistic, but I did think his odd pastime spoke of strength and patience. Replacing Luce as "Moses," as he once jokingly put it, was not easy. Luce had been the de facto owner of the company and essentially did what he pleased. He kept the struggling *Sports Illustrated* alive for more than a decade, accepting huge losses before it finally became a success. No chief executive of a public company could have been that cavalier. Though only an employee, however well compensated, Donovan managed to maintain much Lucean authority by sheer strength of character and ability. He firmly maintained editorial independence from the business side, known in the Time-Life vocabulary as the separation of church and state.

Donovan lacked Luce's creative imagination, but he encouraged creativity. One of the most devastating things I ever heard him say, in arguing against the promotion of one of my colleagues, was: "He never says anything that did not appear on the editorial page of *The New York Times*." He was admirable both for his intelligence and his integrity. Mark Donovan once summarized his father's philosophy: "The intelligent thing to do is the moral thing to do." He was a shade or two more liberal than Luce. In his "acceptance speech" on being appointed editor in chief, he clearly alluded to *Time*'s frequent Republican slant and declared: "The vote of Time Inc. should never be considered to be in the pocket of any particular political leader or party." There should never be any "wishy-washy confusion as to what we believe," but Time Inc.

should "have no vested interest in any party as such." In several long conversations with me, before Luce's death, he made it obvious that he thought Fuerbringer's *Time* was too narrow politically and no longer as lively journalistically as it had been. He pressed me for ideas about how the magazine might be changed, and he seemed to like some of my notions about more personal, informal writing and more topics to be treated.

I also found that we were very close to each other's views in the political center, and that we were both getting nervous about the course of the Vietnam War. "I simply don't believe that we must win at any price," he said. "I can imagine a price that would be too high."

Donovan's friendly poker face, and his habit of never saying anything more than was absolutely necessary, kept me from knowing just what he was planning to do or how he really felt about me. A hint came through an accident. Time Inc. was once considering buying up some newspaper properties, and Luce had asked me to give him my views of the present condition of newspapers. I sent him a long report that he passed on to Donovan, who sent it back to Luce with a scrawled note: "Thanks. A brilliant memo." Instead of delivering it to Luce, a copy boy mistakenly put the memo in my "in" box, and I read Hedley's note with a flush of pleasure before sending it quietly on to Luce's office. It was the clearest indication I had so far of what Donovan thought about me, but it was still a long way from indicating that he would pick me as Fuerbringer's successor.

Then one day came an invitation to join him for dinner. He had a bad cold, and the silence in the elevator to the top of the Time & Life Building was broken only by his stentorian sniffles. Over the dimly lit table in the private dining room, Hedley talked about every possible topic until I came to the sickening conclusion that this was not going to be a decisive evening after all, but that, with his wife and children away in Florida, he just wanted some company. Finally, after he had finished his first martini and we were halfway through a semiedible cheese beignet produced by Restaurant Associates, he said calmly: "I wanted to talk about the future of *Time*. I have felt for quite a while that along about now we should move Otto and persuade him to pursue newspaper acquisitions—although he is not eager to do that. I would like you to be the next managing editor." Despite my excitement I managed a small bow over the cheese appetizer. He continued, "I hope you will accept," and I very nearly laughed out loud. It seemed to him, he added, that we saw eye to eye on the course of the magazine, but he wanted to stress that he hoped I would run it a bit more loosely than Fuerbringer, without being a prisoner to the machine. He also hoped that I would keep on Keogh as my deputy.

Hedley then excused himself to go to the bathroom, and I rushed to the telephone—once again—to give Beverly the news. Later he said that he thought the usual term for a *Time* managing editor should be the equivalent of two presidential terms, give or take a year. At the end of that period, he observed, I would still be a relatively young man and there would be any number of interesting things for me to do—writing a column, perhaps—but he could not hold out any particular position that might follow. It was his way of saying that I should not count on eventually succeeding him as editor in chief. Later in the evening Beverly, the kids and I celebrated with champagne. The bottle was flat, and I hoped this would not be an omen.

Fuerbringer was clearly displeased by the end of his tenure and by the choice of his successor, but his demeanor was impeccable. On the last night in the office as managing editor, he dropped in to say good-bye, and it proved to be an almost sentimental moment. The managing editorship of *Time*, he said, was a wonderful job, and he hoped that I would perform it in the way Harry had set it up, with total responsibility for everything. He was telling me not to give up an inch of control, a message slightly different from Donovan's. He said: "Harry used to say that the president of the United States must be willing to kill himself in his job—and the same goes for the M.E. of *Time*. One thing about this job is that everybody expects you to know everything—and is furious when you do."

I did not agree with Fuerbringer's assumption of omniscience, but I shared his view of the work in other respects. I told him truthfully that I thought he had done an outstanding job and thanked him for the opportunities he had given me. He almost patted my back, almost shed a tear—just a shimmer of moisture in his eyes—said he was sure I would do a great job and was gone. Obviously I could not be sure that I *would,* but I was extremely confident.

I felt ready for the task. But I am not sure that I was ready for history. In January 1968 came the Tet offensive in Vietnam. In March Lyndon Johnson announced that he would not seek reelection. In April Martin Luther King Jr. was assassinated. In June, Robert Kennedy. In August the Russians invaded Czechoslovakia. Also in August the Democrats held their chaotic convention in Chicago. All in all it was a tragic year, but it was also, in cold-blooded hindsight, a perfect year to become the editor of a newsmagazine.

To SEE YOURSELF as others see you is a notoriously rare and troubling experience. I went through it several times following my appointment. A year later Richard Pollak, a freelance journalist of wide-ranging credentials, published an article in *Harper's* about that appointment and about what he and many other people took to be the significance. It marked, in his view, a major change in what he called "the House Organ of the American Dream." Pollak quoted an unnamed colleague of mine who recalled that during a spell of gout I had carried a black cane, and together with the wide-brimmed hat I sometimes wore, I struck him as having stepped straight out of Proust: "Charles Swann in the flesh." The colleague continued: "Imagine a Jewish copy boy from NYU coming up through all those six-foot-six Yalies. Incredible!"

I did not see myself in the least Swann-like. As for those six-foot-six Yalies, I would never completely share their world, but some had become good friends, and besides, they no longer really personified an increasingly diverse company.

Pollak had more to say. "The managing editor of *Time* may be the single most influential linear journalist in the world. Early each week, like a virtuoso at some prose-producing Mighty Wurlitzer, he sits down, shoots his cuffs and pulls and pushes stops on 105 correspondents from Washington to Nairobi, ninety editors, writers and reporters in New

York and coveys of fact-hunting, mini-skirted researchers, all of whom seem to be recruited from Alexander Portnoy's fantasies. With super-polymathic vision, he distills the labors of these far-flung forces down to 50,000 words on everything from Biafra to Beethoven and by the middle of the following week his judgments are writ for the magazine's twenty-two million readers."

Overwritten, I thought as I read this. Too much hyperbole. But I was certainly aware of the reach of *Time*, of the huge resources at my disposal and of the responsibility I had assumed. In front of me on the desk stood a round, tin pencil cup that, according to *Time* legend, had belonged to Briton Hadden, the co-founder, and had been passed along from each managing editor to the next, as Fuerbringer had casually explained to me. It was a reminder, if I needed it, of how the world had changed since Hadden's day, or since I first came to work on the magazine.

The greatest single force affecting journalism was, of course, television. It was not only slowly strangling *Life*, but it affected all other publications. *Time* used to give a sense of immediacy and reality by describing what the weather was like during a parade or what the crowd looked like. Now the readers were seeing these things as they were happening. The leading prophet of this transformation was Marshall McLuhan, and Pollak's reference to "linear" journalism was a salute to him. McLuhan was a fascinating if chaotic thinker who started with the undeniable proposition that new means of communication change society, the most notable instances so far being the invention of the printing press and movable type. Electronic communications, he argued, were restoring some of the oral tradition that had been displaced by print and with it the personal, tribal way of living in the "global village." He described television as a "cool" medium, because its low definition drew the viewer in and made him a participant; print, on the other hand, was a "hot" medium that was precise and informative enough to make the reader into a mere observer. (I always thought that the labels could just as easily be reversed.) The printed book was "linear," he explained, while television presented information and images at random. Early in his career as a communications authority, McLuhan had vitriolically attacked the Luce publications as purveyors of "hack work, glossy mediocrity and stereotypical order."

Like many print journalists, I was haunted by McLuhan for years and was eager to meet him. I finally did in 1971 during a trip to Canada. I found a tall, lanky man whose dress and manner seemed far more orderly than his ideas; he spoke in staccato, almost military tones. As he showed me and several colleagues around his home base, the campus of the University of Toronto, he displayed his habit of throwing up ideas as effortlessly as a wet dog throws off drops of water. His connections and prophecies were startling: the assembly line was an extension of Gutenberg, and it would disappear, as would automobiles; work, too, would disappear, and so would spoken language, perhaps to be replaced by a kind of universal consciousness. Television had "Europeanized" America, as evidenced by new concern for dance, plastic arts and architecture, complex cuisine and wine.

Even if he never bothered to offer support for his assertions or to paper over obvious contradictions, I found immense pleasure in his intellectual game. He kept returning to the decline of the linear: We have seen the disappearance of the stag line, the party line, the receiving line and the pencil line from the backs of nylons. ("The end of the line," I ventured.) I was surprised that he considered television a threat to the old picture magazines but not to the thriving newsmagazines, which, he said, resembled television as "mosaics" that involved the reader in the making of meanings.

I came away unconvinced on that point. I always felt the newsmagazine was a distant descendant of the encyclopedia and of the eighteenth century's passion for cataloging and listing. The newsmagazine's department structure carried a subliminal message that a pattern existed in the chaos of the world and that the average reader could make sense of history. I was convinced that linear organization was a law of nature. In journalism, I believed, it was more essential than ever, and I would hoot in triumph when I saw television news programs employ, as they often did, one-two-three subject headings superimposed on the confusion of the tube. But television had indeed changed the reader's sensibility.

In the early 1950s Luce had sent passionate memos complaining that *Time* was losing its all-important "sense of summary," partly because summarizing the news did not allow writers and editors to show off. (Besides, he grumbled, most *Time* stories were "too damn long.") He may have been right at the time, but now, summary was no longer enough. *Time* had to get behind and below the surface of the evening news. Moreover, the magazine looked too staid, too constricted, for a TV generation.

Other forces besides television were pressing on *Time. Newsweek,* long a poor second, had become remarkably good. Under the editorship of Osborn Elliott, a happy defector from *Time*, the magazine was beginning to give us real competition. It was often faster when it came to cover choices, offered signed opinion pieces and beat the drums of advocacy journalism. Daily newspapers had become much better in their cultural coverage. And then—gulp!! amazing!! pow!!—there was the "New Journalism."

The form was invented by Tom Wolfe, a young writer of genteel Virginia background who had become a familiar character on the New York scene in his white suits. As I came to know him—we were never friends but friendly dinner party acquaintances—I was struck by his extreme frugality in conversation. He obviously saved his words for his writing and used his slightly absurd, dandyish appearance as effective camouflage from behind which he observed his surroundings with merciless precision, precision that was heightened by an almost surrealist imagination. In his raucous rebellion against what he considered the fake objectivity and "pale beige tone" of conventional journalism, he developed a delirious style that sometimes suggested James Joyce as rendered in a comic strip. He used eccentric punctuation or no punctuation. Fasces of exclamation points struck the reader on the head, and run-on sentences shuttled him commalessly toward some distant period. The sound effects were spelled out ("Eeeeeeeeeeeeeeeeee!"), exposition was at a minimum, while dialogue proliferated, in the repetitive manner of real speech. In "The Girl of the Year," Wolfe recorded a temporary celebrity, "Baby Jane" Holzer, at a rock concert: "Wait'll you see the Stones! They're so sexy! They're pure sex. They're divine! The

Beatles, well, you know, Paul McCartney—sweet Paul McCartney. You know what I mean. He's such a sweet person. I mean, the Stones are bitter—" Wolfe then added in a typical psychedelic flight: "The words seem to spring from her lungs like some kind of wonderful lavender-yellow Charles Kingsley bubbles."

There were other practitioners of the New Journalism, some with greater literary credentials and fewer stylistic quirks, including Norman Mailer and Truman Capote. There were also Wolfe imitators for whom the New Journalism came down to writing themselves into an article, tediously going on about their reaction to the wallpaper or to being kept waiting. Wolfe remained the master. While he was unfailingly polite, I sometimes imagined him as poking me in the ribs and saying: "How are you fellows at *Time* going to keep up with me? I'm skating circles around you."

Time, which in its own way had rebelled against pale beige journalism and drawn attention to itself with an irreverent, idiosyncratic style, had become too stodgy, too familiar. The writers especially needed a chance to let off steam and have their ideas heard. Thus, a few months after I took over I organized a working retreat in the serene atmosphere of Bermuda. I did not take the senior editors along because I wanted the writers to be able to speak—and rant—freely without the inhibiting presence of the "colonels." And rant they did. Years of frustration with the system burst forth. Most of the complaints were about the hierarchical editing structure. The writers were at the bottom, the managing editor on top and the senior editors in between, trying to please the boss or themselves but never the writers whose copy they invariably mangled. At least that is the way the writers saw it. The legendary Paul O'Neil, who by now worked for *Life,* was quoted often. Senior editors, he had written years ago, "are just riding around on the writer's back, shooting at parakeets, waving to their friends and plucking fruit from overhanging branches while [the writer] churns unsteadily through the swamps of fact and rumor with his big, dirty feet sinking into the knee at every step." Ted Kalem was almost as funny and equally scathing. "In most cases," he said, "the senior editors saved a story by amputating an arm, adding a third leg, and producing a monstrosity."

I listened with sympathy and almost nostalgia. When I was a *Time* writer I had felt much the same way about the tyranny of the editors. And when I became an editor I was something of a tyrant myself. Soon after I began editing Luce asked me: "How does it feel to be on the other side of the desk?" The jump from writer to editor is the most difficult move in the word game. Since *Time* editors were promoted from among the writers' ranks, they often confused the two crafts. So did I; I rewrote too much. Most of the writers suffered this with remarkable forbearance, or at least a show of it, but there were exceptions.

One was Brad Darrach, James Agee's successor as *Time*'s movie critic, whose boyish face looked perpetually puzzled when it was not contorted with the pain of writing. Once I heavily rewrote one of his pieces (a personality cover story, not a review, for I tried never to interfere with a critic's judgment). *Time* copy always carried the writer's name in the upper-left-hand corner; in those days without bylines it was the author's only mark of identification. Brad was so enraged by my interference that he blacked out his name on every one of the thirteen copies circulating in the office. On another occasion I sent a critical note requesting changes to Alexander Eliot, the magazine's art critic. In a fury Alex sent back my message torn into small pieces with a terse covering memo: "Your shameful note is entirely unacceptable." In calmer moments, instead of tearing up my notes, he had a more practical way of getting back at me. He would save passages I had stricken from his prose and store them in his desk drawer. When I recognized them again in future stories, I often gave in. Undoubtedly I contributed to Eliot's eventual flight from *Time;* he happily escaped into the clouds of Greek mythology, about which he wrote relentlessly.

It took me a while to learn how to balance my strong convictions about a story against respect for the writer's ideas. I am sure some colleagues thought I never did learn this. But I remember a time when I was home with a bad case of flu and had some copy sent to my apartment, so I could edit it there. The batch contained a short piece that was absolutely perfect. When I read it I experienced a flush of pleasure—on top of my fever—and I felt as good about it as if I had written it myself. There is an old joke about the three greatest lies in the world, one of them being "I'm from the government, and I'm here to help you." The statement that an editor exists to help writers sounds like the same kind of lie, but I had really come to believe that it was true.

At the Bermuda meeting I promised that I would try to "civilize" the editing process by asking editors to work with writers on their stories rather than simply changing them behind their backs.

As the two-day conference wore on, the turbulence of the sixties came through. Many writers, especially the younger ones, felt that the magazine was out of touch. Protesting the prim prohibition against four-letter words, one writer exclaimed: "It's time to get shit into the magazine." (I did not think so for years. Our taboo in these matters was probably not broken until 1971, when the Canadian edition reported that Prime Minister Pierre Trudeau mouthed "Fuck off" in Parliament.)

I also sensed a concern for what I could only describe as the soul of the magazine and of our workplace. I heard overtones of isolation and even loneliness. Some reported bitterly that they had not talked to Fuerbringer for two or three years and worried that I would be equally remote. Late in the evening, over drinks, a talented and eccentric writer named John Koffend said: "I don't want to measure my words. I came to *Time* magazine prepared to fall in love with it. I wanted to feel that everybody I worked with was part of me and I was part of them. But it's getting increasingly difficult for me to feel this. Part of your function, Henry, besides putting out a fifty-cent product, is to stay in love with the people who are in love with you as the M.E."

That remark moved and stunned me. I had not seen love as part of my job description. Now I suddenly realized the full dimensions of what I had taken on. These were organization men (and a few organization women) who longed for more identity, more human contact, just like the people in other large enterprises in corporate America. One big difference was that these were journalists and, as such, more than usually concerned with what their "fifty-cent product" stood for. In my concluding speech I did not exactly promise to love them, although in a way I did. I pledged to know them, talk to them, listen to them and respect them.

We must stop oversimplifying complicated situations, I said, and become both more intelligent and more intellectual, not shying away from theory, history, philosophy. *Time* writing had to become better. I urged the writers to pay more careful attention to language, to read poetry and fiction. I promised greater variety, but I insisted that the magazine still needed a reasonably consistent viewpoint, and as managing editor I had the responsibility to maintain it. "The editor of *Time* must substantially believe in the stories we print," I said, adding: "If there's a *Time* writer who feels that we are constantly and plainly wrong about an issue, he has the duty to come and argue with me. And if a *Time* writer finds that his deepest convictions are constantly violated by what *Time* prints, he should not work for us. I don't want mercenaries—we don't necessarily pay well enough to get mercenaries anyway."

After we returned from the pink stucco Eden of Bermuda, I moved quickly to carry out my planned changes, many of which were in the works already. I encouraged longer and more complex stories that made greater demands on the reader. I experimented with poetry and fiction. To mark the reopening of the Belmont Park racetrack, we commissioned the classicist Rolfe Humphries, a racing fan, to contribute two columns of verse ("Riders up! the bugle sounds First Call . . ."), and we printed a short story about religious persecution by Alexander Solzhenitsyn. Such literary flights did not become permanent fixtures in *Time*, but they served as a signal that we were willing to surprise. We began to print essays by outsiders.

One of the most important changes was not apparent to the reader and had to do with our correspondents. I had long felt that it was intolerable to use their work without giving them any say about what appeared in print. With Dick Clurman's eager agreement I instituted a system under which edited stories were wired back to the correspondents for their comments and corrections. I maintained that "New York" had the ultimate responsibility for what appeared in the magazine and sometimes even had a more balanced view of a local situation than a correspondent, who might have developed, as they say in the diplomatic service, "clientitis." But I set down the simple rule that, except in rare situations, the judgment of the correspondent should prevail. The "play-back" system was not foolproof, and it could lead to lengthy wired arguments late on closing night, but it gave correspondents a much greater voice in the magazine. The other major change, introduced very gradually, involved bylines for writers.

For a long time I was not convinced that bylines held any great advantage for the reader, who was accustomed to putting his trust (or mistrust) in *Time* as a whole rather than in an individual writer. Colleagues who opposed bylines argued that readers of *The New York Times*, for example, a paper in which almost all stories were signed, were still likely to be more impressed by "the *Times* says" than by "Clyde Farnsworth says." But I had come to feel that our journalists were entitled to a greater display of their own identity and that younger readers, especially, would welcome having names attached to stories. It would reduce the feeling of faceless anonymity that seemed to be so widely resented in our society. Criticism and essays were the first to carry bylines; the rest of the magazine followed much later in 1980. It was difficult to put bylines on news stories to which so many hands besides the writer in New York contributed. *Newsweek* resorted to multiple credits, of which I made fun at first; I wrote a letter to Oz Elliott that I signed approximately: "Henry Grunwald, with my secretary, Maureen Mingle, copy boy Don Sweet and J. P. Finch in the mailroom and Postmaster General Bailar in Washington." But eventually I agreed that *Time* should adopt the same system.

Max Ways once told me: "Whenever a new editor comes in on a newspaper and starts changing the layout, you can be sure he has no real ideas." I disagreed, at least where *Time* was concerned. I had the sense that the world was refusing to fit into our departments and sections. I felt that people and events and ideas must be allowed to struggle and push into new shapes in our pages, both physically and intellectually. Thus I started to tinker, at first rather clumsily, with *Time*'s makeup, widening headlines, using larger pictures and different typefaces. Over the next several years at least three art directors would struggle with the basic dilemma of being more flexible and exciting and yet maintaining order. We did not fully achieve this until Walter Bernard's redesign in 1977.

The idea of cataloging reality, no matter how chaotic, remained crucial in my mind. The tragedies, disasters, shocks and confusions of 1968 gave me a sometimes almost desperate sense that we had to hang on, close to Toynbee's prescription "Hang on and pray." I was not given to prayer, to my regret, but I clung to reason, thin reed though it might be. Our efforts to chronicle, as rationally as possible, the enormous events around us obviously could not hold the country together, but, in a small way, perhaps helped to combat a growing sense of chaos.

CHAPTER TWENTY-SIX

WHEN I SAW THE PICTURE, something clicked in my mind—the picture of the American embassy in Saigon with a large hole in its massive wall. It was far from the most shocking in a number of famous breath-stopping photos—the nude little girl running to escape a napalm attack, the South Vietnamese police chief shooting a Viet Cong prisoner with a pistol pressed against his head. But the sight of the very core of American power in Vietnam being invaded by the Viet Cong guerrillas—it took six hours to dislodge them—seemed like a symbol of disaster.

The attackers struck throughout the capital. They had brought men and weapons in from the countryside, some of the arms concealed in coffins supposedly destined for funerals. On the lunar New Year, or Tet, January 31, 1968, breaking a truce they had agreed to, the Viet Cong simultaneously hit more than a hundred cities and towns. Inevitably the offensive was compared to a vast, grim pinball machine with names flashing on everywhere, familiar place names like Da Nang, Khesanh, Pleiku, Da Lat and Qunagtri, and Hue, the ancient Vietnamese capital. Even sympathetic observers conceded that the Viet Cong acted with extreme brutality, killing many civilians. The Communists suffered huge casualties, and they were eventually driven out of the places they had seized; the United States and South Vietnamese counterattacks often inflicted more damage than the original strikes, which gave rise to one of the war's most infamous remarks. Describing the battle to break the VC's grip on Ben Tré, an American major said: "It became necessary to destroy the town to save it." Strictly speaking, the Tet offensive was a military failure. But the attack demonstrated the North's tactical brilliance, its willingness to take any number of casualties, its determination to carry on. I had felt all along that the war could not be won outright, but Tet persuaded me that stalemate and compromise would cost far more than I had thought and indeed might be impossible. Until now, public opinion polls had consistently shown majority support for the war; afterward the pattern was reversed. Most Americans simply wanted to get out. That did not necessarily mean that they embraced the peace movement and everything it stood for; white ethnics, reported Father Andrew Greeley of the National Research Institute, were finding it hard to "support peace if it meant that they must also support the Black Panthers, Women's Lib, widespread use of drugs, free love, campus radicals, long hair and picketing clergymen." Nevertheless antiwar passion kept rising.

Lyndon Johnson saw himself increasingly beleaguered and betrayed. Our correspondents kept canvassing public figures and found few who still supported the war. Even that once relentless hawk, Dean Acheson, had turned against it.

I heard the news of Johnson's decision not to run for reelection in the rather incongruous setting of Jamaica, just as Beverly and I were heading for the airport to return to New York after a vacation. "Your president says he won't stand again," the desk clerk said. It took me some time to understand what he meant, and not only because of his rich Jamaican accent. There had been speculation that Johnson might bow out, but I had not believed that a man who seemed to live and breathe and hungrily feed on power would give it up voluntarily.

Lyndon Johnson posed a dilemma for me. I never met him more than casually, but I felt a visceral dislike for him. I remembered listening to his inaugural address and being moved by his words about the poverty he had seen in his youth along the Padernales and his hopes of uplifting the nation.

Like almost everybody else, I had been swept along by his early performance in the White House when, after the shock of the Kennedy assassination and with waves of sympathy to buoy him along, he had propelled an extraordinary amount of legislation through Congress. What put me off was his crudeness and his bullying. The vignettes kept coming: pulling up his shirt for photographers to display his scar from a gall bladder operation; ordering aides in midconference to join him in his bathroom while he was relieving himself. In the eyes of his admirers all this only made him larger than life and even lovable, but I saw these incidents against a background of duplicity, vengefulness and paranoia, especially concerning the Kennedys and what he considered the eastern Establishment. He kept complaining about the press but tried to woo it, if not bribe it; he told a group of correspondents that if they only treated him right, he would make big men of them. When he spoke about hoping to end poverty and racial discrimination, he undoubtedly meant it; but most of the time, fairly or unfairly, I thought him blatantly calculating, with his oddly artificial smile and his seductive, syrupy tones. I sensed his Texas giantism: everything he did had to be the greatest, the biggest, including his role as social benefactor and champion of the downtrodden. In retrospect the combination of vast, open-ended social programs and the win-at-all-costs pursuit of an undeclared war inflicted incalculable damage on the nation.

My feelings toward him gradually mellowed. I was fascinated by his huge, rather clumsy hands, constantly reaching, prodding, pushing. Eventually I saw something pathetic about those hands, because as he grew more beleaguered and tense, he did not seem to know what to do with them. I started to feel sorry for him when he became, virtually, a White House prisoner, unable to move about his country without running into waves of hate.

My last memory of him dates from the 1969 *Apollo 11* launch at Cape Kennedy, which lifted the first men to the moon. In the carnival atmosphere that filled the days and nights before the launch, there were dozens of events, including one hosted by *Life* that featured the German rocket-pioneer Wernher von Braun, some intoxicated off-duty astronauts and Norman Mailer, who crashed the party (he would later publish a brilliant book, *Of a Fire on the Moon*). At one of the many dinners I spent some time with Lyndon Johnson, who seemed physically diminished, not quite filling out his shirt and suit. He was mellow, almost gentle, talking about the promise of space flight; no longer raging, he was Lear in uneasy repose.

Lyndon Johnson, war abroad and civil strife at home were overshadowed by the momentous moon shot. Before dawn one morning, together with several correspondents, I visited the vehicle assembly building, that huge vaulting modern cathedral. A Saturn 5 rocket, 363 feet tall, white, beautiful and mysterious under the floodlights, made me and the other human figures seem almost ludicrously small. But on launch day, from the observation stand three miles distant, the rocket itself seemed puny, a vehicle of incredible hubris. The atmosphere among the spectators was festive, raucous and yet apprehensive. We waited. Ignition. The rocket seemed to tremble, straining to lift, the earth reluctant to let it go before finally releasing it; I had tears in my eyes. As I followed the inexorable climb and the missile grew smaller and smaller in the sky, I had a feeling of being left behind.

I was utterly impatient with the people who argued that space exploration was an unnecessary and expensive stunt. Yes, it was possible to look at the moon over Harlem or Watts and conclude that not a single life, not a single dwelling below, would be improved by landing men on its bland surface. But such a view, as I wrote in *Time,* seemed as narrow to me as the doubt and ridicule that accompanied the seafaring explorers of five hundred years before. They not only immeasurably widened the constricted Old World, but gave man a new view of himself. Something similar, I felt, would happen as a result of this step into space. Amid all the easy talk of revolution, here was a truly revolutionary act. This was Western man at his most typical—reaching for the moon.

Those were rather extravagant thoughts considering what the United States had gone through during the year leading up to *Apollo 11.*

Five days after Johnson announced his withdrawal and spoke of reconciliation in the country came the first of two assassinations, in almost unbelievable succession. They stained the atmosphere; lines from Eliot's *Murder in the Cathedral* kept echoing in my mind: "Clear the air! clean the sky! wash the wind!" It would be a long time before the air seemed even remotely clean once more.

Again the replay of John Kennedy's murder, again the sudden shots out of nowhere, again the blood and the desperate struggle to preserve a flickering life, again the obscure killer whose very insignificance seemed outrageous, again the funeral witnessed by the nation. In Memphis, where he had gone because of a labor dispute involving black sanitation workers, Martin Luther King was killed by a sniper's bullet on a motel balcony. It was fired by an escaped petty convict named James Earl Ray, who pleaded guilty to the murder but later claimed that he was innocent and had been framed. No one missed the obvious and painful irony that the preacher of nonviolence was mourned in violent black riots in more than one hundred cities. Again, as with the death of John F. Kennedy, *Time* did not put the victim on its cover (these were the last few weeks of Otto Fuerbringer's tenure); instead the choice was Lyndon Johnson, to personify a moment of national crisis. While the White House and the Capitol were ringed protectively by U.S. troops, Johnson pleaded for calm and Hubert Humphrey spoke of the shame of the nation. The night before his assassination Martin Luther King preached a sermon in which he said that he was not afraid of death: "Like anybody, I would like to live a long life. . . . But I'm not concerned about that now. I just want to do God's will. . . . He's allowed me to go up to the mountain . . . and I've seen the promised land! I may not get there with you, but . . . we as a people will get to the promised land."

Robert Kennedy often expressed a similar fatalism and a similar refusal to fear death. Only weeks before, he had mused: "If anyone wants to kill me, it won't be difficult." He often quoted Edith Hamilton: "Men are not made for safe havens." Alongside Nelson Rockefeller, Hubert Humphrey and Eugene McCarthy, Robert Kennedy walked in Martin Luther King's funeral procession, behind the casket on an old farm cart drawn by two mules. Two months later Robert Kennedy's own funeral service took place in New York's St. Patrick's Cathedral in the presence of many of the same mourners. Later, in Arlington National Cemetery, he was buried next to his brother, at night, in a subdued ceremony without rifle volleys or taps. In the public mind Bobby had finally emerged from John Kennedy's shadow and grown into a striking and puzzling figure in his own right. I had always considered him slightly comic compared with JFK, nervous, jumpy, eager, almost puppylike. But this impression faded; he was more complex than that. Bullying witnesses as assistant counsel of Joe McCarthy's Senate committee; running down all obstacles and opponents as manager of his brother's election campaign; sending FBI agents to hostile reporters' homes while he was attorney general—that was one Bobby Kennedy. The other Bobby was the champion of the poor and helpless, the idealist who wanted to transform a too harsh society. In both roles he was unpredictable. As a populist he wanted to tax the rich; as a free enterpriser he wanted the government and business to collaborate in creating jobs and get people off welfare: "Under our present welfare laws," he said, "we almost force poor people to produce illegitimate children. I think that's unacceptable in the United States."

Hays Gorey, a *Time* correspondent who knew him well, believed that both sides were genuine: "No one who has seen Bobby Kennedy on the Indian Reservations of Arizona or Idaho," wrote Gorey, "no one who has seen him in the stinking hovels of Appalachia, no one who has seen him take the hand of a starving negro child in the Mississippi Delta, accuses him of acting. Neither he—nor any other politician—could be that good an actor." But, Gorey added, "Robert Kennedy is a man you can go to the well with, but while you are standing at the well with him, you would want to keep a wary eye out—lest you find yourself accidentally or otherwise at the bottom."

More than a year before he was killed, Kennedy, then a New York senator, came to meet with a small group of *Time* journalists. I waited for him in the lobby of the Time & Life Building and was astonished that he arrived alone, looking rather forlorn. To get to the private meeting rooms one had to take an express elevator and then, for the last two floors, change to an excruciatingly slow local. "When I have a little time," said Kennedy with a twinkle, "I'll come back and fix your elevator system."

He kept his humor during the meeting at first but grew increasingly intense as he spoke about Vietnam, his high-pitched voice growing hoarser, one hand chopping into the other. He dismissed the domino theory: "Vietnam is only Vietnam. It will not settle the fate of Asia or of America, much less the fate of the world." He observed, not for the first time, that America could not be the policeman of the world and that American power cannot be a substitute for the will of the people or the government of another country. "Otherwise," he said, "we'll get ourselves embroiled in a whole series of Vietnams."

At one point he was asked about his future political plans. He shrugged and repeated what he'd said in the past. "I don't know what I will be doing a few years from now," he said. "Even tomorrow is so far away. I don't know whether I will still be alive."

By May 1968 Bobby Kennedy was still alive and running hard for the Democratic nomination. *Time* prepared a cover story on him, and correspondent Bonnie Angelo, who was with the Kennedy campaign in Oregon, later recalled that Bobby and his entourage were alarmed because they felt that in the past the magazine had been nasty about him. I had just taken over as managing editor—this was my first issue—and I went to great pains to see to it that our story was fair. Kennedy, I heard, was surprised and relieved. I was pleased by a note from Loudon Wainwright, a splendid, warmhearted *Life* writer who adored the Kennedys. The story, he wrote, was "alarmingly fair to the subject. . . . Gracious."

It was with a sickening and unbelieving sense of déjà vu that I prepared, a scant two weeks later, to do another cover story on Bobby Kennedy, after his assassination in Los Angeles. Without hesitation I ignored the tradition that had kept John Kennedy and Martin Luther King off *Time*'s cover.

Of all the expressions of grief and outrage, I found most apt the words of Boston's Cardinal Cushing: "All I can say is, Good Lord, what is this all about? We could continue our prayers that it would never happen again, but we did that before."

To the cardinal's haunting question one answer came quickly from many sides: America is sick, psychotic, indelibly marked by the original sin of violence. At home and abroad there were rising doubts about the stability of American society and about its capacity to deal with its furies. I felt that the most urgent task for *Time* was to face up to these doubts and if possible to dispel them.

As if to exonerate the United States, we took pains to trace the murderer to the distant and special hatreds of the Middle East; the killer, Sirhan Sirhan, an immigrant from Jordan, saw Robert Kennedy as a champion of the despised state of Israel. But it was not really possible to shake off a nagging sense of guilt or to shift its burden to some exotic, alien zone any more than it was possible to blame John Kennedy's death convincingly on Moscow or Havana. While I sincerely rejected the view that all America was incurably sick, I nevertheless felt that something was terribly wrong. That feeling was reinforced by the very language that had come to fill the air. In Dallas, Assistant District Attorney William Alexander snarled on a TV show, "Earl Warren shouldn't be impeached—he should be hanged!" H. Rap Brown was heard to cry: "How many whites did you kill today?" Lyndon Johnson was routinely denounced as a mass murderer. No one could draw a direct line from verbal overkill to real assassination, but perversion of free speech made murder seem more ordinary, less forbidden, and "kill" just another four-letter word.

THE SUMMER OF 1968 was intensely political. Richard Nixon had just been nominated by the Republicans in Miami, and Hubert Humphrey was nervously preparing for the Chicago convention of a grimly divided Democratic Party. Suddenly foreign events burst in: the Soviet Union invaded Czechoslovakia. Alexander Dubcek, onetime factory worker and lifelong loyal Communist, had become head of the Czech Party. He had rebelled against the old, hard-line hacks and attempted to carry out a Marxist reformation. For eight months he and a group of like-minded comrades had tried to build "Communism with a human face," granting freedom of the press and of assembly and allowing opposition parties to function. The "Prague Spring" brought heady gusts of freedom.

Moscow watched with mounting alarm. After futile attempts to pressure Dubcek into limiting his reforms, the Kremlin decided to send in the Red Army, plus units from other Warsaw Pact countries.

I almost found the event a relief from the raucous and dubious battles at home. The invasion provided a clear-cut villain on the outside, a simple moral issue. It was also the kind of event that *Time* was perfectly equipped to report; it happened on a Tuesday night and thus gave us almost a full editorial week to pull our cover story together by press time on Friday night. (I became so attuned to our editorial rhythm that for years, even after leaving *Time,* I found myself automatically noting the day on which big news broke and calculating how much time the magazine had to cope with it.) We had several correspondents in Prague who circumvented the communications blackout; office drivers from Vienna and Berlin raced to the border to pick up the dispatches. Film from a troop of photographers came out much the same way, and the pictures were startling: students looking not very different from American antiwar protesters demonstrating against the Soviets and swarming over Russian tanks. For a change, signs proclaimed "Russia Go Home!" rather than "America Go Home!"

But the outcome was inevitable: restoration of a conservative Communist regime and another two decades of Soviet control in Eastern Europe. Dubcek's naive belief that Communism could somehow be combined with freedom kept reappearing. It animated the "Euro-Communists" of the seventies, whether they sincerely believed it or merely used it as a tactic. It also animated Mikhail Gorbachev. After he instituted glasnost, a joke made the rounds that sharply expressed his eventual failure. Question: "What is the difference between Dubcek and Gorbachev?" Answer: "Twenty years."

. . .

Dr. Benjamin Spock, who had long since emerged from the nursery to become a leading opponent of the war, joined others in the peace movement to equate the Soviet invasion with U.S. intervention in Vietnam. It was, I thought, an outrageous equation. But the image of Soviet tanks in Prague helped to defeat—narrowly—a strong antiwar plank at the Chicago convention. Hubert Humphrey was on a cruel political rack, pulled between the need for support of his chief's war policy and the desire to win over the peace faction.

The convention shaped up as a major battle, with antiwar protesters streaming toward Chicago. Mayor Richard Daley, who ruled the city like a highly efficient warlord, marshaled thousands of policemen and National Guardsmen to maintain law and order. "No one," he pledged, "is going to take over the streets." In an attempt to keep up the city's cheerful spirit, he ordered lampposts painted Kelly green. But the old beery, jolly atmosphere I remembered from previous visits was now hard to find. (A taxi and phone strike did not help.) Wherever you turned, there were helmeted cops. Hotels were heavily guarded, and the rank old auditorium at the stockyards was an improvised fortress, with armed policemen patrolling the roof. Planes were banned from the airspace overhead. *Time* ran a piece outlining how "the compleat delegate" should be equipped: "goggles to protect the eyes from teargas and Mace, crash helmet from billy clubs, bricks, etc., all-purpose bail-bond credit card (if arrested), air mattress (in event of prolonged incarcerations) . . . bottled water (should yippies manage to turn on the Chicago water supply with a lacing of LSD . . .)"

I had laughed over this story and okayed it, but in view of what was to happen it may have been too farcical. Not that farce was absent from Chicago; yippie spokesman Abbie Hoffman got his four police tails to buy him dinner but was arrested for wearing a four-letter word on his forehead.

The young protesters I saw in Grant Park and elsewhere hardly seemed very menacing. At first the scene almost suggested a carefree outing. Things quickly turned more ominous, as many protesters were coolly determined to provoke trouble in the spirit of Tom Hayden, who had announced: "We are coming to Chicago to vomit on the politics of joy, [and] . . . face the Democratic Party with its illegitimacy and criminality." Some of the protesters threw bricks and nail-studded golf balls at police, but mostly they hurled words at the "pigs"—as Daley later noted in prim indignation—"the foulest of language that you wouldn't hear in a brothel house." On the whole the cops were restrained, until demonstrators in Grant Park hauled down an American flag; then the police started to throw tear gas. Driven from the park, the demonstrators regrouped in front of the Hilton Hotel. When they ignored a warning to leave, the police, on orders, let go; plainly relieved at having been finally unleashed, they attacked with clubs and fists. They drove demonstrators, as well as bystanders, against the walls of the hotel, smashing into anything and anyone. I found myself caught in the crush, feeling both panic and disbelief, pictures forming in my mind that did not become fully clear until later, like developing film: the contorted features and straining neck muscles of the cops, the fear and pain of the victims, blood trickling down enraged faces and, more than anything else, surprise. I managed to slide back into the hotel, luckier than some colleagues; during the week several *Time* correspondents were hit by tear gas and Mace, and a *Life* reporter was badly beaten by cops.

Later I talked to Joe Boyce, the black *Time* correspondent who had been a Chicago policeman. It turned out that six hundred fifty protesters had been arrested, one thousand injured and, as far as anyone knew, no one had been killed. Did that constitute a police riot, as so many people were calling it? "That's too simple," replied Joe. "I used to teach 'acceptable force' when I was at the Police Academy, and some of those cops did follow the lessons. But there had been days of taunts, and it boiled over. Young people didn't realize the ferocity of the animal they awakened. I saw a changed America, I saw white cops beating white kids. A lot of it was class hostility. Here were these college kids who were free to travel, could choose where they wanted to stay and hire lawyers when they were arrested, and they came up against these blue-collar policemen who were making about $6,500 a year."

Meanwhile the delegates were locked in their own fights. Superficially the scene still resembled the jamboree that had so delighted me twenty years before. But the convention was now embroiled in the angry quarrel over Vietnam. Most of the conventioneers wore the neat costumes of middle-class, middle-aged prosperity, but there were also many with beards and love beads. There were more blacks than usual and more celebrity delegates—Paul Newman, Shirley MacLaine, Warren Beatty, Arthur Miller and Rafer Johnson—lending glamour to the antiwar forces. Two figures were dramatically absent, leaving noticeable vacuums. One was Robert Kennedy, whose New York and California delegations seemed bereft and restless. A filmed tribute to Bobby stopped the convention cold, as delegates sang chorus after chorus of the "Battle Hymn of the Republic" and wept for what might have been. The other was Lyndon Johnson, who had wisely decided against making an appearance in the hall but was still largely in control of the convention through the Daley machine.

At times the control threatened to fail. Television brought the images of the turmoil outside into the hall, amid mounting indignation. Senator Abraham Ribicoff of Connecticut was making a nominating speech for George McGovern when his dapper frame and finely contoured face seemed momentarily convulsed with anger; he discarded his text and, looking straight at the Illinois delegation and its leader, Richard Daley, denounced the "Gestapo tactics in the streets of Chicago." Daley struggled to his feet, face red, heavy jowls quivering, his suet mountain of a body leaning toward the podium, and shouted back at Ribicoff through a cupped hand. His exact words were not audible, but lip-readers later rendered them as "Fuck you, you Jew son of a bitch, you lousy motherfucker. Go home." After a succession of other speakers attacked Daley and his cops, it was Daley who went home, striding from the hall surrounded by security men.

There was never any real doubt that Hubert Humphrey would be nominated, but it was a victory badly marred. "Chicago" would long remain a one-word summary of the Democratic Party's near fatal divisions. I called on Humphrey in his twenty-fifth-floor suite at the Hilton, from where he could hear the tumult in the street below and even get an occasional whiff of tear gas. I remembered first meeting him years before when he was the progressive, ebullient young mayor of Minneapolis. Unspoken, but clearly present in his mind, was the puzzlement over how he had now become a villain to liberals and an embodiment of the old conventional order. He was jovial, bouncy and upbeat, but at times his perpetual smile was replaced by tight lips, suggesting anger, and his cheerful eyes would wander into the distance, looking hurt. "There may be a tendency to conservatism in the country right now," he said. "If you let the country move that way, it will. I have no intention of letting it." But he would find that he could not stop it. In his acceptance speech he would plead for national unity and proclaim a new day, but both would elude him: with only lukewarm support from Lyndon Johnson, who kept belittling him in private, he was nevertheless manacled to Johnson's war record.

I returned to New York to edit our convention report, which indignantly condemned Daley and the Chicago police. I then went off to Martha's Vineyard and started to think about the wider significance of the chaotic week. For my colleagues who would put out the next issue in my absence, I dictated some reflections. Like Joe Boyce, I thought that class was a significant element behind the violence. "In a sense Daley's cops represented vast numbers of blue-collar workers who made it into the middle class, a special American achievement," I said. "It represents yesterday's success of the American system. The people who back the cops see in the protesters an attack on their status, security and values. That is why so many Americans seem to be siding with the cops against 'the kids.' So we must ask to what extent a society, and the police who more or less represent it, should be expected to keep cool when faced with the kind of provocation we witnessed in Chicago. The answer must be: to a very large extent indeed. Our society must learn how to withstand, ignore or deflect such provocations, because otherwise it becomes too easy for small numbers of 'activists' to create large-scale trouble. Thus the discipline of a National Guardsman in standing still for two hours while being insulted and abused, the skill of policemen in handling a mob with minimum violence, become symbols of a society sure of itself. On the other hand, the club-swinging rage of so many of Daley's cops indicates a society's fear and vulnerability."

. . .

In the aftermath of Chicago the most obvious trend was a backlash against protest and disorder, the emergence—or reemergence—of a Main Street conservatism. One survivor of the Chicago debacle was Richard Daley. Many predicted his political demise, but his power base in the city was unshakable. When I went to see him in 1975 he was still very much in power. The antiwar protesters who had jeered him had mostly faded away, and hardly anyone still called those Chicago policemen "pigs." Most American cities were in permanent crisis, but not Daley's Chicago. His political machine was the last of its kind, but it still worked—corrupt, but not too corrupt, and highly efficient.

A massive Humpty-Dumpty who had avoided his big fall, Daley was enthroned behind a desk covered with huge ledgers, working on his city budget. He clearly enjoyed it and seemed virtually unmarked by a stroke he had recently suffered. He was patronizing about New York City's desperate financial troubles and lectured smugly: "The city must learn that you can't put out more than you take in." He brushed aside memories of the convention ("that's all past") and instead went further back, to the Chicago of his childhood, which he made sound idyllic. He recalled the house near the stockyards where he grew up and where he still lived. That led to talk of school. The teachers' unions were pressing him hard, asking for more money, but he largely blamed the unruly young for causing trouble. "In the old days," he mused, "it was a wonderful thing to be a teacher. Now look at the situation: kids have no respect."

It was an embarrassing cliché, but not to Daley. Yes, he was an anachronism. The city was changing and would change more after his departure, not least because its blacks rose to political power, something that Daley had been able to postpone for so long. But that fleshy, red-faced figure, secure behind his ledgers, still represented something enduring in American life, a force that continued to contend with, and alternate with, the rages of Chicago 1968. It was the force of Middle America.

PART SEVEN

BACK

FROM THE

BRINK

CHAPTER TWENTY-SEVEN

THE TERM "MIDDLE AMERICA" was coined around 1967 by the astute columnist Joseph Kraft, who, ironically, was a Harvard-educated eastern intellectual. He was a friend of mine, and I knew that he was sympathetic toward the Middle Americans but unsentimental. He defined them as having recently moved from just above the poverty line to just below the level of affluence.

The home of Middle America was no longer Main Street, which now seemed too rural and empty to be a valid symbol, but Elm Street—according to the political analyst James Reichley of *Fortune*. Elm Street was the quiet residential avenue in middle-size American communities where the local gentry lived. It was the values and fears of Elm Street that shaped Richard Nixon's campaign for the presidency. He had actually never lived there, having moved almost directly from near poverty in California to a successful career in Washington. But he embodied Middle America, with his modest origins, his obvious diligence and ambition.

After his bitter defeat for the governorship of California in 1962, he seemed to be gone from politics. ("You won't have Nixon to kick around anymore.") When he moved to New York and joined a prominent law firm, he established himself in a Fifth Avenue apartment in the same building as Nelson Rockefeller, who symbolized everything Nixon distrusted and envied. He made money for the first time in his life and told a *Time* correspondent that he was a quarter-millionaire. (He added: "I wonder what Nelson Rockefeller is worth?") In the never-ending exercise of monitoring and analyzing Nixon's psyche, most journalists and associates claimed that he had relaxed and grown, but when I saw him around town occasionally, I still found him strained, not at ease with himself or others. He was usually half-friendly toward me because of my old Whittaker Chambers connection and half-chilly because he distrusted *Time*. The Luce publications had been too enthusiastic—in his view—about John Kennedy and Nelson Rockefeller to suit him. But Nixon was clearly planning to reclaim a political career, and he dutifully wooed us by coming to lunch a few times. He obviously prepared for these occasions, although there was at least one glitch. Shaking hands with a number of Time Inc. journalists, he reached Jack Jessup, *Life*'s eloquent and erudite editorial writer. "Hello, Jack," said Nixon. "Tell me, did you rebuild your house in Connecticut after it burned down?"

"Yes, and thanks for asking, sir," replied Jessup. "That was ten years ago."

During the lunches Nixon usually concentrated on foreign affairs. He was then making many trips abroad and later complained that he "traveled around the world alone with his briefcase [and] got no coverage." Thus he was eager to display his knowledge. At first he uttered familiar information as if he were imparting great new insights. However, his expertise grew, and he became less obvious. He was awkward, both physically—I often worried that he would bump into a chair or potted plant—and socially. His humor was strained and his enthusiasm or indignation sounded hollow.

By summer of 1967 *Time* was planning a cover on Nixon, but after some reporting the story did not seem compelling and was postponed. He was highly irritated. But an unknown Nixon mole inside *Time* passed along the off-the-record opinions of various politicians about him; at least, commented his aide William Safire later, we knew who our friends and enemies were.

Nixon had emerged as an unofficial spokesman for the Republican

Party, once again getting out his briefcase and crisscrossing the country to speak in support of various candidates. Gradually he became a logical contender for the 1968 presidential nomination. My personal choice was Nelson Rockefeller, whom I liked not so much because of his professional friendliness ("Hiya, fella"), but because I found him solid and courageous. I was drawn to his centrist political philosophy, the very quality, of course, that the true conservative believers among Republicans loathed. They also loathed—irrationally, I thought—his eastern Establishment flair. He had been devastatingly rebuffed by the party four years before, losing the nomination to Barry Goldwater, and now he seemed unable to make up his mind whether or not to try again. Emmet Hughes, who was working for him on and off, told me, "He's just not in the mood to scramble after the nomination. He wants them to come to him. It won't happen that way, but I can't budge him." In the end, some major Republican backers sent a virtual ultimatum to Rockefeller through Hughes, and he declared his candidacy. But Nixon was easily nominated. He was not loved by the Goldwater wing or the Rockefeller wing of the party, but he was acceptable to both.

On the surface he campaigned as a moderate, but there were many signals to Middle America, and especially to the South and the border states, that he intended to be tough on law and order, on welfare cheats, on radicals. He pledged an honorable compromise and peace in Vietnam without providing many details. Nixon was perfecting his famous style of giving with one hand and taking back with the other: peace but not surrender in Vietnam, an end to discrimination but not too fast. I could not help but admire his skillful balancing act, which was symbolized by the selection of a running mate, Spiro Agnew, the son of a Greek immigrant restaurant owner who had made it to Elm Street.

Agnew had been a reasonably good governor of Maryland for two years, and he had a relatively liberal record—he won the governorship with black support. But behind his heavy-lidded eyes and his immobile face, which gave him a permanently dreamy air, more was stirring than most people realized. Some months after Martin Luther King's assassination and the riots that followed, he blamed the violence on "the permissive climate and misguided compassion of public opinion. It is not evil conditions that cause riots, but evil men." He remarked: "When you've seen one slum, you've seen them all." He attacked "phony intellectuals who don't understand what we mean by hard work and patriotism." It was increasingly clear that these were not outbursts of temper, but carefully calculated messages to the Right and especially to the followers of Alabama's George Wallace, who was running for president in a fetid cloud of anger and hate.

I watched Wallace with a mixture of disgust and disbelief, tempted to write him off as a regional aberration, but realized quickly that he had to be taken more seriously. He was blatantly segregationist, but he also appealed to fears that were not strictly racist. And he took the appeal north. "The people of Cleveland and Chicago and Gary and St. Louis will be so goddamned sick and tired of federal interference in their schools," he said, "they'll be ready to vote for Wallace by the thousands." Thousands of people did indeed vote for him, especially blue-collar workers who felt ignored and mistreated. In the end, Wallace won 13.5 percent of the popular vote. Humphrey wound up with a remarkably strong 42.7 percent versus Nixon's 43.4 percent. Nixon's margin was breathtakingly narrow, but he had fought his way back from two bitter defeats and had finally achieved the presidency. Not for years would Richard Nixon again carry his own briefcase.

I DECIDED THAT *Time* should greet Nixon's election with a special section, and I gave it the title "To Heal a Nation." It seemed that after years of war in Vietnam and a war of sorts at home, assassinations, riots and the relentless drumbeat of protest, this graceless and often divisive politician had a chance to bring reconciliation and reform. I assigned the project to Robert Shnayerson, a versatile writer and editor. He was so taciturn that even when he spoke, his mouth seemed tight-lipped. I found his thinking somewhat Talmudic, often circling problems rather than attacking them head on, but his intellect intrigued me. Even though he was politically to the left of me, we spurred each other on, and an article that had been planned to run for six pages was pushed by us to a formidable twenty, most of it very hard going. The piece, really a tract, started by noting how troubled Americans were about their country and quoted the British historian Sir Denis Brogan as saying, "This is not going to be the American Century."

To some this seemed like apostasy, a new managing editor's declaration of independence from Henry Luce. But it was meant only to shake the reader to attention. We presented an impossible laundry list of reforms and innovations, ranging from a criticism of the U.S. Constitution to revenue sharing, mass transit and fixing the post office. In hindsight some of our pronouncements were rather absurd, as when we asked, naively, why America's genius for organization—as demonstrated in the Manhattan Project and the Marshall Plan—could not be applied to ending poverty or traffic jams. When Donovan read an early draft he thought that our recommendations would bankrupt the Treasury, leading us to scale back our own Great Society. Actually the piece was properly skeptical about how much government could accomplish and suggested incentives to bureaucrats for liquidating rather than expanding their programs. The piece ended with a plea for individual effort and a renewed sense of community.

I doubt that Richard Nixon ever read our recommendations or that a great many readers stayed with them all the way through. But I was glad we made the effort.

As it turned out, Nixon had an agenda almost as ambitious as ours, and for all his conservatism he believed in a strong, activist government. He proposed a guaranteed annual income to replace myriad, complicated welfare programs and even suggested national health insurance. He sometimes invoked conservative icons to justify his position. "You know that Bismarck started health insurance in Germany," he once told me during an interview with that habit he had of portentously stating the familiar. Later he would invoke Disraeli's benevolent Toryism. I don't believe he was motivated by deep conviction. Rather, he acted to gain popular support and because he failed to understand the costs that would be involved. He did not know very much about economics, as he would prove in 1971 when he imposed wage and price controls. He was inclined to subordinate economics to politics and foreign affairs. In a conversation years later he said: "The American economy is so strong it would take a genius to ruin it, whereas one small mistake in foreign policy could blow up the world."

VIETNAM WAS STILL Nixon's principal problem and torment. He was far more determined than Johnson to get out and far more prepared to seek a settlement short of victory. But months after peace talks had started in Paris, a settlement was still naggingly elusive.

Early in 1969 I returned to Vietnam with a *Time* "News Tour," a special invention that was part promotional gimmick and part legitimate fact-finding trip. *Time* would ask about two dozen leading businessmen and a few academics to travel to interesting areas, to meet assorted leaders—invariably including kings, presidents and prime ministers. Another two dozen *Time* executives and journalists usually went along, plus support troops. The businessmen, who of course included *Time* advertisers, shared the expenses with Time Inc. The style of the tours was lavish: chartered 707, a specially printed newspaper, the *Daily Bugle*, to keep up with news back home. The pace was breathtaking (twelve hours in a country was not unusual). Businessmen coveted the invitations and worked hard at playing journalist. As usual, some of America's biggest corporations were included: General Motors, AT&T, Westinghouse, Philip Morris, Goodyear, Standard Oil and General Foods, among others. Seagram was represented by its ebullient and irreverent president, Edgar Bronfman. A crisis erupted once when it was discovered that the traveling bar was stocked with competing spirits. Several Time Inc. executives quickly rectified the situation.

Vietnam was the centerpiece of a tour that covered eight Asian countries. I remember getting up at 4:30 A.M. in Saigon, preparing for a field trip and trying groggily to shave when I became aware of regular, dull, booming noises. I thought at first they were caused by the erratic plumbing or some other dysfunction of the Hotel Caravelle, then realized that the sounds were caused by "incoming"—rockets being fired at the city by Communist forces. A big new offensive had started, and the U.S. authorities only reluctantly allowed our tour to proceed.

This time nobody was drawing strategic diagrams on menus, but everybody seemed to be waving very professional-looking pointers, from the top U.S. brass to the last Vietnamese colonel in a dusty hill outpost. Pointers were all stabbing at maps—glossy maps on rollers or smudged, crumpled maps tacked up on cork boards—to show that the war was going well, or at least much better. Yet sooner or later the pointers drew attention to the big continuing problem, the fact that men and supplies kept streaming south. At MAC-V Headquarters at Tan Son Hut air base, General Creighton Abrams sat in the vast briefing theater, listening to subordinates give a routine situation report.

He had replaced Westmoreland seven months before, determined to rely on speed and small units rather than on massive deployment. Clearly bored by the briefing he suddenly bounded to his feet. Striding back and forth, waving a huge cigar rather than a pointer, he came across as a frustrated optimist. "We kept interdicting, especially the First Cav, but then three or four months later, thousands did make it into the area around Saigon." He grew so animated that large patches of perspiration showed on his fatigues. "We shouldn't talk about reducing our commitment here," he argued, "without seeing the other man's money."

The big new word in his briefing and in almost any conversation in Vietnam was "pacification," which used to be known as "the other war" but was more and more "the real war." It sounded simply like the latest and most elaborate version of the old program to establish security in the countryside. In charge of that effort was William Colby, formally called deputy to Abrams for "civil operations and revolutionary development support," a CIA veteran. He described grandiose aims and cited absurdly precise statistics. (Of the hamlets, 79.2 percent were relatively secure.)

The most firmly if not wildly optimistic figure in Vietnam seemed to be President Nguyen Van Thieu, a U.S.-trained but unspectacular military man whose bland, boyish face was unmarked by decades of war and political intrigue. It was up to the Communists to make significant concessions in Paris, he said, but speculated that instead they might just fade away. "They do not want to admit to the people of North Vietnam that they have lost the war, after ten years of propaganda saying they were winning it."

"What's he been smoking?" muttered one group member as we filed out.

As usual, things looked different outside Saigon. At Cam Ranh Bay, the huge American base about an hour's flight time from Saigon, Admiral Elmo Zumwalt proudly displayed his "brown-water" navy, designed to intercept Viet Cong supplies throughout the Mekong River Delta. For all of Zumwalt's energy and fervor there was something surreal about the scene; strapped into inflatable life vests and packed into swift Hovercraft that were painted with gaping dragon teeth to frighten the enemy, our group looked a little like tourists at a seaside amusement park. The river flotilla suggested ingenuity and determination, but just how effective was it? I was acutely aware of the limits of such a visit, so carefully arranged by the military and *Time*'s own correspondents. I felt a kind of guilt at never seeing close up the wounded and the dead on both sides, never experiencing the hardships of the G.I.'s in a hostile and incomprehensible land.

In hindsight, one encounter illustrated the deceptive reality of Vietnam. I met Pham Xuan An, a wiry, studious-looking Vietnamese with a perpetually startled look who had been a *Time* correspondent in Saigon for three years. Partly educated in the United States, he was one of the best-informed, best-liked journalists in the city and was treated as an oracle even by *Time*'s competitors. He would remain with *Time* until the fall of Saigon. I had a long talk with him over a scarred desk in the crowded and cluttered Saigon bureau, located in a dilapidated, barbed-wire-encircled building. He was not complimentary about the Thieu regime, which he considered corrupt. Years afterward I was stunned, as were all my colleagues, when it turned out that An had been a dedicated Communist since 1944, when he was eighteen years old, and had risen to the rank of colonel in the People's Revolutionary Army. No one ever suspected him—in fact, there were rumors that he worked for the CIA. He later claimed, convincingly, that he never fed any disinformation to *Time*. But with access to top-level U.S. military briefings, he had plenty of information to pass on to his Communist superiors. "They wanted the same thing from me that *Time* wanted—accurate reporting," he would recall later. He had learned loyalty from Americans, he said, and was simply being loyal both to *Time* and his country. "I knew we had to get rid of the foreigners, even the foreigners I love so much."

A curiously double-edged postscript to the Vietnam visit was provided by Prime Minister Lee Kuan Yew when the group traveled to Singapore. He spoke with the arrogance of a man who is never in doubt and who had, moreover, successfully outlawed the Communists in Singapore while building a prosperous and stable, if autocratically ruled, city-state. He felt that the United States had made too big an effort ("You're overcommitted, for God's sake") without really understanding the enemy. The world, he lectured, is divided into communities that can discipline themselves and those that cannot. "Victory" was impossible against forces so disciplined and so elusive—unless the United States resorted to a mercenary force of perhaps one hundred thousand Americans. Such a force would eliminate the influence of the volatile young and of "those teachers" (snarling at this point) who encouraged them to evade the draft. A believer in the domino theory, Lee was convinced that America must hang on. "If you do throw this away, then you throw the whole of Southeast Asia away." Whatever its flaws, the message had an undeniably bracing effect. That is partly why we returned to the United States with a somewhat exaggerated belief that perseverance could still bring about a standoff and a settlement.

Nixon had agreed to meet the *Time* travelers and received us in the Cabinet Room. At the huge, coffin-shaped table the president listened intently, his hands folded across his chest. I was impressed by his refusal to fall for optimism. "It is possible to go to Vietnam," he said, "and talk to Abrams and Thieu (who is very poised) and come away with a good feeling. But do you really think there has been that much improvement?" He seemed almost to enjoy the difficulties that required all his political skills, trying to give hope for peace to America while remaining tough with North Vietnam. "I assure you," he said, "we are playing a game that is very calculating and very cool."

As it turned out, the game did not go well.

. . .

The war kept tearing at America. Beyond the question of when and how the United States would get out, there was another question: how the United States would explain the war to itself and what it would do to the country's political and social fabric. I tried to write an essay entitled "On Admitting Error about Vietnam."

"It is no longer possible to argue that the U.S. involvement was anything but a mistake. But what kind of mistake? And only a mistake? The U.S. has never really had to admit a drastic national error. To admit error over Vietnam is unusually bitter, given the effort, the money and the lives expended. The U.S. was not motivated by desire for conquest or material gain; our entry into the war was essentially an act of faith, part of a long and complex battle with Communism. The mistake did not lie in trying to sustain South Vietnam against subversion and attack from Hanoi, but in a miscalculation about what it would take. But it was just that—a mistake of the kind, however grievous, that governments and nations do commit. Many of the radical anti-war protesters are thinking in a curiously puritanical way; they cannot accept a mistake but insist on turning it into crime or sin. The protesters seem to want not only an end to the war but an act of contrition by authority.

"The Nixon Administration has implicitly admitted the error—not of its own making—but not in so many words. A recognition of error remains important, partly for its cathartic effect. The U.S. is in danger of being driven, for years to come, by two rival myths: on the Left, that the war proves the fundamental evil of American society, on the Right that our military was deprived of victory by liberal betrayal. The two sides can come together, if at all, only if the error is admitted and faced."

I held the draft of the essay (condensed in the foregoing) for a few weeks. The administration, after all, was engaged in the immensely intricate business of extricating the United States without losing all public support. Amid the rush of events I never did run the piece, but I strongly believed in what I had written, and it informed the way *Time* would treat Vietnam and the aftermath.

Just how premature I had been in my hope that the two sides in the conflict at home could be reconciled became vividly clear to me in a movie made a few years later. It was called *Hearts and Minds* and was the work of Peter Davis, a young writer-producer of films and television programs. It was powerful and contained much truth, but truth artfully arranged. The film's basic technique was juxtaposition. An American pilot talking about the thrill of seeing something explode versus a Vietnamese peasant woman weeping in her bombed-out house. ("My daughter is dead. I will give you her beautiful shirt. Take it back to America and throw it in Nixon's face.") Lyndon Johnson pledging victory alongside a near crazed American football coach yelling: "Don't let them beat us!" The rational, analytic statements of U.S. government officials echoed against the long monologue of a disabled black veteran: "You don't want to hear about it, but I'll tell you about it [until] you siddown and puke on your dinner." But a great deal was missing. There was hardly a suggestion that the Communist guerrillas could be brutal, that many South Vietnamese were sincere and passionate anti-Communists, that the North was heavily supported by the Soviet Union and China. The spokesmen for American patriotism in the film came across as foolish; references to God and country were included for ironic effect. It was precisely the kind of divisive mythmaking that I had deplored in my unpublished essay.

THE DIFFICULT TASK of winding down the war was increasingly in the hands of Henry Kissinger. My first impression of him went back some years, to Martha's Vineyard. Beverly and I often took our children to the Island Country Club to swim. Much in evidence around the pool was a stocky man with a heavy German accent and an imperious manner. He seemed to be constantly busy reading or writing, and he kept commanding a club employee to fetch additional papers. It sometimes seemed as if he were reading even while splashing in the pool. I did not really get to know Henry Kissinger on those occasions, but I knew about him: Harvard professor of government, adviser to Nelson Rockefeller and author of *Nuclear Weapons and Foreign Policy*. In that book he discussed the frightening possibility of nuclear war, how to prevent it, but also how to prepare for it. It was widely assumed that Kissinger was the inspiration for Dr. Strangelove, Stanley Kubrick's wildly amusing caricature of a Germanic, bomb-rattling and plainly mad strategist. After Richard Nixon hired Kissinger as his national security adviser (at Clare Luce's suggestion), I saw him fairly often. Always preoccupied with press relations—concerning not only his personal reputation, but the public's view of the war—he held frequent, off-the-record news briefings. In addition he was in the habit of giving special background interviews to selected journalists, including Hedley Donovan and myself. He bore no resemblance to Strangelove, except possibly in his accent. (Later I met his brother, Walter, a successful businessman who spoke with hardly a Teutonic trace. When I asked Walter, as did many other people, how it happened that unlike his brother, he had no accent, he replied: "The difference is that *I* listen.") During the small talk before and after our sessions, Kissinger showed a lively interest in the world of corporate power, inquiring whether Hedley and I had come down from New York in a company plane and, if so, just what make and model. (It happened to be a Gulfstream II.) He was on his way to becoming a celebrity—divorced, he seemed to spend much time with movie stars and other glamorous women. His badinage with reporters was welcomed in Washington as relief from the rather grim Nixon White House. (Reporter: "Why do you give so few interviews?" K: "Look what mystery did for Greta Garbo." Reporter: "What do you do to relax?" K: "I crochet.") He had developed his self-deprecatory humor, and in our conversations he made frequent references to his spectacular lack of brevity and his desire to influence the press. He would say things like "Let me tell you what I would like you to print, and then we can start haggling."

When it came to substance he was invariably grave, and his deep, rumbling baritone seemed to carry, if not notes of doom, echoes of the risks and problems he was coping with. The basic dilemma was that the administration had decided on gradual troop withdrawals and "de-escalation" of the war while trying to achieve a negotiated settlement. As a result, Hanoi had little incentive to make concessions; it could simply wait until American withdrawals and American disgust with the war would make the U.S. position in Vietnam untenable. In the seemingly interminable stalemate at the Paris peace talks, the United States insisted that it could not simply pull out, thus sacrificing the Saigon regime to the North. Hanoi insisted on just that. "We cannot be responsible for all eternity for the survival of the Saigon government," said Kissinger. "What we can do is leave it in a condition where, with good conscience, reasonable people can say, 'They ought to be able to do it.'" And if not, if Saigon were to fall anyway, Kissinger said repeatedly, there should be at least "a decent interval."

Kissinger was thus involved in a multidimensional chess game. As he explained it, he had to persuade Hanoi that it had something to gain by negotiating, Saigon that it need not fear a sellout, half of American public opinion that we were not cutting and running and the other half that we were really withdrawing. But the chess game had even further dimensions. He was constantly trying to adjust himself to Nixon's swings in policy and mood, which oscillated between pragmatism and rage. He tried to persuade the hard-liners around Nixon that he was just as tough as they, while vainly trying to persuade his former Harvard colleagues that he was really working for peace. That partly explained his growing reputation as two-faced. Moreover, Kissinger saw a measure of duplicity as inevitable in diplomacy, and he tended to suspect people's motives. He reminded me of a famous anecdote about Talleyrand, who, when he got the news that the czar had died, remarked: "I wonder what he meant by that!"

The administration was often accused of being unpredictable, to which Kissinger responded typically in one of his briefings: "On most levels one wants to be predictable, but if the other side gets the idea that we're so predictable, that our course is so fixed that we will not be affected by anything they do and they can slowly bleed us, then their planning becomes very easy. So, unpredictability is not always harmful."

The administration's least predictable move was the 1970 invasion of Cambodia. That neutral country, whose frontier was a mere thirty-five miles from Saigon, had long provided supply depots and sanctuaries for the Communists. They had not been eliminated by U.S. bombing raids, which, typically, the administration had kept secret. Fear of antiwar protests prompted Nixon to use the kinds of deceptive tactics that Lyndon Johnson had begun with his Gulf of Tonkin resolution. The bombing having failed, Nixon and Kissinger decided to send in ground troops. The move was precipitated by the fact that Cambodia's ruler, Prince Sihanouk (*Time*'s old friend "Snookie"), was overthrown by a coup during his absence in France, where the obese monarch was taking the cure. In one of his most bellicose moods Nixon was determined to "blow the hell out" of the Communist sanctuaries. One night, an aide later recalled, Kissinger received a phone call from Nixon, who sounded drunk, and turned the phone over to his crony Charles ("Bebe") Rebozo, who said: "The president wants you to know if this doesn't work, Henry, it's your ass."

The action produced a tremendous uproar of protest about widening the war. I felt that the war had already been widened by the Communists, who had broken out of their sanctuaries and were driving to seize the government. But I was appalled by Nixon's apocalyptic rhetoric. *Time* was highly critical, pointing out that "he not only failed but failed disastrously" either to secure Cambodia or to intimidate Hanoi. I could never agree with critics that the United States was responsible for genocide in Cambodia by enabling the fanatical Cambodian Communist faction the Khmer Rouge to come to power. Chances are the Khmer Rouge would have taken over anyway.

In explaining Cambodia and other crises, Kissinger always spoke calmly, more in sorrow than in anger, even if *Time* had just taken shots at the administration. He had a manner of treating a journalist as an intellectual equal, a form of flattery that was sometimes hard to resist. He often complained that in his grueling job he had no time to read anything but official papers and that he was compelled to live on his "intellectual capital." If so, I thought he had plenty of capital to spare. I became fascinated by the way his mind worked. Even in his more Machiavellian moments he was still the professor. He spun general principles out of specific situations. He rarely discussed a move, political or military, without forecasting the likely reactions and the reactions to the reactions. He always anticipated attacks on his positions by his trademark phrase: "Reasonable people can disagree, but . . ." He never lost his ability of seeing the other side's point of view. "The North Vietnamese have not fought for twenty-five years," he said, "in order to give away at the conference table what they didn't give up on the battlefield."

Again and again in his briefings he came back to the domestic opposition. "The unrest on the campuses has very deep, maybe even metaphysical causes. It is the result of the modern bureaucratic state, of the sense of impotence that is produced in the individual about decisions that he does not know how to influence." He blamed much of the situation on academics ("my colleagues and myself") who had spent thirty years "debunking" the system. "The academic community has taken the clock apart and doesn't know how to put it together again." On another occasion he deplored the revolt against all authority: "If confidence in the president, any president, and all our institutions is systematically destroyed, we will turn into a group that has nothing left but a physical test of strength and the only outcome of this is Caesarism. If that happens, it will not be upper-middle-class college students who will take this country over but some more primitive and elemental forces."

The notion of Caesarism in America struck me as exaggerated, an echo of Kissinger's European experience. I shared that experience, of course (we are about the same age and came to the United States at about the same time), but I always had a more optimistic view of American society and what it could withstand. His unease about American stability, I thought, also conditioned his view that a precipitous retreat from Vietnam would not only damage U.S. credibility throughout the world, but would have disastrous consequences within the country. "Are you influenced by Germany after World War One and the stab-in-the-back legend?" I once asked him, referring to the widespread notion among Germans at the time that the defeat had been caused by domestic opposition and treachery. He denied that he was thinking about that precedent except in the most theoretical terms, but I was not so sure.

By mid-1970 I said in a *Time* essay that if the president declared the war to be a mistake and announced a much faster exit, the country would go along. But I conceded that there was room for argument. While no decision about Vietnam could have been taken in the Nixon White House—or any other White House—without regard to its effect on the voters, I did not agree that concern for the impending 1972 elections dictated the Nixon-Kissinger timetable and negotiating strategy. I believed that they were genuinely convinced, rightly or wrongly, that a premature departure would seriously damage America.

Time was indirectly involved in the Cambodian conflict through a brief but dramatic incident. A talented young journalist named Robert Sam Anson had been assigned to the Saigon bureau. He was a fervent antiwar partisan who developed a particular passion for Cambodia. Dick Clurman had been replaced as chief of correspondents by Murray Gart, an excellent, experienced correspondent who handled his staff in a manner that would have impressed Patton. After Anson returned to Saigon from a Cambodian assignment, Gart read his files and found them so heated and unbalanced that he instructed the Saigon bureau chief never to send Anson back into that theater. Through a glitch, the order was ignored. Anson headed back to Cambodia and was promptly captured by the North Vietnamese. To get him released we decided to make as much noise as possible, through press releases and cables to various officials, in hopes of persuading the Communists that they had an important prisoner and they better be careful with him. Gart had the idea of appealing to Father Theodore Hesburgh, president of Notre Dame, where Anson had studied. "I knew he remembered Bob Anson as the biggest pain in the ass that ever got to the Notre Dame campus," as Gart put it. Nevertheless, Hesburgh volunteered to appeal to the Vatican, which still had links to Hanoi; Sihanouk also helped. After more than three weeks Anson was released. Later, when we had learned Pham Xuan An's true identity, it seemed more likely that it was he who had really managed to spring Anson, who extolled his captors: "The treatment there was really marvelous. They treated me first as a friend, and after a while we really got to be brothers," he told interviewers. "I didn't feel like I walked out of San Quentin, because the atmosphere was not like a prison, it was like a home." Before leaving that "home," Anson gave an antiwar statement to the Communists for use on their radio. Although it was never broadcast, his words and actions were outrageous for a professional journalist. He offered to quit to avoid embarrassing *Time*. But none of us knew what it was like to be held captive in the Cambodian jungle, even by "brothers," so we decided to keep him on, if only—as one of Anson's least favorite officials might have put it—for a decent interval. But not in Vietnam. All along he had protested against the way his reports were being edited—including his account of his Cambodian experience—and after working in New York for eighteen months, he quit. I sometimes argued with him about Vietnam and enjoyed the exercise, but I came to understand how Father Hesburgh must have felt about him.

IN THE AFTERMATH of the Cambodian invasion, the antiwar movement—and the anti-antiwar backlash—reached a climax on May 4, 1970. It happened at Kent State University after three days of student demonstrations in the normally placid town of Kent, Ohio. The fatal chronology has remained familiar: Governor James Rhodes, who refers to protesters as "worse than Brown Shirts," calls out the National Guard; when the student demonstrators refuse to disperse, some throwing rocks, the Guardsmen loose an apparently coordinated volley of rifle fire. In a few moments four students are killed and ten wounded.

The spectacle of unarmed students being shot down by American troops, many of them of the same age and background as their victims, was stunning; I felt that something snapped in the public mind.

I went to Kent State ten days later at the start of a three-week trip through the Midwest. The university had been shut down and evacuated immediately after the debacle. The gently sloped green campus was deserted except for some men with tape measures and sketch pads who were still trying to map the shootings: half a dozen stakes in the ground with white tags to show where bullets struck; a chalked outline of one body, already beginning to fade; a red cross painted on the ground to mark the place where another student was killed. Not far away were the women's dormitories. Through the uncurtained, trustingly unprotected windows, I saw the scenes of hasty departure. The bunk beds were unmade, pillows and blankets on the floor; irons stood upended between containers of Sea Mist spray starch and Love cosmetics. Snapshots of boyfriends—who could have been among the dead, the wounded, the rioters, the bystanders or possibly the Guardsmen—were tucked in mirror frames. One of the beds carried the sign "Welcome to Cloud 9." I kept looking for clues to what happened and why, but the answers were not to be found on the silent campus.

In nearby Akron I attended a service conducted by the well-known television evangelist Rex Humbard at his Cathedral of Tomorrow, a huge, circular edifice with glass-and-marble walls surrounding five thousand seats and a vast stage hydraulically lifted or lowered. Under a one hundred-foot-long cross, suspended horizontally from the dome and flashing red, white and blue light, the Reverend Humbard preached eloquently on the importance of parental love and guidance in the home. His handsome wife, Maude, sang "What a Friend We Have in Jesus," backed by country guitars and a choir. Later she discussed the events at Kent State: "I would rather see my sons dead, dead in their caskets, than to see them tear down the flag or insult their country like those kids at Kent." In other circumstances I might have been moved by such passion, but now I was troubled by the flash of hate and the unforgiving spirit. A very different note was struck across town, in a half-deserted union hall, by a black shop steward representing the rubber workers, then on strike. "I hear a lot of the guys on the picket line saying that shooting was too good for those kids at Kent. But I tell them, if this strike gets ugly, why, that same Guard could be coming after us."

During past trips I had always felt that America was constantly swaying between "This is the greatest country in the world" and "How are we doing?" But if that suggested a note of uncertainty, I always found reassurance: in America's energy, ingenuity, humor, common sense, and in the sheer size of the land, which seemed to dwarf all quarrels. This time these old talismans did not work as well as before. I thought of Disraeli's "two nations," not divided by wealth and poverty as in nineteenth-century England, but by two opposite views of reality. Within every state, within every community and within many individuals there seemed to be a conflict between the open and the closed mind, between attempts to understand or merely to condemn.

I saw this in El Dorado, Kansas, where I stopped off next. I had chosen it for its name: it's pronounced El Do-*ray*-do, but I thought its symbolic significance was irresistible. It was Elm Street: a town of thirteen thousand people, solid houses, well-kept lawns and a handsome junior college standing like a graceful fortress on the windy Kansas plain. El Dorado had a gleaming, computerized newspaper plant to keep up with the outside world—not that it really wanted to keep up. The paper's editor, Rolla Clymer, said: "If we had our way, we'd build a fence around this town." He represented a new type of isolationist, who did not so much want to withdraw from foreign countries as from New York, which seemed more menacing than the jungles of Indochina or the wiles of Europe. In the country club, with its placid hilltop views, I met with a group of leading citizens who reflected El Dorado's bitter confusion about the war. As elsewhere, there was the tendency of turning the conflict into a morality play: honor, freedom, the American future versus crime and shame. People still spoke of making a stand against Communism, but they were increasingly unsure that Vietnam was the right place. Even the fiercest hawks were now inclined to see our involvement as a mistake. There was the usual indignation against the protesters who burned draft cards or the flag. One civic leader observed: "Well, maybe we need something of the police state; maybe we do need a little repression." But a few in the group also defended the young and argued that they must be heard: "They have some valid points," said the Methodist minister Melvin Short.

I next revisited my old Main Street—Sauk Centre, Minnesota. The place looked remarkably unchanged since I had seen it a quarter century before, slightly larger (the population had increased by a few hundred), slightly cleaner and shinier. Most of the old Main Street landmarks had remained, except there were now two drugstores instead of one, and neither attracted many teenagers, who preferred to be out driving around. The First State Bank stood, unchanged, as a monument to modest solvency, and Ben DuBois was still chairman of the board, holding court behind his rolltop desk in the middle of the lobby. Ben was eighty-five (he would not retire until his death at ninety-six) and opinionated as ever. Most of the members of the Economists' Club were also still alive, and Ben assembled a rump session at the Waldorf Cafe. He was vehemently opposed to the Vietnam War. "A tragic mistake," he called it, "a damn fool mistake." Everyone was shocked by Kent State. A few of Sauk Centre's young men were serving in Vietnam, but war and demonstrations seemed remote. The Midwest and the country might have passed Sauk Centre by, but I was still touched by its durability and fundamental decency.

Later in Minneapolis I again felt the temblors of protest. At the University of Minnesota a student strike was in progress. In front of the student union a rock band was playing. Inside, coeds sold pamphlets—Marx, Marcuse, Che. Everywhere the calls to specific action: organize transport, line up pickets. In times of stress, concrete actions, even trivial ones, bring a sense of relief. There was much talk of revolution—the word was repeated like an incantation. They scarcely had any idea what revolution involved. When I told them that I thought they were really calling for radical reform, they brushed aside such distinctions. "What difference does that make?" asked one of the strike leaders. "Those are just labels." I tried to argue that such labels had made big differences in the past, but they were impatient with any allusion to history. To them history had begun just yesterday. There was much talk about human rights versus property rights. When I mentioned violence—"trashing," for instance—one woman student said with utmost sincerity: "But that's not violence. That's just about property, not about people." She failed to realize that for millions of people, acquiring and keeping property was a very human right indeed.

I was almost absurdly grateful when people announced that they wanted peaceful change; that used to be a minimal attitude in a democratic society. Now I found myself wanting to rush up to anyone abjuring violence and shake hands with a fellow moderate. Most of these young people, I decided, not for the first time, wanted the impossible and wanted it right away. But I also knew that as Americans we must be careful about what we dismiss as impossible. There were moments when

I was touched by their passion and wondered with a pang whether they knew something I did not. I tried hard to build an intellectual bridge to the young. Infuriating though I often found them, I felt that they were calling America beyond the ordinary life of nations. They were echoing, unconsciously, American exceptionalism, the belief that the country must live up to a special destiny. "That is why," I wrote in *Time,* "within reason, we must cherish them."

A few days after she read this Clare Luce called, as she did occasionally. "I see you're defending the radicals," she said in her silvery voice, more ironic than accusatory.

"But Clare," I replied, "I defended them only in the sense that in their own way, like Harry, they want this to be a great country."

"It doesn't work, Henry," she said. "I can't buy that argument and I don't think Harry would, either."

CHAPTER TWENTY-EIGHT

AFTER KENT STATE it was as if the country had looked into an abyss and drawn back with a shudder. Many disillusioned activists went into hiding or moved into the mainstream. Many were haunted by the contradiction of using violence to fight violence. Andrew Kopkind retreated to rural Vermont for a long stretch of self-imposed silence. "Just about everybody went crazy in their own way," he told me later. "It just all seemed as though it had fallen apart."

The country was never free of the sounds of Vietnam, but its temper changed. Norman Mailer, the literary godfather of the sixties, was part of the different, more complex climate. A long feud between Mailer and *Time* began, as he later explained to me, with a savage review of his second novel, *Barbary Shore*, which the magazine described as "paceless, tasteless, graceless." He was particularly incensed because the reviewer, of course, was not identified, and he felt "that everything that's cowardly and nasty in a writer can come out when you don't have a byline." Politically he considered *Time* to be "the spiritual leader of the Cold War," a conflict in which he felt the United States had, at best, half a case.

"For me in those days, *Time* magazine was the equivalent in the literary world of the CIA," he said. In *The Prisoner of Sex* he suggested that he had married Jean Campbell, Luce's former mistress, partly to strike back. He recalled that the protagonist of one of his stories had referred to his "sexual instrument" as the "Avenger." With his marriage, wrote Mailer in his inimitable way, he "whammed nothing less than a Retaliator in and out of Vengeance Mews."

Reporting the famous March on Washington, *Time* had been particularly rough on him; the story had him drunkenly staggering about the stage at a rally, mumbling, spewing obscenities and describing his desperate search for a toilet: "I'm like LBJ. He's as full of crap as I am."

Soon after I took over as managing editor, I decided it was time for a truce, and I wrote to him suggesting a meeting. To my surprise, he agreed. Mailer walked into the Brussels Restaurant with that strange rolling gate suggesting a wary prizefighter, a diffident and engaging smile on the ruddy face beneath the Brillo hair. We realized quickly that we would like each other much better than we had anticipated. He thought me less of a hawk than he had expected, and I found him less radical than I expected. In fact, I thought him deeply conservative— left-conservative, as he put it. He declared himself bored by Marxism, but his conservatism was not so much political as instinctive and atavistic.

Mailer grew heated on the subject of plastics, of all things, a bugaboo of his for years. The mere touch bothered him. "Our generation in America had a certain dream of getting to that suburban garden party where they would drink champagne on the lawn. An astonishing number of them got there—and they're drinking champagne from plastic glasses. They're getting 80 percent of what they thought they were going to get. Not 100 percent. Or take the kids. I think plastic is one of the reasons they grow up so bad. Have you ever seen them with plastic toys in their mouths? I think some of their senses are numbed at an early age and that interferes with learning. I think that God gave us all the materials with which to build a world. And we don't have to add plastic to that." Not only a conservative, I thought, but a crank conservative.

We finished the lunch close to four o'clock in a haze of martinis and Bordeaux, vowing to keep in touch. Mailer compared us later to "logrollers from separate villages who bob and smile at one another when occupying the same log." We were still slightly wary. He described me once as a "sophisticated cigar," which I took as a compliment, although I'm not sure he intended it that way. Gradually we became friends (if not "roaring friends," as he carefully put it). That happened partly because, as he came to dinner parties at our house, he developed a great liking for Beverly. He found her more open, less self-conscious, than me, and he concluded, as he explained, that if she loved me, there had to be more to me than he had first assumed.

"You know, I had a great debt to you," he said, "because my life has been an attempt to get out of ideology. Meeting you introduced a complexity I'd been holding off for years. Which is that you can disagree profoundly with someone and still have reasonable personal relations with them."

Much later Mailer and I reminisced about the sixties. We were both drinking mineral water, not martinis. He had grown stouter, grizzled and patriarchal and in many ways even more conservative. "I remember the period not as a happy time, but as a lively time that was also full of fear and foreboding. There was this arrogant philosophy that no one over thirty was worth listening to. I happened to be over thirty, so I didn't like that too much. Most of those middle-class kids didn't know what they were doing. So I concentrated on Vietnam and didn't get into the other stuff." One of the disasters of the sixties, he felt, was that the black movement began to be separated from whites. Another result of the sixties was political correctness, which he said he loathed. As for feminism, "I was just out to sea on it. I didn't realize how powerful a movement it was, until it came up and hit me in the face."

IT DID NOT hit me in the face but kept poking and prodding me. The images of the long-legged goddess bestriding the world, and of the all-American bitch so dear to middlebrow literature, had faded. Instead there were the new feminist guerrillas manning the barricades—many of them pedantic enough to object to the use of "manning." In a near fatal trend toward self-caricature, they advocated "herstory" instead of history and "girlcott" instead of boycott. Feminine endings were swept away—sculptor, not sculptress, for Louise Nevelson—but in *Time* I managed to hang on to actress and waitress. I also resisted chairperson and, especially, the idiocy of "chair."

Among the fiercest of these militants was Kate Millett, a sculptor and college instructor who had published an explosive book, *Sexual Politics*, of which her former thesis adviser at Columbia University remarked: "Reading it is like sitting with your testicles in a nutcracker." In it she argued that "patriarchy," including the family, must be destroyed. She claimed that there was little biological difference between men and women with the exception of the specific genital characteristics. That, I thought, was quite an exception. We put her on *Time*'s cover, and she sternly looked out at the reader from under unruly dark hair. (Her mother, though a proud supporter of her daughter's views, complained that "Kate's missing the boat if she appears . . . without her hair washed.")

Hardly any of the women I knew shared the more radical feminists' views, but the atmosphere changed. Facing a woman across a desk or a dinner table, I found myself wondering if she considered me an enemy. Once, I stepped aside in an elevator to let a woman colleague walk out first. She said: "Oh, cut it out, Henry. This is bullshit."

I came out of a tradition in which women were seen at the center of a mystery, the mystery of birth and rebirth, an earthy and inescapable reality. Anatomy might not be destiny, as Freud had put it, but its essential conditions would not change unless and until humanity regularly reproduced itself in laboratories. Still, in an era when technology had virtually eliminated the importance of physical strength, when everything from childbirth to housework had been radically eased, women could and should do practically everything men did.

While I sincerely believed this, I was slow to act on it at *Time*. In the early 1970s the magazine had six women writers in a total of nearly sixty writers and no women senior editors. Responding to a question from a group of *Time* women about what the future might hold, I wrote a memo asserting that "any talented writer, male, female or otherwise will be happily considered for employment. There are no limits to careers for women at *Time*, up to and including senior editorships (or

managing editorships for that matter). I must add in candor that I have
not met many women who seem to have the physical and mental energy
required for *Time* senior editing. (Of course, I have not met too many
men who fill that bill either.)" It was a highly patronizing statement,
and I was embarrassed by it in hindsight. I atoned, partly by appointing
two female senior editors, Ruth Brine and Martha Duffy.

But "the women" were becoming increasingly restive. I discussed the
situation regularly with an informal women's committee and was taken
aback when, without warning, they filed a complaint with the New
York Division of Human Rights, charging discrimination on *Time* and
all the other Time Inc. magazines. Several editors including myself
appeared for a preliminary hearing, alongside the women's delegation.
We faced one another across a large square table. It was odd to see
colleagues as adversaries. To my relief, the examiner returned the case
to us for direct negotiations between the company and the employees.
After a weary eight months we reached a settlement with the state and
the women's group, in which Time Inc., in effect, said that we hadn't
done anything wrong but wouldn't do it again. We pledged more opportunities for promotion and invited women who wanted to write to volunteer for regular tryouts. We promised that editors and others would
"act as talent scouts" and be on the lookout "for signs of good writing
among the female staff." One sardonic researcher remarked: "Maybe we
have a television show here; move over, Arthur Godfrey, here comes
Henry Grunwald's *Talent Scouts.*"

But progress was slow, partly because disappointingly few women had
volunteered for writing tryouts. One writer I hired from the outside was
B. J. Phillips, who had worked for the *Atlanta Constitution* and *The
Washington Post*. She had a deserved reputation as a tireless, uncompromising reporter. I assigned her to write politics and later (after she
returned from a four-year stint with *Ms.* magazine) I made her our
sports editor. As something of an anomaly at *Time*, she felt under constant critical scrutiny. ("I could feel eyeballs on my back. A lot.") She
looked like my idea of Huck Finn, an impression reinforced by the blue
jeans she wore constantly and deliberately. ("I was every day in-your-

face with the clothes.") She broke that dress code on one occasion when the governor of her native state, Jimmy Carter, came to lunch, and she stunned her colleagues by appearing in Calvin Klein velvet knickers. Once, when she went on a two-week vacation, her editor, Jason Mc-Manus, and several colleagues plastered her entire office, including the ceiling, with nude photographs from *Playboy* and other sources. When she returned she was faced, as she put it, with "more tits than the world had ever seen." She did not say a word to anyone but next day walked casually into McManus's regular story conference and sat down in her accustomed place, topless.

But despite such hazing she spoke of *Time* warmly. It offered, she said, "the best editing, the best conversation, the best quality of mind. People denigrate group journalism, but they don't understand. There was a wonderful sense of camaraderie, a sense that you were doing something extraordinary together, a band of brothers and an occasional sister."

I wished that she could have been with me when *Time* and I were taken to task by the emerging feminist leader Gloria Steinem. We squared off on a talk show hosted by the engaging Dick Cavett (who had been a copy boy at *Time*). I was preceded by a pair of trained otters, a hard act to follow. As for Gloria, she was dazzling looking, with cascading hair, articulate and sharp. She recalled once having applied to *Time* for a job and being told that she could be only a researcher, not a writer.

I made some rather sexist remarks, calling our female employees "a great delight" and adding, "Some of my best friends are women." It happened to be true, but I said it for a laugh and got it from a sympathetic audience.

Generally Steinem attacked women's conventional role in society. I invited her to contribute a piece to *Time* about what life would be like if women's liberation won out. In a two-page article she outlined her vision. All careers would be open, and a woman who chose to be "her husband's housekeeper and/or hostess would receive a percentage of his pay determined by the domestic-relations courts." Half the country's legislators, she predicted, would be women, along with "a woman president once in a while." This would reduce the country's "machismo problems" because it would do away with "the old-fashioned idea that manhood depends on violence and victory." No more "domineering wives, emasculating women and 'Jewish' mothers. No more unequal partnerships that eventually doom love and sex." There might even be fewer homosexuals, she suggested, "with fewer overpossessive mothers and fewer fathers who hold up an impossibly cruel or perfectionist idea of manhood."

Most of this struck me as a rather preposterous fantasy. But Steinem sounded reasonable compared to Millett and some other feminists who were asserting that all sex was rape, marriage was slavery for wives and society was a male conspiracy to subjugate women. A debate at Manhattan's Town Hall, a year later, is still remembered by some as a defining battle in the war between the sexes. Billed as "A Dialogue on Women's Liberation," it pitted leading feminists against their archvillain Norman Mailer. I went to Town Hall in the spirit of attending a gladiatorial fight. I rooted for Norman but fully expected him to be mauled if not dismembered. Among the combatants was Germaine Greer, one of the best-known feminists, whose book *The Female Eunuch* had argued that, contrary to the stereotype, women's sexuality is not passive. Like an avenging angel in mod clothes, she vibrated with inner fury. ("Do you suppose," I whispered to Beverly, "that anybody ever dares to tell her 'You're beautiful when you're angry'?") Next there was Jill Johnston, a journalist for the *Village Voice*, a militant lesbian who appeared in black from head to toe, her long hair mostly hiding an unadorned face. A sharp contrast was provided by Diana Trilling, writer and critic (and wife of the literary sage Lionel Trilling), impeccable in dress and manner, good-natured and fair. Finally Jacqueline Ceballos, president of the New York chapter of NOW (National Organization for Women), whose reputation for militancy was belied by her Junior League appearance. As for Mailer (I don't recall what *he* wore or how long *his* hair was), he was on his best behavior but wary. He somehow suggested Prince Paris coping with the goddesses on Mount Ida.

The audience, with a sizable admixture of vocal feminists and a sprinkling of celebrities, was unruly and very much part of the action. There were a few sensible arguments, I thought, advocating equality for women, including equal pay. An early skirmish occurred when Greer complained that in our society women were either menials or goddesses or both and Mailer retorted: "Why can't women be goddesses and slobs at different times of the day?" Diana Trilling spoke reasonably about feminism not being a single movement: "We don't all want the same things." She attacked the feminist line that there was no such thing as a vaginal orgasm and hence men were not necessary in bed, remarking with good humor: "I would hope we'd be free to have such orgasms as we're individually capable of." Occasionally Mailer lost his temper. "Hey, cuntie, take it easy," he yelled back at a heckler at one point. What terrified him about the women's movement, he remarked, was its lack of humor.

Humor was provided, though not intentionally, by Jill Johnston, who proclaimed: "All women are lesbians except those who don't know it yet. All men are homosexuals. We're not liberated women, we're lesberated." Suddenly a woman ran up from the audience, jumped on Johnston, began kissing and fondling her, and the two fell to the floor and rolled about on the stage.

At the end the audience filed out of the hall, half-angry, half-amused. Beverly was mostly amused. "Well, Norman survived," she said. "But there were moments when I wanted to go up there and slug a couple of those dames."

To FURTHER EXPLORE the conflict, and to exploit it, I launched a new section in *Time* called The Sexes. We assembled a rather motley round-table, including Kenneth Tynan, the brilliant British critic and impresario of *Oh! Calcutta!* (a mixture of salacious skits and nudity that I found amusing and not especially erotic). Dapper, slightly effete, Tynan looked like something out of Evelyn Waugh, with conversation to match. He offered a memorable defense of pornography: "I think it's an absolute social necessity in the case of some people who are ugly and old and lonely." Then, possibly remembering the audiences that were packing *Oh! Calcutta!*, he added: "But that does not mean it should only be for the ugly, the old and the lonely."

Curiously enough, Jacques Levy, the director of *Oh! Calcutta!*, struck an almost puritanical note when he observed, "When a society's civilization is about to crumble, it immediately returns to the expression of sexuality as the only thing left to somehow titillate and excite." The last word unquestionably belonged to the actress Shelley Winters, then forty-six, who was quoted in an accompanying story on stage nudity: "I think it is disgusting, shameful and damaging to all things American. But if I were twenty-two with a great body, it would be artistic, tasteful, patriotic and a progressive, religious experience."

Women's liberation and sexual freedom were legacies from the sixties to the seventies. The movements were part of a larger phenomenon: the cult of the self, the gospel of personal fulfillment.

The "human potential movement" had emerged in the sixties and kept going. At its shrine in Esalen, near Carmel, California, thousands of people, mostly middle class, came to "get in touch with their feelings and with each other." In one exercise, the "hero sandwich," thirty-five people cuddled in one tight row, regardless of sex. Corporations sent their executives to get sensitivity training, and (at a comparable institution near Washington) State Department employees, including ambassadors, were similarly sensitized. The ultimate endorsement of Esalen came in the form of a Ford Foundation grant.

In a spirit of prurient curiosity I visited Sandstone, an establishment similar to Esalen, with a much crasser emphasis on sex. I was accompanied by a young reporter from *Time*'s Los Angeles bureau, David DeVoss. The first sight to greet us was a pair of young women, nude, sitting on top of an ivy-covered wall, waving cheerfully. Inside, more nude people relaxed on sofas and armchairs. The one area we were not shown was the basement "ballroom," which, we had heard, was outfitted with wall-to-wall mattresses. Our host was Sandstone's founder, John Williamson, a portly, youthful, soft-spoken man in shorts and a jersey, who was eager to tell us about Sandstone's philosophy. It was a new kind of community, he explained, in which people were free to do anything they pleased as long as it was not offensive and hurtful. The human body is good, and open affection and sex are good. He talked about the therapeutic value of it all, the casting out of guilt, and quoted from the Sandstone brochure: "Here, a person's mind, body and being are no longer strangers to each other." The underlying theme was that the greatest enemy of a happy society was inhibition, which I doubted. We had reached a point, to my mind, where a little more inhibition was overdue.

On our way back to Los Angeles I asked DeVoss what he thought the difference was between Sandstone and Esalen. Sandstone, he replied, only thinly rationalized its eroticism. Esalen was saying "We're sitting here nude to save the planet."

ACCORDING TO ONE estimate, America now had approximately two thousand settlements, some admittedly tiny, devoted to alternative life-styles (in the increasingly fashionable phrase), some merely hedonistic, some trivial, some serious. Across the United States people were taking up spiritualism, prophecy, I Ching, witchcraft and Satanism. The phenomenon ranged from well-organized and well-financed churches of devil worship to commercialized mysticism. Episcopal bishop James Pike, whom I had known as a serious, if unconventional, churchman, claimed to have communicated with his dead son through a medium.

Time went so far as to assert: "There is a genuine realm of magic, a yet undiscovered territory between man and his universe."

All this really amounted to a quest for alternate religions. One of these new faiths centered on the conviction that growth was bad, that mankind would destroy itself unless saved from unlimited development. Closely related to this no-growth gospel was environmentalism, which had taken hold of the country's (and *Time*'s) consciousness. Many people, I noticed, began to pronounce the word "earth" with a tremulous reverence. The globe, hurtling on its lonely way through space, was our only home, and we must protect it, cherish it and, yes, even worship it. The emerging ecological gospel was turning an important commonsense warning into a vision of the apocalypse. Contrary to its antitechnology bias, I felt that if we were to cope with such problems as waste and overpopulation, we would need more rather than less technology and growth.

Most of the assumptions that had been dominant for so long—progress, reason, science—were being questioned. Freudian psychology seemed to have shrunk into mere formula, physics dissolved into metaphysics, and religion was teetering between empty ritual, social action and mysticism.

I tried to have *Time* address these currents in a four-part series entitled "Second Thoughts About Man." It turned out to be somewhat vaporous. Mortimer Adler wrote me that it was "undigested and unadulterated balderdash"; one installment in particular was "the most nauseating compilation of rubbish I have ever read." (He and I remained friends anyway.) But the series at least illustrated the current intellectual and emotional turbulence and the proliferation of substitute faiths. Their apostles often wound up on the cover of *Time*, instead of the theologians of the Luce era.

They included such figures as Barry Commoner, the environmentalist who crusaded against everything from atomic fallout to wasteful refrigerators; B. F. Skinner, the behaviorist who wanted to control mankind into salvation or Robert Coles, the humane student of children and the poor. Nevertheless I began to notice an odd phenomenon. It was no longer easy to find individuals to personify what was significant in American society. Many subjects had grown too large and too complicated, too much the result of group effort and trends. We used symbolic illustrations for such topics as the threat of heroin, growing American inefficiency, the old in America, the generation gap, skyjacking, campaign financing, nutrition.

As for Vietnam, the dominant faces were still Nixon's and Kissinger's. The medley of all those other subjects was a kind of escape from the inescapable war. It was coming to an end, but the end was agonizingly slow.

CHAPTER TWENTY-NINE

S HE WALKED INTO MY OFFICE IN KHAKIS, her face bare of makeup, more angular and plainer than I remembered it from the screen. Only a few years before, Jane Fonda had appeared as Barbarella, a futuristic sex object; now she was the Joan of Arc of the antiwar movement. Amid much public outrage she traveled to North Vietnam. She inspected damage inflicted by American bombing on what she considered nonmilitary targets, including the dikes and pumping systems of Haiphong harbor. She broadcast messages urging U.S. pilots to "consider what you are doing," which in the reports at home sounded very much like an appeal to desert. Back in the United States she was greeted by shouts and signs of "Hanoi Jane!" "Red pinko!" "Commie slut!" Although I considered her actions outrageous, I invited her to visit *Time*.

"You should know what is going on and should print more about it," she said. "I cried every day I was there. I cried for America. The bombs are falling on Vietnam, but it is an American tragedy. When asked if she was seeing only one side of the issue, she replied: "There are no both sides in this."

Jane Fonda was part of the last big wave of protest. Nixon kept withdrawing American troops, while the bombing of North Vietnam continued, eased off, was stepped up again. Convinced as I was that even the end of the war would not end the national divisions over Vietnam, I tried to maintain some kind of dialogue, however limited, with the antiwar movement. So I asked David Greenway, one of *Time*'s Boston correspondents, to gather some antiwar critics who flourished in the academic communities of Cambridge.

Murray Gart, the chief of correspondents, and I joined Greenway, a journalistic veteran of Vietnam, for a dinner that included Edwin Reischauer and James Thomson, two noted Asia scholars then teaching at Harvard. The most arresting figure at the table was Daniel Ellsberg, a fellow at MIT. He was, as Greenway later put it, on a high, almost hysterical, waving his arms as he spoke and making rational debate nearly impossible.

At the end of the evening Ellsberg asked Gart and me if we could give him a lift home. During the drive he pressed on me a large sheaf of papers. They were, he said, writings about Vietnam, some of which, he thought, *Time* might find of interest. I tossed the papers to Murray Gart and forgot about them. Shortly afterward, *The New York Times* printed, in seven pages, the first installment of a secret Pentagon report about Vietnam that had been leaked to its editors. When the leaker identified himself on television as Daniel Ellsberg, a terrible suspicion seized me. I phoned Greenway in a mild panic. "David," I said, "the other night in the car, Ellsberg gave us a bunch of stuff. Murray is away, and I can't find it now. You don't suppose they were the Pentagon Papers and we didn't know what we had?"

Ironically Ellsberg was then hiding out from the rest of the press in a cabin Greenway owned in the Boston area. After a few minutes Greenway called back. "You can relax," he reassured me. "Those were not the Pentagon Papers, just some articles Ellsberg hoped you might publish."

The Pentagon Papers were the product of a massive study, commissioned by Defense Secretary Robert McNamara before he resigned in 1968 and carried out by a Rand Corporation team, to determine just how the United States had become, and stayed, entangled in the war. Ellsberg, who had worked for Rand and was a McNamara protégé, had converted from hawk to dove. He felt that the public should know about what he considered criminal mistakes and misrepresentations that had dragged the United States into the war. The classified documents were strictly historical and involved no current military or diplomatic actions. Nevertheless the Nixon administration sued to stop future installments on national security grounds, only to be overruled by the Supreme Court. The justices found no threat to warrant "prior restraint" of publication. I could see why Nixon was furious about the massive leak— although, as *Time* pointed out, the government was going to absurd extremes in stamping even innocuous material "secret." But Nixon and his people crossed a line when they tried to discredit Ellsberg by sending a team of undercover operatives to burgle the offices of Ellsberg's Los Angeles psychiatrist, hoping (vainly, as it turned out) to find damaging information about him. According to the polls, a majority of the public sided with the press on the issue of the papers, although many people failed to see why it was permissible to print stolen government documents. *Time* asked editors around the country what they would have done if the documents had been offered to them. The vast majority said that they would have been somewhat disturbed about ignoring the "top secret" classification but would have published anyway. As for me, if Ellsberg had really offered me the Pentagon Papers that evening, I would have used them.

The incident illuminated the growing siege mentality that was developing in the White House and raised the long-standing war between Nixon and the press to new levels of bitterness. Agnew kept attacking in public—"Some newspapers are fit only to line the bottom of birdcages . . ."—while Nixon fulminated in private or semiprivate. His frequent sounding board, or wailing wall, was my erstwhile rival, Jim Keogh. After my appointment he had let it be known that he considered it a mistake but accepted it. He worked loyally for a while as my deputy, but after the 1968 election he decided to join the White House staff as a speechwriter for the president. (He later became head of United States Information Agency.) At a farewell dinner I gave for him with the magazine's senior editors, Keogh sounded bitter. He knew, he said, that we had all voted for Humphrey (not true) and not to expect any favors from him once he was in the White House. Nixon often discussed journalists with Keogh. In his *Diaries* Haldeman quoted the president: "They all suffer from excess intellectual pride, totally self-centered, hence can't admit they're wrong and can't tolerate being proven so. Thus their hatred for [me] who's proved them wrong so often. Also none has integrity . . . The intellectuals of the Left are actually a new group of fascists." Keogh told him: "Most young journalists are activists, feel they have a mission, not to report but to influence." Nevertheless Nixon was furious that he failed to make Man of the Year after his 1968 election.

The selection of *Time*'s Man of the Year was never a democratic process. Nominations by readers were carefully tabulated, all editors and bureau chiefs were invited to submit suggestions, but somebody had to make the final choice. That somebody was the managing editor, whose decision, of course, was subject to ratification by the editor in chief. Donovan and I decided that it was Nixon's turn in 1971. We requested an interview to run with that story, and Nixon received us in the Oval Office, where we found him markedly relaxed, in a blue blazer, pleasant flames crackling in the fireplace. It was not an interview to make headlines. Looking toward the following year's elections, he predicted that Vietnam would not be an issue because we were getting out but suggested, rather airily, that the Democrats would find *something*. Could the main issue be his personality? I asked. The lack of charisma often cited by his critics?

His reply was pure Nixon, defensively aggressive. It was a legitimate question, "in a way," thanks to "our superheated media." A lot of people wanted a "flamboyant" leader, but maybe "when you really have a crunch, when it is really tough, when the decision made in this office may determine the future of war and peace," it might be better to choose an "individual who is totally cool, detached and with some experience. Now I am not describing anybody, of course. . . ." The last was said with a rather satisfied half-grin.

We had asked to tape the interview and were assured that the U.S. Army Signal Corps would take care of it. Shortly after we left the Oval Office, we were informed by crestfallen aides that the taping had gone wrong; all that was audible was the crackling fire. We managed to reconstruct the interview from memory and notes. Later, when it became clear during Watergate that Nixon's private taping system had missed nary a compromising word, I sent Hedley a note: "Where was that crackling fire when they needed it?"

As it turned out, the Democrats did not pick a candidate for the 1972 election who could be mistaken for flamboyant or charismatic. He was Senator George McGovern of South Dakota, who had once been described by Robert Kennedy as "the only decent man in the Senate" and who was also probably the most earnest. The Miami convention that chose him was shaped by new Democratic Party rules he himself had helped to write after the 1968 Chicago melee. The reforms broke the old party machinery, greatly enhanced the role of primaries and opened up the convention to new kinds of delegates, especially more blacks and women. The McGovernite convention organizers kept out the delegates controlled by Chicago mayor Richard Daley (who sensed what was coming and did not even go to Miami).

McGovern's acceptance speech was delayed until nearly three A.M. by procedural bickering and a series of mock vice-presidential nominations (Ralph Nader, Cesar Chavez, Archie Bunker and Dr. Benjamin Spock). He promised that ninety days after his election all American troops and prisoners of war would be back in the United States. He made the return from Vietnam into a kind of chorus: "From secrecy and deception in high places, come home, America. From the prejudice of race and sex, come home, America. . . . Come home to the belief that we can seek a newer world. . . ."

I felt that the come-home device of the speech (which he had largely written himself) was strained and awkward. Meeting him at breakfast a few days earlier, I found his voice somewhat whiny and his gray face reminiscent of oatmeal. His speech, however, did contain flashes of real passion, which led *Time*'s Hugh Sidey to describe this son of a Wesleyan minister as "St. John the Baptist on Collins Avenue. He believes devoutly in the prescription of the Bible. There shall be no war. Feed the hungry. Minister to the sick. Take from the rich and give to the poor." His agenda struck me as the closest thing to European social democracy I'd ever heard proposed in the United States by a major political party.

He misjudged Middle America, though its virtues seemed embodied by his life: youth in a tiny prairie town, service as a bomber pilot in World War II, honorable years in the Senate. His social program violated Middle America's continuing belief in the work ethic and individual initiative. Even voters of modest income opposed his proposal for taxing away all or most inheritances above half a million dollars. McGovern was puzzled: "I don't know whether people still think they will win a lottery or what."

He favored busing, sounded mild on law and order and was described by his enemies as the triple-A candidate: abortion, amnesty and acid. Ever since the New Deal, the Democrats had succeeded by running against the Great Depression. Now economic security, while still highly important, was no longer the voters' main concern; in a sense, it was emotional security. The big conflict was over social problems, values, standards. In this conflict McGovern failed, rejected as the embodiment of the sixties.

His disastrous defeat by Richard Nixon was further assured when it became known that his running mate, Senator Tom Eagleton, had once had shock therapy for depression. McGovern pledged publicly to support him "1,000 percent" and then dropped him. While tricky Richard Nixon appeared remote and statesmanlike throughout the campaign, honest George McGovern emerged as a vacillating radical.

MEANWHILE THE PARIS peace talks were dragging on. *Time,* and the rest of the press, carefully followed the alternating positive and negative bulletins, reporting any and all sightings of Henry Kissinger in Paris. Obviously the war would be over sooner or later, and *Time* prepared a special supplement. It was written, edited and set in type, to be used at the right moment. We kept updating the stories. On October 26 Kissinger remarked on a television news conference: "We believe that peace is at hand." Cynics suspected that Kissinger was trying to influence the election, a little more than a week away. I did not think so, if only because such a maneuver would have been too risky and might backfire. Kissinger had made his "peace" remark on a Thursday, which did not leave me much time before our Friday-night closing. We tried desperately to find out whether the long expected cease-fire was really at hand. All the hints we gathered were inconclusive but tantalizing, and I finally took the plunge and ordered our Vietnam finale onto the press. The following Monday we would be out with twenty pages and a cover proclaiming "The Shape of Peace." I was nervous when I told Donovan on the phone late Friday night of my decision. He greeted the news with the longest silence I ever heard from that master of silences. "I see," he finally said, clearly skeptical.

His skepticism proved to be right. The negotiations fell apart again, partly because Thieu objected to some of the concessions made by the United States, partly because the North Vietnamese procrastinated and partly because Nixon did not want to seem weak at the last minute. He let it be known that he was angry at Kissinger for having been too optimistic. Nixon and Kissinger then ordered the famous "Christmas bombing" of the North to get Hanoi back to the peace table.

Still, we decided to go ahead with an earlier decision to make Nixon and Kissinger joint Men of the Year for 1972. In addition to Vietnam, it had been an extraordinary year for this strange pair. Nixon's mission to China, prepared by Kissinger's secret trip to Beijing in July 1971, plus the Moscow summit with Leonid Brezhnev ten months later, drastically changed the international terrain.

The approach to "Red China," which for decades had been treated by the United States as an untouchable plague zone, was extraordinary for many reasons. It required a certified anti-Communist like Nixon to make it politically acceptable in the United States. "Nixon-in-China" became for me, as for many others, a permanent political maxim. The agreement to put the paralyzing issue of Taiwan to one side took not only negotiating virtuosity on Kissinger's part, but the courage to defy the dwindling illusion that Chiang Kai-shek's heirs on Taiwan still represented the legitimate government of China. The ghost of Chiang's great supporter still lingered in the Time & Life Building, and I asked myself how Harry Luce would have felt about the deal. My hunch was that, however reluctantly, he would have approved of it. In conversations during the years before his death he showed himself resigned to the reality of Communism in China but predicted that it would not last. It was, he argued, contrary to the essential Chinese character. In the late fifties he had urged Secretary of State John Foster Dulles to allow American journalists into China, and he continued to plead for maintaining communications with Beijing. He also displayed a certain pride in any sign of Chinese power and unity, even if these happened under Communist rule.

The accord with Beijing and the widening détente with Moscow meant that Nixon and Kissinger were successfully exploiting the long-standing rift between the two Communist capitals, following balance-of-power strategy that was second nature to Kissinger. The United States has always distrusted the balance-of-power concept, as well as "power politics," but to my mind there was no other kind of balance and no other kind of politics. The use of power need not imply lying and cheating, but, on the other hand, it could not be replaced in the real world by the mere radiation of virtue.

Both Nixon and Kissinger were specialists in power. In his long career Nixon had learned how to maneuver the interests of voting blocs; through study and instinct Kissinger understood how to maneuver the interests of nations. They complemented each other. Kissinger scrupulously gave Nixon credit for American foreign policy, although he sometimes distanced himself from the boss to suggest that he was trying hard to keep the impulsive Nixon under control. Nixon, in turn, was apt to rant about Kissinger (as about everyone else). According to rumors, confirmed much later, he sometimes even threatened to fire "the Doctor." But Nixon needed Kissinger and knew it.

The news that he was to share the Man of the Year title with Kissinger infuriated Nixon. As we were preparing the cover story, Kissinger phoned me, asking to be left off the cover. "Henry," I said, "people usually ask me to be put *on* the cover."

"I know," rumbled Kissinger. "But the president is really upset."

Kissinger next appealed to Hedley Donovan—twice. "I told him," Hedley reported to me later, "that if he didn't stop pressuring us, we would put him on the cover alone."

When Kissinger described the president as really upset, he was not exaggerating. Nixon issued instructions, as Haldeman later recalled, that Kissinger was not to see people from *Time* under any circumstances, "that I'm to order him to do no interviews, social, return calls or anything to *Time*. And he told me to call the White House operators to turn those calls off to Henry, which, of course, I can't do."

A week after the inauguration the Vietnam cease-fire was finally signed. The terms differed only in detail from the near accord reached the previous October. Hanoi agreed that the Vietnamese government would stay in power and that the South's future would be settled by internationally supervised elections, concessions the North had refused for years. On the other hand, the United States agreed that North Vietnamese forces could stay in the South, pending further negotiations, which obviously made the future of the Saigon regime extremely dubious. But it now had what Nixon and Kissinger had insisted on all along: a chance, just a chance, for survival. The inevitable question was whether the United States could have obtained the same terms much earlier, saving thousands of lives. I thought not. But *Time*'s answer, based on the consensus of our correspondents, was a careful "maybe." Kissinger argued that a significantly earlier deal was made impossible by Hanoi's intransigence, and later some North Vietnamese leaders confirmed this to Western scholars and journalists.

Ultimately, of course, the North broke its agreements, launched a massive offensive against the South, and the U.S. Congress—understandably—refused any further American help. When the cease-fire was signed even the pessimists did not foresee that final, ghastly tableau two years later when the last American helicopter took off from the roof of the U.S. embassy in Saigon with Vietnamese desperately hanging on to the craft as it lifted slowly away from the scene of America's worst defeat. Certainly no one could have imagined that this image would one day become the high point of a wildly successful London-Broadway musical. (I could imagine my father, the author of that earlier, more innocent Saigon musical, *Dschinah,* comment: "Tasteless! Trivializing history!")

. . .

TRYING TO MAKE sense of the constant crises and surprises of Vietnam and compressing them into about fifty magazine pages was, to me, a stunningly exciting job. It was also difficult and complex.

Two quotations about the business of editing have stayed in my mind over the years. One is from Carlyle: "Is not every able editor a ruler of the world?" The other is from Henry Adams: Editing "was a dog's life when it did not succeed and little better when it did." I certainly never agreed with Adams's bleak view, nor with Carlyle's inflated notion of my work. But I did rule *Time* with an extraordinary degree of independence. As was his custom with new managing editors, Hedley Donovan had observed me closely for about six months, reviewing each issue story by story—"grading your papers," as Tom Griffith put it. After that I was cut loose, but Donovan still commented on the magazine and was kept informed by me of any major projects, cover stories and staff changes. I found that Donovan, the very model of a tempered, balanced thinker, was apt to complain that *Time* essays suffered from too much balance, too much on-the-one-hand, on-the-other-hand ball bouncing. He could also be rather puritanical and was indignant about some very explicit passages in a cover story about Marlon Brando in *Last Tango in Paris* (which drew a record number of protest letters and canceled subscriptions). I suggested that readers were not likely to imitate the Brando character's sexual practices because they had read about them in *Time*. Donovan demurred.

But I was able to persuade him that it was absurd to continue the traditional split setup, in which the Time-Life News Service, headed by Murray Gart, did not report directly to the managing editor. Donovan decreed that henceforth the news service would be part of *Time*, but in large institutions such matters are never settled by decree, especially not if they involve a personality like Gart's. He had come to time after various newspaper jobs from Hawaii to Kansas and had performed admirably in several major bureaus. He could be a good companion, but his entire body seemed tense with combative instincts, and often his eyes assumed a hard gleam that conveyed the sheer pleasure of resistance. During months of negotiations he fought for every inch of auton-

omy he could retain, piling on several new conditions for each concession he made. I developed intense sympathy for Henry Kissinger and his
arm wrestling with Le Duc Tho, North Vietnam's chief negotiator. An
agreement was finally achieved, on paper, but in practice Gart and the
news service remained recalcitrant. We reached a working relationship
that might be described, charitably, as creative tension.

I also had to get along with the publisher of *Time*, who was responsible for all business matters. Advertising circulation, newsstand revenues,
printing costs and the like for years had been a nebulous area to me, as
to all editorial employees. That comfortable ignorance was swept away
quickly when I became managing editor. My instructor in these black
arts was James Shepley, the publisher when I took over. He was a
former correspondent and Washington bureau chief who had made the
rare transition to the business side. He had worked as an aide to General
George Marshall during and after World War II and in Richard Nixon's
unsuccessful presidential bid in 1959. Both as a journalist and an executive, he was brash, impatient, rude, explosive, sharp, honest and, to my
mind, altogether admirable.

Shepley was succeeded by Henry R. Luce III, Harry's son. I had come
to like "Hank" and his warm, irrepressible second wife, Claire, who
often talked to me about how he really should succeed his father as the
boss of the whole outfit. But despite his large, inherited stockholding,
the board of directors did not see it that way. Hank had worked in
various jobs around the company and had served as a good bureau chief
in London. But his intelligence and ability were hidden by a shell of
formidable awkwardness, aggravated by Claire's death from cancer.
When he became publisher he tried at first to interfere with editorial
matters, sending me critical notes about various stories. Despite my
affection for him I could not tolerate this. I asked him to stop the
memos. He took it in good part, and we remained on friendly terms.

My most frequent contact with the publisher came at budget time,
when editorial costs were under scrutiny. During the early years of my
tenure this was rarely a big problem. In those flush days I could afford
to be somewhat casual about money matters, especially expense accounts. My attitude, I suppose, was typified by one episode I remember

with some pride. A *Time* team captained by Jason McManus took part in the regular softball games among New York publishing firms. McManus's secretary, DeWitt Smith, took it upon herself to provide amenities for a decisive game against *Newsweek*. She appeared in Central Park in a rented limousine, bearing a silver tea service and a catered spread of shrimp, smoked salmon and white wine, along with linens, china and glasses (no Styrofoam, she insisted). The object was morale building, and it worked. The *Newsweek* team, with a few six-packs of beer and no food, lost six to one. When an outrageous expense account reached Dick Seamon, the editor whom I had put in charge of such matters, he brought it to me. "I'm damned if I'm going to okay this," he said. "All this fancy food! A tea service! A rented limousine—and here's the last straw, a traffic ticket for the limo!"

"But Dick," I said, "we won."

I learned to like the "managing" part of being managing editor well enough. But I sometimes resented the time it took away from editing, just editing. I came to understand, more clearly than I had before, that there were two kinds of editing: micro and macro, to borrow from the economist's vocabulary. Microediting involves phrases, meanings, clarity, structure. Macroediting involves subject matter, events, trends in the news and in journalism, including the entire personality of a publication. While I had mellowed considerably since those early days when I kept rewriting copy, I never got over a certain zeal for microediting. Colleagues sometimes referred to it unkindly as fiddling with stories. I tried as best I could to be a guardian of the language by hacking away at what I considered jargon and clichés. My marginal comments, I fear, often consisted merely of "Ugh! Ugh!" which one irritated colleague termed "the American-Indian school of editing."

Everybody could use editing; in a series we once ran I found a contribution from Marshal Tito badly in need of work, and I offered to edit it myself or have him make some changes; both suggestions were indignantly refused. I did not exempt myself; on one occasion, when I wrote a short insert in a story, I was dissatisfied and sent it on to a colleague, asking him to edit it. The word around the office was that this was excessive even for "HAG."

I could rarely read anything without a pen or pencil in my hand and often scribbled changes in the printed copy of the magazine. I was once caught, on an airplane, editing a story in *Newsweek.* I have even been known to correct misprints in hymns during weddings and funerals.

Ultimately I learned that editing was a matter not of making statements and asserting opinions, but of asking questions. One of the things I always found exciting about working for *Time* was that you could ask any question and expect to get an answer. I was constantly amazed to find, going through newspapers, how many questions remained unanswered in every article and every paragraph. I developed an almost physical connection with news. Certain events, certain ideas for stories, announced themselves, literally, in my pulse or in the pit of my stomach.

I usually began to put the magazine together by reading through the sheaf of suggestions from our correspondents around the country and the world. Late the week before, editors had drawn up preliminary story lists, and now, on Monday and Tuesday, they would come to my office to discuss them. Correspondents had already received "queries"; now others followed, outlining the expected story and asking for specific reporting.

As soon as replies from the correspondents came in on Wednesday and Thursday, writers started their stories. These went to the senior editors to be worked over. That copy reached my desk in heavy waves on Thursdays and Fridays. I would read it, often scribbling detailed suggestions for changes. When I found it necessary—and this was not rare—I would meet with the senior editor and writer and request a revised version, sometimes with twenty-four hours to spare before closing time, sometimes with much less than that. Meanwhile I would be shown pasteups of the layouts prepared by the art department. I would usually request changes, trying to balance the conflicting claims separating the makeup and production people from the word people. On Friday the stories I had already seen would reach me a second time with changes in place. Thus I saw every piece of copy twice, with the exception of a few departments that I had turned over to a deputy and saw only the second time around.

After Keogh's departure I appointed a new deputy, Edward Jamieson. He was brilliant and hardheaded but also modest; he was apt to stress that he had gone to Boston University and not to Harvard. His manner was formal, and he was never seen without a necktie; he was once reported as "streaking," meaning that he had been spotted without his jacket. I came to rely on his solid judgment and to delight in his wicked sense of humor, which flashed out from behind his reserved manner. When the gifted photographer and writer Jill Krementz worked briefly for *Time,* she seemed to some rather excitable. "Delirium Krementz," Ed called her. Eventually I appointed a second deputy, Dick Seamon, a former marine pilot and reserve lieutenant colonel noted for his fascination with technology and his belief in military discipline. He was forever campaigning to get people to work early and firmly believed that only train commuters were well informed because they had enough time to read the paper. (Dick lived in Long Island, near the notorious retired gangster Frank Costello, whom he had befriended and whom he fondly called "Uncle Frankie.") He was a no-nonsense editor who resisted my frequent attempts to get the latest possible information into a story. We often argued about the nature of the newsmagazine. *"Time* is a synopsis," he would say. "And that is enough for the readers. We don't have to try to be up-to-the-minute." I disagreed.

Putting out the magazine still required the same late hours that Priscilla Baker had complained of so many years before. Indeed, the increasing complexity of our layouts and the more thorough reporting I insisted on kept everyone at work even later. I was occasionally accused, with some justice, of aggravating the situation by pondering certain stories longer than strictly necessary.

The week's most demanding effort usually involved the cover story. Its subject was apt to be dictated by major news events. But more often we had innumerable choices, and I liked to think that our selections had become less conservative than in the past. One of my preoccupations was trying to avoid the same cover as *Newsweek.* Correspondents frequently fed us rumors—sometimes accurate, sometimes false—about what "the competition" was doing. Occasionally we managed to trap ourselves in this game, as when both magazines came out simultaneously with a cover on Bruce Springsteen. Once, Jim Shepley took me aside and told me that he could get me regular information on *Newsweek*'s cover choices, presumably through a mole. I rejected the offer. The only sensible thing to do was to make our own decisions without looking over our shoulders.

Normally a cover story would be reported some weeks ahead of time, but events often dictated a "crash" cover requiring a new illustration, new reporting and new writing within a few hours. On such occasions I found myself mouthing that oldest of *Front Page* clichés, "Stop the press," and I must confess that it thrilled me. Even in routine weeks I sometimes ordered two different cover stories, allowing me to choose late in the week. This was not popular with the staff, and it was expensive, as the "business side" never failed to point out. I did not make my mind up quickly or easily, and I would argue that nothing is more expensive than a quick but wrong decision. Nevertheless, in the spirit of self-criticism I asked Seamon for an embroidered sampler he had shown me that read: "The Editor's indecision is final."

Closing the magazine was complex and required long hours of waiting. These were eased by alcohol, which was provided to the staff, along with dinner, on late nights. When some people overdid the drinking, we rationed the liquor supply to one bottle per department. Over the years the staff doctor and I had to cope with several cases of alcoholism. I reluctantly made a rule for myself never to have a drink on closing night before the last piece of copy had left my desk. Other kinds of stimulants could be found. On one occasion, it happened to be my birthday, a copy boy placed a large, handsomely carved box on my desk. I opened it and found twenty or thirty tightly rolled marijuana cigarettes. "It's really good stuff," said the copy boy.

"I'm sure it is," I replied, "but I can't accept this. For one thing it's illegal, and for another it's too expensive a gift."

"It's not a gift, we're just trying to educate you."

There was nothing like the rhythm of words and pictures finally fitting into a pattern. I could sense the editorial floors humming like a well-functioning machine, except, of course, that it was a machine made up of people—people for whom I felt the special closeness that comes with shared, hard work and the vertigo of late hours. Beverly and the children, while more or less resigned, often complained. On my late nights the children were asleep by the time I came home to our apartment, although Beverly usually waited up for me. When Lisa was about eleven, she wrote a poem that expressed her view of my job in pitiful terms.

The Managing Editor

The papers stretched before him in a maddening array
He tried to figure out if he should use the art display
He looked up from his papers when his conscience would permit
Regarding clock and wristwatch when an interval seemed fit
His secretary buzzed him on his fancy telephone
His wife, on the extension, urged him to come home
Saturday was creeping in his bones, under his skin
And, before he knew, hallucinations would begin
Peace talks, war talks, Nixon and his economic freeze
He wondered just which piece of land the Arabs next would
    seize
He packed up all his troubles in his black attache case
After giving thought to who would win the presidential race
He stepped outside, the rain was pouring, not a cab in sight
And he asked the good lord why he had to work so late at
    night.

Lisa did not realize that far from complaining to God or anyone else about my brutal hours, I rather enjoyed them; they were part of the extraordinary excitement of running *Time*, an excitement unknown to civilians who lived by a conventional clock and calendar.

True, our work was disposable. I once visited a magazine wholesaler in New Jersey and saw a huge shredder, two stories tall, with conveyer belts carrying returned magazines toward big blades rising and falling. The cutting edges came down—slash—on *Time* and *Newsweek*—slash—on the *National Review* and the *Nation*—slash—*Penthouse* and the *Christian Century*. Here we all were, equal and companionable under the knife, as those shiny pages were cut into long curling strips and piled slowly into indistinguishable mountains of paper. Here it was not dust to dust but pulp to pulp. Yet all of it would be recycled. That was a symbol of our craft that involved constant renewal. As the old issues died the new ones were already closed and on the way to the newsstand.

CHAPTER THIRTY

ONE OF OUR WASHINGTON CORRESPONDENTS, Sandy Smith, had phoned saying, mysteriously, that he wanted to talk about something important.

I had never met Sandy, but I knew that he had been an investigative reporter on Chicago newspapers before coming to *Life* and then *Time*'s Washington bureau. He worked largely on his own, virtually underground. Everyone else was clamoring for bylines, which I had begun to use in the magazine, but Sandy never wanted his name or his picture in *Time*. Publicity, he said, would put off his good sources in the FBI, the CIA and the Mafia.

I found him a pleasant, bearlike man who blinked frequently, as if unaccustomed to light. His conversation was interspersed with chuckles, suggesting knowledge of nefarious and possibly amusing secrets.

"I smell something very fishy in this Watergate business," he said, "and I don't think you guys up here are taking it seriously enough. I've been talking to my people over at Justice and a lot of other places. Somebody is trying to keep the FBI from going after this. There have been calls from the CIA trying to wave them off. National security, they claim. It would take somebody with real clout to pull this."

Sandy wanted to keep on digging, but he wanted to feel that "New York" would pay attention.

It was not gullibility that kept many of us from grasping the significance of Watergate in the early stages. On the contrary, it was sophistication. Any observer of American politics was accustomed to a certain
amount of dirty tricks. Surely past administrations had used wiretaps for
political reasons. But why would important people in the White House
run the risk of exposure and scandal? It had been clear, well before the
election, that McGovern was going nowhere. But Nixon had barely
squeezed past Humphrey in 1968, so he might well have tried to seize
every advantage in 1972.

At first *Time*'s reporting lagged behind that of other news organizations. Under its dynamic editor Ben Bradlee, who was backed by one of
the best and most courageous publishers, Katharine Graham, *The Washington Post* was way ahead of everybody else in covering Watergate. But
soon our Washington bureau became more aggressive. The most prolific
digger was still Sandy Smith, but he was not alone. Virtually the entire
bureau pitched in, and correspondents later recalled the experience with
the nostalgic glow of veterans. Staffers worked practically around the
clock (so much so that Hugh Sidey, then the bureau chief, politely
requested a pay increase for his people). Hays Gorey, who was covering
the special prosecutor's office among other assignments, recalled, "We
talked to each other in a way we never had before. We helped each
other out." To some extent our reporters, and the rest of the press,
served as conduits of information from the FBI, the Justice Department
and even from grand juries.

I began to sense the exhilaration of a detective story slowly unfolding.
Years later I could still feel the excitement of clues coming to light,
connections emerging, pieces of the puzzle fitting together. But I could
also still remember the chill caused by the ominous question of what all
this might prove about the president of the United States. Our stories
were excruciatingly careful and constantly pointing out that there was
no evidence of the president's direct involvement. The rest of the press
was equally reluctant to accuse him. Hugh Sidey believed that Nixon
had known about the break-in all along and possibly even planned it.
"Few things happen in that White House," he said, "without Nixon
knowing about it." Certainly his closest aides, such as John Mitchell,

would not have kept anything like the break-in from him. Besides, he thought that this was the way the game was played in Washington, that either he would do it to the Democrats or they would do it to him. But our stories only blamed Nixon for creating an atmosphere in which the Watergate transgressions were possible. My own hunch was that he might well have said in effect, "Do what's necessary," without him getting directly involved. It was impossible to foresee that Watergate would grow and spread and cover the landscape like an eruption of monstrous pods, devouring the presidency.

THE COUNTLESS SUMMARIES and replays of Watergate, published later, gave the impression of a well-constructed drama, revelations following each other almost logically in a straight line to the inevitable end. In fact, the story unfolded slowly, in a zigzag pattern, amid doubt and disbelief. As I write this, trying to retrace that pattern in my mind, I once again encounter the weird cast of characters that might have populated a novel by Richard *(The Manchurian Candidate)* Condon. There was G. Gordon Liddy, one of the original "plumbers," who had broken into the office of Ellsberg's psychiatrist and helped plan the Watergate burglary. Liddy was forever trying to demonstrate to himself and others that he was not afraid. He had eaten a rat at the age of eleven (cooked) and, in the most famous episode, held his hand over a candle flame without flinching. There was Howard Hunt, Liddy's fellow plumber, former CIA agent and author of suspense novels *(One of Our Agents Is Missing)*. He made a point of noting that he had once worked for *Life* and *The March of Time* (confirming, among other things, my suspicion that roughly every third person in America has at one time or another been employed by Time Inc.).

The identity of the characters and their misdeeds began to blur. Was it McCord (James McCord, the former CIA agent and White House consultant) or Magruder (Jeb Magruder, that is, of the Committee to Re-elect the President) who accused John Mitchell, the former attorney general, of having been in on the Watergate planning. Or both? As for Chuck Colson, special counsel to the president, was he Nixon's evil genius? What most people were sure about was that Colson had said he would walk over his grandmother to help Richard Nixon. What connected most of these characters was brimming pipelines of money—including hush money for the Watergate burglars. Was the chief paymaster Nixon's lawyer, Herbert Kalmbach, or Maurice Stans, the undersecretary of the Treasury, with his safe that contained a million dollars in cash? Just what was the role of Howard Hunt's wife, who was killed in an airplane crash carrying ten thousand dollars in cash? There was no doubt about Tony Ulasewicz, a retired New York cop who distributed money to people he never saw by leaving packets of one-hundred-dollar bills in building lobbies or luggage lockers, often finding it difficult to "get rid of all those cookies."

Behind all of them loomed H. R. Haldeman and John Ehrlichman, the most powerful men in the White House next to the president. I thought of them as Fafner and Fasolt, the two monstrous giants in Wagner's *Ring* who guard the treasure of the Nibelungs.

After ten months of denials what had become known by the catch-all label "the cover-up" began to break down. The president's earlier statements, his press secretary, Ronald Ziegler, declared in a memorable phrase, were "inoperative." Then, stunningly, Haldeman and Ehrlichman themselves became inoperative. As they were increasingly implicated in the cover-up, Nixon forced them to resign. In effect, he put the blame on them while still calling them "the two finest public servants I have ever known."

At the same time he fired his bright young counsel John Dean, who had been acting as his designated point man for the defense.

In *Time*'s Washington bureau Hays Gorey decided to go after Dean. Gorey had a mild, almost sweet manner that hid a hard, inquisitive mind. People trusted him because of his gentleness. He kept phoning Dean's lawyer, Robert McCandless, who finally agreed to meet him. "He told me to bring my car. We wound up in Alexandria with McCandless telling me turn here, turn there. Then he got out and told me to wait, and there was John Dean!"

But Dean was not yet ready to talk. Gorey returned that evening bearing a bottle of wine and flowers for Dean's wife. Dean found that he liked Gorey and made clear what he was after. He wanted immunity from prosecution. So far, Archibald Cox, the recently appointed special prosecutor for Watergate, had refused to grant it. Dean and his lawyer thought that an interview in *Time*, framed the right way, might help. Gorey brought Dean to talk to me a few days later in New York. I found him tense but controlled, not looking quite as young as in his photographs. He was thirty-four, with an innocent, fresh-faced air. Gorey did not yet fully trust him—"I felt I always had to watch myself with him"—and Dean certainly did not fully trust *Time*. Dean explained that if he talked on the record, he wanted the magazine to plead for his immunity.

"We can't do that," I said. "And even if we did, I don't believe it would help you much."

He said that he and McCandless thought it would. "Can you at least tell me how you would characterize my immunity request? Could you call it 'justified' or something like that?"

"I can't commit myself about just exactly what we would say in a future story. But I think 'interesting' might be a reasonable characterization."

That did not satisfy Dean. I finally agreed that we might call his case "persuasive." In conversations with Gorey, Dean was still careful and doled out information in installments. Nixon, he said, in effect had lied when he'd announced that Dean had made a full report on Watergate exonerating all "presently employed" White House staffers. Dean claimed he had made no such report. He also let us know that Nixon had confronted him with two documents, one a virtual confession that Dean alone was responsible, the other Dean's resignation. Dean had refused to sign either, forcing Nixon eventually to fire him. Dean also said he had lots of evidence to implicate others, notably (as he had already told the Justice Department) John Mitchell. He kept pitching us to plead his case for immunity, threatening that if indicted, "I will probably never testify. Maybe everyone will have to wait until I'm an old man and write a book."

As it turned out, the public did not have to wait for the book. With limited immunity (he would plead guilty to a single count of conspiracy) Dean appeared before the Senate Select Committee investigating Watergate. Meeting in the grandiose Senate Caucus Room 318, under four glittering chandeliers hanging from a gilt-and-blue ceiling, the committee became a riveting national television attraction. It rivaled the spectacle of the Army-McCarthy hearings that had taken place in the same chamber nearly two decades before. The chairman was North Carolina senator Sam Ervin, a folksy, shrewd country lawyer who quoted the Bible a lot and constantly used down-home parables to illustrate his points.

Dean testified for five days, fluent and unruffled, wearing horn-rimmed glasses (instead of his usual contact lenses) that gave him an earnest, studious appearance. His pretty wife, Maureen, sat just behind him, looking, on the television screen, as if she were made of porcelain. Gorey stayed close to Dean, occasionally dropping by his house in the evening. "Mo" cooked hamburgers, gave her husband a rubdown, and they reminded each other to say their prayers before they went to sleep. He talked a lot about telling the truth for the sake of the nation, and while that was plainly self-serving, he did tell the truth—about his own involvement, about Nixon's and about the others'.

As I followed all this, my strongest reaction was disbelief. There was nothing surprising about Nixon's paranoia. It was a lifelong trait, demonstrated in casual conversations and in serious policy moves. He saw himself surrounded by relentless foes who could not begin to be enumerated in the "enemies list" kept updated at the White House. (When it became public in June 1973, I was surprised that no one from *Time* was on it.) Nixon's attitude was strengthened by events: years of demonstrations and riots, vilification of authority and denunciations of America. He also knew that he evoked an intense, visceral hostility in many people. As Kissinger once put it, even a paranoid may have real enemies. But what really baffled me was not Nixon's bunker mentality, but his belief that he could somehow convince the nation that he had not known, had been duped or was not responsible. According to the polls, at least half the country did not believe him. Nixon loyalists regarded the whole business as a liberal conspiracy to undo the last election. But the people who really troubled me were not the ones who believed that

Nixon was blameless, but the ones who thought the whole thing was not very important. Yes, some laws had been broken, technically, but there had been no "real crimes." (After all, no one was killed.)

To clarify my own thinking, I wrote some lengthy notes: "The ultimate and unspeakable corruption of Watergate would be if the American people were to decide that it does not matter. The ultimate and unspeakable act of corruption by the President, no matter what else he did or did not do, would be to confirm the American people in that corruption."

Should Watergate be allowed to overshadow Nixon's accomplishments in foreign affairs? After arguing with myself for a dozen pages, I concluded that, historically, Watergate might prove to be more important than the opening to China, détente with the Soviet Union and other successes, because it involved the character of America.

Feeling that way, I continued to let *Time* go all out. Before it was over we ran more than thirty cover stories related to Watergate. *Time* staff members, working in nonpolitical areas, began to complain to me that their sections were being squeezed by the Nixon saga. Some subscribers also felt that we were indulging in overkill, but to judge from the volume of reader mail and the booming newsstand sales, the vast majority felt otherwise.

Week after week the Nation section was almost suffocated by a paper flood of reporting. Its senior editor, Jason McManus, who had started at *Time* as Common Market correspondent in Brussels, was just the man to cope coolly and efficiently with information overload. He organized the material with an engineer's eye and refused to be rattled by the almost permanent crisis emanating from Washington. At times he also resisted late-breaking news that would interfere with an already laid-out section. An editor of exactly the opposite inclination was Marshall Loeb, who had been handling "Business" and whom I assigned to fill in for McManus while he was away for six months supervising the launching of a European edition. Thereafter, during the remainder of Watergate, Loeb moved in and out of the Nation section. An irrepressible journalist from Chicago, he did not recognize that anything was impossible. Tearing up a story or a section at the last moment to make room for new information delighted him. I was certain that if I asked him on closing night to produce a ten-page history of the world, he would nod, mutter his trademark "Sure, sure, sure" and set to work. He was relentless in the demands he made on himself and on his staff, who both admired and dreaded him.

One of the functions of our Watergate stories was recapping events that grew so complicated that keeping track of them resembled trying to trace the pattern of an electronic circuit board. That became the specialty of Ed Magnuson, who was to write most of our Watergate stories. He had spent a decade on the *Minneapolis Tribune*, where he often covered municipal scandals and corruption. It proved to be a good preparation for Watergate. Eyes squinting when he was trying to judge some new, sensational fact, "Mag" quietly, methodically prepared large wall charts of events and connections.

By far the most sensational revelation to appear on those charts was that Richard Nixon had taped every conversation in the White House for almost two years.

The revelation came from a witness before the Ervin committee, whose name had not yet even been mentioned. He was Alexander P. Butterfield, administrator of the Federal Aviation Administration and former aide to Haldeman. A meticulous bureaucrat, he looked a little like Elmer Fudd, but he was sharp and even possessed a sense of irony, rare in Washington. During a routine examination a junior member of the Ervin committee staff asked Butterfield, casually, whether meetings in the president's office were ever recorded. "Oh, God," replied Butterfield, holding his head, "I was hoping you wouldn't ask that." As he later testified publicly, there was a recording system in the White House, and Nixon had automatically taped his conversations. It suddenly appeared that all the testimony, all the speculation about what Nixon knew or didn't know, might be settled once and for all.

I believed that Nixon must have thought the tapes would somehow exonerate him—but then why did he fight so tenaciously against releasing them? There was never a satisfactory answer. After a long delay the U.S. Court of Appeals ruled that he must turn over the tapes to Judge John Sirica. He refused. Six days before, in October 1973, the Yom

Kippur War had broken out. There was concern that the USSR would become involved. Nixon used that as an excuse; in times of international conflict, he argued, the United States must not be seen as weakened by a constitutional crisis. He proposed a "compromise," offering to supply summaries of the pertinent tapes, their accuracy to be verified by a single, trusted senator, John Stennis, who was seventy-two and hard of hearing. Nixon carefully explained that special listening devices would be provided. It was a bizarre, almost surreal scheme, suggesting a desperate if not unstable state of mind. When Archibald Cox, the Watergate special prosecutor, refused the "compromise," Nixon, enraged, ordered him fired on October 20, 1973. The number three man in the Justice Department, Solicitor General Robert Bork, carried out the execution. I was surprised, for Bork was no Nixon loyalist. I had met him in Washington a few weeks before. Sharp, sardonic, Mephistophelian in appearance thanks to his goatee, Bork was rough on his boss. When I asked him what he thought Nixon's chances of survival were, he replied: "The president shouldn't be worried about surviving, he should be worried about a criminal indictment!" But Bork now carried out Nixon's order; as he later explained, he felt that a president could not be faced down in public by a subordinate official.

My first reaction to the news of the "Saturday Night Massacre" was: "Why do these things have to happen on weekends?" Other Watergate explosions had been similarly timed, and so here we were, once again, compelled to rip open the issue that had already gone to press. (Running a magazine can sometimes provoke rather parochial reactions.) But there was no way to miss the significance of what had happened. Nixon was now plainly out of control. Even loyal Republicans condemned him. "Impeachment" had been hesitantly mentioned for several months (*Time* had first discussed the possibility in April 1973), but now twenty-three bills were introduced in the House of Representatives.

For some weeks Hedley Donovan and I had been talking about the possible need for *Time* to make a formal statement on Watergate and Nixon. Traditionally *Time* carried no editorials. These were confined to *Life* or *Fortune*. After *Life* was "suspended" in December 1972 there were suggestions around the company that *Time* should now have an editorial page. I had argued strenuously against this because I did not think that we should abandon *Time*'s old recipe of blending information, interpretation and judgments. But strictly as an exception, Hedley and I agreed, *Time* should run an editorial calling for Nixon's resignation. But could we responsibly do that if the alternative was Spiro Agnew?

Our relations with Agnew had been turbulent. Before the 1972 election a *Life* editorial had suggested that Nixon should drop Agnew as his running mate for some better-qualified candidate. Agnew was furious. At a lunch in the vice president's suite in the Executive Office Building, next to the White House, Agnew confronted a group of us, including Hedley Donovan and Hugh Sidey. I asked him why he felt that he had to conduct his continuing war against the press. He fixed his sleepy gaze on me and said with contempt: "Mr. Grunwald, you are so naive." He went on to say that this was not one of "your usual Time-Life lunches. I am not here to be interviewed but to tell you some things that are on my mind." He complained about our coverage of him, reading from a list of uncomplimentary passages. He specifically cited the *Life* editorial and its statement that he was not intellectually qualified to be president. "My IQ happens to be 130. Is it for *Time* to decide who is qualified to be president?" he went on to berate us.

Hedley was indignant and said later that he had been on the point of walking out. Instead he'd looked at Agnew across the table and said: "Mr. Vice President, you work for us. You're a public servant. The reason we say these things about you is that we believe they are true and we have a responsibility to tell our readers."

As for the *Life* editorial, no insult was intended. Said Donovan, "There are any number of people, including friends and members of my family, of whom I think very highly, who are not qualified to be president."

After listening to Hedley in grim silence, Agnew changed the subject and started talking about the tapestries on the wall. Hedley later described his "some of my best friends" argument as rather jesuitic, but he obviously liked it. In the plane going home afterward he turned to me and said: "Henry, I have great regard for you, but I wouldn't want you to be president." I replied that barring a constitutional amendment, the issue was academic, as I had not been born in this country.

In the very suite in which we were having lunch with Agnew, he had earlier received cash payoffs in plain envelopes, if subsequent charges were true. The charges were part of the case against Agnew that federal prosecutors in Maryland would bring involving bribery, extortion, kickbacks and tax evasion that had begun while he was governor of Maryland. Agnew at first furiously protested his innocence, but in a plea bargain negotiated with the Justice Department he pleaded no contest and resigned. "I'm not surprised," said Nixon to an aide. "All those Maryland politicians are like that." Two days later he nominated Agnew's replacement, Gerald Ford of Michigan, the House minority leader, who enjoyed a reputation of being impeccably honest, not to say square. Several weeks later, with Ford's confirmation virtually assured, Hedley phoned me. "I guess it's all right to go ahead now," he said.

I had decided to write the Nixon editorial myself, and I had labored over it for several weeks, in secrecy. How strange, I thought, that three decades ago I had arrived in this country as a young refugee, in whose eyes the figure of the president of the United States was, if not God-like, certainly exalted. And here I was now arguing for a president's resignation. But despite a momentary pang, I felt I had the right to do this, as an American and a journalist. Colleagues who did not know me very well thought that, given my European background, I regarded Watergate cynically. The contrary was true. I did not think I was naive about the purity of American politics, but I wanted the United States to be, and believed it to be, an essentially decent country. Thus, Watergate hurt. It was in this spirit that I wrote and rewrote the editorial, updating and sharpening my arguments. Hedley edited my draft, strengthening some points and adding others. The piece was retyped so often that one long-suffering copy reader sent a note to my secretary: "This has been done 800 times. Check with HAG on final, final version." Although the business executives of Time Inc. would not normally be consulted on an editorial decision, in this case Hedley discussed our project with Andrew Heiskell, the board chairman, and Jim Shepley, by then president. They were enthusiastically for it. Ralph Davidson, a hearty, shrewd, but cautious executive who had risen from advertising sales to succeed Hank Luce as publisher of *Time,* was against it. "Perhaps for the good of the country Richard Nixon should step down," he wrote to me, "but should *Time* say so?"

Time said so in the issue of November 12, 1973, under the headline "An Editorial—The President Should Resign."

Nixon, the article argued, "has irredeemably lost his moral authority, the confidence of most of the country and therefore his ability to govern effectively. . . . If he decides to fight to the end, he faces impeachment by the House, for he has indeed failed his obligation under the Constitution to uphold the law. But even if he were to be acquitted, the process would leave him and the country devastated. . . ." Months of legal deliberation would leave the nation paralyzed, and so the "wise and patriotic course is for Richard Nixon to resign, sparing the country and himself this agony . . . Nothing can be found in U.S. history even remotely approaching the skein of events that the word Watergate no longer defines or contains. . . . One cannot think of any organization, public or private—including some dictatorships—where a Chief Executive could survive in office after such a performance. . . . An American President must be given the widest freedom of action." Even bad mistakes by him, even serious conflicts with the other branches of government, do not justify his removal but, the editorial argued (echoing the notes I had written to myself earlier), "there is a limit beyond which even such 'permissible' offenses . . . become intolerable. And the situation changes fundamentally when the effect of the President's action . . . is to subvert the constitutional system itself. . . . The nightmare of uncertainty must be ended. A fresh start must be made."

We released the text on Sunday evening, November 4, the day before *Time*'s issue appeared on the newsstands. It created a major stir. Most of the staff was taken completely by surprise—and delighted. TV and the papers gave the news big play. *The New York Times* also published an editorial calling for Nixon's resignation on that Sunday (I had not known about this in advance), but our stand drew special attention, considering *Time*'s past Republican coloration and the fact that this was the first editorial since its founding.

Some of my colleagues had a long-standing date with General Alexander Haig, Nixon's new chief of staff, at the White House the next day. The editorial, he said, was like "being hit in the face with a cold fish."

Public reaction was strong. Following the news reports, and without even reading the editorial, hundreds of angry callers besieged our switchboard. Within ten days 2,500 letters, mostly critical, had poured in, the largest initial reaction to any *Time* story so far. The prize winners, in my judgment, were Mr. and Mrs. David Moylan, of Roanoke, Virginia, who wrote: "You are hereby directed to stop publishing. You are under citizen's arrest for sedition, treason, subversive activities and other high crimes. . . ."

Another reader who was almost as vehement was Clare Boothe Luce. From her residence in Hawaii she wrote: "Fifty-year-old *Time* has written its first editorial. It demands the resignation of the President. The 70-year-old widow of Henry R. Luce, *Time*'s founder and its Editor-in-Chief for 43 years, is now writing her first letter to *Time*. And it condemns that editorial."

"Publishing your letter," I wired her, "will unquestionably lead to widely and gleefully publicized stories about a feud between you and the editors of *Time*. It will be exploited by people not necessarily in sympathy with the President, you or *Time*." She got the point and grudgingly withdrew the letter.

But that was not the end of it. She denounced the editorial in press interviews and sent another letter, this one not intended for publication. It was a remarkable document. She took off from speeches Hedley and I had made at *Time*'s fiftieth anniversary celebration (like the bash of a decade before, it was again held at the Waldorf, but without the cover celebrities). We both alluded to Watergate, but I also ambitiously proposed a new agenda for the seventies and said, among other things, that we must help reinvent liberalism on a more realistic basis. Hedley spoke about the moral issues raised by Watergate and asked rhetorically, "How could this happen? What went wrong here?"

In fourteen steaming pages Clare provided her answer. "How could Watergate *not* have happened, given the general moral condition of the country? It is the great liberal fallacy of our times to hold that public virtue can exist in a society where private morals and ethics are . . . at worst, non-existent. . . . For example there is today no consensus on the morality or immorality of abortion. The culture of a nation-society is all of a piece. It is like a great lake . . . pollute it anywhere, and every drop . . . becomes dirtier.

"Today we live in a culture where power, money, sex are the dominant values. Anything is . . . okay if it works, pays off, makes money, pleases the customer, satisfies voters, sells on the newsstands. . . . Where there are today no major poets, playwrights or novelists. Where *The Sensuous Woman* stays and stays at the top of the best-seller lists. Where Marlon Brando makes the cover of *Time* for being a pain in the ass . . . where the leading characters in the best-read novels are . . . Mafia Godfathers, hit men, cynical spies, seedy private eyes, grifters, drifters, hucksters, hustlers, copulators, homosexuals and masturbators. Where film producers find their plots in torture chambers . . . prisons, brothels and toilets. Where people cue up from Waikiki to Broadway to see a movie about a woman whose clitoris is in her throat, which she keeps stuffing, like a Christmas goose, with random penises . . . where editors of the nation endlessly deplored the brutalizing effects of the war in Vietnam on American youth, but see little connection between the growth of crime and violence among the young and the TV fare. . . . Where teenie-bopper singers let their pricks hang out for the dear little girl screamers, become millionaires overnight—and commit drug-soaked suicides . . . where editors inveigh against heroin and marijuana but ignore American's no. 1 drug problem, alcoholism because . . . there's so much money in liquor advertising. And without advertising, how could we editors afford to tell the people about the *fundamental* immorality of the Nixon Administration? In passing, Harry . . . was honest enough to say that *Time*'s taking of liquor ads was one of the sins he had committed as a publisher and a journalist. 'And God will damn well punish me for it,' said Harry (a knowledge which occasionally drove him to drink).

"It's a culture . . . where everybody does agree that God is dead—assuming He ever existed. . . .

"This is the Power-Money-Sex (and maybe death) oriented culture, which produced Nixon and Watergate. . . . I took some hope from Grunwald's banquet remark that 'We must help to reinvent liberalism.' It does rather need to reinvent . . . a new concept of 'integrity. . . .'

"Where were the watchdogs of the Republic when Lyndon Johnson . . . was using his White House connections to make himself a millionaire? It seemed to me that their keen noses could not or would not pick up the spore of corruption when it was dropped by a Liberal. . . .

"Although I am more than a little disgusted with the hubris of America's only Untouchable Institution, the Press . . . it may well be the last hope of American Democracy. . . . It is providing, though in unconstitutional ways, some of the checks on the power of the Executive . . . but it must exercise that power in the direction of restoring the power of the Congress. It must not, as is now the case, revel in its newfound position as the Fourth Branch of Government and take on itself the job of forcing the President to resign. . . .

"The Liberals . . . had better get on pretty fast reinventing liberalism. . . . And, as Harry would have done, saying a few *mea culpas* for the darkness throughout the land that has so inevitably led to Watergate."

I could not help being swept along, almost physically, by the cadences of her anger. "She sounds like Savonarola," I said to Hedley. I thought she had told some undeniable truths about life in America. But he and I agreed that it was a long way to Watergate from Marlon Brando's notorious buggery in *Last Tango in Paris* or Linda Lovelace's marathon fellatio in *Deep Throat.*

"I think I will write her," said Hedley, "that I didn't vote for Linda Lovelace but for Richard Nixon."

Where Clare's letter was ultimately hollow, or even outrageous, was in blaming everything and everybody for Watergate. There were countless people, including politicians, who did not behave like Richard Nixon and his crew. On other occasions she had affirmed the principle of individual responsibility, both as a Republican and as a Catholic. Now she seemed to be sweeping aside individual responsibility in a random barrage of blame aimed at "society." If she at least partly exempted journalists, she did not stop her attacks on the press, including *Time.*

She wrote again the following April, and this time I ran her letter without argument. Quoting a critical comment about our Watergate coverage by TV's Harry Reasoner, she denounced us for our "phobic Watergate reporting" and "editorial overinvestment in the destruction of the President."

ONE OF THE more engaging reactions to our editorial came from Walden T. Yale of Springfield, Illinois, and was accompanied by a construction made from recording tape that he nominated as "Thing of the Year," instead of Man of the Year. "Please hang it on the wall of *Time,*" he wrote, "as a reader's tribute to a most courageous staff and publication."

As it happened, we had chosen Judge John Sirica as Man of the Year for 1973. He was presiding over the trials of the Watergate defendants and was increasingly seen as the force that kept the case going. The son of an immigrant barber, Sirica had tried three times before getting his law degree at Georgetown, supporting himself as a welterweight fighter and boxing coach. A Republican, he went into private practice and was appointed to the federal bench in 1957 by Eisenhower and acquired a reputation of being fair but tough, hence his nickname, "Maximum John." Before I went to meet him in Washington with a group of colleagues, Hays Gorey warned me: "You will probably find him corny and maybe something of a hack. He speaks in platitudes, but he's totally sincere. He is very serious about his duty and can't be pushed around." When we told him that he was being considered for Man of the Year, he was flustered and delighted. He didn't want to presume, he said, but could he tell his wife? Amid all the more or less sophisticated power players swirling around Watergate, it was refreshing to meet someone so unassuming; yet he had real power and held the future of the president in his fighter's hands.

Nixon dropped the "compromise" and turned over some tapes to Sirica in response to his subpoenas. Some were missing, the White House said, and offered other tapes, as if they were somehow interchangeable. Then it became known that one recording covering an apparently key conversation between Nixon and Haldeman contained an eighteen-minute gap. Nixon's longtime secretary, Rose Mary Woods, said that she must have caused at least part of the blank when she reached for the telephone with one hand and accidentally hit the record button with the other and, at the same time, kept her foot on the operating pedal. Several secretaries in the Time & Life Building tried to reenact this and, after many contortions, decided it was impossible. So did a panel of audio experts in Washington.

By then Nixon had appointed a new special prosecutor, Leon Jaworski, a highly successful Houston trial lawyer. There had been rumors that Jaworski, a Republican, had been handpicked by that great Nixon ally, John Connally, and would prove to be tame. But if anything, he turned out to be tougher even than Archibald Cox.

Early in February 1974 Jaworski met with us in the conference room of *Time*'s Washington bureau. Inevitably the conversation turned to the tapes. "Let's suppose, hypothetically, just hypothetically," said Jaworski in his soft Texas voice, "that we have come across evidence that the president of the United States had committed an impeachable offense. What do you think the president will do?"

"He will resign," said Ed Magnuson.

Several people around the table laughed. Jaworski shook his silvery head. "Well, let's not laugh at that. Let's just think about that for a moment. Suppose," Jaworski continued, "the president knows we have this tape which is damaging, knows we have this information. Wouldn't he think this is a good time to get out and give a self-sacrificing speech and say he was doing it as a magnanimous gesture?"

We were all stunned by Jaworski's frankness, not to say indiscretion. The next day Jaworski's press secretary phoned to say that rumors of the meeting had begun to circulate in Washington and to please protect his boss. Eventually Jaworski explained that he had gone out on a limb so that *Time* would not let up, that we were on the correct course and should not fear to press on. Unless we knew which way events were moving, we could easily be misled.

. . .

THROUGHOUT WATERGATE NIXON carried on his foreign policy quest. Kissinger further strengthened relations with China, maneuvered with Moscow and practiced "shuttle diplomacy" in the Mideast. All this was aided by the fact that other countries, especially in Europe, could never take Watergate quite seriously. They could not believe that what to many seemed like a trivial episode might actually bring down an American president.

Henry Kissinger emerged as just about the only force for stability in the White House. Although it was revealed that during the U.S. involvement in Cambodia he had approved FBI wiretaps to catch leaks, he was not tainted by Watergate. There had been constant infighting and policy differences between Kissinger and Secretary of State William Rogers, whose authority was being steadily demolished. Kissinger threatened to resign if he didn't get Rogers's job. At length Nixon decided that he had no choice and forced out his old friend Rogers. In September of 1973 Kissinger became secretary of state.

Nixon continued to hang on with incredible tenacity. Scores of White House officials had gone to jail or were on the way there. Top former cabinet members were under indictment, and Nixon himself, it was learned later, had been named an unindicted co-conspirator by the Watergate grand jury. The House Judiciary Committee, under Representative Peter Rodino, held hearings to determine whether the president should be impeached. And still Nixon held fast.

The endgame began in July 1974, when the Supreme Court unanimously upheld the earlier ruling by the U.S. Court of Appeals that Nixon must deliver the tapes to Sirica. For a while there was only silence from the White House. I couldn't understand it and kept asking colleagues: "What are they doing? They must have anticipated that this might happen."

"No," said Jason McManus, "they're in total disarray. They didn't think it would come to this."

Then Nixon made his most devastating admission: six days after the break-in he had discussed it with Haldeman and agreed on plans to cover it up. He had forgotten all about that conversation, he said, until he reviewed the tapes. But most people saw his earlier assertions of innocence as brazen falsehoods. "There are only so many lies you can take," said Barry Goldwater, "and now there has been one too many. Nixon should get his ass out of the White House—today!"

That sentiment became nearly universal. And so, August 9, 1974, at long last, the resignation speech. Here was the same dark, jowly face, the same deep and hollow voice—but not the strained smile—that had been familiar for more than two decades. Leon Jaworski had been correct in anticipating what Nixon might say. He announced, in effect, that he was resigning for the good of the nation. He could have fought on to be vindicated, he declared, implying that he might have won, but that would have been a huge distraction from important business, and the country deserved a full-time president. He had lost his political base in Congress, he said, as if describing some parliamentary mishap, and admitted no guilt, only mistakes. He was composed, dry-eyed and without bitterness. He finished with a plea for unity. His farewell to the White House staff the next day was very different. He cried. He rambled. He talked about his father (a great man, though he never amounted to much) and his mother (a saint). He said he had never ducked responsibility, a line that must have evoked bitter laughter from millions who watched him; it did from me. It was impossible not to feel sorry for him, yet compassion was overwhelmed by embarrassment at his self-pity and self-deception. "Those who hate you don't win, unless you hate them," he said, "and then you destroy yourself." He may have actually believed that, but surely hate and suspicion were what destroyed him.

The most poignant moment came when he stepped into the helicopter that was to take him to exile. He turned at the door and waved in an awful parody of the victory salutes that had followed past triumphs.

The spectacle of Nixon's resignation and departure did not produce the kind of national bond in a watching nation that had been evident, for instance, at John Kennedy's funeral. What had died here was not a man, but only a man's ambition—or, to be fair, a man's promise.

The great cliché in the aftermath was that the system had worked—and it was true. In many other countries a comparable chain of events would have remained hidden or else sent soldiers and tanks into the streets. For a special *Time* issue on the resignation, I had solicited a contribution from historian Henry Steele Commager: "In a few years we will look back on [Watergate] with a certain pride because we did not in fact succumb to what happened. . . . Watergate was . . . an attempt to subvert the Constitution, but the Constitution survived. It was an attempt by the President to put himself above the law, but in the end it was the law that imposed its magisterial authority upon the President. . . ."

This issue of *Time* carried the picture of a smiling, solid president, Gerald Ford, on its cover under the banner "The Healing Begins." Not until the issue was off the press did the irony strike me: five and a half years ago we had introduced the Nixon era with the heading "To Heal a Nation."

AFTER NIXON'S RESIGNATION most people had assumed that he would fade away forever. But again he defied such predictions. Step by step he planned his reemergence from disgrace. He was interviewed on TV by David Frost. He published a book, *RN: The Memoirs of Richard Nixon.* He brushed Watergate aside as a blunder, never conceding that he had lied about it. When, during the writing of his book, aides urged him to admit more, he was enraged. "If I do that, I can never come back to public life," he said.

I saw him for the first time since his resignation in 1986, when a group from *Time* was invited to have dinner with him at his spacious house in Saddle River, New Jersey. Surrounded by Oriental artifacts, he was as serene as Nixon ever could be. He displayed a meticulous knowledge of baseball prospects and an equally detailed grasp of American politics, state by state, if not precinct by precinct. He was proud of his Bordeaux (Château Lafite-Rothschild 1961) and affable about his pre-Castro Cuban cigars ("Here, grab a few"). Nixon had apparently learned to live with his past. Since I always found it hard to forgive myself for mistakes or failures, I had to admire the way he seemed to have adjusted to what must have been the constant, haunting memory of his disaster.

As part of his campaign to build contacts with journalists, he started sending me little notes when he saw some article of mine in print. So one day in 1990 I asked to see him. He shared a small building with Perillo Tours in New Jersey, its forecourt displaying a marble copy of Michelangelo's David. I had brought a tape recorder. "I don't trust those things," said Nixon without any hint of irony. His face was fleshier than I remembered it, and he was slightly stooped. He relaxed in a boxy armchair, and we started to talk world affairs. There were the familiar sweeping judgments, mostly smart, occasionally off the mark. Gorbachev: he would survive. Yeltsin? "A clown." The cold war? "They lost it, but we haven't won it yet."

Condescension often broke through the statesmanlike surface. "The Poles, I have great affection for them and all the rest, they're very good at music and very good at poetry and very good at drama, but they're not worth a damn versus the Germans. They fight better than the Italians, but they aren't well organized." Listening to his rambling was disorienting, a little like watching an old home movie, real but not quite real.

I went back for another visit in 1993. This time we talked more about America, which he insisted must still be a world leader. But without the Soviet threat how could people be persuaded to make the necessary effort? "We have to be taken to the mountaintop and shown what we need to do. Anything that makes the world a little richer, a little better, a little freer and so forth, serves our long-term interests. If the American people get totally obsessed with materialism, we're in very deep trouble. I think what the country needs—is maybe a religious revival." Whittaker Chambers, he said, knew that, and it was too bad that he wasn't around now to write about it. I recalled, silently, what Chambers had told me about Nixon years before—that the man lacked conviction and vision.

He started to reminisce. He recalled the Luces. Jim Shepley. "That wonderful *Life* editorial writer whose house burned down" (Jack Jessup's fire was still lodged in Nixon's mind). Actually he thought his relations with *Time* had been pretty good, except, of course, during Watergate. "I always considered you to be a very tough-minded, hard-nosed editor. A straight shooter, no bullshit." I was surprised by his need at this late date to project goodwill, but I had to ask him how he had felt about our editorial advocating his resignation. "It was a blow, but not unexpected. You were not the first or the only ones. I think the *Omaha World Herald* had the most impact on me, coming from where it did."

So much for the eastern elitist media.

Fifteen months later I attended Richard Nixon's funeral at his birthplace in Yorba Linda, California. The event was impressively well organized, with assembly points for the guests, shuttle buses and color-coded passes. I was struck by the contrast between the simple Nixon family house, so often evoked by him to certify the virtuous modesty of his origins, and the imposing presidential library that had been built nearby. There were apparitions from the past, including Spiro Agnew, whom I had not seen for twenty years and who, in my imagination, was on furlough from some low-security prison (actually he looked smug and comfortable). It was eerie to see the lineup of the four former presidents: Gerald Ford, his ruddy features, as usual, unmarked by time; Jimmy Carter, his still-boyish face an odd contrast to his white hair; Ronald Reagan, immobile and waxen; George Bush, serene and healthy, no longer the haggard, unhappy campaigner.

As the flag-draped coffin was carried into place, the band struck up "Hail to the Chief" the last time for Richard Nixon and then "America: My Country 'Tis of Thee." The sweetness of the song contrasted sharply with the recollection of a man who could be called many things, but not sweet. The eulogies, of course, evoked only his accomplishments, barely mentioning "mistakes" and "controversy." Bill Clinton, decades removed from his four predecessors, slid gracefully over Nixon's dark side when he urged that he should be judged on nothing less than "his entire life and career." Watergate was a word unspoken. The sudden roar of the jet fighters in their flyby pierced my ears and moved me strangely, as did the twenty-one-gun salute and the three rifle volleys, which reminded me, however incongruously, of the poignant last line of Hamlet: "Go bid the soldiers shoot."

Was the Nixon funeral a lie? Yes, like most funerals, but not completely. His offenses were not mentioned, but they would not be forgotten. The praise for his accomplishments was exaggerated but not undeserved. As for the panoply, it seemed appropriate for any man who had been elected president twice by the people. I took it as a tribute, not mainly to the individual, but to democracy, that tremendous gamble that elevates heroes and scoundrels or a mixture of the two and cuts them down again.

Chapter Thirty-one

Less than a year after Nixon's resignation I accompanied *Time*'s Los Angeles bureau chief, Dick Duncan, on an odd visit to the writers' workshop at Terminal Island federal prison. I spoke to a group of about thirty convicts who were interested in writing and journalism. Gordon Liddy was part of the workshop but boycotted the session because he felt that *Time* had been nasty to him. Watergate, however, was a big topic. Why were they so interested? I asked. One angelic-looking girl (I later heard that she was a notorious dope dealer) replied: "Because you guys have the real power. Look what you did to Nixon."

Most Americans felt that way: the general view was that the press had brought down a president. Actually Congress had done as much as the press, if not more, but after Watergate I never again felt quite the same way about journalism. I believe this was true of most people in the field.

Americans have usually been ambivalent about the press. Defenders of journalism love to quote Thomas Jefferson, who declared that if he had to choose between a government without newspapers and newspapers without government, he would choose the second. Less well-known is his later statement that he was "infinitely happier" since he stopped all his newspaper subscriptions. He urged editors to divide the news into four categories: the truth, probabilities, possibilities and lies. There had usually existed among the public, the government and the press a certain jovial disrespect, what one writer, Paul Weaver, called "an atmosphere of amiable suspiciousness." By the time of Watergate that mood was a lot less amiable. The American press was far better and more responsible than it had ever been before; it also was taken—and took itself—far more seriously, almost, as Clare Luce had put it, as a fourth branch of government. Many people found it difficult to accept the basic paradox about the press: it is a profit-making enterprise without formal professional rules and regulations, yet it performs an essential public service. Again and again people asked journalists, "Who elected you, anyway?" My own answer invariably was: "Nobody—and that's how it should be." I liked to cite Irving Kaufman of the U.S. Court of Appeals, the bantam, aggressive jurist who had presided over the Rosenberg trial. He compared journalists to judges: "They sustain democracy, not because they are responsible to any branch of government, but precisely because, except in the most extreme cases, they are not accountable at all. . . . Thus they can check the irresponsibility of those in power." But it was the irresponsibility and power of journalists that troubled many. Speaking at a judicial conference chaired by Kaufman, I told the assembled judges: "I wish I could take some of you off the bench and give you a reporting assignment. Let's assume that we've had a tip about kickbacks in Pentagon procurement. Let's also assume that a direct inquiry only brings stout denial of wrongdoing. You are supposed to find out the facts. But suddenly you are without the authority to summon witnesses, to have them testify under the disciplines of contempt or perjury or to compel the production of documents. I think you would be quickly frustrated by the power and resourcefulness of government to hide, evade and manage the facts."

Legal challenges to the press were mounting, many of them centering on the right of journalists to keep sources confidential. Most laymen and many judges failed to understand that right. The use of confidential sources is often abused by reporters who don't press hard enough for on-the-record statements and by sources who snipe from behind the protection of anonymity. I discouraged the use of blind quotes in *Time*. But the practice remained essential to get information from people who fear for their jobs or their safety. I did not feel that journalists could claim an absolute privilege to keep sources confidential. But, I argued in a letter to our readers published in *Time,* exceptions must be rare, such as in cases where a "reporter had essential information on a violent crime or a matter of overriding danger to the national security." But subpoenas against newsmen, many of them obvious fishing expeditions, kept being issued; sometimes police searched newsrooms for reporters' pictures and notes. The Supreme Court under Warren Burger was not too sympathetic toward the press on that issue but suggested that Congress might write legislation to protect journalists' rights to confidentiality. A number of states had already passed "shield laws." The concept made me uneasy. I feared that such laws, though well intentioned, would wind up restricting journalists' rights by the very act of listing them. In the end there was no choice but to accept, more or less gratefully, whatever protection was offered by shield legislation.

Perhaps the most important legal issue involving the press centered on a 1964 Supreme Court decision, *New York Times* v. *Sullivan.* In it the Court held that a public official could not prevail in a libel suit unless actual malice or reckless disregard of the truth was proved. Most laymen failed to understand why the press should ever go unpunished for printing an untrue statement. The Court's answer, in effect, was that public officials were in a privileged position, with plenty of resources to fight back. Threat of libel might keep journalists from printing what they consider the truth. *Sullivan* was an immensely important decision for America's free press, but in the seventies it was being whittled away in various court cases. Moreover, by introducing a concept like "reckless disregard," it made a journalist's state of mind a legitimate subject for inquiry. Paradoxically, an editor's conscientious question about accuracy ("Let's make sure this is really true") could be used in court to show "serious doubts." The same was true of casual notes. In the past I might well have scribbled some rude remark about a politician in the margin of copy for the benefit of colleagues ("What a jerk!" "How silly can you get?"). Now I restrained myself, to avoid any suggestion of "actual malice" in some possible libel suit.

One of the things that disturbed me most was the wrongheaded notion of the infinitely diverse U.S. press as a single institution. That notion, it seemed to me, was abetted by the increasing use of the word "media," which I loathed. It suggested that all purveyors of information were the same—one big blob. This was particularly true when the word was used barbarically, in the singular—"the media is . . ."

One generalization, however, was valid: Many journalists were trying to relive or re-create Watergate. They wanted to be Bob Woodward and Carl Bernstein, *The Washington Post*'s Watergate reporters, celebrated in the movie based on their book, *All the President's Men.* This helped push the press into a new, almost permanent adversarial role toward government and other centers of power. On the other side it prompted public figures, even more than usual, to blame everything that went wrong, and especially their own mistakes, on the wicked "media." One might say, paraphrasing Dr. Johnson on patriotism, that bashing the press had become the first refuge of scoundrels.

Some weeks after Nixon's resignation, I pointed out to the staff that the press must retain its investigative function while avoiding reflexive and mindless hostility toward government. It would be a difficult balancing act. Our work would be less exciting than it had been during the long crisis. We would have to deal with many mundane problems requiring explanation and analysis. The greatest sin of the American press, I argued, was not bias or negativism, although these were real enough. It was, rather, shallowness.

THE RESENTMENT AGAINST the press was only part of a much larger crisis of confidence in American society and its institutions. Two presidents, Johnson and Nixon, had lost—to different degrees—the trust of the country. A report by the Public Agenda Foundation showed that trust in government had dropped to 33 percent from 76 percent a decade before. A reaction set in, among politicians and journalists, that led to a near obsession with public virtue. Sunshine laws, those that opened government meetings to the public, piled up. Ethics rules multiplied. Disclosure forms for new appointees became absurdly complicated. Special prosecutors were called for at the drop of an accusation. Whatever good may have been done by this wave of ostentatious morality, it led to vast hypocrisy. Minor infractions were pursued amid much publicity, while major ones continued behind ever more ingenious camouflage. America moved into an era of Pecksniffery.

Repairing the Watergate damage did not prove easy. Gerald Ford, fairly open and candid, nevertheless jolted the country by issuing a full pardon for Richard Nixon. On balance I thought Ford was right in sparing the country any further Watergate turmoil. In several conversations and interviews at the White House, I never heard him say anything extraordinary, but neither did I hear anything stupid and outrageous. His face serene, his hands usually clutching an empty pipe, he talked prosaic common sense. He was resigned to the limitations of his office if not of himself: "The president can't turn a switch and everything changes." He was smart about his old home, Congress, and the "floating" coalition of Republicans and Democrats he tried to work with. Yet he had lots of trouble on the Hill, especially in foreign and defense policy, even though he retained Henry Kissinger as secretary of state. The Strategic Arms Limitation Talks (SALT II) ran into furious conservative opposition.

At home Ford was beset by the worst recession since the late thirties, and he faced a lingering energy crisis. The problem had started before Ford became president; the United States was simply consuming and importing too much energy. Then, in retaliation against American help for Israel in the Yom Kippur War, the Arabs imposed an oil embargo. Suddenly there were gas lines. The shock was severe, almost like cutting off water or air. Americans had long assumed that cheap gasoline was a God-given right. Now rationing loomed. The whole idea of conservation—driving less, turning down the thermostat, not lighting buildings at night—was an affront to the United States.

Later, when I traveled through the West and Southwest, the energy shortage had eased temporarily, but its effects lingered. The country was fractious; it seemed to resemble a large jigsaw puzzle whose pieces, stubbornly, would not fit together. In the Southwest people said, "Why should we produce all this oil and gas and ship it up to the Northeast, where people don't want to drill for oil to spoil their precious beaches?"

In Arizona there were complaints that the state and its copper mines were, in effect, a "colony" for the East. Opposite poles were represented by two states, Oregon and Texas. Oregon was an island, an idyll of advanced social legislation, participatory democracy (the initiative and referendum were used frequently), and passionate opposition to uncontrolled growth. Oregonians were devoted to "livability." They did not seem to be particularly aware that this clean and pleasant condition was made possible, at least in part, by the dirty, sweaty, industrial East, which they abhorred. Oregon politicians kept complaining that the state's timber resources were not adequately cared for by the federal government, to the point where I could imagine them arguing for "one tree, one vote."

In contrast, Texas remained raucously antiunion, antiwelfare, antiplanning or even antizoning. It was infatuated with power, its civic religion being individualism in its fiercest, Darwinian form. Texas, it seemed to me, was to the rest of America what all of America still was to the rest of the world.

Later, in California, I had breakfast with Tom Hayden, the sixties radical now gone almost straight and running for the Democratic nomination for the Senate, who could not resist expressing the energy battle in Vietnam terms. Deregulating natural gas, he argued apocalyptically, "would lead to the destruction of this country in order to save it."

Not everybody shared such doomsday visions. Still, the energy problem was turned into a morality play, once again illustrating that unique American talent for giving practical problems an almost religious cast. The nuclear reactors of Los Alamos were treated by environmentalists as dark, satanic idols, while the solar and thermal energy plants of Arizona were seen as pure and almost holy.

As I moved along my Western itinerary, I kept encountering the suspicion that the current sharp recession was not just temporary, but the sign of a deeper economic disorder. A widespread litany, at least outside Texas, concerned the country's need to lower its expectations. Probably its most magnetic exponent was California governor Jerry Brown. I met him at his regular Los Angeles hangout across the street from the Paramount Studios, El Adobe Café, a casual Mexican restaurant that served a very good arroz con pollo, his favorite dish. I found myself agreeing with very few of his ideas but was nevertheless drawn to his intensity. His quick mind and Jesuit education showed in the nimbleness of his arguments and his sense of history. Considering his attacks on materialism and progress, I asked him at one point whether he was not really running a counterreformation; he replied without missing a beat, "Sure, in a way I am." He whipped out pad and pencil and jotted down numbers to show that California simply could not afford to spend more money on education or on old-age benefits.

What Brown's rather cruel pencil pointed to was obvious: the American economy and the American government could not provide everything that everybody wanted. That had long been a theme of conservatives, but it was striking that the message now came from a liberal. But I believed that in the long run America simply could not accept a negative slogan like lower expectations.

Another constant refrain was the need for leadership. This thought was behind a rather ambitious *Time* project in 1974. I proposed that we find two hundred people who showed enough accomplishments and promise to provide leadership in the future. The number was arbitrary, as was the age limit (forty-five). *Time* correspondents and other staff members took well over two months to conduct their search and produced five hundred nominations. There followed a lengthy winnowing process, with heated arguments rattling back and forth. Was this mayor worthier than that congressman, this college president less tarnished than that foundation head? Leah Gordon, *Time*'s chief of research, called it "a surreal blizzard of paper." The final selection, with short profiles of each, was in hindsight more than respectable, but not consistently prophetic. The list included ten governors, twelve U.S. senators, twenty-one congressmen and fifteen mayors. Some of their careers would be snuffed out within a few years, but most advanced or at least endured. (At this writing none of the original choices has made it to the White House, although many of them tried: Ted Kennedy, Jack Kemp, Joseph Biden, Jerry Brown, Lamar Alexander, Ross Perot, Pat Buchanan. A few years later we rounded up another fifty names, which included William Jefferson Clinton of Arkansas, at thirty-two the youngest governor in the United States.) At least two of our choices wound up in jail: City Councilman Matthew Troy of New York, and Marion Barry, who became mayor of Washington, D.C. Reaching beyond elected officials, we selected the likes of Ralph Nader, Alan Dershowitz, Barbara Walters, Joan Ganz Cooney, Vernon Jordan, Billie Jean King, Carl Sagan, Saul Steinberg, Gloria Steinem. In September 1976 we invited all two hundred to a conference in Washington to discuss the nature and prospects of leadership. The most frequently quoted definition was Harry Truman's famous line about a leader being someone who makes people do what they don't want to do and like it.

But another less well-known quote from Truman was perhaps more thought provoking: "The C-students run the world." Few of the conferees felt that they deserved a C in leadership, but they conceded that America as a whole seemed to lack it, and they were not sure that they could provide it. Why not? They blamed a long list of factors as obstacles to leadership: The country's sheer size and complexity. A hostility toward excellence. The press (of course), with its tendency to tear everyone down. Lack of privacy for public figures ("the proctologist's view of leadership," as Missouri governor Kit Bond put it). The erosion of values and the splintering of consensus. Finally they blamed history—the great, stimulating crises of depression and war were missing. Many of the complaints about obstacles amounted to a cop-out, I thought. But the popular cry for leadership was also something of a cop-out, an excuse for people not trying harder themselves. Leadership requires followership.

Someone quoted French political scientist Bertrand de Jouvenel, who divided leaders into two categories: *dux*, literally leader, and *rex*, literally ruler. The first is the inspirational activist and innovator, while the second is the organizer and manager. The two types are sometimes present in the same person, but not often.

That distinction seemed to be pointing, coincidentally, to a man who was then running for the presidency, Jimmy Carter. This moralist and engineer, preacher and administrator, was seen by his followers as both *dux* and *rex*.

• • •

I STARTED TO FOCUS on Carter in 1971, when we were preparing to do a cover story on the New South. For the cover we considered several governors under whom the region was moving away from segregation and stubborn, hard-shell provincialism. Our correspondents were leaning toward Carter, and we invited him to visit *Time* in New York. He was slight of build, with penetrating blue eyes that seemed almost to pop out of their sockets when he made a point, when he was pleased or angry. His soft, southern voice had a way of drooping at the end of a sentence, which after a while could become rather depressing. He was fiery when he talked about the South's need to stop discriminating against blacks, although that attitude had gotten him into trouble with unreformed segregationists. He insisted that most whites now agreed with him.

"I know my people," he said repeatedly, "and I speak what is on their minds."

Our cover story, he said later, gave him his first national exposure. (During the presidential campaign, when *Time* criticized an anti-Carter story in *Harper's* magazine, its editor, Lewis Lapham, rather absurdly accused us of leading a conspiracy to get Jimmy Carter elected.) I visited him in 1974 in Atlanta; by now he was running hard for the presidency. I found him in his chrome-and-black-leather office, sitting against an incongruous blue damask backdrop. It had been installed to cover a marble wall that had made him and his visitors look as if they were sprouting antlers when photographed. In our conversation he emphasized efficiency, telling me about how he had eliminated or consolidated a huge number of government departments. ("It had gotten so that every time I opened my closet door in my office, a new state agency would fall out.") He spoke eloquently about zero-based budgeting. "We mustn't just work with the current budget and keep adding to it. We must start from scratch every year." The concept was new to me at the time, and I was impressed. As the contest for the 1976 Democratic nomination developed, his rivals and the press scrutinized Carter's record, including what had seemed like a defense of Lieutenant William Calley when he was sentenced to life imprisonment for his part in the My Lai massacre. Other blemishes, real or imagined, were seized on by

Carter's political opponents, mostly liberals—in the spectrum of Democratic presidential aspirants, Carter was a conservative. In a sense he provoked the attacks by his promise to the people, "I will never lie to you."

In July I sat in the press gallery of New York's Madison Square Garden and thought at times that I had wandered into a revival tent. The convention echoed with the old-time religion and a more or less unified Democratic Party line. In a stirring acceptance speech Carter carefully balanced conservative and liberal themes. "Americans," he said, "have emerged from their recent ordeals as idealists without illusions, realists who still know the old dreams of justice and liberty."

The following month it was Jerry Ford's turn in Kansas City. I had always been frustrated by the remoteness of our staff in the Manhattan offices from most of the events they were writing about. This time I abolished that remoteness by taking the Nation staff to Kansas City and having all the convention stories written on the scene. The copy would be sent on its way into the layout and production process via fax machine, which was then still a novelty. It was an exhilarating experience. Editors, writers, researchers, photographers, layout staffers and messengers, most of them accustomed to separate cubicles, now shared one big workroom in the Kansas City Municipal Auditorium. A special kind of excitement accompanied the questions shouted from desk to desk, the information exchanged and the ideas instantly shared. I wished we could have bottled that atmosphere, like Arthur Bryant's barbecue sauce, and taken it back to New York.

Jerry Ford's nomination was a near certainty, despite a challenge by California's Ronald Reagan. Old animosities flickered. At one point Nelson Rockefeller, Ford's vice president, grabbed a Reagan sign from a delegate who, he claimed, had shoved it in his face. Another delegate retaliated by ripping out Rocky's floor telephone. At a coffee session the next day the *Time* staff presented Rockefeller with a shiny white duplicate instrument to commemorate "the Battle of the Telephone." Rockefeller had announced that he did not want to be Ford's running mate. He was sick of the whole business of being vice president, he told us. It wasn't worth all the battles, all the maneuvers. The choice eventually was Senator Robert Dole of Kansas. When he joined the *Time* group for breakfast, he had not yet been chosen. It was my introduction to his already famous acerbic style. He described Jimmy Carter as "sort of a southern-fried McGovern or Humphrey," a mass of contradictions and evasions. He was equally rough with the GOP, which he described as a party in mothballs. Despite Dole's tough talk I found something fragile about him, an impression perhaps caused by the World War II injury that had maimed his right hand; he used it awkwardly, like a broken wing.

SOME WEEKS BEFORE the election I went to see Jimmy Carter in Plains, and he took me to a Sunday morning service at the Plains Baptist Church, a serene white wooden building. We sat in Carter's regular third-row pew; he enthusiastically joined in singing the hymns. It was more than the usual politician's dutiful visit; brother Jimmy was at home here, and no one in the crowded church made a fuss about him, despite the presence of several Secret Service agents who tried, not very successfully, to be inconspicuous. In his campaign speeches he promised America a government as good as its people, and he kept asking the voters to trust him. There was so much talk about trust and love that I was reminded of the wonderful Gershwin musical *Of Thee I Sing,* in which a presidential candidate, lacking any safe issues, campaigned on a platform of love.

After Nixon and Watergate the candidate as saint (sort of) appealed to a great many people, but the image also alienated quite a few. There were questions about his competence, especially in international affairs. Once, during a short hop on his campaign plane, he startled me by saying rather casually that, among other things, America should pull its troops out of South Korea. I began to worry about how, as president, he might deal with the world. Ironically, during one of their televised debates, it was in foreign affairs that Carter scored a big advantage over Ford. During an exchange about Eastern Europe, Ford declared passionately, "I don't believe that the Poles consider themselves dominated by the Soviet Union. Each of those countries is independent and autonomous. . . ." Ford apparently meant to say that the United States did not accept Soviet rule in Eastern Europe as permanent, but the statement came out sounding as if Ford were stupidly denying the obvious: that the satellites were satellites.

During a conversation with me a week and a half before the election, Henry Kissinger suggested that Ford had taken a remark by Carter on Eastern Europe as an attack he had to turn back. That, he said, was typical of Ford's stubborn character. "If someone tells Ford that he had got out of bed at eight o'clock that morning, and he is already sitting at his desk, Ford will still nevertheless deny that he has got out of bed." As for Carter, said Kissinger, he was spouting liberal clichés about a moral foreign policy without recognizing the dangers of making commitments that could not be followed up. Several of his foreign policy advisers, added Kissinger, were "congenital mediocrities." He did not put Zbigniew Brzezinski in that category but had reservations about him, too. "Zbig" was likely to be national security adviser if Carter were elected. Kissinger thought that Brzezinski, though intelligent, moved with whatever foreign policy concepts were fashionable at the moment, was given to gimmicks and had not yet proved his loyalty to Carter. "But," added Kissinger, "everything that can be said about Brzezinski could have been said about me in 1968."

THE ELECTION ASIDE, 1976 was lit up by the bicentennial celebrations. Among the grand spectacles was the visit by Queen Elizabeth II, descendant of the king who had provoked the American Revolution. More than seven thousand new citizens took the oath of allegiance, and a million people converged on Philadelphia to watch a reenactment of the signing of the Declaration of Independence. The climax was provided by the "tall ships," 212 sailing vessels from 34 nations cruising into New York Harbor and up the Hudson. *Time*'s own contribution to the bicentennial came in print. We had the notion of putting out a special issue, as if *Time* had been published in July 1776. The cover, of course, was Thomas Jefferson, and the central news event was the signing of the declaration (we duly noted that Jefferson was disappointed by the revised and edited version of his original, copies of which he sent to friends). Another story speculated about the next stage in the War of Independence, including "the coming Battle for New York"; we quoted a contemporary on New Yorkers who were "magnificent in their pride and conceit." Under the supervision of my ingenious and scholarly colleague, Otto Friedrich, with the guidance of the noted University of Virginia historian Robert Rutland, a staff of a dozen writers and twice as many researchers transposed most of our usual departments into the eighteenth century. In Economy we raised the question of whether the colonies, lacking industry, would have the strength to sustain a new nation. Under Ideas we provided an answer from the free-market gospel of Adam Smith (not neglecting to mention that, as a child, he had been kidnapped by Gypsies). In Press we noted that newspaper reporters were generally unedited and unpaid, which led, among the staff, to many wry comparisons with the present. The People section relied heavily on foreigners, who seemed racier than the locals; there was the Marquis de Sade, in flight from the French police for various abominations, and the recklessly extravagant, strawberry blond Marie (Mme. Deficit) Antoinette, whose mother, Austria's empress Maria Theresa, accurately foresaw "disaster."

The issue was more than an amusing stunt. It illustrated the near miraculous growth of the nation from its small beginnings, the grandiose yet prudent vision of the Founders and the continuity of some of its conflicts. In a concluding article we pondered the future of the experiment. "Man might be created equal, even as the Declaration avers," we wrote, as a *Time* essayist might have two hundred years before, "but he soon creates his own inequalities. . . . Perhaps the greatest peril . . . is that contending groups, properly encouraged to strive for their self interest, will do so with such heedless vehemence that the needs of society as a whole will be forgotten." We noted another danger. Reason, as expressed by the people's will, was the unprecedented foundation of the new republic, and someday reason might "lose the religious and moral grounding it has today."

CARTER'S PRESIDENCY COULD not capture or personify the buoyant mood of the bicentennial celebration. The promise that he would be both *dux* and *rex*, both manager and inspirer, soon faded. He was bedeviled by high inflation, caused by some factors he could not control, such as world oil prices, and others he could have avoided, notably sharp increases in the minimum wage and Social Security taxes. He got off on the wrong foot with Moscow by making unrealistically ambitious demands. Carter deserved credit, however, for settling the future of the Panama Canal and, later, bringing Israel and Egypt together at Camp David. Despite an irritating headmasterly preachiness, he also helped make human rights an international issue. In a *Time* essay I argued that perhaps we were all expecting too much of Jimmy Carter—and indeed of all our presidents.

To repair his image the White House arranged a series of small dinners for the press. It was *Time*'s turn first. In July 1978 I found myself in the family quarters, along with a group of colleagues and our wives. Carter was just back from a Western economic summit in Bonn, and a few days before, *Time* had printed a Hugh Sidey column reporting that the European leaders' attitude toward the president "ranged from doubt to contempt." Carter asserted plaintively that this just wasn't true. "I like all of them and they like me," he insisted, warmly referring to "Helmut" (for Schmidt) and "Valéry" (for Giscard d'Estaing). He hoped for a summit with Brezhnev (not yet "Leonid"). Much of the time Carter was defensive. Yes, he admitted, his relations with Congress were uneasy, but, after all, its own leadership could not control that recalcitrant body, so how could he? Rosalynn Carter, who followed his every syllable like a stage prompter, broke in as she did repeatedly during the evening: "Jimmy, tell them about the big effort we're making with congressmen, taking them to the theater and all," she said.

I told the president that a frequent criticism was that his advisers formed a rather narrow, closed circle and that perhaps he should get more outsiders into the White House. This nettled him. He listened to a great many people, he said, and had an excellent cabinet. But as for his close advisers, he knew them. They knew him. He needed their loyalty. As he said this, he seemed almost to be pleading.

I came away with the impression that he was finding everything far more difficult than he had expected, but that he remained totally dedicated and stubborn. These qualities might yet win out in the end, but, more probably, we were indeed expecting too much of him. Most of the time Carter was relaxed and gracious, but he lacked presence and inspired no awe. Two of my colleagues actually patted his arm as we stood talking after dinner. Earlier Rosalynn had taken the wives on a tour of the sleeping quarters. "I knew they were unpretentious people," Beverly said later, "but I didn't expect them to be *that* unpretentious. In her bathroom I saw her laundry hanging up to dry."

As we said good night, Carter showed us the Truman balcony, which he and Rosalynn especially enjoyed. Standing there in the moonlight, he said that despite all the difficulties of his job, "I love it, I can't wait to get up every morning." Unfortunately he never managed to convey that exuberance to our group, let alone to the country.

In the summer of 1979 Carter held a six-day brainstorming session at Camp David, to which he shuttled politicians, businessmen, sociologists and a sprinkling of religious leaders. All came away impressed by his seriousness, and some thought he was quite optimistic. But what really stood out in their reports were Carter's doubts and worries. There was much love for America and much hate of the government, he told his visitors ("not just me, but I'm part of it"). In William James's phrase, he called for the "moral equivalent of war" against the energy crisis. But that appeal, he said, had been ridiculed. Moreover things would get worse: "The only trend is downward." The standard of living would decline further. Recalling hours spent with Leonid Brezhnev at a recent summit, he drew an incredible parallel. "The problems we face in the Western world are the same as the ones faced in the Eastern world, general malaise." In a major speech a few days after the Camp David meeting, Carter tried to give the energy problem a spiritual dimension. Winning that battle, he said, "can also help us to conquer the crisis of the spirit in our country. It can rekindle our sense of unity, our confidence in the future. . . ." It did not happen, at least not in Carter's presidency. He never used the word "malaise" in that speech, yet that is the tag by which it was remembered.

CHAPTER THIRTY-TWO

THE ENERGY CRISIS that so persistently haunted the Carter presidency and the country made the Middle East synonymous, in the American mind, with trouble. I made several trips in the mid- and late seventies to the oil-producing Gulf States and found myself in the midst of sheer fantasy, a cosmic joke. Here were some of the world's most obscure and, from a Western point of view, most backward countries, now vital to the survival of the most advanced societies. The West's need for Mideastern fuel had made the oil states so rich in a few years that their governments literally did not know how to spend their profits. The gleaming palaces and international hotels rose alongside the remnants of old mud houses. The riches showering down—or more accurately gushing up—created the impression of a fairy tale. As a sort of counter–fairy tale I imagined a mad scientist who finds a way to run our machines on Coca-Cola, returning these statelets to their former insignificance. I remember those implausible oil states in a series of vignettes.

In Oman, essential to the security of oil traffic in the Gulf, Sultan Qabus bin Said had built himself a vast modern palace with Disneyland touches; a reflecting moat spanned by a bridge covered in Astroturf. Across the bridge came the slight, black-bearded sultan wearing *dishdash* and a silver dagger to entertain visitors at high tea.

In Kuwait I was delayed by a monstrous traffic jam, caused by a public hanging of three murderers in the Safad Square that drew a large audience. Despite such archaic customs Kuwait had one of the world's more munificent welfare systems.

In my hotel room in Saudi Arabia I found, along with a stack of tourist brochures, a copy of the *Protocols of the Elders of Zion*. It seemed incredible that an internationally important regime would stoop to using a notorious forgery from tsarist days about an invented Jewish plot to dominate the world. It was a reminder that at least part of the Saudi leadership lived in severe intellectual isolation. That was true even of King Faisal. His deeply furrowed face was sullen, even sour, but he emanated dignity. Still, when he said that Israeli intransigence might hurt Jews everywhere and that he did not wish to see that, he hardly sounded convincing. Although I knew that he was highly suspicious of both Jews and journalists—I wondered how he might regard me in my double capacity—I felt some sympathy for him. I had heard that he often took his prayer rug to the seashore to meditate in silence and that he suffered from ulcers. Ruler of a vast realm with a tiny population, vulnerable to all neighboring states, the king depended heavily on U.S. support. ("We are pinning all our hopes practically on our friends the Americans.") At the same time he was paying protection to everyone in sight, including radical governments and the PLO. We were meeting in his vast, chair-lined audience chamber, in which he still received even the humblest petitioners in his regular *majlis*, a reminder that his country was suspended between tribal traditions and the computer age.

For all its fantastic aspects, the role played by oil was at least measurable, in tonnage and prices and potential reserves. The overarching Arab-Israeli conflict was not. "Blood is thicker than oil," an Israeli editor once told me, making the point that, on balance, the supply of energy was less significant in the region than the supply of passion.

I had seen Israel for the first time in the late sixties, intensely curious about the country Uncle Alex had described as a miracle in the desert. My first impression of it was unsettling. Soldiers were everywhere, and the conversation was predominantly about past battles and possible future ones. It was two years after the Six-Day War, which had ended in a crushing defeat for the Arabs, but there was no peace. I found that Israelis saw the whole world through their own inverted telescope, judging every event according to whether it would help or hurt their country. But I recognized a certain bracing simplicity in the situation. Hardly anywhere else, certainly not in the United States, were people joined in so clear and overriding a goal: Israeli survival. I felt as if I had wandered into a large family, a claustrophobic *mishpokhe* where everybody seemed to know—and quarrel with—everybody else. It was odd to be surrounded entirely by Jews, and I missed the variety and the contrasts of American life. Yet I had to admit that there was also something comfortable about it. In the West even the most assimilated Jews were never quite free of the questions, on meeting a stranger, "Is he Jewish? How does she feel about Jews?" Here those questions never came up.

I discussed this with my old friend Rinna, whom I saw for the first time in many years. She was in charge of public affairs for the Weizmann Institute and was married to one of its brilliant physicists, David Samuel. He was a grandson of Lord Samuel, who had been high commissioner to Palestine. This made her Lady Samuel, but she did not use the title. "My being a viscountess," she said, "must be some ghastly celestial mistake." She had lost none of her sardonic humor, even though Israel, as she observed, was not "celebrated as a land of laughs. Milk and honey, yes. Blood, sweat and tears, yes. But the big guffaw, no." But when she playfully referred to Israel as "Iz," it was not to demean it, and when she spoke of Israelis as "my people," she might sound ironic, but she was serious. Although Rinna had spent so much of her life in Britain and the United States and spoke Hebrew with a strong English accent, she was unshakably loyal to this old, and new, nation, feared for it and hoped for it and would not think of living anywhere else.

As for me, I did not feel that Israel was, in any sense, *my* country. Yet I believe that no Jew can set foot in Israel without reexamining, at least in passing, just where he belongs, just who he is. I was still skeptical about Zionism, about the wisdom and feasibility of reversing two thousand years of history. But such skepticism was easier at a distance. Here on the ground, Israel was an overwhelming reality.

That reality was still not accepted by most Arabs. Reality meant something quite different to the Arabs than to a Westerner. This became very clear when I met Gamal Abdel Nasser, the colonel who had made himself dictator of Egypt. The Egyptian elite considered him vulgar, but his soldierly, unpretentious manner appealed to the masses. He was widely seen as the leader of the Arab world, and his voice was heard all over the Middle East on ubiquitous transistor radios.

When Hedley Donovan and I went to see him in 1969 at his modest Cairo house, he seemed to have recovered from his defeat in the Six-Day War. He was cocky and cheerful, laughed a great deal, emitting something between a hiss and a giggle. In a verdant backyard birds chirped serenely. Before there could be a peace settlement, he insisted, the Israelis have to give up all the occupied land, including Sinai. (The United Nations Security Council had passed Resolution 242, calling on the Israelis to withdraw from "occupied territories"; with deliberate ambiguity it did not say "the" or "all" occupied territories.) "Israel says she will not leave the occupied areas until we sit down with her to talk peace. But we refuse to sit. If we sit now, we sit as defeated people, sitting only to capitulate." Egyptians had obviously been demoralized by the defeat, but in an odd leap of logic Nasser presented this as an asset. "We are against a big increase in morale because it might bring pressure from the people for military action that could be unwise." Once or twice during the conversation he referred to Israeli prime minister Golda Meir, who, he said, was the only Israeli "with real balls." He laughed uproariously as he said it, slapping his thighs and uttering an Arabic phrase, which, the interpreter told us afterward, was a curse he refused to translate.

A few days later, in a Spartan conference room in Jerusalem, I saw Golda Meir. As she entered she was accompanied by an aide carrying a purple leather box filled with Israeli and American cigarettes, plus a battery-operated lighter, which I mistook at first for a recording device. I had met her before when she was foreign minister. (On one occasion she came to lunch at the Time & Life Building and my secretary ordered pork chops, which she consumed without protest.) She had seen press reports of our interview with Nasser and said with mild sarcasm, "I understand you bring me special regards from my neighbor. He wishes me well, I'm sure." Reminiscing about Nasser's behavior immediately after his defeat, she said, "In that great speech of his, when he seemed prepared to take the blame on himself, there was a moment when we thought, perhaps foolishly, Well, maybe this is a turning point, because maybe he realized he did not accomplish what he wanted and brought so much sorrow and death. Not to the Israelis—I never expected him to feel sorry for us—but his own people. But he recovered very quickly and became true to himself again."

Many people, including Israelis, thought that greater flexibility by Israel following its victory could have produced a settlement. But Golda was not interested in flexibility or compromise. "I am sorry, but suicide we will not commit," was one of her favorite mantras. "If we lose a war, for us that is the last war. Then we are not here anymore."

Talking about the Palestinians—although in her mind there were no Palestinians, only Arabs—she insisted that they had not been driven out of their homes when Israel was founded but had left voluntarily (a dubious point). Her stubby fingers gripping a cigarette, her voice rising in anger, she recalled how the Arab countries had deliberately kept the refugees in camps. I had visited such camps, with the endless rows of prefabricated houses, where people lived in a terrible limbo. "For twenty years the textbooks used in those camps, printed with United Nations money, have been full of hatred of Israel. There were wonderful arithmetic examples like 'There were five Israelis, we killed three, how many were left?' Now, the little boy who was five when he learned that lesson is twenty-five and maybe a Fatah commando, but we are asked to give them a free choice to come back."

Any conversation in the Middle East involved history lessons. Inevitably, Golda recalled how in 1947 the United Nations had decided to partition Palestine and to internationalize Jerusalem. But the Arabs attacked the new state. "Not one single power in the world to whom

Jerusalem is holy lifted a finger to defend the holiness of this city when the Arabs shelled it. After the Jordanians occupied East Jerusalem, we could not come to the Wailing Wall. The Arabs threw the living Jews out of the holy city, and then they turned to the dead ones. They took the gravestones out of the cemeteries and paved roads with them." Then, in an attempt at calm, she said, "But this is the past." I would learn that nothing in the Middle East is ever really past.

THE COUNTERPOINT BETWEEN Nasser and Golda Meir stayed in my mind. The pattern changed only in excruciatingly slow ways. The next time I traveled to the area was in 1975, a little over a year after the Yom Kippur War, in which Israel had come close to defeat. Nasser had died of a heart attack and been replaced by Anwar al-Sadat. He impressed me as a remarkably serene man who nevertheless knew the risk he was running in talking peace. He combined fatalism with an urgent desire for action. While he reiterated some of the standard demands for an Israeli pullback, he was willing to go a long way to achieve what he called "eternal peace."

No one could guess that within less than three years Sadat would make his dramatic trip to Jerusalem that eventually led to a peace treaty between Egypt and Israel. But his language and tone were new. "I am not asking the United States to break its special relationship with Israel. But I am now your friend. Treat me as a friend also." Regarding further peace talks, he pleaded: "At heart I am willing, I am willing. But make it easy for me."

Meanwhile, on the Israeli side, Golda Meir had been replaced as prime minister by Yitzhak Rabin. I remembered him from his days as Israeli ambassador to the United States, when he invariably accompanied Prime Minister Meir on her visits, sitting silent and glum while she talked. He seemed less passionate than his predecessor, less visionary than his counterpart in Cairo. His bulk—he was trying to give up smoking, he explained, and had gained twenty pounds—contributed to an air of stolidity. Sounding sorrowful rather than angry, chewing his words as if they tasted bitter, he said: "No Israeli leader can come to the Israeli people after twenty-six years of conflict and four wars and say 'I believe the other side has good intentions, but I can't say what those intentions are.' "

Next day at lunch in a new mess hall at Ramat David Air Base, Shimon Peres, Israel's defense minister, uttered the same message in a quite different manner. Israel was ready to give up land for a political settlement but must not again jeopardize its security. That was standard, but he added: "Our hearts are torn." During many later meetings I always found Peres more flexible than Rabin, more intellectual, more cosmopolitan—he liked to sprinkle his conversation with witticisms and French phrases. But he was also more nervous. His nearly poetic vision of a Middle East in which Jews and Arabs would share land, water and prosperity developed only gradually. The most stunning transformation would occur in Rabin. The stolid and seemingly unimaginative soldier became a visionary of peace and a martyr to that cause.

WHEN I RETURNED to the Middle East in 1978, the new prime minister was Menachem Begin. He soon proved more intractable than any past Israeli leader. Encountering him at a dinner in the Knesset, in front of the Chagall tapestries depicting Jewish life in the Diaspora, I saw him as a mixture of Old Testament prophet and finicky lawyer. In his view, he explained, the famous UN Resolution 242 did not apply to the West Bank or, as he had begun to say, Judea and Samaria, thus nailing down his claim to biblical real estate. The Arabs there could have "administrative autonomy" but nothing approaching sovereignty. After dinner he walked over to the windows overlooking the Bethlehem Hills and said with his angry squint: "Where else in this world, in modern history, has it been known that the Parliament House of an independent nation is within the range and danger of enemy fire?"

In Cairo Sadat was discouraged, disappointed that, as he saw it, Begin had not responded to his overture in the same spirit. He also felt that the United States was not doing enough to back him. But he was determined to keep looking for an agreement that both Israelis and Arabs could accept. "I still consider this mission a sacred mission," he said. "There is no way to go back. I have accepted my fate."

His fate was his assassination. In 1978 Sadat, along with a fiercely reluctant Menachem Begin, signed the Camp David Agreement, Jimmy Carter's greatest foreign policy achievement. The accord, which returned the Sinai to Egypt, was cheered by most of the world. Some Israelis were worried. Rinna Samuel wrote me that she was hardly comforted by "the Camp David gestalt," but "beggars can't be choosers." Much stronger opposition came from Islamic fundamentalists in Egypt who raged against peace with Israel. At a parade commemorating the Egyptian army's early successes in the 1973 war, Sadat was gunned down. His vice president, Hosni Mubarak, who sat next to him, was only slightly wounded. Within days Mubarak assumed the presidency and cracked down on dissidents. I saw him one month afterward. He was stocky and low-key, a pragmatist who had spent years handling problems for his boss. Mubarak lacked Sadat's vision and flair, but he pledged convincingly that he was committed to carrying on Sadat's policies. The assassins, he said, represented only an isolated few. "We are a nation of believers, who value human life very highly."

FOR ALL THE Middle East's excruciating complexity, there were certain fixed points. One was represented by King Hussein of Jordan. He had been seventeen when he came to the throne, and his survival since then seemed almost miraculous. His country was staggered by more than a million Palestinian refugees who had little in common with the native population. For all his occasional mistakes, Hussein maneuvered brilliantly among hostile Arab states, the Israelis (with whom he maintained secret contacts) and the United States. He was meticulous, from his uniform to his speech, with "sir's" and "permit me's" punctuating his arguments. Like all other Arab leaders, he would complain about Jewish influence in the United States leading to one-sided support of Israel. Once, when Washington wanted to sell Stinger missiles to Jordan and ran into opposition, Hussein said bitterly, "If I had known that the president would have to go before the United Jewish Appeal to get approval, I would not have sought it." But I always found him rational and reassuring.

Another permanent fixture in the Middle East, and just as much of a survivor as Hussein, was Syrian president Hafez al-Assad, whom I first met in 1975. His thin, oddly pliable body gave the impression of a cobra being propped up in a high-backed chair. Assad was so affable that one had to remind oneself that he ran a brutal dictatorship backed generously by Moscow. More virulently than Hussein, he attacked the power of the Jewish-influenced media and financial institutions in the United States. "Why," he asked me, "is it not required to tell the American Jew that he should only be an American Jew in the same way as an American Christian or an American Muslim?" I maintained that U.S. policy toward Israel had widespread support far beyond the Jewish community.

My most bizarre encounter with Assad would come in 1986. I happened to be in London when he sent word he wanted to see me on an important issue. I was surprised (we had met only twice before), and I was fairly sure that his aim was propaganda. But I was curious and flew to Damascus. As it turned out, Assad wanted to deny charges—widespread and well founded—that Syria was involved in international terrorism. He countered with a long, numbing recital of what he considered Israeli terrorist acts tolerated by the United States. Then he turned to a trial going on in London in which a Jordanian with a Syrian passport was accused of attempting to blow up an Israeli jetliner by planting a time bomb in the carry-on bag of his pregnant Irish girlfriend. The man claimed that he had help from Syrian authorities. Assad indignantly denied this and insisted that it was all an Israeli plot to discredit Syria, and he supported his story with much fantastic speculation. At one point Assad complained that the U.S. attitude toward the Middle East was divorced from reality. Yet for all his shrewdness I began to wonder about his own sense of reality. Referring to relations between the United States and the Soviet Union, Assad remarked that only an extraterrestrial force could make peace between the superpowers. He went on to tell me about his long-standing interest in UFOs, which he took very seriously.

. . .

An argument often heard from Arabs, and from some Israelis, was that in the missile age territory no longer matters. Perhaps the most vocal opponent of that view was Ariel ("Arik") Sharon. This was my first impression of him: He was standing on a small West Bank rise called Hirbet Zufin, near Qalqiliya, overlooking Tel Aviv, Herzliyya and the Mediterranean. On two easels he had propped up several maps, which flapped in the breeze. With the inevitable pointer he explained to a group of American visitors: "Our main problem is the depth of the country"—or, rather, its lack of depth. "From where we stand it is only eight miles to the sea." Sharon rejected the notion that strips of land no longer matter as a defense. "It's very different when you can see the targets."

A brilliant commander who led the dash across the Suez Canal in the 1973 war, Sharon was now minister of agriculture, but crops were the last thing he worried about. He was a strong advocate of keeping buffer zones against the Arabs and putting Israeli settlers in the Sinai and on the West Bank. "We can take risks, but we cannot risk our existence. We are not going to trust anyone except ourselves."

As he spoke swarms of bees attacked the visitors. "Don't move. They won't bite," he said.

"The hell they won't," replied an American industrialist. "They got me twice on that advice."

The fabled Moshe Dayan, hero of the Six-Day War, was no more eager than Sharon to give up territory, but his tone and emphasis were quite different. At a dinner at the Israel Museum in Jerusalem he spoke about the need to negotiate with the Palestinians (though not the PLO). I remembered meeting him some years before when he walked me and several colleagues through his garden filled with exquisite antiquities, his good eye gleaming as if to make up for the lost vision in the other. He talked of the country's permanent state of siege but was also eloquent about the benign and tolerant Israeli rule in the occupied territories. "We must help the Arabs to become modern, to catch up with the rest of the world." He sounded like nothing so much as an enlightened

British colonial administrator, a member of the Jewish raj. He confirmed my growing belief that the conflict between Jews and Arabs was not merely over disputed land and history, or between religions, but a confrontation of culture. Israel was the West. The Arab countries, the impoverished ones as well as the few rich enclaves, were part of the "underdeveloped" world. "Underdeveloped" might be a patronizing Western word, but most Arabs I knew accepted the term. That gap between cultures, I thought, would have to close or at least narrow if there was ever to be peace.

THROUGHOUT THE REGION the Palestinians were an insistent presence. They came in different forms. Many were the highly educated administrators and economists on whom governments depend. Many were the hapless refugees still festering in the camps. Many were guerrillas, whom the radical regimes supported and the moderate regimes feared. Many were academics, journalists, businessmen. Politically they ranged from extremism to relative—very relative—restraint. Together they formed a kind of Greek chorus accompanying the Middle East's tragic action. I met them in dilapidated shacks on the West Bank and in air-conditioned offices. After listening to them repeatedly, I developed a distinct aversion to the word "justice." "All we want is simple justice," they said over and over again, as if justice were simple.

I especially remember a meeting in the basement of Amman's Intercontinental Hotel with a group of Palestinian activists. "The one person in the world without an entity is the Palestinian," said Sari Nasir, a professor of sociology. "We are terrorists because we want to go home. Don't make it difficult for us or we'll turn into psychotics." That condition already seemed close at times; Nasir hinted that someday "any group," including the Palestinians, might be able to use a nuclear bomb. The Reverend Elia Khoury, a Christian Arab, was more moderate: "We are willing to share the country with them." That included Jerusalem. But Israel vowed that the city would never be divided again. To both sides Jerusalem was a battle cry, a prayer, an assertion of destiny.

Everywhere in the world at Passover, Jews express the hope "Next year in Jerusalem." In the city itself the Jews say instead, "Next year Jerusalem rebuilt." The man who did as much as anyone to rebuild Jerusalem was its mayor, Teddy Kollek.

He was probably the most popular Israeli, whom, it sometimes seemed, half the world considered a close friend. He had tried hard to make Jerusalem into a place where Jews and Arabs could live together in peace. His plans included common playgrounds and other joint facilities. Under his administration the Jewish Jerusalem expanded, with vast new apartment complexes looking like fortresses. But he proposed a system of boroughs in which Jewish and Arab citizens could have autonomy.

Teddy Kollek was born in Vienna, like myself, although more than a decade earlier. We discovered a few similarities in our backgrounds; his father, too, had been of Hungarian origin and served in the imperial army. Teddy, too, disliked school and worshiped the pseudo-American novels of Karl May. But, among other differences, Teddy was better than I had been at sports and at being Jewish. An ardent Zionist from his earliest years, Kollek went to Palestine in 1934 with his family. He was soon active in facilitating Jewish immigration and buying arms for what would become Israel. I first met him in New York in the late forties when he visited my friend Rinna. I remember him as a lithe figure with reddish blond hair and a face half-puckish, half-cherubic, sitting on the floor, looking upward and talking with total confidence about the future of Israel. When I saw him again three decades later, his spirit had not changed. At breakfast early one morning in the Mishkenot Sha'ananim Restaurant overlooking the valley of Hinnom, the traditional site of Gehenna, he looked down on the city as if he owned it—which in many ways he did. At other times, walking with him or riding in a minibus with the mayor next to the driver, tour guide's microphone in hand, I realized that he literally knew every stone. He could talk about Jerusalem's history, layer by archaeological layer, and about his plans for new museums, new parks. In between he could point out to aides that a streetlight was out or a tree dying.

For me, Jerusalem was not a matter of inspiration at first sight. I was put off by what seemed like a clutter of unrelated views. I was not especially moved by the Wailing Wall, and I was not, at least at first, capable of the act of imagination that was necessary to evoke the Temple. The Church of the Holy Sepulchre struck me as depressing, small, dark and offensively split up into segments by rival Christian denominations. As a shrine, I found the Dome of the Rock the most impressive, with a soaring dignity. But what was ultimately captivating was the total picture made up of a thousand details spread out between the luminous hills, a mass that could not possibly combine into harmony and yet did. Mythical sites took on reality. The Mount of Olives had always been merely a symbol from the Gospels, but here it was, a real place, green and sloping gently toward that other sacred abstraction, the Garden of Gethsemane. Its silent olive trees stunned me and at the same time strangely soothed me.

The fact that all three great monotheistic religions found a spiritual home in Jerusalem, Kollek once said, could not be a coincidence. Jerusalem, he explained, is "conducive to meditation and thought and wonder at the meaning of life." For centuries these three faiths had moved their adherents to fight each other, but Kollek believed that they could also inspire people to live together in brotherhood. The thought reminded me of a classic play by the eighteenth-century German poet Gotthold Ephraim Lessing, called *Nathan the Wise*, which I had been taken to see as a child. It was about a sultan, a Christian Templar and a Jew, and its message was brotherhood. In a famous passage Nathan tells the story of a father who was supposed to leave a magical ring to his favorite son. As he could not make up his mind which of his three sons was his favorite, he promised it to each of them and had a jeweler make two copies indistinguishable from the original. After his death the sons quarreled about which one had the true ring and took the case before a judge. "Let each one believe his ring to be the true one," secure in the knowledge that the father loved each son equally, said the judge. "I bid you in a thousand, thousand years to stand again before this seat. For then, a wiser man than I will sit as judge upon this bench and speak."

. . .

For a while, at least, the Arab-Israeli conflict was overshadowed by an extraordinary event: the Iranian hostage crisis. On November 4, 1979, a mass of "students," with the encouragement of the Iranian government, stormed the U.S. embassy in Teheran and seized some sixty American diplomats and embassy employees. Less than a year before, Jimmy Carter had been in Teheran as the guest of Shah Mohammed Reza Pahlavi and toasted his country as "an island of stability." In that respect Carter followed the example of Richard Nixon, who had regarded the shah as a kind of royal subcontractor for U.S. interests in the Gulf and allowed him to buy unlimited amounts of U.S. arms. As a fierce anti-Communist, the shah was seen as a reliable ally against the Soviet Union and other threatening forces in the region. In an area that was full of monarchs, sultans, sheiks and mere dictators of motley background and lavish taste, the shah was special. The "King of Kings" seemed to have stepped out of an ancient Persian tapestry into the age of missiles and jets (he piloted one himself). Alongside his lovely and jewel-encrusted empress, he roamed among five palaces in Iran and luxurious residences in Europe and the United States. In 1971 he had celebrated the 2,500th anniversary of the Persian empire—he traced his lineage somewhat dubiously to Cyrus the Great—in an extravaganza at Persepolis, to which all available heads of state were invited, including one emperor, eight kings and a cardinal, plus assorted presidents and prime ministers. The $100 million jamboree did not do much to highlight the shah's social conscience, although it was carefully pointed out that as part of the celebration he had also built new schools and highways. The shah tried hard to modernize his country, carrying out land reform in the "White" (meaning bloodless) revolution and giving women the right to vote. In a 1975 conversation he told me that he considered himself superior to Atatürk as a reformer. I had heard that underlings often kissed his hand and foot, but there was none of that as aides ushered me and Karsten Prager, who covered the region for *Time*, into the sparkling Mirror Hall, his office in Teheran's Niavaran Palace.

His heavy horn-rimmed glasses gave him the air of a serious business executive. For a ruler who had been put back on his throne by the CIA after a coup in the early fifties, and was being relentlessly courted by the United States, he was arrogantly critical of America. He lectured me about America's moral decay and our lavish consumer society, an odd charge from this rather lavish consumer. By then his autocratic regime was rattled by protests and occasional acts of terrorism. He put it all down to a handful of desperate extremists.

"What can they sell our people? Our farmers own their land. Our workers can buy shares in factories. Studies are free. . . ." He was scathing on the subject of liberal intellectuals: "They will accept any-thing that comes from the other side. Anything that is Communistic, that is nihilistic, is okay. One by one, countries are going to fall. I am talking about French so-called intellectuals, Swedish so-called intellectu-als, Dutch so-called intellectuals . . . No doubt there is an intellectual international. They all work for Marxism. They penetrate everything."

It was a rather paranoid exaggeration. Iran's intellectuals were indeed complaining about the regime's arbitrary and often harsh rule, but the shah chose to overlook other opposition: the growing middle class, busi-nessmen, hard-pressed bazaar merchants, all of whom felt that they were not getting enough of a share in Iran's prosperity. Above all, there was discontent from the Shiite Mullahs, who saw the shah's moderniza-tion of Iran as decadent and blasphemous. The prophet of the religious opposition was a black-robed cleric with a permanent epic scowl, the Ayatollah Ruhollah Khomeini, the spiritual leader of some thirty-two million Iranian Shiites. He had been exiled by the shah for political agitation and had been living in Iraq until 1978, when the ever-hospita-ble, ever-mischievous French allowed him to settle near Paris, from where he waged a campaign of hate against the shah. His preachments were recorded on tape and the cassettes smuggled into Iran, where they were widely circulated.

Meanwhile the United States remained hopeful about the shah's fu-ture. At the initiative of Time Inc.'s president, Jim Linen, who had cultivated the shah (he had a decided weakness for crowned heads), the company helped set up an educational publishing firm in Teheran to produce textbooks. It was profitable, but its principal benefit from my point of view was that Joan Manley, the head of Time-Life Books, journeyed to Teheran once a month to check on operations and returned with large quantities of caviar, which she generously shared. Alas, the caviar—and much else—soon came to an end.

The press, including *Time,* had been slow to recognize the weakness underneath the regime's hard carapace. But by the mid-seventies we were turning skeptical. One report from our Washington bureau suggested, "Because the shah is a U.S. creation, there is willful schizophrenia among U.S. policy planners," split between advocates of a soft or hard line in dealing with the Iranian dissidents. The shah himself vacillated. Opposition mounted amid riots, reprisals, casualties. In the end the shah fled the country and went into restless exile. Few of the heads of state, who had enjoyed the Persepolis spectacular a few years before, wanted the political liability of letting him into their countries. By then it was known that he was suffering from lymphatic cancer, and on the urging of David Rockefeller and Henry Kissinger, Jimmy Carter allowed the shah into the United States on humanitarian grounds. While the shah was undergoing treatment at New York Hospital, Khomeini raged against the United States, "the mother of corruption," and denounced the American embassy in Teheran as a "nest of spies and intrigue." That was the cue for radicals to strike at the embassy. Thus the long hostage crisis began.

There was something absurd and surreal about the very idea of taking hostages, I thought, a reversion to the dark ages of ambush and ransom. But Teheran wanted to humiliate America. In that it succeeded. The hostages were bound, blindfolded and paraded by their captors. The militants' garbage was wrapped in the American flag.

Americans watched an endless series of diplomatic forays and limited sanctions, none of which worked. Hopes kept rising, only to sputter again. Yellow ribbons sprouted on trees, flagpoles, car antennas. At Christmas 1979 the White House tree remained unlit, except for the star on the top. Walter Cronkite ended each broadcast with the statement "And that's the way it is . . . the fifteenth, [or fiftieth, or two hundred thirty-fifth] day of captivity for the American hostages in Iran."

Time made Khomeini its Man of the Year for 1979. The man assigned to cover him was Bruce Van Voorst, a tough, able correspondent who had worked briefly for the CIA before turning to journalism. Van Voorst obtained a rare interview with Khomeini at his residence in Qom. It was a notably modest house, but one of its four rooms was permanently fitted out as a TV studio with floodlights and cameras. With barely a nod to his caller, Khomeini sat down cross-legged, stared at the floor and launched into a diatribe against the United States for first installing the shah in Iran and then giving asylum to this "murderer." If the facts "penetrate the Zionist-imperialist propaganda screen," Americans "will have a change of heart about us and reciprocate our amicable attitude." Van Voorst asked some hard questions, for instance: "Sometimes you issue *elamiehs* telling the people what to do, and then, when you want to avoid responsibility, you reply you can do nothing, it is in the hands of the people or the students. Aren't you trying to have it both ways?" Khomeini dodged, accused, condemned, called for justice and made some fantastic statements, suggesting that the United States had bombed Hiroshima for profit. He called on U.S. voters not to reelect Carter because his "continued presidency is a danger for America."

The selection of Khomeini as Man of the Year provoked the mother of protests from readers. Many misunderstood the symbolism, thinking we were honoring an outrageous villain rather than merely noting that he was responsible for the most striking news event of the year. Soon afterward American newsmen were expelled from Iran and not much information was provided by journalists of other countries. *Time* was lucky to have a special source in Iran. His name was Raji Samghabadi, the former managing editor of Teheran's English daily, who had taught himself the language by reading *Webster's Collegiate Dictionary* and T. E. Lawrence's *Seven Pillars of Wisdom.* He joined *Time*'s Teheran bureau in early 1979 and stayed on after our other correspondents had to leave at the end of that year. He was warned not to work for the magazine, so his name never appeared on any of the stories he sent. He filed to the *Washington Star*, hoping the Iranian authorities would not discover that it was owned by Time Inc. Then, as the crisis was coming to an end, in November 1980 Raji was arrested, along with other journalists, by members of the Islamic Guard. He was told that all "spies" would be executed. At three A.M. Raji was taken from his cell and ordered to sign a confession of espionage. He refused. He was taken to a courtyard where a firing squad awaited. Again he was ordered to confess. Again he refused. He was blindfolded, the rifles sounded and he waited for the pain. It never came; he had not been shot. He was dragged back to his cell and then moved from place to place. Raji assumed that his captors had simply grabbed anyone they thought might provide a valuable confession. When they failed, they abandoned him. After six days he was able to make his way to New York via Pakistan and France. In New York, working the phones, he put together eyewitness reports from his extensive network in Iran. I found him tireless, ebullient and passionate about what was happening in his country. "Khomeini rode in on a tide of hatred against the shah," Raji said. "But he betrayed the people and did things one hundred times worse than the shah did. Khomeini stole the revolution and the hopes for the future."

Meanwhile, in complete secrecy, Carter was planning a desperate operation to rescue the hostages. It proved to be a disastrous failure. In Washington, at two A.M., Carter called for the text of John Kennedy's remarks announcing the collapse of the Bay of Pigs mission. By seven A.M., using similar language, Carter went on television to tell the nation of the debacle. Secretary of State Cyrus Vance, who had opposed the action, resigned in protest. The president tried to carry on and prepared for that fall's elections. But the Carter presidency, and the hopes for a second term, died in the wreckage of "Operation Eagle Claw." The failed mission seemed to symbolize everything that was wrong with Carter's style of governing. There were the typical flaws in planning, the mixture of caution and desperate daring, excessive micromanagement by the president and—perhaps most of all—bad luck. The very qualities that Americans had always counted on, whatever else might go wrong— technical ingenuity and military competence—failed. After more diplomatic maneuvering the hostages were finally released on January 20, 1981, hours after Ronald Reagan was sworn in as president.

PART EIGHT

PARTINGS

AND

RENEWALS

CHAPTER THIRTY-THREE

WHILE THE CARTER PRESIDENCY was winding down and Reagan was moving toward the White House, I had been running *Time* against the backdrop of a company slowly transforming itself. One portent of change was cable television. Home Box Office was launched one night in the winter of 1972 in Wilkes-Barre, Pennsylvania, where 365 people had been persuaded to subscribe at $6.00 per month. The early programming consisted mostly of second-rate movies, sports, including the roller derby and bowling, and such attractions as the Pennsylvania Polka Festival. A tentacled giant would grow from these modest beginnings. (By 1980 cable revenues would overtake print revenues in Time Inc.)

Another business expansion actually seemed more important and, to many in the company, more ominous. In 1973 Time Inc. merged with Temple Industries, a huge, Texas forest products concern. The connection happened through a pulp and paper company, Eastex, which Time Inc. had long owned. It seemed like an odd union to most of our employees, to Wall Street, and to the press. Everybody half assumed that "Texas" was taking over *Time* and that the chairman of what had become Temple-Eastex would wind up running Time Inc. The *Fortune* offices displayed humorous signs evoking a woodsy future: "Vice President for Leaves, Twigs and Bark," "Branch Manager." Newspaper stories described Arthur Temple, accurately enough, as the king of a vast forest realm that he ruled from tiny Diboll, Texas, a company town of 3,557. He was a University of Texas dropout who loved hunting, fishing and making money. At a lunch I arranged with the editors, he asked shrewd questions and disclaimed any intention of interfering with the magazines. He did not know anything about publishing, he said, although, he added with a grin, he owned the *Diboll Free Press,* circulation 4,200.

Temple was a tall, massive man who often wore a hat indoors, chewed cigars and was noted for picturesque speech. He might advise against a deal by saying "A man can eat only so many beans" or warn against a difficult decision with the words "We'd better pull that snake out on the road and see how long it is before we try to kill it." But behind his rustic folksiness he was sophisticated and socially progressive. On his periodic visits to the Time & Life Building I found him thoroughly refreshing, providing a breeze of outside air in the sometimes close corporate atmosphere. But investors never accepted pulp and publishing as a good fit, and Time Inc.'s stock suffered. The magazine employees blamed many tough, unpopular management decisions on "the Texans."

That was unfair. The magazine business had problems of its own. An ever-increasing share of advertising dollars went into television, and the cost of publishing kept mounting. The circulation of *Time* and our other magazines grew reassuringly, but it became necessary to entice subscribers with "bonuses," such as umbrellas, shower curtains, beach floats and clock radios, a deplorable tactic.

A particular demon in the eyes of the *Time* publishing staff was the W. R. Simmons Research report, which gauged the number of times each copy of the magazine was passed along to other readers. *Time*'s "pass-along" number was frequently lower than *Newsweek*'s. My business colleagues tried to explain this by asserting that *Time* was a more interesting magazine. But Madison Avenue did not quite buy the image of the *Time* reader clutching his copy and refusing to hand it over to wife, children or friends.

To find out more about the readers' likes and dislikes, some of our

circulation people arranged for "focus groups." Although I never believed in that device or other market surveys, I was heartened to find
that many readers understood the virtues of the newsmagazine: "They
tell you what happened Tuesday wasn't important, but what happened
Thursday *was* important." "They put it all together. The whole story in
one shot." The news itself was variously described as "bad," "depressing," "repetitious," "tedious," "ghastly."

But we had to supply serious news, no matter how "depressing," and
we had to add information not readily found elsewhere. That was expensive, requiring large numbers of people. Undoubtedly the numbers
had grown too large. I had to make cuts.

In late 1973 a group of writers and researchers sent me a petition
charging that "the company has been financially strangling the editorial
side." They felt that their salaries, once considerably ahead of the rest of
the industry, no longer compensated them adequately for their hard
work and long hours and that staff reductions were hurting the quality
of the magazine. At a meeting Andrew Heiskell spelled out some of the
economic facts of life: inflation, pressure from Washington to hold down
prices, including advertising rates, and the need to make a decent profit
to satisfy shareholders. Over the next two years I talked regularly to the
writers' group. I would point out that, as someone had calculated, *Time*
still had eight people behind every page printed. Moreover, working
conditions were hardly spartan. Apart from amenities (food, transporta-
tion home), the company offered exceptionally generous fringe benefits.

But a more important issue was at stake. For years the Newspaper
Guild and the company regularly negotiated salary increases. These
were across the board up to a certain level; above a cutoff point management was free to use its discretion in awarding or not awarding raises.
As the 1976 contract talks approached, the guild was pressing hard for a
higher cutoff point. Management proposed lowering it, with a certain
sum set aside for raises to be given strictly on merit. Negotiations with
the guild were being conducted by the "business side," but I strongly
concurred that we should have a chance to reward good performance
rather than being tied more and more to automatic raises; virtually

every other editor in the Time & Life Building vehemently agreed. Most lower-paid employees disliked the idea, and much of the staff sympathized. Guild membership increased sharply.

On June 2, 1976, most of Time Inc.'s editorial employees walked out. It was the first strike in the history of a generally benign and paternalistic company. It happened against the backdrop of a shrinking union movement that was still fighting against automation and for featherbedding. The guild was weaker than it felt. Its new members were enthusiastic on the surface but lacked staying power or union traditions. Some were so naive as to think that the strike pay, provided by the guild, would equal their normal salaries. (It was actually $45 per week.) Joe Ferrer, a thoughtful writer who was active with the guild and trusted on both sides, said later: "We felt we were right; we believed in the justice of the cause and thought that alone would help us prevail."

The union's aim was to stop at least one of the Time Inc. magazines from coming out. But our publications were printed in Chicago and elsewhere in nonunion plants, and no other unions, including the Teamsters, honored the strike call. Senior editors turned to writing, their copy going straight to me or to my assistant managing editors, eliminating a whole layer of editing. Hedley Donovan became a replacement writer in "Nation"; Jim Shepley wrote "Law" stories. Secretaries filled in as researchers or computer operators.

It was a strange experience to cross the picket line of people I had worked with for years. Should I look stern and solemn? Should I smile—or would that seem to belittle their earnest stand? I tried to look neutral and waved. Some of them jeered, but without much passion. The picket signs were half-humorous: "Time Marches Out," "Time Marches Backward." Several strikers walked their dogs on the line. But there were also real flashes of anger. Most nonstrikers worked exceptionally hard, but overall the stripped-down system of writing and editing meant that the magazine went to press faster than usual. On closing night the first week I left at the unbelievably early hour of nine P.M., leading some guild members to assume that I was faking it, as psychological warfare.

There was a certain sense of triumph when the first issue during the strike appeared on time. But when we started working on the third, a measure of fatigue had set in. By then the strikers had lost heart. After eighteen days the guild gave up and accepted the contract we had offered in the first place. The strikers returned to work in a body. Very little bitterness remained, although complaints about long hours and worries about quality persisted. Ironically the strike had demonstrated that, far from being understaffed, the magazine could do very well with fewer people and with a simpler structure. Among other strike-inspired changes I loosened the rigid territorial divisions among sections; when the Education writer was not busy in his regular department, for instance, he might fill in at Law. I explained this in a lengthy memo, which provoked a parody from an unknown humorist on the staff: "Art critic Robert Hughes has already volunteered to do back-up stories on astrophysics. Movie critic Jay Cocks will back up Russian expert Pat Blake in covering Solzhenitsyn and, as many of you already know, Senior Writer Mike Demarest is filling in Thursday nights in the cafeteria."

In the following months the magazine felt easier to handle, more maneuverable. Business was good; *Time* and the entire company were thriving. But I knew that my tenure must soon come to an end. In 1977 I began my ninth year as managing editor, amounting to the "two presidential terms, give or take a year," that Hedley Donovan had forecast. When he'd made me managing editor he had warned me not to expect anything beyond that position. But through the years his manner suggested that I figured in the plans he had to be making for his mandatory retirement in 1979.

So I reluctantly prepared for my exit. But who would succeed me? The obvious choice seemed to be Jason McManus, whom I had appointed assistant managing editor in 1976. He had become indispensable for his cool intelligence and his organizational gifts, which he had displayed during the long Watergate siege. He had a talent for making his staff happy, or at least contented. Few people knew about Jason's beginnings. His first career choice was the Presbyterian ministry, and while he was a student at Davidson College he was given a small church as an apprentice minister in suburban St. Louis. For thirteen weeks he wrote the sermons and conducted the services but discovered that this was not his calling. "If you want to change the world," he observed later, "it is not a huge leap from the pulpit to the press." I did not believe that Jason particularly wanted to change the world, but I thought he would make a good managing editor.

Hedley Donovan had other ideas. As sometimes happened, he was in the mood to do something unconventional. Early in 1976 he had startled me by suggesting that Ray Cave, executive editor of *Sports Illustrated,* come to *Time* as an assistant managing editor. Such transplants from one Time Inc. magazine to another were rare. It was obvious that Hedley wanted to put Cave in the running to be the next managing editor. I hardly knew him but was familiar with his reputation: hard-shelled, somewhat dour, enterprising. I was not exactly delighted by the prospect of somebody taking over the magazine who had never had any experience with *Time*. But Hedley made it clear that he would not insist on Cave as my successor if I objected after working with him for a while. On that basis I saw no reason to resist Cave's move to *Time*.

He was met by considerable suspicion from the staff, but he and I functioned well together. He was highly skilled in the techniques of making magazines, had an excellent eye for illustrations and a sharp, unconventional news sense. A graduate of St. John's in Annapolis, the "Great Books college," he was not as narrowly focused on sports as I expected. He had been an investigative reporter for the *Baltimore Evening Sun* and observed, without striking any heroic pose, that he had been drawn to this kind of reporting by "a high level of annoyance at things being done to the citizen." But he felt that, since Watergate, investigative reporting had become too much of a fad. He had a somewhat formal manner, perhaps because his father had been a West Pointer and a brigadier general. He was prickly and seemed to take positive delight in arguing and disagreeing. But I found him intriguing and refreshing.

In June 1977 Hedley told me that he wanted me to work with him as his second deputy, alongside Ralph Graves. The former managing editor of *Life,* an admirable journalist and executive, Graves might well be the next editor in chief. But I knew that Hedley always wanted more than one choice available to him. In September I moved upstairs and Ray Cave became managing editor of *Time*.

Leaving *Time* was unsettling. It was my home professionally and in many ways personally. I knew it the way a manager knows his factory or a captain knows his ship. I knew its moods and temper, its virtues, its faults and bugs, I knew what it could and could not accomplish. Above all, I knew its people. As a newcomer years before, I had been captivated by the characters I met. Now I was still captivated by them, though many of the original set had been replaced over the years. In my last months at *Time* I found myself leafing through an imaginary album and making my good-byes.

The most poignant good-bye was to Johanna Davis. She had first appeared at my door in the late fifties when, recently out of Wellesley, she applied for a job—any job—at *Time*. I happened to need a secretary, and the personnel department sent her to me. Across my desk I saw flowing brown hair that made her round face look narrower than it was, warm, blue eyes and an ironic smile that seemed older than her twenty-two years. She was short and on the pudgy side. She knew no shorthand but had been—I was carefully told—the typing champion of Southern California (120 words per minute). I thought that her background coincided nicely with some of the entertainment sections I was then editing.

Johanna was the daughter of Herman Mankiewicz, author of *Citizen Kane* and other notable films. I realized within minutes that she was frighteningly bright, and like almost everyone she met, I was instantly enchanted. I hired her. Josie was steamily involved with Peter Davis, the young television and film producer who would later make *Hearts and Minds*, the documentary about Vietnam that I found so troubling. Peter seemed to be in the office constantly, not to mention on the telephone, and they were soon married.

Given her brains and wit, I saw to it, in due course, that she was promoted to researcher and then writer. Josie was a natural humorist, with herself as the heroine and butt of her stories. She could make an anecdote out of buying detergent and a major adventure of going to the hairdresser. Looking at an ancient Japanese screen in a living room, she would improvise an uproarious story about what was depicted, explaining that the men on their knees were measuring the palace for linoleum. She was full of marvelous stories about her Hollywood childhood and about her parents, Herman, the Casanova of the commissary, and his long-suffering wife, always known as "Poor Sarah." She recalled Halloween in Beverly Hills, when she was sent out trick-or-treating in a limousine. The chauffeur would walk to the front door of various mansions, carrying an ornate paper bag, and white-gloved butlers would fill it with elegant candies while she waited in the car under a chinchilla lap robe. The point, she said, was that she never did anything for herself that somebody else could do for her. That was why, she would explain, hilariously, she never masturbated. When she was at the Westlake School for Girls in Los Angeles, a famous institution attended by all Hollywood princesses, she even found someone special to do a difficult geometry assignment for her: She wrote to Albert Einstein. ("I think you will agree it is the hardest thing!") The great man sent the solution by return mail, providing her with a typical Josie punch line: he forgot to put a stamp on the envelope.

Her stories for *Time,* over which she agonized, were usually as amusing as her conversation, often with a sharp edge of insight. In a piece about "cocktail kissing" she wrote: "The kiss as greeting has moved out of the domain of theater and show business circles where everyone has already kissed everyone else and only the handshake denotes abiding love." Josie's humor conveyed the half-hidden message that life was okay, after all, even in its more awful moments. She radiated warmth, and she was an instinctive confidante. There were times when Josie's friends worried about her state of mind—for instance, when she spent months covering every surface in her apartment with contact paper.

In 1973 she published a short, widely praised novel called *Life Signs* about a young woman much like herself who, pregnant with her second child, is cracking up under the strains of motherhood, marriage, New York life and an idiotic therapist. Musing about how childbearing and child raising was driving so many women of her generation to the brink of insanity, the heroine reflects: "Motherhood's not going to get me. It would be like dying in a subway crash, you'd end up just one name in a huge list of victims. If I go under, it's going to be in some special incredible catastrophe." A year after her book came out, Josie was standing on the sidewalk in front of her house on Charles Street in Greenwich Village. Next to her was her eleven-year-old son, Timothy. Two taxis collided and one of the cabs mounted the sidewalk, hurling her against a metal mailbox. She was dead on arrival at the hospital. Her son was unhurt. It was indeed a special, incredible catastrophe—insufferably casual, brutally random. My reaction, even more than grief, was rage.

ANOTHER OF MY rather bittersweet farewells was for Essie and Alwyn Lee. She was chief of research at *Time;* he was a book reviewer. But their job designations hardly summed up this extraordinary pair. She was a strapping, regal woman, with a melodious but sarcastic laugh. He was a thin, sharp-beaked man, the remnants of youthful good looks only slightly diminished by a perpetually furrowed forehead and an occasionally sour expression, due as much to various ailments as to his outlook on life. They were both irreverent, but she was also ebullient and maternal, loved to cook and create comfort. He was sardonic but a good and loyal friend, wondrously erudite, original in his thinking and bardic in his conversation. Her speech was elliptic, with many gaps, as if she assumed that you knew all the names and situations she was alluding to and that you shared with her many uproarious secrets. His speech was precise, detailed and evocative, suggesting that you were ready to share with him a deep understanding of the human condition.

I knew Essie as a researcher long before she was promoted to chief. As principal guardian of the magazine's accuracy, she had a sharp eye for the false and the bogus. She was a fierce defender of her "girls" and their craft; when an editor referred to them as mere fact checkers, she remarked icily: "When I need a checker, I'll go to the supermarket." One of her favorite expressions to describe a funny situation was, "What larks!" For several weeks, on closing nights, she would gather some researchers and copy readers in the office lounge, put Chubby Checker

on the record player and insist that they teach her the twist. Taking off
for a weekend, she might say, "If anyone wants me, tell them I'm on my
way to buy a bikini and then I'm going to Thumbsville." Thumbsville
was her name for a massage.

One of my first memories of Alwyn has him chopping wood at their
farm at Croton-on-Hudson, hacking away ferociously, sweating in the
sun. It was among his favorite ways of relaxing. After a while he politely offered me the ax and invited me to take a whack, too. I was not
very good at it, and he gently retrieved the lethal instrument from my
inexpert hands.

They were both Australian, with solid middle-class backgrounds. At
Melbourne University Harry Alwyn Lee was a gifted student, passionate
about politics (he joined the Communist Party) and unruly. He went to
work for an encyclopedia but never got much beyond "Fleas, Performing." As a reporter for the *Melbourne Herald* he was once assigned to do
a story on a leprosarium near Victoria. The piece contained the memorable sentence " 'Conditions at Coode Island are disgraceful,' a leading
leper said today. . . ." His editor did not appreciate this parody of
journalese, but Lee was irrepressible. On another occasion, to liven up a
dull news day, he invented a maddened pack of savage Alsatians swim-
ming the Murray River and terrorizing northeastern Victoria. The wife
of the *Herald*'s publisher happened to be devoted to Alsatians, and Lee
was soon looking for other work. In 1939 the Lees left Australia and
headed for the United States, stopping off in Mexico. There Lee interviewed the exiled Leon Trotsky. He was amused to find that Trotsky
was raising rabbits in his garden but could not bear to have them killed.
He might be "the author of *In Defense of Terrorism*, organizer of the
Red Army," wrote Alwyn, but "his rabbits live in peace." Soon afterward
Trotsky was assassinated with an ice pick by one of Stalin's agents.
Alwyn's faith in Communism had begun to fade before that, and now he
grew into a staunch anti-Communist, like Whittaker Chambers, whose
close friend he became. During World War II Alwyn was a war correspondent for his old paper, the *Melbourne Herald*, and covered the
landing with the U.S. Fifth Amphibious Corps on Red Beach, at Iwo
Jima. He was later wounded at Okinawa.

Back in the United States Alwyn published short stories, essays and reminiscences. I eventually brought him to *Time*. Editing his book reviews required an unusual amount of pruning and rearranging, but it was worth it. He wrote with often startling insights and deep, uncompromising seriousness. On the side, Alwyn was forever composing a long mock-heroic and bawdy poem in iambic pentameter, partly autobiographical but mostly an attack on Australian culture. The work would never be finished or published, but friends were allowed occasional glimpses. In one passage he evoked the raucous Australian cocktail hour: "So speech that none can analyze nor parse / As Horse's arse communes with horses arse."

Alwyn was notoriously thirsty—he would sometimes pour vodka over his morning cornflakes. I once found him passed out under his desk in the office, and a reliable eyewitness, the writer John McPhee, claims that I knelt down by his side and cried, "Speak to me, speak to me!" (I don't recall uttering that cliché.) More typically, Alwyn did his drinking at Glennon's, a cozily ragged Third Avenue saloon with layers of mold on the ceiling. The owner-bartender was Jimmy Glennon, an erudite man with a large repertory of Latin quotations and Irish anecdotes. I spent quite a few happy and instructive hours there listening to Alwyn, trying to get a word in occasionally. On one legendary night a fellow drinker took out his glass eye, dropped it in his beer and said to Alwyn, "Will you drink to my eye?" Alwyn removed his false teeth, dropped them in his own beer and declared, somewhat gummily, "An eye for an eye, a tooth for a tooth."

After a lengthy bout with pancreatic cancer Alwyn died in Rome in 1970. Essie lived on for more than two decades; she died in London in 1992 at the age of ninety. Theirs had been an often rocky but very close marriage. Just how close I did not fully realize—they were never publicly demonstrative in their affections—until years later when I read a letter Alwyn had written to Essie the night before the landing on Iwo Jima. It was supposed to be delivered to her if he were killed. He kept the letter, and it eventually found its way to his old friend the writer Alan Moorehead, whose son John showed it to me. It alluded to something that Alwyn had only occasionally touched on in our talks: how being in danger in World War II had given him a sense of identity and had helped him overcome the fear that he might lack courage. The letter was unguarded, without his critical avoidance of emotion. "I have loved you in the way I do at this moment—in my heart and soul and for always," he wrote. "It is something to know one thing as certainly as I do this. You know perhaps better than I do why I had to come out here. Without doing that, the thing between us might have shorted in the end, but now it is complete; and there are worse things to regret than death. . . . All the good things come back to you, my dearest. I remember everything in all the years between us and you are fresh and clear and lovely now in my mind and for always. I would like to have walked in the hills again with you as we used to back in Australia and held your hand, and have you speak to me again. . . ."

IN MY IMAGINATION the Lees formed a special trio with Robert Hughes, another "mate" (as he would put it) to whom I was sorry to say good-bye. Hughes, however, was very much alive, and we would remain friends. Like Alwyn, Hughes was Australian, brilliant, a marathon talker, a painter and poet before turning to journalism and criticism. They were friends, though Hughes was much younger and politically far to the left of Alwyn. Hughes appeared in my office one day in 1970, and I see him dressed in a black leather jacket. But that is a trick of memory, because Hughes was an enthusiastic, part-time biker. He undoubtedly wore an entirely respectable suit. I was looking for a new art critic at the time, and one of my colleagues had noticed Hughes's writing in British journals. I had read a batch of clips forwarded by our London office and a book titled *Heaven and Hell in Western Art.* How was I to resist someone who could write, "God did not live in Hampstead and was not expected to act like a liberal"?

I invited Hughes to fly to New York for an interview and quickly hired him. He was a shock to the *Time* system. Once he terrified a researcher by entering her office swinging a Samurai sword. He kept unpredictable hours, could never be reached on the phone, was feuding constantly with the tax authorities on both sides of the Atlantic and drove our bookkeepers to rage with his vague and belated expense accounts. I was bombarded with complaints, all of which I dismissed. I laid down a flat ruling: Hughes was so good that he should be allowed to get away with almost anything. I enjoyed his irreverence. One evening he was waiting for an elevator in the Time & Life Building. The door slid open, revealing Henry Kissinger and myself riding down from a meeting. "Ah!" said Hughes loudly. "If it isn't Tweedledum and Tweedledee!"

He was too elemental a force to tie down. I gave him great latitude to take time off for his books and television series, including *The Shock of the New* and *The Fatal Shore*, his history of the founding of Australia (which he referred to as "Kangaroots"). I often thought that he might quit, but he always returned from his outside adventures. He liked his base at *Time*, he explained. He tended to write mostly about what he wanted, but he was conscientious regarding any assignment he took on. One of the few complaints I ever had from him concerned a stunning collection of Japanese art bought by New York's Metropolitan Museum. Hughes and our reporters had a hard time pinning down the facts about the transaction and about the mysterious and reclusive seller. "I have relished every chore I have had to do for *Time* in the last five years, *except* this one," Hughes wrote me in a memo. "I would rather compose distichs in Lacadaemonian dialect on the length of Tom Hoving's peter. . . ."

Hughes's copy might be late, but it was impeccable and required virtually no editing. His knowledge of art and culture seemed boundless, but his criticism was never oppressively academic. He had a hypnotic, evocative way of describing what he saw on a canvas. He could praise and blame with equal enthusiasm, but he was especially devastating about contemporaries. On Jasper Johns, whose work he actually admired: "One went to it like Oedipus to the Sphinx. Ask it the wrong question and it would bite one's beak off." In a long poem composed of Alexander Pope–ish couplets, published in the *New York Review of Books*, he satirized the New York art world, including pretentious collectors, gallery owners, critics and artists. Julian Schnabel, whose work famously included heavy impasto and broken crockery, was skewered in thin disguise: "And now the hybrid child of Hubris comes / Julian Snorkel, with his ten fat thumbs; / Ad nauseam, he babbles, honks and prates / Of Death and Life, Careers and Broken Plates."

His conversation was much like his writing. He was performing constantly, using more arcane words than anyone this side of Bill Buckley, and he spoke in bon mots that sounded rehearsed. Some undoubtedly were. Later, when he published *The Culture of Complaint*, friends realized that many of his philippics against contemporary society ("A polity obsessed with therapies and filled with distrust of formal politics; skeptical of authority and prey to superstition; its political language corroded by fake pity and euphemism") echoed past harangues. He once asked me—quite seriously, I thought—whether I could help him become the first journalist to join a space mission and go to the moon. I was at a loss about how to engineer this. I regretted that, because if Hughes had made it, our image of the moon would never have been the same again.

M Y DEPARTURE FROM the magazine was marked by the inevitable parties. One was a full-dress, changing-of-the-guard banquet. Another, which I remember more warmly, was a smaller office bash. In my own parting remarks I talked about the exhilaration of editing *Time* and was sufficiently carried away to use a line from the movie *Patton*, when George C. Scott surveys a battlefield and says of combat: "God, I love it so." I *did* love it and missed the excitement of running a weekly news-magazine ever after.

Having turned over the Briton Hadden pencil cup to Ray Cave, I moved to my new office. It was only nine stories away from the *Time* editorial floor, but the distance was vast. I found the prevailing quiet overwhelming; the thick rugs seemed to be covering the walls as well. There was no sign of the heavy human traffic, the drive and tension I was used to at *Time*. After a few months on the thirty-fourth floor, Ralph Graves had observed that the view was superb and that it was nice to have people come in and dust the plants. But he felt that this "finky floor," as one secretary called it, was too remote. "Editors should be more involved," he wrote in a memo. "There are too many empty offices up here. Some are used for picnics at lunch, which is better than not having them used at all." But he thought that the empty spaces added "to the Frank E. Campbell atmosphere."

Ralph's title, which I now shared, was corporate editor. When my name appeared under that designation, Teddy White wrote me: "Jeezus Christ—what a title! It makes you sound like an institution, like the director of the President's Science Advisory Office."

Our duties as corporate editors involved whatever chores Hedley Donovan felt like turning over to us. We each supervised a number of the magazines. We also dealt with various administrative matters, including salaries, and stayed vaguely in touch with the company's cable and film operations. We were what Ralph called "gentlemen in waiting," understudying Hedley while he made up his mind which of us should get his job.

Ralph had grown up in the Philippines, the stepson of Francis Sayre, the U.S. high commissioner, served in the air force during World War II and a few years later landed a job as a research trainee at *Life*. He gradually rose on the masthead as a correspondent and editor, worked with the great photographers (including Margaret Bourke-White and Alfred Eisenstaedt) and became managing editor in 1969. Along the way he also wrote several novels. His most memorable achievement was the famous special issue that carried the photographs and names of all Americans killed during one week of the Vietnam War. In 1972 he had the misfortune of presiding over the death of the weekly *Life*, which neither he nor anybody else could have prevented.

On the thirty-fourth floor he and I worked amiably together. I found myself once again in the same situation I had been in when I was pitted against Jim Keogh for the managing editorship of *Time*, except that I felt closer to Ralph and thought he had a much stronger claim to the job. I wanted it and planned to quit if I did not get it, but there was hardly any tension between us; we never maneuvered against each other. Later in a speech I summed up my view of him this way: "Ralph is imaginative without being flaky; forceful without being mean; efficient without being pedantic, human without being soft; and he eats a lot without getting fat—which is unforgivable."

About a year after my arrival on thirty-four, Hedley summoned me to lunch. In his best poker manner he had given me no indication of whether he was leaning toward Ralph or me. I had the instinct, later confirmed, that Andrew Heiskell favored Ralph, who, he thought, would get along better with the business side, but it was Hedley's decision. With six months to go before his mandatory retirement, Hedley declared, he was planning to put my name to the Board of Directors as his successor—if I was willing. It was a replay of the occasion a decade earlier when he had offered me the managing editorship of *Time*. Once again I echoed his formality.

"I'm very pleased and very flattered," I said. "And I'm very much aware of the enormous responsibility. But, yes, I'm willing." I was fifty-six.

Hedley said he would welcome maintaining some connection with Time Inc., perhaps as a consultant. "But that of course will depend on whether you want to make use of me." Until moments before, he had been the omnipotent boss on whose word my professional fate depended. The reversal in our roles was stunning.

As for Ralph Graves, said Hedley, he would be my deputy, with an upgraded title, editorial director. After Ralph heard the news he walked into my office and said: "Congratulations."

"Thank you," I said. "It could have been you just as easily." I took a bottle of vodka from my office refrigerator and poured two drinks. I told him—sincerely—that I was relieved and delighted he would be my deputy. Years later he confided that he had been momentarily disgruntled and considered looking for some other job in the company but couldn't think of one. It was a measure of his extraordinary character that he felt apologetic about this entirely understandable reaction and considered it bad form.

Among the messages I received on my appointment, my favorite was a wire from Bill Buckley: "Congratulations! Together we can rule the world." I wired back: "Thanks for including me." The changing of the guard required yet another banquet. Hedley made a thoughtful and graceful farewell speech in which he humorously mentioned that people had often compared being editor in chief to being pope. I responded with a long cherished quote by Pope Leo X: "Let us enjoy the papacy now that God has given it to us." But I warned my assembled colleagues that I would try to keep myself and them permanently dissatisfied with our performance. Beyond that pep rally assurance I made some predictions about the world we would be reporting in the coming decade. "For the balance of this century we face incredible nationalistic and even tribal feuds and hatreds that we somehow thought had been left behind," I said. "We face both in the U.S. and in the world a bitter battle over resources, a growing demand on the goods of society, which—at least for the moment—industrial civilization seems unable to meet. . . . We face a serious test of American power abroad and of the market economy and of democracy itself at home. We face a real danger to our system in the alarming rise of single-issue politics and an increasing stubborn unwillingness to compromise. . . ."

MY CHILDREN AND Beverly were in the audience. Amid all the celebration we heard, each in our own way, the voice of fear. The summer before, during what had begun as one of our routine vacations on Martha's Vineyard, Beverly had undergone a mastectomy. The prognosis was good, and she was cheerful and apparently strong. We had never thought much about the future except in vaguely pleasant anticipation. But now we were beset by apprehension, and the years ahead were a haze of uncertainty.

CHAPTER THIRTY-FOUR

THE UNCERTAINTY ABOUT THE FUTURE turned my attention back to the past. I found myself looking more closely at what we had always taken for granted: the years of marriage, the children's growing up. In Beverly's vision this was a Family on a Hill. It was the best, the closest, the most loving anywhere, as she perceived it. To a large extent I shared that perception. My career came first, but after that, the family took precedence over all other claims to our attention and loyalty. Outsiders were allowed in as guests, but only a few of them became intimates. When she was in first grade Lisa was startled that another girl told her: "You talk about your family too much." Peter, Mandy and Lisa made up nicknames for each other and called themselves the "Poose, Moose, Loose Foundation." The spoof name (which persists to this day on birthday greetings and other family correspondence) symbolized our clannishness.

The clan was at its closest during vacations in Martha's Vineyard, which became a happy ritual. Beverly loved gardening there, despite the sandy soil close to the beach, and produced masses of daisies apparently on sheer faith. Scrabble was the great evening entertainment, with the season score carefully kept. (She usually beat me, largely thanks to her knowledge of obscure two-letter words.) On Sundays, whether in the Vineyard or New York, the children would be spread out on our bed, reading the papers. "Only in our family," Mandy said later, "would this be considered our primary sport." Mandy also recalled that Beverly and I made the children believe "Wherever you were, whatever you were doing, you'd prefer to be with us. You'd come home from incredible trips and tell us it would have been so much better if we had been there, too." We meant what we said. But perhaps by reveling in our closeness we created a kind of emotional cocoon.

The family was a small sovereignty with invisible frontiers, and Beverly put me at its center. I made no effort to resist. Her rules, as the children later recalled, were plain: Daddy works hard. His job is important. When he comes home, we must be neat and pleasant. He works late hours and must catch up on his sleep on weekends; no noisy little friends to be invited on Sunday. At the dinner table, Beverly made it clear, the children were supposed to be interesting or amusing, and they were. We pressed them hard to do their best. And Mandy remembered that her mother "taught me nothing was impossible. She had blind faith in those she loved."

Mandy was tall, energetic, stylish, loved parties and dancing but could be fiercely angry in the face of what she considered injustice. Lisa was brooding, dramatic, dressed in black much of the time and was a natural writer; in the family she was known as "BYP" for budding young poet. Peter was charming and precocious; he wrote, directed and produced a commercially released short subject when he was sixteen. He was also formidably logical, and it was hard to win an argument with him, although I continued to try. "I was not so much raised as edited," he once remarked. While that referred to me, Beverly did her share of editing.

While the children were small she tried to outlaw certain television programs, including *The Three Stooges,* which she felt might encourage them to hit each other more than was reasonable, and *I Love Lucy,* which she feared might give them the wrong idea of marriage, what with Lucy always bamboozling her husband.

Her own ideas about marriage were conventional. She had made a decision to put aside her career ambitions and to concentrate on husband and children. But she still wrote and occasionally contributed book criticism to *The New York Times*. Once she reviewed a work titled *After Nora Slammed the Door*, in which the author, Eve Merriam, argued that leaving the doll's house was only half the battle and that the modern Noras must have significant careers and substantial incomes. Beverly tackled the thesis with a vehemence that eventually made me wonder whether she was trying to justify her own life. "Many women are happy and fulfilled in being 'just housewives.' If they are intelligent and sufficiently propelled, they need not stagnate. . . . Surely, Mrs. Merriam, money isn't everything. And what about love? You never mention it. Happy marriages do exist, you know."

But Beverly did not try to live in a doll's house. She avoided frilly dresses and wore the simplest cosmetics. Once when a friend persuaded her to let herself be made up professionally, she came home looking great, but within a few minutes, plainly embarrassed, she washed her face clean. She did not spend much time looking at herself in the mirror. But when she did, it was with an air of confidence. "This is who I am," she seemed to be saying. She was always herself, whether she was talking to the president or a handyman. I never knew her to be jealous of looks or money or talent in others, never heard her being malicious. She had an instinctive sense of fairness. At times she could be smug— never about herself, but about me and the children. Among our best friends were Patricia and Fred Painton, she a former *Fortune* researcher and he a *Time* writer based in Paris. Despite the distance we were very close. Fond as Beverly was of Pat, she could never resist boasting about the accomplishments of our children during those long telephone conversations between New York and Paris or Martha's Vineyard and Cape Cod, where the Paintons had a summer place. Pat was driven to retaliate by talking up the merits of her own two gifted daughters. "It was like a family competition," Pat told me later. "Mostly, it was about the children, but not entirely. Whenever I would tell Beverly on the phone that it was raining on the Cape, she would reply: 'Oh, we're having bright sunshine over here.' "

As our children grew older, Beverly began thinking about working again. We had become friendly with John Fairchild, and when he approached her about writing for *Women's Wear Daily*, she was delighted.

For three and a half years she wrote a regular feature called "Getting Around," which included personality profiles. I was very proud of her work. She was an excellent, sympathetic interviewer. She always wrote at the last minute, sometimes pulling all-nighters, but her copy was sprightly and full of shrewd observations. She wrote about whatever intrigued her on the New York scene. As a demon shopper, she had a vendetta against incompetent sales clerks who did not know their stock, which inspired a piece called "Death of a Saleswoman." She wrote about auctions (possibly her favorite pursuit). She wrote about fortune-tellers, teachers of charisma and taxi drivers. In her profiles she dealt with people she had not known but admired—Jorge Luis Borges, Louise Nevelson, Truman Capote. Some of them became friends, but above all, she liked to write about those who were friends already. One of the closest was Beverly Sills, who called herself Beverly No. 2. We both loved her as an artist and a life force. Given that radiant voice, which might have been enough, it was always surprising to find that she had an excellent business brain and great shrewdness about people. She was a tireless talker and had none of the usual prima donna pretensions. She would write notes, make phone calls and even eat snacks until moments before she had to make an entrance. She had no stage fright in an opera house or, as far as anyone knew, in life. She and her husband, Peter Greenough, had a severely retarded son and a daughter, Muffy, who was born deaf. Beverly found it particularly sad that her daughter would never be able to hear her sing. But she and Peter overcame (or at least hid) their pain and devotedly helped Muffy to lead a normal life. I have never heard Beverly Sills complain. "People plan and God laughs," she would say. But she laughed, too.

Beverly No. 1 and Beverly No. 2 were presently joined by a third club member, the sculptor Beverly Pepper. I once observed the three Beverlys lunching at a French restaurant in New York, giving off laughter and an aura of strength. We had first met her through her husband, Bill Pepper, a quirky and scholarly journalist who for many years was the Rome bureau chief for *Newsweek*. She, too, was an effusive talker and story-teller, with an indomitable sense of humor. She was also a ferociously dedicated artist. Her small, slender frame surprisingly contained all the pent-up force of her huge, steel sculptures, which stand in cities all over the world. With Bill she shared (when they were not traveling) a fabulously restored fourteenth-century palazzo at Todi in Umbria. Theirs was a marriage embodying both love and tension, their conversation a dazzling fugue of mutual interruptions.

Other friends were Mike Wallace, in whom Beverly brought out a warmth, almost gentleness, that belied his inquisitorial persona, and the fey, brilliant Benjamin Thompson, who rebuilt—really, reinvented—Boston's Faneuil Hall area, later New York's South Street Seaport and Baltimore Harborplace. More than any other architect I knew, he built for comfort and joy. (He would eventually design a new house for me on the Vineyard.) And then there was Jerzy Kosinski.

A letter from Jerzy was instantly recognizable by the envelope. It always bore a variety of colorful, multishaped stamps, proclaiming things like "Urgent!" "Special Handling," "Official Business," "Top Secret." They were a signature and a game of changeable identity, a game he liked to play most of the time. One foggy evening, disembarking from the ferry at Martha's Vineyard, I was met by an apparition with a silver tray bearing a martini. "Madame thought you would like this," said the fellow, and it took me a few moments to realize it was Jerzy, who was staying with us, impersonating a butler. He enacted so many roles and played so many tricks on life that it became notoriously difficult to decide which of them were real and which invented. He sometimes claimed that his great novel *The Painted Bird*, the harrowing story of a little boy's brutal and nightmarish fate in Nazi-occupied Poland, was autobiographical; later it turned out that it was largely fiction. But, more often than not, I believed his stories. He had escaped Communist Poland, he said, by forging letters from nonexistent academics that eventually fooled the authorities into letting him travel to America to accept an invented fellowship. Jerzy told this tale with such a humorous twinkle that people often wondered if it were really true. His progress when he came to America sounded fantastic: odd jobs as a chauffeur and paint scraper, study at Columbia toward a Ph.D. in sociology, marriage to a very rich woman. But it had all happened. When he first told me, before I knew him well, that he was a crack skier, I was skeptical, because I had thought of him as bookish rather than athletic. But then I found out that he was indeed accomplished at the sport. And polo? Could this spindly, middle-aged man really be a polo player? All doubts disappeared when I watched him in a match in Santo Domingo, riding and swinging the mallet creditably if not brilliantly.

We had met at the house of a mutual friend, the *Time* correspondent Friedel Ungeheuer, and his wife, Barbara. Kosinski had what he called a "Gypsy face"; I thought it looked more like the face of a witch, with piercing eyes and a hooked nose, yet oddly attractive. I was instantly drawn to his warmth, his intensity and his humor, and we quickly became friends, which is rare in one's middle years. He was restless and, as a houseguest, always had to keep busy, polishing the car or twirling his "Comet" on the beach. This was a contraption he had learned to make in his childhood: a tin can with nail holes, stuffed with burning twigs or moss, whose heat could be regulated by swinging it from a wire. The "Comet" could serve as a lantern, a weapon or a cook stove.

He was generous with advice, which could sometimes be eccentric. He encouraged Lisa in her efforts to write poetry but also startled her once by declaring that if she wasn't writing in a given month, it was because she was either not happy enough or not unhappy enough. "If I knew only you and not your parents, I would have arranged a truly destructive love affair for you," he told her. "Your mother would say, 'I think Lisa may commit suicide,' but I would know you would commit ten great poems."

We became so close that it was always slightly surprising to discover that he had other friends who, in turn, seemed a little jealous when we talked about our ties to him. Everyone wanted to own Jerzy, but no one did. And no one knew all parts of him. There was the man who lectured at Yale and the one who haunted the S&M clubs and transvestite bars. The man who enchanted all children and the one who evoked in his later novels a brutality suggesting his favorite painter, Hieronymus Bosch, mechanized. He was eloquent about the horrors of the century, but, given his ironic humor and his game playing, he seemed to shy away from tragedy. Later we had to wonder whether he was merely hiding from it.

In 1982 he was the target of a scurrilous article in the *Village Voice* claiming that much of his literary output had been ghostwritten. I knew that he had often hired copy editors to go over his manuscripts, but no proof of the accusations was ever offered and I was certain that they were false. The article also alleged that Kosinski had CIA connections, a replay of Polish Communist disinformation. Jerzy was desperately troubled by the episode and told me that Polish agents were watching him in New York. I was never sure whether he was merely imagining this, but the whole affair left him permanently unsettled. When I visited him in his ski retreat in Switzerland in the fall of 1983, he showed me a manuscript for a novel with which he hoped to retaliate against the attacks on him (it eventually turned into the almost unreadable *The Hermit of 69th Street*). Over dinner early in 1991 I found him even more eccentric than usual. He had a scheme for building small, individual shelters on wheels for the homeless that sounded like movable coffins. In May 1991 he stepped into his bathtub and pulled a plastic bag over his head. He had been worried about his health. But not even his wife, Kiki—for years his companion, secretary, public relations agent, and the anchor of his life—could offer a convincing explanation of why he killed himself.

WHEN THE FIRST symptom of Beverly's cancer appeared in 1978, neither of us could quite believe that it was "bad." She had never seemed fragile. Fear of falling made her uncertain on stairs and escalators, but aside from that she seemed invulnerable. Her perennial optimism existed along with a kind of fatalistic superstition, especially about health. She would never use illness as an excuse to get out of some commitment, because she was sure that the lie would come true. She also deeply distrusted doctors—which perhaps should rank not as superstition, but as rational skepticism. When she was told she had cancer and that without surgery she would be dead in six months, she insisted: "I will be dead in six months *with* surgery; they will botch me." That was her most frequent word for what doctors did: they botched people. After fervent pleas by myself and the children, she reluctantly consented to the mastectomy, and she quickly recovered her vitality. She continued her column and resumed her normal life, marching up and down New York's avenues with seemingly undiminished vigor. We spent time with our friends, most of whom did not even know that she had been ill. She kept up her usual interest in my work, which at that time involved two very different people: Kissinger and Castro.

WHEN HENRY KISSINGER left the State Department after Carter's election, he and his wife, Nancy, took an apartment in New York. The descent from his extraordinary position was difficult, he later recalled, although more than any other exile from power I have known, including former presidents, Kissinger managed to maintain his celebrity status. The international consulting firm he set up, Kissinger Associates, was quickly successful, and, as he noted proudly, hardly a foreign statesman passed through New York without calling on him. It was impossible to go to the theater or the opera in his company without drawing a small crowd. Although he was politically out of favor with both the Right and the Left, he was widely popular, especially with businessmen. He once took me as his guest to the Bohemian Grove, that notorious all-male enclave near San Francisco, where once a year executives, politicians and other notables gather for serious seminars and collegiate high jinks. Wandering with him among the various "camps"—and stopping occasionally to urinate against the tall majestic trees, as was the quaint custom of the club—I found that people kept coming up to him to shake his hand, clap him on the back. Curiously enough, for all his sophistication he was almost naive about the impact of what he said. He was apt to make very unflattering remarks about people whom he praised in public. He was always surprised when, inevitably, his words got back to them and he had to deal with their anger. He was extremely thin-skinned and considered anything short of complete agreement an attack.

Years later he was furious about a biography by my former colleague Walter Isaacson. "Why are you so angry?" I asked him. "I thought the book was quite balanced, rather down the middle."

Kissinger growled: "What business does he have being down the middle about me?"

I had approached him while he was still in office, suggesting that, if and when he wrote his memoirs, I wanted *Time* to print excerpts. In the late seventies he was hard at work writing, and I was occasionally allowed to look at the growing manuscript, always behind closed doors in his office. It was a fascinating work, and I was somewhat surprised that he was an excellent, graceful writer with a distinct gift for bringing characters to life. Time Inc. paid him $2 million, which covered serial rights in *Time* and publication of the book by Little, Brown, a Time Inc. subsidiary. The manuscript he turned in, for volume one alone, came to more than 1,500 proof pages. At one point representatives from Little Brown and his foreign publishers and syndicators met in a large conference room in the Time & Life Building to discuss the final details of their contracts. "Never in the history of publishing," I observed, looking around the room, "have so many paid so much for so much."

Kissinger was paranoid about leaks from the manuscript, and for that matter, so were we. I was therefore rather nervous when I took it with me to Martha's Vineyard to get some ideas about how to excerpt it for *Time.* I carried it in a box that was too large for me to take into the cabin of the small commuter plane, so I had to check it. When I claimed the package on arrival, it could not be found. The vision of having to tell Kissinger that I had lost his entire book months before publication was too horrible to contemplate. I called the local police, and the box was eventually located, having been misplaced in a remote section of the airport. The memoirs, titled *The White House Years,* were duly published, to considerable fanfare, as was the second volume two years later. In his *Doonesbury* strip, Garry Trudeau saluted the publication of *Years of Whitewash.* There followed an imaginary interview with me.

Q: Mr. Grunwald, isn't your magazine's fascination with Kissinger beginning to turn into an obsession?

A: No, I think it's something rather more special. My editors and I have become the keepers of the Kissinger flame. . . . His view of history, to which we hold all the rights, is gospel—unexamined and immaculate.

Q: So it's more like an organized religion?

A: Right. In fact, we're applying for tax-exempt status.

In the fall of 1979 Fidel Castro came to speak at the United Nations. He gave a party for New York journalists at Cuba's UN mission and asked our good friend Barbara Walters, who had established a rapport with him during a visit to Cuba, to help him with the guest list. Leaving our apartment that evening, I decided not to take along my usual supply of cigars. "Castro's bound to offer some," I said to Beverly.

I was wrong. During the entire long, long evening an aide slipped large Cohibas to the Maximum Leader but not a single one to the guests. I mentioned this to Barbara later, and she, in turn, reported my complaint. Thereafter the Cuban ambassador to the United Nations sent me, every month, a box of Cohibas. Cuban cigars were banned by the U.S. trade embargo. After a year or so, calculating the considerable street value of these superb cigars, I asked the ambassador to stop the shipments. (I am not sure to this day whether that represented integrity or sheer stupidity.)

At dinner that evening I found Castro as personally engaging and voluble as advertised. In his impeccably tailored fatigues and combat boots, he was larger and bulkier than I had expected. In a nonstop monologue he made his case for why Cuba deserved a seat at the UN Security Council and why the United States should lift the embargo. A few months before, CIA surveillance had spotted a Soviet force of three thousand near Havana. The Carter administration, which was trying desperately to round up congressional support for the Strategic Arms Limitation Treaty with Moscow, felt it had to be seen as tough and needlessly exaggerated the incident. In the end Carter declared himself satisfied that the brigade represented no menace. The brigade, Castro insisted, had been there for seventeen years only to train Cubans, and furthermore, he was sure the CIA knew it. "The CIA knows everything. It knows if you have a girlfriend," he said to one of the guests.

Toward the end of the evening (dinner was not served until eleven P.M.) Castro happened to be chatting with Beverly and asked her, somewhat surprisingly, if she liked lobsters. She said she did. "I have to leave at dawn tomorrow, and I have all these lobsters left over, good Cuban lobsters," said Castro. "May I send you some?"

"Of course," said Beverly, delighted. As it turned out, the lobsters never came. What did come was an invitation for us to visit Castro. With Dick Duncan, then *Time* chief of correspondents, and his wife, Cherie, and the photographer David Kennerly, Beverly and I set out for Cuba.

I had never seen Havana in its corrupt-romantic heyday. There were scarcely any traces of that left. The city, clearly suffering from the U.S. embargo and from Socialism, was run-down—even the palm trees somehow seemed dusty. A handful of new hotels were drab, full of tourists from Eastern Europe, who should have felt right at home. There was no evidence of discontent with the regime except for the long lines of Cubans in front of the Swiss embassy, which housed the U.S. Interest Section, there to apply for American visas. On what was once known as the Isle of Pines, now called the Isle of Youth, we were shown a major attraction: a former prison consisting of several large, circular buildings, the empty cells eerily surrounding huge inner spaces dominated by slender watchtowers. The place was to be a museum as a memorial to the evils of Fulgencio Batista's dictatorship. Our escort was an ebullient politician, Roberto Ogando, the local "Head of the People's Power," who next took us to the hospital wing. There the young Castro, as a prisoner of the Batista regime, had been kept isolated so that he would not incite the other prisoners with his revolutionary rhetoric. Beverly looked around the small but clean, bright room with its white mosquito-netted bed and declared: "This looks a lot more comfortable than the kind of place in which they kept Solzhenitsyn." The remark did not endear our group to our guide. Nor did a notation that Kennerly wrote in the visitors' book: "This is the greatest prison I have ever been in. . . ."

Elsewhere on the island we were shown several schools where third world students, mostly African, were being indoctrinated. One was reserved for recruits from Angola, where Cuban troops were fighting alongside the Marxist government in a bitter civil war with UNITA, the anti-Communist guerrilla force led by Jonas Savimbi and aided by South Africa. At one point I found myself surrounded by a hostile crowd of Angolans who were berating me for American policies favoring Savimbi.

"The whole world knows that America is against Angola," said one of the students.

" 'The whole world knows' is not a sufficient argument," I replied. "A lot of people might say 'The whole world knows that the Soviet Union is a repressive dictatorship.' But you would not accept that as a sufficient argument, either."

This absurd attempt at logic only inflamed the students, who turned ugly, starting to shove and wave fists. Roberto Ogando hastily extricated me from the melee.

The tense episode contrasted with our meeting with Castro, who personified bonhomie. Duncan and I had been told to bring our wives, and no sooner had we walked into his office in Havana's Palace of the Revolution than Castro asked Beverly: "Did you get the lobsters?" He was highly upset when she said no and instantly instructed aides to look into the lapse—and kept returning to the matter of the lobsters with almost Queeg-like persistence.

We lounged on large cowhide-covered sofas, ample supplies of cigars and daiquiris on the marble table. In his hypnotic Spanish Castro spoke interminably about the achievements of his revolution, the progress in health care and education, in supposedly wiping out unemployment, poverty and prostitution. America should help Cuba, he argued, and should not be afraid of revolution, which was necessary throughout Latin America to give people a better life. "Revolutionaries have a moment of great fever and passion, combined with a lack of experience. So you have to be very patient with them."

As he spoke he had a habit of putting his index finger against his nose, a gesture usually accompanied by the word *pienso* (I think) followed by a long disquisition. He was eloquent on the subject of all the money the world was wasting on armaments. It was a few days before Christmas, and he said: "If Santa Claus asks me whether I want the hydrogen bomb, I say no, I don't want it! Can you imagine if we had a bomb here, or ten bombs? What do we need them for? They will solve nothing."

Castro defended Cuba's "nonaligned" status despite his dependence on the Soviet Union. If it weren't for support from other countries, "we would have died here like Numantia,* in ancient times."

After two hours, rather weary by now, Duncan and I made a motion to leave, but Castro held us for another hour and fifteen minutes. I could not help liking him, in spite of what he stood for. He was a mixture of passion, shrewdness, sincerity and Party-line nonsense. I thought he was preposterous when he said: "I tell you that never, never has the Soviet government tried to tell Cuba what it should do." Russia, he insisted, was the freest society in the world and only wanted peace. Six days later the Soviets invaded Afghanistan.

The next evening, our last in Cuba, we were in the comfortable government guest house when we heard a commotion outside and several soldiers with submachine guns appeared. They were followed by Castro, who, in turn, was followed by other soldiers carrying a large wooden box. He pointed to his slightly sunburned forehead and said: "Look at my tan. I've been out diving for lobsters all day to make up for the ones you didn't get in New York." He had brought his chef, who was also his bodyguard, he explained, and if we were willing, the man would be glad to cook us some of the lobsters for dinner. There followed another hour's conversation, in the middle of which Castro got to his feet and said: "Let's see how the lobsters are doing." He stalked into the kitchen, sweeping Beverly and Cherie along, holding forth on the right way to cook his catch: add pepper, salt, spices and lemon juice and broil, not boil, for fifteen minutes. In a story in *The Washington Post*, he explained, the writer Sally Quinn had gotten the recipe wrong: she had said twenty minutes. Presently he shook hands all around, said

---

* A Celtic-Iberian settlement in Spain, Numantia held off various invaders for sixty years before being taken by the Romans in 133 B.C.

good-bye and left with his soldiers. The lobsters were good but a little tough.

DURING THE CUBA trip Beverly had complained of backaches. Back home, her doctor was not alarmed and claimed that X-rays did not suggest anything other than some normal back problem, a pinched nerve. He ordered muscle relaxants, long bed rest. She did not improve. Only after three months did further X-rays and a bone scan deliver the dreaded news: her original cancer had spread to her bones and liver. We knew what that meant, of course, but clung to artificial hope. I was enraged at her original physician, who had taken so long to reach the true diagnosis. Her new doctor, an oncologist, was reassuring without promising anything. He gave us all the statistics about possible remission, and of course we seized on the positive side of the odds. There would be chemotherapy. No reason not to travel, he said, and we made plans to go to one of Malcolm Forbes's famous balloon meets in Normandy and to China. But she was never able to make those trips. She accepted the loss of her hair caused by the chemotherapy and joked about her wig. She tried to pretend to herself that her energy was undiminished; but it was ebbing quickly. I remember her walking up Madison Avenue, attempting to maintain her usual march tempo, but struggling and slowing as if fighting against an invisible wall.

We went to Martha's Vineyard that summer, as usual. As she always had in the past, Beverly fussed about her lawn, her shrubs, her beloved daisies, and, as always, she berated the rabbits that were eating them. "Look at him, he's growing fat on my daisies," she would cry. She would order Peter or me to chase the marauders away, but as soon as we picked up a stone to hurl, she would say: "Don't hurt them. They're kind of cute."

The year before, we had started an expansion of our house, and while the work was still going on, we stayed in a cottage we owned nearby. Every day Beverly and I would walk over to inspect the builder's progress. Her particular joy was a new tiled bathroom with a huge tub, and Mike Wallace, laughingly, fully dressed, stretched out in it to show its dimensions. I knew that she would almost certainly never use that bathtub and would never see the rebuilt house finished. But we didn't talk about that. She discussed her treatments and her symptoms with the children and me. She did not hide her anger at what was happening to her and her stubborn, irrational conviction that if only she had not had that mastectomy, things would still be all right. But she would not mention the prospect of her death. The children and I would allude to it among ourselves without really facing it. But we bent to her powerful will and pretended, when we talked to her, that she would recover. She refused to talk about her illness, even to her closest friends, even to her sister, Sally. Nor did she let me tell my sister, Meta, although they loved each other. In long and innocuous telephone conversations, she still explained about back problems that kept her in bed.

Our friends and family shrank from the force field of privacy that she maintained. None pressed her for the truth, not even that practiced and insistent interviewer Barbara Walters. During one of her hospital stays Beverly encountered Barbara, who was visiting another friend. What was Beverly doing here? she wanted to know. "Oh it's nothing serious, everything is under control," replied Beverly, and Barbara did not go further. I would take long walks on the beach in Martha's Vineyard, literally talking to myself about what the future would be like, but I never talked to her about it. She wanted it that way, and I had to admit it was easier as well for me.

Throughout these nightmare months I continued doing my job, of course, finding escape in the office routine. Early in the fall I took a brief trip to China. I was uneasy about leaving Beverly, but *Time* was setting up its first bureau in Beijing. She urged me to go, and if I had insisted on staying home, we both would have had to admit why. Things were opening up in China to the point where I was even encouraged to visit Tibet, occupied by the Chinese since 1950 and long off limits to foreigners. High on the oxygen thoughtfully provided in large pouches for outsiders, I wandered about Lhasa, its Jokhang Temple seemingly floating up into the sky, but on the inside gloomy and oppressive, at least in my present mood. I spent much time buying trinkets from furtive hawkers—free enterprise was creeping in—to bring back to Beverly.

Back in New York and at my desk, I followed the news, as always. The year was full of death, perhaps no more than usual, but it seemed so at the time. Countless people killed in Afghanistan, in the Iran-Iraq war, in El Salvador's civil war. So many killed by earthquakes in Algeria and Italy that there was a shortage of coffins. John Lennon murdered. In between all this, there were reports of new developments in recombinant DNA research, hailed by the press as promising a possible cancer cure. Too late for Beverly, I thought. But it was a reminder of that old, if by now slightly frayed, American optimism in the face of all obstacles, including the ultimate one. I had long had the impression that to many Americans death was an affront, a disorder that somehow should be fixed.

AGAINST THIS MELANCHOLY backdrop, politics seemed more unreal than usual. Jimmy Carter had been renominated after a challenge by Teddy Kennedy. Shortly before Kennedy formally announced his candidacy, Bob Ajemian, our Washington bureau chief, and I had dinner with him at his house in Washington. He was scathing about Carter, whom he considered weak, indecisive, inept. The country simply could not go through another four years of drift. Yet Kennedy himself was strikingly incoherent when it came to specific policies. He was vague about inflation, then a key issue, rambling on about guidelines and cooperation between management and labor. On energy prices he simply supported continued controls. He kept saying, "I could bore you to death with details," but, in fact, he supplied very few.

Ajemian, who knew him well, was struck by his incoherence and nervousness, belied by his ruddy good health. I had seen him soon after Chappaquiddick, when he actually had appeared firmer and more coherent than now. I was hoping to find a touch of that old Kennedy magic, but it was not easy to detect. I reminded him of a line in one of his recent speeches in which he had said that people didn't want much—

only simple things like jobs, prices they could afford, reasonable interest payments, decent education, safe streets and standing tall among nations. When I suggested that "only" was hardly the right word for this agenda, and that it was far from simple, he would not concede the point. It really was simple, he insisted, adding, "It can all be done." Leadership was the answer, he kept saying, leadership.

I asked the inevitable question: Given what had happened to his brothers, what about the danger of assassination if he ran for president? He replied that he had weighed the risks. "I love life and my family needs me, especially my children. But I feel the country needs me, too. Besides, as my father used to say: 'Home holds no terror for me.' " It took me a minute to realize that by "home" he meant death.

SOME WEEKS BEFORE, Beverly had started on an experimental procedure involving blood transfusions. During one of her regular hospital treatments, she went into cardiac arrest and was revived by an emergency team. Mandy, who was with her that day, summoned me from the office in a panic. "I thought I would be the last person to see her," she said later. Beverly's doctor took me aside to ask me whether I wanted him to continue to resuscitate her. I automatically said yes. Hope is not rational but an instinct, a habit.

A day or two later she was in a hospital room, sitting on the bed, cheerfully dangling her legs and watching television. After she came back to our apartment, the final siege began. Lisa was away at college, Mandy and I were working during the day; we took turns looking after her at night. Peter, who was at home struggling to write a novel, was alone with her much of the time. He developed an obsession about justifying the margins of his pages, perhaps an unconscious attempt to maintain a sense of order and control. He also kept careful notes about her symptoms and her medication, supposedly for the doctor, but really to establish a routine that created an illusion of normalcy. He made lists of "good signs"—she had more appetite this morning, her eyes were clear, longer periods between the onset of pain. We rigged up a buzzer between the bedroom and my study, where I tried to work at night, so that Beverly could call me when she needed help. Eventually, over her protests, I hired nurses.

One night, after Lisa came home for Christmas vacation, Beverly talked to her about the future. I quote from Lisa's journal: " 'Remember if I die, I would want Daddy to be happy,' Mommy said. What she meant was she didn't want him to be lonely, she wanted him to re-marry. She didn't get into details about marriage or another woman but I think she was trying to make it clear to me that she didn't want him to stop his life. This was the first time she ever made even the most glancing reference to dying. We talked about love. I asked her what it would have been like if she had married anyone but Daddy. She said 'good but not great.' But how did you know I asked. She said, 'I don't know.' I said you knew he would love you, would be successful? 'Success never figured into it much. I never thought about it much, just wanted to be with him. If you love someone they give you strength, energy, you want to make them proud.' "

Another evening, Lisa and I talked. My own recollection of the conversation is vague, and I again quote from her journal. "We were both near tears. Daddy said bitter things about the purpose of life. I said 'think how awful it would be if there was no suffering, no death to push against. No one would do anything; there would be no drive.' He said he used to believe that but not right now, maybe he will again someday."

The children and I went through a few motions at Christmas, including presents, and that turned out to be almost more painful than ignoring the holiday altogether. New Year's Eve was the worst. We had always been together on that occasion, with the children returning by midnight from wherever they were for champagne and a little dancing. We halfheartedly thought we might re-create the usual scene, but Beverly was too sick to get out of bed. She was disoriented and kept asking what was making all that noise; it was the fireworks in Central Park.

In the meantime Ronald Reagan had been elected and everyone was giving parties for him—*the Washington Post*'s Katharine Graham, *Newsweek*'s George Will—and I felt that Time Inc. must not be left out and arranged a large dinner for January 6 in Washington. I introduced the president-elect in a haze. Immediately after the dinner I flew back to New York and scribbled a note to myself on the plane. Intoxicated by exhaustion, alcohol and altitude, I wrote: "Death is an outrage. It is intolerable for me to go on. And yet what is the alternative, unless one commits suicide?"

Beverly died three days later. She had been semiconscious for some time. One of the last things I heard her say was: "Nurse, you're folding that sheet all wrong." The words were delivered in her old strong voice and in a tone she might have used on an incompetent salesgirl.

It had been thirty years since the men from the funeral parlor had taken away my father. I had the preposterous, momentary illusion that the same men had come for Beverly. They were quiet and efficient and handed me the wedding ring they had removed from her finger. We had been married for twenty-eight years. Mandy, who had a way of taking charge in a crisis, tried to herd the rest of us into the kitchen so that we would not have to watch the final moments. But I wanted to see and I stood there staring at the black body bag as the men moved it through the door.

Mandy, still taking charge, made lists of friends to call about the funeral. I had the strange impression that she had assumed her mother's role, displaying the same care and efficiency with which Beverly used to organize a party. At the memorial service Peter and Mandy reminisced about her, Lisa read a poem she had written and Mike Wallace read tributes from many colleagues and friends. Barbara Walters evoked the image of Beverly that everyone shared: "Dark hair flying, bright eyes shining, caftans, aglow, touching, talking, always kind and, my God, the epitome of the word 'alive.' "

THERE IS LITTLE time for mourning in modern American life. I was asked out to a dinner party scarcely two weeks after Beverly died. Even though I knew that people were trying to be kind, I was a little un-nerved. They were rushing things, I thought, feeling the need for a pause, a transition. But I went. I was miserable, trying to make cheerful, or at least casual, conversation. I had always assumed that Beverly, given her formidable strength, would outlive me by many years. Now I had to accept that such calculations are nonsense. Also, that we're not really allowed pauses and transitions.

Among the many condolence letters, one especially stayed in my mind. It was from my old colleague Douglas Auchincloss, who had left the magazine years before. He wrote: "In dying, those we love do leave us a legacy, a built-in awareness of our own death—and that is certainly a great gift indeed." I was puzzled: in what way was this awareness a gift? Yet I did find an odd comfort in it, and I gradually came to understand why. I felt guilty, of course, that I was alive and Beverly was dead, and this survivor's guilt was assuaged by the reminder of my own inevitable death.

CHAPTER THIRTY-FIVE

AT THE DINNER TABLE ONE NIGHT I had told Beverly and the children that if Ronald Reagan became president, we would move to Paris. I didn't mean it, of course, but I was really concerned about whether, intellectually, he would be up to the job. Like so many others, I underestimated him. I first became aware of Reagan during those long-ago sessions on Forty-second Street, when I taught myself English from the screen. He was the kind of actor my father described as *brav*, or nice, decent, adequate. *Time*'s first significant political mention of Reagan had been in April 1961, the result of a "suggestion" from Luce, who had been struck by Reagan's talks as a spokesman for General Electric. "I really had to push the editors hard to get that story in," he groused later. The piece summarized Reagan's message about the excesses of government and described him as "boyish of face and gleaming cf tooth." I did not take him very seriously, given my old prejudice against performers using their prominence as a political platform. I was startled when he was elected governor of California.

I met Reagan once in Sacramento but got my first real look at him at a *Time* lunch in June 1980. He was, yes, still boyish of face and gleaming of tooth at sixty-nine, and his views had not changed much, either. But he was far more coherent than I had expected. He had some refreshing observations. On the prospect of having to choose a cabinet, he

528

wanted successful people for whom government service would be a sacrifice. "The trouble with the Carter administration is that for everybody they got in, it was a step up. They never had it so good." Did he see a chance that, if elected, he might actually break up the bureaucracy? "Maybe this is one place where my age is an advantage. What the hell do I have to lose?"

Reagan's campaign speeches were brimming with mistakes and misstatements, carefully chronicled by the press, including *Time*. His statistics were often close to fantasy, zeros were added or dropped casually. In one typical instance Reagan claimed that it took the government $3.00 in overhead to deliver $1.00 to a needy person; the correct figure was not $3.00 but $.12. Reagan almost always went right on repeating such mistakes. It didn't matter. His basic line fitted the country's emotional needs: so did his personality. In contrast with both Nixon and Carter, Reagan was cool, relaxed, self-confident. He knew who he was. During a brief trip to watch him campaign, I found him so serene and above mere details that I told a colleague: "Perhaps he should be running for king and not for president." The press kept saying that he was a good actor. But the secret of his appeal was not his acting skill, but his conviction. He clearly believed what he said. With four more years of Jimmy Carter as the alternative, I somewhat nervously voted for Reagan. (I had always been registered as an independent and voted for candidates of either party.)

I wondered how Ronald Reagan would look in the White House. I saw him there, a few months after his inauguration, with a group of international businessmen. In the Blue Room, with its vibrant satin curtains, French Empire furniture and bronze Hannibal clock on the mantel, he looked as if he had always lived there. In a voice sometimes cracking because of hay fever, he was folksy without losing dignity. Describing his intention to shrink the federal role, he used the kind of verbal play he liked: "We're doing this by just changing one little two-letter word; we're changing control *by* government to control *of* government." As for Moscow, there would have to be linkage between arms control and other issues. Our adversaries, he added, would have to find out "that there is a price the West will not pay to go on in ease and comfort." This was the quintessential Reagan: simple, direct, sweepingly general, any menacing message delivered in unmenacing tones.

If Reagan kept to generalities, David Stockman, speaking to the same group, was, if anything, overwhelmingly specific. The brilliant, youthful, former divinity student and congressman was head of the Office of Management and Budget (OMB) and chief oracle of the supply side doctrine. Stockman spoke with a combination of evangelical fervor and statistical grasp. He outlined what he called the dominant Keynesian illusions, chief among them being the "money illusion." The United States had accumulated $300 billion worth of new deficits since 1977, he said, which in effect transferred to the public sector vast resources that could have created growth and investment in the private sector. Stockman denounced subsidies and other devices to manage demand and defended Reagan's programs for cutting taxes as well as social spending. Talking rapidly, suggesting a handsome movie star trying to look serious by wearing glasses, Stockman dazzled his foreign listeners—and alarmed some. "He scares me to death," said one. "I do not see that man at all wavering from his principal view."

Before the end of that year, Stockman wavered. He confessed in an *Atlantic Monthly* interview that he had churned out phony budget projections, playing with the figures to achieve the desired outcome. Reagan was furious, and Stockman apologized publicly, but, amazingly, he was kept on at OMB despite his heresy. He was thought to be indispensable. No one else seemed to have anything like his command of every last digit. But I had the impression that he used figures so glibly, they did not sound real and that numbers were a kind of poetry to him.

Before long Reagan was forced to modify some of his tax cuts and make other budget concessions. Larry Barrett, our White House correspondent, reported that the best, if not the only, way to persuade the president to change course was to convince him that a shift was only tactical and did not really violate his basic policies. Most of the time this was the case. He never gave up his core convictions, and people sensed that.

Unlike many of his critics, I did not think that Reagan was merely engaged in a sentimental con game, promising to revive an irretrievable past. He did not cause but embodied profound changes that had taken place in American society, a reaction against trends that had begun with the New Deal and had grown into too much of a good thing. Yes, there was a lot of nostalgia for the old values, real or imagined, a lot of patriotic bombast (which appealed to my old immigrant loyalties even as I recognized the hokum). But Reaganism had serious intellectual underpinnings, loosely described as neoconservatism. That trend was expressed by, among others, two men I knew and liked. One was Irving Kristol, an all-purpose intellectual, lecturer and editor. The other was Daniel Bell, a self-described right-wing Social Democrat who had been labor editor of *Fortune* before leaving to teach sociology at Columbia and Harvard. Kristol spoke with smooth irony, Bell with a passionate growl. Together they founded the *Public Interest*, a journal that tried to find serious solutions to the political-economic-social problems besetting the United States. (Norman Podhoretz, before he himself turned conservative, called it the suggestion box for the capitalist class.) Kristol, reluctantly accepting the label, explained that a neoconservative was a liberal mugged by reality. The neos differed from old-line conservatives by stressing economic growth rather than mere frugality. The welfare state, Kristol believed, could not be abolished, but its intrusive paternalism could be curbed. Whenever possible, free market solutions should be found, as, for instance, housing vouchers for the poor versus government-sponsored public housing. I was particularly struck by Bell's distinction between treating people equally and trying to make them equal. Liberals, he suggested, demanded not merely equality of opportunity, but equality of outcome. In its extreme form, it seemed to me, this meant that the just society must compensate people for all inequalities, including natural ones, which would amount to playing God. Reagan was apt to carry with him and quote from articles in the *Public Interest*, as well as from *Commentary*, edited by Podhoretz. If these men were not the Reagan brain trust, their ideas—often carried to the president by William Buckley—pervaded the administration.

· · ·

SOON AFTER REAGAN'S inauguration, each of the Time Inc. magazines published a series of articles under the collective heading "American Renewal." I had launched the project well before his nomination. For once, I thought, our separate magazines might undertake a joint effort and address the country's problems, each from its own perspective. Some of my colleagues considered the idea overly ambitious. "Pretentious," Otto Friedrich called it. But it was very much in the Time Inc. tradition, and I persisted. An art director designed an identifying symbol—an upward-thrusting arrow. (This inspired *National Lampoon* to publish a parody issue entitled "Let's Get It Up, America!")

Most of our recommendations—by the magazines' own staffs and many outside experts—were quite sensible, if hardly original. Most could be described as neoconservative. We were critical not only of government, but of business, complaining that it was not doing enough to promote efficiency and growth. I set overall policy but did not try to force editors into positions against their judgment. We usually reached agreement after some dickering but failed on affirmative action, to which *Fortune* was more strongly opposed than I. The result was a straddle. We raised objections to it but asserted that "some measure" of it should remain. In a kind of keynote essay Lance Morrow, one of the finest writers on *Time*, exhorted: "Americans need to focus now on a different form of expectation: not what they expect for themselves in the way of entitlements, but what they are entitled to expect from one another in the way of social behavior."

The foreign policy plank was written by Strobe Talbott. He had come to *Time* as a summer intern in our London bureau before going on to study Russian literature at Oxford as a Rhodes scholar. By now he was diplomatic correspondent in the Washington bureau. He made a specialty of reporting on arms control (about which he wrote three books), and I followed him, sometimes out of breath, through the theological thickets of throw weight and first strike capacities and the conundrums of how many warheads could dance on the head of a missile. I enjoyed his thin-lipped humor and admired his awesomely methodical mind. I was more hawkish about Russia than he, and we often argued the fine points of his stories. He once accused me of "solution mongering." When I edited an article that analyzed some problems, he pointed out that I usually asked: "But what is to be done?" Yet his contribution to "American Renewal" positively bristled with suggested solutions, many of them quite stern. (A little over a decade later Talbott would have to monger a great many solutions, and not just journalistically, when he became deputy secretary of state under his onetime Oxford roommate Bill Clinton.) The most important requirement, his article concluded, as to restore an American sense of strength and self-confidence.

THERE WAS A great deal of self-confidence about foreign policy in the early Reagan White House, but not much expertise. The president was surrounded by what had come to be known as "the troika"—presidential counselor Edwin Meese, who functioned as an all-around policy adviser; James Baker, the chief of staff; and Michael Deaver, deputy chief of staff. A group of Washington correspondents and I once played the game of trying to cast this trio in the *Wizard of Oz*. Meese, who was rather disorganized and bumbling, some of us thought, was the scare-crow, who needed a brain. Baker, a hard-edged efficient political opera-tor, was the Tin Man, who needed a heart. Mike Deaver, a smart, tireless public relations man, could be seen as the Cowardly Lion be-cause he rarely took a strong stand beyond protecting the boss's image. The Wizard, of course, was Reagan.

The three were ill informed about foreign policy, which in their view came down mostly to a hard line against the Soviets. Secretary of State Alexander Haig, having worked for Nixon and Kissinger and served as NATO commander, knew more about foreign and security policy than any other high official in the administration. But the troika did not trust him. He was too assertive, even self-promoting, and he was suspected of not always being firm enough in dealing with Moscow. He was hardly a soft-liner, but he tried to avoid being needlessly provocative. "We shouldn't unnecessarily poke sticks into the polar bear's cage," he once told me. Apart from any policy differences, Haig was near paranoid about attacks on his authority. Behind his forced composure, one could sense the steam rising. He repeatedly complained that "guerrillas" in the White House were out to get him. He kept threatening to resign and did it once too often.

He was replaced by George Shultz, who had served as secretary of labor and head of the Office of Management and Budget under Nixon. I knew him as a man of contagious calm. For the time being, it seemed as if the State Department had been taken over by Buddha. But his serenity was soon disturbed by Defense Secretary Caspar Weinberger, an aggressive advocate of Reagan's arms buildup.

Listening to him in his huge Pentagon office, with its bust of General MacArthur and a rather incongruous Titian self-portrait behind the desk, I found myself virtually hypnotized. Weinberger spoke in a low purr, like a smooth machine that could not be stopped. He went on without pausing for breath or punctuation, arguing for a seemingly unlimited arms buildup. He was especially agitated about Central America. He and others in the administration wanted to destabilize Nicaragua's Sandinista regime, which was supporting Marxist guerrillas in neighboring El Salvador. Shultz did not necessarily disagree with the aim but was infuriated by Weinberger's tactics and accused him of pursuing his own foreign policy. Over breakfast in Washington one morning I was amazed to hear the normally imperturbable Shultz positively rant at the Pentagon, which had recently carried out big military exercises in Honduras, just across the Nicaraguan border. Such actions, surrounded by a lot of belligerent talk, were hurting the United States. "Things have gotten out of control," fumed Shultz. "You never know what these crazy kooks are going to do next." Couldn't he talk to Weinberger? I asked. "He won't listen," Shultz replied. As for the president, he couldn't very well go to him to settle every dispute between himself and Cap.

I came away with the uneasy feeling that Shultz, whose intelligence and character I admired, was at a loss about what to do in Central America. Actually events there were a sideshow. The main battlefield of the cold war was still Europe. It is sometimes difficult to remember that the contest with Moscow was far from over and that one of its key elements was the allegiance of the Europeans. Three major, interrelated trends were at work: the emergence of the European Community, disputes over the role of NATO and unrest in the Eastern bloc. Each of these trends was important to the U.S. position in the world. On many trips, sometimes with *Time* News Tours, I tried to observe these trends and the main players in the continuing, complex interaction between America and Europe.

I WAS ESPECIALLY INTRIGUED by the prospect of a united Europe, which now seemed possible not because its people had suddenly become virtuous, but largely because after centuries of fratricidal war they were exhausted. Having grown up with the knowledge of Europe's bristling frontiers, I was excited to see people freely crossing back and forth, and especially the young roaming the whole continent as if it were their playground.

The man who had fought harder for European unity than anyone else was Jean Monnet, whom I had long admired as a practical visionary. He had started his career as a brandy salesman for the family business in cognac. ("The great thing about making cognac," he often said, "is that it teaches you above everything else to wait.") Amid the postwar ruins he conceived the Coal and Steel Community between France, Germany and other Western European countries, which grew into the Common Market. I did not meet him until he was eighty-four, in 1973.

Sitting behind a claw-footed desk in his Paris study, overlooking the chestnut trees on the avenue Foch, he sounded like a prophet, without illusions. Repeating one of his notable maxims, he said: "Union among men is not natural. Necessity is always required." Monnet clearly had the United States in mind as a model for the future Europe. The idea still evoked much skepticism.

One of the fiercest doubters was André Malraux, the novelist (*Man's Fate*) and political activist who had moved from Marxism to passionate Gaullism. (Most Frenchmen and tourists knew him as the minister of culture who had cleaned the grime off Parisian buildings and monuments.)

I called on him, with a *Time* correspondent, early in the seventies at the Château Vilmorin, near Paris. (It belonged to the family of his late companion, the writer Louise de Vilmorin.) His two cats, Fou Rire and Lustré, kept climbing over his visitors. Malraux was pale, with obviously dyed black hair and deep, sunken eyes, and as he spoke his face and body were contorted by a rather ghastly twitch. (He attributed this to an illness contracted years ago in China.) Europe, he said, had once been at the center of things, but that time was gone forever. "I don't deplore the idea of Europe, I think it's a lie, the last of the great myths." Was there no leader around whom Europe could unite? *"Cher monsieur,"* he replied ironically, "we're not finishing our novels these days, and God isn't putting the finishing touches on great men." He was equally skeptical about the United States, which he felt lacked a sense of destiny. This was before Nixon's trip to China, and Malraux accused him of maneuvering "as if he were the president of Luxembourg." The attitude was typical of French arrogance toward the United States, which I resented even though I believed that in the long run a strong France was vital to American interests even if that strength involved some anti-American posturing. Many Europeans, including Frenchmen, now lived more comfortably, as well as more safely, than many Americans in our big cities. But few grasped that the United States had coasts and horizons, dreams and duties, far beyond Europe's.

One who did was President Georges Pompidou, the former banker and professor devoted to business and to poetry. He told me in 1973: "There is too much talk about U.S. weakness. I think too many of your countrymen are starting to believe this. But that is wrong. America is a great country." Even though he had often baited the United States, I believed he meant this.

The day after that interview I made a sentimental pilgrimage to the apartment building on the rue des Eaux near the Seine in the sixteenth arrondissement, where my parents and I had lived as refugees. The building looked much the same—the typical gray facade with its forbidding iron shutters. I tried to explain to the concierge that I had once lived there and that my family and I had fled our apartment back in 1940 when the Germans invaded. She was unsympathetic. No, she could not possibly show me our old apartment. I was on the point of telling her that yesterday's young refugee had just interviewed her president, but the adult in me suppressed the impulse.

I F THE FRENCH often made trouble for U.S. policy, the Germans were publicly more compliant but difficult in their own way. Their ambiguity was typified by West German chancellor Helmut Schmidt, a remarkable politician whom I tried to see on most of my European trips. A conservative Social Democrat, he was a staunch free-marketeer and anti-Communist. Alternately ingesting snuff and puffing on menthol cigarettes, his voice raspy and his eyes rheumy, he would grade the American performance. In the Carter years he complained about U.S. weakness, and in the Reagan era he would complain about U.S. irresponsibility. Like most Europeans, he wanted the United States to be tough but not too tough. In part his attitude was explained by pacifist strains in his own party and the emergence of a new political force, the Greens.

Environmental zealots, the Greens were against not only the stationing of U.S. missiles in Europe, but Germany's membership in NATO, capitalism, industrial civilization, economic growth and, of course, nuclear power. The best-known Green leader was Petra Kelly (her last name was that of her American stepfather). She was a frail woman in her thirties. When I saw her in Bonn in 1982 she reminded me of an undernourished Jane Fonda. She had a kind of Bavarian charm, but her confused ideas were a mixture of feminism, Marxism, pacifism and Gandhi-ism. She spoke passionately about civil disobedience. "Would two hundred thousand Germans sitting on the track before Auschwitz have prevented Hitler?" The Greens became important in other countries as well, but Kelly and her movement symbolized for me a special, irrational and unstable German idealism that I always found alarming.

P ROTESTERS IN THE West were able to agitate freely while condemning the society that gave them this freedom. Andrei Sakharov and a few other Soviet dissidents pursued their cause under constant surveillance and in danger of jail or worse. In the mid-seventies I went to see

Sakharov. (The authorities tolerated occasional visits by foreigners.) His seventh-floor, two-room Moscow apartment was crammed with overflowing bookcases and fading photographs of dissident friends. Sakharov was tall, stooped, wearing a loose sweater and run-down slippers. He sipped tea spiced with sliced green apples and stared at the floor as he spoke. He recalled that when he started to design the H-bomb, he believed that he was working for peace, for a balance of power in the world. But he became increasingly alarmed by fallout and contamination from atmospheric nuclear testing and by the way the Soviet regime was brandishing the weapon he had helped build. He knew that his call for a general amnesty for political prisoners would not be heeded, but he felt he must reiterate it through whatever channels he could find. Ironically he called himself Andrei Blazhenny—a Russian word that connotes both sainthood and madness.

It was extraordinary to see this aging, somewhat fragile, harassed man defying a formidable police state, using as his weapon his uncompromising and indomitable conscience.

His image stayed in my mind when, a little later, I attended a concert of the Leningrad Philharmonic, which provided a different but equally powerful reminder of the strength of individualism against collective power. Amid the gleaming white columns and under the glittering crystal chandeliers in the great rectangular hall, the orchestra performed Mozart's *Requiem*, and I was so affected that, back in my hotel room, I wrote down some thoughts about it. "What did this Soviet, middle-class audience, listening with stiff and respectful attention, make of these words? 'Lord have mercy on us, Christ have mercy on us'—did this still mean anything after almost 60 years of relentless efforts to stamp out religion? As for the music, it suggests harmony and order, but an order based on the subtle interplay of individuals. It makes obeisance to God but also extols man. It is the music of Europe, written at a time when Europe was shedding the last vestiges of feudalism. Today Communism propagates a new feudal order, without the nobility or spiritual consolations of the old." I was being, as I soon realized, too gloomy. The new feudalism was not winning.

In 1979 the Kremlin had granted *Time* an interview with Leonid

Brezhnev. He had been in power by then for fourteen years, noted for his high lifestyle—elaborate elk hunts, a fleet of fast, expensive cars, luxurious dacha, all of which reminded Henry Kissinger of *The Great Gatsby*. Several *Time* colleagues and I faced Brezhnev across the huge conference table in his rather bare Kremlin office, its walls covered with off white silk. We had been instructed to submit questions in writing in advance. His answers were handed to us in an elegant dark red leather folder that had the appearance of a bound state treaty. Brezhnev read out the answers, which were translated by the only aide at his side, the smooth, silver-haired Leonid Zamyatin, information chief for the Politburo and an old hand at dealing with Westerners. When he finished reading his last answer, Brezhnev laboriously started to get up. I lifted my right arm, rather brusquely, I am afraid, and reminded him that we had been told that he would take some questions in addition to the written ones. Resignedly Brezhnev resumed his seat, and the interview continued for a while. Overall, he said nothing really remarkable. He blamed certain forces in Washington for trying to undermine détente, denied that Soviet and Warsaw Pact forces constituted a threat to Western Europe. He grew most animated about China ("I am sick and tired of talking about it") and compared America's approach to Beijing with Western appeasement of Hitler. He insisted that the Soviet Union wanted nothing but "peace, peace and, once again, peace!" banging his fist on the table. At seventy-two, and long reported to be ailing, he spoke haltingly, his speech slurred and his face contorted, plainly the result of a stroke. When he inscribed a book for us, he used the pen with great difficulty. Clearly he would not be around much longer, and he seemed the very embodiment of a moribund empire.

UNDER THE BANNER of "Solidarity," Polish workers began an extraordinary campaign to bring about reform of the country's hopelessly inept and bankrupt command economy. The symbol of that movement was an electrician named Lech Walesa, who led a strike at the Gdansk shipyard that proved to be the beginning of a revolution.

When I visited Warsaw in May 1981 Walesa had become a political celebrity. My colleague Dick Duncan and I met him in a dim hotel bar, where he gustily drank champagne. He refused to answer political questions ("I'm only a labor leader"), and after a short while we had to leave. Walesa said, "If you could come back, I will tell you what questions to ask, and we could have another conversation." We did have that other conversation a few months later. By then Walesa's stocky, peasant figure and walrus mustache had become familiar to most of the world. He had proved himself a shrewd tactician who had won legal status for Solidarity and maneuvered the regime into loosening its political grip. He often used homely metaphors that reminded me of Chance, the gardener, in Jerzy Kosinski's *Being There.* Denying that other Communist countries had anything to teach Poland, he said: "Every nation has its own special conditions. You can't grow oranges in Poland." Arguing that definitions and labels are misleading, he mused: "If I put water in a champagne bottle, it's still water." He took pains to point out that he was not trying to defy Moscow but acknowledged that he was engaged in a dangerous test of strength with the Polish government. "We can be defeated, and half of us could be shot," he said, "but we also know how to smile and hold our fork properly." In his lapel he wore a small picture of the Black Virgin of Czestochowa. Whenever he was in trouble he would pray, "Queen, Mother of God, save me."

In December 1981 the Polish prime minister, General Wojciech Jaruzelski, imposed martial law and jailed Walesa. He suppressed all free politics and expression in the country. But he could not fix the disastrous economy or prevent the eventual collapse of his regime.

My trip to Poland brought an echo from the past. Mira Michalowska, the researcher who had been a friend in my early years at *Time,* was back in her native Poland. She had lived all over the world with her diplomat husband, who was now retired while she wrote and translated books. Her still pretty face and smile showed her ironic attitude toward life more than ever. "We haven't chosen the best place to grow old in," she said wryly. "But come to think of it, we didn't exactly choose it. Nobody but nobody understands this strange country." She had little good to say about the Polish or Soviet regimes or, for that matter, about U.S. policy, which she felt still took Communism too seriously.

"Do you remember," I asked her, "you warned me not to come too heavily under the influence of Whittaker Chambers?" I recalled that as early as 1957, after the uprising in Hungary and the antigovernment demonstrations in Poland, Chambers had foretold the eventual crackup of Communism in the satellites. On the plains of Poland and Hungary, he had written to William Buckley, "a new force of destiny" was emerging, amounting to a "revolution against the Revolution."

The mention of the long-forgotten name of this anti-Marxist prophet startled her. "That seems like a million years ago," she said.

In 1983, AFTER bitter political opposition from the Left, in various countries, NATO finally deployed intermediate-range nuclear missiles to balance Soviet weapons already in place in Eastern Europe. It was a significant turning point in the cold war, and no one had fought harder for it than Margaret Thatcher. She had become a political phenomenon, a gorgon to her enemies and a female Churchill to her admirers.

The Tories were still in opposition when I had met her for the first time in London. I was racked by a severe hangover when she arrived for our breakfast meeting at eight A.M. She was impeccably dressed and coiffed and so cheerful that I cringed like Bertie Wooster on one of his desperate mornings after—without Jeeves around to provide a curative potion. When I talked with her some years later at 10 Downing Street, I began to suspect that despite Reagan's reputation as a true believer, he was a Doubting Thomas compared to her. She spoke in a fluting voice that contrasted with the resounding brass of her message. Norman Mailer once told me that he considered her sexy, a feeling I could not share.

Her campaign to transform British society was in full force. She talked about how she wanted every Briton to be a property owner someday and how the unions must be routed. The Labor Party, she said, was no longer an underdog. "Indeed, you might say that the underdogs are those who are held to ransom by the monopoly of the unions and the public sector." For years labor had allowed fanatic left-wingers to infiltrate its ranks and to rise to the top. "All bad philosophical movements start from the top—from the upper middle classes—not from the bottom." I never knew anyone whose words were so free of doubt or qualification. When I mentioned that Ronald Reagan had often been criticized for his bellicose rhetoric toward the Soviets, she rallied fiercely to his defense: "People keep saying that about Reagan's rhetoric. I say, 'Show me the paragraphs.' It's one of those legends that become lodged in people's minds."

It was more than a legend. "They reserve unto themselves the right to commit any crime, to lie, to cheat," summed up his view. Détente was still a dirty word for most certified Reaganites. I was certainly no dove myself, but I felt that bluster would not get results. The threat of military force always had to be kept in reserve, but I thought that what we also needed were cleverness and guile. I made that point later in a speech in New York at the Foreign Policy Association, which, somewhat fancifully, I called "Ulysses vs. Matt Dillon." Soon after Brezhnev died I began to believe that Reagan's Matt Dillon approach might change, and I came to this realization in a rather odd way.

My children gave me a surprise party for my sixtieth birthday, in December 1982. The evening was exuberant, with a large cast of friends. I did not feel sixty, and in my reply to many toasts, I advanced the theory that everybody has one ideal age that remains fixed regardless of the calendar; mine, I said, was somewhere between forty and forty-five. Suddenly there was a stir, and a vast birthday cake was wheeled in on a trolley by, of all people, Nancy Reagan. I had met her casually a few times before, and she appeared that evening at the instigation of Mike Wallace, an old friend of hers. In the commotion surrounding her entrance, the First Lady managed to back into the cake and a vast quantity of chocolate attached itself to her. There ensued a bizarre moment when Oscar de la Renta dropped to his knees and nimbly removed the layers of frosting from her Galanos dress.

Afterward she and I talked. The president was traveling in Latin America at the time, and our conversation turned to foreign policy. "I resent so many people talking about Ronnie as a warmonger," she said. "He is not. He really wants peace. He's just a very good poker player." She insisted that our relations with Moscow would soon look very different. I was surprised by the passion in her voice, and I understood that she was quite deliberately conveying a message. She was clearly determined that "Ronnie" be remembered in the future as a man of peace. I knew that Reagan listened to her, and I assumed that he was also beginning to be concerned with his place in history. I remembered that conversation over the following years, when Reagan was starting to emphasize peace and cooperation, sometimes evoking the Bible.

A FEW MONTHS after Reagan's overwhelming reelection in 1984, a stunning change occurred in Moscow. Succeeding three elderly and ailing leaders who died in office, Mikhail Gorbachev became the new boss of the Soviet Union. *Time* submitted a request for an interview. Late in August 1985 the Soviet embassy informed me that *Time*'s team was expected in Moscow within forty-eight hours. My colleagues and I saw Gorbachev in the same Kremlin room in which we had met Brezhnev more than six years earlier. The contrast was striking. Gorbachev was fifty-four, vital, magnetic. He moved gracefully, greeting each of us individually, and had obviously been well briefed. "I see that you are not only editor of *Time*," he told me, "but of six other magazines. And then your company has all those television stations. Aren't you afraid of antitrust?"

In front of him on the baize-covered table was a sheaf of typewritten notes marked up in different colors. We had again been asked to submit written questions, and Gorbachev handed us the answers in a folder— green this time, not red. "You see," he joked, "we're not trying to export revolution." He then agreed to answer questions but made an opening statement that took fifty-four minutes. Since the whole interview was supposed to take an hour, I tried once or twice to interrupt him, without success. But he extended the time. His deep voice might shift from a whisper to strong, assertive tones that cut through the big room. His hands moved eloquently, pointing, stabbing, gently thumping the table in a kind of modified karate chop. His deep brown eyes stared at us, as if compelling our attention, but he smiled easily. In a skull session preparing our questions, we had decided that our objective was not to bait

Gorbachev—I never thought of an interview as a bullfight—but to draw out, as best we could, his ideas and character.

Despite his personal charm he took a hard line on U.S.-Soviet relations, blaming Washington for continuing strains. His first meeting with Ronald Reagan was to take place in Geneva in November, and he complained that the U.S. administration was looking on the event like "a bout between some kind of political 'supergladiators' with the only thought in mind being how best to deal a deft blow at the opponent." He also showed touches of humor. If Washington kept dismissing every Soviet proposal as mere propaganda, he said, why not retaliate in kind? "We have stopped nuclear explosions. Then you Americans could take revenge by doing likewise. You could deal us yet another propaganda blow by suspending the development of one of your new strategic missiles. And we would respond with the same kind of 'propaganda.' "

I came away with the major impression that Gorbachev was deeply confused about how to handle his domestic economy. He projected more but better central planning, the strengthening of many state industries. But he also pledged decentralization as well as "initiative and a spirit of enterprise." It was obvious that he had no intention of really uprooting the Soviet system but merely hoped to improve it by tinkering with it. When he rather vaguely mentioned the need to use "such tools as profit, pricing, credit" to increase efficiency, I doubted that he knew what he was talking about. He seemed to regard such capitalist features like gadgets that could be bolted onto the existing Soviet economic machinery to make it run better. There was something naive about this, an impression strengthened by his earnest statement that he would curb alcoholism by reducing the production and sale of vodka.

"It will never work," muttered Felix Rosenthal, a Russian member of our Moscow bureau, as we critiqued the interview afterward. The real extent of Gorbachev's miscalculation about the chances of reforming Communism would become clear later. In the meantime he was tremendously appealing for his accessibility and quickness of mind. And thus, I thought, he might make a formidable opponent.

During the interview Gorbachev showed himself plainly worried about Reagan's Strategic Defense Initiative ("Star Wars"), boasting that the USSR could counter it—without mentioning the ruinous cost that this would impose. Gorbachev, like other critics of SDI, kept talking about the "militarization" of space, as if it were somehow sacrosanct. I considered that a phony argument. At the same time, I could not accept Reagan's view that full-fledged SDI would be purely defensive and no threat to the USSR. I thought that it represented, as I wrote in *Foreign Affairs,* an attempt "to transfer the task of peacekeeping from the precarious calculus of threat and counterthreat, from the area of human will, to a more or less automatic regime of laser beams and mirrors in orbit." (After the collapse of the Soviet Union and the increase of nuclear weapons in many less predictable countries, the case for SDI would become much stronger.)

At the Iceland summit in 1986 Reagan tried to persuade Gorbachev to accept SDI in exchange for eventually abolishing all nuclear weapons. Gorbachev refused. But the meeting proved that SDI was a powerful lever that had moved Gorbachev to offer significant arms control concessions. It also displayed Reagan's deep, instinctive distrust of the balance of terror. The notion of abolishing nuclear weapons entirely may have been naive and even dangerous, but it also revealed in the old cold warrior an abhorrence of war that surprised many.

"I<small>T IS NOT YET</small> clear where Gorbachev is going, or how far." The words were spoken by Deng Xiaoping, whom I saw a few months after the Gorbachev interview during a *Time* Newstour of Asia. Gorbachev was a quarter-century younger and had risen in a relatively tranquil political career. Deng had been part of Mao Tse-tung's revolution and survived three periods of political disgrace. During the insanities of the Cultural Revolution he worked in a tractor factory and waited on tables. Deng was more self-effacing than Gorbachev, or at least pretended to be, making jokes about his age (he was then eighty-one) keeping him from doing very much. That was patently untrue, and no one doubted that he was, in fact, what the Chinese press called him: the country's "Paramount Leader." He was tiny, less than five feet, and perched in a huge armchair, he seemed even smaller. From time to time during our meeting he discreetly used the big brass spittoon near him. He was willing to go much farther than Gorbachev in economic reform. He had already virtually abolished the collective farm system, allowing profits and private ownership in the countryside. ("If you want to bring the initiative of the peasants into play, you should give them the power to make money.") Several times I asked Deng how this fitted in with Socialism, and he blandly denied that there was any conflict. I began to realize his American capitalist visitors were more preoccupied with ideology than he was. Deng's famous maxim was "It doesn't matter if a cat is black or white as long as it catches mice." He casually conceded that some people in some regions would grow rich more quickly than others, but that could not be helped. "Other roads will only lead to poverty and backwardness, and I think this is the only road toward prosperity China can take." Change in the cities and in industry would be more difficult than in the countryside, he admitted. China was a strikingly different place from the country I had seen five years before; there had been nothing like the well-stocked food and vegetable markets, the neat, new houses, the humming village industries, the signs of foreign influence from rock music to computers.

Deng had transformed the lives of his people more emphatically than any other world leader, while Gorbachev's reforms were still only vague promises. The biggest difference between them was that while Deng was more radical in moving toward free market economics, he was not willing to move very far toward freedom in politics. Gorbachev, whether from idealism or from a failure to understand the nature of power, or both, would try to loosen the political system ahead of the economic system. That would eventually lead to his downfall. At a banquet after our interview with Deng I saluted China's new openness to the world and its openness to itself, in the sense that it was facing past mistakes. I invoked Henry Luce's lifelong love of China and suggested that though he was strongly opposed to Communism, "if he were here now, he would be greatly excited and rather proud of what China is accomplishing in becoming a modern economy." As I reached the traditional closing "Ganbei," I was not as confident as I must have sounded of Harry's pride. I may have taken the founder's name in vain.

CHAPTER THIRTY-SIX

As TIME INC. CHANGED, so did the position of the editor in chief. Many areas were now beyond his responsibility and competence—television, forest products. Many colleagues worried about that, notably Jerry Korn, the formidable editor of Time-Life Books, who argued passionately that just about everything should be under my control. "Jerry, let's face it," I told him. "I can't edit trees."

Hedley Donovan had spent months before his retirement trying to formalize the editor in chief's new role. He wrote and rewrote a "Constitution," which he persuaded the board of directors to adopt. The editor in chief would continue to report directly to the board rather than to the chief executive, a situation that not all directors favored. The board would delegate its responsibility for editorial quality to the editor in chief; it would not supervise him regularly but could replace him if his performance was judged unsatisfactory. He would have special responsibility to express his concern "if non-publishing activities of Time Inc. seemed to be in conflict with editorial positions" or if "the good name of Time Inc. publications might be affected." The editor in chief and the chief executive officer would be jointly responsible to the board "where their responsibilities intersect." It was this intersection that later caused many accidents.

Usually the issue was how much money could be spent—on new

547

projects, for instance. This had been no problem while Hedley Donovan and Andrew Heiskell were partners. Heiskell was an urbane, cosmopolitan executive who tended to rely on his own shrewd judgment more than on statistical projections. For years, while he moved up in the corporation he had the reputation of being a lightweight, partly because of his good looks and his bon vivant tastes. (Lunching with him, one could always count on a decent bottle.) He had a way of saying serious things in an offhand manner, avoiding solemnity and jargon. In a typically casual way he had tossed out the idea for *People* magazine. He and Hedley dealt with problems by wandering into one or the other's office and talking until they reached agreement. A year younger than Hedley, Andrew did not have to retire until 1980, when he reached sixty-five. During our relatively short partnership, when I was made editor in chief, he and I could not achieve the same rapport that had existed between Hedley and him, but we got along well.

Soon after my appointment I proposed the launch of a new magazine about science. The idea came from *Time*'s Leon Jaroff, who had dealt ably with science as a writer and editor for years, and from Sydnor Vanderschmidt, the magazine's science researcher. For much of the public science was still a forbidding subject. Nevertheless I enthusiastically drafted a prospectus full of trumpets and drumrolls. ("Science is the most important force in our lives. The computer garbles your bank statement: Science. We try to find alternate fuels: Science. Women by the thousands have mastectomies: Science. Radiation hurts: Science. Radiation heals: Science. It intrudes everywhere—in the sky and under the skin, in one's house and in one's brain.") The publishing staff sent out the usual test mailing, and the results were mildly favorable but not conclusive, as these things rarely are. It took a final decision by the CEO to commit the necessary money. "Let's do it," said Heiskell. It would not have happened that way after his exit, for the atmosphere changed.

Andrew Heiskell had long brooded over who should succeed him. Once, during a corporate retreat at Lyford Cay, he walked about with me and rattled off possible names. In the end he chose Dick Munro, who had been successfully in charge of the company's TV and cable operations. Colleagues told me later that Munro was uneasy with me, even afraid of me, although I was not aware of it. We did have different interests and enthusiasms. In a dinner toast he once said: "I don't take Henry to the ball game and he doesn't take me to the opera." But I sensed compassion in him. While Beverly was dying, he told me that he was praying for her.

A former marine, (he was wounded three times in Korea and won the Purple Heart), Munro was politically liberal and personally macho. Short and muscular, Munro had a habit of rolling up his shirtsleeves, crossing his arms and slinging his necktie over his shoulder, a gesture that quite unreasonably irritated me. He peppered almost any statement with incongruous, tough-guy obscenities.

After he became CEO we occupied offices in opposite corners of the thirty-fourth floor, separated by no more than fifty feet. It was a walk not often taken. In the "Church and State" Time Inc. tradition Munro felt that he had no business commenting on editorial matters, not that I would have been particularly receptive. But, at his invitation, I participated for years in his weekly meetings with his senior executives, at which all company affairs were discussed. Endlessly discussed. Munro would preside in his jovial fashion, imposing little order and usually treating the participants to shoe shines from Jimmy, a Time Inc. institution.

Munro surrounded himself with a trio of bright, energetic, younger executives. They were Kelso Sutton, head of the magazine group; Gerald M. Levin, chief of the company's video operations and Nicholas J. Nicholas, the chief financial officer. I liked Sutton's voracious appetite for books and his bouncy good humor, although I eventually detected much anger underneath. He was apt to make needling suggestions ("Why don't you fire that guy?"), and he often let his enthusiasm overcome his judgment. Nicholas could be typecast as a financial wizard; numbers seemed to be dancing behind his metal-rimmed glasses. But he was far more than a high-level accountant and had a sharp analytic mind. He often alienated people with his sardonic smile and abrasive manner. Levin was ostentatiously calm, with a sense of humor so understated that it was apt to be invisible and a mustache that gave him the air of wearing a disguise. He was invariably and accurately described as thoughtful, and it was not difficult to imagine that he might have become a rabbi, a calling he had once considered, or an academic. The conventional view was, as a colleague put it, that Levin had his eyes on mountaintops while Nicholas was good at fighting through the swamps. The reality was more complex. Nicholas was not as tough as he looked and Levin a lot tougher. In 1986, after some serious mistakes in managing HBO, Levin found himself sidelined. He was put in charge of strategic planning, a move that seemed terminal. But he would later achieve a spectacular resurrection.

Munro juggled the talents and ambitions of these three men and, in that same year, finally named Nick Nicholas president and chief operating officer, in effect designating him as his deputy and successor. It had taken him six years to make that choice. In my view he had a hard time with decisions. (He felt the same way about me.) Above all, as he later admitted, he did not enjoy his job. He had announced when he took over that he would retire in ten years when he reached sixty, and I sometimes got the impression that he could hardly wait.

The business world was haunted by takeover artists. To protect top managers, "golden parachutes" had become widespread. Munro instituted that device for himself and other officers. *Fortune* decided to run an article about parachutes and listed leading American executives who were thus equipped. J. Richard Munro was ninth from the top, with a $3 million severance package. (My own parachute was considerably lighter.) I approved the story before it went to press and warned Munro about it. Embarrassed by what in those days still seemed like a lavish deal, Munro decided to cancel all the contracts, including his own. Better protection than parachutes or "poison pills" might be provided by a preventive merger, creating a new company too big to be raided. My business colleagues feared the "barbarians at the gate" but at the same time had a hankering to join them. Huge media combinations were being created, and Munro and company kept looking for partners. There were discussions about joining up with a beleaguered CBS or with the immensely profitable Gannett Newspaper Group, headed by the flamboyant Al Neuharth, inventor of *USA Today*. Gannett looked tempting, but in the end Munro decided that the "cultures" of the two companies could not mesh. He considered Gannett unscrupulous and a little tacky. (Years later, when Munro championed the merger with Steve Ross's Warner Communications, he would seem less fastidious.)

If it was the age of the corporate raiders, it was also the age of the MBAs, whom American business treated almost as shamans. They were involved in America's own version of perestroika, with "downsizing" the almost universal catch phrase. Munro brought in a consultant, Bruce Hiland, and eventually made him vice president for administration. Most of Hiland's recommendations were sensible enough. He freely dispensed management maxims, the best of which I thought was "Smart is cheap. Effective comes dear."

The company now was straddling two eras. The buttoned-down ghosts representing paternalism and a kind of high-minded casualness were not quite gone; the new hardheaded professionals were not yet confident or competent enough to make Time Inc. into the supermodern communications giant they dreamed of.

It did not take an MBA to realize that the company had to be shaken up. We were not really at home in the new world of communications. I felt, for example, that Time Inc.'s cable operations should present news and information programs, but the prevailing view then was that no money could be made in that area. I continued to believe that Time Inc. and not Ted Turner should have created CNN. Perhaps, I once told a group of colleagues, Time Inc. needed a sort of internal raid. Just such a move had been advocated by Nick Nicholas. In a report written with Bruce Hiland, he argued that the company's businesses—roughly one-third each, in publishing, cable and forest products—failed to add up to a clear identity. In due course the forest products businesses were sold off. New projects, the report suggested, should be developed systematically and not by "adhocracy."

ONE RESULT OF adhocracy involved the *Washington Star.* Once the capital's dominant paper, it had been sliding downward ever since the mid-fifties. In 1978 Heiskell and Donovan decided to buy it. The *Star* came at a bargain price of $20 million. Its circulation was only about a third of the mighty *Washington Post.* The company pledged to spend $60 million over five years to turn it around. Hedley told me: "We will not try to overtake the *Post.* We will only try to maintain a niche in Washington." The niche proved to be a dead end. The *Star* was put in the hands of Time Inc. executives who had little or no grounding in the newspaper business. Afternoon papers like the *Star* were disappearing all across the United States, and distribution in the Washington area was difficult and costly.

When I became editor in chief I also became a director of the *Star,* but beyond that I functioned mostly as an adviser; according to the Donovan Constitution, the paper was semiautonomous. Even so, during my regular visits I enjoyed the newspaper atmosphere. "Hot off the press" was a phrase not yet dead in our language. There was something special about holding a fresh newspaper in your hand: the coarseness and crackle of the newsprint, even the occasional smudge of ink, suggesting speed and excitement. Under Murray Gart, who had been moved from the Time-Life News Service to become its editor, the *Star* was more than respectable. Ben Bradlee of *The Washington Post* described it as the best afternoon daily in the United States. But the *Post* was so dominant that readers and advertisers saw scant advantage in the *Star.* A little over three years after the acquisition all of us came to the reluctant but unanimous conclusion that the paper had to be folded. We were short of the promised five years but, at an $85 million investment, well above the $60 million we had pledged. I had the painful experience of joining Munro, Shepley and Gart in a Washington press conference to explain our decision. Reaction to the closing was bitter. Mary McGrory, who had been a *Star* columnist for more than thirty years and was still youthful in her liberal passions, complained that "people we did not know made mysterious decisions about our fate" and compared Time Inc. executives to "Roman generals who came to the provinces."

In the meantime we had launched our science magazine, *Discover,* with Leon Jaroff as editor. It was intended for an intelligent, general audience, between the highly abstruse *Scientific American* and the jazzy, sensational *Omni. Discover* won big acclaim from advertisers and readers—circulation grew from an initial four hundred thousand to eight hundred thousand by 1982. Nevertheless the magazine would have to perform even better to become profitable. I blamed much of its commercial failure on my business colleagues, who in seven years saddled it with four publishers, one of them a mail-order specialist without magazine experience who had performed badly at Time-Life Books. But editorially too the magazine was not as strong and imaginative as it should have been. In 1984 I reluctantly replaced Leon Jaroff with one of the best, most inventive and most literate editors in the building, Gilbert Rogin, who had been running *Sports Illustrated* with great panache. Jaroff was understandably bitter and mistakenly convinced that I had acted under pressure from the business side. He went back to *Time* to write and edit excellent science articles. But he remained unreconciled. I learned that he habitually referred to me as the JVP, which, colleagues thought, stood either for Jewish Viennese Prince or Jewish Viennese Prick.

Rogin did a dazzling job, but business did not markedly improve. Munro lost patience. In seven years the company had invested $70 million. I recalled that *Sports Illustrated* had lost $100 million (in 1987 dollars) before turning a profit. I pleaded with the board of directors that *Discover* deserved at least two more years, but I lost. The magazine was sold in 1987 and at this writing is being published profitably by the Disney Company.

M Y BUSINESS ASSOCIATES were lusting for a different kind of magazine. They wanted another blockbuster weekly like *People*. Kelso Sutton pushed for a television magazine that could compete with the hugely successful *TV Guide*, which was only just beginning to carry cable listings and was very cumbersome. I did not consider the idea very interesting journalistically, but I thought that such a magazine could provide a highly useful service.

For managing editor of *TV Cable Week*, I chose Dick Burgheim, formerly of *Time* and *People*, a show business enthusiast. Editorial offices were moved to Westchester to avoid high Manhattan rents. I worked hard on the project, editing articles and even capsule reviews.

Surveys and focus groups were favorable—and about as reliable as the research that preceded the launch of the Edsel. In a publishing innovation the magazine would be sold not directly to subscribers, but through cable system operators, who would receive a cut. Most of them declared themselves enthusiastic, but they were not required to make any firm commitments. In a memo to Munro, Sutton and myself, Ralph Graves warned of the high risks. "What worries me most about this project is the sheer number of different gambles involved, every one of which we have to win." Among the gambles were the "hazardous" dependence on the cable operators and competition from free guides. He compared the whole enterprise to Russian roulette. It was a prophetic memo, and to my lasting regret, I did nothing to back it up. Amid fanfares of promises and skyrockets of publicity, the launch proceeded—and within weeks the vessel ran aground. The magazine cost subscribers nearly $3 per month, and the operators quickly realized that they could do better selling the customers additional cable services instead. In only five months the losses mounted to nearly $50 million—half the $100 million investment that had been budgeted to stretch over four or five years. After twenty-five issues the magazine was folded. A postmortem concluded that in future there would have to be a better balance between experienced executives and "fast-track young tigers." In my view the problem was not with young tigers or old tigers, but with dumb tigers, myself included. In a memo to Munro I pointed out two ironies. The project had been animated not by any strong editorial passion, but by a business concept; paradoxically that ultimately made for bad business. Moreover, if Ralph's warning had been heeded, he would not have earned thanks for avoiding a costly mistake but been blamed for blocking a great and profitable opportunity.

A different kind of postmortem was provided by Christopher Byron, a *Time* business and economics writer whom I had assigned to *TV Cable Week*. He published a book called *The Fanciest Dive*, which was inaccurate in many details and full of mean-spirited schadenfreude—but we deserved it. One episode was almost worth the price of the book. While we had located the editorial offices in Westchester to save money, various executives, including myself, often commuted to White Plains by company helicopter, in the style of the times. During one meeting there I found myself late for an appointment in Manhattan. As Byron tells it, I burst out of the conference room and told the first secretary in sight to get me a helicopter. The young woman later said: "I didn't know what he was talking about—I thought maybe it was some new Galleria delicacy, some triple-scoop dessert with a propeller on it."

TV Cable Week's failure affected our self-image and morale. For years afterward the company was torn between the desire to recoup and the fear of another failure. Various projects appeared on the drawing board, and one, *Picture Week*, was seriously tested, with encouraging results. But in the end the risk of a costly launch was judged too great.

By then magazine development had grown into a corporate absurdity, with two separate units under separate publishing chiefs, supposedly to achieve creativity through internal competition. Eventually the structure was mercifully abolished, and the business of inventing magazines would not resume for some years. A piece of jargon constantly used by publishing types was that new publications had to be "market driven." Well, of course, magazines are businesses. On the other hand, markets don't just exist, they must be created. Looking back, I am stunned by the sheer amount of paper and the cacophony of committee arguments. We were not so much market driven as bureaucracy driven. Rather than start new publications, many in the company felt it was less risky to buy existing properties (in 1985 Time Inc. had acquired Southern Progress Corporation, which profitably published good and unexciting home magazines, among others) and to bankroll outside entrepreneurs. Very much aware that the previous regime of Donovan and Heiskell had produced *People* and *Money*, I was greatly frustrated by the lack of similar accomplishments on my watch.

MY MAIN TASK was to maintain the quality of the existing publications and, if possible, to improve it. I missed the hands-on editing, the direct contact with the staff. The thirty-fourth floor seemed very far away from the action. So, following a precedent established by Luce and Donovan, I sat in for the managing editors of various magazines for two or three weeks. The staffs regarded these visitations with some nervousness but, as far as I could tell, welcomed the attention I paid and the questions I asked.

I began with *Fortune,* which I considered one of the most intelligent magazines anywhere. The spirit was clubby and a little academic, suggesting faculty meetings more than newsroom action. The conversation was languid, but the ideas were sharp and backed by solid information. Opinions were markedly less liberal than on the other magazines, where it was extremely difficult to find conservatives. After much agonizing, *Fortune* had recently switched from monthly to a biweekly to be more current (and profitable). Under its managing editor, Robert Lubar, a transplant from *Time,* it was still trying to adjust to its new rhythm. Many staff members, and readers, missed the old *Fortune,* which had been seen as a kind of business bible; when it treated a subject, usually at great length, there was nothing left to say about it—or so its fans and editors believed. The new *Fortune* ran shorter pieces and fewer surveys of broad cultural phenomena, emphasizing company news and investment strategies. Yet the notion was still strong among editors that getting a story right was more important than getting it early, and the magazine still did not seem current. I believe *Fortune* eventually overcame that failing, but I never forgot that working late on my second day there, I wanted to watch the evening news and could not find a television set.

The atmosphere at *People* was as different as the subject matter—and the vocabulary. When *People* writers spoke of a split, they didn't mean stock but marriage, and gross referred not to profits, but to the latest antics of J. R. Ewing. I was intrigued by the new ways of referring to unmarried couples—"live-in lover" seemed especially popular. Some of the names that reached my desk were puzzling (the Captain & Tennille? Mackenzie Phillips?). But most of the cast of characters consisted of mainstream celebrities, along with quite a few politicians, businessmen, artists and writers, ranging from cellist-conductor Mstislav Rostropovich to the master chronicler of bird life, Roger Tory Peterson. The managing editor, Dick Stolley, combined irreverence with professionalism, and so did his staff; they were intensely earnest in trying to find a new angle on Elizabeth Taylor or making lists of the most beautiful, the most boring, and so on. I had a very good time "guesting" at *People,* as the magazine might unfortunately put it, and realized, more so than I had before, that it was not just a celebrity album, but a kaleidoscopic reflection of American life.

Knowing my limitations, I did not sit in at *Sports Illustrated* (although its managing editor always thoughtfully gave me a preview of the annual swimsuit issue). I did eagerly return for a stint at *Time* in the spring of 1983, an event Ed Jamieson dryly referred to as "the Second Coming." Ray Cave, always a clean-desk man, had left his office in pristine condition, and I knew I would have to mess it up before feeling at home. He had installed sleek new furniture, but the "squawk box," connecting this office with all the senior editors, was still there, as well as the Briton Hadden pencil cup.

After six years I had to rediscover the *Time* routine. The late hours seemed a little more tiring; I sometimes had the uneasy sense that the system, once second nature, was now running me. But by the end of my visit I was again on top of it. There were the inevitable worries about whether the era of the newsmagazine was passing, but I thought that *Time,* under my successor, provided much evidence that it was not. The month was an exercise in nostalgia. I reveled in the renewed camaraderie with many old colleagues, and I had glimpses of the brash yet shy copy boy I had been, the ambitious writer, the managing editor who thought there was no better job than running *Time.*

A few writers had started working on computers rather than typewriters, and a wholesale switch would occur within two years. After decades of leaning over copy as it came out of the typewriter or lay on my desk and under my pencil, I found it strange to face the screen. The words seemed to stare back at me almost as equals, abolishing my dominant position. (Eventually I would become infatuated with the near magical ease of the word processor.) I had my most striking impression of the new technology when I walked into *Time*'s large central computer room, whose big mainframes were driving copy-processing, bookkeeping and various other functions. Lights flashed on panels, their meaning mysterious to the layman. Behind its glass walls, the room was cool, antiseptic and silent. I thought I heard a low hum, an occasional click from the machines, but that was more imagined than real. The soft steps of the people who worked there evoked the stocking feet in Oriental shrines. I recalled how Henry Adams described walking into the Hall of Dynamos at the Great Exposition of 1900 in Paris. In that superb chapter from *The Education,* titled "The Dynamo and the Virgin," he saw the huge, barely murmuring machine as a symbol of infinity: "as a moral force, much as the early Christians felt the Cross." Eventually, he wrote, "one began to pray to it." I was not tempted to pray, but I did feel that I was in the presence of a new force. Was it, in Adams's words, a moral force? I was not sure. I did understand that the force was not material like the dynamo's; physical power was being replaced by intellectual power. Would Adams, if he were here now, write a chapter on "The Computer and the Virgin"?

Quite apart from these guest appearances I regularly reviewed the story lists for all our publications, reading particular articles before press time, often proposing changes. I talked at length to all the managing editors on everything from future cover subjects to the line and tone to be taken on issues. But I spent more time on what was obviously our most important magazine. While I was working on this chapter I received a large cardboard box from Ray Cave filled with copies of my memos to him while he was managing editor. It was, he explained, only a sampling of the total. The subjects ranged from policy (arms control, the contras) to minute matters of style and language. I wondered in retrospect how Ray had borne up under the barrage, but he assured me that it had been very helpful. As Ray was notoriously frugal with flattery, I took his assurance gratefully at face value.

MY SINGLE MOST painful experience involving *Time* was the libel suit by Ariel Sharon. The case had its origin in the 1982 Israeli invasion of Lebanon. Three months after the invasion Lebanon's president-elect Bashir Gemayel was assassinated. He was the leader of the country's Christian Phalangist faction, which had been engaged in an on-and-off civil war with Arabs and Palestinians. After the assassination Israeli defense minister Ariel Sharon ordered the Phalangist militia to enter the Palestinian refugee camps at Sabra and Shatila, ostensibly to keep order. The result was a massacre in which seven hundred to eight hundred Palestinian civilians were killed. Amid the outcry that followed, a commission of inquiry under the president of the Israeli supreme court, Yitzak Kahan, investigated the event.

The report was devastating to Sharon. It concluded that he was "indirectly responsible" for the killings because when he ordered the Phalangists into the camps, he should have realized what would happen. He should not have disregarded, said the report, the serious consideration "that the Phalangists were liable to commit atrocities." Sharon vehemently attacked the report, protesting that it placed the "mark of Cain" on his forehead, but he was forced to resign as defense minister (he remained in the cabinet in another capacity).

Time ran a cover story summarizing the report. Halfway through the eight-page article was a paragraph reporting that Sharon had paid a condolence visit to the Gemayel family. *Time* had "learned," said the story, that Sharon had "reportedly discussed with the Gemayels the need for the Phalangists to take revenge for the assassination of Bashir." This did not seem especially remarkable. Given the circumstances, it would have been odd if revenge had *not* been discussed. In fact, General Rafael Eitan, chief of staff of the Israeli army, testified that he had warned Sharon just before the Phalangists went into the camps that "they are seething with the feeling of revenge, and there might be rivers of blood." But both Sharon and his ally, Prime Minister Menachem Begin, vehemently proclaimed that *Time* had accused Sharon of instigating murder. Moreover *Time* had said that the details of the Sharon conversation were contained in a secret Appendix B to the commission report, and Begin denied that this was so—"a lie," he said. Highly damaging was the fact that *Time*'s publicity department had issued a press release about our story to the effect that Sharon had "urged" the Phalangists into the camps. This was true, of course, but the release was widely misreported in Israel as saying that Sharon had urged the killings. If we had issued an immediate statement that our story had never said that, we would have saved ourselves an enormous amount of grief. In fact,

Cave and I had discussed making just such a statement, but I first wanted to see whether we could learn more about Appendix B.

The disputed passage in our story was a condensation of an earlier report from our correspondent David Halevy, who had concluded, after talking to confidential sources, that the information about Sharon's conversation with the Gemayels was in Appendix B. We realized that he could have misunderstood or been misled, in the furtive atmosphere where informants risked prosecution under Israeli law. But all we really knew for certain, then, was the fact of Begin's and Sharon's denial. With all due respect, both were politicians badly damaged by the Kahan report; Sharon especially was fighting for his political future and the chance to be prime minister.

We asked for access to Appendix B, but we were turned down by Israeli authorities on security grounds. While we were still pondering this dilemma, Sharon sued for libel five days after the *Time* issue went on sale in Israel, eventually demanding $50 million.

From that moment on anything we might say became a legal matter, and the advice from our lawyers was not to say anything yet. Besides, even if reference to the exchange between Sharon and the Gemayels was not contained in Appendix B, that did not disprove it had taken place. The contents of the conversation had been outlined to Halevy by several confidential sources, among them an Israeli intelligence official who read from notes taken at one meeting. Another key confidential source was an Israeli general who told Halevy that he had access to notes about a slightly earlier meeting at which Sharon said that Bashir's murder was a "Syrian-Palestinian conspiracy" requiring some reaction or retaliation. "Dudu" Halevy was an Israeli, a lieutenant colonel in the Israeli army who had once had close ties to the Labor Party. He had often admiringly reported on Sharon as a military man. But he made no secret of the fact that he disapproved of his policies and of the West Bank occupation, which he felt would corrode Israel in the long run. In sixteen years as a *Time* correspondent, Halevy had made one bad slip involving what seemed to have been a false report on Begin's health. (We retracted that article.) But the rest of the time he had been a reliable reporter who broke some major stories.

Lawyers began to take depositions in New York from the principal characters in the case, including Sharon. He felt himself rudely treated by our chief counsel, Thomas Barr of Cravath, Swaine & Moore, and was also dissatisfied with his own lawyers, to the point where he nearly withdrew the suit. I did not believe that the case would ever come to trial, and neither did my colleagues and our lawyers. Sharon, we reasoned, was a foreign politician, objecting to a passage that we felt was at worst ambiguous, who had been condemned in his own country for his role in the Lebanese massacres. He might not be exactly "libel proof," as one of our legal team put it, but he had a longtime reputation for ruthlessness in Israel, and worse things had been printed about him than our report. As our lawyers later argued, in a plea for summary judgment, the case should be dismissed under the "act of state" doctrine, meaning that the events in question were acts of a foreign government and could not be adjudicated by a U.S. court. Moreover, the Israeli government blocked access to certain witnesses and documents we considered essential. Tom Barr observed: "I don't see why Qaddafi can't sue here too and then say that every piece of evidence is a state secret." In the meantime one of Sharon's own lawyers proposed a settlement statement that Sharon angrily rejected. Later a revised statement was approved by Sharon and was submitted to us. I requested what I considered minor changes to underline the absence of malice on *Time*'s part. But Sharon rejected that version, too. At that point our lawyers were still convinced that the case would be dismissed.

We were stunned when Judge Abraham Sofaer rejected our plea for summary judgment. Soon afterward Sofaer asked me to come to see him. I went to his chambers with Ralph Davidson, chairman of the Time Inc. board, and Tom Barr. I had not met Sofaer during all the preliminary legal maneuvering. He was a highly intelligent, former law professor with huge spectacles that seemed too large for his youthful face. He made a strong pitch for settlement, suggesting we might have a very hard time in the trial ahead and urging me not to stick up for David Halevy. There was a hint that Halevy was a bad apple and that I should not jeopardize *Time* as a whole for this one correspondent. I told Sofaer that I was perfectly willing to retract the error on Appendix B (provided it became clear that we *were* in error) and also to issue a statement that our story was not intended to imply that Sharon had deliberately instigated revenge. But Sofaer made it clear that was not good enough. We needed somehow to retract the story itself. This I refused to do. Halevy, I said, was sure of his sources. Of course he might have been misled by them, but we did not know this. It was not up to us to prove that our story was accurate, but up to Sharon to prove it was false. This was true in law, but it became clear all too soon that it would not convince public opinion or the jury. The trial proceeded.

Most of the top executives on the business side of Time Inc. had advised that we settle, but the decision was left to me by them and by the board of directors. I was reluctant to settle for several reasons. It was a long-standing, firm Time Inc. policy to fight all libel suits, unless we were convinced we were wrong. Any other course, we felt, would merely encourage frivolous litigation. I was concerned about the increase of libel actions, bizarre suits and the ballooning of monetary awards by juries.

Many of these were later reduced or nullified by appeal courts, but the cost of litigation could be crippling. In recent years the average libel judgment had grown to $2 million. By comparison the average malpractice award was $700,000, suggesting that juries found the press worse than bad medicine. Especially troubling were politically motivated suits by public officials and the erosion of the all-important *Sullivan* rule. In a case often linked with the Sharon suit—it was tried in the same federal courthouse at the same time—General William Westmoreland had sued CBS for saying that he had falsified estimates of enemy troop strength. CBS eventually settled by issuing an ambiguous statement, and both sides claimed vindication. But the motivation behind the suit struck me as alarming. Dan Burt, Westmoreland's lawyer, had said openly: "We are about to see the dismantling of a major news network."

Against this background I considered it important not to back off just to avoid trouble. There was also another reason: Sharon's violent propaganda campaign against *Time*. He kept talking relentlessly, in press interviews, on TV, in speeches, about the "blood libel" committed by *Time* not only against him but against Israel and the Jewish people. The

With Henry
Kissinger (left).
"Tweedledum and
Tweedledee," said
Robert Hughes.
(Oscar Abolafia/
Time magazine)

Time's foreign-born staff
posing for a special
issue on immigration,
July 8, 1985.
(Ted Thai/*Time*
magazine)

With candidate Ronald Reagan during the 1976 campaign in Kansas City. (© Michael Evans)

With Nancy Reagan at my surprise sixtieth birthday party. She was the biggest surprise.

(© Carl Mydans)

Norman Mailer toasting me. From left, Pat Buckley, Lisa, Roger Rosenblatt, Lou (Mrs. Ralph) Davidson.
(© CARL MYDANS)

With Lisa, Mandy and Peter at their party for me.
(© CARL MYDANS)

With Beverly No. 2 (Sills).
(PERSONAL COLLECTION OF HENRY GRUNWALD)

With Shirley MacLaine in her current incarnation, 1985. (© TONY RUTA)

In my thirty-fourth-floor office, in front of my cartoon wall. Middle row second from left, a David Levine caricature which *New York* magazine used for a mock *Newsweek* cover of me. Lower right, my whimsical motto.
(PHOTO © 1980, NANCY S. KESSLER/TIME INC. PICTURE COLLECTION)

Interviewing Gorbachev in the Kremlin, 1985. Next to Gorbachev, Georgi Arbatov.
(© RUDI FREY, *TIME* MAGAZINE)

Louise.

(PERSONAL COLLECTION OF
HENRY GRUNWALD)

Faithful reader Harry.

(PERSONAL COLLECTION OF HENRY GRUNWALD)

Reviewing the Honor Guard as the new American Ambassador in Vienna.
(CHRIS NIEDENTHAL, *TIME* MAGAZINE)

How not to smile: presenting
my credentials to President
Kurt Waldheim.
(© BERNHARD J. HOLZNER/TIME
INC. PICTURE COLLECTION)

With Louise at the Lippizaner stud farm at Piber. (PERSONAL COLLECTION OF HENRY GRUNWALD)

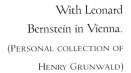

With Leonard Bernstein in Vienna. (PERSONAL COLLECTION OF HENRY GRUNWALD)

The Marine gunnie presenting the American flag
to me as I am about to leave Vienna.
(PERSONAL COLLECTION OF HENRY GRUNWALD)

With my father's bust in
Vienna's Alfred Grunwald
Park. (PERSONAL COLLECTION
OF HENRY GRUNWALD)

Time article, Sharon declared, was "one of the most terrible things that has been done to the Jewish people." *Time* was one of the "centers of anti-Semitism existing these days in the world." These outrageous and absurd changes infuriated me.

I attended the trial often but not daily, making my way through the gauntlet of photographers at the Foley Square courthouse. The event had drawn so much attention and so many spectators that the proceedings had to be moved to a larger courtroom. Both sides used visual aides profusely—huge maps to illustrate part of the fighting in Lebanon, big blowups of the *Time* story and the Kahan report. The diminutive Sofaer sometimes seemed to disappear below the bench but ran things with authority, often intervening in the questioning of witnesses. Tom Barr, rugged and aggressive, prowled the courtroom as if stalking Sharon. A brilliant lawyer with vast experience in corporate litigation, Barr had successfully defended IBM in an epic thirteen-year antitrust action, but this was a very different case, and he was absent from the trial for part of the time because of illness. Barr's opponent was Milton Gould, a deceptively friendly, cozy-looking veteran trial lawyer who combined a folksy style with heavy irony. He ranged from the jocular, as when he said of Sharon, "He may be fat, but he's not crazy," to the portentous, evoking Voltaire's famous slogan, which he rendered as "Stamp out infamy." (Voltaire was referring to the Catholic Church but Gould to *Time* magazine.) Barr dwelled at length on Sharon's reputation for brutality, charging that his "enormous personal ambition skates the very edge of psychosis." Gould, on the other hand, naturally presented him as a military hero, a "farmer when he was not fighting Israel's enemies," and led Sharon through an account of his humble but cultured family (his mother never wore shoes, but his father played the violin).

I recalled my first meeting with Sharon, years before on the West Bank, when he gave that bad advice about the attacking bees. Since then I had seen him again, during a Mideast trip, in his Jerusalem office and at lunch in the Time & Life Building. He had spread out his inevitable maps in the dining room to illustrate once again Israel's precarious military position. I suppose I must have asked some provocative questions because, when I had to leave the lunch early, I heard him say ironically to the remaining group: "A tough guy, isn't he?" Not nearly as tough as he, I thought when I observed him in the courtroom. Walking to his place, Sharon moved with a prizefighter's gait that reminded me of Norman Mailer. He conveyed barely contained energy in the thrust of his body and his solid features. On the stand Sharon was sometimes rambling but highly articulate, polemical, constantly repeating the theme of "blood libel."

Much of the trial turned on *Time*'s operations, on our ways of reporting and checking, on the nuances of words. Misconceptions and distortions about all this abounded in the questioning by the Sharon lawyers. Again and again, sitting in court and waiting for my turn to be called, I wanted to cry out: "No, no, that's not what happened, that's not what we did, that's not what we meant!" The author Renata Adler later reported that *Time*'s journalists as witnesses were indifferent to the truth and "looked like people whose mind it had never crossed to be ashamed." That was outrageous, but in fact many of *Time*'s witnesses were too defensive, too ill at ease. Halevy was an especially poor witness under sharp attack from Gould and was goaded into making political statements against Sharon. Uri Dan, Sharon's press adviser (who also happened to be the *New York Post*'s correspondent in Israel), reported in his book, *Blood Libel,* that the general had urged his lawyers not to call me as a witness. "Don't examine Grunwald," he said. "He might well strengthen *Time*'s case. We've got to remember that if Grunwald, a Jew, has managed to make it to the top, and to survive there for so long, he's a tough nut to crack." It might also have occurred to Sharon that his charges of anti-Semitism against *Time* might be undermined by me. I was nevertheless called to testify. While I was on the stand I was suddenly face-to-face with Sharon, who sat on a front bench, arms crossed, eyes glaring. The main points of my testimony involved a defense of the use of confidential sources and a reaffirmation of my opinion of Halevy as a reliable reporter. According to Dan, Sharon complained bitterly that both the judge and Milton Gould were treating me with "kid gloves . . . it's a shame, a disgrace."

In December 1984, while in Paris on business, I received a phone call from New York. Our lawyers had once again worked out a settlement proposal, and they, as well as most of my colleagues, thought we should accept it. It was now almost two years since Sharon had begun his suit. I was virtually alone in keeping the case going and constantly felt the pressure of that responsibility. Only twice in my life have I suffered from insomnia—after Beverly's death and now, during the final months of the trial. Reluctantly and somewhat wearily, I agreed to the proposed settlement. The text was substantially what Sofaer had asked for months before. In effect, it did not merely reiterate that we had not intended to accuse Sharon of instigating the killings, nor did it merely retract the mistake about Appendix B, but it said that we had "no information" on which to base the disputed paragraph. On the airplane back to New York next day, I brooded about the statement. We had come this far; would it be better to stay the course? I particularly focused on *Sullivan;* whatever else the jury might find, I was sure that it would not find "actual malice" and that this would be important to *Time*'s reputation. Back in New York I reopened the matter and asked our lawyers if they could get agreement to a few changes in the proposed statement. Thereafter the entire settlement effort fell apart.

In the meantime Judge Sofaer had written to Justice Kahan, asking him to examine Appendix B and to answer three questions concerning the reported conversation. Early in January came his reply that there was no mention of a conversation about revenge. Our Israeli counsel expressed "substantial and material reservations" about this answer, among other reasons because it did not cover an additional body of secret testimony originally given to the commission. After the release of the Kahan reply, we printed a retraction of the Appendix B error. The effect on the jury and the public could not have been more damaging. While we still considered this error distinct from our basic information, it obviously undermined our credibility as a whole. Later, a former Israeli ambassador to Washington, Ephraim ("Eppie") Evron, told me of a conversation he had with Kahan before he died. Kahan had been greatly astonished that an American judge would negotiate with a foreign government about the details of evidence. Within the narrow questions put to him by the American court, Kahan said, he could have given no other answers.

The jury had to rule on three questions: was the story defamatory, was it false and was it published with malice? Only if the jury's answer was yes to all three questions would we lose. The story was defamatory, Sofaer told the jury, if it was read to say that Sharon "consciously intended" or "actively encouraged" the killings. We did not think that the story said that, but the jury disagreed. The jury also found the story false, obviously with the Appendix B error in mind. Under Sofaer's instructions each of these verdicts was announced separately. The process took ten days, creating maximum, protracted publicity. It also created maximum tension and anxiety in myself and my colleagues. Waiting for each installment of the jury's decision was a grim ordeal. On the third question, regarding malice, the jury found *Time* innocent, and we thus won the case. But it was a dubious victory. The jury made a special statement "that certain *Time* employees, particularly correspondent David Halevy, acted negligently and carelessly."

Most press commentators severely condemned *Time*. Steven Brill wrote an article in the *American Lawyer* under the headline "Say it Ain't So, Henry!" in which he accused us of lying and simply making up the story. The piece was rabid in tone and contained many inaccuracies and misconceptions. Anthony Lewis of *The New York Times*, who had earlier written in defense of *Time* and denounced the Sharon suit as a political maneuver, now castigated us for arrogance in not admitting error. Richard Clurman, former chief of the Time-Life News Service, published a severely critical book, *Beyond Malice*, in which he took us to task for, among other things, hyping our story through the use of the words *"Time* learned," which he felt was bragging about a mere "tantalizing tidbit"—and on this he was right. Renata Adler worked two *New Yorker* pieces into an overwrought book about the Sharon and Westmoreland cases, *Reckless Disregard*, in which she accused *Time* of legal and journalistic shams. The condemnations by Clurman and Adler were especially painful to me because they were friends, but I knew that they wrote from conviction and without "actual malice." Many press critics were self-righteous and animated by an open desire to denigrate the *Time* "system," as they saw it. In retrospect it would have been wiser if I had tried harder for an early settlement. Throughout I focused on *Time*'s vindication under the *Sullivan* rule rather than the damage that could be done to us on the way there.

The case had dragged on for more than two years. In the meantime my work continued much as usual and my life rather differently.

CHAPTER THIRTY-SEVEN

Being a widower in New York at sixty was an odd experience. To "date" or "go out" at that age seemed slightly absurd, but it was certainly preferable to being alone. I became a rather busy "extra man" around town, and kind friends frequently tried to throw me together with desirable (in their eyes) eligible women. I preferred to make my own choices, and some of my experiences were warm and memorable. Then one evening at a large dinner I met a woman who struck me as exceptionally pretty. Her fine, piquant features, resembling one of those sleek, Egyptian cat sculptures, were enhanced by a small bandage on her upper lip, which formed a kind of beauty spot (it was the result, I later learned, of minor surgery). She was introduced as Louise, and I didn't quite catch her last name—in the party din it sounded like Melando or Machado, the latter vaguely familiar to me. Her face stayed in my mind, and a few days later I went to the *Time* morgue (by now politely known as the editorial reference department) to see if we had a file on her. As soon as I saw the picture of China Machado, identified as a well-known model, I realized that she was not the woman I had met at the party. Since I was then "seeing" the hostess of that evening, I felt that it would be tasteless to ask her the identity of the woman with the bandage. But a few months later, at another party, there she was again. She turned out to be Louise Melhado, and I found her delightful.

We started going to the theater and the opera. "I was flattered that you called me," she said years later. "You would phone me a week in advance and in the meantime you had been to China or had dinner with Margaret Thatcher."

We talked a lot, easily. She was that rarity, a native New Yorker, had gone to Spence, dropped out of Briarcliff College to go to work for *Vogue*. She started there as a secretary and became a fashion editor, working for several years under the legendary Diana Vreeland. "I was her pet," she once said. Louise had worked hard but managed to have a great time, running from Seventh Avenue to the magazine to various shoots, making friends with photographers like Horst and Penn. At night she went dancing, sleep being unimportant. At twenty she married tennis champion Dick Savitt (as a *Time* cover subject he had taken her to that anniversary bash at the Waldorf in 1963). The marriage broke up after two years. They had a son, Bobby, who grew up to be almost as good a tennis player as his father and as charming as his mother. Louise spent the sixties at considerable distance from the counterculture. She managed to combine the roles of a young mother and a popular girl about town, a permanent fixture on the best-dressed list and always in the right columns with the right people. In 1970 she married Frederick Melhado, a New York financier who was divorced with two young sons. I had met him briefly before I knew Louise and found him exuberant and amusing. The marriage lasted ten years. They remained friends, and the Melhado boys stayed very close to her.

When Louise and I met she had been divorced for five years. I realized that she was a version of those debutantes I had read about in the papers in my early twenties, an incarnation of that dream creature my friend at *Time* had named "Cicily Smythe-Heatherstone." Well, not quite. On our first trip together to St. Maarten, several months after we met, she surprised me by producing a large paper bag of sandwiches. She did not trust the airline food, even in first class. "You have to understand," she said, "that I have a refugee mentality." I took that as a joke, but when she told me her family's history I learned that there was at least a trace of truth in it.

Her maternal grandfather, Louis Adler, had come to the United

States from Russia as a young boy, alone. He had left home because his widowed father had married a woman Louis could not abide. That grandfather was the refugee in her background. Until she told me about him, I had not realized that she was Jewish. After his arrival in New York, in classic immigrant fashion he went to work in a shirt factory at $3 a week. One day when he found that his pay envelope contained $5, he took it to his boss, thinking a mistake had been made. "Poor me," he said later. "How was I to know that it was a raise?" "Poor me" became his nickname.

The American dream scenario took over: Louis ended up as a major real estate developer. On Seventh Avenue he constructed two outstanding buildings, 530 and 550, at the heart of the garment district, which would become part of his granddaughter's beat as a *Vogue* fashion editor. There were other buildings, including the U.S. Customs Court (he finished that project ahead of schedule and under budget and astounded the government by returning the remaining money). He was an intense American patriot, impatient with unassimilated Jews. "They're in America," he would say. "They should be Americans." Setting up a charitable foundation on his seventy-fifth birthday, he said that he wanted to repay his country "in a small measure."

Louise's paternal grandfather, Herman Liberman, came from much older, German immigrant stock. The Libermans had been in America for several generations, had made money on Wall Street, were part of what Stephen Birmingham called "Our Crowd"—and what Louise came to refer to as "Mayfair Judea." Like most of that set, the Libermans looked down on recent immigrants, especially from Eastern Europe, and were not delighted when Herman Jr. married Ruth Adler, daughter of the former shirt maker from Russia. But such snobbery was overcome by the considerable Adler fortune, and by Ruth herself. According to all accounts she was beautiful, smart, an outstanding student at Wellesley, witty, ironic. Louise's father was on the floor of the stock exchange, dashing, a ladies' man. After their divorce Ruth remarried twice. She had a weak heart and died when she was only forty-nine.

Herman's eccentric hobby was to walk through every Manhattan street (502 miles) and take photos of all houses of worship he passed, beginning with the Shrine of Our Lady of the Rosary at State Street and Minuit Plaza. In seven years he photographed 889 churches, synagogues, mosques and Buddhist and Hindu temples. He died of lung cancer in 1973.

I was immensely drawn to Louise's joie de vivre, which seemed to reflect what I'd heard about her mother. As we came to know each other better, I realized that she had far deeper qualities than were apparent from her sometimes flippant manner, which she described as her butterfly side. One evening over dinner she told me earnestly that the most important quality in people was goodness. She knew that it was difficult, she continued, for successful men to be good—"their ego, their power, their minions bowing at the waist, get in the way. But you never seem to have lost your goodness." The word and the thought were curiously old-fashioned and touching. Later she told a friend about me: "He didn't take me to the World Series or Wimbledon, and he didn't look like Sidney Poitier, so he must have had some secret." The secret, she explained to me eventually, was that I was so nice. "Freddy Melhado laughed me into marriage. You niced me into it." At an earlier stage in my life, I might have felt put down by this description, but now I gladly accepted it. "Besides," she added, "there were one or two other traits in your favor."

The marriage did not happen all that quickly. I was concerned that I was nineteen years older, and Louise must have been, too, although she gallantly argued that this didn't matter. I was also troubled by something else: while I had made what seemed like an outrageous amount of money for a journalist, she was a lot richer. But I knew that I loved her and wanted to be with her. We started to share Louise's apartment, just around the corner from mine. One day I wrote a letter proposing marriage and left it for her to find. We were married on May 1, 1987, in a small ceremony at our apartment. My son, Peter, was my best man. Bobby Short played (he was an old friend of hers, and she had asked him on a sudden inspiration only the night before). We started our honeymoon in Moscow, which she had always wanted to see.

In many ways she and I are an odd couple, but our contrasting character traits complement each other. She is invincibly gregarious, while I tend to be reserved. She can converse with a Trappist monk or a totem pole, while I must make an effort with strangers. The telephone is a way of life to her, an extension of sociability, while I consider it strictly an instrument of communication. She cannot wait to discard things— newspapers, letters—while I find it painful to throw anything away. Her generally cheerful mood can quickly swing to the opposite, while I tend to be even-tempered. She is impatient, while I have gradually acquired patience. She hates new gadgets (for years she mourned the passing of the dial telephone), while I dote on them. She is a formidable organizer who could run an army (a friend nicknamed her Norma Schwarzkopf) and a relentless advance planner who starts Christmas shopping in February, while I have to force myself not to put things off. She makes quick, firm judgments on almost anything, while I ponder. She is generous with advice (usually preceded by the signal words "Let me tell you something . . ."), while I hesitate to offer counsel.

I discovered early on that she was insecure about not having finished college (when we met she was taking courses on Irish playwrights and art history). Yet she has an excellent mind, an impressive, detailed knowledge of art and an immense appetite for history, from ancient Egypt to Bismarck's Germany. She has great taste and is not exactly averse to luxury, but she also enjoys the simplest pleasures, such as food at coffee shops, an inclination I do not understand. A diamond ring delights her no more (and possibly less) than a good-looking piece of junk jewelry bought at a flea market, and she does not hesitate to bargain. "If I buy a dozen of these, shouldn't there be a dollar off each?" She has a huge gift for friendship. "Perhaps I could have had the big career," she once said, "but my friends are my career."

When she first met my children she was put off by their memories of the Family on the Hill. How could a new wife fit into this picture? She created a new picture and invited them into it. They understood that she was very different from their mother, and they accepted her on her own terms. They also saw that she was making me happy. Louise and I established a balance between our lives, symbolized by our sharing her house in Southampton, where she had spent summers since childhood, and mine in Martha's Vineyard, where my family and I had vacationed for nearly three decades.

M<small>Y CAREER AT</small> Time Inc. was approaching its end. I was due to retire on December 31, 1987. My last two or three years seemed more than usually filled with outside activities—speeches, panels, conferences. There was a round of festivities involving anniversaries of one magazine or the other. There were *Time* cover exhibits ranging from London to Hollywood, where I enjoyed seeing some old acquaintances, notably Shirley MacLaine. We had first met in 1959, when *Time* did a cover story about her. She had declared then: "But it's too soon!" Now she said: "The first time they just showcased my face. For the '84 cover they showcased my entire body. Maybe when I'm sixty-five they'll photograph my mind." Her mind would have made quite a photograph. I remembered having dinner with her in New York when she was her usually irrepressible, upbeat self. Halfway through the meal she said that she was finishing another book. I asked politely what it was about, and she replied as nonchalantly as if talking about acting or travel: "Oh, it's about my past lives." I thought she was joking but soon realized that she was in dead earnest about having been, among many other incarnations, a Spanish infanta, a Russian ballet dancer, an eleven-year-old Inca boy with a gift of the third eye. A Mongolian bandit she encountered in an earlier life, she said, was actually her mother. I told her that people would think her crazy (I did myself), but she was sublimely unconcerned. The book, of course, became a best-seller and established her as America's leading time traveler.

"You're having all these celebrations," a friend of Clare Luce's told me one day. "Don't you think you might do something for Clare?" She was then eighty-two and feeling a little frail, I gathered, and could use an acknowledgment of who she was and had been. I arranged a dinner for her in Washington's F Street Club. The guests included the president and Nancy Reagan. Clare hardly seemed frail and was beautiful and witty as usual. At her behest somebody had tracked down my old friend

Lucian Heichler to get background information for the inevitable toast. He recalled that soon after my arrival in the United States I told him: "I've always wanted to be a writer and now here I am in this country where I don't know the language!" Clare noted that I had overcome that hurdle and added: "While he was learning it millions of native-born Americans were becoming increasingly unable to use *their 'Mutter-sprache'* [mother tongue] correctly." She ended by toasting three Henrys, her husband, her stepson and myself—"Henry the father, Henry the son and Henry the Holy Ghost." It was certainly the only time that anyone compared me to a part of the Trinity.

The dinner was really a farewell. Louise and I saw her several times afterward, but she died of cancer in 1987. She was combative and flirtatious almost to the end. Living in a sense between eras, she was a feminist who nevertheless relied heavily on strong men. Looking back, I realized that her versatility—journalist, playwright, politician, proselytizer—meant that she had not pursued any one career to the fullest. But the mixture was stunning.

ONE OF MY major preoccupations in those final years was to arrange for my succession, which, under the Donovan Constitution, was up to me. Ralph Graves, two years younger than I, had decided to retire early in 1983. To replace Ralph as my deputy, I moved up Ray Cave and appointed Jason McManus managing editor of *Time.* If I were to follow the Time Inc. tradition of choosing the next editor in chief from within, the selection, in my view, came down to these two. Cave was the more imaginative and energetic editor, who had done an excellent job on *Time* for eight years, but his personality had become even more abrasive. On the thirty-fourth floor, far from settling calmly into the outwardly serene atmosphere, he became very combative toward the business side. McManus had a far better way with people. In September 1986 I lunched with my fellow directors (the editor in chief was then a member of the board). I offered my views of the two contenders, making it fairly clear that I would recommend McManus but not giving a final commitment. I thought I would do so about midyear 1987, which I considered a fairly standard timetable. Munro, however, wanted the decision sooner because he was terrified that I might pick Cave. More and more often he dropped into my office, asking for my decision. I resented the pressure. Munro started a campaign against Cave with the board that was offensive and unnecessary. On April 16 I told the board and Munro of my decision to name McManus.

I looked toward my retirement with some dread. My work had been so much a part of my life, my identity, that I wondered who I would be without it. Louise told me later, "You started talking about this from the moment we met." After their exits Donovan and Heiskell had kept consulting contracts, office space and secretaries. But Munro, in a display of business machismo and cost-cutting prowess, was impatient with such arrangements. He would later ask Heiskell to pay rent for his office space. As for me, I was offered an office for one year, and McManus invited me to contribute occasional essays to *Time*. I would do so later. But I made other plans, negotiating with a newspaper syndicate to do a column and talking to publishers about books that I might write. Then in June 1987 came a call from the White House. On the line was Howard Baker, Reagan's chief of staff, whom I had known casually for years. We exchanged pleasantries until, in his amiable, butterscotch voice, he said: "I'm calling to ask whether you might be interested in a diplomatic assignment."

I was surprised but asked: "What have you got in mind?"

"Vienna," he said.

THIS WAS THE penultimate year of the Reagan era. Looking back over 1987, I realized that it constituted a kind of summing up of trends and portents. A continuing political puritanism, with the press playing Cotton Mather: Gary Hart, a promising presidential candidate, was brought down by the revelation that he had been cheating on his wife. (What made the incident reprehensible was that he had positively challenged the press to catch him and then complained when it did.) The substitution of fear for morality: the AIDS epidemic caused a new appreciation of monogamy or even abstinence. Failing that, there was "safe sex" and condoms advertised for the first time on TV. The growing laboratory approach to the creation of life: the legal fight for Baby M (claimed by her surrogate mother, who had been artificially inseminated) and the bizarre issue of whether frozen embryos stood to inherit their donors' property. The rise and fall of Wall Street: the Dow peaked at 2722 on August 25 and lost 508 points on October 19, the worst drop in history. The decline was not permanent, but it damaged forever the image of those youngish Wall Street operators who became instant multimillionaires. Yuppies may not have been all that different from any other ambitious, rising generations, but I sometimes suspected that real estate had actually replaced sex as the major yuppie passion. After the October crash the designer water began to taste bitter and many BMWs had to be sold or were repossessed.

Ronald Reagan was widely seen as the patron saint of the yuppies, presiding over what had already become known as the "decade of greed." Everything from the horrendous savings and loan scandal (bipartisan in origin) to the wave of takeovers and leveraged buyouts to Michael Milken's junk bond schemes to ostentatious bar mitzvahs was blamed on Reaganism and its celebration of profit. I thought that was a considerable oversimplification. Unquestionably some Reagan policies and much rhetoric contributed to the atmosphere. But as author Charles Murray put it later: "You can't have sustained, sizable economic growth without producing something very like the phenomena that have gotten journalists so upset about greed and selfishness. Economic growth means that a lot of people get rich." The outcries about greed also overlooked the unprecedented increase in charitable giving and the turbulence caused by worldwide trends, including the evident failure of the welfare state and the continued growth of the global market. Still, the age-old questions of where legitimate gain ends and excessive greed begins and how capitalist incentives can be blended with a measure of social justice would torment the United States well beyond the eighties.

I had always kept my distance from all administrations, beyond what I considered legitimate contacts to gain information and impressions, and was hardly close to the Reagan White House. But after Nancy

Reagan's surprise appearance at my birthday party, we were occasionally in touch. She seemed to enjoy talking politics with me, sometimes on the phone, sometimes at a public function. She was smart and well informed. She had been criticized, especially during her early years in the White House, for being extravagant, capricious and too close to a glitzy Los Angeles crowd. She herself felt, she once told me, that she served as a kind of whipping girl for critics who did not dare attack the popular president. As for her influence in the White House, she had worked for the rather belated dismissal of Don Regan, Reagan's abrasive and obtuse chief of staff between 1985 and 1987. She also wanted Reagan to get rid of Ed Meese and failed, as she did in trying to persuade her husband to soften his stance against abortion. On policy in general, she did not push her own agenda but passed along the views of the pragmatists like James Baker and Michael Deaver. Fiercely protective of "Ronnie," she recognized the danger of his overoptimism and tried to provide balance.

On the occasions I saw Reagan himself, he was, as usual, charming and serene. Delivering the first of a series of speeches sponsored by *Time* at Illinois's Eureka College, from which he had graduated half a century before, he was eloquent on the subject of freedom and the decline of statism. He quoted Jean-François Revel, F. Scott Fitzgerald and Whittaker Chambers. But what I found most memorable was his easy presence on that small, elm-shaded campus, speaking in the gym that had been named for him and mingling with students and alumni afterward over the coffee urn. As I stood talking to Reagan, recalling my past connection with Whittaker Chambers, people came up to him easily; he managed to be both presidential and unpretentious. Some years later, at a farewell party given for the Reagans by Katharine Graham, I collided with Nancy and dropped my drink to the floor. Instantly, out of the corner of my eye, I saw a dark-clad figure stooping to pick up the glass. I was thinking, Kay really has a well-trained staff, when I realized that it was the president.

I never found it easy to talk to him about issues because he was given to repeating his famous anecdotes or pat formulas. At one White House dinner he stunned me by saying in all earnestness: "Do you realize that if every business in America could be persuaded to add only one worker, there would be no unemployment?" Another time, defending himself against charges that he had run up the deficit spectacularly, he said: "The president doesn't spend money, Congress does." True enough, but hardly the whole story. Nevertheless he was far shrewder than his critics allowed. His vagueness about facts, his reliance on those prompt cards, were familiar. Thus it always came as something of a surprise when he showed that he knew what he was talking about and, above all, what he wanted. Anatoly Dobrynin, the longtime Soviet ambassador in Washington who had dealt with six U.S. presidents, would later write that Reagan was no figurehead: "He grasped matters in an instinctive way but not necessarily in a simple one, and Americans often failed to realize the complexity of his character."

True, he was apt to ignore details, and this became something of a defense in the Iran-contra scandal that marred his second term. It was obvious that despite denials, the top people in the White House knew what was going on. I was also sure that Reagan himself must have had at least an inkling. I suspected that he had tried not to know too much and that his staff involved him as little as possible. Reagan later made an extraordinary statement that managed to assume and shirk responsibility at the same time. "A few months ago," he said, "I told the American people I did not trade arms for hostages. My heart and best intentions still tell me this is true, but the facts and evidence tell me it is not." He was instrumental in bringing about a new relationship with the Soviet Union, partly thanks to Gorbachev, but also thanks to his mixture of toughness and accommodation.

Domestically, on balance, I now felt that he had accomplished, at best, half a revolution. He succeeded only in a limited way to curb government power and spending, cutting discretionary programs but unable or unwilling to tackle middle-class entitlements and other sacrosanct categories in the budget. But, like Margaret Thatcher in Britain, he did manage to change the terms of the economic and political debate.

He restored the aura and authority of the presidency (not permanently, as it would turn out). As the first two-term president since Eisenhower, he was often compared with Ike and would leave office with a 5 percent higher approval rating. "Ike came into office with the status of a genuine national hero," commented political scientist Richard Neustadt, "and merely had to preserve that aura. Reagan came in only with what he had on his back and had to create his stature." I touched on this point during a social lunch with Nancy Reagan early in 1987. She was talking about "Ronnie's" successor and made it clear that she did not much care for George Bush. She wished it could be Paul Laxalt, senator from Nevada and a great Reagan friend, although she realized he had no chance. Referring to the subject of Reagan's unfinished agenda, I said: "I sometimes think it will take a Democratic president to carry out your husband's program. Or, if not exactly his program, some set of conservative policies."

"You are talking about the Nixon-in-China principle," she said. And I agreed. "Well," she continued, "I hope you're wrong." I remembered this conversation years later when a Democratic president, Bill Clinton, proposed cuts in government spending and welfare reform of the kind Reagan could never have gotten away with.

WHEN I RECEIVED that phone call from Howard Baker, I immediately suspected Nancy's hand, although I had not made the slightest effort to gain such an appointment or even hinted at it. I felt I could not be considered for an ambassadorship because I lacked political clout and certainly was not a contributor to the Republican Party (or to the Democrats, for that matter). Much later I learned what had happened. One day, without my knowledge, my friends Dick Clurman and Mike Wallace were talking about what I would do after my retirement. The idea came up (they were not sure who thought of it first) that I might make a good ambassador to Austria, a post that was then vacant. Mike called his friend Nancy and suggested it to her.

Initially I was skeptical about Baker's offer. Vienna was a minor post. Moreover it promised trouble; U.S.-Austrian relations were vexed by the

controversy over President Kurt Waldheim, and Jewish organizations
were much concerned about who would be the new American ambassador to his country. It could be argued that under the circumstances a
Jew, and a refugee from Austria at that, was not the right choice because
of what might be called a conflict of emotional interest. But acting on
that objection would disavow my status as an American citizen and as a
reasonably dispassionate observer. After two weeks of thinking about it,
and discussing it with Louise and my children, I decided that a return to
my native city, from which I had been expelled by the Nazis, was too
compelling to turn down. As a colleague of mine, Ron Sheppard, wrote
to me: "The symmetry is extraordinary."

Given the Waldheim situation, I was under strong pressure from the
White House not to discuss the pending appointment. I had planned to
resign as editor in chief after it was official. But when the news leaked,
Munro, McManus and others felt that I should quit immediately, and I
did so in mid-August. The continuing Waldheim controversy still caused
me some misgivings. One of the people I consulted about it was Elie
Wiesel. "You must do it," he said. After a serious talk in which he
argued that I could make a difference in the job, he added jokingly:
"Besides, it will be great for a book."

I moved out of my office to make room for my successor, Jason
McManus, and established temporary quarters on another floor. It felt
remote, like exile. I spent most of my time trying to clean out and
organize my files, which was a hopeless task. My whole career seemed
jammed into rows of metal cabinets, most of the folders marked more or
less neatly by date and subject, others marked in cryptic scrawls—"first
drafts," "speech notes," "souvenirs." Nostalgia rose from the file drawers
along with the particles of crumbling paper. I found it irresistible to
browse. A copy of my first personnel record as a part-time copy boy. My
early *Time* stories, clipped and pasted in a scrapbook—a practice I gave
up after a few years. Records of raises and promotions. A batch of
medical reports from the company doctor, regularly, year after year,
recommending some weight loss. Ribald doggerel by my long-ago colleague Roger Hewlett ("Oh, Bishop Sheen, Oh Bishop Sheen. You're the

best man in a dress I've ever seen . . ."). A long memorandum to
Robert Manning, for many years a *Time* writer and editor, trying to
explain why I had mangled (in his view) his cover story on Ernest
Hemingway; it was, I suggested, too worshipful. Memos arguing policy
points. Memos correcting grammar. Memos in salute of departing colleagues, the office equivalent of obituaries. Pictures and more pictures:
myself in Vietnam wearing fatigues and in China struggling up the
Great Wall; hanging on to a reindeer in Lapland; drinking at office
parties; interviewing American presidents (one photo showed me with
Gerald Ford as I impatiently and unforgivably looked at my wristwatch). Budgets. Masses of clips on the Sharon case. And "notes to
myself" on countless topics. I was in danger of keeping up this browsing
for days. Fortunately practical matters intervened, especially filling out
endless forms in preparation for becoming a cog in the federal government.

At the inevitable transition dinner marking Jason's ascension and my
departure, amid all the good fellowship and nostalgia I pronounced a
few warnings. I suggested that publishing magazines mostly for advertisers was wrong and that it was equally wrong to bribe customers to
buy magazines by giving away cameras, telephones and other premiums.
I paid tribute to my business colleagues for never trying to tell me what
to print or not to print but suggested that the church-state system was
not working, especially when it came to new ventures, because we
lacked a unified vision. I also recalled that I had attempted to keep our
magazines in the political center, in contrast with the occasionally shrill
conservatism of our past. I urged my successors not to go to the opposite
extreme and become automatically liberal, because a predictable magazine is a boring magazine. "We are all editors," I said. "We edit when
we tell our children what happened at the office today or what a new
movie was like or what a witness said at the latest congressional hearings. . . . After all these years as a journalist, I am more awed than
ever by the responsibility we have in editing reality, in what we leave
out and what we include. . . ."

Apart from such solemn notes there was a lot of hilarity during the evening, especially about my new venture. Stefan Kanfer announced: "I was the one who found the ad that Henry answered, which is why we're here tonight. It was in *Stern* and reads: *'Wenn Sie das lesen können, dann können Sie eine gute Stellung im Ausland bekommen,'* which means: 'If you can read this, you can get a good job overseas.' And he did."

I was not necessarily leaving journalism forever, but I kept thinking a great deal about the craft I had chosen—or that had chosen me. Ever since I had given up my ambition to be a playwright, I had been happy to be a journalist. It was great work, a pass to all the world, almost never boring, rewarding curiosity and enterprise. It was also important to democracy. But two qualities about journalism had often disturbed me. One was superficiality. Yes, there were specialists, but most reporters and virtually all editors had to be generalists, knowing a little about a lot. I had often felt uneasy passing judgment on stories about nuclear physics or the validity of the Laffer curve. Sometimes I yearned to be a full-time, thoroughgoing authority on something—Renaissance bronzes or the Middle Ages. But if I had really wanted to be that kind of an expert, I told myself, I would have tried it.

Another aspect about journalism that troubled me was the feeling that proximity to statesmen, politicians, artists, all kinds of celebrities, somehow put one on a par with them. This was a dangerous illusion. A journalist must never forget that he is only an observer and, almost by definition, an outsider. Deep commitment to a cause is laudable in anyone else, but in a journalist it is not permissible. We are supposed to try to be objective, however elusive that goal. We are also in a hurry. We concentrate on a subject, an event, a personality, for a while and then move on. I was especially aware of this because of my personal history. For years after coming to the United States I felt myself something of an outsider. So the outsider role of a journalist gave me a kind of protective coloration. It allowed me to be in a place or in a situation for professional reasons. I thought that perhaps this suggested a parallel with show business. The performer must have an almost tangible contact with the audience, but he still remains remote and in a sense protected. All of journalism contains elements of show business, not because it is artifice, but because it must seize and hold the public's attention. As a performer, as an editor-showman, I had had quite a good run, along with some flops. I knew, as I moved to other work, I would miss the audience. I would miss the smell of the printers' ink and the roar of the press.

PART NINE

ENCORE

IN

VIENNA

CHAPTER THIRTY-EIGHT

"M̲r̲. A̲m̲b̲a̲s̲s̲a̲d̲o̲r̲ T̲a̲n̲t̲a̲m̲o̲u̲n̲t̲!" said George Shultz in a cheery voice over the telephone. The expression sounded like a character out of Gilbert and Sullivan. Shultz was telling me that my nomination was about to be official and that I would soon hear from the president to that effect. I asked him whether, given the Waldheim situation, there might be opposition from U.S. Jewish leaders. Shultz did not think so but advised me to talk to some of them.

Waldheim. I remembered him well from his time as UN secretary general, when the greatest threat he seemed to represent was boredom. I found him pleasant enough but without imagination or unusual insights. He was sometimes criticized as being too pro-Arab. Having returned to Austria at the end of his two terms as secretary general, he ran for president in 1986 on the ticket of the Conservative Volkspartei (People's Party). The Austrian president is largely a figurehead, but his election does give an indication of popular sentiment. During the campaign, with the Socialists trailing, incendiary charges emerged in the Austrian and afterward the U.S. press. During World War II, it was reported, Waldheim had been attached to German army units in the Balkans that had been guilty of atrocities, including deportation of Jews. Waldheim had apparently falsified, or only partly stated, his record. In his defense, Waldheim said that he had been a mere lieutenant acting mostly as a translator, without any command authority, and that he had not been involved in or aware of any war crimes.

Thereafter the Austrian election campaign took on a nasty, occasionally anti-Semitic, tinge. Many Austrians who were proud of Waldheim's international prominence resented what they regarded as outside—especially Jewish—interference in their election. But many others believed the charges. When Waldheim insisted that he had never been a party member but had felt obligated to join a Nazi youth group and a riding club, a leading Socialist politician observed: "I guess he means to say that he has never been a Nazi, only his horse was." The remark inspired a well-known Austrian sculptor, Alfred Hrdlicka, to construct a large wooden horse wearing a Nazi cap. A group of left-wing Socialists began to take it to Waldheim rallies, which annoyed him to the point of tears. In the United States the case against Waldheim continued to be propelled by the World Jewish Congress, which consisted of a small headquarters group in New York and fifty member organizations of varying size in other countries; it was headed and largely financed by Edgar Bronfman, the chief of Seagram. I remembered him from those *Time* News Tours, and other occasions around New York, as fun loving, affable and bright; but now he had emerged as a serious Jewish leader who was received with deference by heads of state. As the Waldheim controversy grew, a relatively unfamiliar term appeared: watch list.

In the decades following World War II the press occasionally reported that a suspected onetime concentration camp guard or other former Nazi was found in some cozy U.S. suburb. But nothing much happened until an earnest, ambitious young congresswoman from New York, Elizabeth Holtzman, grew indignant. In 1978 she introduced an amendment to the U.S. immigration law. It barred from admission to the United States any alien who ordered, incited, assisted or otherwise participated in the persecution of any person during World War II because of race, religion, national origin or political opinion. Such people were to be placed on the "watch list" of undesirable aliens, requiring a joint decision by the Justice and State Departments. Since the amendment's passage it had been applied in only a handful of cases. Following the accusations against Waldheim, there was great pressure in Congress and elsewhere to put the Austrian president on the list. In the Justice Department the Office of Special Investigations, charged with tracking down war criminals, started a year-long inquiry into the Waldheim record. Judge Abraham Sofaer, by now reincarnated as the State Department's legal adviser, read the report early in April 1987 and concurred with its recommendation that Waldheim should be cited. "Do it," George Shultz said, according to notes taken by aides. "It's long overdue." Shultz felt that Attorney General Ed Meese was moving too slowly and expected the State Department to keep Waldheim off the list on foreign policy grounds. "No way," said Shultz. "That would be a travesty." The U.S. ambassador to Vienna, Ronald Lauder, had been largely left in the dark. In May he went to see Shultz to complain and insistently asked who had written the report and when. Shultz told Lauder he should get his information from the legal adviser's office, and as Shultz recollected it, asked him to leave.

The watch list decision was widely resented in Austria, and it helped Waldheim win a decisive majority (53.9 percent). During the run up to the election, in June 1986 *Time*'s international edition had published a Waldheim cover story, which I read before it went to press. The story was cautious about the evidence as it was then known. To my mind the affair ranked very low among world events. But as the story pointed out, it mattered greatly to Austrians, who felt that not only Waldheim but their country stood accused of trying to conceal their role in the horrors of Nazism. *Time*'s cover line was "The Art of Forgetting."

I met with Edgar Bronfman and several associates, including Israel Singer, secretary general of the World Jewish Congress, U.S.-born son of Austrian refugees and graduate of a rabbinical school. Bronfman was thoughtful and sounded more moderate than some of his associates. The issue, he argued, was not Waldheim personally, but the danger that whitewashing him would trivialize the Holocaust. Austria, he said, had never really faced up to its past. But there was general agreement that a distinction must be made between Waldheim and his country. The group, I found, was extremely hostile to anyone who even mildly defended Waldheim. That included Simon Wiesenthal, whom I had sought out when he visited New York. The famous "Nazi hunter," aging but indefatigable, said that he considered Waldheim not a war criminal but a liar. Those criticized also included an old acquaintance of mine, the noted publisher George Weidenfeld, a fellow Viennese who had been in school with Waldheim at the time of the Anschluss. When, as a Jew, Weidenfeld could no longer attend classes, young Waldheim regularly brought him the assignments so he could keep up his studies. Weidenfeld was convinced that Waldheim had not been a Nazi. Bronfman and Singer were scathing about both Wiesenthal and Weidenfeld and equally negative about several Jewish organizations. Rabbi Marc Tanenbaum, one of the leaders of the American Jewish Committee, was described as "two-faced like Talleyrand," and Singer dismissed his ideas with a Viennese slang word *Schmee* or, roughly, malarkey. (When I saw Tanenbaum, he, in turn, described Singer as a *yeshiva bocher*—a boy in a Jewish religious school—suddenly translated into the world of power and private jets, with kosher meals.) Such internecine bickering did not change one fact: the Jewish community approved the watch list decision and so, apparently, did a majority of the U.S. public.

Early in December I went before the Senate Foreign Relations Committee for my confirmation hearing in Room 419, Dirksen Senate Office Building. Given the number of ambassadors that had to be confirmed every year, I marveled at the flow of ceremonial words that filled the occasion. I had been prepared for the hearing by my State Department handlers, but I chose to write my own introductory statement. I had been tempted to say that Austria was an important unimportant country but thought better of it. Austria, I said instead, was more significant than its size indicated because of its geopolitical location at the crossroads of East and West and especially at this moment of tremors in Eastern Europe. I suggested that Austria was a Western success story because of its solid economic recovery after World War II, its establishment of viable democracy and, not least, because it was the only place the Soviets ever left voluntarily (after the conclusion of the state treaty in 1955). On the subject of Waldheim, I briefly used the formula that I had discussed with Shultz and others in the State Department: despite the irrevocable watch list decision, I would work to maintain our traditional warm relations with Austria, based on many common interests.

The quizzing by the senators was mild. The only discord was provided by Jesse Helms. Peering at me through his round glasses that gave him a perpetually astonished look, he began by recalling a 1981 *Time* cover story that noted there were few books in his living room. Our reporters, he said sarcastically, had overlooked the fact that there was a library upstairs. "So tell them to come back, and I will lend them any books that I have." He then confronted me with a *Foreign Affairs* article in which I had been partly critical of Reagan foreign policy and had written that in certain situations it was necessary to make deals with the Russians, trading concession for concession. Helms thought this signified a dangerous compromise of America's moral role in the world, and we fenced about that for a while. He then launched into a general, rambling attack on the Soviet Union, stressing the case of the Korean Airlines plane that had been shot down by the Russians, killing 269 passengers, an act he described as premeditated murder. He had almost been on that plane himself, he related dramatically, before switching to another flight. For a while both planes had been on the ground in Alaska, and he had met many of the doomed passengers, including two little girls from Rochester, New York, whom he'd held on his lap. It was a fairly gripping story, but it was hard to see what it had to do with me or Austria. Given Helms's habit of browbeating witnesses or holding nominations hostage, he was tame. He even wound up with a rather sensitive flourish: "I know it must be a sentimental journey to go to Austria, even though America is your country. But you are bound to have some feelings about the land of your forebears."

Before I could start that journey, I had to take an unsentimental trip through the State Department maze. Each State Department office felt it had to leave an imprint on a new ambassador, from management, which provided lectures on efficiency, to security, which detailed the dangers of terrorism (I was fitted for a bulletproof vest, which I would never wear). Among the other agencies, Commerce was eloquent on the need to help U.S. business abroad, and the CIA offered a briefing that included a display of rather simple James Bond–ian gadgets, such as a boot containing a microphone. I assumed that more sophisticated stuff was withheld, despite the elaborate security clearance I had undergone (the FBI had even sent agents to Martha's Vineyard, asking neighbors, among other things, whether they had ever observed me drunk). Along with useful advice and sensible rules from the State Department, there were ludicrous instructions: "Report any cohabitation with a foreign national within one month of the date cohabitation begins. . . . Relationships involving continuing romantic or sexual intimacy without cohabitation are reportable when the employee determines that it is, in fact, a continuing relationship."

The most important part of my preparations involved the Justice Department report on which the watch list decision was based. I called on its principal author, Neal Sher, the director of the Justice Department's Office of Special Investigations. He was forty, born after the gruesome events in which he was now steeped, and he struck me as intense and driven. In his mind there was no statute of limitations for war criminals. "The passage of time," he had said, "does not mitigate what they have done." I had to get special permission to see his report. Only a few copies existed, one of them in a safe in Abraham Sofaer's office.

We had an odd reunion, reminiscing about the Sharon case. Sofaer was a little hazy about it, like a general not quite remembering the details of a long-ago battle. I was not allowed to take the Waldheim document from the office and read its two-hundred-plus pages in two sittings, taking notes. It was a painstaking description of the several German military units in which Lieutenant Waldheim had served between 1942 and 1945 in the Balkan theater and the operations these units had carried out. They included reprisals against partisans, execution of civilians, deportation of Jews and others. The report's main effort was to tie Waldheim personally to these atrocities.

As I read I was struck by two aspects. One was a polemical tone and occasional sarcasm, especially about the defenses that Waldheim had advanced, which struck me as unusual in a legal document. The other was the frequent use of phrases such as "it is difficult to escape the conclusion," "it is entirely possible" and "he may well have." Nevertheless the report was thoroughly persuasive that "there can be no legitimate doubt that Waldheim's role as an interpreter, staff intelligence

officer, and staff operations officer . . . was in no way insignificant."
While there could be questions about his involvement in specific actions,
there was ample evidence that he transmitted orders, handled documents and attended briefings that made him aware of what was going
on. I concluded, and this was later confirmed by legal experts I consulted, that there was no adequate proof that he was a war criminal by
Nuremberg standards, nor did the report claim he was. But he clearly
"assisted or otherwise participated" in persecution as stated by the
broadly worded Holtzman amendment. The same was undoubtedly true
of hundreds if not thousands of other officers in the German army, but
they did not happen to become secretary general of the UN or president
of Austria. The most telling fact was this: If Waldheim's Balkan service
was as harmless as he claimed, there would have been no reason to
systematically suppress that part of his military record. He later said
that the facts had always been on file at the Austrian Foreign Office, but
he consistently omitted them in accounts of his career. Waldheim got
away with this not by cleverness, but because he benefited from bureaucratic inattention and his almost overwhelming ordinariness. There was
simply nothing menacing in this former lieutenant—whom unkind critics described as looking like a headwaiter. When Waldheim sought a job
at the Austrian Foreign Office his application went to an overburdened
denazification commission whose reports were endlessly delayed; impatient, the foreign minister, after a desultory check of his own, finally
went ahead and appointed Waldheim as a career foreign service officer.
His acceptability was assumed from then on.

In January 1988 I was sworn in by George Shultz, with Nancy Reagan making another surprise appearance. In his remarks Shultz told the
story of former senator Mike Mansfield, then ambassador to Japan, who
on one occasion had placed his hand on a globe, covering the outline of
the United States, and said: "This is my country." I responded: "I felt
that way when I first set foot on these shores nearly fifty years ago, and
I feel that way as I leave for Austria."

Louise, my children and a few friends were present. Sadly missing
was my sister, Meta. She had been overjoyed at the news of my appointment. As she and her husband spent half of each year in Vienna, we had

both looked forward to being together there, revisiting some of our old haunts and dissecting the current scene. Just before Thanksgiving, Meta died in her sleep of a heart attack. We had been very close, and I had always taken comfort in her love and her goodness. I was devastated by her death, which would shadow my entire time in Vienna.

FIVE DAYS AFTER my arrival I found myself in front of the old Imperial Burg, now the residence of the Austrian president. A detachment of the Guards Battalion was lined up, and the duty officer shouted: "Honor Guard, Attention! Present arms!" The band struck up a march. One of the instruments was a large drum, carried by a pony. I learned later that the Austrian army had two ponies, Donner and Blitz (Thunder and Lightning), and on this occasion it was Donner's turn. I thought he looked a little bored. In morning coat and striped trousers, involuntarily beating time to the march tempo with the gloves I carried, I strode past the row of parade-straight, steel-helmeted soldiers, their heads turning and their eyes following me as I passed. They were barely out of their teens, but I could not help thinking—however unfairly—that they looked no different from the Austrian Storm Troopers whom I had seen and feared in my youth. The duty officer shouted again: "Excellency, Captain Bruno Gebauer requests permission to withdraw." Accompanied by the embassy's deputy chief of mission and the political officer, I was then led upstairs, crossed several magnificent reception rooms and faced Waldheim, who was smiling expectantly while photographers flashed away. I presented my "letters of credence," omitting, as suggested by the State Department, the customary personal greeting from the president of the United States. My daughter Mandy, a political consultant, had told me: "Daddy, when you shake hands with him, don't smile. You shouldn't be photographed that way." It is remarkably difficult to keep a neutral face when confronted with an insistent grin. But I realized that I managed it when I saw the photograph of the meeting, in which I looked stern, if not grim. People in America and Austria mentioned that picture to me for years, and I became convinced that it did more than a dozen speeches to signal the official U.S. attitude. Back downstairs I stood at attention for the Stars and Stripes and the Austrian national anthem. I had expected the lovely old Haydn melody but found that it had been replaced by what struck me as a slow, boring tune (I was shocked to discover later that it was by Mozart, whom I worship).

On the way back to the embassy I watched the streets through the car windows, finding them both familiar and strange. I had been in Vienna briefly several times since that first postwar trip, when the city still showed scars of war and despair. On each visit after that it had appeared a little more prosperous, and now it looked affluent, comfortable, resolutely untragic. I kept thinking about those young soldiers and about their fathers and grandfathers, part of the generation that had helped drive me and my family out of the country and so many others to death. Now I was riding in the embassy limousine, with the American flag fluttering in front. But there was little time for such musings. I had to get down to work.

I REMEMBERED THE famous saying by the seventeenth-century poet and diplomat Sir Henry Wotton: "An ambassador is an honest man who goes abroad to lie for his country." But he added that a journalist is a "dishonest man who stays at home to lie for himself." I thought of this canard as I began to experience the differences between my past and my present occupations. As an ambassador it is not absolutely necessary to lie—in fact, it is dangerous—but it is advisable not always to tell the whole truth. Journalists usually say more than they know, while diplomats are expected to say less than they know. As a journalist my main task was to get information. That was my task as an ambassador as well (for a far more limited audience). But unlike a journalist, an ambassador also has to be a government spokesman, a pleader for policy, an influence peddler.

Diplomacy was big business in Vienna. Among many other international institutions Vienna housed a branch of the United Nations; the Conference on Security and Cooperation in Europe (CSCE), which was trying to write a treaty about collective security and human rights, among other issues; and the group that had for fifteen years been fruitlessly negotiating Mutual and Balanced Force Reductions (MBFR) with the Warsaw Pact. It was widely known as the oldest established diplomatic crap game in the world. Each of these had its own U.S. representative, with ambassadorial rank, functioning independently but using the U.S. embassy for support. The embassy itself had a staff of about 350, including officers for the Defense, Commerce and Agriculture Departments, the Drug Enforcement Agency, the Immigration Service and others. Most of them were crammed into a large but rather cozy building of simplified baroque style. It had originally served as the Consular Academy, one of whose students had been Kurt Waldheim. (The ambassador's residence, half an hour away, was a bunkerlike villa built in the 1930s by a Jewish banker. Its best features were a large garden and its proximity to the lovely Schönbrunn Park.)

The heads of the various embassy sections plus a few other senior officers constituted the "country team" with whom I met regularly in a sound- and bug-proof room known as "the Bubble." The deputy chief of mission, Michael Habib, a wise and seasoned foreign service officer, would begin by mentioning the major issues to be discussed, and then the others would report on what, if anything, was new in each area. I suppose I conducted these meetings much like *Time* story conferences, making suggestions, asking questions and pressing for more information.

The "stories" we produced were the reporting cables to the State Department. It took me a while to accept that they would not result in anything as concrete—or satisfying—as a printed magazine. At best they might influence the decision or help shape a policy. It was also part of the ambassador's job to make calls on other envoys and Austrian officials. After two or three weeks Mike Habib took me aside and told me gently: "I gather that you ask a lot of serious questions during your courtesy calls. But you see, these are not interviews. There is supposed to be a lot of small talk." For a while I took his warning to heart, and when I called on the ambassador from Beijing I made a point of talking about food and asked him if he knew of any good Chinese restaurants in Vienna. The answer was no. Hearing about this later, Louise never allowed me to live it down. ("This is diplomacy?")

More than I had realized, I was in public relations. I wondered to what extent ambassadors were still necessary, in an era when presidents and prime ministers could pick up the telephone and talk directly to each other. But presenting the best case for one's nation seemed more important than ever. The State Department sent daily press guidance, but I often relied on my own experience. I had frequent discussions with my staff about how to comment on a particular move by the U.S. or the Austrian government and whether to issue a press release or arrange an interview or a lunch with selected editors. In my past career this was often known as "news management," but I took to it without qualms. In no time at all I began to refer to the press as "they." The moment I had arrived at the Vienna airport and told the phalanx of reporters, "No comment now," I realized that I had crossed to the other side.

Many of the journalists I dealt with were intelligent and able. But their resources were limited and, moreover, most European journalists do not exactly make a fetish of accuracy, preferring opinion and speculation to facts. I had the advantage of knowing German, although I had not used it for decades. When I had to make speeches I wrote them in English and had them translated, so I could deliver them in accurate German.

THE VIENNA EMBASSY was unusually intriguing because for years the city had been an unofficial headquarters for the cold war. The old antagonists were still in place, still maneuvering and plotting against each other. Thus in many ways my most fascinating duty involved dealing with the CIA, whose Vienna station was one of the largest in the world. The Agency took up a sizable, tightly secured part of the embassy building. Every morning an Agency employee would bring the daily CIA briefing to my office. I would read it while he sat in front of my desk. When I was finished he took it away again. Often, this precaution struck me as unnecessary; much of the material seemed to repeat diplomatic reporting, if not newspaper stories.

The CIA employees, most of whom had diplomatic cover titles, were in a sense nonpersons; they mingled infrequently with other embassy staffers, although everyone knew who they were. I found them on the whole more interesting and more intellectual than the foreign service types but also more nervous, high-strung and unpredictable. In this last respect the station chief was untypical; he was calm, almost serene, soft-spoken with a midwestern solidity about him. He was totally dedicated to the United States, to the Agency and, not incidentally, to his nearly model family. Louise referred to him with a set of private initials she reserved for very few people: BOA, meaning Best of America. Techni-cally he was my subordinate, but he functioned on his own. We had regular meetings, in another, smaller "Bubble," and he briefed me on current activities, usually reading from handwritten notes on a sheet of yellow legal paper. In theory he informed me about anything I needed to know, with special attention to the possibility that CIA activities might go wrong and embarrass the embassy and the United States. I liked and trusted him, but he was the sole judge of what to tell me. His briefings were long, detailed and absorbing. The action ranged from surveillance, in many ingenious ways, of foreign diplomats or agents, to wooing new recruits, to the reception of defectors from the East bloc, some of whom were walk-ins who would suddenly appear at the em-bassy. It was to this station chief, at a Christmas party in 1986, that marine sergeant Clayton Lonetree had turned himself in; he had sold details about the Agency's Vienna operations to the KGB.

The most spectacular Viennese espionage case broke in 1989, when I was told by our station chief that Felix Bloch, who had been the number two man at the embassy until a few months before I arrived, had been selling secrets to the Russians. Phone calls from the State Department on a secure line informed me that so far only the secretary of state and two or three other officials knew about this, but that the case was bound to become public soon and I had better prepare the Austrians.

The news was astounding. I had met Bloch several times and had found him to be the very image of an impeccable foreign service officer. After seven years in Vienna he was extremely popular, even beloved, and was an old friend of Foreign Minister Alois Mock. When I went to brief Mock, he at first insisted that there must be some misunderstand-ing. I convinced him otherwise, and tears came to his eyes. After the news became public most Viennese were incredulous and suspected that

Bloch was the victim of some dark plot. The fact was that the CIA had picked up a reference to Bloch in a telephone surveillance of a suspected Russian agent. Later Bloch was secretly photographed exchanging briefcases with a man in a Paris bar. Bloch claimed that he was a stamp collector and that the briefcases had contained stamps. No evidence was ever produced that would stand up in court (under U.S. law, for example, it would have been necessary to prove what was inside Bloch's briefcase, and that was impossible). But there was no doubt in the mind of anyone familiar with the details that Bloch was guilty. Among other things, the investigation revealed that for years he had patronized, usually on Saturday mornings, a Viennese prostitute who specialized in leather and whips. One assumption was that the Russians had discovered his habits and blackmailed him into spying for them. Bloch never came to trial but was ultimately dismissed by the State Department.

I HAD TO RESIST the temptation to become too fascinated by the CIA's activities, by espionage and the lingering *Third Man* theme. As U.S. ambassador I had to be, among other things, a kind of master of ceremonies for the American community, which involved commencement speeches at the American School, Thanksgiving sermonettes and throwing out the first ball at games between American and Viennese students who were just discovering our national pastime. (Once, when I attempted to throw the ball, the catcher remained at home plate. My pitch was considerably short.) I also served as godfather to the embassy staff, many of whose troubles—divorce, alcoholism, delinquent children, accidents—wound up on my desk. Problems were often presented to me by the "gunny" (gunnery sergeant), who was in charge of the marines guarding the embassy. Young and away from home, they were constantly getting into scrapes with Austrians who had to be pacified.

Another headache was that under pressure from Congress, the State Department was repeatedly asking embassies to cut costs. I thought that the United States must be the only nation that is so hostile and niggardly toward its foreign service.

The State Department bureaucracy could be exasperating. Routine decisions moved slowly. Background information from Washington was hard to come by, and I greatly missed the *Time* library and research service. The regular personnel reports from my own section heads made it sound as if I were presiding over a collection of Achesons and Kennans. When I tried to tone down some of the habitual superlatives, I was told that I did not understand the language, in which superb meant good and good meant mediocre. But I liked and respected most of the foreign service officers I worked with, who were diligent and dedicated. They were hardly original or daring, but those qualities were not encouraged by the system.

Among the embassy's greatest assets were the Austrian employees, ranging from highly experienced political and economic analysts to traffic managers. Two of the stars were Waltraud Lenzhofer, the protocol chief, who combined tact with endless knowledge about every potential embassy guest; and Horst Kainz, my driver, who knew every shortcut, every office, every restaurant and, I believe, every secret in the country. Louise insisted that he really ran the embassy.

FORMER COLLEAGUES SOMETIMES came to Vienna, often on the way to Eastern Europe, and asked me what Austria was really all about. I usually told them that it was about history. In World Wars I and II the country had been crushed by history, but since then it had managed to escape it in significant ways. The process began when Austria was certified Hitler's first victim by the Allies, thus being spared harsh retribution for its role in the Nazi horrors. The country also eluded the later phases of the cold war when the Soviets withdrew, and it avoided or at least mitigated some of the bitter ideological conflicts between Right and Left that raged elsewhere in Europe. Austria was still divided between "Red" and "Black," I would explain, between the Socialists and the conservative People's Party, with its traditional, now quite loose, links to the church. But the division was buffered and codified in a pact known as Social Partnership. Appointments to jobs, from the cabinet to labor unions to practically every other organization, had to be balanced between the two major parties. The parliament was vocal enough, but the big decisions were worked out quietly among so-called chambers representing business, labor and agriculture.

This system made for stability, but it was also stifling. The free market was limited by rules and regulations almost reminiscent of medieval guilds. Keeping a shop open in the evening or on weekends was virtually impossible because no one was supposed to gain an advantage over a competitor. Envy of other people's success was endemic, almost a civic principle. In spite of all this Austria was remarkably prosperous. But the system was beginning to creak.

Austria reflected trends that were evident elsewhere. One was the crisis of Socialism and of state-run enterprises. The situation was personified by the former and the present chancellors. Bruno Kreisky, now grizzled and ailing, had governed the country from 1970 to 1983 with so much panache that he was nicknamed the Sun King. Kreisky gave Austria a higher international profile, largely through his controversial attempts to build bridges between Jews and Arabs. He also presided over a burgeoning economy—while it lasted. Franz Vranitzky, who became chancellor in June 1986, was strikingly different. Where Kreisky was short, stocky, pugnacious but captivating, a bon vivant, Vranitzky was tall, affable but reserved and somewhat austere (his wife once confided that he buttoned even the top buttons of his polo shirts). Kreisky was an old-style Socialist who once told me passionately that state-run enterprises should be kept going even if they lost money, to preserve jobs. Vranitzky, a pragmatist who had headed one of Austria's major banks, knew this notion could no longer prevail. He began very gradually to shrink the inefficient public sector. Kreisky resented that bitterly, complaining that Vranitzky had abandoned the Socialist faith. "He's a banker and talks like a banker. You can't expect anything else from him." But I found Vranitzky to be a politician of real stature. Too many others were what the Austrians call *klein-kariert* (literally "small checked" or "narrow"). Like elsewhere, people were turning against both major parties, which were seen as fat, comfortable and ridden by bureaucracy and corruption.

A citizen of the country that produced Watergate, the Iran-contra affair and the S&L disaster had to be careful in judging other people's misdeeds. But the Austrian variety could be highly colorful. A prime example was Udo Proksch, a sloppy, unprepossessing con man who managed to acquire that national treasure, Demel, the peerless confectioner. He also captivated several of Vienna's most attractive and aristocratic women. At the same time he seduced politicians and bamboozled them into supporting his bizarre schemes, such as quick-cast plastic tanks for the army and an enterprise to bury people upright (to save space). In 1977 a ship he had chartered exploded in the Indian Ocean with a loss of six lives. The cargo supposedly was a nuclear processing plant. It turned out later that it was only scrap and that Proksch had arranged the explosion to collect millions in insurance money. After years of investigation Proksch fled and was eventually caught and convicted of murder.

The scandals contributed to growing disillusion with the old political establishment. The chief beneficiary of that trend were the right-wing Free Democrats, a small party reshaped by Joerg Haider. At thirty-nine he was slim, attractive, with an outdoor, athletic air. He was highly articulate and effective on television. He talked about appointments by merit rather than party fiat, reducing the budget, modernizing the country. Often offensive—he called the postwar Austrian state a monstrosity—he found favorable things to say about Hitler's employment policies and was widely seen as a neo-Nazi. Kreisky referred to him as half a Fascist. Haider told me that he was not really a German nationalist but used that rhetoric to satisfy "the old folks." It was hardly a reassuring explanation. After several more meetings with him I felt that calling him a neo-Nazi was too simple. I saw him as a populist, radical opportunist who gladly appealed to whatever lingering pro-Nazi sentiment existed but would also appeal to anything else that might lead him to power.

A big issue at the time was whether Austria should join the European Community. Many Socialists saw it as a capitalist plot, and many businessmen and farmers feared competition. But leading politicians and progressive entrepreneurs, who looked toward the West, favored membership. The matter really involved Austria's identity. Its long established neutrality was for many people an attitude toward life. Officially the United States took no position, but I privately argued that Austria had to join the global marketplace and reenter history.

Our government was not shy in pushing its views on other issues. One of them was terrorism. Wide-open Austria had been the scene of several attacks, and there was evidence implicating the large Libyan embassy in Vienna. Washington wanted to see that embassy reduced, and I would periodically take this request to the minister of the interior. He was one Karl Blecha, a man of radiant insincerity who kept making promises without much follow-through. But on the working level Austrian police cooperated well with us in containing terrorists. I moved about with two plainclothesmen assigned by the Austrian government. I am not sure how effective they would have been in the unlikely event anyone came gunning for me, but I felt quite secure.

Washington had other problems with Austria: "tech transfer," involving the shipment of advanced technology to the East bloc; money laundering by drug dealers behind the screen of Austrian bank secrecy; a proposal by Austria's miniarmy to buy defensive missiles from Russia. I pressed Austrian authorities to accommodate Washington on all these issues. But I occasionally felt that our government—especially self-important middle-level officials in Justice, Commerce, and other departments—was being rather arrogant toward a sovereign country, regarding Austria if not as a banana republic, at least as a whipped cream state. The Austrians often dragged their feet—an art at which they are highly skilled—but by and large they were remarkably cooperative.

THE OVERRIDING PROBLEM was Waldheim. My role was to insist on the irrevocability of the watch list decision, while at the same time assuring the Austrians that we had the friendliest feelings toward them. According to the ground rules worked out between the State Department and myself, my contacts with Waldheim were to be limited to formal protocol occasions. Chances were, I was told, he would try for other meetings and especially photo opportunities to convey the notion that the United States had relaxed its attitude toward him. At Vienna's Opera Ball, as if symbolizing the opposed political camps, Waldheim and Chancellor Vranitzky occupied opposite boxes, and I carefully avoided the president's. I felt awkward and rather silly, but I knew that appearances mattered. One of Waldheim's top aides, Georg Hennig, visited me, suggesting occasional private meetings with his boss to discuss the world situation. I declined. Later, during a winter outing held by Foreign Minister Mock for the diplomatic corps, Louise happened to share a toboggan ride with Hennig. There was instant press speculation that this might signal a change in U.S. policy about Waldheim. At one point Mock, a Waldheim loyalist, suggested to me that Washington's treatment of Waldheim could have serious consequences and might drive Austria into Moscow's arms. It was an unconvincing and uncharacteristically clumsy move by Mock, whom I had come to know not only as an obsessively hard worker, but as an experienced professional. But I understood his frustration. Waldheim was ostracized not only by the United States, but by virtually all Western countries. His foreign travels were limited mostly to a few Arab nations, and other heads of state avoided Vienna. His isolation was interrupted briefly in June 1988 by a visit from Pope John Paul II, who attended a reception (among other ceremonies) for the diplomatic corps. I had seen this pope only at a distance before, and now, like everyone else, I felt enveloped by the warmth and intensity he radiated. Carefully watching the pope as he moved along the large circle of envoys, shaking hands, an Austrian journalist claimed to notice that he lingered for a few extra moments with me, the Israeli chargé d'affaires and the French ambassador, who had scandalized many people by bringing his mistress to Vienna. "His Holiness," reported the journalist, "paid special attention to two Jews and a man living in sin."

The Waldheim controversy was a kind of civil war in the Austrian conscience. A great many people thought Waldheim was contemptible and should resign. Others argued heatedly that he was not a war criminal and that he had done nothing they or their fathers would not have done. Talk about him was endless, to the point where Louise said: "A real holiday in Vienna would be a week without one word on the subject."

During my first conversation with Chancellor Vranitzky, he volunteered his views on Waldheim. He blamed Waldheim for having made many serious errors in not understanding the nature of his own difficulty. "Waldheim," said the chancellor, "had used the phrase 'I have only done my duty' in referring to his service in the Wehrmacht. It was a bad statement. If Waldheim had said that he had joined the German army because he had to or because he was forced to, like so many of his generation, out of fear, it would have been universally understood."

Soon after this meeting came the publication of a report by an international commission of historians that had been proposed by Waldheim and whose head, a noted Swiss scholar, had been approved by him. But the report was a blow to Waldheim's cause. Waldheim, the historians found, "attempted to let his military past slip into oblivion and as soon as that was no longer possible, to whitewash it." The commission found no evidence of his direct, personal guilt for war crimes but concluded that he had been "in proximity" to war crimes, "incriminating measures and orders." Vranitzky commented wryly, "It is not enough for the president of Austria to be simply not a war criminal." In contrast there was the view expressed earlier by Michael Graff, secretary general of the People's Party, that Waldheim was all right if there were no proof that he had killed six Jews with his own hands. Graff was forced to quit.

Perhaps the most intriguing Waldheim champion I met was Hans Dichand, the legendary head of *Neue Kronen Zeitung,* Austria's largest newspaper, read by at least half of the population. It was a tabloid full of crime, sex and superficial news (my all-time favorite headline: "19 Little Circus Dogs Save Their Mistress from Being Raped!"). The paper had a marked tinge of anti-Americanism and especially fulminated against the watch list decision. Dichand turned out to be affable and, considering his wealth, eccentric in his dress; one would have hesitated to donate his overcoat to the Salvation Army. Waldheim had just made a speech in which he'd apologized for the Nazi horrors in words Dichand found inadequate. "The Holocaust is not something to say you are sorry for—that's an expression one might use for stepping on someone's foot." Nevertheless he defended Waldheim ("We really didn't know anything about these things") and added that Waldheim may simply have had a hard time remembering after all these years. "I was in the navy on many ships, and I can't remember their names today." It was, I thought, a preposterous comparison.

The Waldheim speech Dichand criticized was part of a major commemoration of the Nazi takeover on March 12, 1938. It was a rare act of public penance. Walking through Vienna, I found myself transported back to the grim days of the Anschluss; everywhere—on posters, in shop windows and bookstores and in special exhibitions—there were images of German troops marching in, of Viennese crowds cheering, of Jews being beaten or arrested, of concentration camps. In dozens of ceremonies in public halls, churches and theaters, Austrians, of all stations and parties, held observances that were impressive and often moving.

Just about every politician made a speech or issued a statement. After much bitter infighting, Waldheim was persuaded not to take part in the formal ceremony at the Hofburg but made his speech on television. While rejecting "collective guilt"—as did virtually every speaker—he apologized for Nazi crimes committed by his countrymen and admitted that "many of the worst hangmen of National Socialism were Austrians." He did not refer to his own role but recalled that on the day the Germans marched in, when he was nineteen, his mother wept and that on the following day his anti-Nazi father was arrested by the Gestapo.

Perhaps the most remarkable words of the commemoration were spoken by Viktor Frankl. A Jewish psychiatrist who had spent three years in concentration camps, he became famous for his work, especially *Man's Search for Meaning*, in which he outlined his "logotherapy" involving treatment through emphasis on the total meaning of existence. (The book became an international best-seller but ironically was hardly noticed in Austria.) Frankl now spoke of reconciliation. He recalled his parents and his wife, who had died in the camps, but he said, "Do not expect words of hate from me. . . ." He also recalled Austrians who, at the risk of their own lives, had helped Jews during the Nazi years, including himself and a cousin. To him Vienna was "the home of such wonderful people." He continued: "There exist only two human races: decent and indecent. We must accept the fact that the decent ones are always in the minority." He concluded: "I encourage all men of goodwill to extend their hands for a greeting, across all boundaries and tomb-stones of the past."

Many of Frankl's fellow Jews, and others, could not share his forbear-ance. Later I invited him to lunch at the embassy and found him a strangely contradictory figure. Nearly eighty-five and frail, he happily recalled the young people who had crowded about him after his speech with tears of gratitude in their eyes. But he harshly condemned the younger generation in general for lacking standards and honor. Discuss-ing the United States, he asserted that "America imports the best of European culture but exports the silliest like blue jeans." (I felt I had to defend blue jeans.) At the same time he said he liked McDonald's. As for the Anschluss commemoration, he thought it had not done much good because it represented overkill.

He was partly right. The issue, it seemed to me, was not what Austri-ans called *Vergangenheitsbewältigung,* or coming to terms with the past, but coming to terms with the present and the future. As Simon Wiesenthal put it: "We should stop trying to convert old, ingrained anti-Semites. Only by providing in-depth information to the younger genera-tion can anti-Semitism be eliminated." With that in mind, the Educa-tion Ministry was preparing teaching materials about the hitherto largely ignored Holocaust. A stunning exhibit at the Chamber of Labor called "Youth under the Swastika" illustrated the whole ghastly brain-washing apparatus of the Hitler era, which corrupted children in the guise of false patriotism and pernicious "glory." I saw schoolchildren, to whom Nazi horrors were presumably as unreal as Grimm's fairy tales, being taken to this exhibit en masse. No one could be sure if they understood. Nevertheless I was impressed by the effort to inoculate the young against the poisons of the past.

Another kind of commemoration took place later with the dedication of a monument against war and Fascism by Alfred Hrdlicka, the Waldheim horse sculptor. It was located near the center of the city, behind the opera house and opposite the famed Albertina museum. Opponents of the project had argued furiously, but in vain, that it should be placed more or less out of the way, on the site of the former Gestapo headquarters. The work was a strange, disorienting group of abstract and representational stone sculptures, brutal and ugly at first sight. Its most arresting component was a kneeling bronze figure of an old man scrubbing the ground. It was an evocation of the Jews who, after the Anschluss, had been forced to scrub away (often with toothbrushes) anti-Nazi slogans that had been painted on the sidewalks. This figure drew even louder protests than the monument as a whole. Many Viennese did not want to be faced with this ugly reminder of inhumanity in the midst of their city. Some Jews were also offended because they did not want their people depicted as eternal victims. A young Jewish matron we knew said: "I don't want my children to see Jews that way."

The issue of anti-Semitism in Austria nagged at me throughout my stay. After I arrived in Vienna, I received scurrilous letters attacking the United States and Israel. "What a dirty and vicious Jewish character you have! Certainly you must be aware that your brothers, the bloodthirsty Jewish bastards Shamir, Rabin, Sharon and similar thugs, are slaughtering innocent and helpless Arab women and children." "How did it happen that you, a Jew, became the U.S. Ambassador to Austria? Was there no other qualified person?" One quite different letter came from a Viennese Jew who was indignant that I had taken the post and suggested that I resign and "tell the U.S. Government to send a Texas cowboy." (The suggestion was partly prophetic because my successor would be Roy Huffington, not a cowboy, but an oilman from Texas.) The two or three dozen such letters were outweighed by the warmly welcoming messages.

I discussed the treatment of Jews with Paul Grosz, a quiet, modest furrier who was head of Vienna's tiny Jewish community. Since the country's Jewish population had shrunk from two hundred thousand before the Anschluss to less than ten thousand people out of seven and a half million, it was very nearly anti-Semitism without Jews. This suggested that some Austrians needed the Jew, real or imagined, as a devil figure. Grosz thought that most Austrians honestly believed that they were not anti-Semitic, largely because they defined anti-Semitism as beginning only at the gates of Auschwitz. On balance, Grosz thought the situation was not as good as Austrians believed, but not nearly as bad as outsiders assumed. I came to agree with that judgment. But the evidence was contradictory. One public opinion study, for instance, reported that the percentage of Austrians who would feel "disgust" on shaking hands with a Jew had declined from 18 percent in 1976 to 7 percent in 1987 but was rising again. When my friend A. M. Rosenthal, former executive editor of *The New York Times* and now a columnist, visited Vienna, a notoriously nasty writer for *Kronen Zeitung* made great sport of referring to him as "Rosenthal, Rosenbaum, and Rosenberg."

On the other hand, there was no official or institutional discrimination. Anti-Semitic utterances could be punished by law. While people would obviously wear their most benign faces when dealing with the U.S. ambassador, I became convinced that anti-Semitism was no worse—and perhaps better—in Austria than in many other countries, notably Hungary and Poland or, for that matter, Germany, which was often favorably compared to Austria. Among the people who led me to that belief was Vienna's able mayor Helmut Zilk, a boisterous showman and a courageous foe of all prejudice. Another was the former archbishop of Vienna, Franz Cardinal Koenig. I had met him some years before in New York when I was among several people he asked for advice on how to mount a campaign for nuclear disarmament. Within the limits of Catholic doctrine Koenig was a liberal. He was a luminous but quiet man, sophisticated but deeply humane. The church in Austria had often played a part in spreading or not resisting anti-Semitism; Koenig admitted this sorrowfully and fought hard to prevent the recurrence of this tendency. Anti-Semitism, he said, was wrong, not only on moral grounds but because Christians are the "spiritual children of the tribe of Abraham."

The real problem, I thought, was not anti-Semitism as such, but the wider forces of xenophobia, distrust of the outside world, and isolation. That isolation was apt to be reinforced by a haunting preoccupation with the past. A cosmopolitan financier once remarked: "Our troubles go back to that damn treaty." I was startled because I thought he was referring to the State Treaty of 1955, which released Austria from occupation. "No, no," said the man, who was in early middle age, "I'm talking about the Peace Treaty of Saint-Germain in 1919."

The lost Austro-Hungarian empire lingered like the phantom pain of an amputated limb. An elderly designer told me about his father: "He was a cook, you know. He worked for Crown Prince Ferdinand, the one who was assassinated at Sarajevo in 1914. Ferdinand died with my father's chicken in his belly." The Habsburgs still had a considerable place in the Austrian imagination. The head of this ghost dynasty was Otto von Habsburg, the seventy-five-year-old son of the last Austro-Hungarian emperor, Karl, and great-grandnephew of Franz Josef, who had ruled for nearly seventy years before his death in 1916, in the midst of the war that destroyed his empire. Otto had lived in the United States during and after World War II, and I remembered the letter my father had once written him because of his alleged Hollywood connections. In fact, he could not have been less touched by show business. When he came to lunch his clothes might have been seen as a costume—loden coat, dark-green-and-gray Austrian suit—but they were natural on him. He was serious and modest. He lived in a small town in Bavaria and worked diligently as a member of the European parliament. We talked about Austria's chances of entering the European Community and the possibility of a United Europe. I asked him whether he had any thought that the monarchy might someday be restored. "Absolutely not," he said without a trace of resentment. On the other hand, he remarked, "Nothing is as small-minded and wrong and foolish as to try to erase a phase of one's own history."

A year later the Habsburg phase came to life as if statues suddenly began to move and old portraits started to speak. The occasion was the funeral of Otto's mother, Zita, Austria's last empress, who died at ninety-six, having lived in exile much of her life. One hundred fifty thousand people came to sign the condolence books by her coffin. As Louise and I sat in St. Stephen's Cathedral, the Mozart *Requiem* rising into the vast, dark space above, we knew that we would never see such a spectacle again. One hundred twenty clergy participated in the ceremony, wearing vestments that had not been used since Emperor Franz Josef's funeral. Tyrolean marksmen in lederhosen and feathered hats carried the coffin, which was draped in the empress's standard, showing all the colors of her former lands. Most of the Socialist ministers avoided the funeral, bowing to a tradition of their own: the conviction that the Habsburgs had stood for feudal repression. Socialist youths distributed leaflets listing the evils of the old order—child labor, the seventy-hour week—but hardly anyone paid attention. In a drenching rain we followed with a mass of people behind the black hearse. The cortege stopped at the Capuchin Church, located above the seventeenth-century Habsburg crypt. An ancient ritual was reenacted. A representative of the family knocked on the door, seeking entrance for Zita, empress of Austria, queen of Hungary, queen of Bohemia, Dalmatia, Croatia, Slovenia, Galicia and on and on. From inside, the prior responded: "We do not know her." The request was made again and denied again. A third knock, a third question: "Who seeks entry?" This time the response was: "Zita, a mortal, sinful human being." Then the door opened. After a short service the empress was taken to the crypt below to be placed among the 142 coffins, with their crowned death's-heads, of the House of Habsburg.

CHAPTER THIRTY-NINE

IN VIENNA I continued an old habit of clipping newspaper stories. There were the obvious folders marked politics, economics, foreign policy, and so forth. But one was labeled "soul." In Britain or France I might have used the less ethereal term "national character." But there was something in the Viennese atmosphere that suggested the word "soul"—and it was not merely the memory of Sigmund Freud, who until recently had been shamefully ignored by his native city. That folder included an essay in Vienna's leading newspaper beginning with the sentences "It has been said about the Austrians that they cannot wait to get the years between kindergarten and early retirement behind them. On the other hand they are not quite sure whether they are more inclined toward nostalgia than toward a love of death." There were reports that Austria had the second highest suicide rate in Europe (after Hungary), that the country ranked low in sexual activity, that culture was an escape for people, a kind of opium for the middle class. There were articles about the dismissal of the manager of the Staatsoper—the Viennese had always cared more about who ran the opera than who ran the country. There were black-bordered death notices with the name of the deceased fortified for eternity by every title and honor ever received (Professor, Doctor, Doctor, Doctor). Headlines like "Are We a Nation of Crooks?" In addition to the clips I had included some other mementos, notably a Christmas poem by an Austrian TV executive that read in part: "In these festive days lies abound / when almost everyone knows dark secrets of his neighbor / when neither remorse nor good intentions melt the ice."

What did this kaleidoscope suggest about the Austrian soul? I thought I saw defensiveness, repressed emotion, trivialization of big matters and magnification of the trivial, insecurity of one's place (hence the mania for titles) and a dark streak beneath the cheerful surface. Austrian culture had long suggested melancholy mixed with pleasure, the skull beneath the fleshy skin, rage lurking behind the charm. I sometimes observed that anger flashing out momentarily after endless smiles and flattery. The anger was often directed inward. Many Austrians bitterly resented criticism, yet they also savagely criticized themselves. While I was in Vienna the hallowed Burgtheater produced a play by one of Austria's most famous writers, Thomas Bernhard, a relentless misanthrope. The play was called *Heldenplatz,* for the square in front of the Imperial Palace where thousands of Viennese had cheered Hitler. It consisted mostly of soaring prose arias of hate. "Austria is a stage where everything has rotted and fallen apart, despised nation of millions of forgotten people, millions of weaklings and madmen . . . a sewer without spirit or culture spreading its stench throughout Europe. . . . The President is a liar, the Chancellor is a stock-speculator [who] drives up in his million dollar car and babbles about comrades. . . . Today's university professors are unbelievably primitive; their ignorance is beyond words. . . . Again and again you are fooled by Austria, but you cannot forget that you are living in the most vicious of all European states. . . ."

That was a bizarre distortion. Despite the understandable outcry against it, the play was performed repeatedly. When I attended a few people walked out, but most of the audience merely cowered beneath the interminable waves of insult. I kept thinking about Austria's endless capacity for self-flagellation, always accompanied by a strange ambiguity. Bernhard died in February 1989, having forbidden all further performances of his works on Austrian soil. Yet in the final passage of his 1984 novel, *Woodcutters,* the narrator expresses his love-hate in a torrent of repetitive, hypnotic prose: "As I ran I reflected that the city through which I was running, dreadful though I had always felt it to be and still felt it to be, was still the best city there was, that Vienna, which I found detestable and had always found detestable, was suddenly once again the best city in the world, my own city, my beloved Vienna, and that these people, whom I had always hated and still hated and would go on hating, were still the best people in the world: I hated them, yet found them somehow touching—I hated Vienna, yet found it somehow touching—I cursed these people, yet could not help loving them—I hated Vienna yet could not help loving it. . . ."

I CERTAINLY DID NOT hate Vienna. Did I love it? The word was too strong; a more accurate term would be "affection." People kept asking me how it felt to be home again, and I had to keep telling them—perhaps sounding a little too insistent—that Vienna was not my home. The city did reach out to me. The very street names, dimly remembered, formed an evocative litany. But the names of people mostly evoked loss. No relatives were left and only two or three friends of my family. Teta had long since died. But there was my old school. A few years before, I met in New York with several former classmates who had emigrated to the United States, and one of my friends suggested that our old Vienna gymnasium, which had thrown us out more than two years short of our graduation, really owed us some sort of symbolic reparation. A letter was dispatched to the Austrian authorities, and after some bureaucratic delays and some prodding, our group was invited to come to Vienna. Half a dozen of us made the trip and gathered in the once dreaded building amid speeches and the school choir to receive "honorary" diplomas. (I was also handed copies of my old report cards, all bad.) The students who witnessed the ceremonies were somewhat baffled by what it was all about, but in a discussion many of them said they wanted to learn more about the roots of Nazism.

Soon after I came to Vienna as ambassador I decided to have another reunion. This time the Jewish refugees who had returned to Austria for the occasion were joined by a group of non-Jewish former classmates, most of whom had been drafted into the German army. They were professional men, retired or nearing retirement. Louise and I had them all to dinner at our residence, and it was, inevitably, a shock to see that the sixteen-year-olds of half a century ago had turned into unrecognizable elderly men. We exchanged the usual reminiscences about teachers, grades, pranks and plans we had made for the future. What had become of that future was mentioned only gingerly. It loomed like a dark gap between us, for we had been on different sides of a terrible war, swept up by different fates. Inevitably I wondered what would have become of me if there had been no Hitler and no war and I had remained in Austria. I suspected that my life would have been comfortable and unexciting.

Another way in which Vienna reached out to me was through memories of my father. People kept sending me sheet music of his songs, old programs and pictures. A writer, Hans Weigl, who as a very young man had worked with my father and had since become a distinguished literary figure, recalled the lyrics on which they had collaborated. Vienna's Festival Weeks opened with a concert in front of the City Hall of songs that had been forbidden during the Nazi years, including those of my father's. I saw several performances of his operettas. A plaque in his memory was placed on the apartment building where we had lived, and the city of Vienna named a park for him. I knew that this probably would have never happened except for the accident that his son was now the American ambassador in Vienna. Whatever the motivation, I was touched by the tribute and commissioned a bust of him to be placed in the park. "In a sense he never left Vienna," read one newspaper comment. "It was Vienna that was absent for a while."

With some nostalgia, I showed Louise my childhood haunts. But she, in turn, made me see the city through new eyes. Insatiably curious about the stones and forms of history, she toured Vienna with a young museum curator, century by century, and soon led me to things I had never paid attention to before. The National Archives displaying the Treaty of the Congress of Vienna and the U.S. Friendship Treaty with Austria signed by Andrew Jackson. The huge, simple, serene theater, designed early in the century by the great Otto Wagner, for the inmates of the insane asylum Steinhof. Every hidden corner and treasure of the Schoenbrunn Park, including the fake Roman ruin that seemed to cast a special spell. The out-of-the-way St. Marx Cemetery, overgrown and full of lilacs, with graceful female figures of grief in permanent sleep. Before long she knew more about the Habsburgs than most Viennese and was as familiar with them as with the tribes of New York. She knew the great collectors and the great builders in the dynasty, their triumphs and scandals, their table manners and their sexual habits. She could tell you which archduke had been a transvestite (Ludwig Viktor, nicknamed "Lutzi-wutzie"). Or who had married whom (recalling the famous maxim "Let others fight wars; fortunate Austria conquers by marriage"). One of her favorite stories, which few Austrians had heard, involved Empress Maria Theresa, who in her later years grew so fat that a special elevator had to be built in the Habsburg crypt so that she could visit the sarcophagus of her late, beloved husband. Two days before she died the elevator broke and, weary and sick, she said: "Oh, just leave me down here."

But Louise seemed to know just as much about the living because she somehow inspired people to tell her things. "Everybody has a story," she would say. "Everyone seems to have a relative who was in a concentration camp—or ran one." She developed her own nomenclature for the people around us. The embassy staffers were "Foggies," for Foggy Bottom. Austrian officials were the "Ballies," for Ballhaus Platz, the location of the Chancellory and Foreign Office. Other ambassadors were the *"Chères"* for *"Chère Colleagues"* the customary French phrase for fellow diplomats. The surviving members of the nobility were the "Aristos," who were often the most amusing and cosmopolitan. One of our favorites was Prince Karl Schwarzenberg, the scion of an ancient family, who looked like a tall Proust and was given to good works and eccentric gestures; at a French reception celebrating Bastille Day, he carried a white lily in memory of the unfortunate Bourbons. At our parties we mixed them all up together, with journalists and artists invited with minimum concern for political animosities.

Then there were the fairly constant visitors from the United States for whom Louise served as a tireless guide. They included congressional delegations, which hit Vienna with the regularity of comets. Many friends also came, including Beverly Sills, who was shopping for a production to take home to the New York City Opera (it proved too expensive). Mortimer Adler gamely wandered through an exhibit of the Austrian philosopher Ludwig Wittgenstein's works, a reminder of Vienna's turn-of-the-century intellectual brilliance now sadly vanished. Perhaps the grandest emissary from the United States was Leonard Bernstein, who came twice to conduct the Vienna Philharmonic. The orchestra and the city loved him, and he reciprocated (with occasional reservations). He was exhilarating and seemingly indestructible. Louise and I watched him rehearse in the magnificent, gilded Musikvereinssaal to the point of exhaustion. In his dressing room later, Louise observed disapprovingly that there was no shower. "Shower?" said Lenny. "I don't even have a toilet, just this little washroom. But all the great conductors in the world have peed in this sink."

The Viennese adored Louise, and I adapted John Kennedy's line: "I am the man who accompanied Louise Grunwald to Vienna." In New York we had spoken about the ambassadorial life with Bill Luers, a superb "Foggie," and his wife, Wendy. Louise and I were vastly amused when Wendy quite casually spoke about "the time we were ambassador in Prague." Yet soon after we arrived in Vienna Louise caught herself making a similar remark to me—and rightly so, I felt. An ambassador and his wife are a partnership, and Louise did more than her share. She was solicitous of the embassy staff, especially the CIA complement. Always fascinated by espionage, she hinted heavily that she would like to be recruited, but in vain. Once she invited the station chief and his family to an Easter egg hunt in our garden; the spymaster found not a single egg. When he left for another assignment, she decided to give an unprecedented party in our residence for all the Agency employees. The high point was a reading from Dickens by an actress in nineteenth-century costume.

"How did you know that I loved Dickens?" asked the station chief.

"Oh, an ambassador from one of the Eastern bloc countries told me," said Louise. The station chief blanched until he realized that she was joking.

. . .

THE COLD WAR was still no joking matter, even though it was plainly losing its old ferocity. Ambassadors from West and East mingled politely but still warily. My Soviet opposite number was Gennadi Shikin, a walking caricature of the beefy KGB type. Shikin's behavior was an indicator of events in Moscow. Initially dour, he softened gradually as glasnost proceeded back home, and eventually he became downright cozy. He even munched hot dogs at our Fourth of July reception. In January 1989 the long-running CSCE negotiations finally wound up with an agreement emphasizing a human rights agenda, including freedom of religion, information, and travel in the thirty-five participating countries. For the conclusion of the conference George Shultz came to Vienna, accompanied by a massive entourage that took up an entire hotel floor. With the end of Reagan's second term only days away, it was a kind of farewell trip for Shultz. He was in high spirits, dancing exuberantly at a ball at City Hall. Just before leaving, he took his staff (as well as Louise and myself) to Demel's for a high-calorie good-bye feast.

Seven weeks later Shultz's successor in George Bush's new administration, James Baker, arrived. The occasion was the overdue burial of the old MBFR negotiations and the opening of a new conference, Conventional Arms and Forces in Europe, originally known as CAFE, which sounded frivolous and was replaced by CFE. I met him at the airport, and during the drive to town he invited suggestions about U.S. policy in Europe and made it clear that, rather than relying on the State Department bureaucracy, he would run his own show. (That is precisely what he eventually did, with a small inner circle of aides.) He also wanted some specific information. The name of the foreign minister— M-o-c-k—did that rhyme with Coke? No, I said, it rhymes with cock. A more startling question followed. Did they speak German in Austria or some other language? German, I said, suppressing my astonishment, for I had always known Baker to be thoroughly informed.

That is indeed what he showed himself to be two days later when he had his first face-to-face session with the Soviet foreign minister, Eduard Shevardnadze. It took place in our residence, where years before, John

Kennedy had faced the bullying Nikita Khrushchev. The meeting proceeded in the dining room under the benign and attentive gaze of George Washington in a Gilbert Stuart portrait on the wall. Baker was completely on top of his brief. So was Shevardnadze, who struck me as a slightly melancholy presence across the big green table. Baker pressed for more progress by the Soviets on human rights, and Shevardnadze was reassuring and accommodating. There was some sparring on other matters, including disarmament, but I found the whole encounter remarkably mild. One of the few ominous notes came when Baker complained about a recent killing at the Berlin Wall where East German border guards were still shooting at people trying to escape. He urged Moscow to use its influence to stop this inhumane policy.

The incident at the Wall was a jarring anachronism in the new atmosphere, an atmosphere largely credited to Gorbachev. The West seemed hypnotized by him. In his travels to Paris, Bonn and Rome, he talked peace and cooperation. His favorite theme was the "Common House of Europe," which the USSR and the rest of the continent would share. America and Canada should be included, too, Gorbachev said, but not very convincingly. Reading the State Department cables, I realized that Washington was worried about all this undermining the solidarity of NATO. Many politicians and journalists argued that we needed to match Gorbachev's vision with one of our own. I thought that was wrong because we indeed had a vision, and he was, in effect, trying to duplicate it. The "House of Europe" appeal should be turned back on him, I felt, by spelling out precisely what admission to the "house" would require—real progress toward pluralism and the free market. In a speech at Innsbruck University I suggested that Gorbachev, in dealing with the outside world, was turning failure into success: by frankly admitting the disastrous condition of the Soviet economy, he was convincing many people that a new, better, democratic Soviet Union was as good as accomplished. I described him as an interim figure whose "revolution" had not gone nearly far enough, because he still wanted to repair the system rather than replace it. Many in the West had a hard time accepting this; when I said that Marxism was dying, the students in my audience roundly booed me.

The people living in the Soviet satellites believed that the system's death throes would be slow and that it was still dangerous. They kept escaping to the West in a continuous flow. Austria, more generous than other countries, had since 1945 accepted six hundred thousand as immigrants, despite grumbling from xenophobes. Many others moved on, some to Israel. But most wanted to go to America, and it was part of the U.S. mission's job to grant visas. Long lines of Hungarians, Czechs and Poles sat waiting for their interviews in the modern, functional anteroom of the consulate general. I recognized the Sunday-best clothes worn to make a good impression, the clutched envelopes of documents, the nervous, whispered exchanges. Several times I sat unobtrusively in the back of the interview room, listening as families told their stories to a consular officer. They were supposed to show that they were not simply seeking better living conditions but would be persecuted if they went back to their own countries. There were long stories accompanied by letters and news clippings, but the cases were difficult to judge. The presumption, however, was that in a Communist country almost everyone was in danger. I could not help thinking that nothing on this scale had been done by the world for the Jews escaping the Holocaust. But I sympathized with these newer refugees, remembering my own long-ago experience when the visa to the United States was the ultimate hope.

GLASNOST AND PERESTROIKA were having contagious effects in the satellites. I asked to see the cable traffic from U.S. missions in Budapest, Prague, Warsaw and Moscow and met with journalists and politicians traveling back and forth. Old Party bosses were deposed and replaced by younger, ostensibly more liberal men. Repeatedly the Old Guard resisted the sweep and was overwhelmed. Early in 1988 Hungary lifted travel restrictions for Austria and thousands of Hungarians streamed across the border to go shopping in Vienna for television sets and VCRs and everything else in sight, causing tremendous traffic jams. (The mayor thoughtfully provided extra parking spaces.) The shoppers drove back home, their purchases often strapped to the roofs of their cars as taunting reminders of capitalist prosperity.

As I write this, I see on my desk a piece of black, jagged barbed wire that I keep as a souvenir. It is a reminder of the extraordinary days when the iron curtain collapsed. To enhance Hungary's image in the West, the Budapest government began dismantling 215 miles of wire fence along the Austrian border, and several people brought me pieces of it. East Germany became the instrument of the curtain's final collapse. Its citizens were allowed to travel freely to other satellite countries, given a long-standing agreement that the "fraternal" authorities would keep them from crossing into the West. That arrangement was beginning to break down. Despite the disappearance of the wire the Hungarian border with Austria was still technically closed, but it was now lightly guarded and hundreds of East Germans made their way across. East Germans also began moving into Bonn's embassies in East Berlin, Prague and Budapest, hoping somehow to get to West Germany. Soon afterward Hungary formally suspended the long-standing agreement that had barred escape. Early in September the big exodus began. In one thirty-six-hour period ten thousand refugees came across and boarded trains provided by the Austrian government for the trip to West Germany. Austria now was not only a way station for a great migration, but a listening post as news and rumors and speculation flowed in.

As the months went by the whole embassy and much of Vienna focused on the refugee exodus. On November 9, at midnight, the once unthinkable happened: the Wall was opened and triumphant Berliners began to dismantle it. Only a year and a half before, Ronald Reagan had stood at the Wall and challenged the Communist rulers on the other side to tear it down. Many dismissed this as an empty, provocative gesture. Now it was reality.

THE NEW REALITY was difficult to grasp. As the year came to a close, Jim Baker convened a meeting of America's European ambassadors in Brussels. Around the large conference table there was an almost palpable wonder at the situation and worry that everything was happening too quickly. Baker spoke about a new architecture for Europe, but his designs were sketchy. The chief topic was the future of Germany. Jack Matlock, the U.S. ambassador in Moscow, reported that there was some talk there about German neutrality as the price of reunification. Everyone agreed that that was out. Vernon Walters, the magisterial diplomat-of-all-work who was then our ambassador in Bonn, was convinced that reunification would happen anyway. But no one was sure how or on what terms. It was hard to believe that Moscow would allow East Germany to become part of NATO. A few of us believed that it might just be possible. But Moscow would need a fig leaf—a whole hedge of fig leaves, I thought—in the form of security guarantees or some sort of Europe-wide defense system. No one foresaw what would happen in less than a year—Germany's swift reunification, with strong American backing, and the collapse of the Warsaw Pact.

B<small>Y THEN</small> L<small>OUISE</small> and I had decided to go home. I had been reappointed by George Bush and certainly could have stayed on at least until the end of his term. But at the outset we had made up our minds to leave after two years, and much as we enjoyed our time in Vienna, we saw no reason to change that plan. When the Viennese heard about our impending departure, many were hurt and incredulous. "What have we done to drive you away?" was a typical question. Few believed that we—or perhaps anyone—would want to leave Vienna voluntarily. Rumors circulated that Louise or I was gravely ill, or that I was headed for another assignment, or, on the contrary, that I had fallen into disfavor with the Bush administration. Horst, the sophisticated driver, was one of the few who understood. "I suppose," he said, "after two years things begin to repeat themselves." That was at least part of the explanation. I felt that I had largely accomplished what I was supposed to do: take the strain out of the atmosphere between Washington and Vienna. Perhaps the nicest testimonial to that came from the doorman at the Pallavicini Palace, where many public functions took place. "Mr. Ambassador," he once told me. "We're so glad to have you here. There's such a calmness about you."

We missed our children, even though they had visited us. Lisa was married by now to a *Wall Street Journal* editor, Stephen Adler, and had published her first novel. Mandy was thriving as a political consultant, and Peter had co-produced his first feature film. Bobby Savitt was working in the family real estate business. Louise and I wanted to be closer to them. We also missed America. It was unsettling to read and hear about the United States at long distance. I found myself pained every time I saw stories about scandals, crime and drugs in the United States. I was particularly shaken by the case of the "Central Park jogger," a woman executive on Wall Street who was raped and left for dead by a band of teenagers "wilding" in the park. It sometimes sounded as if American society as a whole were wilding: more and more children having children, a million people in jail, an insane, unstoppable torrent of privately owned guns. There was no major crisis, but enough trouble for me to feel that I should be back home. That was no doubt irrational—I could hardly make a difference by being in New York—but it was a powerful instinct. I never felt more American than I did in Austria. I longed for the special freedom, openness and speed of U.S. life, for the feeling of being part of the big world that seemed remote in Vienna.

During my many farewell calls I found much concern over the future. Chancellor Franz Vranitzky worried that Austria might be lumped together with the nations emerging from Communist rule in a kind of Eastern European grab bag.

The ailing Bruno Kreisky was troubled by the prospect of German reunification, referring to those East German crowds that had been calling for *"Ein Volk, Ein Reich"* ("One People, One Realm"), echoing the old Nazi slogan. "I don't like young people who yell," said Kreisky, "regardless of what it is they yell."

For these very experienced men, the collapse of Communism—so long fought for and hoped for—was not a source of unalloyed triumph. On the contrary, it suggested many new threats. Among the most severe was the reemergence of nationalism in the Soviet republics and in Eastern Europe, from Ukraine to Yugoslavia. As the heavy lid of Communist rule was gradually lifted, old ethnic and tribal animosities were bursting to the surface. Vienna's newspapers seemed haunted again by the names of those old tribes—Serbs, Croatians, Macedonians, Slovenes, Montenegrans. The components of that artificial state, Yugoslavia, were struggling for independence. Balkan watchers predicted that before long there would also be trouble from the Bosnians. "Bosnia-Herzogovina" were words I had uncomprehendingly heard as a child when grown-ups talked about the start of World War I. "Sarajevo" was another such word. It seemed implausible that these names once again were echoing ominously in our minds. I was tempted to write an article to be called "From Sarajevo to Sarajevo." I had long been convinced that the nation state and the conventional idea of national sovereignty were fading. Events in the Balkans suggested that I was wrong, or at least premature. Even in Western Europe the dream of unity seemed to recede.

My oddest farewell call was on Kurt Waldheim. He had never given up trying to overturn the watch list decision. After George Bush's election he had sent a handwritten letter to him. It was addressed in the typical Austrian fashion of insisting on titles even when the greeting is personal: Dear "Mr. President, Dear George." Waldheim recalled how they had come to know each other when Bush was U.S. ambassador to the United Nations and pleaded to be taken off the list. The letter was referred to me for a suggested reply. The request had to be turned down, and I proposed that it be answered by the Justice Department.

When I saw Waldheim in his splendid quarters, which were eerily silent and without signs of much activity, he said that he had been deeply hurt by this handling of his message through channels. "Mr. Ambassador," he said, "you are familiar with American media and American politics. Is there anything you can advise me to do to reverse the watch list decision?"

I once again explained the Holtzman amendment and the symbolic significance the case had assumed. "Mr. President," I replied, "the only advice I can give you is to do nothing."

I left him, a rather forlorn figure, in the gilded emptiness of his office.

Our departure from Austria inspired mixed feelings. Despite its faults I admired much about this country: its ability to survive, its patience, its diligence, its democracy, however flawed. Muddling through was always a great Austrian talent, but I felt it had done better than that. I would miss some of the friends we had made, would miss the enchanting scenery and the great music that seemed to be everywhere, in concert halls, churches, in the very air.

I would miss the remnants of an old civilization, surrounded though it was by contradictions. These never struck me more deeply than during one of our last trips outside of Vienna, when we went to Mauthausen, the notorious concentration camp about ninety miles from the capital. I had visited it before for commemorative ceremonies but had not had a close look. Besides, Louise wanted to see it, too. Atop a steep hill amid pleasant farm country it looked like a gray fortress with its watchtowers and massive ironbound gate. It had been built from granite quarried by prisoners who carried the stones up a long "stairway of death." Nearby were many monuments built by countries whose citizens had been imprisoned in the camp—Russia, Poland and others. The camp buildings had been preserved as a museum. It did not offer the harrowing human details we had seen at Auschwitz—the discarded suitcases and eyeglasses, the heaps of hair cut from the heads of inmates. But the torture cells were there at Mauthausen, whitewashed and ghostly, the crematorium ovens and the large gas chamber, the photographs of prisoners staring down from the walls. I knew that, but for extraordinary good fortune, my picture or that of my family might easily have been among them. More than one hundred thousand people died here by gas, shooting, hanging or exhaustion. I felt what I always did when I contemplated the Holocaust: a stunned and complete inner silence, an overwhelming vertigo, caused by the mind's inability to comprehend.

After Mauthausen Louise and I had decided to visit nearby St. Florian. The famous monastery, founded in the Middle Ages and rebuilt in the seventeenth and eighteenth centuries as a glorious monument to the Baroque, was encrusted with history. It was named for a Roman officer who had been converted to Christianity and martyred in 304 A.D. The ceiling frescoes in the abbey depicted the Austrian victory over the

Turks in 1683. Above the main altar fourteen panels showed (among other scenes) the Passion and the martyrdom of St. Sebastian, the work of Albrecht Altdorfer, a contemporary of Dürer and a master of the Renaissance union between the human and the divine. Anton Bruckner had served as organist here for most of his life and was buried under the great gold-and-white organ.

Mauthausen and St. Florian: no juxtaposition could have been more jarring. It represented a height and a depth of Western civilization, its glory and its most abysmal crime. The contrast was Austria, it was Europe, it was humanity.

Soon afterward I said good-bye to the embassy staff. The marine guards lined up in formation, flanking the staircase leading to the exit, and at the bottom the gunny presented me with the American flag that had stood in my office. I was very moved. It was the end of a long journey and a reaffirmation of my loyalty, of my home. Maybe America had nothing like St. Florian, but surely—and blessedly—it had nothing like Mauthausen, either.

AFTERWORD

IT WAS A ROUGH REENTRY. The shock began on the way to Manhattan from the airport with the sight of the filthy, garbage-strewn embankments along the highway. The image stayed with me like a splinter in the eye. It was a reminder that New York, for all its riches, was unable to meet some of its most basic needs. As Louise and I settled back into the city, our excitement at being home was dimmed by the crumbling streets, the fear of crime, the homeless sleeping on the sidewalks.

TV news projected nightmares, and not only in New York: drugs everywhere, outbursts of racial hate, the almost surreal reports of small children being killed by stray bullets on their front stoop. None of this was new. I had seen it all before I left; I had observed it at a distance from abroad and it was one of the reasons why I had wanted to come home. But after two years away I now experienced it with a sharp, new clarity. It hurt badly. At times it was heartbreaking.

I remembered my arrival half a century ago as a young refugee. Could this still be the magical place I had first seen, which I somehow, unreasonably, thought of as *my* New York, my America? I have been troubled by that question ever since my return.

The answers are unsettling. Race is still the most depressing specter. The fight against segregation has been replaced in large part by black self-segregation and reverse racism. The insistence on racial and ethnic identity has led to a destructive new tribalism reminiscent of Europe's fratricidal past (and occasionally still its present). Instead of Europe becoming Americanized, I feared that the United States was becoming Europeanized—or balkanized. The American civic religion—stressing unity over diversity, requiring mutual accommodation—is eroding, along with its intellectual underpinnings. I am infuriated by the people who mindlessly dismiss Western culture as a mere regional tradition, ignoring the fact that it offers universal truths. I am distressed by ethnic communities often aggressively bent on avoiding English—with the help of bilingual education and ballots. This disturbs me not merely because I recall my own frantic efforts to learn the language of my new homeland, but because I know the corrosive conflicts caused by multiple languages in other countries.

The constant demands for new "rights," far beyond the "inalienable" ones envisioned by the Founders, or more recent reformers, are rarely accompanied by notions of responsibility or duty (an almost forgotten word). An ingenious system of checks and balances is often an instrument of deadlock while politics is drowning in money. The liberating spirit of the American school that had so inspired me when I first experienced it has degenerated into near chaos, producing generations of illiterates or semiliterates at the very time when new technology requires highly educated citizens.

Many of our problems are caused by good intentions carried too far. We started out by trying to protect people against extreme want and ended up by creating a welfare state that showers the middle class with extravagant entitlements, keeps the underclass in permanent dependency and subsidizes an epidemic of illegitimate children unmatched anywhere in the industrialized world. We began with the wonderful desire to establish decency and banish hate but drifted into new forms of censorship. We fought for more justice, but now every imaginable injustice and disorder is blamed on some conspiracy, creating a cult of the victim.

•   •   •

AFTER A LIFETIME in journalism, observing the endless wars, mass murders, brutalities and the infinitely varied forms of deceit, I find it impossible not to believe in the existence of evil. That is a heavy word, and Americans have a difficult time dealing with the concept. Some of us seek to banish it by various forms of orthodoxy and publicly dictated morality. Others try to ignore it or define it out of existence by resorting to pragmatism and relativism. I thought those philosophies were destructive back in Sidney Hook's class, and I still do. I am not a fundamentalist, but I believe that a society without a set of fundamental values cannot endure. Often it seems that such values are vanishing and the very term is widely derided.

I am not sentimentalizing the past or succumbing to the disorienting drug of nostalgia. In many ways this is a much better country than it was a half century ago. People live longer and are healthier. The implements of technology are in almost everybody's hands. Conditions that once were casually condoned, including racial discrimination, are no longer acceptable. Poverty, which used to be seen as more or less inevitable, is now considered an outrage. Notions of what a decent society owes its citizens have vastly multiplied. For that very reason the stubbornly remaining areas of want and misery are seen as intolerable. Democratic capitalism has been so successful that a scholar described it as the perfect system and proclaimed it to mark "the end of history." That was a vast exaggeration—we are still caught up in angry struggles over how to share prosperity—but we have created more wealth for more people than seemed possible only a few decades ago.

Given such unmistakable progress, I remain incurably optimistic about America. While the United States may never recover the preponderance it enjoyed after World War II, it could remain the leading power economically, politically, militarily and intellectually. In that sense the next century could again be America's—if we want it and if we are willing to commit ourselves to extraordinary effort, determination and discipline. Those are big ifs. But there is at least some reason to believe these goals are attainable.

Alongside the decay and conflict, I see the irrepressible drive, the jackhammer energy, the ambitions as high as the builders' cranes, the still dazzling opportunities seized with endless ingenuity. I see the Main Streets and Elm Streets, often outraged by radical change, but—so far—able to bend to it without breaking; the countless civic groups, committees, associations, drives for every conceivable cause, all caught up in the perennial American passion for improving the nation.

America has an unmatched capacity for renewal. It has shed its skin again and again to reemerge with new life. It rebuilt itself after the Civil War and Reconstruction; it reformed itself after the cruelties of the nineteenth-century industrial surge and the excesses of the robber barons; it picked itself up after the Great Depression; it achieved at least partial healing after the bitter national split over Vietnam and the counterculture's nihilism.

America remains spectacularly flexible. It may not be classless, but it has fewer class barriers than any other society past or present. It has no permanent ruling caste, and the ranks of power and success are still remarkably open to newcomers—as they were to me—from every layer of society and every country in the world. Despite the mean-spirited and panicky new wave of anti-immigrant feeling, I believe strongly that immigration must and will continue to make its powerful contribution. It has always been a source of fresh energy and enthusiasm as millions discover America anew and in a sense rebuild it in every generation.

ONE OF THE things that has always struck me about Americans is how rarely we resort to blaming problems on human nature, on "that is the way it is." When things go wrong we may blame the government or various conspiracies or nasty foreigners and occasionally even ourselves. But we do not shrug and say, "That's life." I find this rejection of fatalism exhilarating, but it can also mean unrealistic expectations.

America is a living essay in freedom, but the essay is often confused. We are obsessed with freedom, yet we remain baffled by it. We have created the freest society in the world, yet we long for stability. We have freed ourselves of most traditions and constraints, yet we are alarmed by disorder. We profess to believe in the free market, yet we resent its inevitable, painful ups and downs. Do we sufficiently understand the age-old question of what freedom really means: giving as well as taking, obligation as well as liberty? We want everything: individual sovereignty as well as social harmony, equality as well as privilege. The most exciting fact about America is its refusal to recognize limits. The most dangerous fact about America is its refusal to recognize limits.

In this contradiction lies the heart of America. It is not stability but struggle, not serenity but effort.

Ultimately the issue is not that the United States harbors racism, extremism and other universal disorders. It is rather how hard and how persistently we try to overcome them. I believe we try harder than any other people.

I said at the outset of this book that my love of America is not uncritical. But I do love this country, this country that can endlessly fool itself and be fooled and yet retain a saving common sense; this materialistic country that is constantly involved in moralistic struggles and spiritual yearnings; this smug country that is relentlessly self-critical. I am grateful that my life has been intertwined with it.

There is a passage in *The Brothers Karamazov* that has always remained in my mind. Ivan insists that he cannot accept divine harmony if it has to be paid for by suffering of innocents. "I hasten to give back my entrance ticket," he declares. "I most respectfully return Him the ticket." In a moment of great despondency while my first wife, Beverly, was dying I sat with my children, talking of my life, and recalled the quotation. "You can't return the ticket," I said, pounding the table. "You can't return the ticket."

Looking back, I would not want to return the ticket if I could. Not the ticket to my life nor the ticket to America.

SOURCES

SOURCES

The principal source for this book is my memory, supported by extensive contemporary notes, correspondence to and from me, articles I wrote, speeches I made and interviews in which I participated. I was also able to draw on *Time* archives and files.

Many friends and former colleagues generously shared their recollections, and others helpfully supplied information and advice. Among them were Bonnie Angelo, Robert Sam Anson, Douglas Auchincloss, Laurence I. Barrett, James Bell, Jesse L. Birnbaum, Margaret Green Boeth, Fifi Booth, Joseph N. Boyce, Pamela Sanders Brement, Ruth Brine, Ray Cave, John Chambers, Richard Clurman, Shirley Clurman, Alastair Cooke, David DeVoss, Marta Fitzgerald Dorion, Pat and Dave DuBois, Peter Duchin, Vivi S. Duffy, John T. Elson, Lawrence Ferlinghetti, Josè M. Ferrer III, Dean Fischer, Judy Friedberg, Otto Friedrich, Otto Fuerbringer, Murray Gart, Frank Gibney, Leah Gordon, Hays Gorey, Ralph Graves, Paul Gray, Brooke Hayward, Lucian Heichler, Bruce Hiland, Ivy Hildebrand, Alger Hiss, Robert Hughes, Margaret Hyland, R. Edward Jackson, James Jackson, Stefan Kanfer, James Keogh, Henry Kissinger, Andrew Kopkind, Marshall Loeb, Andreas F. Lowenfeld, Henry Luce III, Edward F. Magnuson, Norman Mailer, Frank Mankiewicz, Robert P. Marshall Jr., Peter Bird Martin,

Frank McCulloch, Joseph A. McGowan, John McPhee, Frank B. Merrick, Emily Mitchell, John Moorehead, James Murray, Burjur Nargolwala, Patricia Neils, Bruce Nelan, Jane Nelson, Richard M. Nixon, Dorothy O'Keefe, Eric Pace, Douglas Pike, B. J. Phillips, Victoria Sales Rainert, Rozanne Ridgway, Roger Rosenblatt, Rinna Samuel, Kathleen Shortall, David J. Scheffer, Ronald Z. Sheppard, George P. Shultz, Hugh Sidey, Dave Simpkins, Robert M. Steed, John Steele, Bryan B. Sterling, Jean Sulzberger, Georges Temmer, Jack E. White, and Donald M. Wilson.

For general background and confirmation of details I relied on *Time* and also drew on a number of books, notably the three volumes of the Time Inc. company history (the third volume was prepared under my supervision). A partial bibliography follows:

Adams, Henry. D. W. Brogan, intro. *The Education of Henry Adams.* Boston: Houghton Mifflin Company, 1961.

Adler, Renata. *Reckless Disregard: Westmoreland v. CBS et al. Sharon v. Time.* New York: Alfred A. Knopf, 1986.

Allen, Frederick Lewis. *The Big Change: America Transforms Itself 1900–1950.* New York: Bantam, 1965.

Baines, Jocelyn. *Joseph Conrad: A Critical Biography.* New York: McGraw-Hill Book Company, 1960.

Baldwin, James. *The Fire Next Time.* New York: Dial Press, 1963.

Barrett, Laurence I. *Gambling with History: Ronald Reagan in the White House.* Garden City, N.Y.: Doubleday & Co., 1983.

Bell, Daniel, et al. *Writing for FORTUNE: Nineteen Authors Remember Life on the Staff of a Remarkable Magazine.* New York: Time Inc., 1980.

Benda, Julien. *La trahison des clercs (The Treason of Intellectuals)* New York: William Morrow & Company, 1928.

Bernanos, Georges. *The Diary of a Country Priest.* New York: Carroll & Graf Publishers, 1992.

Bernhard, Thomas. *Heldenplatz/Thomas Bernhard.* Frankfurt am Main: Suhrkamp, 1988.

―――. *Woodcutters.* Chicago: University of Chicago Press, 1989.

Bingham, June. *Courage to Change: An Introduction to the Life and Thought of Reinhold Niebuhr.* New York: Charles Scribner's Sons, 1972.

Book of Common Prayer, and Administration of the Sacraments, and Other Rites and Ceremonies of the Church. (According to the use of the Protestant Episcopal Church in the United States of America. Together with the Psalter or Psalms of David.) 1928/1662 version. New York: Oxford University Press, 1944.

Brammer, Julius, and Alfred Grünwald. Libretto. *Die Herzogin von Chicago.* Music by Emmerich Kálmán. Leipzig: W. Karczag, 1928.

Brooks, John. *The Big Wheel.* New York: Harper & Row, 1969.

Buckley, William F., Jr., and Charles R. Kesler, eds. *Keeping the Tablets: Modern American Conservative Thought.* (*American Conservative Thought in the Twentieth Century,* rev. ed.) New York: Perennial Library/Harper & Row, Publishers, 1988.

———. *Wind Fall: The End of the Affair.* New York: Random House, 1992.

Burnham, James. *The Managerial Revolution.* Bloomington, Ind.: Indiana University Press, 1960.

Busch, Noel F. *Briton Hadden: A Biography of the Co-Founder of TIME.* New York: Farrar, Straus and Company, 1949.

Camus, Albert. Justin O'Brien, trans. *The Myth of Sisyphus and Other Essays.* New York: Vintage International, 1991.

Carnegie, Dale. *How to Win Friends and Influence People.* New York: Simon & Schuster, 1952.

Chambers, Whittaker. *Cold Friday.* New York: Random House, 1964.

———. "Ghosts on the Roof." *Time,* March 5, 1945, 36–37.

———. *Witness.* New York: Random House, 1952.

———. William F. Buckley, Jr., ed. *Odyssey of a Friend: Letters to William F. Buckley, Jr.: 1954–1961.* New York: Putnam, 1969.

Clurman, Richard M. *Beyond Malice: The Media's Years of Reckoning.* New Brunswick, N.J.: Transaction Publishers, 1988.

———. *To the End of Time: The Seduction and Conquest of a Media Empire.* New York: Simon & Schuster, 1992.

Commager, Henry Steele. *The American Mind: An Interpretation of American Thought and Character Since the 1880's.* New Haven, Conn.: Yale University Press, 1950.

Commission on U.S.-Soviet Relations. *The Soviet Challenge: A Policy Framework for the 1980's.* New York: Council on Foreign Relations, 1981.

Davis, Johanna. *Life Signs.* New York: Atheneum, 1973.

De Beauvoir, Simone. H. M. Parshley, trans./ed. *The Second Sex.* New York: Knopf, 1953.

Dickstein, Morris. *Gates of Eden: American Culture in the Sixties.* New York: Basic Books, 1977.

Dobrynin, Anatoly. *In Confidence.* New York: Times Books, 1995.

Donovan, Hedley. *Right Places, Right Times.* New York: Holt and Company, 1989.

Dos Passos, John. *The Big Money.* New York: Harcourt, Brace and World, 1936.

Dostoevsky, Fyodor. Constance Garnett, trans. *The Brothers Karamazov.* New York: The Macmillan Company, 1912.

Eliot, T. S. *Murder in the Cathedral.* New York: Harcourt Brace, 1935.

Elson, Robert T. *The World of TIME INC.: The Intimate History of a Publishing Enterprise 1923–1941.* New York: Atheneum, 1968.

Fanon, Frantz. Jean-Paul Sartre, pref. *The Wretched of the Earth.* New York: Grove Press, 1965.

Feibleman, Peter S. *Lilly: Reminiscences of Lillian Hellman/Peter Feibleman.* New York: Morrow, 1988.

Frankl, Viktor E. *Man's Search for Meaning,* rev. ed. New York: Simon & Schuster, 1984.

Friedan, Betty. *The Feminine Mystique.* New York: Norton, 1963.

Friedrich, Otto. *City of Nets: A Portrait of Hollywood in the 1940's.* New York: Harper & Row, 1980.

———. *The Grave of Alice B. Toklas.* New York: Henry Holt, 1989.

Geismar, Peter. *Fanon.* New York: Dial Press, 1971.

Gill, Brendan. *A New York Life: Of Friends & Others.* New York: Poseidon Press, 1990.

Gitlin, Todd. *The Sixties: Years of Hope, Days of Rage.* New York: Bantam Books, 1993.

Goodman, Paul. *Growing Up Absurd: Problems of Youth in the Organized System.* New York: Random House, 1960.

Gorer, Geoffrey. *The American People: A Study in National Character.* New York: W. W. Norton & Company, 1948.

————. "Justification by Numbers." *American Scholar,* July 1948, 280–286.

Grunwald, Henry. "Main Street 1947." *Life,* June 23, 1947, 100–114.

————. "Quality of Life behind the Soviet Statistics." *Fortune,* March 1964, 146–147, 206–217.

————. "Thoughts on Trouble in El Dorado." *Time,* June 22, 1970, 18–21.

————. "Down with 'Media." *Time,* June 7, 1971, 56–57.

————. "Don't Love the Press, But Understand It." *Time,* July 8, 1974, 74–75.

————. "The Morning after the Fourth: Have We Kept Our Promise?" *Time,* July 14, 1975, 19–20.

————. "Loving America." *Time,* July 5, 1976, 35–36.

————. "Arguing with South Africa." *Time,* June 27, 1977, 32, 37–38.

————. "Are We 'Destroying' Jimmy Carter?" *Time,* May 15, 1978, 97–98.

————. "The Press, the Courts and the Country." *Time,* July 16, 1979, 74–75.

————. "The U.S. and Europe: Talking Back." *Time,* June 30, 1980, 26, 29.

————. "New Challenges to Capitalism." *Fortune,* May 7, 1990, 138–144.

————. "The Second American Century." *Time,* October 8, 1990, 70–72, 73–75.

————, ed. and intro. *Salinger, A Critical and Personal Portrait.* New York: Harper, 1962.

Halberstam, David. *The Best and the Brightest.* New York: Ballantine Books, 1992.

————. *The Powers That Be.* New York: Alfred A. Knopf, 1979.

Haldeman, H. R. Stephen E. Ambrose, intro. *The Haldeman Diaries: Inside the Nixon White House.* New York: G. P. Putnam, 1994.

————, with Joseph DiMona. *The Ends of Power.* New York: Times Books, 1978.

Hayden, Tom. *Reunion: A Memoir.* New York: Random House, 1988.

Hellman, Lillian. Garry Wills, intro. *Scoundrel Time.* Boston: Little, Brown and Company, 1976.

Herzstein, Robert E. *Waldheim: The Missing Years.* New York: Arbor House/William Morrow, 1988.

Higham, John. *Strangers in the Land: Patters of American Nativism.* New York: Atheneum, 1963.

Hodgson, Godfrey. *America in Our Time, From World War II to Nixon: What Happened and Why.* Garden City, N.Y.: Vintage Books, 1978.

Hook, Sidney. *Marxism and Beyond.* Totowa, N.J.: Rowman and Allanheld, 1983.

Hughes, Robert. *Culture of Complaint: The Fraying of America.* London: Oxford University Press, 1993.

————. *Heaven and Hell in Western Art.* New York: Stein & Day, 1968.

International Commission of Historians Designated to Establish the Military Service of Lt. Kurt Waldheim. *The Waldheim Report: Submitted Feb. 8, 1988, to Federal Chancellor Dr. Franz Vranitsky.* Copenhagen, Denmark: Museum Tusculanum Press, University of Copenhagen, 1993.

Jessup, John K., ed. *The Ideas of Henry Luce.* New York: Atheneum, 1969.

Judis, John B. *William F. Buckley, Jr.: Patron Saint of the Conservatives.* New York: Simon & Schuster, 1988.

Kanfer, Stefan. *A Journal of the Plague Years.* New York: Atheneum, 1973.

Karnow, Stanley. *Vietnam: A History.* New York: Viking Press, 1983.

Kirkendall, Lester E. *Premarital Intercourse and Interpersonal Relations.* New York: The Julian Press, 1961.

Kissinger, Henry. *White House Years.* Boston: Little, Brown and Company, 1979.

————. *Years of Upheaval*. Boston: Little, Brown and Company, 1982.

Kraus, Karl. *Die letzten Tage der Menschheit*. Frankfurt am Main: Suhrkamp, 1992.

Kristol, Irving. *Neo-Conservatism: The Autobiography of an Idea*. New York: The Free Press, 1995.

————. *Reflections of a Neoconservative*. New York: Basic Books, 1983.

Lessing, Gotthold Ephraim. Bayard Quincy Morgan, trans. *Nathan the Wise: A Dramatic Poem in Five Acts*. New York: F. Ungar Publishing Co., 1955.

Lewis, Sinclair. *Main Street*. New York: Harcourt, Brace and Company, 1920.

Lynd, Staughton. *Intellectual Origins of American Radicalism*. New York: Pantheon Books, 1968.

Macdonald, Dwight. *Against the American Grain*. New York: Random House, 1962.

MacLaine, Shirley. *Dancing in the Light*. New York: Bantam, 1985.

Mailer, Norman. *The Prisoner of Sex*. Boston: Little, Brown and Company, 1971.

————. *The White Negro: Superficial Reflection on the Hipster*. San Francisco: City Lights, 1957.

————. *Why Are We in Vietnam?: A Novel*. New York: G. P. Putnam's Sons, 1967.

Manchester, William. *The Glory and the Dream: A Narrative History of America, 1932–1972*. Boston: Little, Brown and Company, 1973.

Marcuse, Herbert, with Robert Paul Wolff and Barrington Moore. *A Critique of Pure Tolerance*. Boston: Beacon Press, 1965.

————. Douglas Kellner, intro. *One-Dimensional Man: Studies in the Ideology of Advanced Industrial Society*. Boston: Beacon Press, 1991.

Martin, Ralph G. *Henry & Clare: An Intimate Portrait of the Luces*. New York: G. P. Putnam's Sons, 1991.

Matthews, T. S. *Name and Address: An Autobiography by T. S. Matthews*. New York: Simon & Schuster, 1960.

May, Karl Friedrichs. *Winnetou der rote Gentleman*. Freiburg, L. B., F. E. Fehsenfell, 1893.

McLuhan, Marshall. *Understanding Media: The Extensions of Man.* New York: McGraw-Hall Book Company, 1964.

McLuhan, Marshall, and Quentin Fiore. *The Medium Is the Message.* New York: Random House, 1967.

Miller, James. *Democracy Is in the Streets from Port Huron to the Seige of Chicago.* New York: Simon & Schuster, 1987.

Millett, Kate. *Sexual Politics.* Garden City, N.Y.: Doubleday & Company, 1970.

Morton, Frederic. *A Nervous Splendor: Vienna 1888–1889.* New York: Penguin Books, 1980.

Munson, Gorham. *The Awakening Twenties: A Memoir History of a Literary Period.* Baton Rouge: Louisiana State University Press, 1985.

Neils, Patricia. *China Images in the Life and Times of Henry Luce.* Savage, Md.: Rowman & Littlefield, 1990.

Niebuhr, Reinhold. *The Self and the Dramas of History.* New York: Charles Scribner's Sons, 1955.

O'Neill, William L. *A Better World. The Great Schism: Stalinism and the American Intellectuals.* New York: Simon & Schuster, 1982.

Oshinsky, David M. *A Conspiracy So Immense: The World of Joe McCarthy.* New York: Free Press, 1983.

Peale, Norman Vincent. *The Power of Positive Thinking.* New York: Prentice-Hall, 1952.

————. *The True Joy of Positive Living: An Autobiography by Norman Vincent Peale.* New York: William Morrow and Company, 1984.

Plato. B. Jowett, trans. *Plato's The Republic.* New York: Modern Library, 1941.

Pollak, Richard. "TIME: After Luce." *Harper's,* July 1969, 42+.

Prendergast, Curtis, with Geoffrey Colvin. Robert Lubar, ed. *The World of Time Inc.: The Intimate History of a Changing Enterprise. Vol. III: 1960–1980.* New York: Atheneum, 1986.

Renault, Mary. *The King Must Die.* New York: Random House, 1958.

Riesman, David, with Nathan Glazer and Reuel Denney. *The Lonely Crowd: A Study of the Changing American Character.* New Haven, Conn.: Yale University Press, 1951.

Rosten, Leo. *The Education of H*y*m*a*n K*a*p*l*a*n.* New York: Harcourt Brace, 1937.

Saroyan, William. *Love's Old Sweet Song*. Music by Paul Bowles. Words by Saroyan. New York: Chappell, 1940.

Schwarz, Egon. *Keine Zeit für Eichendorff*. Königstein/Ts.: Athenäum, 1979.

Shaw, Bernard. *Man and Superman: A Comedy*. Westminster, London: A. Constable, 1903.

Spiel, Hilde. *Vienna's Golden Autumn: 1866–1938*. New York: Weidenfeld & Nicolson, 1987.

Spock, Benjamin. *The Common Sense Book of Baby and Child Care*. New York: Duell, Sloan and Pearce, 1946.

Swanberg, *W. A. Luce and His Empire*. New York: Charles Scribner's Sons, 1972.

Talese, Gay. *Thy Neighbor's Wife*. New York: Ivy Books, 1993.

Weinstein, Allen. *Perjury: The Hiss-Chambers Case*. New York: Alfred A. Knopf, 1978.

Weyr, Thomas. *Reaching for Paradise: The Playboy Vision of America*. New York: Times Books, 1978.

Whyte, William H. *The Organization Man*. New York: Simon & Schuster, 1956.

Wolfe, Tom. *The Kandy-Kolored Tangarine-Flake Streamlined Baby*. New York: Farrar, Straus and Giroux, 1965.

———. *Radical Chic*. Toronto: Doubleday Canada Ltd., 1970.

PERMISSIONS

Permissions

Lyric excerpts from *The Duchess from Chicago* by Alfred Grunwald reprinted by permission of Weinberger, Vienna. See page 13.

Lyric excerpts of "The Waltz of Old Vienna" by Irving Berlin. Copyright © 1939 by Irving Berlin. Copyright © Renewed. International Copyright Secured. Used by permission. All Rights Reserved. See page 86.

Excerpt from "Choruses from 'The Rock' in *COLLECTED POEMS 1909–1962* by T. S. Eliot, copyright 1936 by Harcourt Brace & Company, copyright © 1964, 1963 by T. S. Eliot, reprinted by permission of the publisher. Printed in Canada with permission of Faber and Faber, Ltd. See page 174.

Four lines from "HOWL" FROM *COLLECTED POEMS 1947–1980* BY ALLEN GINSBERG. Copyright © 1955 by Allen Ginsberg. Reprinted by permission of HarperCollins Publishers, Inc. See page 268.

Six lines from "AMERICA" FROM *COLLECTED POEMS 1947–1980* BY ALLEN GINSBERG. Copyright © 1956, 1959 by Allen Ginsberg. Copyright Renewed. Reprinted by permission of HarperCollins Publishers, Inc. See page 269.

INDEX